Biological Diversity

Biological Diversity

Frontiers in Measurement and Assessment

EDITED BY

Anne E. Magurran

Professor of Ecology & Evolution,
University of St Andrews, UK

and

Brian J. McGill

Assistant Professor, School of Biology and Ecology
& Sustainability Solutions Initiative, University of Maine, USA

OXFORD
UNIVERSITY PRESS

OXFORD
UNIVERSITY PRESS

Great Clarendon Street, Oxford OX2 6DP

Oxford University Press is a department of the University of Oxford.
It furthers the University's objective of excellence in research, scholarship,
and education by publishing worldwide in

Oxford New York

Auckland Cape Town Dar es Salaam Hong Kong Karachi
Kuala Lumpur Madrid Melbourne Mexico City Nairobi
New Delhi Shanghai Taipei Toronto

With offices in

Argentina Austria Brazil Chile Czech Republic France Greece
Guatemala Hungary Italy Japan Poland Portugal Singapore
South Korea Switzerland Thailand Turkey Ukraine Vietnam

Oxford is a registered trademark of Oxford University Press
in the UK and in certain other countries

Published in the United States
by Oxford University Press Inc., New York

British Library Cataloguing in Publication Data

Data available

Library of Congress Cataloging-in-Publication Data

Biological diversity : frontiers in measurement and assessment / edited by
Anne E. Magurran and Brian J. McGill.
    p. cm.
ISBN 978–0–19–958067–5
1. Biodiversity. 2. Biodiversity—Monitoring. 3. Biodiversity conservation.
I. Magurran, Anne E., 1955–   II. McGill, Brian J.
QH541.15.B56B587 2010
578.7—dc22   2010029049

Typeset by SPI Publisher Services, Pondicherry, India
Printed in Great Britain
on acid-free paper by
CPI Antony Rowe, Chippenham, Wiltshire

ISBN 978–0–19–958066–8 (Hbk.)
     978–0–19–958067–5 (Pbk.)

1 3 5 7 9 10 8 6 4 2

Contents

Part V Applications

List of Contributors

Scott A. Bonar, USGS Arizona Cooperative Fish and Wildlife Research Unit, 104 Biological Sciences East, University of Arizona, Tucson, AZ 85721, USA

Stephen T. Buckland, Centre for Research into Ecological and Environmental Modelling, University of St Andrews, The Observatory, Buchanan Gardens, St Andrews, KY16 9LZ, UK

Anne Chao, Institute of Statistics, National Tsing Hua University, Hsin-Chu, Taiwan 30043

Robin L. Chazdon, Department of Ecology and Evolutionary Biology, University of Connecticut, Storrs, CT 06269-3043, USA

Steven L. Chown, Centre for Invasion Biology, Department of Botany and Zoology, Stellenbosch University, Private Bag X1, Matieland 7602, South Africa

Robert K. Colwell, Department of Ecology and Evolutionary Biology, University of Connecticut, Storrs, CT 06269, USA

Sean R. Connolly, ARC Centre of Excellence for Coral Reef Studies, and School of Marine and Tropical Biology, James Cook University, Townsville, QLD 4811, Australia

William K. Cornwell, Departments of Botany and Zoology, and Biodiversity Research Centre, University of British Columbia, 6270 University Blvd., Vancouver, BC, Canada V6T 1Z4

Melanie Culver, School of Natural Resources and Environment and AZ Cooperative Fish and Wildlife Research Unit, USGS, University of Arizona, Tucson, AZ 85721, USA

Thomas P. Curtis, School of Civil Engineering and Geosciences, University of Newcastle Upon Tyne, Newcastle Upon Tyne, NE1 7RU, UK

John Donoghue II, University of Arizona, Department of Ecology & Evolutionary Biology, P.O. Box 210088, Tucson, AZ 85721, USA

Maria Dornelas, ARC Centre of Excellence for Coral Reef Studies, James Cook University, Townsville, QLD 4811, Australia and CESAM, Department of Biology Universidade de Aveiro, Campus de Santiago, 3810-193 Aveiro, Portugal

Jeffrey S. Fehmi, School of Natural Resources and the Environment, 325 Biological Sciences East, University of Arizona, Tucson, AZ 85721, USA

Robert Fitak, Genetics GIDP, University of Arizona, PO Box 210476, Tucson, AZ 85721-0476, USA

Kevin J. Gaston, Biodiversity and Macroecology Group, Department of Animal and Plant Sciences, University of Sheffield, Sheffield, S10 2TN, UK

Nicholas J. Gotelli, Department of Biology, University of Vermont, Burlington, VT 05401, USA

Fangliang He, Department of Renewable Resources, University of Alberta, Edmonton, Alberta, Canada T6G 2E1

Peter A. Henderson, Pisces Conservation Ltd, IRC House, The Square, Pennington, Lymington, Hants, SO41 8GN, UK

Hans-Werner Herrmann, Arizona Research Laboratories, Human Origins Genotyping Laboratory, University of Arizona, Tucson, AZ 85721, USA

Lou Jost, Via a Runtun, Baños, Tungurahua, Ecuador

Yue M. Li, University of Arizona, Department of Ecology & Evolutionary Biology, P.O. Box 210088, Tucson, AZ 85721, USA

S. Kathleen Lyons, Department of Paleobiology, National Museum of Natural History, Smithsonian Institution, Washington, DC 20560, USA

Karen Magnuson-Ford, IRMACS Centre & Department of Biological Sciences, Simon Fraser University, 8888 University Dr., Burnaby, BC, Canada V5A 1S6

Anne E. Magurran, School of Biology and Scottish Oceans Institute, University of St Andrews, St Andrews, KY16 8LB, UK

Brian A. Maurer, Department of Fisheries and Wildlife, Michigan State University, East Lansing, MI 4882, USA

Robert M. May, Department of Zoology, University of Oxford, South Parks Road, Oxford, OX1 3PS, UK

Melodie A. McGeoch, Centre for Invasion Biology, Cape Research Centre, South African National Parks, P.O. Box 216, Steenberg 7947, South Africa

Brian J. McGill, School of Biology and Ecology & Sustainability Solutions Initiative, University of Maine, Deering Hall Room 202, Orono, ME 04469 USA

Norman Mercado-Silva, USGS Arizona Cooperative Fish and Wildlife Research Unit, 104 Biological Sciences East, University of Arizona, Tucson, AZ 85721, USA

Arne Ø. Mooers, Department of Biological Sciences, Simon Fraser University, 8888 University Dr., Burnaby, BC, Canada V5A 1S6

Stuart E. Newson, British Trust for Ornithology, The Nunnery, Thetford, Norfolk, IP24 2PU, UK

Lise Øvreås, Centre for Geobiology and Department of Biology, University of Bergen PB7800, N-5020 Bergen, Norway

Michael L. Rosenzweig, University of Arizona, Department of Ecology & Evolutionary Biology, PO Box 210088, Tucson, AZ 85721, USA

Candan U. Soykan, Biology Department, San Diego State University, 5500 Campanile Drive, San Diego, CA 92182-4614, USA

Angelika C. Studeny, Centre for Research into Ecological and Environmental Modelling, University of St Andrews, The Observatory, Buchanan Gardens, St Andrews, KY16 9LZ, UK

Karl Inne Ugland, Section of Marine Biology and Limnology, Department of Biology, University of Oslo Pb. 1064, Blindern, N-0316 Oslo, Norway

Mark Vellend, Departments of Botany and Zoology, and Biodiversity Research Centre, University of British Columbia, 6270 University Blvd., Vancouver, BC, Canada V6T 1Z4

Peter J. Wagner, Dept. of Paleobiology, National Museum of Natural History, Smithsonian Institution, Washington, DC 20560, USA

Evan Weiher, Department of Biology, University of Wisconsin - Eau Claire, Eau Claire, WI, USA

Chi Yuan, University of Arizona, Department of Ecology & Evolutionary Biology, PO Box 210088, Tucson, AZ 85721, USA

Foreword

The only portrait in the Council Room of the Royal Society in London is one of Joseph Banks, whose powerful presence still seems to dominate the room. Banks was President for an astonishing 42 years, from 1778 to 1820. These were, moreover, turbulent years: the French Revolution, the Napoleonic Wars, and subsequent post-war unrest in Britain (including the Peterloo massacre). Less commonly appreciated is the fact that these were also turbulent years within this old-established and influential scientific society. Up until the later years of the eighteenth century, 'science' essentially meant mathematical and physical science. Banks was a botanist (he studied briefly under Linnaeus), and influential members of the Royal Society deprecated him as being not so much a scientist as a gardener (albeit a politically well-connected one).

Underlying all this is the astonishing fact that the first stirrings of systematic interest in cataloguing the diversity of other living things with which humans share the planet came a full century after the foundation of the Royal Society in 1660 and Newton's providing a fundamental understanding of the laws of motion, along with the inverse square law of gravitational attraction. The corresponding date for Linnaeus' binary codification in De Rerum Naturae (which recognized a global total of around 9000 species of plants and animals) is 1758. In many ways the legacy of this century-long lag still lingers.

Today the global total number of distinct species of eukaryotes (never mind the viruses and bacteria, where there are essential differences in the definition of 'species') that have been named and recorded is probably around 1.6–1.7 million, with roughly 15,000 being added each year (May 2007). Part of the uncertainty derives from lack of synoptic databases for many groups, which compounds difficulties in resolving synonyms—the same species independently found, and then named and recorded, in two or more different places by different people. Today's true total of distinct eukaryotic species is estimated to lie in the range of 5–10 million, with figures as low as 3 million or as high as 100 million being defensible. These lamentable uncertainties result partly from what a management consultant would call inefficiencies in the distribution of the relevant workforce. Although the taxonomy of taxonomists is itself poorly documented, rough estimates suggest it is approximately evenly divided among vertebrates, plants, and invertebrates (Gaston & May 1992), but there are around 10 plant species, and at least 100 invertebrate species (possibly more than 1000), for each vertebrate species. The labour force is even more inefficiently divided if one considers the research literature on conservation biology. Here an analysis of the 2700 papers published in Conservation Biology and Biological Conservation between 1979 and 1998 showed 69% devoted to vertebrates, 20% to plants, and 11% to all invertebrates (with half of these being lepidoptera, which appear to have the status of honorary birds) (Clark & May 2002). And conservation action, as indicated, for example, by the World Wildlife Fund's Annual Report, is almost wholly devoted to charismatic megavertebrates. This is understandable in view of public attitudes, but arguably unfortunate in terms of preserving ecosystem functioning; the argument that protecting vertebrate biodiversity will more-or-less automatically also preserve invertebrate biodiversity does not survive close examination (Prendergast et al. 1993).

The present volume is, of course, focused on advances—along with remaining areas of ignorance—in our understanding of patterns of biological diversity: what is there and how best to measure and characterize it. The broad range of relevant topics covered in the book is clearly and succinctly set out in Magurran and McGill's introductory Chapter 1, and so I make no effort to duplicate it in this Foreword, but I cannot resist re-emphasizing how many aspects of this quest for understanding began much more recently than Linnaeus. In particular, note that the first published study of the important issue of species' relative abundance (SRA) is only 100 years old (Raunkaier 1909).

Quite a few of the chapters deal with various "indices", aiming to reduce the often complex details of the relative abundance of species in a defined area or ecosystem to a single number (or, rarely, a couple of numbers). For purposes of quick assessments or comparisons, this is understandable, and often sensible. However—and here I am riding one of my hobbyhorses—I believe that whenever possible it is better to use the full distribution of SRA. Condensing this information, often the fruit of much labour, into a couple of indices such as mean and variance (or something equivalent) may seem convenient, but the loss of detail can easily result in important features of the relevant community assembly being overlooked. Particularly pernicious, in my view, is the so-called Shannon-Wiener diversity index, $H = -\sum_i p_i \ln p_i$ (with p_i the number of individuals in the ith species, as a fraction of the total). Whilst entrancingly tempting in its resonance with information theory, by taking logarithms to get the Shannon-Wiener index one is greatly compressing the data (remember the difference between 100 and 1 000 000 is less than a factor of 10 once natural logarithms are taken), and thereby significantly weakening the discriminatory power of the index. If one must use simpler indices, at least avoid those based on logarithmic transformations of the data (May 1975).

Another thing to keep in mind when considering patterns of abundance in relation to threats to biodiversity is that rarity does not necessarily imply endangerment. Nor does great abundance necessarily imply robustness: witness the passenger pigeon. This point was first emphasized, with telling examples, in Rabinowitz's classic paper 'Seven Forms of Rarity'. It is worth emphasizing again (Rabinowitz 1981; Rabinowitz et al 1986).

The pressures currently being inflicted on natural communities of plants and animals are huge, and increasing. Since Darwin published the *The Origin of Species* roughly 150 years ago, human numbers have increased sevenfold, and the energy use per person has increased by a similar factor, resulting in a 50-fold increase in our overall impact on our planet's ecosystems. Vitousek et al.'s (1986) estimate that humanity takes to itself, directly or indirectly, roughly 40% of terrestrial net primary productivity has recently been validated by satellite images of the land area modified by us (Sachs 2008). Even more extraordinary, of all the atmospheric nitrogen fixed in 2008, 55% came from the Harber-Bosch chemical process rather than the natural biogeochemical processes which created, and which struggle to maintain, the biosphere (Sachs 2008).

All this has consequences for the services that natural ecosystems deliver to us. Such ecosystem services are not counted in conventional measures of gross domestic product (GDP), although rough estimates of their value puts it comparable with, or greater than, the global GDP of conventional economics (Constanza et al. 1997). The recent Millennium Ecosystem Assessment (MEA) classifies these various ecosystem services under 24 broad headings (Millennium Ecosystem Assessment 2005; see also May 2007). Of these services, 15 are assessed as currently degrading, four improving (these mainly relate to food production), and we do not understand the remaining five well enough to evaluate them.

Not least among the areas where we need deeper understanding of the origins and maintenance of biological diversity is how might humans alter habitats and ecosystems to provide for their needs, but do so subject to constraints which preserve both particular individual species and key elements of ecosystems. This will not be easy. Many purists will flinch at the prospect. The alternative, however, would seem too often to be a mosaic of degraded habitat, increasingly threatening dedicated reserves, with all the tensions thus entailed. Terborgh's (1983) *Five New World Primates* is a pioneering work in this arena.

In summary, the present book could not be more timely. It gives a comprehensive and authoritative account both of what we do know, and what we do not. As such, it provides a toolkit of useful information and techniques, and also a guide to areas requiring further work.

Robert M. May
Zoology Department
Oxford University
Oxford OX1 3PS, UK

Challenges and opportunities in the measurement and assessment of biological diversity

Anne E. Magurran and Brian J. McGill

'When we look at the plants and bushes clothing an entangled bank, we are tempted to attribute their proportional numbers and kinds to what we call chance. But how false a view is this! Every one has heard that when an American forest is cut down, a very different vegetation springs up; but it has been observed that ancient Indian ruins in the Southern United States, which must formerly have been cleared of trees, now display the same beautiful diversity and proportion of kinds as in the surrounding virgin forests.'

—— Darwin, Origin of Species (1859)

1.1 Introduction

By the 1800s naturalists had begun to document a fact that was surely apparent to the earliest humans: that species vary markedly in how common they are. Audubon, for example, noted that bird species in North America differ in abundance by up to seven orders of magnitude (McGill 2006; McGill et al. 2007). Darwin's (1859) reflections on the observation that some taxa are abundant yet many are rare, and that there are geographical differences in the abundances and types of species, shaped his thinking about natural selection. In drawing attention to the 'proportional numbers and kinds' of species in nature, however, Darwin also identified questions that continue to challenge ecologists a century and a half later.

Humans have a strong intuitive sense of the distinction between high diversity and low diversity assemblages, as encapsulated, for example, by the contrast between a tropical rain forest and a monoculture planted for timber. Moreover, the inequality of species abundances that Darwin reported is so pervasive as to have acquired the status of an 'ecological law' (McGill et al. 2007). However, quantifying the biological diversity of a community, assessing differences in this diversity over space or time, and doing so in ways that are useful to those who seek explanations for the natural patterns as well as to the managers and policy makers charged with the sustainable use of wild nature, is by no means as simple as it first appears. The reason for this difficulty is that biological diversity is a multifaceted concept that can be defined and documented in different ways. Being clear about exactly what we mean by biological diversity (or biodiversity) is the first step towards measuring it. Even then the user can be confronted by a myriad measures, some of which will do a better job than others. The goal of this book is to guide readers through the entangled bank of biodiversity measures and provide an up-to-date and accessible account of this important and rapidly expanding field.

1.2 State of the field

2010 marks the United Nations International Year of Biodiversity (UN IYB), an initiative that highlights the growing need to provide informative and robust assessments of biological diversity. The objectives of the IYB are to promote the protection of biodiversity and encourage organizations, institutions, companies, and individuals to take direct action to reduce the constant loss of biological diversity worldwide. However, 2010 is also the target date set by the 2002 World Summit on Sustainable

Development 'for significant reduction in the current rate of loss of biological diversity'. It is by now generally accepted that the 2010 target will not be met, and of course there are many reasons for this, one of which is the ongoing debate about how best to measure biological diversity.

The measurement of biological diversity has resonances with the parable of the blind men and the elephant where one felt the trunk, one an ear, one a tusk and another a leg, only to find that they disagreed about the nature of the creature they had encountered. Quantifying biological diversity is in some ways like trying to measure an elephant (Nanney 2004). An elephant might be described in terms of its morphology or behaviour or neural circuitry, or DNA. Gene expression might be tracked through time or compared amongst individuals. The social interactions in different herds might also be explored. All of these approaches are valid, but clearly different. The investigator needs to specify which aspect of the elephant is being assessed, and then make the case that the types of measures adopted are employed correctly and are suitable for the purpose for which they are bring used. In the same way that there is no single method that entirely captures the essence of elephantness, so there is no one metric that perfectly quantifies biological diversity. A large, and growing, number of diversity measures have been developed (Southwood & Henderson 2000; Royal Society 2003; Magurran 2004). Southwood (1978) (p. 421) wryly noted the 'explosive speciation' of diversity indices and the habit of inventors of new measures to condemn their predecessors. Biodiversity assessment embraces not just the classical measures of richness, evenness, and species abundance distributions but also evaluations of occurrence, range size, and vulnerability as well as functional traits and phylogenetic diversity. It is clear that there can be no single 'best buy' index that will suit all needs. Instead, clusters of measures have been developed to capture a certain aspect of biodiversity, with some of these performing this task better than others. Although it may seem like a disadvantage to have to choose amongst a range of metrics, the ability to examine biological diversity in different ways not only helps ecologists gain a deeper understanding of how ecosystems function, but also sheds light on

issues of practical concern such as the link between diversity and ecosystem services.

The quantification of biological diversity probably began with Darwin, who in 1855 recorded all the plants in the meadow, Great Pucklands, next to his family home at Downe. His list ran to 142 species. It was over 50 years before the first account of the relative abundance of species was published by Raunkaier in 1909. Other early, yet pivotal, papers by Motomura (1932) and Fisher (Fisher et al. 1943) laid the foundations for the investigation of species abundance distributions. Additional insightful and significant contributions (including those by Preston (1948), MacArthur (1960), May (1975), Pielou (1975), Taylor et al. (1976), and Sugihara (1980) followed. These provide the framework within which biodiversity is measured, and still repay careful reading. Two developments that occurred towards the end of the twentieth century, however, shifted the measurement and assessment of biological diversity to a new gear. The first of these was the recognition that biological diversity is a crucial global resource as well as one that is being lost at an accelerating rate, the second the advances in computing power that have fostered substantial improvements in statistical and modelling techniques.

1.3   What is in this book

Although vastly improved analytical and computing resources are of tremendous benefit to ecologists, the rapid development of new methods, the inconsistent and sometimes confusing application of old ones, and the lack of agreement in the literature about the best approach means that users can be bewildered. This book provides an up-to-date account of the methods used to measure and assess biological diversity and places particular emphasis on the practical issues involved in measurement. It extends the discussion in Magurran (2004) and includes many new developments as well as a re-examination of familiar approaches. Our focus is measurement of the variety, abundance, and geographical occurrence of taxa, reflecting the sense in which Darwin used the term 'diversity'. The authors have wide experience of the measurement of biological diversity and have contributed to recent advances. As befits a vibrant field, our contributors do not invariably agree on which metrics and approaches are the best ones, although there is broad consensus about the essentials of biodiversity assessment. The various chapters set out the issues that investigators must consider and explain the advantages and disadvantages of different methods, thus helping the reader to reach a sensible conclusion about the best course of action in their own particular study system.

The book is primarily aimed at those who need to measure and assess biological diversity. We have in mind upper-level undergraduates engaged in research projects, graduate students, and postdoctoral researchers, as well as environmental managers and conservation biologists. Although not designed as a theoretical ecology text, we nonetheless hope that the issues raised in the book will spark the interest of modellers and theoreticians. In each chapter the author(s) describe the state of the field, discuss recommendations and future directions, and end with key points.

The book begins with an overview of the basic measurement issues involved in biodiversity studies. As Scott Bonar, Jeffrey Fehmi, and Norman Mercado-Silva make plain, survey design and methodology play a crucial role in the success—or otherwise—of biodiversity investigations. These are well-known concerns, although they often get much less attention than they deserve; Chapter 2 sets out the points that must be addressed before an investigation can even begin. In contrast Stephen Buckland, Angelika Studeny, Anne Magurran, and Stuart Newson highlight a problem that is potentially of great importance but one that has, until now, been almost entirely overlooked. Most diversity statistics proceed on the assumption that individuals and species have been collected at random from the community of interest and most investigators use these statistics irrespective of whether this assumption is fulfilled. In practice individuals and species often vary considerably in how easy they are to detect. Buckland et al. show how detectability can affect the conclusions drawn from diversity statistics, and provide advice on how to deal with the issues raised, although it is clear that assessing individual and species variation in detectability is easier for some taxa than for others.

The next section deals with the approaches that are sometimes described as measures of 'species diversity'. Although the term 'biodiversity' can mean many things, and is sometimes used in a generic way (EASAC 2009), most scientists, managers, and policy makers identify species richness as a central component. In many ways species richness—the number of species in a given locality or assemblage—is the iconic measure of biological diversity. It is used to identify biodiversity hotspots and plays an important role in conservation planning. Species richness also accords well with our intuitive sense of biological diversity. However, despite its wide appeal and apparent simplicity, accurate estimates of species richness can be remarkably difficult to achieve. This is not just at the global level, where it is still unclear, to within at least an order of magnitude, how many species inhabit the planet, but also at local levels and even for taxonomically well-characterized organisms. The reason for this difficulty lies in the observations of Darwin and Audobon—because most species are rare, an increase in sampling effort will almost always lead to an increase in richness. Fortunately there has been intense interest in recent years in providing solutions to this problem; Nicholas Gotelli and Robert Colwell provide a clear account of the approaches that can be used to make fair comparisons amongst sites where sampling effort differs (which can happen even if the investigator thinks that it is the same) and examine the new generation of non-parametric estimators that can be used to deduce the minimum number of species present in an assemblage.

Although species richness is widely used as a measure of biological diversity, investigators often want to find a means of quantifying Darwin's 'proportional numbers and kinds' in a single statistic. As noted at the beginning of this chapter all communities consist of species that vary in their abundance. However, communities (or localities) can also differ from one another in terms of their proportions of species, that is, in how 'even' their species abundance distributions are. The degree of evenness can shed light on the processes that shape a community's structure or provide a gauge of the impacts on it. There are a swathe of measures that populate the ground between species richness and evenness. These include familiar choices such as the Shannon, Simpson, and Margalef indexes and a host of less well-known ones. Brian Maurer and Brian McGill explore this territory in Chapter 5 and provides guidance on the use of diversity statistics.

Researchers may also want to go beyond an assessment of the diversity of a single site to say something about the larger picture. This might involve drawing conclusions about the distribution of biological diversity amongst a series of communities or examining sifts in diversity across a gradient. Whittaker (1960) first made the distinction between α diversity—the diversity of a site or habitat—and β diversity—the difference in compositional diversity between two or more sites. α and β diversity combine to give γ diversity—the diversity of the landscape. Until recently measures of compositional similarity and β diversity received less attention than methods of assessing α diversity. There has, however, been a marked increase of interest in this topic during the last decade and in Chapter 6 Lou Jost, Anne Chao, and Robin Chazdon provide an overview of this rapidly developing field.

The idea that the number of species recorded increases if a site is surveyed over an extended period has deep roots in ecology and was first formalized by Preston. who argued that species area and species time curves are equivalent. The urgent need—highlighted by the UN's IYB—to quantify changes in ecological communities and to determine whether the rate of biodiversity loss is accelerating or slowing has led to a flurry of research in this field. Anne Magurran reviews methods of evaluating temporal turnover in Chapter 7, but argues that there is still much to be learnt about baseline changes in ecological communities.

A single index of biodiversity limits the amount of information that can be conveyed. An alternative is to examine the structure of a community in terms of its species abundance distribution or spatial patterning in more detail. This is the subject matter of the next section of the book. In Chapter 8 Anne Magurran and Peter Henderson explore the ecological context of commonness and rarity, and discuss methods that can be used to identify and track common and rare species. A species abundance distribution is the formal description of the abundance of the recorded species in a community, as well as a tool that is widely used to compare communities and to test hypotheses about community structure (McGill et al. 2007). Brian McGill examines species abundance distributions in detail in Chapter 9. After summarizing current methods of studying species abundance distributions, he suggests a new way to visually display species abundance distributions that does not suffer from some of the limitations of earlier graphical methods. He also presents a detailed analysis of which quantitative measures behave well under small sample sizes and which measures are truly independent of each other. Based on this he offers some guidelines on which measures to use under several scenarios. One of the main challenges with regard to species abundance distributions is how best to fit them. In Chapter 10 Sean Connolly and Maria Dornelas critically evaluate different approaches for fitting species abundance models to data and examine methods of quantifying goodness of fit. As they conclude, model selection statistics are a promising development and have advantages over traditional approaches such as graphical inspection and comparative analyses of goodness-of-fit statistics.

Whereas some ecologists focus on the distributions of species abundances others are concerned with the spatial placement of species. As Kevin Gaston and Fangliang He argue in Chapter 11, one of the most fundamental units of biodiversity is the presence or absence of a species in a given site, such as habitat patch, an island, or a grid square on a map. They show that simple species × sites ($r \times c$) matrices, in which the presence/absence of different species (in rows r) is given for a set of different sites (in columns c), lie at the heart of many biodiversity studies and are linked to patterns such as species–area relationships, nestedness, and gradients in β diversity. Gaston and He explore occupancy–area relationships, occupancy–abundance relationships, and species–occupancy distributions, and note that a key challenge is to estimate species abundance from occupancy. Brian McGill develops the spatial perspective in Chapter 12 by examining the implications of the spatial structure of biodiversity for management and conservation. New developments in spatial statistics are explored and applied to questions such as 'is there variation in abundance across space?' and 'are there interactions across space?'. The analysis of spatial structure is an example of an area of biodiversity in which new analytical techniques are proving particularly important.

Historically most investigators have used species (or in some cases morphospecies) as their biodiversity currency. However, some ecologists, for example Pielou (1975), were ahead of their time in recognizing that it is possible to increase the information content of biodiversity assessment by including taxonomic or phylogenetic information. This view has been reinforced by growing awareness of the need to conserve biodiversity function and by rapid advances in methodology. Recent developments in this field are discussed in the next section of the book, on alternative measures of diversity. The section begins with a contribution by Evan Weiher on trait diversity. He argues in Chapter 13 that there are four conceptual aspects to trait diversity: the occupation of trait space, functional evenness, functional divergence, and the density of species packing. A rapidly growing set of indices is available and guidance is provided on the choices. As always the approach will depend on one's goal. For example, a multivariate method may be most appropriate if the goal is to assess the amount of trait diversity in a community.

Phylogenetic diversity is another area in which large numbers of metrics are being developed. Much of the impetus behind this rapid expansion is the growing awareness that these measures have an important role to play in both conservation biology and community ecology. Mark Vellend, William Cornwell, Karen Magnuson-Ford, and Arne Mooers provide a conceptual overview of phylogenetic diversity in Chapter 14 and report the results of simulation analyses that examine artificial communities constructed using a range of assumptions about phylogeny structure and assemblage composition. Vellend and coauthors also explore the qualitative and quantitative relationships among metrics and advise on choosing metrics for different purposes. They point out, for instance, that the sensitivity of phylogenetic diversity metrics depends to a large extent on the shape of the phylogenetic tree. Improved phylogenetic information is, of course, underpinned by the revolution in molecular ecology. This means that rather than counting species—or even evaluating traits and phylogenies—investigators can now directly evaluate the diversity of genes. Melanie Culver, Robert Fitak, and Hans-Werner Herrmann discuss these opportunities in Chapter 15. As they point out, genetic diversity can be measured using a variety of molecular genetic markers, each with a different evolutionary rate. Markers have different resolving power, so the choice of marker will depend on the biodiversity question, and the level of resolution needed to address that.

As will already be clear, the methods presented in this book are relevant to a wide range of theoretical and applied questions. The final section, on applications, presents a set of topics and case studies in which diversity measurement and assessment plays a fundamental role. Lise Øvreås and Thomas Curtis argue in Chapter 16 that microbial diversity is the outermost frontier in the exploration of diversity. They note that the traditional species concept is useless in microbial ecology and focus instead on evolutionary relationships inferred from changes in molecules, primarily rRNA. Øvreås and Curtis note the importance of sampling and look ahead to the advent of novel massive parallel sequencing as a means of providing a comprehensive examination of microbial communities. Although advances in microbial ecology are driven by technology, the assessment of microbial diversity is also dependent on statistical techniques, such as the non-parametric richness estimators devised by Anne Chao.

Chapter 17 turns to another problem of considerable contemporary concern, that is disturbance and its impact on ecosystems. Maria Dornelas, Candan Soykan, and Karl Inne Ugland examine the use of biodiversity metrics to measure the effects of disturbance and observe that the sheer number of methods available can make it difficult to select an appropriate measure. This difficulty is heightened by the lack of rigorous comparative studies exploring the merits of the different approaches. They argue that the most appropriate method will vary from case to case depending on the nature of the disturbance but recommend several options, including the use of multiple metrics. The empirical cumulative distribution function is one new method that appears to have considerable merit. Traits-based metrics are also potentially valuable. Dornelas et al. conclude by emphasizing that more theoretical work is needed to understand the effects of disturbances on biodiversity metrics other than species richness.

There are few landscapes in the world have not been modified by humans. Steven Chown and Melodie McGeoch ask, in Chapter 18, how the goals of biodiversity measurement are shaped by this transformation. Biodiversity assessments of modified landscapes such as agroecosystems draw on the techniques discussed in this book and, as elsewhere, the approach adopted in any particular case will depend on the question being posed. However, it may be informative to explicitly address management issues, for example when assessing the biodiversity of a landscape that is a tapestry of modified habitats such as hedgerows and monocultures, or contains fields under a variety of agricultural systems, for example conventional and organic farming. In another context, conservation managers often seek to reduce impacts and reverse transformation. Chown and McGeoch argue that $r \times c$ matrices are a very useful addition to the toolkit of methods used to assess transformed landscapes as they make it possible to explore patterns across different levels of biodiversity, such as genes, traits, and species.

Quantifying the loss of biodiversity is a task that increasingly preoccupies ecologists and conservation biologists. It is also a central goal in palaeontology and investigators who test ideas about extinction in the context of the fossil record use methods that are similar to those employed by conservation biologists. In Chapter 19 Peter Wagner and Kathleen Lyons review current palaeobiological methods for inferring extinction patterns. These extend from 'traditional' methods that use information in stratigraphic ranges to approaches that exploit exact information about distributions of finds within stratigraphic ranges. As Wagner and Lyons show, the fossil record provides data that can be used to test a wide variety of extinction hypotheses.

Michael Rosenzweig has been influential in shaping views about species area and species time curves (Rosenzweig 1995). In Chapter 20 he is joined by John Donoghue, Yue Max Li, and Chi

Yuan in an examination of species density, particularly its use in assessing and comparing sites in a management or conservation context. The attraction of species density in such evaluations is clear. Although, as we have emphasized above, there is no single measure of biodiversity that serves all needs, many practitioners desire a few informative and intuitive metrics, ideally ones that appeal to politicians and policy makers. Species density is an obvious candidate but has a significant drawback in that it does not scale linearly with area. Rosenzweig and colleagues develop estimates of species density that take the curvature of species–area curves into account and highlight its value as a useful indicator of environmental condition.

Our conclusion, in Chapter 21, says that the measurement of biodiversity is growing (and will continue to grow) increasingly more sophisticated. This is to be welcomed as it allows for more nuanced discussions and more refined measures appropriate to specific questions. At the same time, the healthy growth of a tree requires regular pruning. Measurement of biodiversity is no different. Ecologists need to put as much energy into removing unsuccessful measures as we do into developing new measures. Finally, the increasingly complex ability of scientists to measure the multifaceted idea of biodiversity should not be allowed to distract from the societal and policy goals of conserving biodiversity. There is a real concept and relatively simple measures get us close enough to allow policy decisions and assessments to occur.

This book covers a wide range of approaches and reflects the activity and excitement at the frontiers of biodiversity measurement and assessment. We are conscious that there are aspects of biodiversity measurement that we have not dealt with or have mentioned only briefly. These include issues such as population trends, the extent of habitats, the status of protected areas, the fate of threatened or invasive species, surrogate measures (for instance those based on remote sensing), and matters related to ecosystem services such as wild harvests. A single book could not do justice to all this material, and interested readers will find that there is a growing literature that tackles it. However, we stress that the fundamental issues that underpin many of these alternative and broader measures are addressed in the book. For example, a composite indicator or headline index is only as good as the estimates of species richness or species density subsumed within it, and sampling and detectablity issues need to be addressed in every study before robust conclusions can be drawn. As explained at the outset our emphasis in this book is on Darwin's 'proportional numbers and kinds' and we hope that it will prove a useful guide to measuring and assessing this 'beautiful diversity'.

Acknowledgements

We are indebted to our contributors, to Bob May for writing the Foreword, and to Ian Sherman and Helen Eaton for overseeing the publication of the book. In addition we are most grateful to Amy Deacon for drawing the hummingbird vignettes, and to Nichole Engelmann and Malissa Hubbard for compiling the index. We also thank the National Center for Ecological Analysis and Synthesis (NCEAS) for funding a workshop on species abundance distributions that allowed us to first meet, to meet many of the contributors to this book, and to start many discussions on measuring biodiversity. Anne Magurran wishes to thank the University of St Andrews and the Royal Society of Edinburgh. Brian McGill thanks the University of Arizona, School of Natural Resources and the Environment, and his colleagues there.

PART I

Basic Measurement Issues

CHAPTER 2

An overview of sampling issues in species diversity and abundance surveys

Scott A. Bonar, Jeffrey S. Fehmi, and Norman Mercado-Silva

2.1 Introduction

Homer S. Swingle was a pioneer in pond management and professor of fisheries at Auburn University. Results from his scientific research on the principles of fish interactions in lakes and ponds, and methods to improve fish production are used worldwide, and he is credited with improving lives of countless people by increasing the amount of food available to those in developing countries and providing recreational opportunities to a multitude of anglers. His advice was sought by US presidents, prime ministers, the United Nations and countries across the globe (Byrd 1973).

His biological work was groundbreaking, yet there is little evidence that Homer Swingle used sampling procedures when conducting his work. His major works contain no reports of sampling error with his estimates (Swingle 1950, 1952) and his contemporaries have pointed out that he actively avoided subsampling in favor of census. His methods for enumerating a population were simple. At the conclusion of his pond experiments, he would census every fish involved, either by draining or treating the pond with piscicide (fish poison). Being a student on Swingle's piscicide crew meant counting *every* dead fish as it floated to the water's surface in the hot Alabama sun over a 3-day period. Those involved in the third-day pickup were the unluckiest, and often the least senior members of the crew—a smelly task indeed!

While a complete census of all experimental or survey subjects provides the most complete information, few of us have the luxury of counting every

subject in a population to estimate population characteristics. It simply costs too much, takes too much time, or is infeasible in some other way. Therefore we have to sample a portion of the population to estimate diversity or population parameters such as abundance. For example, a marine biologist estimating the number of clams in the Gulf of California cannot hope to count every one—he will expand an estimate calculated from a sample of plots. A plant biologist measuring the biomass of grasses in a field will not weigh every grass blade in the field—she will estimate the biomass through a sample of plots containing grass. A wildlife biologist will not count all mice in a national park to determine relative density of different species. Density will be determined by a subset of captures from different areas.

To ensure the most useful information, a biologist must be familiar with basic sampling issues. Here we discuss some issues that all biologists should know when sampling diversity, abundance, or other parameters. Consideration of these issues allows the biologist to sample in a manner that, while not a perfect reflection of the population, will provide the best representation of the true population as possible.

2.2 State of the field

Successful sampling of plant and animal communities address similar basic issues. In the following sections we discuss considerations that every sampler should understand before beginning a survey.

2.2.1   Setting objectives

Critical to any good survey are clear objectives. These objectives should answer the fundamental questions for the survey. What is needed from the survey? How will the survey data be used? If the sampling design or methodology becomes confusing and complicated, returning to the objectives of the survey can help clarify what needs to be done. Deviating from the objectives of the survey may make the information obtained from sampling much less valuable for answering the original questions.

Explicit objectives can improve the study design. A poorly worded objective for a survey might be: 'Estimate the effect of outflow from the Brandon Chemical Plant on freshwater clams.' More precise would be: 'Estimate the effect of outflow from the Brandon Chemical Plant on abundance, growth, and species diversity of freshwater clams.' Wording objectives as specifically as possible will allow biologists to design a survey that will meet those objectives.

Objectives that drive plant and animal sampling efforts include estimating conservation status, the potential effect of human action or inaction on communities, or, perhaps the most common, comparing a trend in a site over time to adapt management.

There are several other considerations when sampling diversity or abundance which help to define study objectives more clearly.

2.2.2   An important partner: the statistician

Just as a business executive needs the services of a good lawyer and a good accountant, a biologist needs a good statistician. Go to any academic library and scores of books on sampling techniques are available. Which methods should be used to design a survey? Any biologist should have some background of sampling techniques, which may suffice for simple surveys. However, consultation with a good statistician can dramatically improve the sampling design. Finding a good statistician is like finding a good mechanic. The best ones are incredibly busy, and the biologist will probably need persistence to encourage their involvement in a study. However, they can make the difference between a failed study and a study that can provide the most information for the lowest price. Which are the best statisticians for the biologist? They tend to be those who have on-the-ground, practical experience with biological studies in addition to a solid statistical background. One talented statistician at a Pacific Northwestern University in the USA had a solid knowledge of his subject, and had also been a commercial salmon fisherman and an active participant in field projects. The biologist could be assured that this individual would help to design a study that met the statistical requirements, but was also practical and logistically possible.

2.2.3   What species to sample

When sampling plant or animal diversity or abundance, a decision must be made as to which species to sample. At a recent meeting of the Ecological Society of America, Pulitzer Prize winning ecologist E.O. Wilson stated that a person could conceivably spend their entire life studying the species found associated with one tree stump. There are literally thousands of species, from bacteria to mammals, that make their home there—a staggering level of diversity. Practically, there are many species in any given area, so which do biologists sample?

Study objectives can help to identify the species that should be studied and the methods required to study them. Typically there is more interest in some species than others. For example, in plants, sampling may be structured around plants associated with the abundance of food and habitat of an important wildlife species, invasive plants that impact desired plants, or rare plant species of special conservation concern. Plants with neutral or little impact on the survey objectives tend to be discounted. For animals, species of special conservation concern can also be overall drivers of the study, such as those on threatened and endangered species lists. Other species might be indicators of ecological conditions such as the presence of Plecoptera (stonefly) or Chironomidae (chironomid) larvae in streams of varying water-quality conditions. Still others might be important species that drive a community, such as the most abundant picivorous (fish-eating) and insectivorous (insect-eating) fish of a lake community that make up most of the biomass.

Not only species must be considered when sampling, but life stages and size as well. For plants, larger perennial plants are much more likely to be detected than smaller ephemeral plants. (Plant scale differences can be dealt with by changing the plot size as discussed later) (see also Chapter 3). For animals, one must cover all the areas where the different life stages of a given animal (in the case of abundance estimations) or all species (in the case of the estimation of diversity) might be. This may require the use of different sampling methodologies for each stage or require that sampling efforts be carried out in different seasons or at different times of the day. For example, to detect the presence of *Salvelinus confluentus* (bull trout) in Pacific Northwest streams, juveniles are most often sampled near the substrate at night because this is when they are most commonly seen (Bonar et al. 1997). The sampling design and methods for animals with large habitats (or ranges) will necessarily be different from those of sessile animals or animals with very low motility. The size of the species of interest can affect the sampling. It will take a much larger plot to sample a grove of *Sequoiadendron giganteum* (sequoias) than *Bromus tectorum* (cheatgrass).

2.2.4 Where to sample

Where should a biologist sample if he or she wants to know something about an underlying community or population? At first glance, this sounds like a simple question, but it can be complex. Below are tips to help the biologist select from where the sample should be taken.

The *target population* is the population or ecological resource of interest. For example, the target population might be all sea urchins in the waters off San Juan Island, Washington, mule deer on the Kaibab Plateau, or plant communities of the northeast Siberian coastal tundra. The *sampling frame* is the physical representation of the target population. It represents what or where the samples are taken from to characterize the target population. For the above examples the sampling frame might be the littoral zones of the San Juan Island from the shore to 20 m deep at high tide, the Kaibab Plateau, or the

montane and lowland tundra distributed between the Laptev and Chukote Seas, respectively.

For best results, the sampling frame should mirror or represent the target population as closely as possible. For example, say the biologist's objective was to estimate the proportion that each aquatic macrophyte (vascular plant) species contributed to the total macrophyte biomass in Lake Taupo, New Zealand. Because most macrophytes will be found in depths of less than 15 m, a sampling frame consisting of the littoral zone up to a depth of 15 m should adequately bracket the community. However, if the sampling frame consisted only of sampling sites less than 1 m deep, it would not adequately encompass the target population of macrophytes. Sampling in waters less than 1 m deep would potentially overestimate the proportion of shallow water emergent plant species biomass in the entire community and would not meet the research objective.

Sometimes the sampling frame is obvious. The area bounds are established along jurisdictional or management boundaries as specified by the project funding (e.g. Saguaro National Park, Posey County, Indiana, the island of Barbados, or the site of the new subdivision). In some situations defining the sampling frame can be challenging. Perhaps an estimate of *Cancer magister* (Dungeness crab) density is needed for the Pacific Ocean off Washington State, USA. Three boundaries of the sample frame are easy to determine: the frame is bounded on the south at the Columbia River at the Oregon border, at the north at the middle of the Strait of Juan de Fuca on the Canadian boundary, and at the east by the waterline of the Washington coast. However, defining the western limit of the sampling frame, how far offshore to sample, is less clear. *Cancer magister* are not found in the deepest abyss, but become less dense in progressively deeper water. It would make no more sense to sample *C. magister* in a deep ocean trench than selecting sites containing no people (such as a wilderness area) when surveying human population characteristics. Using the biological characteristics of the *C. magister* (it is rarely found in water deeper than 180 m) one can set an outer depth limit to the sampling frame.

The sampling frame may be restricted to where sampling gear can be used effectively, even though the organism may be found outside the frame. For example, a common method to sample freshwater fish in lakes is electrofishing, but electrofishing cannot generally be used to capture fish in water deeper than about 3 m. The sampling frame for electrofishing sites in lakes would include segments along shorelines up to 3 m deep, not transects in deep offshore areas where there would be little chance of catching fish by this method. Often the samples taken from such a frame may not reflect the entire community diversity or abundance, but can provide an important index for trends or similar work.

Because the sampling frame can vary among studies, the frame must be defined and reported in any report or publication. This is especially important if other biologists are not familiar with the type of survey and cannot assume its sampling frame.

2.2.5 Bias, sampling error, and precision

A biologist known by one of the authors wasted 2 years of his working life and 4 years of a study, costing his project sponsors thousands of dollars, because he did not know the fundamentals of sampling procedure. The biologist was tasked with studying how littoral (shallow water) fish populations changed following reduction in aquatic plant communities. He was to record the abundance of various fish species in the littoral zone for 2 years before the plants were removed and 2 years following. The 2 years of samples prior to plant removal had already been collected by others using springtime electrofishing. The biologist had other tasks in the spring, so he decided to collect his electrofishing samples in the autumn. Unfortunately, unknown to the biologist, this was a fatal flaw for his study. Different species and sizes of fish use the littoral zones of lakes in the spring and in the autumn. The sampling conducted pre treatment in the spring could not be compared to the sampling conducted by the biologist post treatment in the autumn because the effects of plant control could not be separated from the effects of seasonal differences in fish use of the littoral zone. The biologist failed to consider bias. Bias, and also the concepts of precision, sampling error, and accuracy should be known by all who collect samples.

The terms sampling bias, precision, sampling error and accuracy are all related to the fundamental question in survey design: 'How well does the sample estimate parameters of the target population?' *Accuracy* is the closeness of agreement between an observed value and an accepted reference value (Locke 1994) and is a function of how much *bias* and *sampling error* is in the sample. Bias and sampling error are often confused, but they are different.

A sample is biased when, to some degree, it does not represent the population from which it was taken. Bias can be subdivided into measurement bias and sampling bias. *Measurement bias* occurs when measurements are taken incorrectly. Perhaps the biologist was sampling lizards and did not set traps correctly, so the abundance of lizards was underestimated. Perhaps a poorly trained crew recorded birds seen in only a portion of the area of interest, biasing the study towards those birds found only in that portion. Perhaps a fish-measuring board started at 5 mm instead of 0 mm, so all fish lengths were overestimated. These are examples of measurement bias, which can be reduced by careful crew training and ensuring sampling equipment is properly calibrated and working correctly. *Sampling bias* occurs when the sample does not include all groups of interest in the population. Stated in another way, this means that a sampling method does not capture all organisms equally. Every sampling method has inherent sampling biases that can affect estimations of animal diversity and abundance (Willis & Murphy 1996; Krebs 1999; Southwood & Henderson 2000)

Sampling or method-specific biases need to be understood to adequately estimate the accuracy of animal diversity and abundance values. Sampling can be biased by organism size. A net used in estimations of fish diversity or abundance, for example, can have a mesh size that very small fishes can escape through, therefore the net is said to be biased towards larger fish, that is it captures larger fish in a disproportionately greater amount than they occur in the population as a whole, so the mean fish length of the sample will be greater than that of the population. Other methods or a smaller mesh size may be effective for capturing smaller fish, but they will have their own limitations (Lyons 1986; Mercado-Silva & Escandon-Sandoval 2008; Rabeni et al. 2009). Sampling can also be biased towards particular species. A trawl might capture smelt effectively because of their schooling behaviour in the water column, but *Micropterus salmoides* (largemouth bass), which are associated with the lake bottom and structure, may be harder to capture, therefore the gear is biased for smelt. Depending on the species, the differing amounts of bias present can be difficult or impossible to measure, and present particular problems when evaluating diversity using species proportions (e.g. Shannon or Simpson's index). Those species which are easier to capture can be overrepresented in the indices (see further discussion of this point in Chapter 3).

Size and species bias are also present in plant sampling, as each sampling method is typically better at detecting some groups of plants than others. In most instances, larger and more persistent plants are much more likely to be detected than smaller, more ephemeral, or juvenile plants. Juvenile plants of species judged important can be especially problematic in that they can be difficult to detect compared to adults because all plants are small early in their lifecycle. Plant scale differences can be dealt with by changing the plot size, as will be discussed later.

Bias can make comparisons with the true population difficult, but there are some ways to account for bias in a study. Ensuring crews are properly trained and biologists are familiar with the amount of bias that may occur using a particular sampling gear aids in the evaluation of the importance of bias in surveys.

If bias is the same over time (trend surveys) or space (for status surveys) the sample data can be used for comparison or to follow trends. A trawl net could be used to monitor fish population trends in a lake over time, under similar conditions, with the understanding that fewer small fish would be captured than larger fish in each sample, but abundance of all might increase or decrease over time. However, if a biologist uses a gill net one month to catch fish and the next month uses electrofishing for trend monitoring, the bias would be different for the two gear types and the samples could not be compared. The biologist would not know if trends in the data were due to the actual changes in the population or just differing gear bias. Similarly, if trawling was conducted in very different habitats, or in different seasons of the year when fish behaviour varied, the biologist would not know if differences in capture rates were due to how well the trawl fished in the different habitats or time periods, or in the actual numbers of fish present. This is the error the biologist made in the example above. The bias of the electrofishing surveys was not the same in the spring as in the autumn in the lake in question.

If the objective is to capture a diverse sample, a combination of methods should be used to cancel out the bias of the different sampling gears as much as possible. This should be tried to collect a wide range of (1) species with different habitat use, (2) species with different behaviour, and (3) different life stages of a given species with a specific size and ethology. The sampling methods selected should cover all possible niches that exist in an ecosystem. Lethal methods such as the application of poison or explosives in fish studies, although they are destructive, may in some cases be the only alternatives to fully sample a community. Still, even these may fail at capturing certain elements of the community (e.g. fish eggs resistant to poison effects, individual fish that die but cannot be captured).

Perhaps the best methods to correct for sampling bias involve double sampling while surveying or conducting preliminary studies that calibrate gear, that is evaluating sampling gear *efficiency* for the studied species under a wide variety of conditions (Peterson & Paukert 2009; Chapter 3). In double sampling a randomly selected subset of samples from the overall survey are sampled twice: once using the sampling method and then using an unbiased population estimator, such capture–recapture for species richness or abundance (Williams et al. 2002) or an occupancy estimator for species detection (MacKenzie et al. 2002). The 'true' population estimates are then regressed against the samples and correction factors are developed for samples in the survey that were not double-sampled (Box 2.1). Gear efficiency studies are more labour intensive than double sampling as they use abundance

Box 2.1 An example of correcting for bias and estimating precision

Microwterus dolomieu (smallmouth bass) are collected using backpack electrofishing at 50 block-netted sites to estimate their mean abundance in a stream. To correct for sampling bias, a randomly selected subset of 15 sites is selected for double sampling. In each of the double-sample sites, *M. dolomieu* catch per unit effort (CPUE) and an unbiased population estimator (capture–recapture estimate) of abundance are determined. Next the abundance estimate is regressed against CPUE to calculate a correction for all samples.

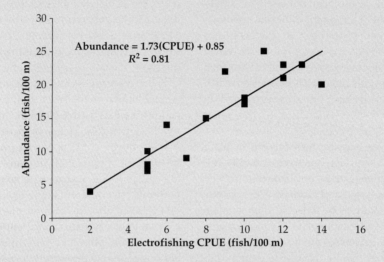

All 50 samples are then converted from CPUE to estimated abundance using the regression equation developed above. How precise is the mean abundance of *M. dolomieu* in this stream? The mean abundance and associated standard deviation of the 50 converted samples can be calculated using formulas from any standard statistics text or computer software. Notice that there is still variability that was not captured during the conversion of CPUE to estimated abundance. More variability could have been accounted for by developing a more labour-intensive gear calibration model, accounting for the effects of habitat complexity and other factors.

estimates obtained through capture–recapture or removal methods (which can have bias associated with them as well) to calculate the efficiency of the gear in a separate study before the survey. Gear efficiency depends on species-specific attributes such as capture avoidance, size, patterns of aggregation, and habitat complexity. Gear efficiency studies help to determine the true rarity of a given species, as some sampling methodologies, being relatively inefficient at capturing a certain species, may give the false idea that a species is less abundant than it actually is (Lyons 1986; Bayley & Herendeen 2000; Longino et al. 2002; Chapter 3). If gear efficiency is not calculated, sometimes a lower threshold of gear efficiency can be used, which is based on pilot surveys or the literature. Bonar et al. (1997) assumed a lower threshold of 25% snorkelling efficiency for encountering the *Salvelinus confluentus* (bull trout) that were present in Pacific Northwest streams. This was used in the calculation of sample sizes needed to detect *S. confluentus* if they occurred in actual densities of less than 0.15 fish/100 m of stream. Even if no correction is used for bias, it is important to understand the limits of sampling methods being used and create correction factors between sampling methods. These could be used to calculate method bias that should be accounted for in data interpretation.

Sampling error is the inverse of the amount of *precision* in an estimate. Unlike sampling bias, sampling error is easily measured, quantified, and reported as *variability, standard deviation, standard error* or some other measure of dispersion. For example, an estimate is needed of fish density in a lake. A trawl net that samples a specific volume of water is used to catch the fish. Fish are spread evenly throughout the lake, and on six sequential trawls 5, 6, 4, 5, 6, and 3 fish are captured, respectively. The average or mean number of fish per trawl sample is 4.8. Here the biologist may have a lot of confidence that the true mean of the fish population available to trawling (excluding any bias) is close to 4.8. Sampling error is low (0.48) and the sample is precise. If the fish are distributed in clumped groups throughout the lake, the six sequential trawls may capture 2, 11, 0, 14, 0, and 2 individuals, respectively. There is more 'spread' or experimental error in the later estimate (with an error of 2.48) and the average (4.8 fish/trawl) calculated from this estimate is less precise. The biologist is less confident that this average represents the actual population mean, again assuming there is no bias.

One way to illustrate precision and bias is by reference to targets (Fig. 2.1). The bull's eye of the target is the true population parameter. For the first target on the left, a tight cluster of samples to the right of the bull's eye is precise (the samples are tightly clustered) and biased (the samples are not centred on the target but are off to the side). A loose cluster of samples to the right (second target) is imprecise and biased. A loose cluster of samples in the middle is imprecise and unbiased (third target). A tight cluster of samples in the centre of the target is precise and unbiased (fourth target).

Now we know our objectives, what species we will sample, where we will sample, and some of the factors that can affect sampling surveys, such as bias and precision, we will discuss how to sample and how much to sample.

2.2.6 How to sample

Nets, plots, traps, bird-calling surveys, dredge samples: what can be used to quantify the animal or plant population? Below we discuss important

considerations about selecting gear types or plots when sampling. Often previous studies or reference books of sampling techniques (e.g. Bonar et al. 2009b) can be used to choose an appropriate method for sampling the species of interest.

The minimum size unit in sampling is called a *sampling unit*. For animal surveys, the sampling unit could be a location for a pit-fall trap set, a transect for sighting birds, or a shoreline length where all frogs are captured. For plants, the sampling unit is often a plot. A subset of sampling units is drawn from the sampling frame in a way to ensure the subset represents the area of interest. Units to be sampled within a sampling frame are usually chosen *randomly*, which means that every sampling unit has an equal chance of being selected. They can also be assigned *systematically*, which means using a random starting point and taking a sample at every *n*th unit. Some type of random allocation of sampling units is almost always preferred, but systematic sampling can be equivalent to random sampling if the ordering of the individuals is independent of the attribute being measured. Descriptions of various commonly used sampling designs, such as simple random sampling, stratified random sampling, systematic sampling, adaptive sampling, and cluster sampling, are provided in sampling texts (Cochran 1977; Williams et al. 2002; Thompson 2004; Scheaffer et al. 2006; Bonar et al. 2009b).

Researchers must be careful to adopt sampling methodologies that will minimize the effects on individuals, populations, and habitat. The humorist Don Novello wrote a comic letter to NASA, which was testing for life on Mars in the mid-1970s by burning a small sample of Martian soil and testing for carbon residue. Novello wrote 'That doesn't mean there *is* life on Mars—that means there *was* life on Mars—You killed it!' In the past, it was common to sample animal populations using destructive techniques. For example, toxicants were widely used to sample fish communities in a variety of ecosystems. Today these methodologies are often discouraged, although they are still in use for a variety of management purposes (Bettoli & Maceina 1996). Techniques that destroy habitats (e.g. bottom trawling for fishes or marcoinvertebrates [Freese et al. 1999]), change animal behaviour, or hurt

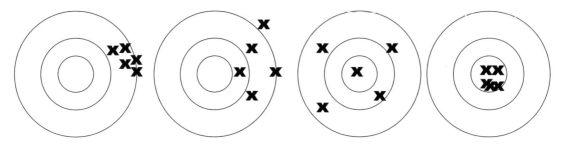

Figure 2.1 Depiction of bias and precision, with centre of target representing true population value. Far left figure shows sample that is biased and precise, sample on second target is biased and imprecise; sample on third target is unbiased and imprecise; sample of far right target is unbiased and precise.

animals (i.e. gill nets [Murphy & Willis 1996]) should also be carefully considered before using. When possible, observation and other sampling techniques that do not involve the taking of individuals may be good options to estimate the diversity and abundance of certain species, especially those easy to identify. However, sometimes it is necessary to take a small number of individuals to provide data to protect the population as a whole.

Pilot surveys are small studies carried out before the initial survey, and are an indispensable component of most surveys. They can be used to help identify the species present, the scale at which organisms occur, and the heterogeneity of populations for sample variance estimates in sample size calculations. For example, in *S. confluentus* surveys, Bonar et al. (1997) recommend that an informal snorkelling survey is used to document presence before extensive time and resources are spent designing an expensive statistically intense study for the reach. Bonar et al. (1993) used pilot surveys to calculate the sample size needed to adequately estimate biomass of aquatic macrophytes.

For animals, motility is perhaps the most important factor that determines which sampling method to use. Sessile or low-mobility animals are usually detectable by a variety of active sampling methodologies and cannot easily evade detection. Although it is clearly possible to capture mobile animals using active methodologies, animals with moderate to high mobility can, and often will, attempt to evade being captured by active methods. Passive methods (e.g. attractants, traps), observation (e.g. direct observation, distance sampling),

or techniques based on animal signs (e.g. food remains, tracks, scats) are often better suited to mobile animals. See Bonar et al. (2009b), Murphy and Willis (1996), and Krausman (2002) for various techniques to sample fish and wildlife populations. Other references such as Hauer and Resh (2006), and Sørensen et al. (2002) discuss sampling invertebrate populations.

For plants, plots are usually the unit sampled, and the biologists must choose a plot shape and plot size. Square, rectangular, and circular plots, and transects (a one-dimensional rectangle (Pueyo et al. 2006)) have all been used to sample diversity. Squares and rectangles can be the easiest to delineate in the field because strings or tapes can be stretched between the corner points. Narrow rectangular plots are often recommended because they can capture more patchiness within each plot, although this will depend on the elongation of the plot and the homogeneity of the site. Circular plots for surveying plants can be difficult to set up in areas with trees and shrubs because plots are usually marked by attaching a string to the plot centre and moving it around in a circle. The movement of the string radius is obstructed by plants above the surveyor's height. Larger plots capture more different landscape elements and plant associations, but lose fine detail. This can be corrected by measuring small and large plants at different scales using nested plot designs (Fig. 2.2), including the Whittaker plot (Shimida 1984) or the modified Whittaker plot (Stohlgren 2007). More methods on determining the appropriate size of the plot will be discussed in the section on how many samples to collect below. See Stohlgren (2007), Bonham (1989),

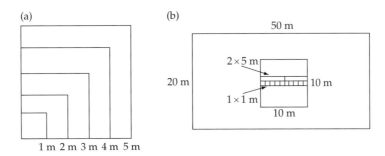

Figure 2.2 Two common nested plot designs. (a) A simple geometric progression of plot sizes typical of a pilot study. (b) A Whittaker plot (Shimida 1984), which is commonly used as well as numerous published modifications (Stohlgren 2007).

and Elzinga et al. (1998) for various techniques used to sample plants.

Detecting rare or elusive species sometimes requires specialized sampling designs (Thompson 2004). For plants that are rare because they are concentrated in a small part of the area of interest (a clump or cluster), use two-stage sampling (e.g. Elzinga et al. 1998). In two-stage sampling, the plot is searched by walking, driving, or remote sensing until the clump of rare plants is discovered, and then the clump is subsampled. Adaptive sampling for plants and animals is similar (e.g. Smith et al. 2004). Here biologists search for a species of interest at predetermined locations and if the species is found, they sample nearby. To search for rare plants, Poon and Margules (2004) recommend stratifying a region of interest using environmental variables and then noting in which strata populations of rare species are known. New searches are then concentrated in similar environments in the same general location or in other geographical areas.

2.2.7   Quantifying the sample

When a sample is taken, what will the biologist measure to quantify abundance and diversity? A measure of abundance is important because diversity is not the same as species richness and depends on the relative commonness and rarity of the species present. There are many options, for example the number of organisms, their weight, the amount of area they occupy, or their presence. Which of these factors are measured depends on the objectives of the study.

Abundance measures tend to be more problematic with plants than with animals because plant growth can exhibit considerable plasticity under different environmental conditions and plants commonly have both asexual and sexual reproduction strategies. With animals, abundance measures are made difficult because of movement, different life stages and sizes, and ontogenic changes. Common choices for measuring abundance include density, biomass, and cover (usually for plants). These data allow calculation of the many diversity indices currently available. Commonly used ones include Simpson and Shannon (Stohlgren 2007).

Density is the number of individuals by species per unit area. The number of individuals is simply counted within each plot. For animals, direct counts are often not possible and a method such as catch per unit effort, mark–recapture, removal technique or distance sampling is used to estimate the animal density in an area (Murphy & Willis 1996; Buckland et al. 2001; Krausman 2002; Bonar et al. 2009b). Sometimes counts of animals in an area are so great that subsampling for density (e.g. zooplankton (Karjalainen et al. 1996)) or using biomass measures are easier (e.g. zooplankton, marine fish (Ware & Thomson 2005)). Some plant types do not fit well into counting density (sod-forming grasses, multi-stemmed shrubs, clonal trees, etc.) because determining which part represents an individual is a daunting and time-prohibitive exercise. Without digging up roots to look for a connection between individuals, it can be impossible to assess observationally which plants are individuals. This problem expands as the total area covered by these plants increases within the area of interest. While each situation is somewhat unique, a rule stating that individuals with known clonal propagation must be greater than a fixed distance apart to be considered individuals (e.g. for bunch grasses a separation of more than 10 cm) will allow data collection despite the uncertainty.

An enticing but less useful alternative is gather frequency data (presence or absence) for each plot and then attempt to convert it to density. While this has had some success in the field (see Bonham (1989) for plants), it remains overly dependent on the assumption that the underlying distribution of organisms is random. However, for plants, as the plot size reaches or exceeds the size of a plant of interest, the density data collected are essentially frequency data, which can add complexity to the analysis. Determining if the plant is in the plot or not can sometimes be difficult because of the plant's plastic growth form. A typical rule is that if an individual plant's basal area is more than half in the plot and rooted in the plot it counts as being in that plot.

Measuring areal coverage is usually conducted for plants and sessile animals such as sponges (e.g. Lauer & Spacie 2004) and coral (e.g. Gardner et al. 2003). Again, because of the growth plasticity of plants, areal coverage measurements can sometimes be problematic. Using cover mitigates some of the difficulties with collecting density as well as being more or less independent of the scale of the plant in terms of the time needed to collect data for a plot—individuals do not need to be enumerated. Cover has been successfully used in many studies of diversity but it can make comparison between studies difficult because small differences in procedure can produce large differences in the data (see the section below). In addition to procedural differences, many vegetation protocols only advise measuring the surface layer of the cover, which discounts or dismisses those species that occur beneath the canopy. This gives disproportionate weight to plants dominant at the time of observation. In some systems, the aerially dominant plant is relatively fixed throughout the season, as mentioned above, yet in other systems it varies from week to week throughout the growing season, which would change the diversity measure based simply on the time of sampling rather than from more substantive differences. A simple fix for this

difficulty with measuring cover is to observe the cover of all species independently of one another, but this takes more time and cannot be done with remote sensing or photography because it requires evaluation of each layer of cover. Remote sensing data can give information valuable to diversity studies in that the vegetation alliance can often be identified, but species other than some large plants and invaders with unique phenology cannot be usually identified (Gillespie et al. 2008). Remote sensing can also help with plot stratification and offer support for inferences about the extent and grain of the field sampling.

Directly measuring the biomass of animals is usually a straightforward procedure and can vary from simple to time-consuming depending on the study. Individuals are weighed (either wet or dry weight depending on the study) and summed for the sampling unit; a subsample from the unit is weighed and a mean obtained that is multiplied by the number of individuals in the unit, or the group is weighed in mass. For plants the biomass option can be very time-consuming because rather than observationally collecting these data, plants are typically harvested, sorted, bagged, oven dried, and weighed.

Conversion between the different measures of abundance between animals can often be conducted through regression or other types of analyses when animals of the same species have similar morphology. The plastic growth of plants (where individuals can mature in a range of sizes spanning orders of magnitude) makes conversion between different measures of abundance problematic. However, there are limited situations where the individual plants are similar enough to make cover density and biomass well correlated. Only evaluation of the actual conditions at the time of data collection can help to determine if a conversion between measures of abundance is well advised.

2.2.8   When to sample

Determination of diversity and abundance in animal communities is heavily influenced by seasonality, time of day in which a sample is taken, and the reproductive stage of a given taxon. Sampling efforts should occur during a season which allows for most taxa to be susceptible to being captured. This includes considerations of migratory behaviour. Similarly, species' diurnal/nocturnal movement cycles should be taken into consideration when planning sampling procedures. Often, entire assemblages are most detectable at a given time of day. It is at these times when samples should be taken to maximize species richness.

Timing is also a very important consideration for plant studies. Each growing season, the range of plants, their density, their distribution, and even their size can be different. Species can colonize or be extirpated from the area of interest in short periods of time. Even within a growing season, the presence of perennial plants waxes and wanes, while this pattern defines the lifecycle of many annuals and ruderal perennials. Within the herbaceous zone, switches in dominance are not uncommon as the season progresses, despite relatively stable plant populations. Some plants mature early and others later. A similar change can occur in woody communities, where dominance changes can seem sudden between seasons as later succession species in the community overtop those that arrived earlier. In deserts, plants can remain dormant in the seed bank for years until suitable growing conditions occur. An overarching statement about the appropriate time period in which to observe diversity is not possible but instead depends on the within- and between-year site variabilities and how they relate to the larger question.

2.2.9   How many samples to collect

The size of sampling error depends on (1) the heterogenity among sampling units in the sample frame and (2) the number of sampling units observed/collected (sample size) (Groves 1989); therefore, the more heterogeneity among samples, the more samples must be taken to estimate the parameter with a given degree of confidence. In addition, the more samples taken the better the chance of collecting rare species. Because of these principles, collecting more small samples is usually better than collecting fewer large samples.

The most precise and accurate estimations of animal diversity and abundance come from intense sampling on a system for a long time period. These studies reveal temporal variation of a species' appearance in collections, and have experienced specialists who can identify the collected species and know which species from adjacent areas might appear in their collections (Longino et al. 2002). More commonly, diversity or abundance studies are of limited duration or geographical scope, and need to employ efficient sampling methodologies that can provide accurate estimates with small sample sizes.

Sufficient sample sizes are obtained in different ways, depending on study objectives. Sometimes sample sizes are previously set based on previous studies. For example, in plant studies, no matter how large the plot size, at least five independent sampling units are recommended to allow enough plots to capture the variability (Stohlgren (2007) recommends seven). In other studies sample sizes are calculated based on the accepted level of error in the estimate and the variability of the parameter estimated through a pilot study, previous study, or, sometimes, an educated guess. The cost of sampling can be a factor in decisions. If developing 99% confidence intervals for an estimate requires 100 000 samples, a biologist might have to accept 95, 90 or even 80% confidence intervals for the estimate if it only requires 30–100 samples and does not substantially affect survey objectives. Surveying references provide overviews of how to assign samples and calculate sample sizes for means, totals, and proportions using common sampling designs, including simple random, stratified random, cluster, and systematic sampling (Bonham 1989; Elzinga et al. 1998; Magurran 2004; Bonar et al. 2009b).

Advances in computer science and mathematics have resulted in substantial progress in the development of monitoring designs for trends that allow the biologist to maximize power by allocating samples over space and time based on the variance structure of initial samples (e.g. King et al. (1981), Gibbs et al. 1998, Urquhart et al. (1998), Urquhart & Kincaid (1999), and Larsen et al., (2001, 2004)). Software programs such as MONITOR (Gibbs 1995) and TRENDS (Gerrodette 1993) are available to help the biologist allocate samples and maximize power in order to detect trends.

Species accumulation curves to estimate the amount of sampling needed for diversity sampling have recently seen increased use. Here, plot size or the number of samples taken is recorded on

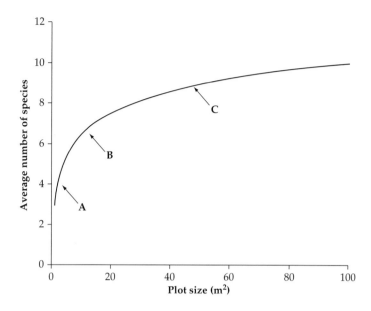

Figure 2.3 A example of a species area curve from nested square plots sampling perennial plants in the Sonoran desert, Arizona in 2007. If the plot area increases from 1 to 10 m^2 (point A), the plot captures twice as many species. Once the plot size increases to 20 m^2 (point B), the plot has doubled in area but only captured one additional species. As the area of the plot continues to increase (point C), the number of new species increases only very gradually as rare species are encountered. An efficient plot area in this example might be 20 m^2.

the *x*-axis and the number of species collected is recorded on the *y*-axis (Fig. 2.3). Increasing the number of samples or plot size initially has a dramatic effect on the number of species encountered (A). However, as more samples are taken or plot size is increased, the curve flattens where more sampling does not result in many more species collected (B). It is at the point where the curve levels that the number of samples to be collected or the plot size is optimized (C). Species accumulation curves

Figure 2.4   A theoretical species area curve for a nested plot as it increases in area. The segment marked A is the traditional species area curve with the line flattening as all common species have been captured and occasional rare species are encountered. As the line enters segment B, the line shows the plot expanding out of the current vegetation association into a different type. For example, in the Sonoran Desert, Arizona, this could be moving from an upland site into riparian vegetation or onto a slope. If a large enough plot could be censused, this stair-stepped pattern would be repeated as the area increases to encompass all of the vegetation associations in the area of interest. In practice, the part of the site represented in segment A would be stratified and sampled separately from that in segment B.

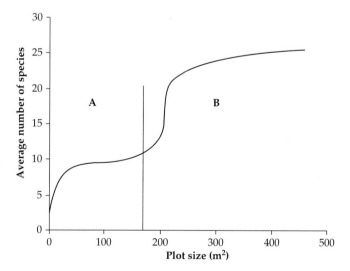

for nested plots occur at different scales and can be more complex (Fig. 2.4).

Given the difficulty of detecting rare species in assemblages, and the limitations that exist in carrying out field surveys to estimate biodiversity, it is often necessary to use statistical techniques that can help in determining the amount of effort that would be necessary to capture the entire diversity. Three methods for estimating species diversity are (1) fitting a statistical distribution to rank abundance data, (2) extrapolating a species accumulation curve to its asymptote, and (3) estimating the asymptotic number of species with non-parametric estimators (Longino et al. 2002). For individual-based (abundance) data, the area under a fitted, lognormal abundance distribution has been used to estimate the total number of species, including undetected rare species (Chao et al. 2009). Other species abundance models such as the log-series, geometric, negative binomial, Zipf–Mandelbrot, and the broken-stick (Magurran 2004) can also be fit to abundance data to estimate asymptotic species richness. Curve-fitting methods, which can be applied to both abundance data and incidence data, extrapolate a fitted function such as the Michaelis–Menten equation or a mixture model out to the asymptote of the species accumulation graph (Soberon & Llorente 1993; Colwell et al. 2004). Other parametric and non-parametric methods are useful in the estimation of biodiversity in a species assemblage (Chao et al. 2006; Chao et al. 2009).

2.2.10   Comparing information from different surveys

The objective of studies on the diversity or abundance of animals is often to compare these metrics through time or from one area to another. Conversion techniques have been developed for comparing data collected using different techniques (e.g. Scheiner et al. 2000; Peterson & Paukert 2009), but these are often labour intensive and can introduce additional error. Methods used at different times or in different areas can also be standardized (Bonar & Hubert 2002; Bonar et al. 2009a,b). By using the same methodology in each sampling effort, it is possible to eliminate the variability introduced by modification of sampling methods, although vali-dation still needs to occur to relate the standardized sample to the true population. Standardization not only refers to the equipment used or how it is used, but also to other aspects of sampling such as timing of sampling, the habitats that are sampled, and effort. Care should be exercised to make data from independent collections as comparable to one another as possible. Standardization is useful even in cases when large-scale time or space comparisons are not the focus of a given study. Today, many databases exist that compile information from a variety of independent studies that were carried out using standard techniques. These often serve as a basis for large-scale studies. Standard methods for animals such as fish (see Bonar et al. 2009b) have been developed, but standard methods of sampling plant diversity have been difficult to develop (Stohlgren 2007) and general methods must be modified for each unique set of questions, abiotic-, biotic-, and budgetary-realities.

2.2.11   Preparing for the field

While objectives are being set, and the survey design developed, there are additional tasks to consider. Often a permit from a natural resource management agency will be required to carry out sample. Always plan enough time to obtain the permit. For example, obtaining federal or state permits to sample endangered species in some areas of the USA can take up to a year, and because diversity or abundance surveys are often used to quantify a species in peril, long wait times can be the norm. After permits have been obtained, the appropriate landowners and natural resource agency personnel should be notified to inform them of specific dates when sampling will take place. If notification does not occur, law enforcement personnel are often called out to the site to investigate the 'suspicious activity' occurring. Field sampling is frequently conducted in remote locations using specialized equipment. Project logistics and the salaries of surveyors are usually the most expensive parts of any project. Checklists should be used to ensure that all field equipment is ready and loaded before the survey, and contingency plans (such as having a spare set of equipment available) for when equipment failure occurs should be developed to avoid unnecessary expense. When surveying a field site, it is important to move quickly and accurately, minimizing unnecessary breaks and ignoring minor discomfort to complete the site on schedule. Above all, the emphasis should be on safety. Surveys should not be continued if dangerous weather conditions develop, sampling equipment poses a risk, or other conditions associated with the sampling are compromised.

2.3   Prospectus

Proper planning of surveys and consideration of fundamental issues such as bias, accuracy, and precision can help ensure a useful, valid study (Box 2.2). Biologists who initiate surveys without considering the basics of survey design risk embarrassment and the outlay of considerable funds with few results. Those who carefully plan their surveys from the start will provide information that can advance science, influence politics, or shape laws and policies.

Box 2.2 Guidelines for sampling

- Develop clear, detailed objectives for the survey.
- Define the sampling frame—select what, where, and how to sample.
- Seek advice from statisticians when designing surveys.
- Consider how bias and sampling error will affect estimates. Correct for bias (calibrate sampling) if possible and maximize numbers of samples collected and allocate samples in time and space to reduce sampling error.
- Incorporate some form of randomization when selecting samples.
- Chose methods to sample that minimize impact to the organisms studied.
- When possible, sample using standard techniques so results among studies can be compared.
- Incorporate time and planning for obtaining sampling permits and conducting safe surveys, and develop contingency plans for when things go wrong in the field.
- When in doubt about survey design or logistics, refer back to survey objectives.

Comparison across large regions and communication among diverse researchers are becoming increasingly important, therefore the adoption and development of standard sampling techniques will play even a greater role in the future, similar to the standard methods already developed for climate science, water chemistry, geology, and medicine.

With the advent of technology, analysis procedures, and automation, many sampling procedures will become easier over time. However, the basic considerations will remain the same. A fundamental knowledge of basic sampling issues will help those surveying for biological diversity, no matter what tools are available in the future.

2.4   Key points

1. Set clear objectives for surveys, with a carefully defined sampling frame.
2. Design the survey, seeking help from a statistician when needed. Define when, where, and how to survey, using methods that minimize mortality to surveyed organisms and incorporate some form of randomness.
3. Precision and bias affect the utility of sampling estimates. Account for the effects of bias by using the same techniques over time to monitor trends, using a variety of gears with different bias to cancel species-related bias for point estimates, or, the best way, by validating sampling techniques with true population parameters. Maximize precision by increasing sample sizes and careful consideration of sample allocation over space and time.
4. Pilot surveys can help define the sampling effort required and identify the logistical challenges the main survey will face.
5. Sample using established standard sampling methods when possible to maximize the comparability of the data among studies. Ensure safe surveys and use field etiquette, including obtaining sampling permits in advance, to maximize survey efficiency.

CHAPTER 3

Biodiversity monitoring: the relevance of detectability

Stephen T. Buckland, Angelika C. Studeny, Anne E. Magurran, and Stuart E. Newson

3.1 Introduction

Most studies that monitor biodiversity are deficient in an important respect: they assume that the captured or observed animals or plants form the community of interest, or at least are a representative sample from it. For single-site monitoring, if the site is small and individuals of the taxa of interest are easily detected, it might not be unreasonable to conclude that the counts correspond to the community of interest. However, for more cryptic species and/or larger sites, complete enumeration of individuals is seldom feasible (Coddington et al. 2009). Most diversity measures assume that the individuals we count are a random sample of the community (Magurran 2004, p136). It might be possible to ensure this if sampling is conducted on a sufficiently large random sample of plots within the site, where each plot is small enough to allow complete enumeration of individuals on the plot. If this is not achievable, we can expect heterogeneity among individuals in probability of detection.

Increasingly, in part due to the change of emphasis for biodiversity monitoring signalled by the 2010 Biodiversity Target of the Convention on Biological Diversity (which states that there should be 'a significant reduction of the current rate of biodiversity loss' by 2010), the focus is on quantifying biodiversity trends within regions or countries, in which case the community should be the entire biota of the region or country. Since we cannot record the entire biota directly, we must sample locations and species (Chapter 2), with the aim of drawing inference on the entire biota. If survey sites or plots are selected according to a randomized scheme, such as the stratified random scheme of the UK Breeding Bird Survey (Newson et al. 2005), the issue of representativeness of sites is addressed. Representativeness of species is more problematic, especially when complete species lists do not exist, and some species and taxa are much more difficult to survey than others. Hence, biodiversity monitoring will always be based on a reduced set of taxa. Within that set, a random subset of species might be an appropriate means of easing the task of monitoring.

Even after addressing these issues, we need to consider the issue of detectability, unless our plots are so small that all individuals can be detected and so numerous that all, or nearly all, species occur on at least one sample plot. We use the term 'probability of detection' for the probability that an individual is recorded. Recording of individuals might be achieved by visual or aural detection, or by capturing them in traps, nets, etc. A combination of methods might be used. Typically, we can expect detectability to vary according to a number of factors, but the one that interests us here is when detectability of individuals varies among species, as this will bias the species proportions used in many biodiversity measures (Yoccoz et al. 2001).

In this chapter, we consider the implications when detectability varies by species, with particular reference to monitoring regional biodiversity trends. We consider some measures of biodiversity that are potentially useful for quantifying trends in regional biodiversity and explore how these measures are affected when the issue of detectability is ignored.

Although our focus is on regional monitoring, there are parallels with site monitoring. For example, we might seek to quantify the biodiversity of a site by sampling a number of small plots within the site. In this case, we do not require that each plot is sufficiently large to reflect the entire biodiversity of the site, but we expect the plots collectively to achieve this. If it is possible to make each plot sufficiently small to allow complete enumeration of the plot, then the issue of detectability of individuals on the sample plots becomes irrelevant. If, however, there are too few plots, many species present in the site will not be detected because they do not occur on any of the plots. Thus we need a large sample of plots, but we do not need large volumes of data from each plot, to quantify reliably the biodiversity of the site. The same issues apply when we seek to quantify the biodiversity of a region by sampling many sites within a region. Note that, for a regional survey, we might adopt a hierarchical sampling scheme, with a representative set of sites through the region and a representative set of plots within each site.

We focus primarily on detectability of individuals in this chapter. However, as alluded to above, there is also an issue of detectability of species: if detectability of individuals of a species is very low, or if a species is so rare that few, if any, occur in the sampled sites or plots, then the species may be undetected (Chapter 4). In statistical terms, if there is an adequate sample of plots or sites, this is not a problem, as unrecorded species will represent a small proportion of individuals in the community; the estimated proportion will simply be zero if no individuals are detected. What constitutes an 'adequate sample' of plots or sites depends on the spatial heterogeneity of the environment and on heterogeneity in the detection probabilities (greater heterogeneity requires a larger sample size in both cases). It also depends on the size of sample plots/sites, especially if the site/region is spatially homogeneous with respect to its biodiversity. (In a very heterogeneous environment, we would prefer a large sample of small plots to a small sample of larger plots, as we need to sample more locations to quantify biodiversity of the site or region. In a more homogeneous environment, there would be less gain from sampling

more locations and more gain from making plots larger.)

3.2 State of the field: which biodiversity measure?

In choosing our biodiversity measures, several considerations must be taken into account. First, we need to choose the component(s) of biodiversity we wish to measure. Buckland et al. (2005) list six criteria that we might like our measure to satisfy (Table 3.1). The non-statistical criteria are related to three components of biodiversity: species richness, species evenness, and abundance. The statistical criteria are that the measure should have good and measurable precision, and have an expectation that does not vary with sample size.

Another consideration is whether trends in biodiversity measures should be sensitive to trends in the rarest species of a community. Rare species are an important positive contributor to species richness, although they make it difficult to estimate (Colwell & Coddington 1994; Chapter 4). However, an increase in the number of rare species reduces species evenness and rare species generally have a negligible contribution to abundance.

If rare species are excluded from analyses, the geometric mean of relative abundance indices, as used by Gregory et al. (2003), has good properties,

Table 3.1 The six criteria proposed by Buckland et al. (2005) for a biodiversity measure.

Criterion	Description
1	For a system that has a constant number of species, overall abundance, and species evenness, but with varying abundance of individual species, the index should show no trend.
2	If overall abundance is decreasing, but number of species and species evenness are constant, the index should decrease.
3	If species evenness is decreasing, but number of species and overall abundance are constant, the index should decrease.
4	If number of species is decreasing, but overall abundance and species evenness are constant, the index should decrease.
5	The index should have an estimator whose expected value is not a function of sample size.
6	The estimator of the index should have good and measurable precision.

meeting all the criteria of Buckland et al. (2005) except one: if the number of species is declining, the index fails to reflect this, as the rare species are excluded. If they are included, zero counts or abundances are problematic. They can be replaced by small positive values to allow the index to be calculated, but its variance is likely to be high when rare species are analysed (Buckland et al. 2005).

Note that 'rare' species are often defined pragmatically to be those species for which few if any individuals are detected by the sampling programme, so that estimation may be compromised, as for the above method using the geometric mean. Ecologically, it seems unsatisfactory for 'rare' to be determined by sampling effort, rather than by, for example, the proportion of individuals in the community that belong to a given species.

Whether rare species are included or not, Simpson's index performs well with respect to five of the six criteria of Buckland et al. (2005). The one criterion for which it fails relates to abundance: if all species are declining at the same rate, the index remains constant. Strictly, its expectation is a function of sample size. If the form of the index used is $1 - D$, where $D = \sum_i \hat{p}_i^2$ and $\hat{p}_i$ is the estimated proportion of the community that is of species i, it can be adjusted to ensure that it is an unbiased measure of $1 - \sum_i p_i^2$, where p_i is the true proportion of the community that is of species i. The adjustment is to multiply the index by $n/(n-1)$, where n is the total number of individuals detected (Lande et al. 2003). However, this assumes that the n individuals detected are a simple random sample of the N individuals (across all species) in the community for which we wish to draw inference. Even if we were interested only in local biodiversity, it is usually implausible that detectabilities or trappabilities will be the same across species. In the case of quantifying regional biodiversity, the correction has even less relevance. As n is typically large, the issue is academic: the multiplier is so close to unity that it makes no practical difference.

The Shannon index also generally performs well with respect to five of the six criteria of Buckland

et al. (2005). Like Simpson's index, it stays constant if all species are declining at the same rate. The Shannon index is also inferior to Simpson's index with respect to the dependence of its expectation on sample size. Its bias is $-(s-1)/n$, where s is the total number of species in the community (and is generally unknown); hence, for large n, the bias can generally be considered negligible. However, if rare species are included in monitoring, and these account for a significant proportion of total abundance, then the Shannon index violates the criterion that its expectation should not be a function of sample size (Lande et al. 2003).

Buckland et al. (2005) proposed a modified form of the Shannon index that satisfies all six of their criteria, provided n is appreciably larger than s. However, it has been constructed simply to satisfy the criteria, without any theoretical foundation, and its performance has not been rigorously assessed. In practice, it is generally preferable to use different indices to reflect the different elements of biodiversity, assumed here to be species richness, species evenness, and abundance. Only if a single headline index of biodiversity change is needed might the modified Shannon index be considered.

A related issue relevant to monitoring regional biodiversity is that of α and β diversity (Chapter 6). Over large regions, much of the diversity will be due to β diversity; that is it arises because species composition and relative abundances differ appreciably among locations within the region. Site-specific diversity measures will reflect α diversity only. By analysing data pooled across sampling locations (in which either species proportions p_i are averaged across sites or counts or estimated abundances are summed across sites), γ diversity is estimated. α diversity is estimated by averaging site-specific measures across sites, possibly weighting by number of individuals detected or trapped at each site, and β diversity is estimated as either the difference between γ and α diversity (additive β diversity) or the ratio of γ to α diversity (multiplicative β diversity). If either the Shannon index or Simpson's index is used, estimated β diversity is guaranteed to be positive using the additive definition and to be greater than unity using the multiplicative definition.

3.3   Detectability: are species counts relevant for monitoring biodiversity?

3.3.1   Individual detectability

All too often, numbers of individuals detected are substituted into equations for measuring diversity with little thought given to whether those numbers give biased estimates of the quantities of interest. Much of the theory underlying biodiversity measures assumes that all individuals in the community are equally likely to be sampled, irrespective of species. In real communities, this will seldom be the case. Some species will be inherently more easily detected or trapped than others. If detectability is not estimated, then biodiversity measures will be biased (see Box 3.1). The theoretical underpinnings claimed for some measures of biodiversity provide little reassurance in reality.

Let us explore the implications if issues of detectability are ignored. We consider the case where we are interested in biodiversity of a region, but the same arguments apply if we are simply interested in a single plot or site. Suppose for a given survey region we have:

s = number of species in the region

N_i = number of individuals of species i in the region, $i = 1, \ldots, s$

n_i = number of individuals of species i detected in the region

π_i = probability of detection of an individual of species i with estimate $\hat{\pi}_i$

$E(n_i) = N_i \pi_i$ = expected number of individuals of species i detected

$\hat{N}_i = n_i / \hat{\pi}_i$ = estimated number of individuals of species i in the region

$p_i = N_i / \sum_{i=1}^{s} N_i$, with corresponding estimate $\hat{p}_i = \hat{N}_i / \sum_{i=1}^{s} \hat{N}_i$

$q_i = E(n_i) / \sum_{i=1}^{s} E(n_i)$, with corresponding estimate $\hat{q}_i = n_i / \sum_{i=1}^{s} n_i$.

When the true N_i are not known, diversity indices such as Simpson's index ($D = \sum_{i=1}^{s} p_i^2$ or transformations of this) and the Shannon index ($H = - \sum_{i=1}^{s} p_i \log_e p_i$) should be estimated by substituting estimates $\hat{p}_i$ of p_i, which requires estimates $\hat{\pi}_i$. Instead, standard practice is to evaluate them by

substituting $\hat{q}_i$ for p_i. If we can assume that $\pi_i = \pi$ for all i, which means that the probability of detection of an individual does not depend on species, then this strategy is justified. The assumption is seldom stated explicitly and almost never criticised, yet it seems unlikely that *any* community comprises individuals that are equally detectable irrespective of species, unless it is possible to enumerate all individuals on plots. If detection is by trapping, individuals of some species are more readily trapped than others; if it is by active searching, individuals of some species are more visible or audible than others. This issue is recognized, for example, in arthropod surveys, where different trapping methods are often used in an attempt to achieve a more representative sample of individuals (e.g. Colwell & Coddington 1994).

If we relax the assumption that all organisms are equally detectable, we can still use the measures of the previous section, but with counts replaced by abundance (or density) estimates. For α diversity, the $\hat{N}_i$ would be estimated for each plot, while for γ diversity they would be estimated for the wider survey region, obtained from a combined analysis of the data from all sites in the region (with appropriate allowance for survey design, e.g. if the sites are a stratified random sample, analysis should be appropriately stratified).

3.3.2   Estimating individual detectability

The problem remains of how to estimate detectability and hence abundance. The preferred approach will depend on the taxa being sampled and the environment they occupy. The simplest solution is to have sample plots that are sufficiently small that all individuals on the plot are detected. In this case the counts are the plot abundance estimates. Equally, abundance values for the wider region from which the plots were sampled are readily estimated. In the case of simple random sampling, the $\hat{p}_i$ are then the same, whether based on counts or abundance estimates. This approach might be feasible with ground beetles, for example, or for large mammals in open habitat. However, the method is inefficient for most taxa because plots may have to be so small that most counts are zero. A further

> ## Box 3.1 If we estimate species proportions by the proportions observed in our sample, are measures based on these proportions biased?
>
> Intuitively, it might seem that we would not introduce bias into biodiversity measures even when the π_i vary among species, provided that π_i is independent of N_i, that is that the detectability of individuals of a species is independent of species abundance. Thus, although q_i may be smaller than p_i for a less detectable species and larger for a more detectable species, we might hope that these biases compensate, so that the distributions of q_i and p_i are the same. Unfortunately this is not the case. We can see this by considering the distributions across species i of $E(n_i)$ and N_i. We would like the distribution of N_i across species to be identical to that of $kE(n_i)$ for some constant k (which cancels top and bottom when q_i is evaluated, giving $q_i = p_i$). Thus we would like the distributions of $log_e(N_i)$ and $log_e[E(n_i)]$ to be the same apart from location (which will differ by the factor $log_e k$). However, $log_e[E(n_i)] = log_e(N_i) + log_e(\pi_i)$, so that $\text{var}\{log_e[E(n_i)]\} = \text{var}[log_e(N_i)] + \text{var}[log_e(\pi_i)] + 2\text{cov}[log_e(N_i), log_e(\pi_i)]$. When π_i and N_i are independent, the covariance term is zero, and $\text{var}\{log_e[E(n_i)]\} > \text{var}[log_e(N_i)]$ except when $\pi_i = \pi$ for all i (in which case $\text{var}[log_e(\pi_i)] = 0$). Thus if π_i and N_i are
>
> independent, the distributions are identical apart from location only when detectability does not vary by species. The two distributions have the same variance when $\text{var}[log_e(\pi_i)] = -2\text{cov}[log_e(N_i), log_e(\pi_i)]$, giving $\text{cov}[log_e(N_i), log_e(\pi_i)] = -0.5\,\text{var}[log_e(\pi_i)]$. If the π_i are very variable, this corresponds to a strong negative correlation between detectability and abundance.
>
> These results indicate that we can generally expect the q_i to be more variable across species than the p_i when detectabilities π_i vary across species. Species evenness takes its maximum value when all the p_i are the same, corresponding to zero variance. As variability increases, evenness decreases. Thus, if we estimate p_i by $\hat{q}_i$, we expect to underestimate evenness and hence biodiversity.
>
> ### Conclusion
>
> Measures of biodiversity that are based on species proportions are biased when these are estimated from samples, unless individuals of different species are all equally detectable.

problem for mobile populations is that an instantaneous count of the plot is needed; if this cannot be achieved, then new individuals may move onto the plot while counting is being conducted, leading to overestimation of density. This overestimation will be greater for more mobile species, generating bias in the diversity measures.

Another solution is to use mark–recapture to estimate detectabilities. The approach tends to be costly and is prone to bias because even within a species, capture probability can be heterogeneous among individuals. This is in part because animals can move on and off the plot, and those with home ranges that are wholly in the plot are much more likely to be trapped than those whose home ranges are largely off the plot. This generates bias in detectability and abundance estimates.

Distance sampling (Buckland 2001) can be an effective way of estimating detectability from sightings surveys (see Box 3.2). For biodiversity monitoring, a problem of distance sampling is

that there are typically too few detections for many species to allow estimation of detectability. However, by pooling data across species and then using multiple-covariate distance sampling with species as a factor (Alldredge et al. 2007; Marques et al. 2007) this difficulty is largely avoided, although the detectability of the rarest species with, say, fewer than 10 detections might have to be assumed to be the same as for similar, more common, species (Section 3.4).

Box 3.3 discusses different methods of detectability and distinguishes between individual detectability and species detectability.

3.3.3 Species detectability

For rare species, $\hat{q}_i$ and $\hat{p}_i$ will be zero if $n_i = 0$. This too is a detectability issue, but relates to the detectability of a species, rather than to the detectability of individuals. Although many methods exist to estimate the number of

Box 3.2 Distance sampling

Distance sampling (Buckland 2001, 2004) covers several related methods in which distances of detected individuals from a line or point are recorded, from which the effective area corresponding to a count is estimated. The most commonly used method is line transect sampling, for which lines are placed randomly in the survey region or, more commonly, a set of equally spaced parallel lines is randomly superimposed on the survey region. An observer traverses each line, recording any animals detected within a distance w of the line, together with their distance from the line. These distances are used to estimate a detection function, which is the probability that an animal is detected, as a function of distance from the line. For the basic method, it is assumed that this probability is 1 at zero distance from the line, that is animals on the line are seen with certainty. Given an estimate of the detection function, we can estimate the proportion of animals detected within a strip extending a distance w from the line on either side. This allows us to estimate animal density by adjusting encounter rates (i.e. the number of animals detected per unit length of line) to allow for animals missed in this strip. Given random placement of an adequate number of lines (or a grid of lines) through the survey region, this density estimate is representative of the whole survey region, allowing abundance within that region to be estimated. Probability of detection π_i of individuals of species i comprises two components, one reflecting the probability that an animal within a surveyed strip of half-width w is detected and the other reflecting the probability that an animal is within a surveyed strip.

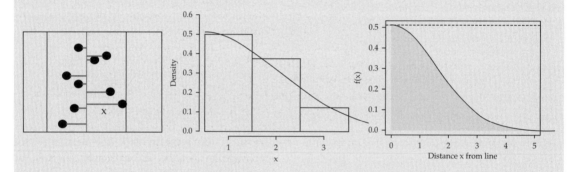

The left-hand plot shows part of a line transect with positions of detected animals shown. The distances x are shown in the form of a histogram with three distance intervals in the middle plot, together with a half-normal detection function fitted to the distance data. For an animal that is within a survey strip, its probability of detection is represented in the right-hand plot by the proportion of the rectangle that is shaded, corresponding to the fitted half-normal function.

This method is used to sample a wide variety of terrestrial, freshwater, and marine animals, as well as some plant populations (e.g. trees in rain forest).

species that are not detected (see Chapter 4), the resulting estimates tend to be particularly sensitive to the assumptions made. Species detectabilities will be even more heterogeneous than individual detectabilities (because individuals of rare species are much less likely to be encountered than individuals of common species), so estimators should accommodate this heterogeneity. Even so, it is a challenging problem to estimate the number of undetected species purely based on data from those species that are detected. Most measures of biodiversity are not unduly affected if some rare species are estimated to have zero abundance. Species richness is an exception to this.

For regional monitoring there are three reasons why a species might not be detected: it might be present on at least one of the sample plots but not detected, it might be present in the region but not on any of the sample plots, and it might be absent from the region at the time of the survey.

Box 3.3 Which methods of estimating detectability might be appropriate for which taxa?

Individual detectability

Distance sampling (Buckland 2001, 2004) is useful for species where individuals are readily detectable from a line or point, at least if they are close to the observer. It can be effective for estimating the detectability of medium and large terrestrial mammals, marine mammals, most birds, many reptiles, many fish and benthic fauna, and plants where individual plants are readily identifiable.

Mark–recapture (Borchers et al. 2002; Williams et al. 2002) can be effective when trapping methods or other methods that involve capture are used. Groups for which probability of capture might be quantified using mark–recapture include small mammals, birds in rain forests, reptiles and amphibians, and insects.

In rare circumstances when animals are trapped, a sufficiently large proportion of the population might be removed to allow removal and related catch methods (Borchers et al. 2002) to be used to estimate the trapping probability of individuals.

Species detectability

The species abundance distribution summarizes the counts of each species observed in a survey, recording the number of species represented by one, two, three, … individuals. To estimate the species richness of a community we need to estimate the number of species represented by no individuals in the sample. There are many possible methods for this (Magurran 2004; Chapter 4). The methods are applicable to any taxon, although estimation of the number of missing species tends to lack robustness when there is no replicate sampling and individuals of different species have different detectabilities.

When there are repeat visits to each of a number of sites, occupancy methods (MacKenzie et al. 2006; Chapter 4) allow estimation of species richness from simple species lists compiled on each visit to each site. Again, the methods are applicable to any taxon.

Rare species, which can account for a substantial fraction of the species richness in a community (Coddington et al. 2009), may be missed during sampling simply by chance. Undersampling is particularly problematical in tropical arthropod assemblages. Species richness estimators offer one solution (Chapter 4) as long as there is no inherent bias in the sampling methodology. However, rare and common species may differ in ecology (for example by occupying different habitats (Magurran & Henderson 2003)). Moreover, most sampling techniques violate the assumption that individuals are captured or recorded at random. A light trap is a classic example of this since not all moth species respond to the light source in the same way (Southwood & Henderson 2000). It is not just species that vary in their responses—male and female moths may react differently to the light stimulus (Altermatt et al. 2009). Heterogeneity in this sex difference amongst species will contribute to bias. Weather conditions can also affect sampling. Holyoak et al. (1997) found that the total number of moths captured by a light trap was positively correlated with temperature and negatively correlated with rainfall, and that the strength of this correlation varied with taxon. Preston (1948) argued that a moth trap is an acceptable method of sampling because, while species vary in their degree of phototropism, it is random with regard to commonness and rarity amongst those taxa that are equally attracted to the light. However, comparisons of diversity amongst sites, or over time periods, in which the detectability of species varies are challenging.

Species might be missed because they are not present at the time of the survey. Temporal turnover in the form of local colonizations and extinctions is an intrinsic feature of all ecological communities (MacArthur & Wilson 1967). Species are gained and lost by island assemblages while seed banks may contain many species that are only occasionally seen in the 'expressed community'. This raises the conceptual issue of who belongs to the community. Should species that have been recorded in the past, and which may re-occur at some point in the future, be included in a species list? In practice of course it is not always easy to determine which form of absence—methodological or ecological—is involved. These issues are discussed further in Magurran (Chapter 7). Box 3.4 looks at ways in which detectability might be addressed in surveys of butterflies.

Box 3.4 How might detectability be addressed in surveys of butterflies?

We use the example of butterflies to illustrate the issues that should be addressed.

In the UK's Butterfly Monitoring Scheme (Pollard 1979), observers walk along transects, placed subjectively through the best butterfly habitat in a site, and record all butterflies entering a box ahead of the observer. Observed species proportions may be biased in such surveys for three reasons: (1) smaller, less active species may pass undetected within the box, (2) conceptually, the method is a snapshot count of butterflies in the box, but for butterflies in flight there will be a flow of butterflies in and out of the box, which biases counts upwards, and this bias is greater for more active species, and (3) the species proportions along the transect may not be representative of the site because the transect is positioned in what is judged to be the best habitat.

The above biases might be removed or at least reduced by placing transects at random through the site and by recording distances from the line of detected butterflies when they are, say, 1 m ahead of the observer (or a distance that is sufficient to ensure that responsive movement of the butterfly does not occur before their position is recorded). By recording the butterfly when it crosses this imaginary line ahead of the observer, bias arising from butterflies in flight is avoided. Detected butterflies that do not cross this line while in sight are not recorded. Line transect methods may be used to analyse the recorded distances, to allow for varying detectability of species, on the assumption that any butterfly on the transect itself will be detected.

The above methods may be workable in relatively open habitats. In more closed habitats, such as rain forest, it may be necessary to use mark–recapture to estimate the catchability of individuals of different species. In this context it is worth noting that bias in the estimates of the probability of capture can be tolerated, provided relative estimates of probability are well estimated. That is, if individuals of one species are twice as likely to be caught as individuals of another, we need to be able to estimate that, but we can tolerate some bias in estimating the actual probabilities of capture.

If species richness is the favoured measure of biodiversity, then species detectability rather than individual detectability becomes relevant. Species-specific counts of butterflies in traps may be used to estimate the number of species present that are not represented in the sample. However, different methods can lead to quite different estimates of this number, that is estimation is not robust.

Given data from repeat visits to multiple sites, occupancy methods are useful for estimating species detectability, and hence species richness (Chapter 11). To apply these methods, we need record only what species were detected at each visit to each site. No counts are needed.

3.4 Case study: the UK Breeding Bird Survey

We consider here the Scottish data for the years 1994–2007 from the UK Breeding Bird Survey (BBS) (Freeman et al. 2007; Newson et al. 2008). Plots of size $1\,km^2$ were selected according to a stratified random sampling scheme, with sampling rate proportional to the number of volunteer observers available. In 2007, 405 plots were surveyed.

The survey of each 1 km square is conducted by line transect sampling. Two parallel transects, each of length 1 km, are defined, and the observer walks along them, recording all detected birds. These are recorded in one of four categories: within 25 m of the line, between 25 and 100 m of the line, more than 100 m from the line, or flying over the site. In common with Newson et al.

(2008), we use here data for the first two categories only.

If it were possible to detect all birds within 100 m of the line, then the combined count for a square out to 100 m would represent all birds in a plot of size $0.4\,km^2$ (width of 200 m (100 m either side of the line) and length of 2 km, corresponding to the two lines at each site). This would give us a direct estimate of density, from which we can estimate the size of the Scottish population of each recorded species, taking account of the stratified random sampling scheme. For a complete count, we would expect three times as many birds of a species between 25 and 100 m of the line as between 0 and 25 m of the line. The observed difference in counts tends to be less than this. We use the two counts to fit a detection function, which assumes that all birds on the line (distance of zero) are detected, and that the probability of detection falls as distance from the line increases. In our analyses, we assumed that the form of this detection function was half-normal.

For each species, a single half-normal model was fitted across years and sites. The dependence of probability of detection on habitat and year was assessed using the multiple-covariate distance sampling (mcds) engine of Distance (Thomas et al. 2010). The size of the Scottish population in a given year of each species was estimated as

$$\hat{N}_i = \sum_r \frac{A_r}{m_r a} \left[\sum_s \sum_j \frac{1}{\hat{\pi}_{ijsr}} \right]$$

where $\hat{\pi}_{ijsr}$ is the estimated probability of detection of the jth detected bird of species i at site s of region (stratum) r for that year, $a = 0.4\,km^2$ is the size of the covered region in a single site, m_r is the number of sites surveyed in region r in that year, and A_r is the size of region r.

We conducted these analyses on species recorded in at least one year in Scotland on BBS squares and classified as 'farmland' species. These classifications are based on Jacobs preference indices, calculated according to Newson et al. (2008). For the rarest species, the detectability was assumed to be the same as for a similar, more common species. The species' common and scientific names are listed in Table 3.2, together with counts and corresponding estimates of the size of the Scottish population in 2007.

For Simpson's index, we define $1 - D_a = 1 - \sum_{i=1}^{s} \hat{p}_i^2$ and $1 - D_c = 1 - \sum_{i=1}^{s} \hat{q}_i^2$. Hence the first estimate is obtained from abundance estimates $\hat{N}_i$, while the second is obtained from mean counts $\bar{n}_i$, where $\bar{n}_i = \frac{\sum_r A_r \bar{n}_{ir}}{\sum_r A_r}$ is a weighted mean count per site of species i to allow for different sampling rates by stratum and $\bar{n}_{ir} = \frac{\sum_s n_{isr}}{m_r}$ is the mean count per site of species i in region r, where n_{isr} is the count of species i in site s of region r. (We consider here γ diversity only; to estimate α diversity, and hence β diversity, we would need to estimate the index for each 1 km square, and average these across squares, weighting by the stratum sampling rates.) Similarly for the Shannon index, we define $H_a = -\sum_{i=1}^{s} \hat{p}_i log_e \hat{p}_i$ and $H_c = -\sum_{i=1}^{s} \hat{q}_i log_e \hat{q}_i$. We

Table 3.2 List of species i comprising the farmland breeding bird community in Scotland. Also shown for each species are the following quantities for 2007 only: estimated mean probability of detection in the surveyed strips $\hat{\pi}_i$, total count n_i, mean of counts per site $\bar{n}_i$ (weighted by stratum area), and estimated abundance $\hat{N}_i$ (in thousands). 'UK' indicates that the estimate $\hat{\pi}_i$ was obtained using UK data, as there were too few detections in Scotland alone.

Species	$\hat{\pi}_i$	n_i	$\bar{n}_i$	$\hat{N}_i$
Red-legged partridge, *Alectoris rufa*	0.51	29	0.053	21.8
Grey partridge, *Perdix perdix*	0.61	35	0.049	16.6
Common quail, *Coturnix coturnix*	0.61	1	0.001	0.2
Common pheasant, *Phasianus colchicus*	0.49	314	0.562	237.3
Common kestrel, *Falco tinnunculus*	0.44	8	0.018	8.5
Corncrake, *Crex crex*	(0.61)	0	0	0
Stock dove, *Columba oenas*	0.47	29	0.021	9.2
European turtle dove, *Streptopelia turtur*	(0.59)uk	0	0	0
Sky lark, *Alauda arvensis*	0.65	1140	2.818	891.8
Yellow wagtail, *Motacilla flava*	0.37uk	2	0.005	3.1
Common whitethroat, *Sylvia communis*	0.32	194	0.438	285.9
Rook, *Corvus frugilegus*	0.78	958	2.000	543.1
Carrion crow, *Corvus corone*	0.64	695	1.219	398.7
Hooded crow, *Corvus cornix*	0.53	43	0.181	69.4
Tree sparrow, *Passer montanus*	0.27	72	0.084	62.4
Brambling, *Fringilla montifringilla*	0.38	1	0.001	0.5
Common linnet, *Carduelis cannabina*	0.38	359	0.869	452.3
Twite, *Carduelis flavirostris*	0.45	17	0.070	33.0
Yellowhammer, *Emberiza citronella*	0.41	411	0.935	482.0
Corn bunting, *Emberiza calandra*	0.43	11	0.005	2.6

also evaluated the geometric mean of relative abundances estimates, using either abundance estimates $\hat{N}_i$ (in which case relative abundance in a given year for species i is taken as the abundance estimate for that year divided by the abundance estimate for 1994) or mean counts $\bar{n}_i$ (so that the relative abundance for species i in a given year is estimated as the mean count for that year divided by the mean count for 1994). To avoid the problem of calculating a geometric mean when any estimates

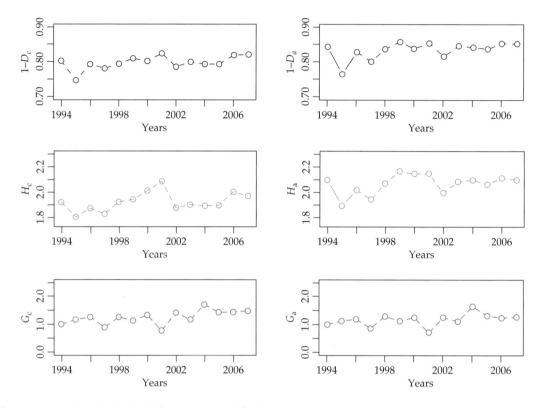

Figure 3.1 Estimated trends in breeding bird biodiversity in Scottish farmland, 1994–2007, assessed using Simpson's index $1-D$, the Shannon index H and the geometric mean G. The indices derived from counts $\bar{n}_i$ uncorrected for detectability are shown on the left-hand side, while those derived from abundance estimates $\hat{N}_i$ are shown on the right-hand side.

are zero, we excluded any species for which there was at least one year during 1994–2007 in which no birds were recorded. These species were red-legged partridge, common quail, corncrake, turtle dove, yellow wagtail, brambling, and corn bunting.

The above indices were evaluated for each year 1994 to 2007 (Fig. 3.1). Tests for linear trend were also conducted (Table 3.3).

As anticipated, diversity as measured by Simpson's or the Shannon index is estimated to be greater when we allow for different detectabilities between species than when we do not (Fig. 3.1). However, the evidence for trend in these indices is largely unaffected (Table 3.3). For the geometric mean based on counts, we obtain evidence of an increase in biodiversity over the time period of the BBS ($p = 0.024$), but if we allow for detectability, the test for linear trend becomes non-significant ($p = 0.126$, Table 3.3).

Table 3.3 Estimated slope of relationship between each of the following indices and year: Simpson's index ($1-D$), the Shannon index (H), and the geometric mean of relative abundance estimates (G). For each index, we show estimate (slope), standard error (s.e.) and the p value of the test of no slope for two cases: estimates calculated from counts uncorrected for detectability (subscript c) and estimates calculated from abundance estimates (subscript a).

Index	Slope	s.e.	p	Index	Slope	s.e.	p
$1-D_c$	0.0024	0.0011	0.058	$1-D_a$	0.0031	0.0015	0.059
H_c	0.0072	0.0047	0.153	H_a	0.0076	0.0050	0.153
G_c	0.0359	0.0139	0.024	G_a	0.0223	0.0136	0.126

3.5 Discussion

Ignoring detectability might not be a major problem if the bias is consistent across time or space. However, if effort varies between times or locations, then bias arising from variable detectability among species will itself be variable, generating bias in temporal or spatial trend estimates in biodiversity. We found clear evidence of bias in estimates of the Shannon and Simpson's indices from the Scottish farmland BBS data, when counts were uncorrected for detectability. In addition, we found that evidence for a trend in relative abundance, as measured by the geometric mean across species, vanished when the relative abundance estimates were corrected for detectability.

The goal of many biodiversity studies is to compare sites or communities that reflect natural variation (such as a successional or altitudinal gradient) or that have been subjected to anthropogenic impacts such as pollution or disturbance (Chapter 17). The localities or samples in such a comparison may differ in a number of ways. For example, the body size of organisms often changes when a site is polluted or a system is over-harvested—indeed the shifting relationship between biomass and numerical abundance is used as a measure of impact (Warwick & Clarke 1994). Body size is likely to influence detectability. Many sampling devices such as gill nets or plankton nets trap individuals within a particular size range so, although it may seem sensible to deploy the same sampling gear when assessing biodiversity at different sites, variation in detectability could generate misleading answers. Behavioural changes in harvested or hunted species (Casas et al. 2009) may also affect detectability.

If detectability cannot readily be estimated as an integral part of a monitoring scheme, it may be possible to carry out experiments at sample locations to estimate detection probabilities, although in some communities, such as speciose tropical arthropod assemblages, this will not be feasible.

In our example, although we have corrected for detectability, we anticipate that some bias will remain. Our analyses assume that birds that are on or very close to the transect line will be detected with certainty, and this is unlikely to be the case for some species, especially nocturnal species. In addition, it is not always possible to follow the ideal transect line, and the actual line covered may be biased towards or away from habitats preferred by certain species. Nevertheless, bias in estimated biodiversity trends can be expected to have been reduced.

Detectability can be particularly difficult to accommodate when most species are represented by very few individuals, so that even if the survey design allows detectability to be estimated, there may be insufficient data for reliable estimation. For single-site monitoring in tropical environments, typically around a third of the species are represented by just a single individual (Coddington et al. 2009). If the focus is on estimating regional biodiversity trends and data are gathered from a number of representative sites through the region, the proportion of species for which there are too few data to estimate detectability is likely to be smaller. This is related to the issue of 'repetitive sampling': repeated sampling of the same units results in more (apparently) rare species than when sampling occurs at the same intensity but where each area is sampled just once (Dobyns 1997; McGill 2003a). However, for highly diverse communities, the number of species with very few detections will remain large. Another strategy to reduce the number of apparently rare species in the sample is to use different trapping methods at each sample location, as a species that is unlikely to be caught by one method may be more likely to be caught by another (Longino et al. 2002). Of course, if the different methods sample different species entirely then, while the community is better represented, the proportion of species with very few detections for the data pooled across the trapping methods will be within the range observed for the separate methods.

3.6 Prospectus

The rising interest in monitoring regional biodiversity, sparked in large measure by the 2010 target, is starting to focus attention on the communities that are to be monitored. In statistical terminology, it is important to define the population (which typically comprises individuals of a number of species within a region in our case) about which we wish to draw inference. In this context, it is important either to ensure that individuals of different species are equally likely to be in our sample or to gather data that allow estimation of detectability by species. Thus we anticipate that the design and field protocols of surveys that are to be used to monitor biodiversity trends will receive closer scrutiny than has occurred to date.

We have shown how to adjust diversity indices when estimates of detectability are available from sample data. With respect to statistical inference, we expect further developments related to estimators and their properties, for when detectability varies among species. A thorough analysis would, for example, estimate uncertainty in the diversity estimates.

Especially when we are interested in monitoring regional biodiversity, our focus is more on a rate of change of diversity (and change in that rate of change) than in a single index value. While only a linear regression model was fitted to the adjusted diversity estimates here to look at trends over time, more sophisticated models such as the generalized additive models used by Buckland et al. (2005) provide greater flexibility, and thus potentially a better fit to the time series generated by the underlying ecological processes.

However, the issue of missing species will inevitably remain a focus of concern and of research, in particular when we are looking at a regional scale. Species might be missing because of seasonal effects at the time of the study or because they are rare and therefore missed in the sampling process. In the latter case, when a large number of plots is sampled repeatedly over time, occupancy methods are likely to prove useful for addressing this difficulty. It remains to be studied more closely how strongly the adjusted indices are affected by this uncertainty about the total number of species. Survey design as well as data analysis should try to take seasonal or other ecological effects into account as far as possible to allow identification of the different effects which lead to missed species in sample data.

3.7 Key points

1. When using diversity measures such as the Shannon and Simpson's indices, researchers are making the implicit assumption that individuals have been sampled at random from the community.
2. In most cases this assumption does not hold as there will be heterogeneity amongst individuals in the probability of detection.
3. If probability of detection of individuals can be calculated for each species, indices can be corrected for detectability.
4. Unseen species are also a detectability issue—in this case the species are too rare to have been detected by the sampling protocols or the protocols are ineffective for detecting the species.
5. The Scottish farmland bird community was used as a case study and detection functions fitted for each species. Estimates of biodiversity made using the Shannon and Simpson's indices were higher when the data were corrected for detectability, and the geometric mean of relative abundance estimates showed evidence of a positive trend for the uncorrected data, but no evidence of a trend for the corrected data.
6. A drawback of this approach is that detection functions cannot be fitted to rare species, so that either such species must be excluded from analysis or similar species must be identified that are assumed to have the same detectability.
7. If not estimated, variable detectability may introduce bias in many comparative investigations of biodiversity, such as contrasts between polluted and unpolluted assemblages and estimation of temporal or spatial trends in diversity.

Acknowledgements

We are very grateful for review comments from Rob Colwell, which led to a much improved manuscript.

PART II
Diversity

CHAPTER 4

Estimating species richness

Nicholas J. Gotelli and Robert K. Colwell

4.1 Introduction

Measuring species richness is an essential objective for many community ecologists and conservation biologists. The number of species in a local assemblage is an intuitive and natural index of community structure, and patterns of species richness have been measured at both small (e.g. Blake & Loiselle 2000) and large (e.g. Rahbek & Graves 2001) spatial scales. Many classic models in community ecology, such as the MacArthur–Wilson equilibrium model (MacArthur & Wilson 1967) and the intermediate disturbance hypothesis (Connell 1978), as well as more recent models of neutral theory (Hubbell 2001), metacommunity structure (Holyoak et al. 2005), and biogeography (Gotelli et al. 2009) generate quantitative predictions of the number of coexisting species. To make progress in modelling species richness, these predictions need to be compared with empirical data. In applied ecology and conservation biology, the number of species that remain in a community represents the ultimate 'scorecard' in the fight to preserve and restore perturbed communities (e.g. Brook et al. 2003).

Yet, in spite of our familiarity with species richness, it is a surprisingly difficult variable to measure. Almost without exception, species richness can be neither accurately measured nor directly estimated by observation because the observed number of species is a downward-biased estimator for the complete (total) species richness of a local assemblage. Hundreds of papers describe statistical methods for correcting this bias in the estimation of species richness (see also Chapter 3), and special protocols and methods have been developed for estimating species richness for particular taxa (e.g. Agosti et al. 2000). Nevertheless, many recent studies continue to ignore some of the fundamental sampling and measurement problems that can compromise the accurate estimation of species richness (Gotelli & Colwell 2001).

In this chapter we review the basic statistical issues involved with species richness estimation. Although a complete review of the subject is beyond the scope of this chapter, we highlight sampling models for species richness that account for undersampling bias by adjusting or controlling for differences in the number of individuals and the number of samples collected (rarefaction) as well as models that use abundance or incidence distributions to estimate the number of undetected species (estimators of asymptotic richness).

4.2 State of the field

4.2.1 Sampling models for biodiversity data

Although the methods of estimating species richness that we discuss can be applied to assemblages of organisms that have been identified by genotype (e.g. Hughes et al. 2000), to species, or to some higher taxonomic rank, such as genus or family (e.g. Bush & Bambach 2004), we will write 'species' to keep it simple. Because we are discussing estimation of species richness, we assume that one or more *samples* have been taken, by collection or observation, from one or more *assemblages* for some specified group or groups of organisms. We distinguish two kinds of data used in richness studies: (1) *incidence data*, in which each species detected in a sample from an assemblage is simply noted as being present, and (2) *abundance data*, in which the abundance of each species is tallied within each sample. Of course, abundance data can always be converted to incidence data, but not the reverse.

Box 4.1 Observed and estimated richness

S_{obs} is the total number of species observed in a sample, or in a set of samples.

S_{est} is the estimated number of species in the assemblage represented by the sample, or by the set of samples, where *est* is replaced by the name of an estimator.

Abundance data. Let f_k be the number of species each represented by exactly k individuals in a single sample. Thus, f_0 is the number of *undetected* species (species present in the assemblage but not included in the sample), f_1 is the number of *singleton* species, f_2 is the number of *doubleton* species, etc. The total number of individuals in the sample is $n = \sum_{k=1}^{S_{obs}} f_k$.

Replicated incidence data. Let q_k be the number of species present in exactly k samples in a set of replicate incidence samples. Thus, q_0 is the number of *undetected* species (species present in the assemblage but not included in the set of samples), q_1 is the number of *unique* species, q_2 is the number of *duplicate* species, etc. The total number of samples is $m = \sum_{k=1}^{S_{obs}} q_k$.

Chao 1 (for abundance data)

$S_{Chao1} = S_{obs} + \frac{f_1^2}{2 f_2}$ is the classic form, but is not defined when $f_2 = 0$ (no doubletons).

$S_{Chao1} = S_{obs} + \frac{f_1(f_1-1)}{2(f_2+1)}$ is a bias-corrected form, always obtainable.

$$\text{var}(S_{Chao1}) = f_2 \left[\frac{1}{2}\left(\frac{f_1}{f_2}\right)^2 + \left(\frac{f_1}{f_2}\right)^3 + \frac{1}{4}\left(\frac{f_1}{f_2}\right)^4 \right] \text{ for}$$

$f_1 > 0$ and $f_2 > 0$ (see Colwell 2009, Appendix B of *EstimateS User's Guide* for other cases and for asymmetrical confidence interval computation).

Chao 2 (for replicated incidence data)

$S_{Chao2} = S_{obs} + \frac{q_1^2}{2q_2}$ is the classic form, but is not defined when $q_2 = 0$ (no duplicates).

$S_{Chao2} = S_{obs} + \left(\frac{m-1}{m}\right)\frac{q_1(q_1-1)}{2(q_2+1)}$ is a bias-corrected form, always obtainable.

$$\text{var}(S_{Chao2}) = q_2\left[\frac{1}{2}\left(\frac{q_1}{q_2}\right)^2 + \left(\frac{q_1}{q_2}\right)^3 + \frac{1}{4}\left(\frac{q_1}{q_2}\right)^4 \right] \text{ for}$$

$q_1 > 0$ and $q_2 > 0$ (see Colwell 2009, Appendix B of *EstimateS User's Guide* for other cases and for asymmetrical confidence interval computation).

ACE (for abundance data)

$S_{rare} = \sum_{k=1}^{10} f_k$ is the number of *rare* species in a sample (each with 10 or fewer individuals).

$S_{abund} = \sum_{k=11}^{S_{obs}} f_k$ is the number of *abundant* species in a sample (each with more than 10 individuals).

$n_{rare} = \sum_{k=1}^{10} k f_k$ is the total number of individuals in the rare species.

The sample coverage estimate is $C_{ACE} = 1 - \frac{f_1}{n_{rare}}$, the proportion of all individuals in rare species that are not singletons. Then the ACE estimator of species richness is $S_{ACE} = S_{abund} + \frac{S_{rare}}{C_{ACE}} + \frac{f_1}{C_{ACE}}\gamma^2_{ACE}$, where γ^2_{ACE} is the coefficient of variation,

$$\gamma^2_{ACE} = \max\left[\frac{S_{rare}}{C_{ACE}} \frac{\sum_{k=1}^{10} k(k-1)f_k}{(n_{rare})(n_{rare}-1)} - 1, 0 \right]$$

The formula for ACE is undefined when all rare species are singletons ($f_1 = n_{rare}$, yielding $C_{ACE} = 0$). In this case, compute the bias-corrected form of Chao1 instead.

ICE (for incidence data)

$S_{infr} = \sum_{k=1}^{10} q_k$ is the number of *infrequent* species in a sample (each found in 10 or fewer samples).

$S_{freq} = \sum_{k=11}^{S_{obs}} q_k$ is the number of *frequent* species in a sample (each found in more than 10 samples).

$n_{infr} = \sum_{k=1}^{10} k q_k$ is the total number of incidences in the infrequent species.

The sample coverage estimate is $C_{ICE} = 1 - \frac{q_1}{n_{infr}}$, the proportion of all incidences of infrequent species that are not uniques. Then the ICE estimator of species richness is $C_{ICE} = S_{freq} + \frac{S_{infr}}{C_{ICE}} + \frac{q_1}{C_{ICE}}\gamma^2_{ICE}$, where γ^2_{ICE} is the coefficient of variation,

$$\gamma^2_{ICE} = \max\left[\frac{S_{infr}}{C_{ICE}} \frac{m_{infr}}{(m_{infr}-1)} \frac{\sum_{k=1}^{10} k(k-1)q_k}{(n_{infr})^2} - 1, 0 \right]$$

The formula for ICE is undefined when all infrequent species are uniques ($q_1 = n_{\text{infr}}$, yielding $C_{ICE} = 0$). In this case, compute the bias-corrected form of Chao2 instead.

Jackknife estimators (for abundance data)

The first-order jackknife richness estimator is

$$S_{jackknife1} = S_{obs} + f_1$$

The second-order jackknife richness estimator is

$$S_{jackknife2} = S_{obs} + 2f_1 - f_2$$

Jackknife estimators (for incidence data)

The first-order jackknife richness estimator is

$$S_{jackknife1} = S_{obs} + q_1 \left(\frac{m-1}{m} \right)$$

The second-order jackknife richness estimator is

$$S_{jackknife2} = S_{obs} + \left[\frac{q_1 (2m-3)}{m} - \frac{q_2 (m-2)^2}{m(m-1)} \right]$$

By their nature, sampling data document only the verified *presence* of species in samples. The absence of a particular species in a sample may represent either a true absence (the species is not present in the assemblage) or a false absence (the species is present, but was not detected in the sample; see Chapter 3). Although the term 'presence/absence data' is often used as a synonym for incidence data, the importance of distinguishing true absences from false ones (not only for richness estimation, but in modelling contexts, e.g. Elith et al. 2006) leads us to emphasize that incidence data are actually 'presence data'. Richness estimation methods for abundance data assume that organisms can be sampled and identified as distinct individuals. For clonal and colonial organisms, such as many species of grasses and corals, individuals cannot always be separated or counted, but methods designed for incidence data can nonetheless be used if species presence is recorded within standardized quadrats or samples (e.g. Butler & Chazdon 1998).

Snacking from a jar of mixed jellybeans provides a good analogy for biodiversity sampling (Longino et al. 2002). Each jellybean represents a single individual, and the different colours represent the different species in the jellybean 'assemblage'—in a typical sample, some colours are common, but most are rare. Collecting a sample of biodiversity data is equivalent to taking a small handful of jellybeans from the jar and examining them one by one. From this incomplete sample, we try to make inferences about the number of colours (species) in the entire jar. This process of statistical inference depends critically on the biological assumption that the community is 'closed,' with an unchanging total number of species and a steady species abundance distribution. Jellybeans may be added or removed from the jar, but the proportional representation of colours is assumed to remain the same. In an open metacommunity, in which the assemblage changes size and composition through time, it may not be possible to draw valid inferences about community structure from a snapshot sample at one point in time (Magurran 2007). Few, if any, real communities are completely 'closed', but many are sufficiently circumscribed that that richness estimators may be used, but with caution and caveats.

For all of the methods and metrics (Box 4.1) that we discuss in this chapter, we make the closely related statistical assumption that sampling is *with replacement*. In terms of collecting inventory data from nature, this assumption means either that individuals are recorded, but not removed, from the assemblage (e.g. censusing trees in a plot) or, if they are removed, the proportions remaining are unchanged by the sampling.

This framework of sampling, counting, and identifying individuals applies not only to richness estimation, but also to many other questions in the study of biodiversity, including the characterization of the species abundance distribution (see Chapter 9) and partitioning diversity into α and β components (see Chapters 6 and 7).

Figure 4.1 Species accumulation and rarefaction curves. The *jagged line* is the *species accumulation curve* for one of many possible orderings of 121 soil seedbank samples, yielding a total of 952 individual tree seedlings, from an intensive census of a plot of Costa Rican rainforest (Butler & Chazdon 1998). The cumulative number of tree species (*y*-axis) is plotted as a function of the cumulative number of samples (upper *x*-axis), pooled in random order. The smooth, solid line is the *sample-based rarefaction curve* for the same data set, showing the mean number of species for all possible combinations of 1, 2, ..., m^*, ..., 121 actual samples from the dataset—this curve plots the statistical expectation of the (sample-based) species accumulation curve. The *dashed line* is the *individual-based rarefaction curve* for the same data set—the expected number of species for (m^*) (952/121) individuals, randomly chosen from all 952 individuals (lower *x*-axis). The black dot indicates the total richness for all samples (or all individuals) pooled. The sample-based rarefaction curve lies below the individual-based rarefaction curve because of spatial aggregation within species. This is a very typical pattern for empirical comparisons of sample-based and individual-based rarefaction curves.

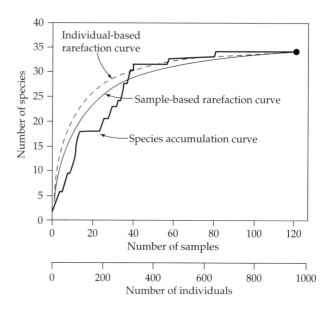

4.2.2 The species accumulation curve

Consider a graph in which the *x*-axis is the number of individuals sampled and the *y*-axis is the cumulative number of species recorded (Fig. 4.1, lower *x*-axis). Imagine taking one jellybean at a time from the jar, at random. As more individuals (jellybeans) are sampled, the total number of species (colours) recorded in the sample increases, and a *species accumulation curve* is generated. Of course, the first individual drawn will represent exactly one species new to the sample, so all species accumulation curves based on individual organisms originate at the point [1,1]. The next individual drawn will represent either the same species or a species new to the sample. The probability of drawing a new species will depend both on the complete number of species in the assemblage and their relative abundances. The more species in the assemblage and the more even the species abundance distribution (see Chapter 9), the more rapidly this curve will rise. In contrast, if the species abundance distribution is highly uneven (a few common species and many rare ones, for example), the curve will rise more slowly, even at the outset, because most of the individuals sampled will represent more common species that have already been added to the sample, rather than rarer ones that have yet to be detected.

Regardless of the species abundance distribution, this curve increases monotonically, with a decelerating slope. For a given sample, different stochastic realizations of the order in which the individuals in the sample are added to the graph will produce species accumulation curves that differ slightly from one another. The smoothed average of these individual curves represents the statistical expectation of the species accumulation curve for that particular sample, and the variability among the different orderings is reflected in the variance in the number of species recorded for any given number of individuals. However, this variance is specific, or *conditional*, on the particular sample that we have drawn because it is based only on re-orderings of that single sample. Suppose, instead, we plot the smoothed average of several species accumulation curves, each based on a different handful of jellybeans from the same jar, each handful having the same number of beans. Variation among these smoothed curves from the several independent, random samples represents another source of variation in richness, for a given number of individuals. The variance among these curves is called an *unconditional* variance because it estimates the true variance in richness of the assemblage. The unconditional variance in richness is necessarily larger than the variance conditional on any single sample.

4.2.3   Climbing the species accumulation curve

In theory, finding out how many species characterize an assemblage means sampling more and more individuals until no new species are found and the species accumulation curve reaches an asymptote. In practice, this approach is routinely impossible for two reasons. First, the number of individuals that must be sampled to reach an asymptote can often be prohibitively large (Chao et al. 2009). The problem is most severe in the tropics, where species diversity is high and most species are rare. For example, after nearly 30 consecutive years of sampling, an ongoing inventory of a tropical rainforest ant assemblage at La Selva, Costa Rica, has still not reached an asymptote in species richness. Each year, one or two new species are added to the local list. In some cases these species are already known from collections at other localities, but in other cases they are new to science (Longino et al. 2002). In other words, biodiversity samples, even very extensive ones, often fall short of revealing the complete species richness for an assemblage, representing some unspecified milestone along a slowly rising species accumulation curve with an unknown destination.

A second reason that the species accumulation curve cannot be used to directly determine species richness is that, in field sampling, ecologists almost never collect random individuals in sequence. Instead, individual plants or mobile animals are often recorded from transects or points counts, or individual organisms are collected in pitfall and bait traps, sweep samples, nets, plankton tows, water, soil, and leaf litter samples, and other taxon-specific sampling units that capture multiple individuals (Southwood & Henderson 2000). Although these samples can, under appropriate circumstances, be treated as independent of one another, the individuals accumulated within a single sample do not represent independent observations. Although individuals contain the biodiversity 'information' (species identity), it is the samples that represent the statistically independent replicates for analysis. When spatial and temporal autocorrelation is taken into account, the samples themselves may be only partially independent. Nevertheless, the inevitable non-independence of individuals within samples can be overcome by plotting a second kind of species accumulation curve, called *a sample-based* species accumulation curve, in which the x-axis is the number of samples and the y-axis is the accumulated number of species (Fig. 4.1, upper x-axis). Because only the identity but not the number of individuals of each species represented within a sample is needed to construct a sample-based species accumulation curve, these curves plot incidence data. This approach is therefore also suitable for clonal and colonial species that cannot be counted as discrete individuals.

4.2.4   Species richness versus species density

The observed number of species recorded in a sample (or a set of samples) is very sensitive to the number of individuals or samples observed or collected, which in turn is influenced by the effective area that is sampled and, in replicated designs, by the spatial arrangement of the replicates. Thus, many measures reported as 'species richness' are effectively measures of species density: the number of species collected in a *particular* total area. For quadrat samples or other methods that sample a fixed area, *species density* is expressed in units of species per *specified* area. Even for traps that collect individuals at a single point (such as a pitfall trap), there is probably an effective sampling area that is encompassed by data collection at a single point.

Whenever sampling is involved, species density is a slippery concept that is often misused and misunderstood. The problem arises from the non-linearity of the species accumulation curve. Consider the species accumulation curve for rainforest seedlings (Butler & Chazdon 1998) in Fig. 4.2, which plots the species of seedlings grown from dormant seed in 121 soil samples, each covering a soil surface area of $17.35\,\text{cm}^2$ and a depth of 10 cm. The x-axis plots the cumulative surface area of soil sampled. The *slopes* of lines A, B, and C represent species density: *number of species observed* (y), divided by *area-sampled* (x). You can see that species density

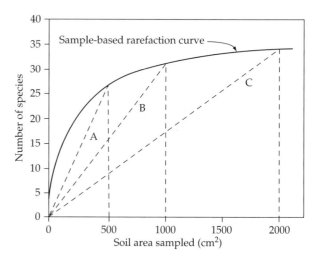

Figure 4.2 Species richness and species density are not the same thing. The *solid line* is the *sample-based rarefaction curve* for the same data set as in Fig 4.1, showing the expected species richness of rainforest tree seedlings for 1, 2, ..., m^*, ..., 121 soil samples, each covering a soil surface area of 17.35 cm² and a depth of 10 cm. *Species richness* (*y*-axis) is plotted as a function of the total *soil surface area* sampled (*x*-axis). Because *species density* is the ratio of richness (*y*-coordinate) to area (*x*-coordinate) for any point in the graph, the *slopes* of lines A, B, and C quantify species density for 500, 1000, and 2000 cm², respectively. Clearly, species density estimates depend on the *particular* amount of area sampled. All of the species density slopes over-estimate species number when extrapolated to larger areas, and species density estimates based on differing areas are not comparable.

depends critically not just on area, but on the *specific* amount of area sampled. For this reason, it *never* works to 'standardize' the species richness of samples from two or more assemblages by simply dividing observed richness by area sampled (or by any other measure of effort, including number of individuals or number of samples). Estimating species density by calculating the ratio of species richness to area sampled will always grossly over-estimate species density when this index is extrapolated to larger areas, and the size of that bias will depend on the area sampled.

Sometimes, however, ecologists or conservation biologists are interested in species density, for some particular amount of area, in its own right. For example, if only one of two areas, equal in size and cost per hectare, can be purchased to establish a reserve, species density at the scale of the reserve is clearly a variable of interest. Because *species density* is so sensitive to area (and, ultimately, to the number of individuals observed or collected), it is useful to decompose it into the product of two quantities: *species richness* (number of species represented by some *particular* number, N, of individuals) and *total individual density* (number of individuals N, disregarding species, in some *particular* amount of area A):

$$\left(\frac{species}{area\ A}\right) = \left(\frac{species}{N\ individuals}\right) \times \left(\frac{N\ individuals}{area\ A}\right)$$

(James & Wamer 1982). This decomposition demonstrates that the number of species per sampling unit reflects both the underlying species richness and the total number of individuals sampled. If two samples differ in species density, is it because of differences in underlying species richness, differences in abundance, or some combination of both? In other words, how do we meaningfully compare the species richness of collections that probably differ in both the number of individuals and the number of samples collected? Until recently, many ecologists have not recognized this problem. The distinction between species density and species richness has not always been appreciated, and many papers have compared species density using standard parametric statistics, but without accounting for differences in abundance or sampling effort.

One statistical solution is to treat abundance, number of samples, or sample area as a covariate that can be entered into a multiple regression analysis or an analysis of covariance. If the original data (counts and identities of individuals) are not available, this may be the best that we can do. For example, Dunn et al. (2009) assembled a global database of ant species richness from a number of published studies. To control for sampling effects, they used the area, number of samples, and total number of individuals from each sample location as statistical covariates in regression analyses. However, they did not make the mistake of trying to 'standard-ize' the richness of different samples by dividing the species counts by the area, the number of individuals sampled, or any other measure of effort. As we have repeatedly emphasized, this rescaling produces serious distortions: extrapolations from small sample ratios of species density inevitably lead to gross over-estimates of the number of species expected in larger sample areas (Fig. 4.2 and Figure 4–6 in Gotelli & Colwell 2001).

4.2.5 Individual-based rarefaction

The species accumulation curve itself suggests an intuitive way to compare the richness of two samples (for the same kind of organism) that differ in the number of individuals collected. Suppose one of the two samples has N individuals and S species, and the other has n individuals and s species. The samples differ in the number of individuals present ($N > n$) and will usually differ in the number of species present (typically $S > s$). In the procedure called *rarefaction*, we randomly draw n^* individuals, subsampling *without* replacement from the larger of the two original samples, where $n^* = n$, the size of the smaller original sample. (This re-sampling, without replacement, of individuals from within the sample does not violate the assumption that the process of taking the sample itself did not change the relative abundance of species). Computing the mean number of species, $\bar{s}^*$, among repeated subsamples of n^* individuals estimates $E(s^*|n^*)$, the expected number of species in a random subsample of n^* individuals from the larger original sample (Fig. 4.1, lower x-axis). The variance of (s^*), among random re-orderings of individuals, can also be estimated this way along with a parametric 95% confidence interval, or the confidence interval can be estimated from the bootstrapped values (Manly 1991).

A simple test can now be conducted to ask whether s, the observed species richness of the complete smaller sample, falls within the 95% confidence interval of s^*, the expected species richness based on random subsamples of size n from the larger sample (Simberloff 1978). If the observed value falls within the confidence interval, then the hypothesis that the richness of the smaller sample,

based on all n individuals, does not differ from the richness of a subsample of size n^* from the larger sample cannot be rejected at $P \leq 0.05$. If this null hypothesis is not rejected, and the original, unrarefied samples differed in species density, then this difference in species density must be driven by differing numbers of individuals between the two samples. Alternatively, if s is not contained within the confidence interval of s^*, the two samples differ in species richness in ways that cannot be accounted for entirely by differences in abundance and/or sampling effort (at $P \leq 0.05$).

Rarefaction can be used not only to calculate a point estimate of s^*, but also to construct an entire *rarefaction curve* in which the number of individuals randomly subsampled ranges from 1 to N. Rarefaction can be thought of as a method of *interpolating* $E(s^*|n^*)$ the expected number of species, given n^* individuals ($1 \leq n^* \leq N$), between the point [1, 1] and the point [S, N] (Colwell et al. 2004). With progressively smaller subsamples from $N - 1$ to 1, the resulting *individual-based rarefaction curve*, in a sense, is the reverse of the corresponding species accumulation curve, which progressively builds larger and larger samples.

Because this individual-based rarefaction curve is conditional on one particular sample, the variance in s^*, among random re-orderings of individuals, is 0 at both extremes of the curve: with the minimum of only one individual there will always be only one species represented, and with the maximum of N individuals, there will always be exactly S species represented. Hurlbert (1971) and Heck et al. (1975) give analytical solutions for the expectation and the *conditional* variance of s^*, which are derived from the hypergeometric distribution. In contrast, treating the sample (one handful of jellybeans) as representative of a larger assemblage (the jar of jellybeans) requires an estimate of the *unconditional* variance (the variance in $s^*|n^*$ among replicate handfuls of jellybeans from the same jar). The unconditional variance in richness, S, for the full sample of N individuals, must be greater than zero to account for the heterogeneity that would be expected with additional random samples of the same size taken from the entire assemblage. Although Smith & Grassle (1977) derived an estimator for the unconditional variance of $E(s^*|n^*)$, it is computationally complex and has been little used. R.K. Colwell and C.X. Mao (in preparation) have recently derived an unconditional variance estimator for individual-based rarefaction that is analogous to the unconditional variance estimator for sample-based rarefaction described in Colwell et al. (2004), and discussed below.

Regardless of how the variance is estimated, the statistical significance of the difference in rarefied species richness between two samples will depend, in part, on n, the number of individuals being compared. This sample-size dependence arises because all rarefaction curves based on individuals converge at the point [1,1]. Therefore, no matter how different two assemblages are, rarefaction curves based on samples of individuals drawn at random will not appear to differ statistically if n is too small. In some cases, rarefaction curves may cross at higher values of n, making the results of statistical tests even more dependent on n (e.g. Raup 1975).

To compare multiple samples, each can be rarefied down to a common abundance, which will typically be the total abundance for the smallest of the samples. At that point, the set of s^* values, one for each sample, can be used as a response variable in any kind of statistical analysis, such as ANOVA or regression. This method assumes that the rarefaction curves do not cross (which may be assessed visually), so that their rank order remains the same regardless of the abundance level used. Alternatively, multiple samples from the same assemblage can be used in a *sample-based rarefaction*, which we describe below.

Rarefaction has a long history in ecology and evolution (Sanders 1968; Hurlbert 1971; Raup 1975; Tipper 1979; Järvinen 1982; Chiarucci et al. 2008).The method was proposed in the 1960s and 1970s to compare species number when samples differed in abundance (Tipper 1979), but the same statistical problem had been solved many decades earlier by biogeographers who wanted to estimate species/genus ratios and other taxonomic diversity indices (Järvinen 1982).

Brewer & Williamson (1994) and Colwell & Coddington (1994) pointed out that a very close approximation for the rarefaction curve is the Coleman 'passive sampling' curve,

$$E\left(s^*\right) = \sum_{i=1}^{S}\left[1 - \left(1 - n^*/N\right)^{n_i}\right], \qquad (4.1)$$

in which i indexes species from 1 to S, and n_i is the abundance of species i in the full sample. As a null model for the species–area relationship (see Chapter 20), the Coleman curve assumes that islands of different area randomly intercept individuals and accumulate different numbers of species (Coleman et al. 1982). The individual-based rarefaction curve is very closely analogous to the Coleman curve (and, although mathematically distinct, differs only slightly from it) because relative island area is a proxy for the proportion n^*/N of individuals subsampled from the pooled distribution of all individuals in the original sample (Gotelli 2008).

4.2.6 Sample-based rarefaction

Individual-based rarefaction computes the expected number of species, s^*, in a subsample of n^* *individuals* drawn at random from a *single* representative sample from an assemblage. In contrast, *sample-based rarefaction* computes the expected number of species s^* when m^* *samples* $(1 \leq m^* \leq M)$ are drawn at random (without replacement) from a *set of samples* that are, collectively, representative of an assemblage (Fig. 4.1, upper x-axis) (Gotelli & Colwell 2001; Colwell et al. 2004). (This re-sampling, without replacement, of samples from within the sample set does not violate the assumption that the process of taking the sample itself did not change the relative abundance of species.) The fundamental difference is that sample-based rarefaction, by design, preserves the spatial structure of the data, which may reflect processes such as spatial aggregation or segregation (see Chapter 12) both within and between species. In contrast, individual-based rarefaction does not preserve the spatial structure of the data and assumes complete random mixing among individuals of all species. Thus, for sample-based rarefaction, $E\left(s^*|m^*\right)$ is the expected number of species for m^* pooled samples that express the same patterns of aggregation, association, or segregation as the observed set of samples. For this reason, sample-based rarefaction is a more realistic treatment of the independent sampling units used in most biodiversity studies. Because sample-based rarefaction requires only incidence data, it can also be used for clonal organisms or for species in which individuals in a sample cannot be easily distinguished or counted.

Operationally, sample-based rarefaction can be carried out by repeatedly selecting and pooling m^* samples at random from the set of samples, and computing the mean and conditional (on the particular set of samples) variance and 95% confidence interval for s^*. On the other hand, $E(s^*|m^*)$ is more easily and accurately computed from combinatorial equations based on the distribution of *counts*, the number of species found in exactly 1, 2, ..., m^* samples in the set (Ugland et al. 2003; Colwell et al. 2004; see Chiarucci et al. 2008 for a history of this approach). Colwell et al. 2004 also introduced a sample-based version of the Coleman rarefaction model, the results of which closely approximate the true sample-based rarefaction curve.

Ugland et al. (2003) provide an expression for the conditional variance in richness estimates from sample-based rarefaction. Colwell et al. (2004) derived an unconditional variance estimator for sample-based rarefaction that treats the observed set of samples, in turn, as a sample from some larger assemblage, so that the variance in S for all M samples, pooled (the full set of samples), takes some non-zero value. This unconditional variance (and its associated confidence interval (CI)) accounts for the variability expected among replicate sets of samples. Based on unconditional variances for two sample-based rarefaction curves, richness can be compared for any common number of samples (or individuals, as explained below). Using eigenvalue decomposition, Mao & Li (2009) developed a computationally complex method for comparing two sample-based rarefaction curves in their entirety. A much simpler, but approximate, method is to assess, for a desired value of m^*, whether or not the two (appropriately computed) confidence intervals overlap. If the two CIs (calculated from the unconditional variance) are approximately equal, for a type I error rate of $P < 0.05$, the appropriate CI is about 84% (Payton et al. 2003; the z value for 84% CI is 0.994 standard deviations). Basing the

test on the overlap of traditional 95% CIs is overly conservative: richness values that would differ significantly with the 84% interval would often be declared statistically indistinguishable because the 95% intervals for the same pair of samples would overlap (Payton et al. 2003).

An important pitfall to avoid in using sample-based rarefaction to compare richness between sample sets is that the method does not directly control for differences in overall abundance between sets of samples. Suppose two sets of samples are recorded from the same assemblage, but they differ in mean number of individuals per sample (systematically or by chance). When plotted as a function of number of samples (on the x-axis) the sample-based rarefaction curve for the sample set with a higher mean abundance per sample will lie above the curve for the sample set with lower mean abundance because more individuals reveal more species. The solution suggested by Gotelli & Colwell (2001) is to first calculate sample-based rarefaction curves and their variances (or CIs) for each set of samples in the analysis. Next, the curves are re-plotted against an x-axis of individual abundance, rather than number of samples. This re-plotting effectively shifts the points of each individual-based rarefaction curve to the left or the right, depending on the average number of individuals that were collected in each sample. Ellison et al. (2007) used this method to compare the efficacy of ant sampling methods that differed greatly in the average number of individuals per sample (e.g. 2 ants per pitfall trap, versus > 89 ants per plot for standardized hand sampling). Note that if sample-based rarefaction is based on species occurrences rather than abundances, then the rescaled x-axis is the number of species occurrences, not the number of individuals.

4.2.7 Assumptions of rarefaction

To use rarefaction to compare species richness of two (or more) samples or assemblages rigorously, the following assumptions should be met:

1. *Sufficient sampling.* As with any other statistical procedure, the power to detect a difference, if there is one, depends on having

large enough individuals or samples, especially since rarefactions curves necessarily converge towards the origin. Although it is difficult to give specific recommendations, our experience has been that rarefaction curves should be based on at least 20 individuals (individual-based rarefaction) or 20 samples (sample-based rarefaction), and preferably many more.

2. *Comparable sampling methods.* Because all sampling methods have inherent and usually unknown sampling biases that favour detection of some species but not others (see Chapter 3), rarefaction cannot be used to compare data from two different assemblages that were collected with two different methods (e.g. bait samples vs pitfall traps, mist-netting vs point-sampling for birds). However, rarefaction can be used meaningfully to compare the efficacy of different sampling methods that are used in the same area (Longino et al. 2002; Ellison et al. 2007). Also, data from different sampling methods may be pooled in order to maximize the kinds of species that may be sampled with different sampling methods (e.g. ants in Colwell et al. (2008)). However, identical sampling and pooling procedures must to be employed to compare two composite collections.

3. *Taxonomic similarity.* The assemblages represented by the two samples should be taxonomically 'similar'. In other words, if two samples that differ in abundance but have rarefaction curves with identical shapes do not share any taxa, we would not want to conclude that the smaller collection is a random subsample of the larger (Tipper 1979). Rarefaction seems most useful when the species composition of the smaller sample appears to be a nested or partially nested subset of the larger collection. Much more powerful methods are now available to test directly for differences in species composition (Chao et al. 2005).

4. *Closed communities of discrete individuals.* The assemblages being sampled should be well circumscribed, with consistent membership. Discrete individuals in a single sample must be countable (individual-based rarefaction) or species presence in multiple samples must be detectable (sample-based rarefaction).

5. *Random placement.* Individual-based rarefaction assumes that the spatial distribution of individuals sampled is random. If individuals within species are spatially aggregated, individual-based rarefaction will over-estimate species richness because it assumes that the rare and common species are perfectly intermixed. Some authors have modified the basic rarefaction equations to include explicit terms for spatial clumping (Kobayashi & Kimura 1994). However, this approach is rarely successful because the model parameters (such as the constants in the negative binomial distribution) cannot be easily and independently estimated for all of the species in the sample. One way to deal with aggregation is to increase the distance or timing between randomly sampled individuals so that patterns of spatial or temporal aggregation are not so prominent. An even better approach is to use sample-based rarefaction, again employing sampling areas that are large enough to overcome small-scale aggregation.

6. *Independent, random sampling.* Individuals or samples should be collected randomly and independently. Both the individual-based and sample-based methods described in this chapter assume that sampling, from nature, does not affect the relative abundance of species (statistically, sampling with replacement). However, if the sample is relatively small compared to the size of the underlying assemblage (which is often the case), the results should be similar for samples collected with or without replacement. More work is needed to derive estimators that can be used for sampling without replacement, which will be important for cases in which the sample represents a large fraction of the total assemblage. Unfortunately, as we have noted earlier, biodiversity data rarely consist of collections of individuals that were sampled randomly. Instead, the data often consist of a series of random and approximately independent samples that contain multiple individuals.

4.2.8 Estimating asymptotic species richness

Consider the species richness of a single biodiversity sample (or the pooled richness of a set of samples) as the starting point in a graph of richness versus abundance or sample number (the dot at the right-hand end of the curves in Fig. 4.1). Rarefaction amounts to *interpolating* 'backward' from the endpoint of a species accumulation curve, yielding estimates of species richness expected for smaller numbers of individuals or samples. In contrast, using this starting point to estimate the complete richness of the assemblage, including species that were not detected by the sample, can be visualized as *extrapolating* 'forward' along a hypothetical projection the accumulation curve (Colwell et al. 2004, their Figure 4). Two objectives of extrapolation can be distinguished: (1) estimating the richness of a larger sample and (2) estimating the complete richness of the assemblage, visualized as the asymptote of the accumulation curve. Once this asymptote is reached, the species accumulation curve is flat and additional sampling will not yield any additional species.

Why should the species accumulation curve have an asymptote? On large geographical scales, it does not: larger areas accumulate species at a constant or even an increasing rate because expanded sampling incorporates diverse habitat types that support distinctive species assemblages (see Chapter 20). As a consequence, the species accumulation curve continues to increase, and will not reach a final asymptote until it approaches the total area of the biosphere. The subject of *species turnover* is covered by Jost et al. and Magurran (Chapters 6 and 7) and *species–area relationships* are the subject of Chapter 20. In this chapter, we focus on the estimation of species richness at smaller spatial scales—scales at which an asymptote is a reasonable supposition and sampling issues are substantially more important than spatial turnover on habitat mosaics or gradients (Cam et al. 2002). In statistical terms, we assume that samples were drawn independently and at random from the local assemblage, so that the ordering of the samples in time or space is not important. In fact, *un*importance of sample order is diagnostic of the kinds of sample sets appropriately used by ecologists to assess local species richness (Colwell et al. 2004).

The most direct approach to estimating the species richness asymptote is to fit an asymptotic mathematical function (such as the Michaelis–

Menten function; Keating & Quinn (1998)) to a rarefaction or species accumulation curve. This approach dates back at least to Holdridge et al. (1971), who fitted a negative binomial function to smoothed species accumulation curves to compare the richness of Costa Rica trees at different localities. Many other asymptotic functions have since been explored (reviewed by Colwell & Coddington (1994), Flather (1996), Chao (2005), and Rosenzweig et al. (2003)). Unfortunately, this strictly phenomenological method, despite the advantage that it makes no assumptions about sampling schemes or species abundance distributions, does not seem to work well in practice. Two or more functions may fit a dataset equally well, but yield drastically different estimates of asymptotic richness (Soberón & Llorente 1993; Chao 2005), and variance estimates for the asymptote are necessarily large. Residual analysis often reveals that the popular functions do not correctly fit the shape of empirical species accumulation curves (O'Hara 2005), and this curve-fitting method consistently performs worse than other approaches (Walther & Moore 2005; Walther & Morand 2008). For these reasons, we do not recommend fitting asymptotic mathematical functions as a means of estimating complete species richness of local assemblages.

Mixture models, in which species abundance or occurrence distributions are modelled as a weighted mixture of statistical distributions, offer a completely different, non-parametric approach to extrapolating an empirical rarefaction curve to a larger sample sizes (or a larger set of samples) (reviewed by Mao et al. (2005), Mao & Colwell (2005), and Chao (2005)). Colwell et al. (2004), for example, modelled the sample-based rarefaction curve as a binomial mixture model. However, these models are effective only for a doubling or tripling of the observed sample size. Beyond this point, the variance of the richness estimate increases rapidly. Unless the initial sample size is very large, projecting the curve to an asymptotic value usually requires much more than a doubling or tripling of the initial sample size (Chao et al. 2009), so this method is not always feasible, especially for hyperdiverse taxa (Mao & Colwell 2005).

Another classical approach to estimating asymptotic richness is to fit a species abundance

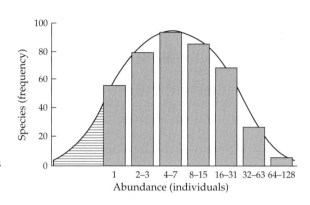

Figure 4.3   Estimation of asymptotic species richness by fitting a log-normal distribution to a species abundance distribution. The graph shows the number of species of ants in each of seven logarithmically-scaled abundance categories (a total of 435 species collected) in a long-term rainforest inventory in Costa Rica (Longino et al. 2002). The number of undetected species (21 additional species) is estimated by the area marked with horizontal hatching, yielding a predicted complete richness of 456 species.

distribution (see Chapter 9), based on a single sample, to a truncated parametric distribution, then estimate the 'missing' portion of the distribution, which corresponds to the undetected species in an assemblage. Fisher et al. (1943) pioneered this approach by fitting a geometric series to a large sample of moths captured at light traps. Relative incidence distributions from replicated sets of samples can be treated in the same way (Longino et al. 2002). The most widely used species abundance distribution for this approach is the log-normal (Fig. 4.3) and its variants (from Preston (1948) to Hubbell (2001)), but other distributions (geometric series, negative binomial, γ, exponential, inverse Guassian) have also been used. The challenges of fitting the log-normal have been widely discussed (e.g. Colwell & Coddington 1994; Chao 2004; Dornelas et al. 2006; Connolly et al. 2009). One of the limitations of this approach is shared with the extrapolation of fitted parametric functions: two or more species abundance distributions may fit the data equally well, but predict quite different assemblage richness. In addition, the species abundance distribution that fits best may be one that cannot be used to estimate undetected species, such as the widely used log-series distribution (Chao 2004).

The limitations of parametric methods inspired the development of non-parametric richness estimators, which require no assumptions about an underlying species abundance distribution and do not require the fitting of either *a priori* or *ad hoc* models (Chao 2004). These estimators have experienced a meteoric increase in usage in the past two decades, as species richness has become a focus of

biodiversity surveys and conservation issues, and a subject of basic research on the causes and consequences of species richness in natural ecosystems. In Box 4.1, we have listed six of the most widely used and best-performing indices. All the estimators in Box 4.1 depend on a fundamental principle discovered during World War II by Alan Turing and I.J. Good (as reported by Good (1953, 2000)), while cracking the military codes of the German Wehrmacht Enigma coding machine: the abundances of the very rarest species or their frequencies in a sample or set of samples can be used to estimate the frequencies of undetected species. All of the estimators in Box 4.1 correct the observed richness S_{obs} by adding a term based on the number of species represented in a single abundance sample by only one individual (*singletons*), by two (*doubletons*), or by a few individuals. For incidence data, the added term is based on the frequencies of species represented in only one (*uniques*) sample, in two (*duplicates*), or in a few replicate incidence samples.

Fig. 4.4 shows how well one of these estimators, Chao2, estimates the asymptotic richness of the seedbank dataset of Figure 4.1, based on sets of m^* samples chosen at random. The estimator stabilizes after about 30 samples have been pooled. When all 121 samples have been pooled, the estimator suggests that 1–2 additional species still remain undetected.

Only four of the estimators in Box 4.1 (Chao1, ACE, and the two individual-based jackknife estimators) are appropriate for abundance data; the rest require replicated incidence data. Most of the incidence-based estimators were first developed, in

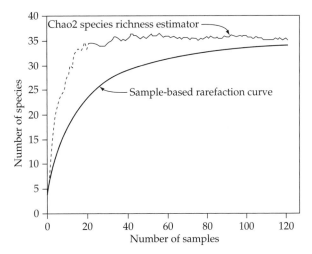

Figure 4.4 Asymptotic species richness estimated by the Chao2 non-parametric richness estimator for the seedbank dataset of Fig. 4.1. Plotted values for Chao2 are means of 100 randomizations of sample order. The estimator stabilizes after only about 30 samples have been pooled. When all 121 samples have been pooled (34 species detected), the estimator suggests that one or two additional species still remain undetected.

biological applications, for capture–recapture methods of population size estimation. The number of samples that include Species X in a set of biodiversity samples corresponds to the number of recaptures of marked Individual X in a capture–recapture study. In species richness estimation, the full assemblage of species, including those species not detected in the set of samples (but susceptible to detection), corresponds, in population size estimation, to the total population size, including those individuals never captured (but susceptible to capture) (Boulinier et al. 1998; Chao 2001, 2004).

Behind the disarming simplicity of Chao1 and Chao2 lies a rigorous body of statistical theory demonstrating that both are robust estimators of *minimum* richness (Shen et al. 2003). ACE and ICE are based on estimating *sample coverage*—the proportion of assemblage richness represented by the species in a single abundance sample (ACE) or in a set of replicated incidence samples (ICE). The estimators are adjusted to the 'spread' of the empirical species abundance (or incidence) distribution by a coefficient of variation term (Chao 2004). The Chao1 and Chao2 estimators also provide a heuristic, intuitive 'stopping rule' for biodiversity sampling: no additional species are expected to be found when all species in the sample are represented by at least two individuals (or samples). Extending this approach, Chao et al. (2009) provide equations and simple spreadsheet software for calculating how many

additional individuals would be needed to sample 100% (or any other percentage) of the asymptotic species richness of a region based on the samples already in hand. Pan et al. (2009) have recently extended the Chao1 and Chao2 indices to provide an estimate of the number of shared species in multiple assemblages.

The jackknife is a general statistical technique for reducing the bias of an estimator by removing subsets of the data and recalculating the estimator with the reduced sample. In this application of the technique, the observed number of species is a biased (under-) estimator of the complete assemblage richness (Burnham & Overton 1979; Heltshe & Forrester 1983; Chao 2004). For a set of m replicate incidence samples, the kth order jackknife reduces the bias by estimating richness from all sets of $m–k$ samples. The first-order jackknife (Jackknife1) thus depends only on the uniques (species found in only one sample) because the richness estimate is changed only when a sample that contains one of these species is deleted from a subset of samples. Likewise, the second-order jackknife (Jackknife2) depends only on the uniques and the duplicates (species found in exactly two samples). Similar expressions for abundance-based jackknife estimators are based on the number of singletons (species represented by exactly one individual) and doubletons (species represented by exactly two individuals; Burnham & Overton (1979)). These estimators can be derived by letting the number of samples m tend to infinity in the equations for the incidence-based estimators.

4.2.9 Comparing estimators of asymptotic species richness

Given the diversity of asymptotic estimators that have been proposed, which one(s) should ecologists use with their data? The ideal estimator would be *unbiased* (it neither over- or under-estimates asymptotic species richness), *precise* (replicates samples from the same assemblage produce similar estimates), and *efficient* (a relatively small number of individuals or samples is needed). Although there are many ways to estimate bias, precision, and efficiency (Walther & Moore 2005), none of the available estimators meet all these criteria for all datasets. Most estimators are biased because they chronically under-estimate true diversity (O'Hara 2005). The Chao1 estimator was formally derived as a *minimum* asymptotic estimator (Chao 1984), but all of the estimators should be treated as estimating the lower bound on species richness. Estimators of asymptotic species richness are often imprecise because they typically have large variances and confidence intervals, especially for small data sets. This imprecision is inevitable because, by necessity, these estimators represent an extrapolation beyond the limits of the data. In contrast, rarefaction estimators usually have smaller variances because they are interpolated within the range of the observed data. However, as noted earlier, the unconditional variance of richness as estimated by rarefaction is always larger than the variance that is conditional on a single sample (or set of samples). Finally, most estimators are not efficient and often exhibit 'sampling creep': the estimated asymptote itself increases with sample size, suggesting that the sample size is not large enough for the estimate to stabilize (e.g. Longino et al. (2002)).

Two strategies are possible to compare the performance of different estimators. The first strategy is to use data from a small area that has been exhaustively sampled (or nearly so), and to define that assemblage as the sampling universe. As in rarefaction, a random subsample of these data can then be used to calculate asymptotic estimators and compare them to the known richness in the

plot (a method first suggested by Pielou (1975), but popularized by Colwell & Coddington (1994)). For example, Butler & Chazdon (1998) collected seeds from 121 soils samples from a 1 ha plot, on a 10×10 m grid in tropical rainforest in Costa Rica, yielding 952 individual seedlings representing a total of 34 tree species (Figure 4.1). Colwell & Coddington (1994) randomly rarefied these data, by repeatedly pooling m^* samples ($1 \leq m^* \leq M$), and found that the Chao2 index (illustrated in Fig. 4.4) and the second-order jackknife estimators were least biased for small m^*, followed by the first-order jackknife and the Michaelis–Menten estimator. Walther & Morand (1998) used a similar approach with nine parasite data sets and found that Chao2 and the first-order jackknife performed best. Walther & Moore (2005), using different quantitative measures of bias, precision, and accuracy, compiled the results of 14 studies that compared estimator performance, and concluded that, for most data sets, non-parametric estimators (mostly the Chao and jackknife estimators) performed better than extrapolated asymptotic functions or other parametric estimators.

In a second strategy for comparing diversity estimators, the investigator specifies the true species richness, the pattern of relative abundance, and the spatial pattern of individuals in a computer-simulated landscape. The program then randomly samples individuals or plots, just as an ecologist would do in a field survey. The estimators are then calculated and compared on the basis of their ability to estimate the 'true' species richness of the region. This kind of simulation can also be used to explore the effects of spatial aggregation and segregation, sampling efficiency, and the size and placement of sampling plots. Brose et al. (2003) carried out the most extensive analysis of this kind to date. In their analyses, which estimator performed best depended on the relative evenness of the rank abundance distribution, the sampling intensity, and the true species richness. As in the empirical surveys (Walther & Moore 2005), non-parametric estimators performed better in these model assemblages than extrapolated asymptotic curves (parametric estimators based on truncated distributions were not considered). One encouraging result was that environmental gradients and spatial autocorrelation (which characterize all bio-diversity data at some spatial scales) did not have a serious effect on the performance of the estimators. These results are consistent with the findings of Hortal et al. (2006), who aggregated empirical data sets at different spatial grains and found that non-parametric estimators were not greatly affected by the spatial scale of the sampling.

O'Hara (2005) took a hybrid approach that used both empirical data and simulated assemblages. He first fit negative binomial and Poisson log-normal distributions to two very extensive (but incomplete) sets of survey data for moths. He used these fitted models to generate sample data for comparing non-parametric estimators, parametric estimators, and extrapolated asymptotic curves. As in other studies, true species richness was greater than predicted by the estimators. In each comparison, only one of the parametric estimators had a 95% confidence interval that encompassed the true richness. The catch is that this method worked well only when the 'correct' species abundance distribution was used. In other words, the investigator would need to know ahead of time that the negative binomial, Poisson log-normal, or some other distribution was the correct one to use (which rather defeats the value of using non-parametric estimators). Unfortunately, in spite of decades of research on this topic, there is still no agreement on a general underlying form of the species abundance distribution, and there are difficult issues in the fitting and estimation of these distributions from species abundance data (see Chapter 10). We hope that future work may lead to better species richness estimators. At this time, the non-parametric estimators still give the best performance in empirical comparisons, and they are also simple, intuitive, and relatively easy to use.

4.2.10   Software for estimating species richness from sample data

Free software packages with tools for estimating species richness from sample data include:

- *EstimateS* (Colwell 2009): http://purl.oclc.org/estimates
- *EcoSim* (Gotelli & Entsminger 2009): http://garyentsminger.com/ecosim/index.htm

- *SPADE*:   http://chao.stat.nthu.edu.tw/software CE.html
- *VEGAN* (for *R*):   http://cc.oulu.fi/~jarioksa/softhelp/vegan.html.

4.3   Prospectus

Estimates of species richness require special statistical procedures to account for differences in sampling effort and abundance. For comparing species richness among different assemblages, we recommend sample-based rarefaction using unconditional variances, with adjustments for the number of individuals sampled. Rarefaction methods for data that represent sampling from nature without replacement are still needed, for small assemblages, as are additional estimators for the number of shared species in multiple samples (A. Chao, personal communication). For many datasets, all existing methods for estimating undetected species seem to substantially under-estimate the number of species present, but the best methods nonetheless reduce the inherent undersampling bias in observed species counts. Non-parametric estimators (e.g. Chao1, Chao2) perform best in empirical comparisons and benchmark surveys, and have a more rigorous framework of sampling theory than parametric estimators or curve extrapolations.

4.4   Key points

1. Biodiversity sampling is a labour-intensive activity, and sampling is often not sufficient to detect all or even most of the species present in an assemblage.
2. Species richness counts are highly sensitive to the number of individuals sampled, and to the number, size, and spatial arrangement of samples.
3. Sensitivity to sampling effort cannot be accounted for by scaling species richness as a ratio of species counts to individuals, samples, or any other measure of effort.
4. Sample-based and individual-based rarefaction methods allow for the meaningful comparison of diversity samples based on equivalent numbers of individuals and samples.

5. Non-parametric estimators of species richness, which use information on the rare species in an assemblage to adjust for the number species present but not detected, are the most promising avenue for estimating the minimum number of species in the assemblage.

Acknowledgements

N.J.G. acknowledges US National Science Foundation grants DEB-0107403 and DEB 05-41936 for support of modelling and null model research. R.K.C. was supported by NSF DEB-0072702.

CHAPTER 5

Measurement of species diversity

Brian A. Maurer and Brian J. McGill

5.1 Introduction

One of the most conspicuous aspects of biodiversity is the fact that individual organisms are organized into relatively discrete units referred to as species. Although there is much variability in what can be called a species, generally a species represents a distinct genetic lineage of organisms that interact with the environment in similar ways and are generally reproductively compatible. For both theoretical and practical reasons, it is often desirable to know how many species are found in a given region of space-time (Chapter 4) and to know something about how abundant each species is relative to others in the same community (Chapter 9). This relatively simple objective, however, becomes greatly complicated because there are so many different ecological circumstances in which species diversity is measured. Because of this there have been a large number of quantities suggested as appropriate measures of species diversity (Box 5.1) (Pielou 1975; Krebs 1989; Magurran 2004). This plethora of indices makes it difficult to evaluate which method is appropriate in what particular circumstances. The most commonly used indices are used primarily because they have been used before, and not necessarily because they provide useful information.

In this chapter we consider the problem of species diversity by focusing firstly on precise definitions of the term. We then describe the necessary statistical sampling theory that follows from the definition. There are two different types of sampling issues, both of which are important to developing an understanding of species diversity. First, there is the issue of how ecological circumstances act as a probabilistic 'filter' in determining which specific species can be found in a region.

We will refer to this as the *ecological sample* in what follows. Second, when collecting data on species abundances within a specified ecosystem, it is often not appropriate to assume that every last individual of every species has been identified. Hence, much field data are subsamples of a larger, unknown community. We will call this the *empirical sample* below. Empirical samples are often used to estimate quantities assumed to represent the unmeasured parameters that describe the process thought to have given rise to the ecological sample (Green & Plotkin 2007).

No ecosystem remains unchanged across space and time. However, there may be ecological conditions that are sufficiently similar that they may give rise to similar levels of diversity. How is it possible to determine whether multiple communities arrayed across space and/or time give rise to an increase in diversity? In other words, given a set of communities that can be sensibly aggregated into a larger entity, is it possible to partition the overall diversity of the aggregate into a component due to within-community diversity and a component attributable to between-community diversity? The former has been termed 'α diversity' and the latter 'β diversity' (Whittaker 1975; Chapter 6). Estimating these diversity components in communities that result from some combination of deterministic and random processes provides a unique statistical challenge.

5.2 State of the art

First it is necessary to define the underlying structure of the statistical population from which the ecological sample of a community is derived. To do this, we start with a definition of a community for which a measure of species diversity is desired.

Box 5.1 Measures of species diversity and eveness

There are a number of descriptors that are based on some concept such as evenness, diversity, or dominance that are not derived from any probability distribution. Of course many of the parameters from probability distributions could fit these goals as well (Box 9.2). The notation used throughout this section is: N_i is the abundance of the ith species after sorting (so N_1 is the abundance of the most abundant species), S is the number of species observed, and N is the total abundance ($N = \sum_{i=1}^{S} N_i$) and p_i is the proportion of abundance for species i ($p_i = N_i/N$). S_i is the number of species with an abundance i, so S_1 is the number of singletons. To provide some order, we have tried to group indices with similar goals and to use a consistent notation.

Number of individuals (N) – Total number of individuals. This is another easily calculated yet powerful descriptor. Note that in neutral theory N is often denoted by J, but we use the more traditional N here.

I. Richness metrics (S)

Richness (S) – Species richness: the total number of species identified in the sample. It is among the simplest descriptors of community structure.

Margalef diversity ($S_{Margalef}$) – Margalef (Clifford & Stephenson 1975) noted that species richness increases with N, and in particular increases non-linearly and roughly logarithmically with N. $S_{Margalef} = (S - 1)/\ln N$

Menhinick diversity ($S_{Menhinick}$) – In a similar vein (Clifford & Stephenson 1975), Menhinick proposed adjusting species richness by the similarly shaped square root of N. $S_{Menhinick} = S/\sqrt{N}$

Chao estimated diversity (S_{Chao}) – Another way to make species richness S comparable between sites with different sample sizes N is to extrapolate to the richness of an infinite sample. Chao (1987) proposed a simple robust estimator for this: $S_{Chao} = S + S_1^2/(2S_2)$.

Chao estimated variance – Although not an estimate of species richness, Chao provided an analytical formula for the variance in S_{Chao} that can be used to place error bars on S_{Chao} ($S_{Chao} \pm 1.96\sqrt{S_{ChaoVar}}$) and is given by $S_{ChaoVar} = S_2[(S_1/S_2)^4/4 + (S_1/S_2)^3 + (S_1/S_2)^2/2]$.

II. Diversity metrics (D)

Diversity is traditionally taken to be a function of both richness and evenness, with less even communities being less diverse than their richness alone would indicate (should a species with only one individual count towards diversity the same as an abundant species?).

Shannon diversity (H' or $D_{Shannon}$) – Shannon's information theory can be used to calculate the information in a community as an estimate of diversity. There is a finite population size version known as Brillouin's index (equation 5.9, main text) which should probably be used but usually isn't. $D_{Shannon} = -\sum p_i \ln p_i$

Simpson diversity ($1/D$ or $D_{Simpson}$) – Simpson noted that $D = \sum p_i^2$ gave the probability that two individuals drawn at random from an infinite community would belong to the same species. This has precedent in population genetics of the probability of getting two alleles the same. As such D is the inverse of diversity and some form of inverse is needed to create a diversity index. Although variations including $1 - D$ (related to the variance within species and to Hurlbert's PIE below) and $-\ln(D)$ (related to the Hill measure H_2) have been used, the most common way (e.g. MacArthur 1972) of converting homogeneity into diversity is $D_{Simpson} = 1/D$.

Hurlbert diversity (1 - PIE or $D_{Hurlbert}$) – Hurlbert (1971) argued that a biologically meaningful measure of diversity is the odds that a given interaction between two species is interspecific (PIE = $1 - D$ = probability of interspecific encounter). With a correction for finite sample size we have $D_{Hurlbert} = 1 - \sum(n_i/N)[(n_i - 1)/(N - 1)]$.

Diversity numbers ($D_{Hill, \alpha}$) – Hill (1973) proposed using information-based criteria to obtain 'weighted' counts of species, based on the degree of dominance. Also see Chapter 6. The weighted counts, H_α, are obtained by choosing an appropriate value of α, with small α weighting rare species most and large α weighting common species most. Note that the Hill numbers are the exponential of the Renyi entropies given in equation 5.6: $H_\alpha = \exp(R_\alpha)$. This set of measures contains many common measures as special cases. $H_{-\infty} = 1/p_S$ (reciprocal of the proportional abundance of the rarest species), $H_0 = S$, $H_1 = \exp(H')$, which some people have argued should be used instead of H' (where H' is the Shannon diversity or $D_{Shannon}$ above), $H_2 = 1/D$ (i.e. $D_{Simpson}$ above), and $H_\infty = 1/C_{Rel}$ (reciprocal of the Berger–Parker index). Kempton (1979) found that α between 0 and 0.5 provided the best discrimination in empirical data known to come from different communities.

$$H_\alpha = \left[\sum p_i^\alpha \right]^{1/(1-\alpha)}$$

III. Evenness metrics (E)

Evenness is a measure of how different the abundances of the species in a community are from each other (Smith & Wilson 1996). A community where every species had the same abundance would be perfectly even. All natural communities are highly uneven, so evenness is a relative statement. Most evenness indices are scaled to approximately run from 0 = maximally uneven to 1 = perfectly even.

Shannon evenness (J' or $E_{Shannon}$) – If diversity is a mixture of richness and evenness, then removing richness should produce evenness. This is the logic behind Shannon's evenness measure; the highest value of $D_{Shannon}$ when all species are equally abundant can readily be seen to be $\ln(S)$ so dividing by $\ln(S)$ will give an index from 0 to 1. $E_{Shannon} = D_{Shannon} / \ln(S)$

Simpson evenness ($1/D/S$ or $E_{Simpson}$) – The same logic applies to Simpson's diversity, giving $E_{Simpson} = D_{Simpson} / S$.

Camargo evenness (or $E_{Camargo}$) – The highest possible evenness is when $p_i = p_j = 1/S$, so Camargo et al. (1993) suggested a direct measurement of deviation from this ideal. $E_{Camargo} = 1 - \sum |p_i - p_j|/S$, where the sum is taken over $i = 1 \ldots S, j = i + 1 \ldots S$.

Smith Wilson evenness (E_{var} or $E_{SmithWilson}$) – Smith and Wilson (Smith & Wilson 1996) reviewed an array of evenness indices and assessed them on some core properties. Two core properties they identified are spanning the whole range 0–1 and being independent of unit of measure (evenness of biomass measured in grams should be equal to evenness of biomass measured in kilograms). They invented an index that performed well on these goals, which they called E_{var}. The formula is based on the variance of log abundances (centered on the mean of log abundances) then appropriately scaled to cover 0–1. $E_{SmithWilson} = 1 - \frac{2}{\pi} \arctan\left[\frac{1}{S}\sum(\ln(n_i) - \mu_{ln})^2\right]$ where $\mu_{ln} = \frac{1}{S}\sum \ln(n_i)$.

RAD beta or NHC evenness (E_{NHC}) – The slope of the rank abundance diagram (RAD) has long been interpreted as a measure of evenness (a perfectly horizontal line would represent perfect evenness). Nee, Harvey, and Cotgreave (Nee et al. 1992) proposed taking the slope of the regression line through the points in the RAD as a measure of evenness. This runs from $(-\infty, 0)$. Some authors (e.g. Smith & Wilson 1996) rescale this to go from 0 to 1 –i.e. $-2/\arctan(\beta)$, but we prefer to keep the simple geometric interpretation β, where β is the OLS slope of log abundance vs. rescaled rank (divide by S so rank goes from $1/S$ to 1). $E_{NHC} = \beta$ as above.

Diversity number ratios (E_{Hill}) – Using diversity numbers H_α (Hill 1973), one can take ratios of different diversity numbers $E_{\alpha,\beta} = H_\alpha / H_\beta$ to express the degree of evenness among species within an ecological sample. The most natural case is $\beta = 0$, then $H_0 = S$, which is the maximal value (i.e. on a perfectly even community with $p_i = N/S$) of H_α for all α. For example, $\log(H_2)/\log(H_0)$ gives Shannon evenness.

IV. Dominance or common species metrics (C)

Dominance is a measure of how much one or a few species dominate the community numerically (McNaughton & Wolf 1970). In some ways it is the inverse of evenness, but it is specifically focused on the right side of the SAD (very common species).

Absolute dominance (C_{Abs}) – The simplest measure of dominance is simply N_1, the abundance of the most abundant species. Although it might seem that N_1 would be so heavily dependent on total abundance N as to be useless, in some systems N_1 can stay surprisingly constant even while N varies. $C_{Abs} = N_1$

Relative dominance (Berger–Parker) (C_{Rel}) – The easiest way to correct for the effects of N is to divide by N, producing p_1 the relative abundance of the most abundant species (Berger & Parker 1970). $C_{Rel} = p_1$

McNaughton dominance ($C_{McNaught}$) – McNaughton (1970) made a more robust measure that was less subject to the vagaries of a single species by looking at the proportional abundance of the two most abundant species (and rescaling to 0–100). A similar index based on the abundance of the three most abundant species was made by Misra and Misra (1981). $C_{McNaught} = (p_1 + p_2) \times 100 = [(N_1 + N_2)/2N] \times 100$

V. High rarity metrics (R)

Rarity – the opposite of dominance metrics – focus on an assessment of rare species. Since abundance is bounded at 1, rarity metrics focus on the number of species with specific abundances in contrast to commonness metrics which focus on the abundance of specific species.

LogSkew ($R_{LogSkew}$) – Skew is the third moment of a probability distribution, measuring asymmetry. Right skew (positive numbers) indicates more probability on the right (abundant) side. Left skew (negative numbers) indicates more probability on the left side. All species abundance distributions are strongly right skewed on an arithmetic

Continued

Box 5.1 *(Continued)*

scale, so the more interesting measure is skew on the log scale. This measures asymmetry relative to the log-normal. A negative number indicates an excess of rare species (McGill 2003). $R_{LogSkew} = \left[\sum (\log(n_i) - \mu)^3 / S \right] / \left[\sum (\log(n_i) - \mu)^2 / S \right]^{3/2} S/(S-2)\sqrt{[(S-1)/S]}$, where μ is the mean of $\log(n_i)$.

% Singletons ($R_{Singleton}$) – A simple measure of rare species is to count the number of singletons. $R_{Singleton} = S_1$

PctRare1% ($R_{1\%}$) – Like the first two dominance measures, $R_{Singleton}$ focuses exclusively on one abundance class, potentially making it a noisy metric. By focusing on multiple abundance classes, this problem can be avoided. The challenge is to define which species count as rare. A simple one is to call any species with an abundance less than 1% of total abundance rare. A major shortcoming of this is that no species can have an abundance less than 1% of N if $N < 100$. This measure is only useful when N is at least several hundred. $R_{1\%} = (S_1 + S_2 + \ldots + S_T)/S$, where T is the largest integer less than $0.01 \times N$.

PctRare5% ($R_{5\%}$) – An alternative, more expansive, definition that can work with $N > 20$ is that a species is rare if its abundance is $< 5\%$ of N. $R_{5\%} = (S_1 + S_2 + \ldots + S_T)/S$, where T is the largest integer less than $0.05 \times N$

PctRareN/S ($R_{N/S}$) – Both the 5% and 1% cut-offs are relative to N only, not S. A thousand individuals with 500 species is bound to have many rare species by these definitions but 1000 individuals with 10 species will be very different. A simple measure that attempts to correct for this is to count a species as rare if its abundance is $< N/S$. N/S gives the average abundance of a species. Because of the strong right skew, the average abundance will be greater than the median (50th percentile) abundance and thus quite large. $R_{N/S} = (S_1 + S_2 + \ldots + S_T)/S$, where T is the largest integer less than N/S

VI. Semi-parametric metrics

Several metrics are not parameters from the probability distributions listed in Box 9.1, but are related to those or other probability distributions.

Fisher's α (α or S_{Fisher}) – The log-series distribution parameter is called c, but as discussed in Box 9.2 for the log-series, α can be calculated as a function of N and c by $\alpha = N(1 - c)/c$. Although typically smaller (sometimes by a factor of 2–10) than S, it is strongly correlated with S. It has been recommended as a sample-size-independent estimator of richness (Rosenzweig 1995).

Lognormal CV – As discussed in the section on the lognormal distribution (Box 9.2) (also see Limpert et al. 2001), the coefficient of variation $CV = \mu/\sigma$ is not a parameter but is perhaps the best single descriptor of shape for the log-normal (making it analogous to the gamma and Weibull shape parameters). A high CV indicates many rare species (high unevenness).

Prop LN μ^*, Prop LN σ^*, Prop LN CV – In the log-normal distribution, both μ^* and σ^* are in units of abundance and scale with increasing sample size N (i.e. $\mu = \log(\mu^*)$ and $\sigma = \log(\sigma^*)$ scale as $\log(N)$). One way to adjust for this is to calculate the log-normal parameters (mean, standard deviation, CV) on the log of the relative abundances, $\log(p_i)$. This removes the heavy dependence on N.

Gambin α – The Poisson-gamma distribution (which leads to the logseries distribution) is discussed in Box 9.2. An alternative sampling distribution to the Poisson is the binomial (Green & Plotkin 2007), where the gamma distribution gives the probability p of the species appearing, which is then passed through binomial sampling. This gives the binomial gamma, which might be a good model for SADs (Ugland et al. 2007). Since the gamma distribution runs to ∞, it is necessary to truncate the right tail (say at the 99th percentile). By scaling without loss of generality so that the maximum value is 1, the binomial gamma or GamBin (Ugland et al. 2007) is well defined with only one parameter, the gamma shape parameter. It has been shown that the GamBin fits many datasets well and that the parameter α may be a good proxy for the habitat complexity from which the community is sampled (Ugland et al. 2007).

m_{logit} and i_{logit} – As discussed in Chapter 9, fitting a sigmoidal logistic function to the empirical cumulative distribution function (ECDF) on a log proportional abundance scale is tantamount to hypothesizing a log–logit probability distribution (Evans et al. 1993; Williamson & Gaston 2005). The logistic function (and log–logit probability distribution) has two parameters: i is a scale parameter and gives the location of the inflection point on the x-axis. In this context, since the inflection occurs at 50% of species accumulated, it gives the median relative abundance on a log scale. Since there are many more rare species than common, this is tantamount to a form of measurement of how many rare species there are. Similarly, m represents the slope of the function at the intercept, and as such is a proxy for evenness. When $m = 0$ every species has different abundance and when $m = \infty$ the logit function becomes a step function and all species are equally abundant. $\text{ECDF}(p) = 1/\{1 + \exp[-m \times (p - i)]\}$, which can be fitted to the ECDF by least squares.

m_{genlog}, i_{genlog}, and a_{genlog} – The logit function assumes that the ECDF is symmetric about the inflection point, which it may not be. A generalized logit with three parameters can allow asymmetry. By the appropriate choice of a three-parameter sigmoidal logit-like function, the parameters m and i can retain their meanings and a single parameter a can describe the degree of asymmetry. $\text{ECDF}(p) = 1/\{1 + a \times \exp[-m \times (p - i)]^{1/a}\}$, which can be fitted to the ECDF by least squares.

Assume that a community can be described by a set of J individual 'sites' occupied by a single individual from one of S species. For some species, an individual may not be a discrete unit, but may exist as a distributed network of 'nodes', such as a tree species that generates above-ground stems from a network of roots. In such situations, it is important to define precisely what part of the network is being counted (e.g. stems). To model this situation, let the random variable X_{ij} be defined as follows: $X_{ij} = 1$ if site j is occupied by species i and $X_{ij} = 0$ otherwise. Since each site can only be occupied by a single individual, it is convenient to combine the random variables X_{ij}, across each species at site j as a single random vector $\mathbf{X}_j$. The limiting distribution of $\mathbf{X}_j$ can be generally considered to be a multinomial distribution with a single observation. Given this general structure, we can calculate the expected value of the random vector $\mathbf{X}_j$ over species as a vector of probabilities $\mathbf{q}_j = [q_{ij}]$, where q_{ij} is the probability that species i is found on site j. Collecting the probability vectors from all sites into a single matrix gives the $S \times J$ matrix $\mathbf{Q}$, which summarizes the probabilities of species distributed across all sites. The expected abundance (N_i) of each species is obtained as

$$N_i = \Sigma_j q_{ij} \qquad (5.1)$$

The vector $\mathbf{N} = [N_1 \; N_2 \ldots N_S]$ is sometimes called the species abundance distribution (see Chapter 9) and has been a major focus of research in ecology for the past several decades. Because of the underlying probabilistic definition of $\mathbf{N}$, it is convenient to consider it as a random vector. An active area of current investigation is the examination of alternative stochastic processes that can model the evolution of $\mathbf{N}$ in space-time (Alonso & McKane 2004; Etienne 2005). Consideration of these models is beyond the scope of this chapter; suffice it to say that the distribution of $\mathbf{N}$ that is most useful is the equilibrium distribution of the underlying stochastic process generating the ecological sample. Here we will use the multinomial distribution to represent this limiting distribution. Finally, it is also useful to consider the *relative* species abundance distribution to be represented by the random vector

$$\mathbf{p} = \mathbf{N}/N \qquad (5.2)$$

where $N = \Sigma_i N_i$.

5.2.1   Species diversity as variance

We are now in a position to consider definitions of species diversity. Diversity is often intended to represent two different aspects of the species abundance distribution. The first is termed 'species richness' or, simply, the number of species in the ecological sample. For reasons that will become evident shortly, the number of species in the ecological sample may not be equal to S (the number of species that have nonzero probabilities of being found in at least one site in the community). In other words, it is possible that n_i might equal zero for some species in a particular ecological sample, even though the species could possibly be found in the community. Let S_e be the number of species with non-zero abundances in a single ecological sample, then obviously $S_e \leq S$ is the species richness of the sample. The other component of species diversity is the degree to which the relative abundances are similar among species. This has been called 'evenness' in the ecological literature, but in actuality the underlying concept of interest is the covariance in relative abundances among species.

There are two sources of variation in relative abundances among species. The first is the variation within a species and the second is the variability among species. The variance within a species is

$$\text{var}(p_i) = p_i(1 - p_i) \tag{5.3}$$

where p_i is the ith element of the vector of relative abundances (**p**). Since relative abundances of species are necessarily correlated, a measure of between species variability is the covariance of the relative frequencies of species i and k, that is

$$\text{cov}(p_i, p_k) = -p_i p_k \tag{5.4}$$

The total variance across all species is obtained by summing equations (5.3) and (5.4) across all species and pairs of species, which gives

$$V = 1 - \Sigma_i p_i^2 - 2\Sigma_{i<k} p_i p_k \tag{5.5}$$

In the two extreme cases when all species are equally abundant or when all species have zero abundance except for one, V reaches its minimum value of zero (no variability among species). Thus, this variance itself is probably not useful as a measure of species diversity because of this. However, equation (5.5) is useful heuristically because it illustrates how the two separate aspects of species diversity, richness and evenness, might be related.

The two terms in equation (5.5) represent different aspects of species diversity. The quantity $D = \Sigma_i p_i^2$ is the familiar metric of species diversity first suggested by Simpson (1949). It has often been called a measure of 'dominance'. In equation (5.5), $1 - D(= 1 - \Sigma p^2)$ represents the total variance attributable to within-species variability. D is well known to be correlated with species richness, and in the context used here it could be considered to be a probabilistic measure of richness. As a measure of species diversity, however, it is incomplete because it does not include information about the variability in relative abundances among species given by the last term in equation 5.5. The last term in equation 5.5 is particularly interesting because it is a measure of the degree to which abundances covary among species. Intuitively, the summed covariances in relative abundances among species capture the essence of the 'evenness' component of species diversity.

To summarize, if species diversity is defined as the number and relative abundances of species within a community, one way to represent it is to partition the total variation in species abundances among species into a within-species component and a between-species component. The within-species component represents the richness aspect of species diversity and the between-species component represents the evenness aspect.

5.2.2 Species diversity as information

In the previous section, species diversity was defined by partitioning the total variance of abundances across all species in the ecological sample. An alternative approach developed in the early 1960s was based on measuring the information content of a long string of symbols developed by information theorists (Pielou 1975 and references therein). The basic idea of the analogy is to view an ecological sample of species as a 'message' with individual organisms as pieces of 'information'. The relevant information is the taxon to which each organism belongs, and the measurement of this 'taxonomic information' is obtained from the relative abundances of species. A general measure of information content per symbol in an infinitely large set of symbols for which some 'code' exists is given by

$$R_a = \ln\left[\Sigma_i p_i^a\right]/(1 - a) \tag{5.6}$$

where a is an arbitrary integer (Hill 1973; Pielou 1975). These are called the Renyi entropies of order a. Different values for a produce different weightings of the information content inherent in the relative abundances of species with low values of a (< 0) weighting in favour of rare species (in the limit $R_{-\infty}$ is a function only of the p_i of the rarest species) and high values of a emphasizing weighting in favour of common species (again R_∞ being a function only of the p_i for the most common species). Three values of a are of particular interest to ecologists. The first, R_0, is simply the logarithm of the number of species in the ecological sample. When $a = 2$, equation (5.6) yields $R_2 = -\log D$, that is, the negative logarithm of Simpson's diversity measure. The final value of interest is the limit of equation (5.6) when a approaches 1, which yields

$$H' = R_1 = -\Sigma_i p_i \log p_i \tag{5.7}$$

This is the well-known Shannon measure of species diversity (Pielou 1975), which is widely used. Hill numbers, which are simply the exponent of Renyi entropy ($H_\alpha = \exp(R_\alpha)$), are also commonly used in ecology (Box 5.1 and Hill, 1973) and Chapter 6, where Hill number H_a is denoted $^q D$.

The appeal of equation (5.6) as a measure of diversity is that it is convenient to define evenness quantitatively. Intuitively, evenness should be greatest if all species are equally common. If this is the case, equation (5.6) yields a value of log S_e regardless of what particular value a takes on. Hence, it is sometimes useful to rescale R_a by dividing it by its theoretical maximum, yielding

$$R_a^* = R_a / \log S_e \qquad (5.8)$$

R_1^* (also denoted J') has been widely used as measure of evenness in the ecological literature.

Pielou (1975) points out that if there is a finite number of individuals in an ecological sample, then the information content per species for that particular sample is

$$H_B = (1/N) \log [(N!)/\Pi_i N_i!] \qquad (5.9)$$

This form of information diversity is related to $H' = R_1$ because as the values of the abundances of species become very large, H_B converges on the Shannon diversity, $H' = R_1$ (Pielou 1975). However, for small collections of individuals (i.e. small, fully censused communities), equation (5.9) is the appropriate measure of information. It has become known as the Brillouin index and takes on values slightly less than Shannon values ($H_B < H = R_1$).

5.2.3 Traditional measures of various types of diversity

Given that species diversity has at least two different general formulations, that is, it can represent a partitioning of abundance in a community into between- and within-species variance components or it can represent shared or mutual information among species, a large number of measurements have been suggested to represent these different aspects of species diversity. Here we survey these measurements and indicate how they relate to our distinction between species diversity as variance and species diversity as information.

We have classified species diversity measurements into six categories based on how researchers have proposed to use them (Box 5.1). The first set of metrics contains those that attempt to express some basic aspect of 'richness'. The idea behind these metrics is to express some aspect of the number of species in the ecological sample. Some, such as Chao's estimators (Chao 1987), attempt to use information from an empirical sample to infer the species richness of the underlying ecological sample.

A second set of metrics used widely in the literature we refer to as 'diversity' metrics and include the most widely used metrics. In this context, diversity is used to mean a combination of both richness and evenness. Simpson's diversity metric is the within-species component of variance discussed above, but also is related to the information concept of diversity. Shannon's diversity metric (H' or R_1) is probably the most commonly used expression of species diversity.

Evenness metrics all attempt to examine how abundance is apportioned among species within a community. The basic concept underlying all of these measurements is that evenness is highest when a community is not dominated by a few species of very high abundance or equivalently that all species have an equal abundance. Low evenness implies that most species in the community are very rare, and consequently may contribute very little to the underlying ecological role the community plays within the ecosystem that contains it.

Dominance metrics are in many ways the converse of evenness. If the scientific objectives of a study focus on the most common species in a community, then dominance measures may be the most appropriate descriptors of species diversity. Likewise, in some studies it may be more important to focus on the rarest species. This might be particularly true in conservation studies where rare species may be of particular interest in determining the value of locations for the conservation of biological diversity. For such studies there are a variety of metrics that focus on the number of rare species found in a community.

Finally, a variety of metrics are based on various parametric or non-parametric descriptions of the probability distribution underlying the apportionment of diversity among species. Some of these metrics are related to probability distributions that arise from assuming a certain type of mechanism underlying the dynamics of abundances among species over time (see Box 9.2 and Chapter 9). Generally, these metrics should be used to fit parameters in specific models that might underlie the structure of a community.

5.2.4 Addressing the difference between the empirical and ecological samples: estimating species diversity components using empirical samples

A fundamental difficulty that has not been addressed up to this point is the nature of the 'object' being measured when ecologists collect information on the abundances of species at a specific location. This 'object' is typically called a 'community', and is defined as all the organisms belonging to a set of species found at a given point in space and time. The existence of such an object in any real sense might be questioned on many grounds (Maurer 1999; Ricklefs 2008), yet there is enough accumulated evidence to suggest that counting organisms of different kinds of species in local regions of space-time is of enormous practical value (Chapters 17, 18, and 20). Here we focus on how to analyse and interpret the data obtained from such counts given that not all individuals can be counted and some species that have appreciable populations in the region may in fact not show up in these empirically derived counts. In practice, nearly all data obtained by ecologists form an empirical sample rather than an ecological sample. It is therefore technically incorrect to calculate a diversity measure (previous section and Box 5.1) on an empirical sample and claim it is the correct value for the ecological sample.

Estimating the number of species, S_e, in an ecological sample from empirical samples assumes that in a local community conditions remain constant enough over the sample period to assume that there are no changes in the relative abundances and incidence of species. If this is the case, then one can assume a 'collector's curve' exists, so that as the total number of individuals sampled increases (the

size of the empirical sample approaches the size of the ecological sample), the total number of species identified begins to asymptote, reaching a theoretical maximum of S_e. S_e is commonly denoted just S, but it is expected in practice to recognize the distinction between the empirical sample and the ecological sample, and use one of the techniques below to estimate this value despite the notational imprecision.

There are two basic approaches to estimating S_e. First, it is possible to assume that some parameterized distribution function can be used as a model for a given species abundance distribution. If this is true, then at least for some statistical distributions, S_e is a parameter (or function of parameters) of the distribution that can be estimated using a sufficiently large empirical sample (Pielou 1975; Magurran 2004). The second general approach is to observe and extrapolate the empirical pattern of accumulation of species as the number of individuals in the empirical sample accumulates. The problem with this approach is that there is no logical way of choosing the sequences with which individuals in the empirical sample are accumulated. If there are n individuals in an empirical sample, there are $n!$ possible ways of accumulating individuals. Estimates of accumulation curves can be constructed either by random sampling (without replacement) samples of various sizes from the empirical sample or by examining the average rate of accumulation using rarefaction (Simberloff 1972). More details on estimating species richness are discussed in Chapters 4 and 20.

Estimating the diversity and richness of ecological samples is limited by the amount of information available on the ecological sample being studied. Generally, both the total number of organisms, N, and the number of species, S_e, in the ecological sample are unknown. If both of these quantities are large, then any single empirical sample may be inadequate to fully characterize the entire ecological sample (Pielou 1975; Peet 1974; Magurran 2004). Empirical samples that are much smaller than the ecological sample are unlikely to contain all species found in the ecological sample. In particular, rare species may show up in relatively few empirical samples.

The solution to the dilemma posed in the previous paragraph is to examine the behaviour of species diversity measurements among many empirical samples taken of the same ecological sample (also see Chapter 9). By taking multiple empirical samples from a single empirical sample, we gain information about the variance involved in the empirical sampling process. If a certain number of sampling units are drawn from the larger ecological sample, then it is possible to calculate measures of species diversity as a function of the number of sample units aggregated (Pielou 1975; Magurran 2004). This assumes, of course, that each sampling unit is drawn from the same ecological sample. On the other hand, if conditions change across space and time, then aggregating sampling units may not be appropriate. This assumption may be problematic if most ecological communities are open systems (Maurer 1999). In the next section we consider how to evaluate whether several empirical samples are drawn from the same empirical sample. It is still common in practice to ignore the distinction between the empirical sample and the ecological sample, and simply calculate diversity statistics (other than richness discussed above) simply on the empirical sample and report them as if they were the true value for the ecological sample. Despite being common practice, this is incorrect (especially for small samples) and the approach just outlined is superior.

5.2.5 Testing for heterogeneity among ecological samples

In the simplest case, suppose two empirical samples have been obtained from a specified location. The question to be answered is whether these two samples can be considered to be samples of a single larger community or whether they are different. The species abundance distribution for each location can written as a vector where $j = 1, 2$ indexes locations. The abundance for species i at location j is given by n_{ij}. The relative abundances are then

$$p_{ij} = n_{ij} / \sum_i n_{ij} \tag{5.10}$$

The index i goes from 1 to S_c, which is the number of species found in at least one of the samples. Note that some of the relative abundances may be zero. Writing the relative abundances as a vector gives two relative abundance vectors $\mathbf{p}_1$ and $\mathbf{p}_2$. Finally, we can calculate the relative abundance vector for the combined two samples as

$$\mathbf{p}_c = \left[\left(\sum_i n_{i1} \right) \mathbf{p}_1 + \left(\sum_i n_{i2} \right) \mathbf{p}_2 \right] \Big/ \left(\sum_i n_{i1} + \sum_i n_{i2} \right) \tag{5.11}$$

Here we assume that each of the abundance distributions can be approximated by a multinomial distribution. If this is the case, then we have two candidate models to describe the data. The first model assumes the two samples come from the same community, hence there is a single multinomial distribution that describes both samples and there are S_c parameters (the actual relative abundances in the single ecological sample). Note that we here assume that $S_c = S_e$, that is, all the species in the ecological sample are found in at least one of the two empirical samples. The second model assumes that each empirical sample comes from a different ecological sample, which means that we would have two different multinomial distributions, each with S_c parameters (the relative frequencies of each species in each of the two different communities). The second model requires twice as many parameters to describe the data as the first model.

To compare such models, we suggest using the information theoretic approach described by Burnham (2002). The approach is based on estimating the log likelihood of each model given the data and substituting the empirical estimates of the parameters into the likelihood function. Interestingly, for the multinomial distribution, the negative log likelihood function for a given data set is simply the Shannon information measure times the number of individuals in the sample. Letting H_{1c} be the Shannon diversity for the combined data, the negative log likelihood for the model assuming only a single ecological sample is

$$L_c = \left(\sum_i n_{i1} + \sum_i n_{i2} \right) H_{1c} \tag{5.12}$$

For the second model, which assumes two different ecological samples, the negative log likelihood (L_2) is obtained as

$$L_2 = \left(\sum_i n_{i1}\right) H_{11} + \left(\sum_i n_{i2}\right) H_{12} \quad (5.13)$$

where H_{11} and H_{12} are the Shannon diversities for each of the separate empirical samples. The log likelihoods for the two models are then compared by calculating the respective Akaike Information Criterion (AIC) for each model:

$$AIC_c = 2(L_c + S_c) \quad (5.14)$$

$$AIC_2 = 2(L_2 + 2S_c) \quad (5.15)$$

The best model is the one which has the lowest AIC. Generally, a difference between AICs of 2.0 or more indicates that the model with the lowest AIC has 'significantly' more support from the data (Burnham & Anderson 1998). Furthermore, it is possible to calculate model weights using AIC differences. The interested reader is referred to Burnham (1998) for further details.

This procedure can be generalized to evaluate whether several different empirical samples come from the same ecological sample. As the number of empirical samples being compared increases, the number of possible models increases rapidly, making it impractical to compute all possible comparisons. In such cases it may be best to use some independent criterion (such as distance between samples) to group empirical samples into a small number of aggregate samples that can be examined using AICs.

The model selection procedure provides a basis for asking questions about so-called 'β diversity'. In the example described above, the first model, which assumes that the two empirical samples are drawn from the same ecological sample, there is no β diversity. The two samples are describing the same relative abundance distribution. The second model assumes that the two empirical samples are drawn from different ecological samples, which implies that there is β diversity (i.e. a turnover in abundances among communities). The degree to which the second model is supported by the data is related to how much β diversity exists between the two samples (Chapter 6). With several sites sampled, it

is also possible to partition diversity into between-site (β) and within-site (α) diversity components (Chapter 6) (Whittaker 1975; Lande 1996; Crist et al. 2003; Crist & Veech 2006).

5.3 Prospectus

While easy to conceptualize, diversity (and evenness) are hard to measure. We present a basic framework here. Several developments are needed to provide a truly firm foundation to the measurement of diversity. First, more attention to and development of methods to account for the fact that collected data are sampled data are needed (i.e. the distinction between the empirical sample and the ecological sample). Second, rather than developing new measures of diversity by ad hoc processes we hope to see a further focus on fundamental ideas like variance and information.

5.4 Key points

1. To properly measure diversity requires recognition that the data usually collected represent just samples (empirical samples) from the actual community (ecological sample), which is in turn a probabilistic, imperfect representation of the potential community.
2. There are a great many approaches proposed in the literature to measure aspects of diversity, including richness, evenness, and the combination (diversity). Most of these approaches have been fairly ad hoc. There are probably at least two or three times as many measures proposed as the ones we cover in Box 5.1. We have tried to highlight the most commonly used and successful measures.
3. We present a uniform framework for building diversity measures. Two of the oldest measures of diversity, Simpson and Shannon, and their corresponding evenness measures, turn out to be directly related to two fairly deep concepts of diversity: variance and information.
4. The best way to use empirical samples to get at the ecological sample is to take multiple empirical samples of the same ecological sample. This provides information about the variability

induced by the empirical sampling process and allows for the development of an asymptotic approach that can then be extrapolated to the properties of the ecological sample. One common method is to plot the measure of interest vs the number of empirical samples and extrapolate.

5. We present a method for testing whether two (or any combination of more than two) empirical samples are drawn from a single ecological sample using the multinomial distribution and likelihood/AIC methods. It turns out that the likelihood is directly related to Shannon's diversity.

CHAPTER 6

Compositional similarity and β (beta) diversity

Lou Jost, Anne Chao, and Robin L. Chazdon

6.1 Introduction

Spatial variation in species composition is one of the most fundamental and conspicuous features of the natural world. Measures of compositional differentiation and similarity quantify this variation. Conservation biologists apply these measures when setting conservation priorities or evaluating regional conservation plans, and ecologists use them to study the homogenizing or diversifying effects of human activities, natural disturbances, or spatial variability of environmental conditions (McKinney and Lockwood 1999; Olden 2006; Vellend et al. 2007). Measures of similarity and differentiation are also essential tools for evaluating the effects of isolation by distance or geographic barriers, and for describing changes in species composition along environmental gradients.

Ecologists aim not merely to describe spatial variation in community composition, but ultimately to understand the causal factors that produce it. Is spatial heterogeneity caused or maintained by disturbances? Do species assemblages converge or diverge in composition over time during succession (Terborgh et al. 1996; Vandermeer et al. 2004)? How do environmental gradients affect the distributions of species (Bray and Curtis 1957; Whittaker 1960, 1972; Tuomisto et al. 1995)? To what extent do compositional differences reflect neutral variation in species abundance due solely to dispersal limitation (Hubbell 2001)? Carefully chosen measures of similarity and differentiation can be connected to appropriate null models to enable hypothesis testing.

In ecology, a general approach to assessing compositional differentiation partitions regional diversity (γ) into within- (α) and between- (β) group components, and derives similarity and differentiation measures from these components. A wide range of similarity, differentiation, and β diversity measures are in common use, reflecting the many ways that assemblages can be said to differ in composition (reviewed by Legendre and Legendre 1998; Vellend 2001; Koleff et al. 2003; Jurasinski et al. 2009; Tuomisto 2010).

Here, we provide a conceptual overview of approaches to quantifying compositional similarity and differentiation. We then discuss the fundamental connection between diversity and compositional differentiation, and show how some of the most important and useful similarity and differentiation measures are directly connected to diversity measures through the concept of β diversity.

6.2 State of the field

Before we can discuss the important approaches in this field, we need to standardize some terms and introduce some mathematical concepts. Our basic unit of analysis is the *assemblage*, the set of individuals exposed to our sampling efforts in a defined area or point. Ecologists generally try to delimit assemblages so that they are spatially uniform in expected species composition. Assemblages can be delimited by uniform habitats, uniform soil types, constant elevational ranges, or host species, and may range in size from a few cubic centimetres of soil to millions of hectares of forest, depending on the biology of the taxa being examined, as well as the question being asked. If an assemblage really is spatially uniform in this sense, ecologists can make many samples throughout the assemblage, and each sample will be a replicate drawn from the same assemblage. When this assumption holds, incidence or abundance data from the replicate samples can be used to estimate the relative abundances of each species in the assemblage (Chapter 4). If the assemblage is not homogeneous in the statistical sense, it can still be characterized by its average properties.

Assemblages are said to have identical compositions if the *relative* abundance of each species in one assemblage is the same as the *relative* abundance of that species in the other assemblages (or, when ignoring abundances, they are identical if the lists of species in the assemblages are the same). Thus assemblages can be compositionally identical even if they differ greatly in density (number of individuals per unit area or volume) or area. This definition separates these logically distinct factors. At the other extreme, assemblages are maximally dissimilar if they share no species. A measure of compositional similarity between assemblages compares the relative abundance of each species in each of the assemblages and returns a summary measure of the closeness of these relative abundances.

A measure of *relative* compositional similarity ranges from 0 to 1, assigning a value of 0 to a set of assemblages that share no species, and a value of 1 to a set of compositionally identical assemblages. Compositional *differentiation* is, loosely speaking, the opposite of compositional similarity. A measure of *relative* compositional differentiation ranges from 0 to 1, assigning a value of 0 to a set of compositionally identical assemblages, and a value of 1 to a set of assemblages that share no species. Measures of compositional similarity and differentiation are really just measures of the divergence between the species probability distributions of each assemblage. Divergence measures play an important role in statistics and information theory, and their properties are well studied (Pardo 2006).

Ecologists use similarity measures to make inferences about their assemblages. These inferences usually conceal implicit assumptions about the mathematical properties of the similarity measure used. If the similarity measure does not have

the required properties, the ecological inferences will be invalid. At least the following three basic properties should be present in any ecologically useful measure of similarity.

The most basic property is that the measure must truly reflect similarity. Similarity is a multifaceted concept, so it is not possible to define it with complete precision. Different similarity measures may legitimately differ in the way they rank sets of assemblages. However, the concept of similarity does have an unambiguous core. It is possible to create a sequence of assemblages whose compositional similarities unambiguously decrease. Suppose we have a set of equally large, perfectly even assemblages (all species equally common), and suppose each assemblage is identical in composition. If we add unique new species to each assemblage, at the same abundances as the pre-existing species, the similarity of these assemblages must decrease. This is an essential part of the meaning of 'compositional similarity', and this core concept will be referred to as 'monotonicity' with respect to unambiguously decreasing similarity. If a measure *increases* from one set of assemblages to the next in this sequence, it is not measuring similarity. Some commonly used similarity measures fail this most basic test. The reverse of this test applies to differentiation measures.

A measure of compositional similarity should not be sensitive to the raw abundances of the species in each assemblage, but only to their relative abundances. This property may be called 'density invariance'. A measure which lacks this property is not measuring compositional similarity, although it may have other legitimate interpretations.

A third property essential in relative similarity and differentiation measures (those that range between 0 and 1) is 'replication invariance'. Ecologists often compare the similarity of a subset of the data (perhaps a particular genus, or age class, or trophic guild) to the similarity of the whole dataset. For example, we may want to know if large-bodied moths are less spatially differentiated in a forest landscape than the moths as a whole. If these part-to-whole comparisons are to make sense, the measure of relative similarity or differentiation must be invariant with respect to pooling of identical subsets. Suppose, for example, that we are studying large, medium, and small moths from two sites. Suppose each set of moths has exactly the same number of species and exactly the same abundances. Each set will show exactly the same degree of differentiation, no matter what measure is used. If ecologists made a part-to-whole comparison, looking at the relative differentiation of small moths compared to that of moths in general, they would have to conclude that the small moths are not exceptional in their degree of differentiation. If we want a differentiation measure to lead to this sensible conclusion, the measure must have the property known in economics as 'replication invariance'. If we have N identical subsets of abundances, and no species are shared between subsets, then the community as a whole should have the same degree of similarity as the individual subsets. Imagine what would happen if this were not the case. Taken to an extreme, every genus in the dataset might show the same high site-to-site relative differentiation, while the community as a whole could be assigned a low site-to-site relative differentiation. This actually happens with some common measures of similarity and differentiation. (Tables 6.1 and 6.2)

6.2.1 Measures of relative compositional similarity and differentiation

Incidence-based measures of relative similarity
Incidence-based measures of relative compositional similarity are based only on the presence or absence of species. These have always been very popular with ecologists. The first incidence-based similarity index in ecology was published at the turn of the last century by Jaccard (1900, 1901), and new ones have been proposed continuously since then. Today, a bewildering number of incidence-based similarity measures are available to ecologists. Hubalek (1982) listed 43 and Koleff et al. (2003) listed 24 incidence-type similarity indices. These papers, along with those of Gower (1985) and Legendre and Legendre (1998), provide comprehensive reviews of incidence-based indices. Table 6.1 presents some important incidence-based similarity measures that are monotonic with decreasing similarity, density-invariant, and replication-invariant. Both the original Jaccard measure and the classic Sørensen measure (Sørensen 1948) are widely used. Both were originally designed to compare two assemblages. They differ only in their perspective. The Jaccard index compares the number of shared species

Table 6.1 A class of incidence-based similarity indices for comparing two assemblages and their corresponding abundance-based versions.

Index	Incidence-based In terms of a, b, c	Incidence-based In terms of S_1, S_2, S_{12}	Abundance-based (See text for details)
Jaccard	$\frac{a}{a+b+c}$	$\frac{S_{12}}{S_1+S_2-S_{12}}$	$\frac{UV}{U+V-UV}$
Sørensen; Dice	$\frac{2a}{(2a+b+c)}$	$\frac{2S_{12}}{S_1+S_2}$	$\frac{2UV}{U+V}$
Ochiai	$\frac{a}{[(a+b)(a+c)]^{1/2}}$	$\frac{S_{12}}{(S_1 S_2)^{1/2}}$	$(UV)^{1/2}$
Anderberg	$\frac{a}{a+2(b+c)}$	$\frac{S_{12}}{2S_1+2S_2-3S_{12}}$	$\frac{UV}{2U+2V-3UV}$
Kulczynski	$\frac{a}{b+c}$	$\frac{S_{12}}{S_1+S_2-2S_{12}}$	$\frac{UV}{U+V-2UV}$
Kulczynski; Cody	$\frac{a}{2(a+b)} + \frac{a}{2(a+c)}$	$\frac{1}{2}\left(\frac{S_{12}}{S_1} + \frac{S_{12}}{S_2}\right)$	$\frac{1}{2}(U+V)$
Lennon et al. (2001) (conditional Sørensen)	$\frac{a}{a+\min(b,c)}$	$\frac{S_{12}}{\min(S_1,S_2)}$	$\frac{UV}{\min(U,V)}$
General	A function of a, b, c satisfying some conditions (see text)	Replace a, b, c by S_{12}, $S_1 - S_{12}$, $S_2 - S_{12}$	Replace a, b, c by UV, $U(1 - V)$, $V(1 - U)$

This table is an expanded version of Table 2 of Chao et al. (2006). Symbols: a, the number of shared species; b, the number of unique species in the first assemblage; c, the number of unique species in the second assemblage; S_1 the number of species in Assemblage 1; S_2 the number of species in Assemblage 2; S_{12} the number of shared species; U and V: see text.

Table 6.2 Some similarity indices for two and multiple assemblages and their properties (density invariance, replication invariance, and monotonicity, given in Section 6.2),

Index	Two-assemblage	Multiple-assemblage	Density Invariance (6.2)	Replication Invariance (6.2)	Monotonicity (6.2)
Incidence-based					
(1) Jaccard	Jaccard (1900)	Koch (1957)	Yes	Yes	Yes
(2) Sørensen	Sørensen (1948)	Diserud and Ødegaard (2007)	Yes	Yes	Yes
Abundance-based					
(1) Horn index	Horn (1966)	Chao et al. (2008)	Yes	Yes	Yes
(2) Morisita–Horn index	Morisita (1959)	Jost (2006)	Yes	Yes	Yes
(3) Additive (based on Gini–Simpson)	Lande (1996)	Lande (1996)	Yes	No	No
(4) Additive (based on entropy)	Lande (1996)	Lande (1996)	Yes	No	No
(5) Bray–Curtis	Bray–Curtis (1957)	Use the average of pairwise similarities or the average distance from an individual assemblage to the centroid	No	Yes	Yes
(6) Percentage Similarity	Renkonen (1938)		Yes	Yes	Yes
(7) Standardized Gower/Euclidean/ Minkowski measure	Gower (1971, 1985)		No	Yes	Yes
(8) Canberra index	Lance and Williams (1967)		No	No	Yes
(9) Correlation coefficient	See, for example, Krebs (1999)		Yes	Yes	No
(10) Normalized expected species shared (NESS)	Grassle and Smith (1976)	Chao et al. (2008)	Yes	No	Yes
(11) Chao–Jaccard and Chao-Sørensen	Chao et al. (2005)	Not available	Yes	Yes	Yes

Formulas

Assume that there are S_i species in the ith assemblage and S species in the combined assemblage. Let $\overline{S}$ denote the average number of species, M_{ir} denote the abundance of the ith species in the rth assemblage, and p_{ir} denote the relative abundance, $i = 1, 2, \ldots, S$ and $r = 1, 2, \ldots, N$. Thus, we have N sets of species abundance $\{(M_{1r}, M_{2r}, \ldots, M_{Sr}); r = 1, \ldots, N\}$ and N sets of the relative abundance $\{(p_{1r}, p_{2r}, \ldots, p_{Sr}); r = 1, \ldots, N\}$.

Incidence-based indices

(1) Incidence-based Jaccard for two assemblages $= S_{12}/(S_1 + S_2 - S_{12})$
   Incidence-based Jaccard for multiple assemblages $= (\overline{S}/S - 1/N)/(1 - 1/N)$

(2) Incidence-based Sørensen for two assemblages $= 2S_{12}/(S_1 + S_2)$
   Incidence-based Sørensen for multiple assemblages $= (N - S/\overline{S})/(N - 1)$

Abundance-based indices

(1) Horn overlap index for two assemblages = equation 6.1
   Horn overlap index for N assemblages = equation 6.4

(2) Morisita–Horn index for two assemblages = equation 6.2
   Morisita–Horn index for N assemblages = equation 6.5

(3) Additive (based on Gini–Simpson index) for N assemblages $= H_\alpha/H_\gamma$, where

$$H_\alpha = (1/N)\sum_{j=1}^{N}(1 - \sum_{i=1}^{S} p_{ij}^2), \quad H_\gamma = 1 - \sum_{i=1}^{S} \overline{p}_i^2 \text{ and } \overline{p}_i = \sum_{j=1}^{N} p_{ij}/N$$

Table 6.2   *Continued.*

(4)   Additive (based on entropy) for N assemblages $= H_\alpha / H_\gamma$, where

$$H_\alpha = -\frac{1}{N} \sum_{i=1}^{S} \sum_{j=1}^{N} p_{ij} \log(p_{ij}), \quad H_\gamma = -\sum_{i=1}^{S} \overline{p}_i \log(\overline{p}_i) \text{ and } \overline{p}_i \text{ is defined in (3)}$$

(5)   Bray–Curtis index for two assemblages $=$ equation 6.6

(6)   Percentage similarity for two assemblages $=$ equation 6.7

(7)   Gower/Euclidean/Minkowski similarity for two assemblages $=$ equation 6.8

(8)   Canberra index for two assemblages $= 1 - \frac{1}{N} \sum_{i=1}^{S} \frac{|M_{i1} - M_{i2}|}{M_{i1} + M_{i2}}$

(9)   Correlation coefficient $=$ correlation of the two sets of abundances $(M_{11}, M_{21}, \ldots, M_{S1})$ and $(M_{12}, M_{22}, \ldots, M_{S2})$. This measure takes value between -1 and 1.

(10) Normalized expected species shared (NESS(m)) for two assemblages:

$$\frac{2\sum_{i=1}^{S} \mu_{i1}(m)\mu_{i2}(m)}{\sum_{i=1}^{S} [\mu_{i1}(m)]^2 + \sum_{i=1}^{S} [\mu_{i2}(m)]^2}$$

where $\mu_{ij}(m) = 1 - (1 - p_{ij})^m$.
NESS(m) for N assemblages:

$$\frac{2}{(N-1)} \frac{\sum_{i=1}^{S} \sum_{j<k} \mu_{ij}(m)\mu_{ik}(m)}{\sum_{i=1}^{S} \sum_{j=1}^{N} [\mu_{ij}(m)]^2}$$

(11) Chao–Jaccard for two assemblages $= UV/(U + V - UV)$
      Chao-Sørensen for two assemblages $= 2UV/(U + V)$

where $U(V)$ denotes the total relative abundance of the shared species in assemblage 1 (2).

to the total number of species in the combined assemblages, while the Sørensen index compares the number of shared species to the mean number of species in a single assemblage. The Jaccard index takes a global view while the Sørensen index takes a local view. Table 6.3 gives some examples. The Sørensen index is a true overlap measure (Wolda 1981): if the two assemblages have the same number of species, the Sørensen index gives the proportion of shared species in each assemblage (i.e. the proportion of an assemblage's species list that overlaps with the species list of the other assemblage).

The Sørensen index is the harmonic mean of the proportion of shared species in the first assemblage and the proportion of shared species in the second assemblage. The Ochiai index is the geometric mean and the Kulczynski–Cody index (Kulczynski 1928) is the arithmetic mean of the two proportions. Because of the relationship between these means, it

is always true that Sørensen index $\leq$ Ochiai index $\leq$ Kulczynski–Cody index.

When the richness of one assemblage is much greater than the richness of the other, both the Jaccard and Sørensen indices are always small. This is an accurate reflection of the difference in species compositions of the two assemblages, but for some applications it can be useful to normalize the measures so that they take the value unity when overlap is as large as it can be, given the respective richnesses of the two assemblages. Lennon et al. (2001) proposed this modification to the Sørensen index, which may be called the conditional Sørensen index. The formula for the conditional Sørensen index is given in Table 6.1. When there are no unique species in one of the assemblages, the conditional Sørensen index always yields a value of 1 no matter how many unique species there are in the other assemblage. Hence, this measure is not informative when applied to two nested assemblages

Table 6.3 Artificial examples with four sets (A, B, C, D) of assemblages illustrating various similarity indices.

Species	Set A Assemblage		Set B Assemblage		Set C Assemblage		Set D Assemblage		
	1	2	3	4	5	6	7	8	9
a	0.125	0.25	0.6	0.55	0.8	0.10	0.75	0.20	0.10
b	0.125	0.25	0.1	0.05	0.1	0.55	0.01	0.15	0.20
c	0.125	0.25	0.1	0.03	0.1	0	0.02	0.05	0.50
d	0.125	0.25	0.1	0.02	0	0.33	0.03	0	0
e	0.125	0	0.05	0	0	0.01	0.19	0	0
f	0.125	0	0.05	0	0	0.01	0	0.4	0
g	0.125	0	0	0.20	0	0	0	0.2	0
h	0.125	0	0	0.15	0	0	0	0	0.08
i	0	0	0	0	0	0	0	0	0.12
Incidence based									
Jaccard	0.50		0.50		0.33		0.33 (See text)		
Sørensen (C_{0N})	**0.67**		**0.67**		**0.50**		**0.60 (See text)**		
Lennon et al.	1.00		0.67		0.67		0.50 (Baselga et al. 2007)		
Abundance based									
Bray–Curtis	0.33		0.53		0.20		0.23 (pairwise mean)		
Percentage	0.50		0.65		0.20		0.22 (pairwise mean)		
Horn entropy (C_{1N})	**0.69**		**0.73**		**0.43**		**0.41 (equation 6.4)**		
Morisita–Horn (C_{2N})	**0.67**		**0.89**		**0.25**		**0.27 (equation 6.5)**		
Chao–Jaccard	0.50		0.61		0.61		Not available		
Chao–Sørensen	0.67		0.75		0.75		Not available		

For each species in the assemblage, the relative abundance is indicated. (For computing the Bray–Curtis index, the total number of individuals is assumed to be 100 in Assemblages 1, 3, 5, 7, and 9, and 200 for Assemblages 2, 4, and 8.)

(see Set A of Table 6.3). See Legendre and Legendre (1998) and Koleff et al. (2003) for the interpretation of the other measures listed in Table 6.1.

Most of these measures were originally designed to compare two assemblages. When more than two assemblages are compared, ecologists have often averaged their pairwise similarities (e.g. Lennon et al. 2001; Vellend 2001). However, the pairwise similarities tend to be correlated, which will cause an inference problem (Diserud & Ødegaard 2007). Aside from the correlation problem, pairwise similarities cannot fully characterize multiple-assemblage similarity when some species are shared across two, three, or more assemblages. A simple example is given by Chao et al. (2008). These problems have motivated the search for multiple-assemblage generalizations of similarity measures that can take global similarity into account.

Although there were measures in the literature that can be regarded as multiple-site Sørensen or related measures, a 'direct' extension of the Sørensen index to simultaneously compare multiple assemblages was first derived by Diserud & Ødegaard (2007). It has the form $(N - S/\overline{S})/(N - 1)$, where N denotes the number of assemblages, S denotes the total number of species in the combined assemblage, and $\overline{S}$ denotes the average number of species per assemblage. This measure is a monotonic transformation of Whittaker's β diversity (see below for details). It is identical to the complement of the 'turnover' measure by Harrison et al. (1992). For multiple assemblages, this generalized Sørensen index provides the overall proportion of shared species from a local perspective. Consider the special case in which each of the N assemblages has S species. Suppose that exactly R species are shared by all assemblages, and the remaining species are unique to their assemblage. This measure then gives the proportion of each assemblage's species that overlap with the other assemblages, R/S The conditional Sørensen index has also been generalized to multiple assemblages (Baselga et al. 2007).

A multiple-site Jaccard index was presented by Koch (1957). It is expressed as $(\overline{S}/S - 1/N)/(1 - 1/N)$, which measures the overall proportion of the shared species in the combined assemblage. In the example of the preceding paragraph, this measure reduces to $R/$(total number species in the combined assemblage). Like the multiple-assemblage generalization of the Sørensen index, it is a monotonic transformation of Whittaker's multiplicative β diversity (Jost 2007). This measure is less useful than the multiple-assemblage Sørensen index because it tends to decline as more assemblages are compared, even if overlap between assemblages is kept constant.

In Table 6.3, Set D includes three assemblages with completely different non-shared species. There are nine species in the whole assemblage, and in each assemblage there are five species, three of which are shared by all assemblages. The proportion of shared species relative to the combined assemblages (multiple-assemblage Jaccard index) is 1:3, whereas the average proportion of shared species in each assemblage (multiple-assemblage Sørensen index) is 3:5. The values for the conditional Sørensen index are also given in Table 6.3.

Each of these measures provides different information about compositional similarity. When choosing a measure, ecologists should think carefully about whether their perspective is local or global. If it is local, the multiple-assemblage Sørensen index is an informative and widely used index, facilitating comparisons across studies. The conditional version of the Sørensen index gives useful additional information, so if diversities differ greatly among assemblages this should also be presented. If the perspective is global, the multiple-assemblage Jaccard index and its conditional generalization could be used, but if the number of assemblages is high, both should be interpreted with caution (see above). When there are many assemblages, it is often easier to convey an intuitive picture of similarity through the Sørensen index rather than the Jaccard index, regardless of whether the perspective is local or global.

A more basic decision is whether or not to use incidence-based similarity measures at all. They are attractive because of the apparent ease of fieldwork, since only presence or absence needs to be noted. When nearly all species in each assemblage can be sampled, they are easily interpretable tools for comparing species lists. In addition, incidence-based measures may be the only alternative available when it is hard to define or count individuals of each species, as in 'uncountable' microbes, colonies of insects, or plant and invertebrate taxa with clonal growth.

In species-rich assemblages, however, intensive sampling efforts are needed to make complete or nearly complete lists of the species in a given assemblage. In practice, similarity measures must be estimated from sample data, so the species richness and shared species richness in the formulas of Table 6.1 are replaced by the observed counts. It is well known (e.g. Wolda, 1981, 1983; Magurran, 2004, p. 175) that all incidence-based indices are biased when sampling is incomplete, and the biases are likely to be substantial for assemblages with high species richness and a large fraction of rare species. The Jaccard and Sørensen indices are often biased downwards (Chao et al. 2006), but could be biased upwards too. The biases exist even in the simplest case when all species are equally abundant. The bias cannot be reduced or removed by using equal sampling fractions, equal sample sizes, or equal effort. Not only the bias but also the variance depends on species abundances (not incidence alone); thus, it is impossible to correct for the bias or to estimate errors without using abundance data. Even when abundance data are available, correcting the bias and assessing variance is not easy. See Chao et al. (2005, 2006) for relevant discussions.

One may be inclined to estimate species richness and shared species richness using non-parametric, low-bias estimators (Chao 2005), plugging these into the formulas in Table 6.1. However, replacing observed values of species richness and shared species with non-parametric estimates is problematic for assessing assemblage similarity. Combining these estimates in the formulas of Table 6.1 unavoidably inflates the variance and often renders the resulting estimate useless.

Finally, and perhaps most importantly, incidence-based similarity measures greatly oversimplify the relationships between assemblages. All such measures regard a maple forest with a few scattered pine trees as identical in composition to a pine forest with one or two maples, even though the two forests are ecologically very different. The relative abundances of species are ecologically important quantities. They should not be ignored, unless there is no choice.

Abundance-based similarity and distance measures
An ecologically more meaningful and informative approach to assessing similarity focuses on the differences in species frequencies among assemblages. This approach is also statistically more accurate and precise than incidence-based approaches. Some authors have adopted a parametric approach to abundance-based similarity measures by assuming that the relative abundances follows a parametric distribution (e.g. Smith, Solow & Preston 1996; Plotkin & Muller-Landau 2002). However, it is almost impossible to test whether a given sample really came from a particular parametric distribution (Chao 2005). We therefore focus on nonparametric indices that do not assume a particular kind of species abundance distribution.

In all the formulas that follow, we assume there are N assemblages, with S total species in the combined assemblages Let M_{ir} denote the absolute abundance of the ith species in the rth assemblage, and p_{ir} denote its relative abundance, with $i = 1, 2, \ldots, S$ and $r = 1, 2, \ldots, N$. Thus, we have N sets of species absolute abundances $\{(M_{1r}, M_{2r}, \ldots, M_{Sr}); r = 1, \ldots, N\}$ and N sets of the relative abundances $\{(p_{1r}, p_{2r}, \ldots, p_{Sr}); r = 1, \ldots, N\}$

Horn and Morisita–Horn overlap measures
The incidence-based Sørensen overlap index has abundance-based relatives. One of the most useful is the Horn (1966) overlap measure, based on Shannon's entropy (Chapter 4). In its original form it compares two assemblages, species by species. To make this clearer, it can be expressed as

$$S_H = \frac{1}{\log 2} \sum_{i=1}^{S} \left[\frac{p_{i1}}{2} \log \left(1 + \frac{p_{i2}}{p_{i1}} \right) + \frac{p_{i2}}{2} \log \left(1 + \frac{p_{i1}}{p_{i2}} \right) \right].$$

(6.1)

This index equals unity if and only if $p_{i1} = p_{i2}$ for all i. When the two assemblages have equal numbers of species and consist entirely of equally common species, the Horn index is equal to the Sørensen index and gives the proportion of shared species in an assemblage.

Another popular overlap measure is the Morisita Horn index, derived by Morisita (1959) and Horn (1966):

$$S_{MH} = \frac{2 \sum_{i=1}^{S} p_{i1} p_{i2}}{\left[\sum_{i=1}^{S} p_{i1}^2 + \sum_{i=1}^{S} p_{i2}^2 \right]} = 1 - \frac{\sum_{i=1}^{S} (p_{i1} - p_{i2})^2}{\sum_{i=1}^{S} p_{i1}^2 + \sum_{i=1}^{S} p_{i2}^2}$$

(6.2)

When the two assemblages are equally diverse and consist entirely of equally common species, the Morisita–Horn index is equal to the Horn index and the Sørensen index, and all give the proportion of shared species in an assemblage. The right side of equation 6.2 shows that the Morisita–Horn measure is based on the squared differences of the relative abundances of each species in the two assemblages. Because of this squared distance, the Morisita–Horn index is dominated by the most abundant species, while the relatively rare species have little effect (even if there are many of them). This makes the measure resistant to under-sampling because the influential abundant species are always sampled relatively accurately. Since ecological processes are often most strongly influenced by the dominant species, this measure is a good measure when looking for functional differences between ecosystems. It may not be appropriate when rare species are important, as in conservation applications. The Horn overlap measure would be more useful in those applications.

C_{qN}, a general multiple-assemblage abundance-based overlap measure
Surprisingly, all the overlap measures we have discussed—the Sørensen index, the Horn index, and the Morisita–Horn index—are special cases of a single general multiple-assemblage overlap measure C_{qN} (Chao et al. 2008):

$$C_{qN} = \frac{\frac{1}{(N^q - N)} \sum_{i=1}^{S} [(p_{i1} + p_{i2} + \ldots + p_{iN})^q - (p_{i1}^q + p_{i2}^q + \ldots p_{iN}^q)]}{\frac{1}{N} \sum_{i=1}^{S} (p_{i1}^q + p_{i2}^q + \ldots p_{iN}^q)}$$

(6.3)

Here q is a parameter that determines the measure's sensitivity to species' relative abundances, and N is the number of assemblages. When $N = 2$, setting $q = 0$ yields the Sørensen index, taking the limit as q approaches unity yields the Horn index, and setting $q = 2$ yields the Morisita–Horn index. Setting $N > 2$ yields the corresponding multiple-assemblage generalizations. The generalized Sørensen index is $C_{0N} = (N - S/\bar{S})/(N - 1)$ and the generalized Horn index can be expressed as

$$C_{1N} = \frac{1}{\log N} \sum_{i=1}^{S} \sum_{j=1}^{N} \left[\frac{p_{ij}}{N} \log \left(1 + \sum_{k \neq j} p_{ik}/p_{ij} \right) \right]$$

(6.4)

The multiple-assemblage Morisita–Horn index can be simplified as

$$C_{2N} = \frac{2 \sum_{i=1}^{S} \sum_{j<k} p_{ij} p_{ik}}{(N - 1) \sum_{i=1}^{S} \sum_{j=1}^{N} p_{ij}^2}$$

(6.5)

For integer values of q between 2 and N, overlap measures C_{qN} have a simple statistical interpretation as the ratio of two probabilities, $^qG_D/^qG_S$. The numerator is the probability that q randomly sampled individuals belong to the same species, given that they did not all come from the same assemblage. The denominator is the probability that q randomly sampled individuals belong to the same species given that they are all drawn from the same assemblage (Chao et al. 2008). This interpretation shows that the value of q determines the 'depth' of the measure: when $q = 2$, only pairwise similarity is considered, but when $q = 3$ the measure also takes into account species that are shared by three assemblages. This measure is density and replication invariant, and monotonic with respect to unambiguously decreasing similarity. Like the multiple-assemblage generalizations of the Sørensen index, C_{qN} gives the true overlap R/S for all orders of q when each assemblage consists of S equally common species, with R species contained in all assemblages and the remainder unique

to single assemblages. In the section on using transformations of β to measure compositional similarity (below) we give an example of the use and interpretation of these measures.

The expected value of C_{2N} (the Morisita–Horn index and its multiple-assemblage generalization) can be predicted under Hubbell's (2001) neutral model of biodiversity, which makes it an important theoretical tool. In Hubbell's neutral model, the community structure depends only on the number of communities N, the number of individuals in each community n (all communities are assumed to have the same size), the migration rate between communities m, and the speciation rate v. After many generations it reaches an equilibrium, and the structure at equilibrium can be predicted from the model parameters. This model is mathematically identical to Wright's finite-island model in population genetics. The expected equilibrium value of the complement of the Morisita–Horn index has been derived for that model (Jost 2008); under the approximation that $1 \gg m \gg v$, the formula for the expected equilibrium value of the Morisita–Horn index itself is $S_{MH} = m/[v(N - 1) + m]$. If similarity between assemblages is much different from this, some causal factors are implicated. C_{1N} (the Horn measure of similarity and its multiple-assemblage generalization) can also be connected to this model under certain special conditions (Sherwin et al. 2006), although a simple analytical expression in terms of model parameters still eludes us.

Bray–Curtis and Renkonen similarity measures
One of the most frequently used abundance-based similarity measures is the Bray–Curtis or 'quantitative Sørensen' index (Bray & Curtis 1957), developed by Bray and Curtis during their pioneering work on plant community ordination. Beals (1984) gives a detailed review of the Bray–Curtis ordination and related techniques. The Bray–Curtis similarity is expressed as

$$S_{BC} = \frac{2 \sum_{i=1}^{S} \min(M_{i1}, M_{i2})}{\sum_{i=1}^{S} (M_{i1} + M_{i2})} = 1 - \frac{\sum_{i=1}^{S} |M_{i1} - M_{i2}|}{\sum_{i=1}^{S} (M_{i1} + M_{i2})}$$

(6.6)

where $\min(M_{i1}, M_{i2})$ denotes the smaller of the two numbers, M_{i1} or M_{i2}. This index reduces to the

Sørensen index if all species in each assemblage are equally abundant. The expression on the right in equation 6.6 shows that it takes the maximum value of 1 if and only if the two sets of absolute abundances are identical, that is, $M_{1i} = M_{2i}$ for all species. This shows that the index confounds density with compositional similarity, so it cannot be considered a measure of compositional similarity. It approaches 0 when sample sizes are very different, whether the assemblages have the same compositions or completely different compositions. For example, suppose every species in a young secondary forest has exactly the same relative abundance as in a primary forest. Suppose the secondary forest has four times as many stems per hectare as the primary forest. Then the Bray–Curtis index will be approximately $1-\frac{3}{5} = 0.4$ rather than unity. If the secondary forest had 10 times the density of the primary forest, the Bray–Curtis index would be about 0.18 instead of unity. If it had 100 times the density of the primary forest, the Bray–Curtis index would be close to 0.02.

In addition to these conceptual problems, the Bray–Curtis index also has some statistical problems when applied to samples. The *observed* absolute abundance for any species depends on the sampling fraction (the ratio of sample size to the total number of individuals in the assemblage), so this index becomes meaningless and performs erratically when the sampling fraction is unequal in the two assemblages (Chao et al. 2006). It also generally has a very large bias in this case (Chao et al. 2006). For these reasons, from both statistical and conceptual perspectives, the Bray–Curtis index cannot be recommended unless sampling fractions are known to be equal. Given the unlikely prospect of establishing such conditions for field data, the Bray–Curtis index seems rarely to be an acceptable choice for such data. Note that equalizing the *number of individuals* (sample sizes) in all samples by rarefaction before calculating the Bray–Curtis index, as suggested by Horner-Devine et al. (2004), does not equalize sampling fractions unless the assemblages themselves can be reasonably assumed to have the same total number of individuals susceptible to sampling.

It follows from equation 6.6 that the Bray–Curtis measure can be interpreted as a normalized Manhattan distance (absolute difference). When there are multiple assemblages, as in the conventional distance-based approach, an average of pairwise Bray–Curtis values is generally used as an overall similarity measure. This approach, unfortunately, ignores information about the species shared among three or more assemblages (Chao et al. 2008).

Renkonen (1938) proposed the following measure of similarity:

$$S_P = \sum_{i=1}^{S} \min(p_{i1}, p_{i2}) = 1 - \frac{1}{2}\sum_{i=1}^{S} |p_{i1} - p_{i2}|$$

(6.7)

This measure is based on the Manhattan distance of the relative abundances of the species in the assemblages, instead of the absolute abundances as in the Bray–Curtis index. It is therefore density invariant, so it is a valid measure of compositional similarity. It attains a minimum value of 0 when two assemblages are completely distinct (no shared species) and it attains a maximum value of 1 if and only if the two sets of relative abundances are identical. Following the work of Renkonen (1938), Whittaker (1952, 1972) and Wolda (1981), this index has become one of the most commonly used measures among ecologists. Gregorius (1987) also suggested its use for a proper genetic distance among populations.

Smith and Zaret (1982) found that in their simulation trials this measure tends to be biased when estimated from sample data, but Wolda (1981) recommended its use if a logarithm transform is applied to species frequencies to reduce the dominance of the most abundant species. This measure suffers from the same disadvantage as the Bray–Curtis index, namely that the analysis for multiple sites can only be based on pairwise comparisons, and thus information about species shared between three or more sites is ignored.

Distance measures
We have seen that the two-assemblage Bray–Curtis and Renkonen similarity indices are complements of some types of normalized Manhattan distance, and the two-assemblage Morisita–Horn index is the complement of a type of normalized Euclidean distance. This use of normalized distance

between assemblages is a natural way to form an index of similarity or differentiation between two sets of quantitative variables. There are many distances, and some common approaches include Euclidean distance, Manhattan distance, Lance and Williams' (1967) Canberra distance, chi-square distance, Minkowski distance, Orlóci's chord distance, and Hellinger distance (Legendre & Legendre 1998; Gower 1985). As indicated by Gregorius (1996), a distinction between 'distance' measures and 'differentiation' measures is that 'distance' refers to a pair of assemblages and obeys the triangle inequality whereas 'differentiation' refers to any number of assemblages but need not satisfy the triangle inequality. A unified class of distance-based similarity measures is the one-complement of the normalized Minkowski distance:

$$1 - \frac{1}{S} \sum_{i=1}^{S} \frac{|M_{i1} - M_{i2}|^p}{R_i^p} \qquad (6.8)$$

where $p \geq 1$, and R_i denotes the range (i.e. the difference of the maximum and minimum) of the ith species abundances. The special case $p = 1$ corresponds to the Gower (1971) similarity index. The special case $p = 2$ corresponds to the similarity index based on the Euclidean distance.

Due to the restriction that 'distance' is only calculated for a pair of assemblages, this approach cannot be directly extended to the case of multiple assemblages. Thus, the information shared by at least two assemblages is ignored in the traditional approach using the average of pairwise distances as the overall dissimilarity. Anderson et al. (2006) modified this approach by considering a multivariate dispersion as the 'β' diversity or a dissimilarity measure. A multivariate dispersion is defined as the average of the distance from an individual assemblage to the 'centroid.' This approach does simultaneously compare the whole set of assemblages because the information shared by multiple assemblages can be incorporated in the 'centroid'.

Indices based on total abundance of shared species
The abundance-based indices discussed above match species relative abundances, *species by species*. That is, the typical similarity indices assess a normalized probability that two randomly chosen individuals, one from each assemblage, belong to *the same* species. Chao et al. (2005, 2006) derived a

class of measures which look at a different kind of similarity, based on assessing the normalized probability that two randomly chosen individuals, one from each assemblage, belong to *shared* species (not necessarily *the same* species). It is simple to convert any incidence-based measure that is replication invariant to its shared-abundance version. Let U denote the total relative abundances associated with the *shared* species in Assemblage 1 and let V denote the total relative abundances of the *shared* species in Assemblage 2. By replacing a, b and c in Table 6.1 with UV, $U(1 - V)$ and $V(1 - U)$, we obtain for each incidence-based index its shared-abundance version, given in the last column of Table 6.1. These indices attain the maximum value of 1 if and only if $U = V = 1$ (even if the two sets of abundances may be different). These two shared-abundance indices are called the Chao–Jaccard and Chao–Sørensen abundance indices in the literature and software packages (e.g. EstimateS by Colwell (2006) and SONS by Schloss and Handelsman (2006a)).

Unlike the ordinary similarity indices that match species-by-species abundances, these measures match the total relative abundances of species shared between two assemblages. In Sets B and C considered in Table 6.3, the total shared species abundances are the same for the first assemblage in each set ($U = 0.9$) and also the same for the second assemblage in each set ($V = 0.65$), yielding the same Chao–Sørensen and Chao–Jaccard shared abundance indices, even though the patterns of abundance for species a and b are drastically different for the two sets. Set C in particular shows that these two indices are quite different from species-by-species abundance-based similarity measures.

One main advantage of these measures is that the under-sampling bias due to unseen shared species can be evaluated and corrected. This class of measures can also be extended to deal with replicated incidence data. The extension of this approach to assessing similarity of multiple assemblages, although conceptually simple, is statistically complicated and is still under development. These measures are designed to be sensitive to rare shared species while still taking abundance into account, so they may make large jumps as more shared species are discovered. They should be used only if their concept of similarity is relevant to the question of interest. For examples of their use and interpretation, see Chao et al. (2005, 2006), Anderson et al. (2006) and Schloss and Handelsman (2006a).

6.2.2 Diversity and compositional similarity

There is an intimate connection between species diversity and compositional differentiation and similarity. If assemblages are identical in composition, pooling them will leave their diversity unchanged. If assemblages are very different in composition, pooling them together with equal weights should result in a total diversity considerably greater than the diversity of any of the assemblages individually. Comparing the diversities of the individual assemblages to the diversity of the pooled assemblages will provide information about their compositional similarity, as long as the pooling gives equal weight to each assemblage. Many of the similarity and differentiation measures discussed above are based on different ways of comparing the diversities of the individual assemblages to the diversity of the pooled assemblages.

Similarity ratio based on diversity measures
Ecologists often use the ratio of mean within-group diversity (the 'α diversity') to total pooled diversity ('γ diversity') as a measure of the compositional similarity of the groups (Lande 1996). If this ratio is close to unity, ecologists infer that the groups must be similar in composition. If the ratio is low, they infer that the groups are highly differentiated in composition.

While this reasoning seems logical, its validity actually depends on the measure used. When the most common measures of complexity are used, such as Shannon entropy (see Chapters 3 and 5)

$$H_S = -\sum_{i=1}^{S} p_i \log p_i$$

or the Gini–Simpson index

$$H_{GS} = 1 - \sum_{i=1}^{S} p_i^2$$

the ratio of mean within-group 'diversity' to total pooled 'diversity' always approaches unity when

within-group diversity is high (MacArthur 1965; Whittaker 1972; Jost 2006, 2007; Tuomisto 2010) even if all the groups are completely distinct (no species in common). This problem arises frequently in practice and can lead to serious misinterpretations (Jost et al. 2010). These 'similarity' measures based on the Gini–Simpson index or Shannon entropy are also not monotonic with respect to unambiguously increasing similarity, so they do not rank datasets correctly in terms of their similarity (Jost et al. 2010). They should not be used to infer compositional similarity across space or time. Because of their non-linearity with respect to pooling of equally diverse groups, they are also dangerously misleading in conservation applications (Jost 2009).

The great mathematical ecologist Robert MacArthur was the first to notice the problems with computing similarity ratios based directly on Shannon entropy or the Gini–Simpson index (MacArthur 1965). He solved the problem by converting these measures to effective number of species. The effective number of species is the number of equally common species needed to produce the observed value of an index. For example, to find the effective number of species for a Shannon entropy of 2.4 (assuming this value of 2.4 was calculated using natural logarithms), we need to find out how many equally common species are needed to obtain a Shannon entropy of 2.4. The answer is 11 species. Shannon entropy is converted to effective number of species by taking its exponential:

$$^1D = \exp(H_S) = \exp\left(-\sum_{i=1}^{S} p_i \log p_i\right)$$

$$= \text{'exponential of Shannon entropy'}$$

while the Gini–Simpson index or heterozygosity is converted by the following formula:

$$^2D = 1/(1 - H_{GS}) = 1/\sum_{i=1}^{S} p_i^2$$

$$= \text{'inverse Simpson concentration'}$$

MacArthur (1965) observed that when the numerator and denominator of the 'similarity' ratio described in the preceding paragraphs is converted to effective number of species, the ratio truly did reflect the compositional similarity of the assemblages, as long as both the within-group mean and the pooled diversity are calculated using equal weights for each assemblage. Pooling with equal weights means not pooling samples directly, but pooling them in equal proportions.

The particular mathematical property which makes some measures behave properly in similarity ratios while others fail is known in ecology as the doubling property or in economics as the replication principle (Dalton 1920; Hannah and Kay 1977). Suppose we make N equally large copies of an ecosystem, each with identical species abundance distributions but with completely different species. The replication principle states that the diversity of the N pooled ecosystems (which share no species) must be N times the diversity of the original ecosystem. This replication principle seems to be implicit in many forms of reasoning about diversity (Hill 1973; Jost 2009). (Replication *invariance*, discussed above, refers to measures that do not change when assemblages are replicated N times.)

Hill (1973) derived a parametric family of diversity measures that obey the replication principle:

$$ {}^{q}D = \left(\sum_{i=1}^{S} p_i^q \right)^{1/(1-q)} $$

This formula gives the effective number of species of all standard complexity and diversity measures (Jost 2007). As discussed earlier, the value of q determines the sensitivity of the measure to species relative abundances; ecologists can either emphasize ($q > 1$) or de-emphasize ($q < 1$) the relative abundances. When $q = 0$, this formula gives species richness. When $q = 2$, it gives the inverse Simpson concentration (Simpson 1949). When $q = 1$ (the value that weighs all species exactly by their frequency), the formula is undefined (because of a division by zero in the exponent), but the limit as q approaches unity exists and equals the exponential of Shannon entropy. Shannon entropy thus can be derived directly from the mathematics of diversity and does not need to be borrowed from other fields. In order to avoid invalid inferences about diversity, these measures should always be used in preference to the raw Shannon entropy or Gini–Simpson index (MacArthur 1965; Whittaker 1972; Routledge 1979;

Peet 1974; Jost 2006, 2007, 2009). Measures of compositional complexity that obey the replication principle are the 'true diversities' of Jost (2007, 2009) and Tuomisto (2010).

When a complexity measure that obeys the replication principle is used in the similarity ratio, with all assemblages weighted equally and with the mean defined in equation 6.9a below, the similarity ratio ranges from unity (complete similarity) to $1/N$ (complete dissimilarity). This range does not depend on their diversities and is easily normalized onto the interval from 0 to 1.

Partitioning diversity into α and β components
As mentioned in the preceding section, α diversity is a mean (not necessarily the arithmetic mean) of the diversities of a set of assemblages, whereas γ diversity is the diversity of the pooled assemblages. γ diversity is at least as great as α diversity, and will exceed α diversity when the assemblages are differentiated. γ diversity therefore has two contributions, one from α diversity and the other from differentiation between assemblages. The contribution of differentiation to the total or γ diversity is called β diversity.

What is the relationship between α, β, and γ? Whittaker (1972) proposed that β be defined through a multiplicative relationship:

$$ \alpha \times \beta = \gamma $$

He applied this relationship to effective numbers of species (species richness, the exponential of Shannon entropy, and the inverse Simpson concentration). He restricted his discussion to the case of equally weighted assemblages, which is the appropriate choice when the goal is to measure compositional similarity.

Lande (1996) proposed instead that β be defined through an additive relationship with α:

$$ \alpha + \beta = \gamma $$

This additive approach is meant to apply to concave measures of diversity and complexity (see Lande (1996) for a definition of concave), such as species richness (see Chapter 4), Shannon entropy (see Chapters 3 and 5), and the Gini–Simpson index. In this approach, α is the weighted arithmetic mean of the diversity or complexity measure of the individual assemblages. β is found by subtracting α from γ. The concavity property ensures that γ is never less than α, so β defined in this way is always non-negative. This approach is superficially similar to the additive partitioning of variances.

These approaches are often respectively called multiplicative partitioning and additive partitioning of γ into α and β components. However, 'partitioning' usually means a *complete* separation of the two components, α (the within-group component) and β (the between-group component). A genuine partitioning of γ into α and β components would place all the within-group influence into the α component, and all the between-group influence into the β component. If the partitioning is complete, the α component provides no information about the value of the β component, and vice versa; they are completely independent components of γ diversity or complexity measure.

When a complete partitioning of γ exists, its form is unique for any given measure. It exists for all standard diversity and complexity measures when assemblages are given equal weights. For species richness ($q = 0$), the complete partitioning is multiplicative: $α × β = γ$. For Shannon entropy ($q = 1$), it is additive: $α + β = γ$. For the Gini–Simpson index, it is neither additive nor multiplicative: $α + β − α × β = γ$. For all effective number of species, or Hill numbers of any order, which are true diversities in the sense of Jost (2007), it is multiplicative: $α × β = γ$ (Jost 2007). The components are:

$$^q D_a = \left(\frac{1}{N} \sum_{i=1}^{S} p_{i1}^q + \frac{1}{N} \sum_{i=1}^{S} p_{i2}^q + \ldots + \frac{1}{N} \sum_{i=1}^{S} p_{iN}^q \right)^{1/(1-q)} \text{(6.9a)}$$

$$^q D_\gamma = \left\{ \sum_{i=1}^{S} \left[\frac{1}{N} (p_{i1} + p_{i2} + \ldots + p_{iN}) \right]^q \right\}^{1/(1-q)} \text{(6.9b)}$$

$$^q D_\beta = {}^q D_\gamma / {}^q D_a \text{(6.9c)}$$

β for true diversities is just the reciprocal of the similarity ratio of the previous section. It ranges from 1 to N, and gives the effective number of completely distinct assemblages; it is a divergence measure between the species probability distributions of the assemblages. It is a 'true β diversity' in the senses of Jost (2007) and Tuomisto (2010). In the special case of $q = 0$, equation 6.9c reduces to Whit-

taker's β diversity $S/\overline{S}$ based on species richness. Investigators using these measures should at least report the values of β for $q = 0, 1$, and 2, in order to give a picture of how differentiation varies between all species ($q = 0$), the typical species ($q = 1$), and the dominant species ($q = 2$). A more complete picture is conveyed by a graph of β diversity from $q = 0$ to $q = 4$ or 5 (beyond this it usually does not change much). This is the β diversity profile. This can be easier to interpret when normalized onto the unit interval to give a similarity profile, as described in the next section (see Box 6.1 for an example).

When assemblage area or size needs to be taken into account, as when measuring regional heterogeneity (Horn 1966) instead of compositional differentiation, a complete partitioning into a measure of mean within-site diversity and a measure of between-site differentiation only exists for measures based on Shannon entropy and species richness (Jost 2007). For the exponential of Shannon entropy, the components are:

$$^1 D_a = \exp \left(-w_1 \sum_{i=1}^{S} p_{i1} \log p_{i1} - w_2 \sum_{i=1}^{S} p_{i2} \log p_{i2} \ldots \right.$$
$$\left. -w_N \sum_{i=1}^{S} p_{iN} \log p_{iN} \right) \text{(6.10a)}$$

$$^1 D_\gamma = \exp \left[- \sum_{i=1}^{S} (w_1 p_{i1} \right.$$
$$\left. + \ldots + w_N \, p_{iN}) \log(w_1 p_{i1} + \ldots + w_N \, p_{iN}) \right] \text{(6.10b)}$$

$$^1 D_\beta = {}^1 D_\gamma / {}^1 D_a \text{(6.10c)}$$

Here the weights w_j are usually taken to be the relative sizes (either in terms of area or total population) of the assemblages. This β ranges from 1 to the weight diversity, which is the exponential of the Shannon entropy of the weights themselves. It takes the latter value when the assemblages are completely different in composition (no shared species). When other measures of diversity are used with unequal weights, it may still be possible to extract information about assemblage differentiation by comparing them to more complicated reference diversities; see Gregorius (2010) for discussion.

Box 6.1 Numerical example: assessing the compositional similarity of trees and seedlings across six sites

We illustrate our multiple-assemblage similarity indices by using the frequency data collected in six forests in north-eastern Costa Rica 2006 by Chazdon and colleagues; see Norden et al. (2009) for details of the six sites. The six 1-ha plots vary in land-use history and in protection from hunting. Two plots are young secondary forests: El Bejuco (EB, 12 years old in 2006) and Juan Enriquez (JE, 12 years old in 2006). Two plots are 'intermediate' secondary forests: Lindero Sur (LSUR, 21 years old in 2006) and Lindero El Peje secondary (LEPS, 29 years old in 2006). Two plots are in old growth forests: Lindero El Peje primary (LEPP, over 200 years) and Selva Verde (SV, over 200 years). The four secondary forests were all cleared, burned, and used for pasture for several years and were subsequently abandoned. Three sites are located within La Selva Biological Station (LSUR, LEPS, and LEPP), and three sites are located 7 km to the west in Chilamate.

Each plot was 50 × 200 m (1 ha). For this example, we consider two size classes of canopy tree species: trees (> 5 cm in DBH) including canopy palms, and canopy tree seedlings (< 1 cm in DBH, but > 20 cm in height). All trees were marked and measured for diameter within a 1-ha plot in each forest. Seedlings were sampled in five strips 2 × 200 m long, running every 10 m (0.2 ha). The number of species and individuals are summarized in Table 6.4. Note that SV old-growth forest has by far the highest seedling abundance; 72% are seedlings of a single canopy palm species, *Welfia regia*. Species richness of trees is significantly greater in the old-growth plots, but seedling species richness is similar (Norden et al. 2009; Table 6.4).

Table 6.4 The observed species richness in four secondary-growth and two old-growth sites (numbers in parentheses denote the number of individuals)

Site	Age in 2006	Seedlings	Trees
EB young	12	65 (3797)	56 (498)
JE young	12	58 (2258)	48 (546)
LSUR intermediate	21	42 (777)	51 (762)
LEPS intermediate	29	47 (1303)	79 (1093)
LEPP old-growth	> 200	53 (1160)	89 (618)
SV old-growth	> 200	54 (5411)	114 (832)
Average number of species		53.17	72.83
Number of species in the six plots		97	184

See Box 6.1 for explanation of EB, JE, LSUR, LEPS, LEPP, and SV.

Table 6.5 β diversities and multiple-assemblage similarity indices (with s.e. in parenthesis) across the six sites for trees and seedlings.

Index	Sizes	$q = 0$ (Presence/ absence)	$q = 1$ (Entropy based)	$q = 2$ (Simpson index based)
β diversity	Trees	2.526 (0.052)	1.982 (0.026)	1.626 (0.037)
	Seedlings	1.824 (0.034)	1.566 (0.011)	1.797 (0.019)
Multiple-assemblage similarity	Trees	0.695 (0.009)	0.618 (0.007)	0.535 (0.015)
C_{qN}	Seedlings	0.835 (0.007)	0.750 (0.004)	0.467 (0.008)

The β diversity formula is given in equation 6.9c and multiple-assemblage similarity in equation 6.3 or 6.12.

Although a specialized group of tree species colonize abandoned pastures and become dominant in early secondary forests, seedling species are more likely to be shared with old-growth forests, due to similar conditions within the shaded forest understory in all plots. We therefore predicted that multiple-assemblage similarity would be lower for trees than for seedlings across the six forest plots.

Here, we assess the compositional similarity indices of trees across the six plots. We then compare the similarity indices for seedlings across the six plots. In Table 6.5 we present the β diversities and multiple-assemblage similarity indices of orders 0, 1, and 2 along with their bootstrapped s.e. for trees and seedlings. We use the observed species and abundance to compute the measures for $q = 0$ and 1 because for these data the under-sampling bias is relatively low so that it would not affect the general 'relative' pattern. For the measures of $q = 2$, we use the nearly unbiased estimators (Chao et al. 2008).

Based on Table 6.5 and the multiple-assemblage similarity profile in Figure 6.1A, for $q = 0$ and 1, the cross-site similarity of seedlings is larger than the cross-site similarity of trees. However for $q \geq 2$, the result is reversed. This is because abundant species strongly influence the assemblage similarity index for $q \geq 2$. This pattern is due to a single species that is superabundant in the SV old-growth forest, *Welfia regia*. When this species is excluded in the comparison, it is clear (Figure 6.1B) the cross-site similarity of seedlings is always larger than the cross-site similarity of trees for all orders. The above

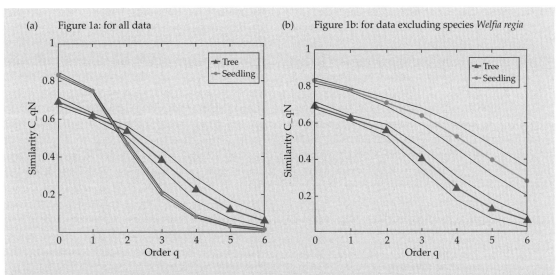

Figure 6.1 The multiple-assemblage similarity profile C_{qN} (for $q = 0 - 6$) and the associated 95% confidence interval: x-axis, order q; y-axis, similarity index C_{qN}. (a) For all data; (b) for data excluding species *Welfia regia*.

pattern is also generally valid for any pair of plots for the three orders.

The results show that, among these six plots, β diversity of trees is higher than for tree seedlings. This pattern reflects the ecological specialization of common trees in secondary vs old-growth forests. In contrast, tree seedlings established in both secondary and old-growth forest are more evenly mixed across the plots and do not show evidence of ecological segregation or differentiation. In the secondary forests, many of these seedlings are colonizing these forests for the first time (Norden et al. 2009). Gradually, these changes in species composition will lead to

differentiation and reassembly of tree species composition as the shade-tolerant species become recruited in larger size classes (Chao et al. 2005). Since the under-sampling bias for the estimates of the measure of order 0 (only presence/absence data are used) generally cannot be corrected and a measure based on abundance data is more informative, it is suggested that the multiple-assemblage similarity index, particularly for measures of order $q = 1$ and $q = 2$ based on abundance data, provides a sensitive and statistically robust metric for comparing compositional similarity of tree and seedling assemblages in forests at different stages of succession (Chao et al. 2008).

The complete partitioning lets us evaluate the multiplicative and additive approaches. Whittaker's multiplicative approach gives the complete partitioning of all effective numbers of species. The additive approach gives the complete partitioning of Shannon entropy but not species richness or the Gini–Simpson index. The additive species richness β is still a useful measure, as shown below, but the additive Gini–Simpson β is confounded with α in a particularly inappropriate way. When α is high, this β necessarily approaches zero, even if all groups are completely differentiated (Jost 2006, 2007, 2008; Jost et al. 2010; Tuomisto 2010). One consequence of this is that additive β using the Gini–Simpson index is not monotonic with respect to unambiguously

increasing differentiation (Jost et al. 2010). It cannot be directly interpreted as a measure of differentiation for a given set of assemblages. It needs to be properly normalized before it can be interpreted (Jost et al. 2010). Hierarchical additive partitioning of this measure gives misleading results as well, since α generally increases at higher hierarchical levels, limiting this β to ever-smaller values as we go up the hierarchical pyramid.

Using transformations of β to measure compositional similarity

β diversity based on complete partitioning is independent of α. However, we may also be interested in measures of the number of species (or effective number of species) by which the assemblages differ; this kind of measure necessarily depends on α. For example, if assemblage weights are taken to be equal, the effective number of regional species not contained in a typical local assemblage is given by $^q D_\gamma - {}^q D_\alpha = {}^q D_\alpha ({}^q D_\beta - 1)$. This is essentially additive partitioning of effective number of species (but taking care to use equal weights when q is different from 0 or 1, and making sure that $^q D_\alpha$ is calculated as above). Economo and Kiett (2008) used this partitioning to investigate the behaviour of Hubbell's neutral theory of biodiversity. Dividing this by $N - 1$ gives the effective number of species unique to a typical local assemblage. This is given by $^q D_\alpha ({}^q D_\beta - 1)/(N - 1)$. These measures should be interpreted with care when comparing regions, since they depend on α diversity.

The β diversities for effective number of species ranges from 1 to N when weights are equal. They can be made into measures of relative compositional similarity by transforming them onto the unit interval. All such transformations inherit the important mathematical properties of this β (independence from α, density invariance, replication invariance, and others). Similarity measures that are transformations of β are not limited to two assemblages. There are many possible transformations of β onto the unit interval, each addressing a different aspect of compositional similarity (Jost 2007; Chao et al. 2008; Tuomisto 2010). A transformation that is linear in the proportion of regional diversity contained in the average assemblage is

$$^q S = (1/^q D_\beta - 1/N)/(1 - 1/N) \qquad (6.11)$$

(Jost 2007). When $q = 0$, this is the multiple-assemblage generalization of the Jaccard index. When $q = 2$ this is the multiple-community generalization of the Morisita–Horn index. The Jaccard and Morisita–Horn measures are members of the same family and are connected by a continuum of similarity measures which differ only in their sensitivity to species relative abundances.

The overlap measure C_{qN} discussed earlier is also a transformation of true β diversity:

$$C_{qN} = [(1/^q D_\beta)^{q-1} - (1/N)^{q-1}]/[1 - (1/N)^{q-1}] \qquad (6.12)$$

This family of measures includes the multiple-assemblage generalizations of the Sørensen index, Horn index, and Morisita–Horn index. All three of these standard indices are measuring the same aspect of assemblage similarity, only differing in the weights they give to species frequencies. The Morisita–Horn index is unique in belonging to both families of similarity measures; it is the both linear in shared diversity and linear in the degree of overlap. It therefore has a wider range of interpretations than other similarity measures. It can be useful to transform the β in equation 6.10c to a normalized measure between 0 and 1, so that we can compare compositional similarity across several sets of assemblages. This transformation generalizes Horn's overlap measure (equation 6.4) to the unequal-weight case:

$$S_{H\_w} = \frac{1}{-\sum_{j=1}^N w_j \log w_j} \sum_{j=1}^N \left\{ \sum_{i=1}^S (w_j p_{ij}) \log \left(1 + \sum_{k \neq j}^N w_k p_{ik}/w_j p_{ij} \right) \right\} \qquad (6.13)$$

We recommend that investigators calculate at least C_{0N}, C_{1N}, and C_{2N} for their data (Box 6.1). They could also use equation 6.12 to graph a continuous similarity profile for a range of q (say, from $q = 0$ to $q = N$). As an example of the use of C_{qN}, consider the assemblage sets A–D in Table 6.3. In Set A, all species in each assemblage are equally abundant, thus the three similarity indices are about the same $C_{0N} = C_{2N} \approx C_{1N}$. In Set B, $C_{2N} > C_{1N}$, implying that the dominant species are more similar than the average species. In contrast, for Sets C and D, $C_{2N} < C_{1N}$, implying that the dominant species are less similar than the average species. C_{2N}, like the Simpson index it is based on, is more sensitive to the dominant species than C_{1N}. We can make comparisons across the four sets because all measures are normalized to the range of 0 and 1. The three similarity indices in both Sets A and B are consistently higher than those in Sets C and D. Based on the Horn index, Set D has the lowest similarity. The proposed indices C_{0N}, C_{1N}, and C_{2N} are featured in the Program SPADE (Chao & Shen 2003a), which can be freely downloaded from http://chao.stat.nthu.edu.tw/softwareCE.html.

COMPOSITIONAL SIMILARITY AND β DIVERSITY

6.2.3   Statistical estimation of assemblage differentiation and similarity

In practice, all differentiation and similarity measures need to be estimated from a relatively small sample taken from each of the study assemblages. Traditionally, species frequencies in the samples are assumed to give good estimates of the species frequencies in the assemblage itself. The sample species frequencies are therefore substituted for the assemblage species frequencies in the theoretical formulas for differentiation and similarity. The resulting estimate is called the maximum likelihood estimator (MLE). This approach is statistically valid only when sample size is relatively large compared to the number of species, so that almost all species are observed in samples. When sample size is relatively small, so that a large fraction of rare species are missed in samples, our simulations show that the MLEs for differentiation indices are generally biased upwards and thus biased downwards for similarity measures. Sampling limitations create challenges for making accurate estimates of differentiation and similarity measures. Moreover, any bias-reduction method valid for estimating α diversity in one assemblage cannot be directly extended to estimate γ diversity. This is because the abundance vectors cannot be simply pooled across assemblages unless the sampling efforts are equal in all assemblages, so that sample sizes reflect assemblage sizes.

The magnitude of the under-sampling bias depends on the diversity order q. For $q \geq 2$, a nearly unbiased estimator exists for any measure based on the Simpson index. Chao et al. (2008) provided such an estimator for the index C_{qN}. Similar estimators can be constructed for β diversity or differentiation measures. For $q = 1$, there exists no nearly unbiased estimator for any measure based on Shannon's entropy. The unseen species have moderate effect on the index. A two-sample jackknife method (Schechtman & Wang 2004) that removes most of the under-sampling bias of the MLE has been applied to Horn's heterogeneity and overlap indices (Norden et al. 2009; Goßner et al. 2009). A coverage-based Horvitz–Thompson approach, similar to that proposed by (Chao and Shen 2003b) for estimating entropy in one assemblage, is currently

under development for multiple-assemblage measures. For $q = 0$, the under-sampling bias could be substantial, especially for highly diverse assemblages. Only an accurate lower bound for species richness (or shared species richness) is feasible (Chao 2005; Pan et al. 2009).

Regardless of how the similarity or differentiation is estimated, the result will always have some statistical uncertainty. Ecologists traditionally quantify this uncertainty by testing their results against the null hypothesis that there is no differentiation, and reporting a P value calculated by randomized resampling. This is rarely an appropriate approach, since the question of interest is not 'Is there any differentiation?'(there will always be some differentiation among natural populations) but rather 'How much differentiation is there?' The problem is one of parameter estimation rather than hypothesis testing. In parameter estimation, statistical uncertainty is expressed by means of a confidence interval. If sample size is sufficient, bootstrapping can be used to calculate an approximate confidence interval around the estimated value of the measure (Chao et al. 2008). If the confidence interval includes 0 (for relative differentiation) or 1 (for relative similarity), then the observations are insufficient to reject the null hypothesis of zero differentiation. If the interval does not include 0, not only can the investigator reject the null hypothesis but he or she will also know the range of magnitudes within which the true population value of the measure lies. This magnitude is the scientifically important aspect of differentiation or similarity. The magnitude of good differentiation and similarity measures can be understood by referring to simpler reference assemblages with the same value of the measure.

6.3   Prospectus

Exciting advances in the mathematics of diversity and differentiation have been made within the fields of genetics, economics, information science, and physics, but these advances are largely ignored outside of the disciplines that generated the advance. In addition the extensive statistical literature on divergence measures (see Pardo 2006) has yet to be tapped by ecologists. Interdisciplinary synthesis of these developments holds great potential. It appears that all disciplines are independently converging on the same concepts, and we would get there faster if each science was aware of the progress made by the other sciences. Order 1 measures (those based on Shannon entropy) have many important mathematical properties not shared by other frequency-sensitive diversity measures, and come closest to the ecologists' intuitive idea of diversity and differentiation (Jost 2007; Jost et al. 2010). If ecologists or population geneticists can derive the expected behaviour of these measures under a neutral model, following the lead of Sherwin et al. (2006), these measures would become the standard in the field.

Standard similarity measures treat all species as equally distinct. Yet in many important ways, an assemblage of rats and an assemblage of mice are more similar than an assemblage of rats and an assemblage of whales. Some recently developed measures take into account functional, phylogenetic, or other kinds of species differences (Graham and Fine 2008; Allen et al. 2009; Cadotte et al. 2009; Pavoine et al. 2009). However, these measures are usually based on additive partitioning of a generalization of the Gini–Simpson index (e.g. Hardy and Senterre 2007). The resulting differentiation measure is not acceptable (Table 6.2, see also Jost (2008) and Hardy and Jost (2008)). Ricotta and Szeidl (2009) have recently extended the diversity of order 2 to take into account phylogenetic or functional differences using multiplicative partitioning. It is

important to extend this measure to other orders, and resolve issues relating to the definition of α diversity.

6.4 Key points

1. The general overlap measure C_{qN} is the best overall measure of relative compositional similarity. It includes the Sørensen, Horn, and Morisita–Horn indices and their multiple-assemblage generalizations, which take global similarity into account.
2. The Morisita–Horn index is especially useful as an abundance-based similarity measure, since its expected value can be predicted from the parameters of Hubbell's neutral model.
3. Some common similarity and differentiation measures (traditional additive β and similarity measures, some distance measures, the Bray–Curtis measure, and between-group component of variance) do not behave as expected and do not necessarily reflect compositional similarity or differentiation.
4. Assemblage differentiation is intimately related to the concept of β diversity. Multiplicative partitioning of effective number of species best captures the notion of β diversity. It can be transformed into the Jaccard and C_{qN} similarity indices, among others.
5. Estimation of differentiation and similarity is statistically challenging, especially for measures based on species richness. Specialized estimators should be used.

CHAPTER 7

Measuring biological diversity in time (and space)

Anne E. Magurran

'....we forget that each species, even where it most abounds, is constantly suffering enormous destruction at some period of its life, from enemies or from competitors for the same place and food; and if these enemies or competitors be in the least degree favoured by any slight change of climate, they will increase in numbers; and as each area is already fully stocked with inhabitants, the other species must decrease.'

—(Darwin 1859)

7.1 Introduction

Communities change through time as well as space. The knowledge that species abundances and identities vary over time helped shape Darwin's thinking when he was developing his ideas on natural selection. It also underpins key ecological concepts such as MacArthur and Wilson's theory of island biogeography (MacArthur & Wilson 1967) and biodiversity models including those proposed by Fisher (Fisher et al. 1943), Preston (1948) and Hubbell (2001). However, although temporal processes are indisputably important in ecology, temporal patterns of biodiversity have received much less attention than spatial ones. In part this is because there are relatively few examples of long time series of biodiversity data. Indeed, in some cases long-term studies have been cancelled by funding agencies because they were deemed to be merely data collection and not cutting-edge science. Events in recent years have proved this view to be short-sighted and one of the most pressing challenges that ecologists face today is being able to detect the signature of anthropogenic activities on biological diver-

sity relative to background rates of change. Darwin recognized that even small shifts in climate will modify community composition and structure, but in the absence of good baseline data it is difficult to distinguish temporal changes in biodiversity that can be attributed to climate change from those that might have happened anyway. The limited availability of this type of information is also one of the reasons why the ambitious goal of the 2002 World Summit of Sustainable Development, to reduce the rate of biodiversity loss by 2010, has proved impossible to meet. A better appreciation of temporal patterns is equally relevant to conservation managers since conservation targets are often set in relation to static benchmarks. Species abundances vary through time, and species will inevitably be lost from or gained by a community or nature reserve. Enlightened conservation planning (e.g. Rodrigues et al. 2000) needs to recognize this and judge the success of management decisions against natural rates of turnover rather than treating species in the same way that curators view a collection of Van Gogh pictures in an art museum.

The temporal changes that all communities experience take one of two forms. First, communities may move from one state to another. This *directional change* can reflect an intrinsic event, for instance when the community undergoes succession. Alternatively, extrinsic factors such as disturbance, pollution, invasive species or a catastrophe can lead to shifts in structure. Of course as Dornelas et al. point out in Chapter 17 it is not always easy to distinguish natural and human imposed disturbance. Second, all communities undergo *non-directional change*. This temporal turnover—the result of immigration and local extinction, as well as variation through time in the abundance of the resident species—is linked to many phenomena that ecologists study, including competition, predation, and population dynamics. The status of a community, that is, whether it is undergoing directional as well as non-directional change, needs to be taken into account in any study that seeks to evaluate change in relation to natural baselines.

It is belatedly being recognized that temporal patterns of diversity deserve much greater attention and for this reason there have, until now, been relatively few attempts to develop appropriate methods. The literature emphasizes methods developed for spatial data and it is often assumed that approaches used to assess diversity in a spatial context can be applied, without modification, to temporal questions. In fact, although this is often fine, there are pitfalls for the unwary user, for example spatial comparisons usually examine different subsets of individuals whereas the same individuals may be sampled repeatedly if a single community is tracked through time. In what follows I draw together information on methods that can be used to measure temporal patterns, provide guidelines on their application, and identify topics that would benefit from further development. The chapter begins by considering timescales of change and the spatial, temporal, and taxonomic boundaries of a community or unit of study. It then presents a brief overview of the different ways in which one can measure diversity, and how temporal measurements fit into this scheme. I distinguish between methods that assess change in diversity over time—this can be change in either the amount of diversity or the composition of the assemblage—from those that combine temporal information to glean insights into the structure of the assemblage. The chapter reviews classical measures of temporal turnover and shows that species time curves can be also be used to assess turnover. It discusses the equivalence of diversity patterns over space and time and briefly examines methods of partitioning of diversity into both spatial and temporal components. In addition, approaches that can be used to evaluate temporal change in species abundance distributions are discussed.

7.2 State of the field: timescales of change and community boundaries

As Preston (1960) observed, the conclusions that an ecologist reaches about biological diversity in a given locality or assemblage will be shaped by the time frame over which data are collected. Preston suggested that there are three main temporal scales: sampling time, ecological time, and evolutionary time. In his view sampling time encompasses the fluctuations that occur in species presence and species abundance, ecological time takes the form of succession, while evolutionary time corresponds to speciation and extinction. Evolutionary timescales are implicit in phylogenetic (see Chapter 14) and palaeontological (see Chapter 19) investigations, while models that seek to explain patterns of species abundance (see Chapters 9 and 10) draw on the features and interactions, such as resource limitation and competition, that characterize ecological time.

Sampling time seems on first glance the least interesting of Preston's three categories, but in practice it can have a substantial influence on the recorded level of biological diversity. There are two interrelated questions to be considered here: how well has the assemblage been sampled and how long has it been sampled for? As Bonar et al. (Chapter 2) and Buckland et al. (Chapter 4) reveal, it can be challenging to sample a community thoroughly. Species may not be equally detectable, they may vary in their diurnal activity levels and different life stages and sexes may have different behaviour patterns.

However, even if it is possible to achieve a fair sample of the species that are present, it is not always easy to decide where the temporal boundaries lie. It is possible, in theory at least, to take a perfect snapshot sample of a community. For instance, it would be feasible, given sufficient numbers of trained assistants, to comprehensively assess the diversity of the herbaceous vegetation in a woodland or of birds on a moorland in a single day. This approach would, however, exclude plant species that flower at a different season or that occur in the seed bank. It also ignores bird species that breed on the moorland but are temporarily absent during migration, while including those migrants flying through en route to their breeding site. There is a distinction then between an *expressed* community and the *potential* community. The expressed community is everything that is present as a given point of time and that can be sampled (assuming no sampling error). The potential community consists of the species that are part of a community when it is evaluated over a longer time period, but not necessarily there at a single point in time. These distinctions matter if we are trying to deduce the richness (or some other measure of diversity) of a community since the species time curve increases with sampling in a similar manner to the species area curve (see section 7.4.1). For example the number of species in a well-documented estuarine fish community (Henderson 2007) is approximately constant from year to year, but rises through time when samples are accumulated (see Fig. 8.5a). It is not clear if the richness of this community is 81 species (the total number detected over nearly 30 years of sampling) or 39 (the average number of species detected in any year). Decisions about temporarily absent species also come into play when species composition is considered. Thus assessments of β diversity, which ask how different two or more localities are in terms of the actual species found there, will depend on which species are considered to belong to an assemblage, which in turn is linked to the time frame over which it is evaluated. These considerations are relevant to estimates of the number of 'unseen' species (see Chapter 4).

One way of dealing with community membership is to use biological knowledge to decide which species belong (Ulrich & Ollik 2004; Ulrich & Zalewski 2006; Magurran 2007). For example, investigations of bird diversity often exclude non-breeding or migratory species. Abbot (1983) argued that it is 'absurd' to include migrants in assessments of temporal turnover. Alternatively, investigators can focus on core species, that is those that occur regularly in the community (Magurran & Henderson 2003). Of course both approaches depend on good background information and may not be possible in poorly documented assemblages.

Ecologists typically define a community as a group of interacting species in a delimited geographical area. Researchers, however, often examine communities that lie within narrow taxonomic boundaries, for example farmland bird species or cichlid fish. The reasons for doing this are usually practical as it is difficult to sample organisms that differ markedly in body size (and would thus require a range of sampling methods), whose life histories occur at a different tempo (such as forest trees and annual herbs), or whose population sizes are not comparable (e.g. microbes and mammals) (see Loehle (2006) and Magurran (2008) for more discussion of these points). Nor is it necessarily straightforward to make inferences about the biological diversity of other taxa on the basis of data from one or a few groups. There has been an extensive debate on the effectiveness of different indicator taxa (e.g. Bibby 1999; McGeoch & Gaston 2002; McGeoch et al. 2002) and in many instances the conclusion that emerges is that some, but by no means all, taxa show similar trends. In one case a study of 14 different taxa in the Brazilian Amazon revealed some groups (notably birds and dung beetles) to be cost-effective and informative indicators, but also found that biodiversity patterns are not correlated across all groups (Gardner et al. 2007).

Policy makers often consider biodiversity across all taxa and may use the term in a generic way without spelling out what is meant by it (EASAC 2009). However, the conclusions that are drawn about biodiversity, such as whether it is being lost or whether conservation management plans are effective, will inevitably be shaped by the way the community is defined. This will include not just spatial and taxonomic boundaries, but also its temporal extent.

7.3 What is being measured?

Biodiversity assessment is a two-step process. The first step involves selecting the measure or measures of diversity that will be used. As noted throughout this book, a range of approaches is possible. 'Classical' diversity measures tend to quantify the total (or mean) number of entities (richness) in the population or to estimate the variability in the relative abundance of these entities (evenness) (see Box 7.1). In addition there are many measures that blend richness and evenness. The well-known Simpson and Shannon indexes are two examples. As Box 7.1 illustrates, the same approach can be

Box 7.1 Biodiversity assessment

Biodiversity assessment is a two-stage process. The first stage is deciding which diversity measure to use, the second is examining that measure of diversity in a spatial and/or temporal context. For example, one might describe the diversity of a sampling locality (depicted as a small shaded cube in the diagram) using the measure of choice and then go on to ask how the diversity of a site changes through a slice of time (represented as the larger shaded section). In both cases it is essential to be clear about the aim of the investigation, and, where relevant, the hypothesis that is being tested.

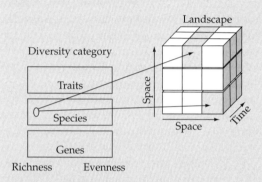

Choosing a measure

In this example there are three 'categories' of interest—genes, species, and traits—each of which captures one aspect of biodiversity. Richness records the number of different types of entity while evenness evaluates the extent to which they are equally represented. They lie at either end of a continuum populated by the many heterogeneity measures that blend richness and evenness. Although investigators generally concentrate on one category of diversity, they can all be measured in equivalent ways. For example, if the focus is on species, biodiversity can be represented as species richness, or by a diversity measure such as the Shannon or Simpson index, or by an evenness index. Alternatively, if genes are the category of interest, diversity might be expressed as allelic richness or heterozygosity. Heterozygosity is statistically

equivalent to Simpson's index. Traits can be treated in the same way. However, while all of these approaches measure biodiversity, the units in which this diversity is expressed, and the insights gained, can differ. Chapters 4 to 10 focus on species diversity measures while Chapters 13 to 16 deal with the alternative currencies of traits, phylogenies, and genes.

Assessing diversity over time (and space)

Investigators often want to go beyond a snapshot measure of diversity at a single site. There are a number of different ways in which temporal diversity can be examined. One approach is to ask how rapidly diversity is accumulated when the time period over which data are collected is extended. Species–time curves (see section 7.4.1) are the best-known example of this, although of course diversity–time curves could be constructed using different measures and these might provide novel insights into community dynamics. A different set of questions asks how much the site (or community) has changed between certain points in time. Turnover indexes (section 7.4.2) and species abundance distributions (section 7.4.3) can be used for this purpose. Alternatively, the goal might be to detect a trend in diversity and this can be achieved by plotting the index of choice against time (section 7.4). Once again this is commonly done using conventional diversity statistics (such as species richness or the Shannon index), but there is no reason why measures that take account of traits or genes could not be used (and might indeed be highly informative). A related, but distinct, question is whether there is a change in this trend (section 7.5).

Other sets of questions might be posed about this landscape. It might, for example, be interesting to know if spatial turnover (classical β diversity, Chapter 6) has changed through time, or whether spatial or temporal turnover is greater, or what the structure of the species abundance distribution is when temporal data are accumulated (section 7.6). The key point is that biodiversity assessment means deciding not just which measure to use, but also being precise about the question that it is being used to answer.

used for different categories of measure, such as genes, species, or traits. However, different measures within a category can yield different conclusions about biodiversity, as can statistically analogous measures in different categories.

The next step is to make inferences about diversity in the wider context. There is a large literature on the virtues and vices of competing diversity statistics but much less attention has been directed to the challenges of drawing robust conclusions about diversity at the landscape scale or across varying time periods from a series of samples. These broader questions can take different forms. For example, one might wish to know how diversity changes through time, for instance in relation to climate change, or along a spatial gradient, such as one related to altitude or disturbance. Alternatively, the goal might be to examine the difference in composition in time or space and to evaluate turnover across landscape scales (see Box 7.1).

7.4   Assessing change through time

7.4.1   Temporal turnover: species time curves

Ecologists have long recognized that species richness increases with sampling duration (Grinnell 1922; Fisher et al. 1943; Preston 1960; Williams 1964). The idea that a species time curve can be used to assess temporal turnover in the same way as species area curves are used to gauge spatial turnover is more recent but is gaining ground (Rosenzweig 1998; White et al. 2004; White 2007; van der Gast et al. 2008). White et al. (2006) examined species time curves from nearly 1000 community time series representing a range of taxa. Their analysis demonstrated the ubiquity of species time curves, showed that they are usually well described by both power and logarithmic functions, and found that when power curves are used the exponent typically ranges between 0.2 and 0.4. Interestingly, lower rates of turnover (denoted by a lower value of the exponent) are associated with higher richness. Shurin (2007) puts forward a number of explanations for this observation. These insights underline the need to take account of timescale in both fundamental and applied work. However Preston's ideas of equivalence in species time and species area curves also have practical implications for those who wish to assess diversity.

Using longterm data from grassland communities Adler & Lauenroth (2003) found, as Preston predicted, that new species are added to the species list more slowly when larger areas are surveyed. Indeed Adler et al. (2005) argued for a general species–time–area relationship using data from eight independent assemblages. Their analysis indicated that species richness is linked to both sampling duration and sampling area. They also found a negative time–area interaction. This means not only that the slope of the species–time curve is lower when larger areas are sampled but also that the slope of the species–area curve is lower when sampling occurs over longer periods. It is thus essential to clearly specify both the area and time period of sampling in an estimate of species richness (Adler & Lauenroth 2003). It also means that, as with estimates of species richness in relation to area (see also Chapters 4 and 20), it is wrong to calculate the number of species present in a shorter (or longer) time period than that over which the data have been collected by simple division (or multiplication). Indeed White et al. (2006) note that, on average, the number of species detected in a 10year period is in the region of twice that recorded in a single year.

7.4.2   Temporal turnover: turnover indexes

An alternative approach is to use an index to capture temporal turnover in species composition. The percentage of species shared between successive time periods is one example (Lekve et al. 2002), the ratio of mean species richness to potential species richness another (Romanuk & Kolasa 2001).

Temporal turnover (t) measures often draw on MacArthur & Wilson's (1967) ideas on the dynamic interplay between immigration and local extinction. Brown and Kodric-Brown (1977), for example, proposed:

$$t = \frac{b + c}{S_1 + S_2}$$

where b is the number of species present in the first census only, c is the number of species present in the second census only, S_1 is the total number of species present in the first census, and S_2 is the total number of species present in the second census. However, as Diamond and May (1977) noted, the census interval affects the estimate of turnover. They proposed an index to take account of this:

$$t = \frac{l + g}{S \times ci}$$

where l is the number of species lost (locally extinct), g is the number of species gained (immigration), S is the total number of species present, and ci is the census interval.

Another common approach is to use similarity (or dissimilarity) measures. For instance, Zamora et al. (2007) used complementarity (a type of dissimilarity measure (Colwell & Coddington 1994)) when assessing temporal shifts in the biodiversity of Mediterranean agroecosystems, while Chytrý et al. (2009) selected the Jaccard index to examine turnover in a successional heathland in the Czech Republic, as did Sepkoski (1988) in his analysis of the diversity of marine macrofossils during the Palaeozoic. Many (dis)similarity (and complementarity) measures—such as the Jaccard index—use presence/absence data. Measures that take account of species abundances are also available. The Sørenson quantitative (Bray–Curtis) and Morisita–Horn measures are examples of these. Turnover measures are reviewed by Jost et al. (Chapter 6). Estimates (viceroy.eeb.uconn.edu/estimates) can be used to calculate some of the more useful turnover measures and as well as a range of other biodiversity statistics.

Similarity measures (and their relatives) have usually been devised to make comparisons between geographical areas. There are few problems associated with their use when assessing temporal turnover, but one exception is the issue of the census interval. Of course if a study examines turnover over identical time periods this is probably not a difficulty (although there are conceivably concerns related to differences in detectability (see Chapter 3)).

Probably the simplest approach is to plot turnover in relation to census interval, as Russell et al. (1995) did in their investigation of temporal turnover in bird communities on islands around Britain and Ireland. Another example of this is shown in Fig. 7.1. As long as there is reasonable sample coverage it is possible to examine the relationship between turnover and census length. Given the dynamic nature of ecological communities an increased gap between samples

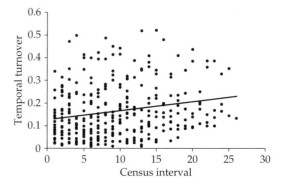

Figure 7.1 This graph shows temporal turnover (measured as 1 minus the Morisita–Horn index) plotted against the census interval for an assemblage of estuarine fish from the UK's Bristol Channel, censused for 27 years. Further details of the study system are given in Chapter 8. Although there is a lot of scatter (this is typical) the trend is for increasing turnover with time.

will normally be reflected in greater turnover. Some localities or communities may nonetheless exhibit higher than expected turnover and this could be related to ecological factors (such as distance from the source of immigrants) or be of management interest (for instance unexpectedly high rates of turnover in a nature reserve).

Plotting values of temporal turnover against census interval is an easy way to visualize change and can be used to make comparisons amongst sites (for example by comparing the slopes of lines fitted to the relationship). Alternatively, it is possible to work from an a priori prediction about the expected pattern of temporal turnover. Russell et al. (1995), for example, developed an equilibrium model (*sensu* MacArthur and Wilson 1967) to explain temporal turnover in their island bird communities. Although this model provided a reasonable fit to the data, it was not entirely satisfactory. Russell and his colleagues then devised an improved non-equilibrium model and used this to compare turnover amongst islands.

7.4.3 Using species abundance distributions to evaluate change

Species abundance distributions (SADs) are an appealing way of examining biological diversity as they provide an overview of community structure and are potentially more informative than a single index (McGill et al. 2007 and see Chapter 9). What SADs do not do, by and large, is to provide information on species composition. This is generally an advantage as it means that communities with little or no taxonomic overlap can be compared. It can, however, be a drawback if the goal is to ascertain how the same community changes through time since the investigator may wish to know if a shift in the abundance distribution is accompanied by a change in composition.

Investigators often want to find out if SADs differ from one another. A straightforward method of doing this is to examine the slope of a rank abundance distribution (Tokeshi 1993; Magurran 2004). For instance, the rank abundance distribution of species present in heavily fertilized plots in the Park Grass experiment at Rothamsted, in southern England (Lawes et al. 1882), has become much steeper through time in response to increased dominance by one or two species and loss of species richness (Tokeshi 1993; Magurran 2004). The Q statistic (Kempton & Taylor 1978; Kempton & Wedderburn 1978)—the interquartile slope, where cumulative number of species is plotted against log abundance—can also be used to make comparisons between assemblages and is less influenced by changes in species richness or the presence of a handful of extremely abundant or very rare species. Another approach is to use the observation that a particular model fits an assemblage to make inferences about its structure. As McGill points out in Chapter 9 (and see also Magurran (2004) and McGill et al. (2007)), a range of models have been proposed to describe and explain SADs. For example, communities at the early stages of succession are often well described by a geometric (Motomura 1932) or log series (Fisher et al. 1943) model, while a log-normal (Preston 1948) model is usually a better descriptor of a mature community (May 1975; Magurran 2004). Connolly and Dornelas (Chapter 10) review the techniques developed for fitting and evaluating SADs but also remind us that care needs to be taken when drawing ecological conclusions from the observation that a certain model provides a good fit.

The above techniques for examining and comparing SADs are well established but may not provide the resolution needed to distinguish temporal tran-

sitions in community structure. Some recent developments that appear to hold promise for temporal analyses include the following:

i It is becoming clear that SADs vary in the extent to which they are multi-modal (Dornelas & Connolly 2008; Dornelas et al. 2009) so tracking changes in modality through time could be informative.

ii The empirical cumulative distribution function (see Dornelas et al. (Chapter 17) for a discussion of this approach) appears to be a useful method of assessing the effects of anthropogenic disturbance on communities and may have general application in identifying changes in SADs through time (and space).

iii Although classical SADs do not consider species identity there is increasing recognition that it can be revealing to do so, and methods that track labelled species using a SAD framework are being developed (MacNally (2007) and Chapter 8). One approach that appears to be particularly promising is the use of rank clocks and the development of statistics that track ranks, such as mean rank shift (Collins et al. 2008).

iv Methods of comparing community composition through time, for example by using the Euclidean distance to measure the difference in composition and structure between pairs of assemblages, are being developed (Collins et al. 2000; Thibault et al. 2004).

v There are some interesting new approaches to modelling and assessing resilience in ecological communities. These may ultimately improve our understanding of the manner in which communities change through time and provide improved methods of assessing this change (Thrush et al. 2009).

7.4.4 Assessing change using biodiversity indexes

There is another simple way of establishing if diversity changes through time and whether this change has a trend, and that it to select a diversity measure (such as the Shannon or Simpson index) and plot it against time (see, for example, Fig. 7.2a). Buckland et al. (2005) provide guidance on tests that can be used to assess the statistical significance of changes

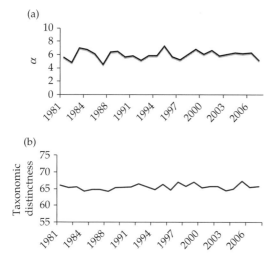

Figure 7.2 A straightforward way of exploring changes in an ecological community is to plot the value of a diversity measure against time. This example uses data from the Bristol channel estuarine fish assemblage (as in Figure 7.1) and shows (a) Fisher's α (Fisher et al. 1943; Magurran 2004), and (b) taxonomic distinctness (Clarke & Warwick (1998) and see also Chapter 14). In this example diversity fluctuates by a small amount from year to year, but does not show an increasing or decreasing pattern through time.

and explain how to extend this approach to examine trends in biological diversity at a regional level.

This method has the merit of being straightforward and intuitive. It will be subject to a decision about which diversity index is most appropriate (see Magurran (2004) and Chapters 5 and 6 for discussion of some options), whether or not species vary in their detectabilities and if this changes through time (see Chapter 3), whether or not sampling protocols are appropriate (see Chapter 2 and Magurran et al. 2010), and so on. Similar considerations apply to the other approaches described in this section. If the goal is to ask if there is a trend in biological diversity other issues come into play, including how the baseline is decided. Some methods, such as the Living Planet Index (Loh et al. 2005) choose an arbitrary year, set diversity at unity, and measure change in relation to that. In the case of the Living Planet Index trends are calculated across each species and then combined. An arbitrary baseline can work well in practice but is ecologically unrealistic as it ignores the inherent variability of natural assemblages. Moreover, the choice of base-

line can have dramatic influences on the conclusions drawn. For example, it can appear that fish stocks have made a substantial recovery if present-day populations are compared with those in the recent past. However, examination of a longer time series can show that present stocks are extremely low relative to their historical levels (Hutchings 2000).

The indexes discussed thus far in this chapter are conventional ones in the sense that their currency is species. There is, however, no reason why other approaches could not be used. For example, one might plot changes in taxonomic distinctness in relation to time (see Fig. 7.2b). Recently, Pavoine et al. (2009) have developed methods for assessing phylo-β-diversity and used these to reveal substantial declines in the diversity of a heavily fished group of rockfishes. This methodology draws on information about phylogenetic and taxonomic diversity (see also Chapter 14) and can be used to evaluate both spatial and temporal diversity patterns. Indexes based on traits and functional diversity (see Chapter 13) are other options.

7.5 Measuring change in the rate of change

The preceding discussion has focused on the methods used to determine whether or not the biological diversity of a community changes over time. Measuring change in the rate of change is an allied but distinct issue. Researchers and managers increasingly wish to know if changes in a community or system are slowing or increasing. The 2010 target, which set out to reduce the rate of biodiversity loss, is an example of this type of question. The slope of a plot of a diversity index against time (as described in section 7.4.4) represents the rate of change in biodiversity (Magurran et al. 2010). The second derivative of the trend line reveals the change in slope and hence measures the rate of change. For example, in a case where biodiversity was being lost, a positive second derivative would indicate an improved situation (that is, a reduction in the rate of loss) whereas a negative second derivative would suggest a worsening scenario. Fewster et al. (2000) and

Buckland et al. (2005) provide methods and explain how uncertainty measures can be calculated.

7.6 Using temporal change to shed light on community structure

Rather than assessing change through time, an investigator may wish to draw on information about the dynamic nature of a community to gain a deeper understanding of its structure. One of the central questions in ecology is why some species are abundant while many are rare (discussed further in Chapters 8 and 9). Temporal data can reveal how the relative abundance of core and occasional species affects the abundance distribution (Magurran & Henderson 2003; Loehle 2006; Magurran 2007). However, as McGill (2003a) cautions, examining a community's structure by the accumulation of many small samples collected through time (or space) can lead to artefacts, for example by giving undue prominence to rare species. Large data sets based on repeated temporal and/or spatial sampling have been widely used to test a variety of SAD-related hypotheses such as Preston's (1948, 1960) veil line. Nonetheless, such data sets can blur the community boundaries (as described in section 7.2 above) and make it difficult to link pattern and process. A more informative approach may be to ask when—and how—a particular SAD is maintained in an assemblage through time (e.g. Thibault et al. 2004).

7.7 Partitioning diversity in space and time

From the preceding discussion it is clear that biological diversity varies through both space and time. It is possible to tease the spatial and temporal components apart to see where most of this diversity is located. Moreno and Halffter (2001), for example, attributed species richness in a tropical bat community to both α diversity (within habitat diversity) and temporal turnover. Whittaker (1960) was first to appreciate that spatial diversity on a landscape (or γ diversity) scale can be partitioned into α and β components. Partitioning methods are receiving growing attention (e.g. Lande 1996; Veech et al. 2002; Crist et al. 2003; Crist & Veech 2006; Jost

2007; see Chapter 6 for a fuller discussion of the issues involved). Until recently the focus has been on spatial partitions but investigators are increasingly considering both space and time in the same analysis (e.g. Tylianakis et al. 2005; Sobek et al. 2009; Tomašových & Kidwell 2009).

7.8 Prospectus

Better methods of assessing temporal patterns and shifts in biological diversity are urgently needed and I believe that there will be much greater emphasis on these topics in the next few years. There are many aspects that deserve more attention but I will briefly mention four that seem important and tractable. First, it would be useful to extend partitioning methods to provide better tools for determining how biological diversity is distributed in both time and space. For example, how much rarity (or commonness) is explained by the nested effects of seasonal, annual, and other cyclic events? Second, many species abundance models are essentially static and thus unrealistic, but could be modified to take account of temporal variation. Third, we still know relatively little about how communities respond to and recover from impacts (McGill 2006). There is growing interest in resistance and resilience (Thrush et al. 2009), particularly in the context of ecosystem function (Loreau 2010) and this will, I hope, stimulate the development of better methods of assessing change in communities and measuring their response to disturbance. Finally, new insights will be gained by moving beyond a single taxon to examine changes in the biological diversity of different groups of organisms in a community through time.

7.9 Key points

1. As has been appreciated for many decades, ecological communities change through time as well as space. There are two types of change: directional change, when a community moves from one state to another (e.g. succession), and non-directional change (the product of ongoing turnover).
2. As Preston observed, change occurs over sampling, ecological, and evolutionary timescales.

3. Investigators may wish to assess the extent of change (temporal turnover), measure change in the rate of change, or draw on temporal information to gain a deeper understanding of community structure.

4. Temporal turnover can be measured by species–time curves, by turnover indexes, by examining changes in species abundance distributions, and by plotting a diversity measure against time.

5. Census interval can have a marked influence on the conclusions drawn and needs to be taken into account in analyses.

6. There is considerable scope for the development of new methods and approaches to measure and explain temporal changes in biological diversity.

7. Policy makers need to appreciate that change is natural and inevitable, and to take account of it in conservation planning.

PART III

Distribution

CHAPTER 8

Commonness and rarity

Anne E. Magurran and Peter A. Henderson

8.1 Introduction

Ecological communities are composed of species, some of which will be abundant while the remainder—almost invariably the majority—are rare. This pattern is so pervasive that it has been dubbed a 'law' of ecology (McGill et al. 2007). To date there is only a single exception to this rule. A bacterium, *Candidatus Desulforudis audaxviator*, is the sole organism inhabiting a goldmine 2.8 km below the earth's surface (Chivian et al. 2008). Although an uneven distribution of species abundances is near universal, the shape of this distribution can vary amongst assemblages. This can be due to the intrinsic features of a community—tropical systems, for example, tend to have high numbers of rare species. However, it may also be influenced by the time frame or spatial extent over which data are collected, as well as sampling methodology and sampling intensity. Small differences in the shape of species abundance distributions are sometimes used to make inferences about the mechanisms that structure a community, for instance to deduce the extent of niche apportionment or to evaluate the impact of disturbance, for example during pollution monitoring (Chapter 17). These assessments will be sensitive to shifts in the proportion of rare species or the balance between commonness and rarity. Furthermore, species may be valued differently depending on their position in the abundance continuum. Much of the functionality in communities, such as the delivery of ecosystem services, may reside in the common species, whereas rare species are often the target of conservation efforts.

Patterns of commonness and rarity raise fundamental ecological questions, but these are issues that are also playing increasingly important roles in management decisions. For example, relative/absolute abundance may be used as a criterion for enacting certain conservation measures (Kunin 1998). Similarly, changes in species abundance distributions may be used a guide for identifying how much human activity has influenced an ecological community (see Chapter 17 for further discussion of these points).

In this chapter we briefly review the different concepts of commonness and rarity, show how the perception of what is rare or common can change with the currency used to measure abundance or the time frame over which diversity is measured, and summarize implications for biodiversity assessment.

8.2 State of the field

Darwin (1859) was well aware that taxa vary in their abundances and commented in *The Origin of Species* that 'rarity is the attribute of a vast number of species of all classes, in all countries'. Contemporary Victorian naturalists, including Wallace and Bates, made similar observations in their writing. However, it was Preston (1948) who, following in the footsteps of Raunkaier (1934) and Fisher et al. (1943), sought a general explanation for commonness and its distribution among species. Commonness and rarity are terms that are in widespread use but which can take different meanings depending on context. As Preston (1948) noted, the term abundance is used in several different ways by ecologists. These include:

1. The total number of individuals of an extant species—*global abundance*.
2. The total number of individuals present, at one moment in time, in a given area (such as a quadrat) or locality—*local abundance*.

3. The proportion of individuals in one species in relation to the abundance of all species in the community—*relative abundance.*
4. The number of individuals recorded or collected—*sample abundance.*

Ecologists typically focus on sample abundance, and often express their data as relative abundance since this facilitates comparisons amongst data sets. Only occasionally do we know the global abundance of a taxon, and often this is because the species has dwindled to a handful of individuals. Local abundance is more tractable, but because it is usually impossible to census every individual in an area, local abundance is usually inferred from sample abundance.

Our focus here is abundance in the sense in which it is used to construct species abundance distributions or to calculate diversity statistics. There are, of course, other ways in which species can be defined as common or rare. Rabinowitz and her colleagues (Rabinowitz 1981; Rabinowitz et al. 1986), for example, proposed that a species' rarity status depends on its geographical distribution, its habitat specificity, and its local population size. Only species with wide geographical distributions, broad habitat tolerance, and large local population sizes are designated as common according to this scheme. All other taxa are rare in one of seven ways. One category of rarity—narrow geographic

distribution, broad habitat specificity, and small local population size—is only occasionally seen (Thomas & Mallorie 1985; Rabinowitz et al. 1986; Magurran 2004).

Species occupancy (see Chapter 11), that is, the number of grid cells or localities that a taxon occurs in, is another approach (Gaston 1994). Occupancy tends to correlate with local species abundance (Gaston & Lawton 1990; Gaston & Blackburn 2000). However, the use of occupancy to deduce species rarity can be biased if occupancy has been measured on a coarse scale (He & Condit 2007).

8.3   Commonness and rarity: ecological context

Species richness is the iconic diversity measure. It is widely used, for example in the designation of biodiversity hotspots, and easy to comprehend, although as is made clear in Chapter 4, accurate estimation of the extent of richness can be challenging. Since species richness measures weight all species equally they are in essence a measure of the number of rare species. This emphasis makes it easy to overlook the fact that a handful of species contribute most of the abundance, even in highly diverse assemblages (e.g. Fig, 8.1). Although some rare species may have a critical role in a community, for example as pollinators, it is increasingly recognized that common species

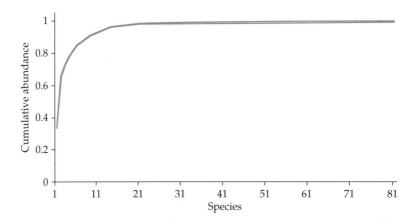

Figure 8.1 A small number of species account for most of the abundance in an estuarine fish assemblage in the Bristol Channel, UK. This community has been sampled monthly for almost 30 years (Henderson & Holmes 1991; Henderson 2007). A total of 81 species have been recorded to date. The graph shows the cumulative relative abundance of species in the assemblage, ranked from most to least abundant.

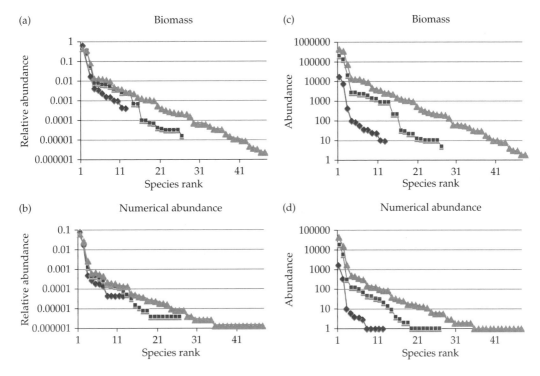

Figure 8.2 Rank abundance or Whittaker plots are a popular way of presenting species abundance data. This graph shows that the shape of this relationship depends on the intensity of sampling, the currency used to measure abundance, and whether the data are presented in relative or absolute form. The data are from an estuarine fish community and were collected in the Bristol Channel, UK, during 167 h of intensive sampling in 1996, by PAH using previously described methods (Henderson & Holmes 1991; Henderson 2007). The three lines on each graph represent the species collected in a 1-h sampling period (◆), a 44-h sampling period (■), and a 167-h sampling period (▲). The number of species sampled were 12, 25 and 47, respectively. Panels (a) and (b) depict the rank abundance plots for relative abundance data when abundance is measured as either biomass (wet weight of fish) or as numerical abundance (number of individuals). Panels (c) and (d) show the equivalent graphs for absolute abundance. Rarity is comparable across the different sampling levels when absolute abundance is used (a single individual or its biomass equivalent is the smallest unit possible). A discrete group of very rare species (singletons and doubletons) are evident with numerical abundance but not with biomass.

contribute significantly to ecosystem function (Smith & Knapp 2003; Gaston & Fuller 2008). Moreover, niche partitioning models typically focus on the most abundant species and ignore the rare ones (Tokeshi 1993) on the assumption that the biological processes that shape abundances act most strongly on the common species. Common species are important from a human perspective as well given that they may provide natural harvests or represent damaging pests. While rare species are particularly vulnerable to extinction, commonness does not necessarily ensure survival. The passenger pigeon *Ectopistes migratorius* is a textbook example of a once abundant species that is now extinct. There are many other cases of previously common species, such as the bison, *Bison bison*, and Peruvian

anchoveta, *Engraulis ringens*, that have undergone dramatic population declines.

Most presentations of biodiversity data, such as rank abundance plots ('Whittaker' plots) or frequency distributions such as 'Preston plots', are drawn to depict relative abundances (e.g. Fig. 8.2). In these the abundance of the most abundant species will inevitably decline as the sample size (or assemblage size) increases (May 1975). For example, the relative abundance of the most abundant fish in the community depicted in Fig. 8.2 falls from 82% when the community has been sampled for 1 h to 73% when it has been sampled for 44 h, and to 67% when it has been sampled for 167 h. These data refer to numerical abundance. The equivalent figures for biomass are 67, 54, and 46%.

Relative abundance plots facilitate the investigation of community structure across assemblages that vary in size and species composition (McGill et al. 2007). However, the untransformed abundance of the same species in nature may show a different pattern. For example, the absolute abundance of the most abundant species in Trinidadian freshwater fish communities is independent of community size, whereas its proportional abundance decreases with increasing species richness (Dornelas et al. in press). This observation has implications for niche apportionment and species packing. It suggests that there is an upper limit in abundance, in numerical terms at least, of species in a community with given environmental characteristics (Lawton 1990). For instance, in Trinidadian streams guppies (*Poecilia reticulata*) are often the numerically dominant species but it seems that resource availability, which will include food and physical space, sets a cap on overall abundance (Magurran 2005).

We still know relatively little about how the abundances of common species vary amongst comparable communities along a gradient, such as a climatic one, but it would be interesting to ask whether any differences that are observed are greater than those that would be expected by chance.

If some species are common, many more are rare. The problem, however, is that ecological surveys can give the impression that extreme rarity is widespread. Coddington et al. (2009) analysed 71 of largest and most ambitious tropical arthropod surveys and found that an average of 32% of species were singletons (Fig. 8.3). The notion that around a third of the species in an assemblage are represented by a single individual does not make biological sense—indeed it is likely that most, if not all, are members of viable, breeding populations. Various explanations have been put forward to explain the preponderance of singletons, particularly those found in rich tropical assemblages. These include habitat specificity (e.g. Price et al. 1995), the presence of vagrant species (e.g. Southwood 1996), the presence of immature forms that cannot be identified (e.g. Longino et al. 2002), and sampling effects, such as the occasional appearance of individuals in traps designed to capture different types of organ-

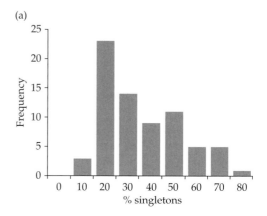

(a)

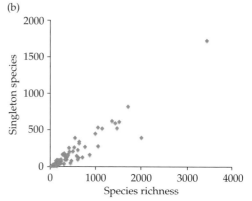

(b)

Figure 8.3 (a) Frequency distribution of the percentage of singletons observed in surveys of tropical arthropods. (b) Number of singleton species in relation to species richness. Data from Coddington et al. (2009).

ism (e.g. Scharff et al. 2003). Coddington et al. (2009) argue that biological hypotheses, specifically small body size, cryptic habitats, male-biased sex ratio, and clumped distributions, cannot explain the observed frequency of singletons. Instead, undersampling bias is the most likely cause. They suggest that the true singleton frequency is probably in the order of 4%. A related problem is that species may vary in their detectability (see Chapter 3) such that some taxa appear to be rarer (or more common) than they actually are in nature.

Many communities hold a small number of living fossils; coelacanths (*Latimeria chalumnae*) and yew trees (*Taxus baccatus*) are two well-known examples. These species, representatives of once dominant taxonomic groups, are almost always rare in abundance and/or highly localized in their distribution. Their rare status may make it more difficult for specialist pathogens, parasites, predators, or herbivores to evolve or maintain populations (in the same way that Apple computers receive fewer attacks from viruses). For example, yew is an ancient woodland tree with few associated herbivores. Kennedy and Southwood (1984) noted that two British oak (*Quercus*) species support 423 insect species. The equivalent figure for yew is six. Additionally there may be adaptations to enable populations to persist at low densities. One key adaptation of plants such as yew is extreme longevity. Thus, although the species may be rare at any one point in time, mature individuals are exceedingly persistent through time. Other instances where species appear to have adaptations that enable them to persist despite being rare include some freshwater fish (Magurran 2009). For example, geographically isolated white-fish species—the pollan, powan, and vendace (*Coregonus* spp.)—have survived in the British Isles since the last ice age while several members of the Good-eid family, for example *Characodon audax* and *Allotoca catarinae*, have naturally restricted distributions in Mexico.

An investigator's perception of which species are rare (or common) can depend on which sites are investigated, the timing and duration of sampling, and the currency used to measure abundance. Species that are rare in one locality may be more abundant elsewhere. Murray et al. (1999) asked whether species of trees that are in the tail of a rank abundance curve are rare throughout their geographical range. They found that 91% of species from dry sclerophyll woodland and 95% of species in temperate woodland were abundant in other places. Similarly, some species that are typically of low abundance, or apparently absent from the assemblage altogether, are exceptionally abundant at certain times. Cicadas are a classic example of such an organism (Yang 2004).

The manner in which abundance is measured can also affect the perception of rarity. Numerical abundance (number of individuals) and biomass are two common metrics. Energy use, which is often inferred rather than measured directly, is another. It is increasingly clear that different currencies lead to different conclusions about the structure of the species abundance distribution, and different

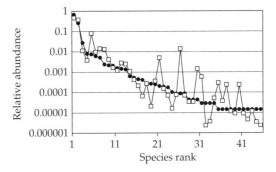

Figure 8.4 Species may have different rankings in alternative currencies. This figure illustrates rank abundance plots for numerical abundance (•) and biomass (□) during an intensive survey of an estuarine fish community (as in Fig. 8.2). Species ranks are based on numerical abundance.

rankings of species in terms of relative abundance (e.g. Saint-Germain et al. (2007), Morlon et al. (2009), and Henderson & Magurran (2010), and see Figs 8.2 and 8.4).

The high level of resources that biodiversity surveys demand (Lawton et al. 1998; Gardner et al. 2007) means that snapshot samples are common. Sometimes, however, longer surveys are possible and it is now well appreciated that biological diversity increases with sampling duration (Preston 1960; Rosenzweig 1995; Thibault et al. 2004; White et al. 2006; Magurran 2007; White 2007; Magurran 2008; see Chapter 7) in an analogous manner to the well-known species area curve (e.g. Fig. 8.5). The increment in species number is to a large extent due to the occasional presence of low-abundance species. In some cases this will be because the numbers of a particular species are so low that it is unlikely to be sampled. In other cases these rare species reflect temporal turnover in species (immigration and local extinction) that all communities experience (MacArthur & Wilson 1967). Repeated sampling at a site is known to inflate the number of rare species (McGill 2003a; Magurran 2007). With the exception of some well-characterized assemblages (e.g. Magurran & Henderson 2003) it is not always easy to identify which rare species belong to an assemblage and which are just 'passing through'. Further research is needed to resolve this important question.

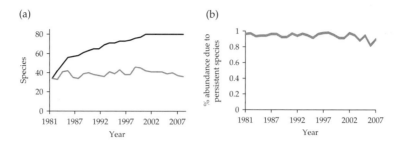

Figure 8.5 (a) Although the cumulative number of species (——) in an estuarine fish assemblage (Henderson & Holmes 1991; Henderson 2007) increases through time, annual species richness (——) remains constant. The rise in total recorded species is due to occasional species, which appear only sporadically in the record and are rare in terms of their abundance. (b) The percentage of overall abundance (number of individuals) in each year of the series that is attributed to species present in all years.

8.4 Assessing commonness and rarity

Identifying common and rare species is a frequent requirement, although not necessarily one that is easy to accomplish. Ecologists, for example, may wish to separate common and rare species when evaluating function. Decisions about the boundaries between commonness and rarity (or frequent and infrequent species) are also required for some of the species richness estimators (e.g. Colwell 2009; Chapter 4). Furthermore, a changing pattern of rarity and commonness (or dominance) can be an important indicator of an environmental impact (e.g. Warwick 1986; Warwick & Clarke 1991).

The most straightforward way of designating common and rare species is in relation to their position on a rank abundance plot. However, it is not always obvious where to draw the boundary between common species and the rare ones. A number of approaches have been suggested. One option is to assign a pre-determined fraction of species to rare and common categories. For example, the lower and upper quartiles in a ranked abundance distribution could be used to identify rare and common species, respectively (Gaston 1994). The disadvantage of this is that some assemblages, such as the tropical arthropod ones mentioned above, have large numbers of rare species (Coddington et al. 2009). A further difficulty is that the quartile approach can classify different species as rare, depending on the currency used. Currency issues also apply to other categorizations of rarity.

A second method is to adopt absolute definitions of rarity, such as singleton status (Magurran 2004). However, as already seen, the presence of singletons may, to a large extent, be a reflection of thoroughness of sampling. By the same token the absolute abundance of the most abundant species will usually be a measure of sampling effort. Complete censuses of ecologically meaningful entities, such as a pond or tree hole community, are one occasion on which the use of absolute abundances would be illuminating.

The third approach is to take account of the ecology of the species, and in particular the extent to which they are core members of the assemblage (Southwood 1996). Magurran and Henderson (2003) found a bimodal distribution of species occurrence in an estuarine fish community. The study has extended over nearly 30 years, with monthly sampling. Some species—the core species—are present in the majority of years in the record. These taxa tend to be abundant. In contrast the occasional species, that is those that appear infrequently, have low abundance. Core species are fish that are associated with estuarine habitats whereas occasional species are predominantly found in other habitats, such as rocky shores. Similar patterns have been detected in other systems, for example forest Hymenoptera and ground beetles (Ulrich & Ollik 2004; Ulrich & Zalewski 2006). Interestingly, core and occasional species leave different signatures on the species abundance distribution. Occasional species are responsible for the long tail of rare taxa; the longer the duration of the sampling the more prominent this tail will become (McGill 2003a).

A fourth, and related, method is to ask if there are clusters of abundance within the species abundance distribution. Ugland and Gray (1982) suggested that the log-normal distribution represents an overlaying of three grouping of organisms, a large group of taxa that are consistently rare, another smaller group of moderately common species, and a third group, the smallest one, with extremely abundant taxa (Gray 1987). Recent research reveals that empirical species abundance distributions can indeed be multi-modal (Dornelas & Connolly 2008; Dornelas et al. 2009). If present, these modes (and there may be more than three) could be used to identify rare and common taxa. In addition, as with the core/occasional partition above, it may be possible to use ecological knowledge of the system to categorize species associated with a particular mode.

Alternatively, one might assign species to different categories of commonness and rarity, and tally the frequencies of the different types or identify them on a rank abundance or other plot. The Rabinowitz approach (Rabinowitz 1981; Rabinowitz et al. 1986) is one option, but others are also possible (e.g. La Sorte & Boecklen 2005), for example distinguishing species that are persistently common, those that experience cycles of alternating high and low abundance, and so on.

A final suggestion is to track the abundance or rank of labelled species (e.g. Murray et al. 1999; MacNally 2007; Collins et al. 2008). For instance, one might be interested in the rank of species of special conservation interest or those of commercial significance such as pests or harvest species, and in how this varies amongst habitats or in relation to climate change. Alternatively, it would be possible to examine the relative abundance, through space or time, of subsets of species, such as the dominant (or rare) fraction of an assemblage. This, of course, requires the development of appropriate null models since it is important to be able to distinguish changes due to anthropogenic activity from those that reflect the underlying ecology (such as turnover) as well as from change that is due to chance or sampling error.

8.5 Prospectus

The characteristic species abundance distributions seen in nature stand out as one of the few ecological laws. Ecologists have been striving to explain these patterns for the best part of a century and have developed statistical, biological, and neutral models for the task (McGill et al. 2007; Chapter 9). However, one of the obstacles that ecologists face in explaining natural species abundance distributions is that competing models can be equally good at predicting empirical patterns. A way forward might be to revisit the Prestonian notion of commonness and rarity, but from the perspective that there are different ways of belonging to one of these categories. Species abundance models could potentially meet this challenge by tracking communities through time and asking, for example, whether species at the rare end of the distribution at a given time point are there because they have persistently low abundance, are migrants or occasionals, are at the downturn of a population cycle, exhibit a characteristic set of traits, or represent a sampling artefact. Linking distributions of numerical abundance and biomass could also provide new insights into what it means to be common or rare.

8.6 Key points

1. Species in ecological communities vary in abundance. Typically, a few species are common, some are of intermediate abundance, and many are rare.

2. The conclusions an investigator reaches about the structure of a community may depend on the currency used to measure abundance and whether abundances are presented as absolute or relative values. The spatial and temporal extent of sampling will also shape the perception of commonness and rarity.

3. High levels of rarity, such as the large numbers of singletons seen in samples of tropical arthropod communities, may be the result of under-sampling or other sampling issues such as variation in detectability. This should be

addressed before other explanations of rarity are sought.

4. Communities may be partitioned in a number of ways, for example by categorizing different types of commonness and rarity, by identifying separate modes of abundance in a species abundance distribution, or by tracking labelled species. Options are discussed but it is noted that this is an area that warrants more research.

5. Historically, analyses of species abundance distributions have ranked species or binned them by abundance. Examination of the different modes of rarity (and commonness) subsumed by such analyses could shed new light on the processes that structure ecological assemblages and help to explain spatial and temporal variation in diversity. The use of different currencies when characterizing rare and common species could also be informative.

CHAPTER 9

Species abundance distributions

Brian J. McGill

9.1 Introduction

A species abundance distribution is a quantitative statement about the difference in abundances between species in a community. In short, it is a statement about the commonness and rarity of species (see Chapter 8). As such, it cuts to the central questions of basic ecological research (the study of the distribution and abundance of organisms: Krebs 1972; Andrewartha & Birch 1984) and of conservation biology (defined by Soule as the science of rarity: Soule 1986). Thus it is not surprising that species abundance distributions are among ecology's oldest patterns, with quantitative measurements as far back as 1909 (Raunkaier 1909) and explanatory models as far back as 1932 (Motomura 1932). Every species abundance distribution ever measured with an adequate number of species (say at least three to five) has shown the same pattern: most species are rare, only a few species are common. In short, 'rare is common, common is rare'.

Perhaps the most useful definition of a species abundance distribution is a vector of comparable abundances representing a community. The idea of 'vector' implies that there is an abundance measure for multiple species. The idea of 'comparable' implies that it is sensible to compare and contrast these numbers. At a minimum comparability requires that the numbers either be true densities or if indices of abundance then that they are estimated in the same fashion across all the species. The idea that they represent a 'community' is the hardest to pin down. Ecologists, despite having community ecology as a central subdiscipline, have never given a truly operational definition to the concept of community. Here we use it to imply a group of organisms that overlap in time and space such that there is a reasonable chance of interaction between the members. The temporal and spatial extent can be quite variable. Spatial extents of as little as $0.25\,\mathrm{m^2}$ are common for grasses and milliliters are common for microbial organisms while communities are sometimes taken to cover entire continents. Similarly temporal extent may range from a point in time (in practice, say, a single day) to millions of years in paleontological applications. The taxonomic extent of a community is also quite variable (ranging from a single genus to entire kingdoms, e.g. all plants). The key criteria seems to be that there is an expectation that the members have the potential to interact with each other and the list of species is in some meaningful way exhaustive (species are not omitted arbitrarily). An extraordinary amount of data have been collected that fit this definition of 'a vector of comparable abundances for the species in a community'. Nearly every dataset with multiple species and abundances (density or indices of abundance) measured qualifies.

There is also an issue of what measure of abundance or what 'currency' to measure. Although number of individuals is by far the most common, this approach has limitations when applied to plants that show clonal growth, and it can also distort results in indeterminate growers, such as plants or fish that can vary by orders of magnitude of size within one species. Common currencies include number of individuals, percentage cover, biomass, and energetic use. It has been argued that energy use might be closer to the actual processes regulating community assembly and therefore should be preferred (Tokeshi 1999). Broadly, the distribution observed is the same for all of these currencies, but subtle and possibly important differences do occur (Wilson et al. 1996a; Chiarucci et al. 1999; Connolly et al. 2005; Morlon et al. 2009).

What might one do with a species abundance distribution? A few obvious applications include:

1. using it to test various models or theories of how communities are assembled
2. using it to identify rare and common species for management purposes (which typically focus on rare species and need quantitative assessments of rarity to justify prioritizing some species over others)
3. using it as an indicator of the ecosystem health of a location
4. to compare two or more locations (or one location across time), for example how do the SADs of two or more communities along a productivity gradient or along a human disturbance gradient change? Such comparisons might be done with any of the goals in points 1–3 in this list in mind.

To date, usage 1 has probably been the most common. A great deal of literature has been devoted to testing theoretical models of community processes using species abundance distributions. Thus Motomura (1932) used SADs to suggest niche preemption. Fisher et al. (1943) and Preston (1948) debated whether statistical arguments leading to log-series or log-normal distributions, respectively, were correct. More recently, literally dozens of other theories of community assembly have been tested by species abundance distributions (Hughes 1986; Tokeshi 1996; Dewdney 2000; Hubbell 2001; Pueyo 2006; Harte et al. 2008). Unfortunately, species abundance distributions have shown little power to either reject theories (Popper 1959; Platt 1964) or differentiate between them (Wilson 1993; Chave et al. 2002; McGill 2003a,b). Even when it can be decisively shown that one theory or model fits a particular location better, very similar locations with very similar groups of organisms are usually fit by a different theory best.

For this reason there has been a call to move away from using SADs for point 1 above, and to move towards a more comparative approach (point 4)(McGill et al. 2007). In general, ecology, and indeed all of science, works better with some form of comparison, whether observational or experimental. It is not reasonable to ask physics to predict that a cloud of gas will condense to form a ball of the exact size and location that we now know as Earth (Roughgarden 2009), but it is reasonable to ask physics to predict what will change in the Earth's motion if a given gravitational attraction from the Sun is applied. Similarly, it may be more realistic to expect ecology to predict how the relative proportions of rare and common species will change as productivity is increased or logging occurs than to predict the precise relative proportions of the abundance of each species at a given location and point in time on Earth.

The 1970s saw a burst of research in this direction. A number of authors explored how SADs changed shape along a variety of gradients, such as succession or productivity (Whittaker 1965; Bazzaz 1975; Hubbell et al. 1999). Fairly strong patterns were suggested. For example, SADs become more even with higher productivity. Work on using SADs as ecosystem indicators was also done (Gray 1979), clearly showing identifiable changes to marine communities as a consequence of pollution. At that time all of the comparisons were done graphically (i.e. by eye-ball). Rank abundance distribution (RAD) plots (log abundance vs rank order) were plotted and their shapes were compared. Unfortunately, this research programme died out quickly without significant confirmation of any of the identified patterns (perhaps in part because they were incorporated so quickly into a prominent textbook and were taken as being well established; Whittaker 1975). In any case, relatively little effort has been made since on comparing SADs to inform about underlying processes or management implications (although exceptions exist, e.g. Wilson et al. 1996a).

9.2 State of the field

Whatever one's goals and whether one uses a single SAD or is comparing SADs as advocated above, there are four basic types of tools to use: visual, parametric, non-parametric, and multivariate. These are described in the following sections.

9.2.1 Visual approaches to SADs

The simplest way to use SADs is to plot them graphically. The ease with which this is done is undoubtedly one of the main reasons for their appeal. There are three main ways to plot the data. The first is to create a histogram. Since the number of unique abundances observed will be a large fraction of the number of species observed, histograms require aggregating or binning the data. There has been great controversy about the best binning method. The simplest way to plot the data is to use an arithmetically scaled axis (Fig. 9.1(a)). Preston (1948) argued for a logarithmically scaled axis (Fig. 9.1(b)) and introduced a method that involved smoothing the data (splitting the number of species found on bin boundaries across two bins). Some have argued for a binning that accounts for the strong skew of the data by lumping the extreme right tail of the data into a single very large bin on an arithmetic axis, which is sometimes referred

to as the $N + 1$ method (Nee 2003). Unfortunately, the results and interpretation of the graphs depends heavily on the binning method used (Gray et al. 2006). In particular, the interpretation of the number of rare species depends on whether an arithmetic or logarithmic scale is used and which exact logarithmic scale. More generally, binning represents a loss of data, which is a statistical no-no when avoidable. More modern techniques for estimating probability density functions (PDFs) such as kernel estimation (Martinez & Martinez 2002) could and probably should be used in preference to binning (see the curved line on Fig. 9.1(a) and (b)). As far back as 1957, MacArthur pointed out these problems and suggested an alternative plotting method, later championed by Whittaker (1965), which has become known as the rank abundance

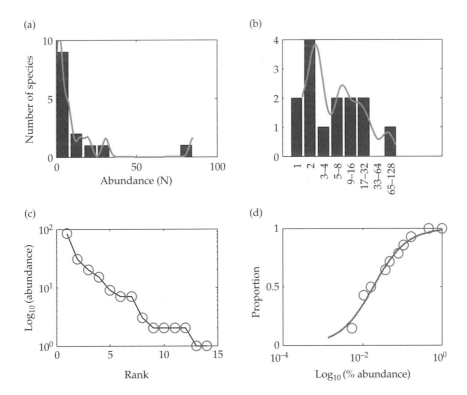

Figure 9.1 Four different ways to plot species abundance data: (a) a histogram (binned) plot on an arithmetic scale; (b) a histogram plot on a log scale (in both (a) and (b) the curved line represents a kernel-smoothed representation of the data); (c) a classic rank abundance distribution; (d) a scaled empirical cumulative distribution function plot (see Box 9.1). The curved line represents a logistic curve fit to the data. This data and the data used in Figure 9.3(a) and (b) are based on trees >1 cm dbh on transects run at Mt St Hilaire nature preserve operated by McGill University as a field station. The data were collected by students in the 2006 Field Methods in Ecology and Behavior course.

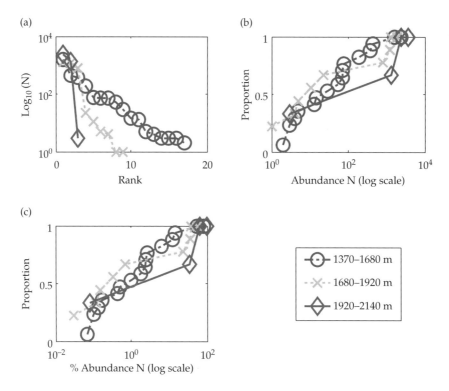

Figure 9.2 Different ways to plot an SAD. This figure is a plot of the data reported in Whittaker 1960. (a) Classic rank abundance distribution (RAD) plot with log N on the y-axis and rank $(1 \ldots S)$ on the x-axis. (b) The empirical cumulative distribution function (ECDF) with log N on the x-axis and proportion of all species on the y-axis. (c) ECDF but with the abundances transformed into percentages of all individuals observed for the given community (here $N =$ 2949, 3342, and 3741, respectively).

plot (Fig. 9.1(c)). In this plot the individual species abundances are sorted highest to lowest. The y-axis is log-abundance and the x-axis is rank (1 = most abundant down to S = number of species for the least abundant). As MacArthur pointed out, this plot has a close relationship to the cumulative distribution function (CDF) used in probability theory to characterize a probability distribution. RADs appear to be easy to interpret. Whittaker (1965) and others have interpreted RADs such as those shown in Fig. 9.2(a) to indicate that low diversity communities are geometric (Motomura 1932), medium diversity communities are log-series (Fisher et al. 1943) and high diversity communities are log-normal (Preston 1948).

Two problems occur with RAD plots. The first is mathematical. Rank is mathematically difficult to

deal with (it invokes the field of order statistics), but the use of a traditional CDF plot would allow for the invocation of a vast array of mathematical machinery developed for CDFs. Secondly, RAD plots suffer from a severe confoundment—by definition the bottom right corner of a RAD occurs at S, the number of species in the community. Thus species with higher diversity will have RADs that are more stretched out along the x-axis (rank) and appear more even. This makes it very difficult to use RADs to provide meaningful comparisons of species distributions across communities with even moderate variations in species richness as the differences in richness quickly dominate all other patterns. A solution to these two problems, called the empirical cumulative density function (ECDF), is my recommended way to plot SADs (Box 9.1 and Fig. 9.2).

Box 9.1 Empirical cumulative distribution function plot

A simple and quick method for correcting for different species diversities between communities is to use a new type of plot (Figs 9.1(d) and 9.2). Specifically, the cumulative distribution function is a plot of the proportion of points with a value (here abundance) less than a given value ($CDF(X) = P\{x \leq X\}$). This is a standard way to analyse probability distributions. When the CDF is calculated from data rather than from a formula, it is called an empirical cumulative distribution function (ECDF). The Kolmogorov–Smirnov statistic calculates the difference between the ECDF and the theoretical CDF (or between two ECDFs).

The CDF is also the integral of the PDF. The PDFs are often plotted for SADs. This means peaks in the PDF correspond to steep upward slopes in the CDF. For example, the Preston plot (1948) is just a PDF on a $\log_2$ scale with binning (i.e. a histogram) used to estimate the PDF from empirical data. However, in comparison to the PDF, plotting the CDF has two distinct advantages:

1. The ECDF is easily estimated. Sort the abundances into increasing order. Use these as the values on the x-axis. Place the ranks (here from lowest to highest abundance, the reverse of RAD) divided by the total number of species on the y-axis. This will give values ranging from $1/S$ to 1. Normally the point (0, 0) is also included to make the graph complete.
2. Because it sums across data, the ECDF is usually more robust (less sensitive to outliers) than the empirical PDF.

The ECDF is also closely related to the RAD (Fig. 9.2). Specifically, the ECDF is generated by flipping the RAD about the $y = x$ line, then rescaling the rank by dividing by S, then inverting the rank axis (smallest to largest instead of largest to smallest). The ECDF has two distinct advantages over the RAD:

1. By rescaling by S the inordinate sensitivity to differences in S allows for useful comparisons to be made between sites.
2. By tapping into traditional mathematical machinery, it should be possible to import new tools into the analysis of SADs.

The improved comparative power of an ECDF over a RAD is demonstrated in Fig. 9.2. The data are from vegetation at different elevations in the Siskiyou mountains (Whittaker 1960). As noted in the main text, this and related data plotted as in Fig. 9.2(a) were used to argue that SADs are fundamentally different at different elevations,

(a)
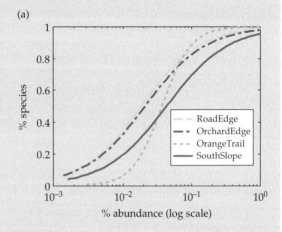

(b)
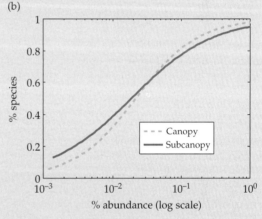

Figure 9.3   Comparisons of SADs using the ECDF plot. (a) Four different plots compared. Data as in Fig. 9.1. We can see that the site at Orange Trail is very different in evenness (the evenness is much higher since the line is more sharply vertical, implying that most species have an abundance of about 4% of the total population). The other sites are broadly similar in this aspect of evenness with species spread out between 0.1 and 10%, but SouthSlope overall has a lower proportion of rare species (the line is shifted down, implying that a given percentile—say 50% of species read on the vertical axis—occurs at a higher proportional abundance, roughly 4% instead of 1%). (b) Two groups of species compared. Here data are summed across all four sites and one SAD is plotted for species primarily found in the canopy, and one SAD is plotted for species primarily found in the subcanopy (shade or early successional). Here it is clear that the subcanopy has more rare species (higher on the left side of the graph).

Continued

9.2.2 Parametric approaches to SADs

The use of the probability-based ECDF immediately suggests that viewing a SAD as a sample from a probability distribution might be useful. To have a reasonable chance of fitting the data, the probability distribution needs to be defined only for positive numbers and to be strongly skewed with a long right tail on an arithmetic scale. The 1940s saw two suggested probability distributions that met these requirements: Fisher's log-series (1943) and Preston's log-normal (1948). Both fit the data reasonably well with the main difference between the two occurring in the prediction for extremely rare species (species with abundances of 1 or 2) (Chapter 10). Preston and Fisher both argued that their approach was superior and this argument has continued unresolved to the present day, with the added complexity of literally dozens of different probability distributions proposed (for extensive lists see Marquet et al. 2003 and McGill et al. 2007). It seems likely that SADs do not contain enough data to decisively decide which one probability distribution is the best fit (if indeed there is such a thing as one distribution to describe all communities) (McGill et al. 2007).

Some probability distributions commonly applied to species abundance distributions are described in Box 9.2. Each distribution will have several (usually one to three) parameters that can be chosen to make the general probability distribution fit a particular dataset (see Chapter 10). These parameters can be interpreted in one of two ways. First, it can be assumed that the

underlying probability distribution and any model that produced this distribution is correct. In this case the parameters can be interpreted in this context. For example, the migration parameter, m, and the speciation parameter, θ, in neutral theory can be estimated to provide the best fit to the neutral theories predicted probability distribution (the zero-sum multinomial or ZSM) and then interpreted according to their mechanistic definitions. Alternatively, these parameters can simply be seen as geometric descriptors of the shape of the species abundance distribution without assuming the underlying model is necessarily true or applicable. In this scenario, for the ZSM, m can be seen as a descriptor of the shape of the left tail of the SAD and the number of rare species, while θ can be seen as a scaling parameter that broadly affects the overall shape and the right tail (McGill et al. 2006). Under either interpretation, these metrics can broadly be called 'parametric' as they are derived as the parameters of a mathematical probability distribution that summarizes the shape of the SAD.

9.2.3 Non-parametric approaches to SADs

Many other numbers or metrics can be used to describe the shape of a SAD that do not derive from a probability distribution. Some of these are intended to measure a specific property of the SAD, such as the diversity or the evenness. Others are just geometric descriptors of the shape of the SAD. An example of the latter is the slope of the RAD (Nee et al. 1992). A number of these measures are summarized in Box 5.1.

Box 9.2 Parametric measure of SAD shape

Parametric measures are the parameters of a mathematically described probability distribution. Such parameters may be interpreted either under the assumption that the probability distribution applies to the data or merely as a useful descriptor of the shape of the data. In the following list, the name of the distribution is given with its parameters following in parenthesis. After some brief comments, a best-practice method for estimation is referenced and the formula for the distribution is given. Some common and useful distributions include the following:

- **Pareto/power (c):** The Pareto or power distribution is based on $p(n) \propto 1/n^c$. The Pareto can be justified as the limit of the log-normal distribution with high variance (Montroll & Shlesinger 1982), as the sole distribution surviving basic transformations (Mandelbrot 1963), as a sign of fracticality (Mandelbrot 1982), or when $c = 1$ as a sign of self-organized criticality (Pueyo 2006). Most SADs fail to be well fit by the Pareto. There are several variants of this distribution and parameter estimation can be tricky (White et al. 2008). I recommend the Discrete Pareto which runs from 1 to N. A simple analytical maximum likelihood estimator exists (if using software that can calculate the harmonic function, $\zeta(c)$).
  $p(n) = n^{-c}/\zeta(c)$
- **PowBend (β, ω):** Pueyo (2006) suggested that the Pareto distribution should apply to SADs but failed because of sample size limitations, in particular the very common species are not accurately represented in their true proportions due to finite sample size. He derived a modified power distribution (the power-bended distribution or PowBend) that bends the distribution down to have fewer large species to represent this. Nominally, the parameter β is the same as the Pareto c, while ω represents the degree of bending. In practice ω ensures a fit to common species, which allows β to fit the rare species portion of the SAD well. Pueyo recommends a four-step programme:

  1. Fit a $1/x$ distribution (i.e. power distribution with $c = 1$ or, equivalently, the powbend with $\omega = 0$ and $\beta = 1$).
  2. If the fit is poor, allow c to vary in the power distribution (or equivalently vary β with $\omega = 0$).
  3. If the fit is still poor, switch to the PowBend and allow ω to also vary.
  4. If this still fails, a log-normal can be fit.

These four steps correspond to using the first to fourth terms in a Taylor power series, and can be used to detect the complexity of the community. Parameters can be estimated by numerical maximization of the likelihood surface. $p(n) = Cn^{-\beta}\exp(-\omega n)$

- **Zipf–Mandelbrot (b, c):** Another modification of the power distribution is the Zipf–Mandelbrot distribution, which contains the power distribution as a special case when $b = 0$. It was first applied to word frequencies and in ecology is interpreted as a sort of successional model where later species have increasingly complex ecological requirements and as a result are extra rare (Frontier 1985). In practice, unlike the Pareto with its excessively rigid one-parameter shape, but like the PowBend, the Zipf–Mandelbrot has a greatly improved fit with two parameters, allowing one parameter (c) to describe fit to common species and the other (b) to describe fit to rare species. Fitting the Zipf–Mandelbrot can be tricky (Izsak 2006). I recommend minimizing a χ^2 goodness-of-fit only on abundances >5 with a careful choice of initial values to speed convergence. $p(n) = (b + n)^c/H(N,b,c)$ where $H(N,b,c)$ is a normalizing constant and is an extension of the ζ function where $H(N, b, c) = \sum(i + b)^{-c}$ and the sum goes from $i = 1...N$.
- **Log-normal (μ, $\sigma\mu^*$, σ^*, cv, cv^*):** The log-normal distribution arises from the central limit theorem on a product of random variables (Limpert et al. 2001). A variety of biological interpretations can fit this description (McGill 2003a; McGill & Nekola 2010). The two parameters are the mean, μ, and the standard deviation, σ, of the (usually natural) log-transformed abundances. However, $\mu^* = \exp(\mu)$ is often reported because μ^* is in units of abundance. Some also transform $\sigma^* = \exp(\sigma)$ to return σ to units of abundance, but this is less common. Clearly μ is a scale parameter (position on the x-axis of abundance), but shape depends on the interaction between μ and σ. The coefficient of variation ($cv = \sigma/\mu$ or $cv^* = \sigma^*/\mu^*$) serves as a shape descriptor, with $cv \ll 1$ indicating a nearly normal shape (even on an arithmetic scale) and the skewness increasing as the cv increases. Parameter estimation is trivial (simply log transform and take the mean and standard deviation).
  $p(n) = \exp[-\log(n/\mu)^2/(2\sigma^2)]/[n\sigma(2\pi)^{1/2}]$

Continued

Box 9.2 (*Continued*)

- **Poisson log-normal (μ, σ, μ^*, σ^*, cv, cv*):** The main problem with the log-normal is that it is a continuous distribution allowing for fractional abundances. One approach is to develop a sampling model (Pielou 1975; Dewdney 1998; Green & Plotkin 2007) (see Chapter 10) where the abstract abundance of a species is given by λ sampled from a log-normal, but the observed abundance is sampled from the Poisson distribution with the one parameter (the average value) given by λ. Parameter estimation requires numerical maximization of the likelihood surface and can be computationally intense as well as requiring some good numerical approximations (Chapter 10, Bulmer 1974).
$p(n) = \int_0^\infty \frac{\lambda^n e^{-\lambda}}{n} p_{LN}(\lambda) d\lambda$ where $p_{LN}(\lambda)$ is the log-normal probability (see above)

- **Gamma (scale, shape):** The gamma distribution is another continuous probability distribution on the range $(0, \infty)$. It is broadly used in mathematics as a general, flexible distribution. Unlike the log-normal, its two parameters are clearly divided into a scale parameter (position on the x-axis) and the shape parameter, with shape again varying from modal to a single mode near $N = 0$. Both the gamma and the Weibull distribution (next) are mathematically more tractable than the log-normal. The gamma distribution is not frequently used for SADs, but occasionally it is used and in some cases found to be the best-fitting distribution (Plotkin & Muller-Landau 2002). There is a simple formula for maximum likelihood estimation (Evans et al. 1993).
$p(n) = (n/\text{scale})^{\text{shape-1}} \exp(-n/\text{scale})/(\Gamma(n)\text{scale})$, where $\Gamma(n)$ is the gamma function.

- **Weibull (scale, shape):** The Weibull is another widely used continuous probability distribution defined on $(0, \infty)$ and therefore sensible for modelling abundances. Again there is a simple MLE formula for estimation (Evans et al. 1993).
$p(n) = \text{shape} \times (n/\text{scale})^{\text{shape-1}} \exp[-(n/\text{scale})^{\text{shape}}]/\text{scale}$

- **NegBin (P,K):** Just as one can make a Poisson log-normal to represent integer sampling from an abstract continuous distribution, one can make a Poisson gamma distribution. This is called the negative binomial distribution. Traditionally, the distribution is zero truncated (the probability of sampling abundance 0 is removed by rescaling). The negative binomial has several different parameterizations and can be confusing. I recommend following the one given by Pielou (Pielou 1975, p. 35–38) along with her estimation method. In this case, P is the scale parameter of the gamma

distribution and k is the shape parameter. One interpretation is that k measures inverse distance from the Poisson distribution ($k = \infty$ gives the Poisson while $k = 0$ is far from Poisson). Thus k has been used in studies of abundances in quadrats to indicate the degree of clumping, but it is unclear how this relates to SADs.
$p(n) = \frac{\Gamma(k+n)}{n!\Gamma(k)} \left(\frac{P}{1+P}\right)^n \frac{1}{(1+P)^k - 1}$

- **Log-series (c):** The log-series is the limit of the negative binomial as k goes to zero (with some mathematical details added) and the zero abundances are truncated (Fisher et al. 1943). It has a single parameter, c. Fisher's α is technically not a parameter of the distribution but is instead an implicit function of the parameters, S and N (specifically $S = \alpha \ln[1 + N/\alpha]$). Fisher's α is generally recognized as a measure analogous to species richness, although in different units. Estimation of c can be done by numerically solving for c in the equation $\overline{n_i} = \frac{c}{-(1-c)\log(1-c)}$. $p(n) = kc^n/n$, where $k = -1/\ln(1 - c)$

- **ZSM (m, θ):** The birth–death–immigration equations of neutral theory can be solved to produce what is known as the zero-sum multinomial (ZSM) distribution (Hubbell 2001; Etienne 2005), although the zero-sum assumption is not critical (Etienne et al. 2007). It has two parameters. Nominally θ is a speciation rate and m is the percentage of individuals migrating from outside the local community. In practice these values are impossible to measure and θ and m are fit by maximum likelihood estimation with the likelihood calculated using complex combinatoric methods (Etienne 2005). This optimization is made even more tricky because there is a long ridge of nearly equal likelihood (Etienne et al. 2006). The parameter θ is strongly correlated with species richness (and is equal to Fisher's α when $m = 0$, in which case the ZSM is the same as the log-series). $p(n)$ has a complex representation (Etienne & Olff 2004; Etienne 2005).

- **Geometric (r):** The first used probability distribution for SADs is the geometric, but ironically it is not actually a probability distribution but a series. The proportion of abundance in each species is a function of its rank, not a random sample from a distribution, and is different from the geometric probability distribution (May 1975). However, it is often still treated as a probability distribution. It has a single parameter, often called k or r. This represents the fraction of the remaining community captured by each successive species. Several approaches for estimation are available (He & Tang 2008) of which I find He and Tang's new method the best.
$n_i = C(k)Nk(1 - k)^{i-1}$, where $C(k)$ is a

normalizing constant $C(k) = 1/[1 - (1 - k)^S]$, N is total abundance and S is species richness.

In summary two groups of distributions emerge. One group contains the Pareto distribution with extensions to create the PowerBend, Zipf–Mandelbrot and the conceptually distinct but mathematically related log-series. The second group contains three continuous functions (log-normal, γ and Weibull) and their Poisson sampling extensions (Poisson–Lognormel, Poisson–Weibull, not discussed here, and Poisson Gamma = negative binomial). The ZSM and geometric stand alone. There are numerous (probably dozens) of other probability distributions that are not mentioned here (Marquet et al. 2003; McGill et al. 2007). The power fraction extensions of the geometric (Tokeshi 1996) are interesting, but currently have no analytical approaches and must be solved by repeated simulation. The log-logistic distribution (the logistic distribution on log abundances) is a little known but valid distribution and is essentially the distribution one assumes when fitting a logistic curve to the ECDF (Fig. 9.1 and section 9.2.1). Since it is primarily a descriptor of visual shape I treat it as non-parametric (Box 5.1), but it has sometimes been argued as a probability distribution outright relevant to SADs (Williamson & Gaston 2005).

9.2.4   Multivariate approaches to SADs

The final approach to dealing with the vector of numbers measured in an SAD is to treat it in its full multivariate nature. This is rarely done with a single SAD (but see, for example, Alonso 2005). With multiple SADs it becomes possible to define measures of dissimilarity distance between communities (over 70 different distance measures have been defined—Legendre & Legendre 1998; Chapter 6—and perform cluster analysis, ordination and other techniques- Clarke & Warwick 2001; Manly 2004). For an example see Figure 17.4. This approach shares with the visual approach the benefit that no data are thrown away. The use of one or a few metrics (parametric or non-parametric) as described in sections 9.2.2. and 9.2.3 involves data reduction, and the multivariate approach has the benefit over the visual approach of being quantitatively rigorous. Yet the multivariate approach has had limited uptake. This is probably largely due to the complexity and training required to correctly perform multivariate statistics. One of the major benefits and reasons for frequent use of SADs is their easy-to-grasp nature. Moreover, our intuition starts to fail in a multivariate world, for example the definition of order falls apart in a multivariate world, but the first three approaches allow for unambiguous statements like there are more rare species in data set X or data set Y is more even.

9.3   Identifying a useful, parsimonious subset of SAD metrics

If one wishes to use the visual or multivariate approaches, then the large number of metrics of SADs is not a problem. Otherwise, the proliferation of dozens of metrics to describe SADs is problematic. Indeed, for SADs with only a few (5–15) species, there are more metrics that can be calculated on it than there are raw data points. Thus there must be redundancy among the diverse metrics. There have been some attempts to identify some metrics as superior to others (Hurlbert 1971; Kempton & Taylor 1974; Smith & Wilson 1996; Wilsey et al. 2005). However, a truly systematic evaluation of both parametric and non-parametric metrics on SADs is lacking. I seek to identify a subset of all metrics that can usefully but parsimoniously describe the essential features of an SAD.

I suggest that there are four properties that a good set of metrics should have:

1. **Efficiency:** No metric will work perfectly on small samples (the shape of the SAD is meaningless with one individual and is nearly as meaningless with 10). However, good metrics should quickly converge to their true values as sample size increases and the standard error should likewise quickly decrease as sample size increases.
2. **Unbiased:** A good metric will not consistently undershot or overshoot the true value when the sample size is small. In other words, the metric

should be on average equal to the true value when many different samples are compared.

3. **Interpretability:** A good metric should be intuitive. It should describe geometric aspects of the SAD that can be easily visualized or that describe factors of the SAD which are biologically relevant or ideally both. Evenness, in its qualitative sense, is an example that has a clear geometric interpretation (close to the horizontal line in RAD or close to the step function ECDF) as well as a clear biological relevance.

4. **Orthogonality:** The first three are properties of individual metrics. Orthogonality is a property of sets of metrics. A set of metrics should contain little overlap or redundancy in what the member metrics measure. In short, the collinearity or correlation between the different metrics should be low. Thus species richness, S, and Shannon diversity, H, have a lot of redundancy, as do H and Shannon evenness, J, but S and J are moderately orthogonal (although it has been shown that even J depends on S and evenness measures other than J show greater orthogonality to S, e.g. Smith & Wilson 1996). I suggest that SAD metrics are currently in the state that landscape metrics were in before Riiters and colleagues (1995) performed their analysis. Over 50 landscape metrics had been suggested, but a factor analysis showed that all the metrics were well described by only six underlying factors.

Factors such as dependency on sample size and orthogonality can be calculated analytically for specific individual metrics or pairs of metrics (Hurlbert 1971; May 1975; Smith & Wilson 1996), but such analytic results are not generally available for most of our proposed metrics, thereby necessitating an empirical approach. To assess which subset(s) of metrics out of all parametric (Box 9.2) and non-parametric (Box 5.1) meet these goals, I performed two simple analyses.

9.3.1 Efficiency and bias

The first analysis assessed bias and efficiency. I took five empirical datasets with more than 10 000 individuals (N): Barro Colorado Island tropical trees (Condit et al. 1996), Winemiller's Venezuelan fish (Winemiller 1990), Fisher's Malaysian moth light trap data (Fisher et al. 1943), Hick's copepod data (Hicks 1980) and one site from Pearson's data on macrobenthos in Loch Linhe (Pearson 1975). Ten replicate subcommunities each of sizes $N = 30, 100, 1000$ and $10\,000$ were randomly sampled from the original community. All 52 metrics (32 non-parametric, 20 parametric) were calculated on each replicate subcommunity and also on the original full community. The latter was assumed to be the true value of the metric for each dataset. Estimated metrics were averaged across the 10 replicates and then calculated as a ratio to the true metric for the full community (so a value < 1 indicates smaller than the true value, > 1 indicates greater than the true value). The results are found in Figs 9.4 and 9.5 and summarized in Tables 9.1 and 9.2.

Overall, it can be seen that small sample sizes give very misleading estimates. Most metrics only began to come close to their true value (even to within ±50%) with at least 1000 individuals sampled and in many cases only with 10 000 individuals sampled. This is problematic as a vast majority of studies of SADs are done with at most a few hundred individuals. Most metrics are also biased. Among the parametric measures, those related to the power distribution (Pareto/Power, Zipf–Mandelbrot and especially the log-series) do the best. Among the non-parametric measures, the classic diversity measures (the Shannon diversity and the closely related pair of Simpson diversity and Hurlbert Probability of Interspecific Encounter diversity measures) have nearly perfect performances converging to the true answer with only a few dozen individuals and being unbiased. The equivalent evenness measures do not fare as well, although the Shannon evenness remains one of the best evenness measures. The non-absolute dominance measures (relative dominance and McNaughton dominance), the percentage rare measures and the intercept from the logit on the ECDF (i_{logit}) all do fairly well (although to have any species that are rare at the 1% level several hundred individuals are needed). Overall the message of this analysis is a sobering one—large samples in the order of 1000 individuals are needed to truly assess species abundance distributions. With

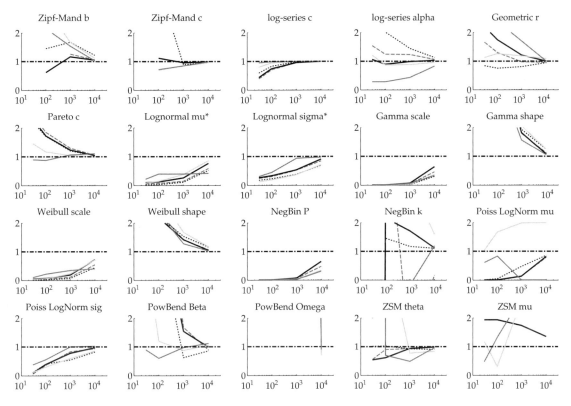

Figure 9.4 Efficiency and bias of parametric metrics. Each line represents the average across 10 replicate draws from a single dataset. The lines give the ratio to the true value, with 1 (the dashed line) representing a perfect match. Values greater than 1 represent overestimates. The x-axis represents sample size, N.

smaller samples, one is best to limit analysis to the Simpson and Shannon diversity measures, the dominance and percentage rare measures and the log-series c and Zipf–Mandelbrot c measures.

9.3.2 Independence of measures

The second analysis seeks to reduce the dimensionality and find orthogonal metrics. Datasets representing 91 communities were analysed, including 21 from Morlaix (different points in time before and after a disturbance: Dauvin 1984), the aforementioned Hicks copepod data, the aforementioned BCI data divided into 10 strips of 5 ha each, 13 communities of macrobenthos from a succession experiment (Arntz & Rumohr 1982), 30 communities of macrobenthos from Loch Linhe and Loch Eil (Pearson 1975), 20 randomly chosen routes from the North American Breeding Bird Survey

with at least 400 individuals (Robbins et al. 1986; Patuxent Wildlife Research Center 2001), and the aforementioned Winemiller fish and Fisher moths. The last three datasets (22 communities) were not exhaustively sampled but instead depended on individuals that approached the counting device or observer. The first five datasets (69 communities) were all exhaustively sampled (every individual in a well-defined area was identified and counted). In addition 55 randomly generated communities (samples from a probability distribution) were created, composed of five replicates of 11 different distribution/parameter combinations (four sets of parameters on the ZSM, three sets of parameters on the log-series and four sets of parameters on the Poisson log-normal). These communities were analysed separately (exhaustively sampled, non-exhaustively sampled and random) and collectively by principal component analysis and k

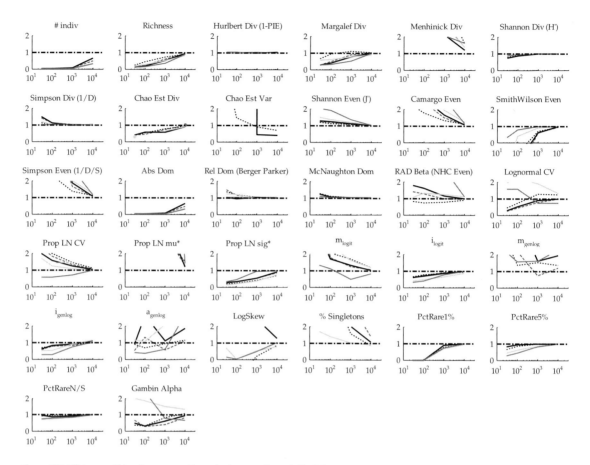

Figure 9.5 Efficiency and bias of non-parametric metrics. Interpretation as in Fig. 9.4.

means and UPGMA clustering where the 52 metrics were treated as measures and the 146 communities were treated as observations. The results are shown in Fig. 9.6 and summarized in Tables 9.1 and 9.2. Simple univariate correlation of all measures with S and N were also calculated (Table 9.3). In general, results from the non-exhaustively sampled communities were less robust than those from sampled communities. It would appear that it is highly desirable to use exhaustive sampling methods whenever possible.

Many measures (Table 9.3) were strongly correlated with S or N or both (echoing the results of the previous section on effects of sample size). However, several measures were largely independent of both S and N, indicating that there is indeed additional information contained in SADs. The metrics most independent of S and N include the slope of the logistic intercept (both the standard, m_{logit},

and the generalized logistic, m_{genlog}), the migration parameter, m, of the ZSM and log-skewness. The logistic slopes can be seen as a measure of evenness while m and skewness more specifically describe proportions of rare species.

The clustering (see Fig. 9.6) produced several useful results. First, three distinct groups of metrics emerged. These groups were robust across all subsets of data, different measures of distance and methods of clustering (hierarchical or K means). One group had measures broadly associated with species richness, including richness per se and various estimators of it as well as diversity measures and Zipf–Mandelbrot b. Another group included evenness measures, including traditional evenness measures, shape parameters of the log-normal, Weibull, gamma and negative binomial distribution, and the slope of the ECDF logit (m_{logit}) and Gambin α. The third group included

Table 9.1 Scorecard of performance for non-parametric metrics.

	Metric	Traditional symbol	Proposed Symbol	Bias (+/0/−)	Efficiency	Tie to S and N	Group	Complexity
Non-parametric								
Abundance ()	Number of individuals	N	N/A	−−	10 000	N/A	N	L
Richness (S)	Richness	S	S	−−	10 000	N/A	S	L
	Margalef diversity		$S_{Margalef}$	−	1000	VH	S	L
	Menhinick diversity		$S_{Menhinick}$	++	10 000	VH	S	L
	Chao diversity estimator		S_{Chao}	−	1000		S	L
	Chao diversity variance		$S_{ChaoVar}$	0	10 000		?	L
Diversity (D)	Shannon diversity	H'	$D_{Shannon}$	0	**30**	VH	D	L
	Simpson diversity	$1/D$	$D_{Simpson}$	0	**30**	H	D	L
	Hurlbert diversity	$1 - D$, PIE	$D_{Hurlbert}$	0	**30**	H	D	L
	Shannon evenness	J'	$E_{Shannon}$	+	1000	H	E	L
Evenness (E)	Simpson evenness	$1/D/S$	$E_{Simpson}$	++	10 000	L	E	M
	Camargo evenness	$E_{Camargo}$	$E_{Camargo}$	++	10 000	L	E	M
	Smith–Wilson evenness	E_{Var}	$E_{SmithWilson}$	−	10 000	L	N	M
	RAD β or NHC	E_{NHC}	E_{NHC}	+	10 000	M	S	M
Dominance or commonness (C)	Absolute dominance		C_{Abs}	−−	10 000	H	N	L
	Relative dominance		C_{Rel}	0	**100**	H	C	L
	McNaughton dominance		C_{McInt}	0	**100**	H	C	L
	LogSkew		$R_{LogSkew}$	0	10 000	**VL**	R	L
	% Singletons		$R_{\%Single}$	+	10 000	M	R	L
Rarity (R)	Percentage rare 1%		$R_{1\%}$	−	1000	VH	R	L
	Percentage rare 5%		$R_{5\%}$	0	1000	H	S	L
	Percentage rare N/S		$R_{N/S}$	0	**100**	M	R	L

Bias is indicated by sign (+ indicates consistent overestimation) with 0 bias being best and in bold. Efficiency represents the approximate sample size required to get an estimate close to the true, full community value; lower values are best and in bold. Metrics that are independent of both S and N are ranked as VL (= very low), low (L), medium (M), high (H) and VH (= very high) with VL and L in bold. Group indicates which of the seven basic categories of measurement the metric is found in. Complexity indicates how difficult the metric is to calculate (L = low, M = medium, H = high). This takes into account the complexity of the formula, the computer skills required and the computational time required. PIE, RAD, NHC

Table 9.2   Scorecard of performance for semi-parametric and parametric metrics.

	Metric	Traditional symbol	Proposed symbol	Bias (+/0/−)	Efficiency	Tie to S and N	Group	Complexity
Semi-parametric	Fisher's α		α	0	10 000	VH	S	M
	Log-normal CV		LNCV	0	1000	L	E	L
	Proportional LN μ^*		%LNμ^*	++	10 000	H	E50	L
	Proportional LN σ^*		%LNσ^*	−	1000	H	N	L
	Proportional LN CV		%LNCV	0	1000	H	N	L
	Gambin α		α_{GamBin}	0	1000	M	E	H
	Slope of logit at inflection		m_{logit}	+	10 000	**VL**	E	L/H
	Intercept of logit at inflection		i_{logit}	0	1000	VH	E50	L/H
	Slope of generalized logit at inflection		m_{genlog}	+	10 000	**VL**	?	L/H
	Intercept of generalized logit at inflection		i_{genlog}	0	1000	H	E50	L/H
	Assymetry of generalized logit at inflection		a_{genlog}	0	10 000	L	?	L/H
	Pareto power c	c	c	++	1000	M	R	M
	PowerBend β	β	B	++	10 000	M	R	H
	PowerBend ω	ω	ω	++	10 000	VL	D	H
	Zipf–Mandelbrot b	b	b	++	10 000	H	D	H
	Zipf–Mandelbrot c	c	c_{ZM}	0	1,000	H	C	H
	Log-series c	x, c	c_{ls}	−	**100**	M	N	M
Parametric	Log-normal μ^*	μ^*, scale	M^*	−−	100 000	M	N	L
	Log-normal σ	σ, shape	σ	−−	10 000	H	N	L
	Poisson log-normal μ	Scale	μ_{PLN}	−−	10 000	L	E	H
	Poisson log-normal σ	Shape	σ_{PLN}	−	100 000	L	N	H
	γ scale	b	Scale$_{\text{gam}}$	−−	100 000	VH	N	L
	γ shape	c	Shape$_{\text{gam}}$	++	10 000	L	E	L
	Weibull scale	b	Scale$_{\text{weib}}$	−−	100 000	H	N	L
	Weibull shape	c	Shape$_{\text{weib}}$	++	10 000	M	E	L
	Negative binomial P	P, scale	P	0	100 000	H	N	M
	Negative binomial k	k, shape	k	0	100 000	M	E	M
	ZSM m	m	m	++	100 000	**VL**	R	H
	ZSM θ	θ	Θ	−	10 000	VH	S	H
	Geometric r	r, k	r	++	10 000	H	N	L

Same notations as Table 2. A complexity of L/H means that it can be easily assessed visually (L) but to compute an actual metric is of high (H) complexity. CV, LNCV, ZSM,

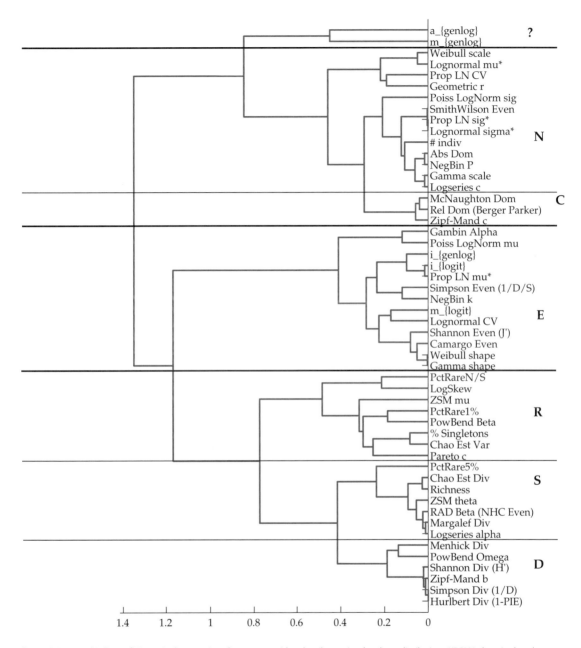

Figure 9.6 Hierarchical tree of 52 metrics (parametric and non-parametric) to describe species abundance distributions. UPGMA clustering based on Spearman Rank correlation distances shown here. Three major groups N/C, E, R/S/D emerge and are repeatable across many datasets and methods. The subgroups (N vs C and R vs S vs D) are less consistent but are useful divisions.

measures broadly related to total community size N, including N itself, scale parameters for the log-normal, Weibull, gamma and negative binomial, the standard deviations (σ) of the various log-normal distributions, the dominance measures, Zipf–Mandelbrot c and, surprisingly, Smith–Wilson evenness. The existence of these three groups was robust. The relationship between the three groups (which two were most closely related) was not robust, varying with data and methods. Similarly, several subgroups within the three groups emerged (Fig. 9.6). These subgroupings were moderately robust across data and methods, although individual measures did switch between subgroups, and the relationships between subgroups often varied. However, because of the overall intuitive sensibility of these subgroupings I am inclined to regard them as real pending further studies. Specifically, three measures of dominance (abundance of common species and here grouped under the label C) always were grouped together within the larger group N. These measures were relative dominance (Berger–Parker), McIntyre dominance and the Zipf–Mandelbrot c. The only consistent subgroup within evenness is three measures (i_{logit}, i_{genlog} and proportionate log-normal μ) that all directly measure the abundance of the 50th percentile species, which might be denoted E50. The richness group had three subgroups, one directly measuring richness and denoted S (such as the Chao estimator, ZSM θ, Margalef diversity, Fisher's a), one closely related group (sometimes intermingling in some analyses) on diversity (D), including the Shannon diversity, the Simpson and Hurlbert diversities and the Zipf–Mandelbrot b. The third subgroup was directly related to numbers of rare species (R), including log skewness, ZSM m, pareto c, PowerBend β, percentage singletons, and PctRare1% and PctRareN/S. Thus in summary, three groups were strongly supported: the N or NC group, the E group (including E50), and the S or RSD group (Fig. 9.6). The subgroups (N vs C and R vs S vs D) were usually found and are intuitive and therefore probably useful.

Principal component analysis was also performed on the same data as the cluster analysis. Results were difficult to interpret and showed variability across analysis methods. However,

Table 9.3 Correlations between different metrics and S (species richness) and N (number of individuals) in 91 communities. Dif = $|N| + |S|$ as a measure of independence of S and N.

	N	S	Dif
$m_{genlogit}$	−0.08	−0.16	0.24
Zero Sum Multinimial m	−0.14	0.25	0.39
m_{logit}	−0.38	0.03	0.41
PowBend Omega	−0.26	0.16	0.42
Log-Skew	0.276	0.16	0.44
Smith–Wilson Evenness	0.43	−0.08	0.51
Poisson Log-Normal μ	−0.07	−0.46	0.53
gamma shape	−0.50	0.05	0.55
Carmago Evenness	−0.54	−0.02	0.56
Poisson Log-Normal σ	0.53	−0.03	0.56
a_{genlog}	0.20	−0.38	0.58
Simpson Evenness (1/D/S) (1	−0.43	0.15	0.58
Lognormal CV	−0.39	−0.21	0.59
% Singletons	0.05	0.56	0.60
Weibull shape	−0.54	0.08	0.62
PctRare N/S	0.51	0.13	0.64
NegBin k	−0.25	−0.39	0.64
PowBend β	0.306	0.34	0.65
RAD B (NHC Evenness)	−0.05	0.62	0.67
Lognormal μ^*	0.326	−0.39	0.72
Gambin alpha	−0.23	−0.50	0.73
Pareto c	−0.06	0.67	0.73
Log-series c	0.40	−0.35	0.74
Weibull scale	0.42	−0.38	0.80
Prop LN CV	0.13	−0.71	0.84
Lognormal σ	0.58	−0.27	0.85
Proportionate Log-normal σ^*	0.58	−0.27	0.85
Proportionate Log-normal μ^*	−0.39	−0.47	0.86
Shannon Evenness (J)	−0.63	0.23	0.86
Geometric r	0.13	−0.73	0.86
PctRare5%	0.19	0.69	0.87
Negative Binomial P	0.88	0.00	0.89
Zipf-Mandelbrot c	0.59	−0.31	0.90
$i_{genlogit}$	−0.62	−0.30	0.93
Absolute Dominance	0.92	−0.03	0.95
Relative Dominance (Berger	0.53	−0.43	0.96
Hurlbert Diversity (1-PIE)	−0.58	0.39	0.97
Zipf-Mandelbrot b	−0.32	0.65	0.97
Simpson Diversity (1/D)	−0.27	0.70	0.97
McNaughton Dominance	0.50	−0.48	0.99
gamma scale	0.82	−0.20	1.02
PctRare 1%	0.40	0.63	1.02
ZSM θ	−0.16	0.89	1.05
N (# of individuals)	1.00	0.05	1.05
S (Richness)	0.05	1.00	1.05
i_{logit}	−0.64	−0.43	1.07
Margalef Diversity	−0.10	0.98	1.08
Logseries α	−0.15	0.95	1.10
Shannon Diversity (H)	−0.46	0.65	1.12
Menhenick Diversity	0.40	0.75	1.15

very roughly, the first axis explained about 40% of the variance and captured large numbers of intermediate abundance species vs large numbers of rare and common species. The second axis captured about 25% of the variance and could perhaps be interpreted as how like the geometric series the data were (with one end of the axis having a steep RAD β, low richness and lots of rare species). The third axis captured about 10% of the variance and represented having high numbers of rare species vs. high numbers of common species.

9.3.3   Overall assessment of useful, parsimonious metrics of SADs

Tables 9.1 and 9.2 summarize these findings and add a column indicating how complex it is to calculate the various metrics. Weighing all of these factors (unbiased and efficient, independent and consistent in meaning, easy to calculate), some recommendations emerge. The best measures depend on your goals. Three scenarios follow.

• **Comparing equal-sized samples from closely related communities:** If the sample size is constant and the communities are directly comparable (e.g. herbaceous plants from a series of 10 × 10 m quadrats) then it is meaningful to directly compare S and N (see Chapter 4). With these simple measures available, it would appear from the three clusters identified that a measure of evenness would add the most and the Shannon evenness or m_{logit} (the latter especially as sample sizes get into the hundreds) would appear best. It is not clear that the Smith–Wilson evenness truly captures evenness since it is clustered in group N and the Camargo and Simpson evenness measures have poor convergence behaviour. One can even imagine doing a simplistic three-dimensional ordination by plotting a scatter plot in the three-dimensionsl space of S, N and E. If additional information is desired, a dominance (C) measure (such as relative or McNaughton dominance) and/or a rarity (R) measure such as log skewness (with more independence from S) or PctRare N/S (with good small sample behaviour) would also make sense. ZSM m works well but

requires very large samples and very advanced computer skills.

• **Comparing unequal samples or samples from unrelated communities:** When comparing data from, say, the tropics and temperate zone or data with different sample sizes, direct comparison of S and N is not meaningful. Gotelli and Colwell (Chapter 4) present methods to make S more comparable. However, it may become desirable to use other measures from the S and N groups. Margalef's diversity or Fisher's a (the latter especially once sample sizes reach into the hundreds) are good, quickly converging representatives of the S group. Representing the N group, the log-series c or the Smith–Wilson evenness have good sampling behaviours but the latter can be confused with an evenness measure and should probably be avoided. The remaining recommendations would be the same as the previous section (Shannon evenness or m_{logit} to capture evenness, E, and then, if desired, a dominance measure, C, and a rarity measure, R).

• **Very small sample sizes (< 100s):** When less than a few hundred individuals are sampled, the gross inaccuracy of most metrics at representing the larger community must dominate goals of independence. In this case, the log-series c, the Hurlbert/Simpson and Shannon diversity, relative or McNaughton dominance, and PctRare5% and PctRare N/S and possibly Shannon evenness (less rapidly convergent than the others, but the best of the E cluster) make the most sense.

9.4   Prospectus

There can be little doubt that sophisticated multivariate analyses are perhaps the most rigorous way of analyzing abundance data. However, the long-standing popularity of simpler (visual and metric-based) approaches to SADs suggests that not everybody can or will make the switch, therefore it is important to pursue a more full understanding of the simpler approaches as well. In this pursuit, a balance is needed between adding new measures that might be better and keeping the number of measures under control. Ecology has tended to see new methods added without old methods decisively removed. Science does not progress this way (Platt 1964). I have attempted here to suggest some new approaches (e.g. m_{logit} and direct measures of rare species by metrics like PctRare5%) as well as to perform some pruning. The results are fairly messy. More efforts are needed in both directions.

In addition, the results have suggested some tantalizing patterns worth pursuing that might ultimately lead us to a more mechanistic analysis. The appearance that Smith–Wilson evenness (called E_{var} by them) does not align with other evenness measures is a surprise and requires more analysis. The fact that the Zipf–Mandelbrot distribution converges quickly and the two parameters are independent suggests that this probability model deserves more usage and understanding. The seeming links between richness (S) and rarity (R) and between abundance/sample size (N) and dominance (C) are provocative. These may prove to be mere artefacts of the limited number of ways one can pack individuals into species, but it is not immediately obvious that they are. Finally, although the results of principal component analysis were very weak, the singling out of the importance of the number of intermediate abundance species is suggestive. Gray noted that intermediate abundant species were the ones that responded most to environmental change (Gray 1979), and Kempton (1979) suggested that metrics focused on species of intermediate abundance had the greatest ability to discriminate between sites. As yet, few metrics have been targeted at this area.

9.5 Key points

1. Species abundance distributions have been widely used because they are easy to measure and have simple methods of analysis (visual and various metrics).
2. I suggest that using a rescaled ECDF (empirical cumulative distribution function) is the optimal way to plot SADs.
3. Most SAD metrics are very inefficient and usually biased. Very large sample sizes are needed. In general, field workers should target sampling 1000 individuals and if this goal is not met, only a few metrics are appropriate.
4. The metrics proposed to date seem to span three broad features, richness/diversity, evenness, and abundance. These three broad groups have some reasonably consistent subgroups, suggesting a total of seven different groupings of metrics: richness (S), diversity (D), rarity (R), evenness (E), with a subgroup focused on median abundance (E50), and abundance (N), with a subgroup focused on relative dominance of common species (C).
5. Three specific scenarios with regards to different types of data are described. All of these scenarios can be analysed visually using the ECDF. When using metrics, different sets of metrics are recommended for the three different scenarios.

Acknowledgements

I thank the working group on SADs held at National Center for Ecological Analysis and Synthesis for many discussions and ideas that clarified my thinking about SADs and to NCEAS for funding this working group. I dedicate this chapter to John Gray, who was one of the leaders of this working group but passed away between our second and third meetings. John was one of those rare individuals who readily spanned the empirical and the theoretical divide in ecology and thought strategically. His 1979 application of SADs to detect the effects of pollution on communities and his 1987 review of SADs were both way ahead of their time. John's personality was as rare as his mind—he was in science purely for the intellectual curiosity and got excited about ideas wherever they came from, even if it was from a lowly graduate student (as I was when I first began interacting with John) or if it contradicted his own ideas. His enthusiasm and kindness are sorely missed.

CHAPTER 10

Fitting and empirical evaluation of models for species abundance distributions

Sean R. Connolly and Maria Dornelas

10.1 Introduction

Identifying and explaining patterns in the commonness and rarity of species has been a fundamental concern of community ecology for nearly a century (Chapter 8). Such *species abundance distributions*, when considered without reference to species identity, are particularly useful to ecologists for two reasons. Firstly, all assemblages have abundance distributions to compare with one another and, secondly, those distributions contain more information than univariate statistics such as species richness or other diversity metrics (McGill et al. 2007). Consequently, ecologists frequently analyse abundance distributions to identify systematic regularities that hold across disparate assemblages and to test ecological theory that purports to explain such regularities.

Nearly a century of investigation has identified both broad-scale similarities and systematic differences in patterns of species abundance. Assemblages with more than a few species overwhelmingly have a frequency distribution of species' abundances that exhibits a 'hollow curve': a plurality of species are represented by one or a few individuals; the number of species represented by increasing numbers of individuals drops off sharply as abundance increases; and there is a very long tail of moderately to highly abundant species (Fig. 10.1a). However, when abundance is plotted on a logarithmic scale, visually identifiable qualitative differences emerge: for instance, in some assemblages, one or more internal modes are present, but in others, no mode is apparent

(Fig. 10.1b). The extent to which these differences represent stochastic variation in the numbers of species in each abundance class, systematic distortion of abundance distributions by sampling effects, or differences in the abundance distributions of the underlying communities is controversial (Hubbell 2001; Lande et al. 2003).

Since Motomura (1932; in Whittaker (1965)) proposed the geometric series to characterize patterns of relative abundance in benthic lake habitats, numerous community models have been used to predict species abundance distributions. Some of these models purport to link abundance distributions to a broad range of other ecological quantities, such as numbers of unobserved species (Connolly et al. 2005), range-size frequency distributions (McGill & Collins 2003), species–area and species–time relationships (Adler 2004), body size distributions (Loehle 2006), spatial and temporal patterns in relative abundance (McGill et al. 2005; Dornelas et al. 2006), and niche similarity (Sugihara et al. 2003). Many such models predict some of these additional patterns, but not others, so species abundance distributions have become the data most commonly used to compare the performance of alternative community models. Using such data to compare models has been criticized recently because many attempts to assess model fit to species abundance distributions fail to identify significant discrepancies between models and data, or to clearly discriminate between the fit of alternative models. However, recent developments in model formulation, model fitting, goodness-of-fit testing and model selection have substantially increased

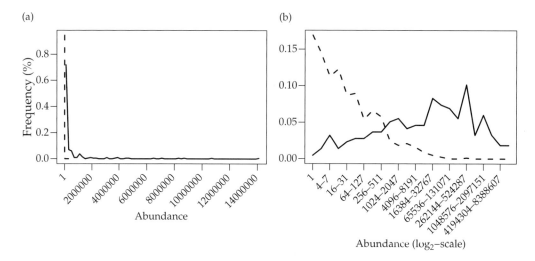

Figure 10.1 Species abundance distributions for the British Breeding Bird survey (Gaston & Blackburn (2000): solid lines) and the benthic fauna of the Ekofisk Oil Field (Gray et al. (1990): dashed lines) on (a) an arithmetic scale and (b) a $\log_2$ scale. Note the strong qualitative similarities between the data sets on an arithmetic scale and the marked differences on the logarithmic scale.

our ability to identify and interpret lack of model fit and to compare the fit of alternative models.

In this chapter, we review and assess traditional and recent techniques for fitting, and for evaluating the fit of, species abundance models. We discuss different approaches for fitting species abundance models to data, for assessing the models' (absolute) goodness of fit to those data and for comparing the (relative) fit of alternative models. Because there has been an increasing diversity of approaches in each of these areas, we describe and critically evaluate these different approaches. We conclude with some advice about the choice of approaches to fitting and testing species abundance models, highlight some important areas for further work, and offer some cautionary words about the ecological interpretation of the results of such analyses.

This chapter focuses on the analysis of numerical abundance (i.e. counts of individuals) because these data have been most intensively investigated and because much of the ecological theory and the more recent statistical modelling is tailored to such data. However, other abundance currencies, such as percentage cover, biomass and energy, have also been analysed (Chiarucci et al. 1999; Connolly et al. 2005). In particular, some theory for abundance distributions, such as niche-apportionment theory, is probably better suited to such alternative metrics (Tokeshi 1990). Recently, Morlon et al. (2009)

proposed a general statistical framework for identifying causal relationships among different abundance metrics, and O'Dwyer et al. (2009) derived the relationships that arise for a neutral model with size-dependent demography. We will return to this topic briefly at the end of the chapter.

10.2 State of the field

10.2.1 Species abundance models

Species abundance models may be theoretical (i.e. derived explicitly from assumptions about the biological factors that generate variability in abundances) or phenomenological (i.e. chosen because they appear to resemble empirical distributions). Stochastic abundance models, such as neutral models (Bell 2000; Hubbell 2001) and the environmental stochasticity models of Engen and Lande (1996a,b) are examples of the former, while the logit-normal distribution (Williamson & Gaston 2005) is an example of the latter. However, most models incorporate both theoretical and phenomenological elements. For instance, niche apportionment models are derived by assuming that a species' abundance is proportional to a randomly determined share of resources along one or more niche axes (Tokeshi 1990). Such models reflect the biological reasoning that species differences in access to resources are the principal drivers of species abundances, and reflect ecological concepts such as pre-emption of niche space. However, a species' share of the available resource pool is either assumed fixed or chosen randomly from a uniform distribution, even though (to our knowledge) a biological argument for these particular values or distributions has never been advanced in the literature. Similarly, Engen & Lande (1996b) show how a log-normal distribution of species abundances can arise in a stochastic model of community dynamics, but elements of the model (e.g. a log-normal distribution of intrinsic growth rates among species) appear to have been chosen more for mathematical tractability than on biological grounds.

In addition to reflecting the processes that generate the underlying distribution of species abundances in the community, abundance distributions in ecological data sets also reflect the processes by which the data are sampled from the community. Some of the earliest attempts to fit species abundance models to data explicitly considered both of these factors. For instance, Preston (1948) proposed that incomplete sampling would produce a truncated species abundance distribution. Subsequently, the role of incomplete sampling was formalised by mathematical models (e.g. Pielou 1975). Such models typically are compound distributions that account for a species' abundance in the community, and in the sample:

$$\Pr(r, n) = \Pr(r|n)\,\Pr(n) \qquad (10.1a)$$

$$\Pr(r) = \sum_n \Pr(r, n) \qquad (10.1b)$$

Equation 10.1a follows from the definition of conditional probability. The first term is the probability that a species has abundance r, given that its true abundance is n; this quantity depends on stochastic sampling effects that cause observed relative abundance in samples to vary around the species' true relative abundance in the community. The second term is the probability that a species' true abundance is n; this depends on the shape of the abundance distribution in the underlying community, and thus on the biological processes that determine that shape. The overall probability that a species has abundance r in a sample (equation 10.1b) is the sum (or integral, if true abundance is a continu-

ous variable) of equation 10.1a over all possible true abundance values, n.

Models of the form given by equation 10.1 reveal that incomplete sampling can cause sample abundance distributions to differ markedly from the underlying community abundance distributions. These effects are somewhat more complicated than simple truncations of the true distribution, as proposed by Preston (1948), but they often qualitatively resemble such truncated distributions (Fig. 10.2). Most such models assume that the data are a random sample from the larger community (e.g. $\Pr(r|n)$ follows a Poisson distribution with a mean proportional to n), but some explicitly consider the effect of non-random sampling of species' abundances. That is, encounter rates for a species during ecological sampling may not be proportional to their true abundances in the community if species differ in detectability or in spatial distribution relative to the sampling scale (Chapter 3). For instance, Engen et al. (2002) examine changes in the shape of species abundance distributions when such non-randomness follows a Poisson log-normal or negative binomial distribution, rather than a Poisson distribution (also see Green and Plotkin (2007)).

10.2.2 Obtaining predicted abundances

Fitting a species abundance model to a sample of species abundances requires choosing a set of parameter values from their ranges of possible values. This requires a method for generating model predictions for each set of parameter values to be considered, and a statistic that quantifies the model's agreement with the data for those parameter values. For many species abundance models, predictions can be generated exactly, by plugging parameter values into a closed-form expression. For example, for a random sample from a gamma distribution of species abundances (Pielou 1975), or as a result of demographic stochasticity with a constant rate of immigration (Volkov et al. 2007), the probability that a species has abundance r follows a negative binomial distribution:

$$p_r = \frac{\Gamma(r + k)}{r!\,\Gamma(k)} \frac{m^k}{(1 + m)^{r+k}} \qquad (10.2)$$

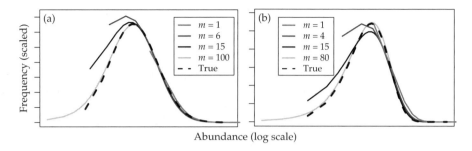

Figure 10.2 Illustration of veil-like effect of incomplete sampling on species abundance patterns. Dashed lines show (a) log-normal and (b) gamma relative abundances for an underlying community; the shaded lines show the (a) Poisson log-normal and (b) negative binomial species abundance pattern expected when sampling from these communities at different levels of intensity. Following Lande et al. (2003), each curve has been rescaled and shifted along the horizontal axis to highlight that, while the pattern resembles qualitatively an 'unveiling' of the underlying abundance distribution, the curves do not superimpose perfectly.

where m and k are the *scale* and *shape* parameters of the underlying gamma distribution.

In other cases, a mathematical expression for a model prediction exists, but a numerical approximation is required to generate a prediction. For instance, the Poisson log-normal distribution arises from Poisson sampling of individuals from a log-normal distribution of species abundances:

$$p_r = \int_{\lambda=0}^{\infty} \left[\frac{\exp(-\lambda)\ \lambda^r}{r!} \right]$$

$$\left[\frac{1}{\lambda\ \sigma\ \sqrt{2\ \pi}} \exp\left(-\frac{1}{2\ \sigma^2} \left[\ln\left(\frac{\lambda}{m}\right) \right]^2 \right) \right] d\lambda$$

$$= \frac{1}{r!\ \sigma\ \sqrt{2\ \pi}} \int_{\lambda=0}^{\infty} \lambda^{r-1} \exp\left(-\lambda - \frac{1}{2\ \sigma^2} \left[\ln\left(\frac{\lambda}{m}\right) \right]^2 \right) d\lambda$$

$$(10.3)$$

where $\ln(m)$ and σ are the mean and standard deviation of the natural logarithm of abundance, respectively. The first square brackets in the top line of equation 10.3 say that the probability that a species has abundance r in the sample is Poisson with rate parameter λ, and the second square brackets say that the rate parameter λ, which is proportional to relative abundance in the community, follows a log-normal distribution. In this case, the integral cannot be solved explicitly, so numerical methods for approximating its value must be applied. In some cases, the numerical calculations can be done (with the aid of a computer) almost as quickly as

evaluating equation 10.2. In other cases, however, the necessary calculations are more cumbersome and can substantially slow down the process of parameter estimation because they may need to be made repeatedly for a large number of different combinations of parameter values.

Some models require stochastic simulation to generate model predictions. Most niche apportionment models fall into this category, as do some stochastic abundance models that do not have analytical solutions (e.g. Bell 2001). This greatly increases the amount of computational time required to generate model predictions. Because each simulated model outcome is subject to stochastic variation, a large number of simulations must be conducted and generally averaged in some way to produce the model's prediction. However, even this averaging process does not completely eliminate stochastic error in model predictions. When the model has parameters that are estimated from data, this complicates the process of finding the parameter values that yield the best fit to the data, as we explain below.

10.2.3 Choosing parameters

Determining how well a model can explain patterns in empirical data often requires that parameter values be chosen from a range of possible values, but this is not always the case. For instance, under the dominance pre-emption species abundance model, the proportion of the available resource pool monopolized by one species is drawn from a uniform distribution: all proportions between 0.5 and 1 are equally likely (Tokeshi 1990). A second species then consumes a similarly determined proportion of the remaining resources, and so forth. There is no parameter that can be varied to make some resource proportions more likely than others.

For models that do have parameters, values for those parameters generally are estimated directly from the data being compared with the model. Several different approaches have been used to estimate parameters, which we review below. Regardless of the particular method, however, such estimates are based on some statistic that quantifies the discrepancies between data and model predictions for a particular set of parameter values. The values of model parameters are then changed until the value of this statistic is minimized. When a model has only one or two parameters, best-fit values can usually be approximated by brute force: calculating the model fit statistic for a range of parameter values and finding the statistic's minimum value (e.g. Fig. 10.3a). However, when calculating model predictions or model fit statistics is computationally

demanding, or when many parameters must be estimated, this approach can be impractical; therefore, contemporary applications typically rely on optimization algorithms to find efficiently the maxima or minima of functions. These algorithms start from an initial set of parameter values and change those values systematically until further changes cease to improve the fit. This is why generating models by stochastic simulation can cause difficulties in parameter estimation: the model fit statistic will be subject to small ups and downs due to stochastic simulation error, and this can cause optimization algorithms to fail (Fig. 10.3b). There is no readily available fix for this problem: researchers must check that any parameter estimates obtained genuinely do give the best fit, for instance by plotting goodness-of-fit profiles (Hilborn & Mangel 1997). Failure to find the best fit can also occur when there are multiple 'local' peaks in model fit, meaning any small movement away from a combination of parameter values causes a reduction in model fit, even though a better fit is possible for a very different set of parameter values (see Etienne et al. (2006) for an example in species abundance

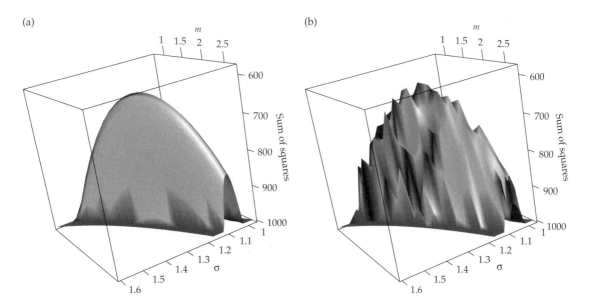

Figure 10.3 (a) A surface plot of the negative sum of squares for the Poisson log-normal, fitted to rank abundance data simulated from a Poisson log-normal distribution with $m = 1$, $\sigma = 1.5$ and $S = 200$. (b) A surface plot of the same model fitted to the same simulated data, but with the expected rank abundance distribution for each set of parameter values generated by averaging the rank abundance distributions for 1000 simulated data sets using those parameter values.

analysis). There is no foolproof way to avoid this, but it is good practice to re-start optimization algorithms from a range of different initial parameter values, to increase the likelihood that all of the local peaks in the model fit are found.

We now turn to several common statistics used in parameter estimation.

Maximum likelihood for species abundances
Contemporary studies frequently fit species abundance models by maximum likelihood methods. This requires deriving, or numerically approximating, the probability that a particular set of species abundance values will be observed, given specific values of model parameters. For instance, equation 10.2 gives the probability that a species will have abundance r in a sample, given that species abundances follow a negative binomial distribution with parameters m and k. The support that an observation provides for a particular set of parameter values, called the *likelihood*, is proportional to this probability:

$$\mathcal{L}(\theta \,|\, r) \propto \Pr(r \,|\, \theta) \qquad (10.4)$$

where θ is a vector of all of the model's parameter values (e.g. $\theta = [m, k]$ for the negative binomial) and r is an observed species abundance. Note that for a species to appear in the likelihood, it must appear in the sample. If one is fitting a model in which some species in the underlying community may not appear in the sample, such as the Poisson lognormal or negative binomial, then the *zero-truncated* form of the model accounts for this:

$$\Pr(r \,|\, \theta) = \frac{p_r}{1 - p_0}, \qquad (10.5)$$

where p_r is the probability that a species has abundance r (e.g. as in equations 10.2 and 10.3). Thus, the denominator is the probability that the species does not have abundance zero, and $\Pr(r|\theta)$ is the probability that a species has abundance r, *given* that it has appeared in the sample at least once. Most commonly, equation 10.5 is extended to account for the entire sample by making the simplifying assumption that species' abundances are statistically independent of one another, and thus the likelihoods for the individual species are multiplied together:

$$\mathcal{L}(\theta|r) = \frac{S_{obs}!}{\prod\limits_{n=1}^{N} \phi_n!} \prod\limits_{s=1}^{S_{obs}} \mathcal{L}(\theta|r_s) \qquad (10.6)$$

Here, S_{obs} is the total number of species in the data set, N is the total number of individuals sampled and ϕ_n is the number of species with abundance n. The fraction is a normalizing constant to account for the number of different ways that the observed species abundances can be divided up among the S_{obs} species sampled (usually ignored, because for any given sample of species abundances, it is independent of the model or parameter values).

In reality, species abundances will not be statistically independent of one another. For instance, in sampling a given area for sessile organisms, if one species is particularly abundant, then there is less space available for another species. One way to account for such constraints is to condition on the total number of individuals that are sampled. In other words, *given* that one has observed a particular set of species abundances that add up to a total sample size of N, what is the likelihood for a particular set of parameter values? This requires normalizing (i.e. dividing) by the probability that the species abundances add up to the observed sample size. Calculating this quantity can be very time-consuming because it requires calculating the likelihoods for all of the possible combinations of S_{obs} species abundances that give a total sample size of N, and adding them up (Etienne & Olff 2004).

Because accounting for such conditioning is potentially cumbersome, it is worth evaluating the robustness of parameter estimates obtained, using the simpler likelihood (equation 10.6), to violation of this independence assumption. To explore this, we compared the bias of parameter estimates obtained using this likelihood when data are simulated in two different ways: in the *Poisson* algorithm, individuals (and thus species) are sampled independently of one another, consistent with equation 10.6; in the *hypergeometric* algorithm, individuals are sampled from the community only until a fixed total sample size is reached (see Box 10.1 for details). We found no differences in the bias of parameter estimates for the Poisson log-normal or negative binomial models (Fig. 10.4): Wilcoxon tests for paired observations confirm no significant differences in bias for any parameter values, for either model ($P > 0.4$ in every case).

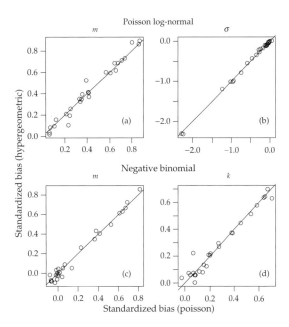

Box 10.1 Analysis of parameter bias due to fixed sample size

For the Poisson log-normal distribution, we first simulated an underlying distribution of species abundances in the community for a particular total number of species, S_{true}, and with a particular standard deviation of log abundance, σ. For the hypergeometric algorithm, we sampled N individuals from this community abundance distribution, where the probability that an individual belonged to species i, p_i, was equal to the species' relative abundance in the community. We then fit the Poisson log-normal distribution to the resulting simulated sample abundance distribution, using the likelihood in equation 10.6. For the Poisson algorithm, for each species in the underlying community, we generated its numerical abundance in the sample by choosing a random number from a Poisson distribution with mean p_iN; thus, total sample size was a Poisson random variable with mean N. Note that, in both algorithms, the number of observed species in the sample can be (and generally is) less than S_{true} because some species have abundance zero. For each bootstrap algorithm, we repeated this simulation 1000 times for each of 27 combinations of parameter values and sample sizes: $\sigma = [1,2,3]$, $N = [100, 1000, 10\,000]$ and $S_{true} = [20, 200, 2000]$. We calculated the mean standardized bias as the difference between the mean parameter estimate (across the 1000 simulations for a particular parameter combination) and the true value, divided by the standard deviation of parameter estimates among those simulations.

For the negative binomial, we followed the same procedure, except that the underlying community abundance distribution was gamma, rather than log-normal, and the parameter and sample size combinations were $k = [0.01, 0.1, 1]$, $N = [1000, 10\,000, 100\,000]$ and $S_{true} = [20, 200, 2000]$. The larger values of N are required for this model to ensure that sufficiently many species appear in the sample for adequate converge of parameter estimation algorithms.

See Connolly et al. (2009) for a detailed description of all algorithms.

Figure 10.4 Comparison of the standardized bias of parameter values for data simulated according to the hypergeometric (fixed sample size) and Poisson (variable sample size) bootstrap algorithms. Each point represents the mean standardized bias for one of 27 parameter combinations for (a, b) the Poisson log-normal and (c, d) the negative binomial. See Box 10.1 for a detailed description of the bootstrap simulations. The large standardized biases (i.e. magnitudes > 1, lower left of panel b) correspond to cases with $\sigma = 3$ and sample sizes smaller than total species richness: in these cases, the proportion of the total number of species that actually appeared in the simulated sample was very small.

These analyses suggest that failing to condition on sample size is unlikely to substantially affect the biases in parameter estimates, at least for these two models. Moreover, it illustrates how this problem can be examined for other models.

Maximum likelihood for abundance classes
Several analyses first place species' abundances into abundance classes and then use maximum likelihood methods to fit model predictions of the number of species in each abundance class against the corresponding observed values (e.g. Hubbell 2001). In general, this approach is likely to be inferior to using the actual abundance values because it removes information from the data that can provide important information about model fit. Because such abundance classes are usually logarithmic in nature (i.e. they get wider as abundance increases),

this loss of information will be particularly pronounced for the most abundant species. This is potentially quite important because the thickness of the tail of highly abundant species is one of the major differences between species abundance models. For these reasons, fitting models to unbinned data should tend to lead to narrower confidence limits on model parameters (and for similar reasons should lead to stronger goodness-of-fit tests and model selection results). However, we have no particular reason to suspect that parameter estimates would tend to be biased when data are binned. Consequently, we suspect that the use of abundance classes probably entails weaker statistical inferences, rather than erroneous inferences.

There is one circumstance in which use of abundance classes for model fitting may be preferable and that is when model predictions must be generated by stochastic simulation (e.g. Hubbell 2001). To calculate likelihood, each observed species abundance must have a corresponding model prediction for the probability that a species has that abundance. When model predictions are generated by simulation, such probabilities must be approximated by running a large number of simulations for a particular set of parameter values and then calculating the average proportion of species that ended up with that abundance in those simulations. However, when the true probability that a species will end up with a particular abundance value is very low, stochastic variation among ensembles of simulations can have a substantial effect on parameter estimation. For instance, substantially different likelihoods may be obtained, depending on whether one, two or three out of 1000 simulations produce a species with a particular species abundance that is observed in the data. Making predictions about abundance classes instead of specific abundance values will tend to make the outcomes of simulations more consistent with one another across replicate runs and therefore stabilize parameter estimates.

Maximum likelihood for rank abundances

Rank abundance distributions differ from normal species abundance distributions by associating a rank with each species' abundance (i.e. the most abundant species has rank 1, next most abundant

has rank 2, etc.). This introduces an additional layer of statistical complexity on top of those relevant to unranked abundance distributions: a species with abundance rank j cannot be more abundant than the one with rank $j-1$, and cannot be less abundant than the species with rank $j+1$. We know of only one maximum likelihood approach to rank abundance distributions (Foster & Dunstan 2009). This approach conditions on the total number of species, the total sample size and the abundances of all of the species with higher rank:

$$\Pr\left(n_j\right) = \Pr\left(N\right)\ \Pr\left(S|N\right)\ \Pr\left(n_1|S,N\right)\ \Pr\left(n_2|S,N,n_1\right)$$
$$\ldots\ \Pr\left(n_S|S,N,n_1,n_2,\ldots,n_{S-1}\right). \quad (10.7)$$

In cases where the probability distribution of abundances, for a species with a particular abundance rank, has a simpler form than the full species abundance distribution itself, this may be a more tractable approach to parameter estimation than one based on fitting to the frequency distribution of species abundances. For instance, under the geometric series model, the abundance of a species is drawn from a probability distribution that depends on the abundances of all species with higher abundances, but not on species with lower abundances. Such models lend themselves naturally to approaches like this one. However, for many models (e.g. the Poisson log-normal, as far as we are aware), no likelihood of the form of equation 10.7 has been formulated for the rank abundance distribution.

Least-squares approaches

Least-squares approaches are often used as an alternative to maximum likelihood in the literature. Most commonly, these methods are applied to rank abundances by finding the parameter values that minimize

$$\sum_{j=1}^{S}\left(n_j - \widehat{n}_j\right)^2, \quad (10.8)$$

where n_j is the observed abundance of the species with rank j, and $\widehat{n}_j$ is the predicted abundance of a species with abundance rank j (Loehle & Hansen 2005; Woodcock et al. 2007). However, least-squares methods have also been used to fit species abundance data categorized into abundance classes (Gray et al. 2005; Pueyo 2006; Volkov et al. 2007).

There are reasons to treat least-squares fitting of species abundance data with considerable caution, particularly when applied to rank abundance data. The statistical theory that supports least-squares estimation holds if three conditions are met: observed values are statistically independent of one another, the variance of this distribution is the same for all predicted values, and the residual variation has a mean of zero. For rank abundance data, the first two of these assumptions are certainly violated, often quite severely, and there is no particular reason to expect the third assumption to be met either. Specifically, every rank abundance is constrained to be no larger than the abundance of the next more highly ranked species, and no smaller than the next lower-ranked species. These constraints make rank abundances highly non-independent. Moreover, the width of this range of possible abundance values tends to narrow substantially from the most abundant to the least abundant species, so the residual variation in abundances will also change substantially as a function of rank. For instance, many species abundance distributions have a large number of 'singleton' species (species represented by only one individual) in an assemblage. In such communities, the lowest-ranked species will be guaranteed to have an abundance of exactly one individual because the next-higher ranked species will also have an abundance of one.

For least-squares fits to abundance classes, the situation is somewhat different. The 'observed' and 'predicted' values are not the abundances of species with particular ranks, but rather the numbers of species falling in a particular abundance class. For this latter case, any statistical non-independence among species is likely to be weaker. Moreover, under random sampling, the stochastic variability around the number of species in an abundance class should approximately follow a Poisson distribution. Provided the predicted number of species in each abundance class is large enough (around five species or more), this Poisson variability should closely approximate a normal distribution. This does not resolve the problem of unequal variances, which violates an assumption of the least-squares approach. However, because the variance and mean are equal for Poisson random variables, the residual variance can be homogenized by dividing each residual by the corresponding expected mean value. This approach is implicit in approaches that minimize Pearson's X^2 statistic (e.g. Doroghazi & Buckley 2008):

$$X^2 = \sum_i \frac{(O_i - E_i)^2}{E_i}, \tag{10.9}$$

where O_i and E_i are the observed and expected numbers of species in abundance class i, respectively. Thus, parameter estimation by minimizing X^2 should have similar properties to maximum likelihood fitting to abundance classes, provided that expected values are not too small.

Separately estimated parameters

Although most species abundance analyses estimate parameters by finding the values that maximize model fit, the parameters of some models can be estimated independently. Generally, this requires that the parameter represent a directly measurable biological quantity. For example, most neutral models explicitly include a parameter to characterize the proportion of new recruits in a local community that arrive from elsewhere (e.g. the migration parameter m; Hubbell (2001)). If there is empirical information about dispersal in a group of species (e.g. the shape of the dispersal kernel), then m can be estimated based on this information (Etienne 2005). Because this approach constrains the possible shapes that a model can take, it makes good agreement between a model and data less likely to occur by chance, and thus more likely to indicate that the model does, in fact, approximate the ecological processes that gave rise to the data. The closest example of this of which we are aware is a study of intertidal dynamics, in which mortality and immigration probabilities were estimated from observed transitions in space occupancy from experimental plots, then used to predict the species abundance distribution from independent transects at the same site (Wootton 2005).

10.2.4 Goodness-of-fit testing

Goodness-of-fit testing involves determining whether a model, once it has been fitted to data, adequately captures the patterns in those data. Often, in species abundance analysis, such assessments are made subjectively, based (for instance) on the apparent visual concordance between observed and predicted values, or on the percentage of variance explained by a model. Formal goodness-of-fit tests determine whether the model's fit to the data is significantly worse than one would expect if the model were true, and, if so, how much worse. In species abundance analysis, such tests have included several conventional tests for frequency distributions (e.g. Kolmogorov–Smirnov, Pearson's X^2 or G-tests). More recently, however, computationally intensive methods have been applied that appear to be better at identifying lack of model fit. The last few years have also seen techniques for unpacking information about model fit to determine how model predictions depart systematically from empirical data. Finally, although not goodness-of-fit tests *sensu stricto*, model fit also can be evaluated by making predictions about patterns other than those used in the fitting procedure. This latter approach is a way of moving beyond a model's ability to describe the data to gain insight into whether the processes that generate the patterns in the data are consistent with those included in the model.

Goodness-of-fit tests are null hypothesis tests: they determine whether or not one can reject the hypothesis that the data were actually generated by the specified model. However, there is a growing recognition among ecologists that models are, by definition, idealizations of nature and therefore that all models can be rejected, given sufficient data and a powerful enough goodness-of-fit test. This recognition has been partly responsible for sparking interest in model selection statistics, which aim to compare model fit relative to other models, rather than relative to the possibility that the model is somehow 'true', as in goodness-of-fit tests. However, the way in which a model fails to fit empirical data can sometimes suggest particular processes, omitted from the model, that may be important in nature (e.g. Dornelas et al. 2006). In addition, some model selection statistics are invalid if none of the alternative models provide a good approximation to the data. Finally, a model's utility for predicting unobserved data depends

critically on how well it characterizes the true underlying distribution. Consequently, the analysis of goodness of fit remains important in the study of species distributions, but there is an emerging shift away from statistical significance per se, and towards quantifying the magnitude of lack of fit and pinpointing the particular features of the data that are poorly approximated by a model.

Subjective methods

Graphical assessment of model fit goes back to the earliest analyses of species abundance distributions (e.g. Fisher et al. 1943; Preston 1948) and is still widespread in the species abundance literature (Ford & Lancaster 2007; Engen et al. 2008). Visual assessments are important for identifying what it is about the data that is responsible for their lack of agreement with a model, but they can be uninformative or even misleading when used in isolation, as can other ad hoc methods such as inspecting r^2 values. The predictions of a species abundance model, except as an extraordinary coincidence, will never match an empirical pattern exactly. Such discrepancies may be due to stochastic effects that are consistent with the model. For instance, a model may predict that the most abundant species includes 60% of the individuals in a community, and this may, in fact, be true of the actual community, but the species may be slightly over- or under-represented in the sample being analysed. Alternatively, discrepancies may be due to the fact that the model poorly approximates the 'true' species abundance distribution. Subjective methods cannot be used to distinguish rigorously between these two possibilities.

Asymptotic tests

Goodness-of-fit tests compare a model fit statistic with a null distribution. If the data are consistent with the model, the model fit statistic should be a random draw from that distribution. Statistical theory has been used extensively to identify statistics whose null distributions have the same basic shape regardless of details of the model, such as parameter values. Several such test statistics have been used in the analysis of species abundance data. For instance, the log-normal and logit-normal distributions have been tested by conducting standard normality tests on transformed abundances (Connolly et al. 2005; Williamson & Gaston 2005); however, this approach is useful only for distributions that can be made Gaussian by transformation. More general tests involve the use of contingency tables comparing observed and predicted frequencies of species in different abundance classes via Pearson's X^2 or similar statistics (Yin et al. 2005; Caruso & Migliorini 2006; Pueyo 2006; Sitran et al. 2009), for which the null distribution is chi-squared. Other analyses have used the Kolmogorov–Smirnov test, but this test is very weak when model parameters are estimated from data, as in most species abundance analyses (Zar 1996).

Parametric bootstrapping
Asymptotic tests are based on mathematical approximations of what the distribution of a particular statistic should be, given particular assumptions about the data. Often, these simplifying assumptions are not well met. For example, the chi-squared null distribution is appropriate only when there are minimum frequencies in each abundance category, so, in practice, species must be placed in abundance classes that often span a large range of abundance values. This removes information from the data and can lead to tests with low statistical power. An alternative approach is to estimate the null distribution directly, by simulating data sets that accord with the assumptions of a particular fitted model and then computing a model fit statistic for each simulation. The frequency distribution of this test statistic across simulations is then used as the null distribution for the model's fit to the empirical data. Such approaches have been termed 'parametric bootstrapping' because one re-samples data from a fitted model to estimate the uncertainty distribution of a statistic, rather than re-sampling from the data itself (Efron & Tibshirani 1993). The disadvantage of this approach is that this null distribution is sample and model specific, and so must be conducted anew for each model and data set under investigation. However, advances in computing power are making such analyses increasingly practical, and its versatility makes it a compelling alternative to more traditional approaches. In biology, for instance, parametric bootstrapping is becoming commonplace in capture–mark–recapture analysis (White et al. 2001) and phylogenetics (Holmes 2003).

In the analysis of species abundances, parametric bootstrapping has been used relatively infrequently, but several different test statistics have been proposed. Tokeshi (1990) first proposed testing model fit by simulation by comparing empirical rank abundance data with comparable data simulated from niche apportionment models, and Bersier and Sugihara (1997) subsequently proposed a test statistic for such analyses. Volkov et al. (2003) and Etienne et al. (2006) use the maximum log-likelihood of the model as the test statistic. Connolly et al. (2005; 2009) used deviance, a test statistic based on the log-likelihood, but normalized to facilitate comparability across sites with different sample sizes and parameter values.

Sample size: species or abundance?
In most species abundance analyses, goodness-of-fit tests make an implicit assumption that species abundance values are sampled, rather than individuals. For instance, the null distribution of Pearson's X^2 test statistic is based on an assumption that the stochastic variability around predicted frequencies of species in an abundance category follows a Poisson distribution. This assumed variability corresponds to a situation in which a certain number of species are sampled, each of which has an abundance label attached to it. Similarly, in some parametric bootstrap analyses, one samples an abundance value for each species observed in an empirical sample (Diserud and Engen 2000; Connolly et al. 2005; Engen et al. 2008). However, in most ecological sampling, a particular area or volume of habitat is sampled, and this sample contains some number of individuals, which in turn have species identities. In particular, a replicate sample might not yield the same number of species because some species that are present in the community do not appear in a given sample, and that number is subject to stochastic sampling variation.

It is possible to develop parametric bootstrap algorithms that simulate this process of re-sampling more realistically than the species sampling approach assumed by most goodness-of-fit tests. Etienne (2007) provides such an algorithm for a neutral model, for which dispersal limitation determines a species' presence and abundance in a sample, and Connolly et al. (2009) provide an algorithm for models that assume random sampling from an underlying community abundance distribution (e.g. Poisson log-normal, negative binomial, etc.). These algorithms lead to goodness-of-fit statistics whose null distributions are substantially narrower, and therefore more powerful at detecting lack of model fit, than analogues based on species sampling assumptions (Connolly et al. 2009: also see Box 10.1). Such differences suggest that, in general, goodness-of-fit tests based on the sampling of individuals may be more powerful at detecting departures from species abundance models than approaches that implicitly or explicitly assume sampling of species.

Multi-pattern testing

Most assessments of model fit compare a model's predicted values with the same data that were used to fit the model. Such assessments tell us whether the model adequately describes the species abundance data. However, frequently the goal of species abundance analysis is to go beyond this and determine whether that good fit indicates that the model approximates well the biological processes that generated the data. One way to do this is to test whether the parameters implied by fit to species abundance data can also explain other characteristics of the assemblage being investigated (McGill 2003c). Most examples of this approach have involved tests of neutral models. For instance, Adler (2004) fitted the neutral model to species abundance distributions of local grassland assemblages, used those parameter estimates, to determine the species–area relationship implied for that assemblage and then compared that prediction with the empirical species–area relationship. Wootton (2005) estimated neutral model parameters from temporal transitions in space occupancy in a benthic community and then tested the model's ability to predict community change when a hypothesized competitive dominant was removed. Dornelas et al. (2006) fitted the neutral model to species abundance distributions of scleractinian reef corals, predicted the frequency distribution of community similarity implied by those estimates, and compared that with the community similarity distribution exhibited by the data.

10.2.5 Model selection

In species abundance analysis, we often wish to know which of several alternative models provides the best approximation for the data, in addition to (or instead of) assessing their absolute goodness of fit. Many studies have compared graphically empirical data with the predictions of different species abundance models. For instance, many of the early analyses that suggest multimodality in species abundance distributions were based on graphical inspection of species abundance distributions (Gray & Mirza 1979; Ugland & Gray 1982). Other approaches are essentially comparisons of goodness-of-fit statistics for different models, such as r^2 values calculated from rank abundance distributions, Pearson's X^2 statistics calculated from frequency distributions of species abundance or statistics calculated from parametric bootstrapping (McGill 2003b; Volkov et al. 2007; Harte et al. 2008; Connolly et al. 2009).

Although approaches like those just described can be informative, they have important limitations. Alternative models may differ in how much uncertainty is associated with their predicted abundance patterns. Models with very flexible forms due to, for example, large numbers of parameters, are more likely to be able to provide good fits to data, even if they would do a poor job of predicting what a new sample might look like. In addition, the model with the lowest r^2 value, or which appears visually to give the best fit, may depend critically on the scale on which species abundances are represented. For instance, for rank abundances considered on an arithmetic scale, apparent model fit will be much more dominated by the model's fit to highly abundant species, compared to when rank abundances are represented logarithmically. Moreover, different models make different assumptions about the sources of variability in species abundance data and thus differ in terms of how much a given discrepancy between the model and data is consistent with a model's assumptions.

To overcome the subjectivity inherent in such ad hoc model selection approaches, biologists in many fields are increasingly shifting towards the use of model selection statistics that have a stronger foundation in statistical theory. Although this practice has not yet become widespread in the analysis of species abundance data, several model selection statistics have been used, including Akaike's information criterion (AIC; Connolly et al. 2005), Bayes factors (Etienne & Olff 2005), Bayesian (or Schwarz) information criterion (BIC; Dornelas & Connolly 2008) and deviance information criterion (DIC; Golicher et al. 2006; Mac Nally 2007). Of these statistics, AIC and BIC are straightforward to calculate, once one has maximum likelihood estimates for parameters, whereas calculation of Bayes factors and DIC are more complicated, sometimes considerably so, because they incorporate prior beliefs about model parameter values. All such model selection statistics, however, quantify the trade-off between the increased uncertainty associated with more complex models and the increased bias (i.e. systematic discrepancies between model predictions and data) associated with simpler models. Moreover, because they are based on likelihood, discrepancy is measured on a natural scale, and thus these statistics do not have the arbitrariness of, for instance, choosing whether to plot rank abundances arithmetically or logarithmically.

Akaike's information criterion
AIC estimates the amount of information that is lost when a model is used as an approximation for the true distribution from which the data have been drawn (Burnham & Anderson 1998). Thus, it provides a relative measure of a model's ability to predict new data sampled from the same true distribution. In many ecological applications, where sample sizes are relatively small, a modified form of this criterion, called AIC_c, is used:

$$AIC_c = -2log(\mathcal{L}_{max}) + 2k + \frac{2\,k\,(k+1)}{n-k-1} \quad (10.10)$$

where $\mathcal{L}_{max}$ is the model's maximum likelihood, k is the number of parameters in the model, and n is the sample size. The first term measures the model's lack of fit to the data in hand, while the second two terms account for the fact that models with more parameters tend to predict the values of new data with greater uncertainty. Notice that the third term becomes very small as sample size (n) gets large, so that, for moderately large sample sizes, AIC depends only on the model's overall fit

and the number of model parameters. Uncertainty about which model is best can also be estimated with AIC by calculating Akaike weights, according to which the probability that a model is the best model is proportional to $e^{-AIC/2}$.

Like all model selection statistics, AIC is controversial. Proponents of AIC typically emphasize the fact that it is an estimate of the information lost when the model is used as an approximation for the true distribution from which the data come, and thus is defensible on objective grounds as an aim of model selection. Critics of AIC most frequently cite the fact that it is not *consistent*, which means that, when one of the models under consideration was actually used to generate the data, the probability that AIC selects this true model does not approach 100% as sample size increases. For extensive discussion of the merits and shortcomings of AIC, readers should consult the relevant statistical literature directly (see Burnham & Anderson (1998) and Taper and Lele (2004) for ecologically oriented discussion).

Finally, it is worth noting that the derivation of AIC at several points uses the model as an approximation for the true distribution from which the data come, and therefore AIC is usually recommended only for models that are good approximations to the truth. Thus, goodness-of-fit testing is an indispensable part of model selection using AIC.

Bayesian approaches
To understand Bayesian approaches to model selection, it is important to recognize that all such approaches involve the application of Bayes' theorem to calculate probability distributions for model parameters:

$$p\,(\theta|y,\,M) = \frac{\mathrm{Pr}\,(y|\theta,\,M)\ \ p\,(\theta|M)}{c} \quad (10.11)$$

$\mathrm{Pr}(y|\theta, M)$ is equal to the likelihood: the probability of observing the data y, if the model, M, with a particular set of parameter values, θ, were true. $p(\theta|M)$ is the probability distribution for the parameters, prior to the data being collected (the *prior*). This prior may be based on previously available independent data, it may reflect subjective belief or (most commonly) is chosen so that its effect on $p(\theta|y, M)$, called the *posterior* distribution, is very small relative to the likelihood. The posterior distribution is an updated probability distribution for the model parameters, in light of the data. Thus, if a particular set of parameter values produces an extremely good model fit compared to another set of parameter values, then the first set will have a much larger posterior probability, relative to the second set, than in the prior distribution. c is a normalizing constant chosen so that the posterior distribution, $p(\theta|y, M)$, is a probability distribution (i.e. so that integrating $p(\theta|y, M)$ over all possible combinations of parameter values yields 1.0). One can think of the prior and posterior distributions as estimating the probability that a particular set of parameter values are the 'true' ones. Alternatively, they may be interpreted as estimating the probability that a particular set of parameter values are the ones that yield the best approximation for truth that is possible for a particular model (sensu AIC; see, for example, Spiegelhalter et al. (2002)).

The most intuitive Bayesian model selection statistic is the Bayes factor (also called the posterior odds ratio) and it is applicable where only two competing models are under consideration:

$$B = \frac{\Pr(y|M_1)\ \Pr(M_1)}{\Pr(y|M_2)\ \Pr(M_2)}$$

$$= \frac{\left[\int_{\theta_1} \Pr(y|\theta_1, M_1)\, p(\theta_1|M_1)\, d\theta_1\right]\ \Pr(M_1)}{\left[\int_{\theta_2} \Pr(y|\theta_2, M_2)\, p(\theta_2|M_2)\, d\theta_2\right]\ \Pr(M_2)}$$

$$(10.12)$$

$\Pr(y|M_1)$ is the probability of observing the data, y, if model M_1 were true. To calculate this, we must first calculate the probability of observing the data, given this model and a particular set of parameter values (θ_1) for that model: $\Pr(y|\theta_1, M_1)$. Then, we average this probability over all of the possible sets of parameter values for the model, weighted according to the prior probabilities for the model parameters. That weighted average is the integral in the numerator and it, in turn, is multiplied by $\Pr(M_1)$, which is the prior probability for the model. Often this quantity is assumed to be equal for all competing models, in which case the Bayes factor just estimates the support provided by the data for the competing models, analogous to a traditional likelihood ratio. In practice, the integrals in equation 10.12 are very hard to calculate,

so Bayes factors are typically only used where a computationally intensive numerical technique, Markov Chain Monte Carlo (MCMC), is applied; this approach can be used to estimate such integrals.

The BIC (Schwarz 1978), although derived from Bayes factors, is much simpler to calculate:

$$\mathrm{BIC} = 2\left[-\log(\mathcal{L}_{\max}) + \frac{k\,\log(n)}{2}\right] \quad (10.13)$$

Here, the penalty term for extra parameters, $k\log(n)/2$, arises in the derivation of BIC as an approximation of the difference between a model's maximum log-likelihood and the weighted average likelihood that appears in equation 10.12. In contrast to the penalty term in AIC, it gets larger as sample size increases. In other words, if sample size is large, then a model with more parameters will need to exhibit a larger improvement in fit to be selected as the best model, compared to what is required if sample size is small. Unlike AIC, BIC is consistent: it selects the true generating model with increasing certainty as sample size increases. Thus, if one of the models under consideration is believed to be true, then BIC should be preferred. However, if one instead believes that the true distribution from which the data come is more complex than any of the models being compared, then there is some disagreement about whether or not it is appropriate to use BIC as a model selection statistic (Burnham & Anderson 1998; Spiegelhalter et al. 2002; Boik 2004). An additional caveat with BIC is that its derivation assumes a very large sample size. There is no correction for small sample size, as with AIC, because if sample size is not large, then, in the Bayesian framework, prior beliefs about the values of model parameters have an impact on model selection.

Finally, DIC is a Bayesian approach based on model *deviance* (Spiegelhalter et al. 2002). Deviance estimates lack of fit as the difference between the log-likelihood of a model and the log-likelihood of a hypothetical model that fits the data perfectly. Formally, DIC is:

$$\mathrm{DIC} = D\left(\bar{\theta}\right) + \left[\overline{D(\theta)} - D\left(\bar{\theta}\right)\right], \quad (10.14)$$

where $\overline{D(\theta)}$ is an average model deviance, weighted according to the *posterior* distribution of the model parameters, and $D(\bar{\theta})$ is the model deviance, evaluated at the posterior mean parameter values. Here, the term in square brackets is analogous to the penalty terms in AIC and BIC because the difference between $\overline{D(\theta)}$ and $D(\bar{\theta})$ will tend to be larger for models with more parameters. When the prior distribution on model parameters is very flat, or there is a very large amount of data, then DIC estimates the same quantity as AIC (Spiegelhalter et al. 2002). However, when parameters are estimated by MCMC methods, DIC can be calculated from the posterior distribution of model parameter values, therefore DIC may be preferable to AIC when the investigator wishes to incorporate prior distributions for parameter values or where the number of parameters or the sample size is not easy to count (as in some hierarchical models and data structures), and thus the value of AIC is ambiguous.

10.3 Prospectus

The analysis of species abundance patterns has been a staple of macroecology for nearly a century. This spans a time period from just after the invention of the likelihood concept, to the invention of computers, of information theory, of the emergence of 'frequentist' and 'Bayesian' approaches as competing schools of thought in statistics, of bootstrapping, and of numerical methods of parameter estimation that make shortcuts such as least-squares unnecessary. Consequently, the tools available for fitting and evaluating models have expanded enormously since geometric, log-normal and log-series distributions were first compared with species abundance data. Having reviewed the range of tools applied in contemporary analysis, we offer some guidelines about how these tools may be utilized productively in the analysis of species abundance patterns and highlight some important areas for further research.

10.3.1 Sampling theory for species abundance models

Sampling distorts the shape of species abundance distributions, often substantially. Therefore, whenever possible, compound distributions that explicitly include both a model for the 'true' underlying species abundance distribution and a model

characterizing sampling from that distribution should be used. However, for some species abundance models, such as niche-apportionment models, such compound distributions have not yet been formulated, and this is an important area for further research. In addition, compound distributions that explicitly characterize the effects of local aggregation at the sampling site, or differences in species detectability, on species abundance data have only been explored in a few studies. Most ecologists do not sample randomly at the scale for which they wish to draw inferences; rather, they are more likely to intensively sample at multiple small sites spread over the broader area of interest. When local aggregation occurs, the abundance distributions at study sites will differ from that of the area as a whole. Consequently, an accessible and relatively general framework for non-random sampling is needed.

In addition, most sampling theory developed to date has focused on counts of individuals and thus is appropriate for numerical abundance data. Accounting for sampling effects in other currencies of abundance (e.g. cover, biomass) is generally lacking, but could proceed in at least two ways. One would be to consider sampling effects at the level of individuals, alongside the infinitely many ways that the continuously varying biomasses of individuals could sum up to a particular observed biomass. The other would be to apply a distribution analogous to equation 10.1, where the first term characterizes stochastic variation in biomass sampled given a particular area, volume or total community biomass sampled. However, we know of no theory, or even empirically documented regularities, that might be used to characterize biomass aggregation, as exists for individuals (e.g. Harte et al. 1999; He & Gaston 2003). This, too, stands as an important challenge for future research.

10.3.2 Parameter estimation

We favour approaches to parameter estimation that utilize maximum likelihood methods wherever possible. In our view, fitting models by eye is unnecessarily subjective and, given the accessibility of software to fit frequency distributions, no longer justifiable. Moreover, except where stochastic simulation is used, binning species abundances before fitting models is not necessary and probably reduces the precision of parameter estimates. More generally, we are wary of least-squares methods for fitting species abundance models because they are supported by statistical theory only under approximate normality and homoscedasticity. In general, these conditions will not be met for rank abundance data, and will only be met for species abundance distributions when abundances are categorized, probably quite coarsely so for the tail of very highly abundant species, and the data or residual variances are appropriately transformed. Nevertheless, despite its strong theoretical foundations, maximum likelihood is not perfect. In particular, maximum likelihood estimates can be biased, particularly for distributions that, like species abundances, exhibit substantial skew (Fig. 10.4; also see Diserud and Engen (2000) and Connolly et al. (2009)). Consequently, we believe that a rigorous, comparative analysis of different approaches to parameter estimation would be informative.

Many species abundance models allow species to have abundances that can be arbitrarily large, but in real ecological samples, quadrat sizes or transect lengths place upper bounds on the total number of individuals that can appear in a sample. To account for this, some researchers have argued for the use of likelihoods that condition on the total number of individuals actually sampled, rather than treating each species' abundance as completely independent of all others, thus implicitly allowing for unrealistically large or small sample sizes (e.g. Etienne & Olff 2005). Although we have not found this statistical independence assumption to increase the bias in parameter estimates (Fig. 10.4; also see Connolly et al. (2009)), we do not know whether this robustness is generally true for species abundance models or what impact it may have on model selection statistics. Further work on this question may help to identify if, and under what conditions, constraints on total sample size have important effects on the results of species abundance analysis.

For species abundance models that are explicitly derived from some ecological theory (e.g. stochastic abundance models), the use of external independent information about the values of model parameters has great potential to strengthen the inferences that can be drawn from fits to species

abundance models (Wootton 2005). This kind of approach can be further developed by explicitly incorporating uncertainty about model parameter values from such independent information. Thus, for a given set of parameter values, there would be two likelihoods: one for the species abundance data, and a second one for the independent data. These likelihoods would be multiplied together to obtain the overall likelihood for the parameters given both data sets. Similarly, in a Bayesian approach, the independent information could be used to construct a prior probability distribution for the model parameter(s). To our knowledge, such approaches have yet to be explored in species abundance analysis.

10.3.3 Goodness-of-fit testing

Failure to find statistically significant lack of model fit indicates only that the investigator has either not sampled enough or has used an insufficiently powerful goodness-of-fit test to detect it. Claims that a model fits data well should be supported by evidence that any lack of fit is small in magnitude, in some meaningful sense, regardless of statistical significance. Similarly, the use of model selection by AIC should be accompanied by evidence that any lack of fit that is present is likely to be small (Burnham & Anderson 1998). Conversely, finding statistically significant lack of fit is a first step to determining what it is about the data that the model fails to capture, and whether this information implicates particular processes, omitted from the model, as important determinants of relative abundance patterns. In this context, we believe graphical approaches to assessing model fit are most useful because they can indicate where discrepancies between models and data are large. When compared with the discrepancies that are consistent with the model's stochastic elements (e.g. as produced in parametric bootstrap simulations), such graphical assessments can be made more rigorously (Connolly et al. 2009). Graphical assessments are also more likely to bear fruit if a variety of representations of model fit are used, including species abundance distributions and rank abundance distributions, and using a variety of transformations of the relevant axes (Pueyo et al. 2006; Etienne et al. 2007b).

Species abundance models make predictions not only about the expected number of species with a particular abundance, but also about the site-to-site variability in relative abundance patterns. This information can also be used in goodness-of-fit testing, when multiple species abundance distributions are available. This idea was first used for replicate samples from the same community (Bersier & Sugihara 1997), but can be extended to sites from different locations that have different species abundance model parameters (Connolly et al. 2009). For data that include multiple species abundance samples, predictions about the variability in species abundance statistics among samples can provide additional information that individual fits cannot.

10.3.4 Model selection

Cross-validation is a well-established, widespread model selection technique that has not been used at all in the analysis of species abundances, to our knowledge. Because it is such an intuitive approach to model selection, it probably deserves some attention. However, the best way to approach cross-validation in the context of species abundance analysis is not immediately obvious. For instance, if one simply eliminates a species, chosen at random, from a dataset and re-fits a species abundance model, then one makes the assumption that the species is the unit that is sampled. This assumption has substantial effects on the results of goodness-of-fit testing (Connolly et al. 2009), so we are wary of giving it critical importance in model selection. Alternatively, however, it may be possible to subsample individuals from within species abundance distributions, or to subsample sites from a collection of replicate sites. For instance, one could randomly sample half of the individuals from a data set, fit a species abundance distribution to those individuals and then test the fitted model against the abundance distribution for the other half. Similarly, where multiple sites are distributed randomly within a larger area, and the species abundance distribution is expected to have the same parameters in each site, then a species abundance model fitted to some of the sites could be tested against the abundance distributions from the other sites.

In general, there is considerable controversy about what approach to model selection is the best one, in ecological or other applications. Therefore, rather than recommending the use of a particular statistic or method, we encourage analysts to understand and take appropriate account of the assumptions that underlie the model selection statistics that they do use. Many applications of AIC, for instance, are undertaken without any attempt to evaluate goodness of fit, despite the fact that one must assume, in order to derive AIC, that the model in question is such a good approximation that it can be substituted for the truth. Similarly, when Bayesian model selection statistics are used, and the prior distribution is chosen for mathematical convenience or on the basis of subjective belief, an assessment of the robustness of a study's conclusions to those priors is important. Finally, graphical analysis of model fit can be an informative complement to formal model selection, just as it is to goodness-of-fit testing.

10.3.5 Conclusions

Parameter estimation, goodness-of-fit testing and model selection are tools for obtaining as good a fit of a model to data as possible—either the data in hand, or a new sample of the same kind of data from the same sampling universe. For most ecologists, however, the goal of species abundance analysis is not to describe variation in relative abundances, but rather to use information about model fit to draw inferences about the processes that drive community structure or dynamics. Rigorous statistical techniques help ecologists quantify how well ecological models characterize patterns in nature, but they are an aide to, and not a substitute for, thinking about the processes that give rise to those natural patterns. Philosophers, historians and sociologists of science have increasingly recognized that the evaluation of models in science often depends on much more than goodness of fit or predictive accuracy. In practice, scientists often evaluate models based in part on how consistent they are with existing, well-supported theory, or on their explanatory power—their ability to provide unified explanations for a large number of patterns that previously required separate explanations (Kosso 1992).

Consider the evaluation of neutral models as an example. Neutral theory offers considerable explanatory power, purporting to explain not only patterns of species abundance, but species–area relationships and even patterns of speciation and extinction in the fossil record (Hubbell 2001). On the other hand, there is considerable empirical evidence for niche differences and life history tradeoffs among organisms. There is also an extensive body of ecological theory, supported by experiments, that links such patterns to species coexistence. Consequently, neutral models, by explaining species coexistence as transient, driven by demographic stochasticity and with species differences playing a negligible role, appears to contradict a large body of ecological theory and data about species coexistence (Abrams 2001; Mazancourt 2001). This may explain why some of the more influential tests of neutral theory have examined how well-known ecological realities omitted from neutral theory drive the very patterns that neutral models seek to explain (Fargione et al. 2003) or assessed the extent to which neutral models really can explain multiple patterns simultaneously (Adler 2004). Those two kinds of tests address these important (albeit subjective) criteria for evaluating models: potential explanatory power and consistency with established and well-supported theory.

Bayesian approaches offer a way to combine these different kinds of considerations by means of prior probability distributions on parameters or prior probabilities assigned to models based (for instance) on their mechanistic plausibility or their explanatory power. However, there will probably never be ways to objectively determine how much to weight to give these different considerations, alongside model fit, when evaluating models. Thus, model evaluation in the broadest sense—the scientific community's judgment about a model's potential to be a productive framework for future research—will probably always involve subjective elements. Indeed, for precisely this reason, we believe that the use of rigorous and powerful statistical tools for assessing model fit is crucial: by providing objective information important to model evaluation, it can help to make the dialogue between theory and data as fruitful as possible.

10.4 Key points

1. Fitting models to species abundance distributions entails considerations about four main issues: obtaining model predictions, estimating parameters, testing the goodness of fit and selecting among competing models.

2. Because sampling affects the shape of species abundance distributions, often substantially, species abundance models should incorporate a sampling theory.

3. We favour maximum likelihood methods for parameter estimation because commonly used alternatives are problematic on statistical grounds. Maximum likelihood will probably perform best when applied to abundances that have not been grouped into abundance classes, unless model predictions must be obtained by stochastic simulation. However, a rigorous comparative analysis of different approaches to parameter estimation has not yet been undertaken.

4. Rigorously quantifying goodness of fit is an important part of species abundance analysis, even if model selection is used instead of classical null hypothesis testing. Parametric bootstrapping is a robust and versatile alternative to conventional goodness-of-fit testing, particularly useful where conventional tests have low statistical power. Graphical analyses complement formal goodness-of-fit testing by helping to identify the features of the data most responsible for lack of fit.

5. Model selection statistics compare models according to different criteria, reflecting philosophical differences about the nature and purpose of statistical analysis, and they should be used and interpreted with these differences in mind. However, all involve a trade-off between how well a model fits the data in hand, and how flexible the model is (i.e. how readily it might fit noise in the data as if it were part of the pattern). Consequently, they offer a stronger basis for comparing the extent to which models capture real patterns in particular empirical data sets, relative to traditional approaches like graphical inspection and comparative analysis of goodness-of-fit statistics.

CHAPTER 11

Species occurrence and occupancy

Kevin J. Gaston and Fangliang He

11.1   Introduction

Arguably, one of the most fundamental units of biodiversity is the presence or absence of a species in a given site (a resource or habitat patch, an island, a mapping unit, etc.). This is evidenced by the fact that simple species × sites ($r \times c$) matrices, in which the presence/absence of different species (in rows r) is given for a set of different sites (in columns c), lie at the heart of probably the vast majority of biodiversity studies (Simberloff & Connor 1979; Bell 2003; Arita et al. 2008; Gaston et al. 2008a). Indeed, some of the most basic patterns which emerge from presence/absence $r \times c$ matrices have long intrigued ecologists, such as species–area relationships, nestedness, and gradients in β diversity.

Summing the presences along a row of an $r \times c$ matrix gives the level of occupancy of a given species, often most usefully expressed in terms of the proportion (p) of the available sites that are actually occupied (or, equivalently, the probability that the species occurs in any one site). This may vary greatly from one species to another, and the question of why some species are widely distributed and others narrowly has long been a staple of ecological discourse (e.g. Darwin 1859; Harper 1981; Rabinowitz 1981; Gaston 1994; Kunin & Gaston 1997). The actual area over which a species is distributed (i.e. the summed areas of the sites at which it occurs) has been termed its 'area of occupancy' (Gaston 1991; Gaston & Fuller 2009), and is important for some, particularly applied, considerations, such as evaluating the risk of extinction that species face in the short term as a consequence of anthropogenic pressures (Mace et al. 2008).

The level of occupancy attained by a species is strongly influenced by the spatial resolution of the occurrence data (i.e. by the size of a 'site'). This is simply because the level of occupancy itself fails to capture other significant features of spatial distribution, particularly the way in which at a fine resolution occupied sites are spatially dispersed. On average, of two species with the same occupancy at a fine scale, that with the more dispersed pattern of occurrences will have the greater occupancy at a coarser resolution (one simple widely used measure of this dispersion is the area contained within the geographically outermost occurrences of a species, its 'extent of occurrence'; Gaston 1991; Gaston & Fuller 2009). Although it is only relatively recently that the analytical form of the relationship between spatial resolution and the observed level of occupancy of a species (Fig. 11.1; the occupancy–area relationship) has come to the fore, the potential significance of spatial resolution on observed patterns of occupancy has been recognized for much longer (e.g. Erickson 1945; Rapoport 1982).

The occupancy of a species is only a crude caricature of the distribution of its individuals. However, the level of occupancy attained across a set of sites is inevitably a function of the number of individuals summed across those sites. Only one site can be occupied when there is a single individual (assuming that sites are defined to be at least larger than an individual), and there is almost invariably some upper limit to the number of individuals that can physically co-occur in a single site, even ignoring all of the factors that can act to disperse individuals more widely (e.g. air and water currents, life history, behaviour). Much attention has been paid to the actual form taken by occupancy–abundance relationships (Fig. 11.1), being motivated initially mostly by the wish to be able to estimate the abundance of a species from its much more readily (and

141

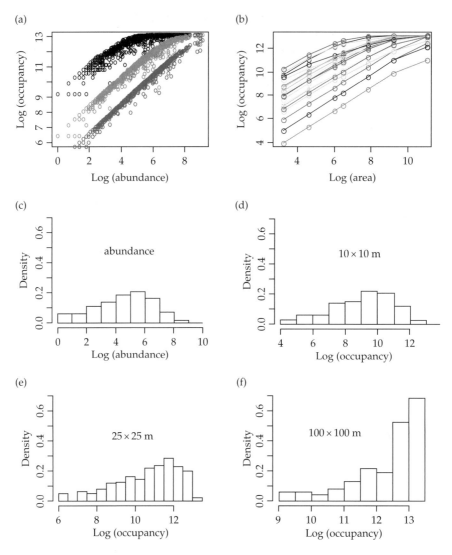

Figure 11.1 (a) Occupancy–abundance curves for 817 tree species from the 50 ha (1000 × 500 m) Pasoh forest plot, Malaysia. The lowermost curve is constructed for the occupancy calculated by cell size $a = 10 \times 10$ m, the middle curve is for $a = 25 \times 25$ m, and the uppermost curve for $a = 100 \times 100$ m. (b) Occupancy–area curves for 20 species randomly selected from the 817 species. (c) The distribution of the abundance of the 817 species, serving as a reference for the occupancy distributions of three cell sizes (d, e, f).

economically) estimated level of occupancy (e.g. Nachman 1981, 1984; Wilson & Room 1983; Kuno 1986; Ward et al. 1986). Although such considerations have in the main concerned agricultural pests (and the need for indicators of when to take control measures against them), more recently they have extended particularly to species of conservation concern (and the need to understand their

population sizes; e.g. Tosh et al. 2004; Sara 2008; Figueiredo & Grelle 2009).

By contrast, the frequency distribution of the occupancy levels of the species in an $r \times c$ matrix (i.e. the distribution of the row totals), the species occupancy distribution (Fig. 11.1), has been subject to investigation by generations of ecologists (e.g. Willis 1922; Gleason 1929; McIntosh

1962; Williams 1964; Anderson 1977; Hengeveld 1990; Gaston & Blackburn 2000). The form of this distribution serves to move consideration beyond the question of why some species are more widely distributed than others to that of why typically a disproportionately high number of species are narrowly distributed, and the circumstances in which this is not the case (e.g. Hesse et al. 1937; Hanski 1982; Gaston & He 2002; McGeoch & Gaston 2002; Storch & Šizling 2002; Gaston 2003). Answers to this latter issue have become increasingly significant with recognition that at broad spatial scales the form of species occupancy distributions may be central to an understanding of many other macroecological patterns and processes (e.g. Gaston 2003; Šizling et al. 2009).

In this chapter we provide a broad review of the present understanding of these three key patterns in the study of biodiversity, namely occupancy–area relationships, occupancy–abundance relationships and species occupancy distributions. In so doing we touch on a wide variety of issues pertaining to the ecology of the occurrence and occupancy of species. Following the bulk of the literature on these patterns, and for reasons of clarity of presentation, throughout we largely ignore the influences of variation in the detectability of individuals of given species or between different species, although clearly these can have marked influences on estimated levels of occupancy and abundance, and in empirical work will often need to be given careful consideration (see Chapter 3).

11.2   State of the field

11.2.1   Occupancy–area relationships

It has long been known that the spatial distributions of the individuals of a species are seldom, if ever, strictly random or uniform. Rather, they are aggregated on multiple spatial scales, with individuals occurring in clusters that are themselves aggregated into larger clusters, which in turn are aggregated into larger clusters still, and so forth. Many methods are available for describing such intraspecific occupancy patterns (e.g. Taylor 1984; Krebs 1999). One key approach is to characterize them in terms of simple models linking occupancy and the area,

a, of a site (here termed occupancy–area relationships, but elsewhere referred to as area–area, p–area or scale–area relationships; Kunin 1998; He & Gaston 2000a; Šizling & Storch 2004). Here sites are assumed to have some characteristic size or scale, usually because species occurrences are mapped onto an equal-area grid, from which cells at a fine resolution can easily be perfectly aggregated to form cells (and thus an occurrence map) at a coarser resolution. This is mathematically convenient, although clearly at odds with the marked heterogeneity of the natural environment and the complexities of the sizes of the set of habitat patches in which most species reside.

A large set of occupancy–area relationships take the general form

$$p = 1 - \left(1 + \frac{ca^z}{k}\right)^{-k} \quad (11.1)$$

where a is the area of the mapping unit, c and z are positive parameters, and k is a real number parameter in the domain $(-\infty, -ca^z)$, or $(0, +\infty)$ (He & Condit 2007). For a given area and k greater than 0, as k increases occupancy also increases (Fig. 11.2). For a given area and k less than 0, occupancy declines as k assumes progressively greater negative values. This embraces many of the more familiar occupancy–area relationships (see section 11.2.2 for more details) as special cases (He et al. 2002), such that

(i) $k \to \pm\infty$ and $c = z = 1$ gives the Poisson model

$$p = 1 - e^{-a} \quad (11.2)$$

(ii) $c = z = 1$ gives the negative binomial model

$$p = 1 - \left(1 + \frac{a}{k}\right)^{-k} \quad (11.3)$$

(iii) $k = -1$ gives the power-law model

$$p = ca^z \quad (11.4)$$

(iv) $k = 1$ gives the logistic model

$$p = \frac{ca^z}{1 + ca^z} \quad (11.5)$$

and

(v) $k \to \pm\infty$ gives the Nachman model

$$p = 1 - e^{-ca^z} \quad (11.6)$$

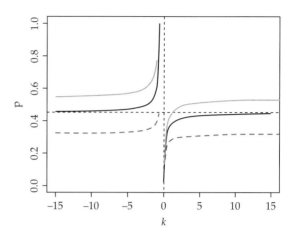

Figure 11.2 Illustration of model (11.1) as a function of aggregation parameter k, where $a = 0.6$. Black curves: $c = z = 1$; grey curves: $c = 1$, $z = 0.5$; dashed curves: $c = 0.5$, $z = 0.5$. The dashed vertical and horizontal lines are the limits of the model. The occupancy p for the horizontal line is $p = 1 - e^{-0.6} = 0.4512$, which is model (11.2).

In all cases, occupancy tends to saturate as the resolution at which this is being documented becomes coarser (i.e. as a increases). The linearized forms of these models, which are therefore often of more value for analytical purposes, are respectively (i) Poisson model: $\log(1 - p) = -a$, (ii) negative binomial model: $\log(1 - p) = -k \log(1 + a/k)$, (iii) power-law model: $\log(p) = \log(c) + z \log(a)$, (iv) logistic model: $\log(\frac{p}{1-p}) = \log(c) + z \log(a)$ and (v) Nachman model: $\log[-\log(1 - p)] = \log(c) + z \log(a)$. Note that the last three of these models share a common form in being functions of $\log(a)$. For a given set of species' occupancy data, the models can be fitted by using either a simple linear regression (with the exception of the negative binomial model, which requires a non-linear algorithm; He & Condit 2007) or a maximum likelihood method (He et al. 2002).

There has been limited comparative testing of these different models for intraspecific occupancy–area relationships, but it seems unlikely that any one of them will remain a consistently better descriptor of the patterns for different species (He & Condit 2007). However, whilst there is no evidence for its inherent superiority, versions of the power-law model ($p = ca^z$) have been particularly widely used in examining occupancy–area relationships. This is because the nested clustering of individuals of a species has led to the view that occupancy patterns can best be understood in terms of a fractal paradigm (e.g. Lennon et al. 2007; Šizling & Storch 2007). Whether one strictly

agrees with this or not, at the very least this may be a useful way to think about the consequences of a habitat hierarchy and/or a hierarchy of the ecological requirements of species in which a region is divided into broad environments defined by climate, within which are areas defined by geomorphology and substrates, divided in turn into patches of macrohabitat each comprised of different subpatches of microhabitat, and so forth (Storch et al. 2008; see also Kolasa et al. 1989).

The fractal model is more typically described as

$$p = p_0 l^{D-2} \tag{11.7}$$

where p_0 is a constant, $l = \sqrt{a}$ (i.e. l is the length of one side of a square mapping unit), and D is the box-counting fractal dimension (Lennon et al. 2007). In a stochastic fractal, the probability that a particular sub-area of a larger occupied area is occupied is a constant (i.e. it is scale independent), and D is therefore a constant (p_0 is also expected to be unity, although an empirical fit often allows it to vary; Lennon et al. 2007). Empirical studies have shown variable fits to a stochastic fractal model (e.g. Kunin 1998; Ulrich & Buszko 2003; Hartley et al. 2004; Šizling & Storch 2004; Lennon et al. 2007). Moreover, whilst a constant D may be a mathematically useful property, there is no necessary reason why it need in reality be constant (Šizling & Storch 2007) and D is often found to decrease with the increase of spatial scale (l) (He & Condit 2007). A variety of approaches have thus been taken to relax this constraint (e.g. Hui & McGeoch 2007b; Lennon et al. 2007; Storch et al. 2008). The approach of generalized fractals seems to be particularly promising (Šizling & Storch 2007; Storch et al. 2008). This retains the essential properties of fractals but does not necessitate strict self-similarity by randomly replacing an original set of areas by sets of smaller patches nested within them following a particular repeated process. Other related approaches to modelling occupancy–area relationships (and often related biodiversity patterns) have also been taken based on simple rules of the occupancy of nested grid cells (e.g. Harte et al. 2005; Conlisk et al. 2007).

11.2.2 Occupancy–abundance relationships

The general model for occupancy–area relationships described above (equation 11.1) is a simple modification of, and was originally derived from, a general model for occupancy–abundance relationships, making the assumption that mean density (μ) in the latter can be replaced by area (a) in the former (He & Condit 2007). Thus the general model for relationships between occupancy and abundance takes the form

$$p = 1 - \left(1 + \frac{c\mu^z}{k}\right)^{-k} \qquad (11.8)$$

or

$$\mu = \frac{k}{c}\left[(1-p)^{-1/k} - 1\right]^{1/z} \qquad (11.9)$$

(He et al. 2002). The associated variance–mean relationship, of considerable ecological interest itself (Gaston 2003), takes the form

$$\sigma^2 = c\mu^z\left(\frac{c\mu^z}{k}\right) \qquad (11.10)$$

where σ^2 is the (spatial) variance in abundance across areas (Holt et al. 2002a).

The special cases of this general model, derived under the same conditions as before (section 11.2.1), are generally more familiar in the context of occupancy–abundance relationships, many having been standard ecological fare for a very long time. The Poisson model ($p = 1 - e^{-\mu}$) reflects the case in which individuals are distributed in space at random, and is widely adopted as a null model for occupancy–abundance relationships (Wright 1991).

However, as we have seen, the circumstances under which this actually occurs are sufficiently scarce that the utility of such a null is very doubtful, and it is usually rapidly dismissed as a fit to real ecological data except when species are very scarce (e.g. Pielou 1977; Taylor et al. 1978; Greig-Smith 1983; Gaston 1994; Brown et al. 1995; Hinsley et al. 1996; Venier & Fahrig 1998). The usual explanation for this outcome is that there are numerous abiotic and biotic reasons why species are unlikely to be randomly distributed. However, it should not be forgotten that because such a distribution is only one among a large continuum of possibilities it may itself be exceedingly unlikely to occur on a simple probabilistic basis (Taylor 1961).

The negative binomial model ($p = 1 - \left(1 + \frac{\mu}{k}\right)^{-k}$) is the most frequently used to describe aggregated spatial patterns of the occurrence of a species (He & Gaston 2000a). However, although a large number of possible causal derivations have been identified, mostly based on the compounding of random processes (e.g. Boswell & Patil 1970; Taylor 1984), its suitability as a general descriptor of the spatial distributions of species has been much debated. Even where the negative binomial provides a reasonable fit to observed distributions of abundances, appropriate values of k are dependent on the mean density (μ; Finch et al. 1975; Taylor et al. 1978, 1979; Nachman 1981; Taylor 1984; Perry & Taylor 1985, 1986; Shorrocks & Rosewell 1986; Hassell et al. 1987; Rosewell et al. 1990; Feng et al. 1993). The negative binomial model has a variance–mean relationship of the form $\sigma^2 = \mu + \left(\frac{\mu^2}{k}\right)$ (Routledge & Swartz 1991; Perry & Woiwod 1992; Gaston & McArdle 1994).

The power-law model ($p = c\mu^z$) (Leitner & Rosenzweig 1997) follows a (positive) binomial distribution describing a regular distribution of species. It has a variance–mean relationship of the form $\sigma^2 = c\mu^z(1 - c\mu^z)$, with $c\mu^z < 1$. The power model is suitable for species of less aggregated or regular distribution, with the level of occupancy for a given abundance being greater than that for the Nachman model (below).

The logistic model ($p = \frac{c\mu^z}{1+c\mu^z}$) (Hanski & Gyllenberg 1997) describes the situation in which the occurrence of individuals of a species follows a geometric distribution (He & Gaston 2000a). Departure from this distribution is captured by c and $z \neq 1$. It has a variance–mean relationship of the form $\sigma^2 = c\mu^z(1 + c\mu^z)$, which is larger than the variance in Taylor's power model (see below), suggesting that the logistic model is appropriate to describe patterns for species having stronger aggregation than that under the Nachman model.

The Nachman model ($p = 1 - e^{-c\mu^z}$) (Nachman 1981, 1984) is suggested as an empirical generalization of the Poisson model with c and $z \neq 1$ representing a departure from the Poisson distribution (He & Gaston 2000b). The Nachman model predicts a variance–mean relationship of the form $\sigma^2 = c\mu^z$. This is Taylor's power function (Taylor 1961). It is the model that has been used most widely to describe intraspecific mean–variance relationships in empirical abundance data, although the generality of its suitability has repeatedly been challenged (Taylor 1984; Sawyer 1989; Routledge & Swartz 1991).

Similar to the occupancy-area models introduced in section 11.2.1, the fitting of occupancy-abundance models to empirical data can be done using linear (or non-linear) regression methods or maximum likelihood methods (He et al. 2002; He & Condit 2007). Occupancy–abundance relationships can be documented on the basis of intraspecific or interspecific data (Gaston et al. 2000). Note that commonly in the latter case, although less so in the former, these are documented with abundance averaged only over occupied sites (μ') rather than over all sites (μ). From an ecological perspective this has been argued to remove the likelihood of an 'artefactual' positive occupancy–abundance relationship arising (occurrence in a smaller number of sites will tend to lead to lower μ simply because the number of individuals is divided by the total number of possible sites). However, in terms of exploring the relationships between different patterns in occupancy and linking these to models in the broader statistical literature, it makes more sense to express occupancy–abundance relationships in terms of μ, as we have done here.

In the case of intraspecific data, an occupancy–abundance relationship is the equivalent of plotting occupancy at a coarser spatial resolution against occupancy at the resolution at which spatial units can only be occupied by a single individual of the species. This can be done with the data points derived either across the same set of sites at different points in time (e.g. Gaston et al. 1998a, 1999b; He & Gaston 2003; Freckleton et al. 2005; Borregaard & Rahbek 2006), or across different sets of sites in different parts of the species' geographic distribution (e.g. Venier & Fahrig 1998; He & Gaston 2003). In both cases, positive relationships are most frequently documented, although not invariably so, with a likely expected weakening for more widespread species (for which marked changes in abundance may be required, both statistically and ecologically, to result in detectable changes in occupancy). The fit of different forms of occupancy–abundance relationships has, however, seldom been tested for intraspecific data (but see He & Gaston 2003; Sileshi et al. 2006).

If intraspecific occupancy–area relationships were sufficiently similar between species, then positive interspecific occupancy–abundance relationships would tend inevitably to follow, as these would equate to plotting the occupancy achieved by a single species at a given coarser spatial resolution according to a particular scaling rule as its abundance varied. In fact, there is doubtless much latitude in how similar intraspecific occupancy–area relationships need to be in order for positive interspecific occupancy–abundance relationships to result. It is thus unsurprising that such positive interspecific relationships have been documented across a wide range of spatial scales, environments (terrestrial, freshwater, and marine), and higher taxa, almost invariably using data points derived for different species across the same set of sites over the same time period (Fig. 11.3; e.g. Gaston et al. 1998b; He & Gaston 2003; Selmi & Boulinier 2004; Heino 2008; Leger & Forister 2009). Indeed, a meta-analysis has shown that typically one-third of the variance in abundance between species is explained by differences in occupancy (Blackburn et al. 2006). The fit of different forms of occupancy–abundance relationships has, again, seldom been tested, although the general model (equation 11.8) tends often to fit very well (Holt et al. 2002a; Gaston et al. 2006).

The formation of occupancy–abundance relationships has most often been explained from the spatial perspective—any factors that would affect the

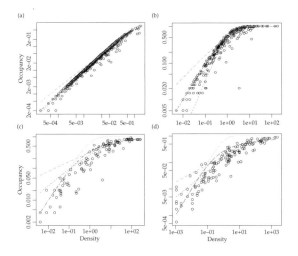

Figure 11.3 Interspecific occupancy–abundance relationships and model fits for four data sets. (a) 817 tree species from the 50 ha (1000 × 500 m) Pasoh forest plot, Malaysia, at cell size = 10 × 10 m (the same data as Fig. 1d); (b) 301 tree species from the 50 ha plot, Barro Colorado Island, Panama, at cell size = 50 × 50 m; (c) 109 bird species from Hertfordshire, England, at cell size = 2 × 2 km (Smith et al. 1993); (d) 131 bird species from south-east Scotland, at cell size = 2 × 2 km (Murray et al. 1998). The four models are Poisson (solid line), Nachman (dashed), logistic (dotted), and negative binomial (longdash). As judged by AIC, the logistic model is the best for (a) and (d), while the negative binomial is the best for (b) and (c).

spatial distribution, aggregation, or randomness in the distribution of the individuals of a species would contribute to occupancy–abundance relationships (Holt et al. 2002a). These might include niche breadth, niche position, and habitat selection (for reviews see Gaston et al. 1997, 2000; Gaston 2003). A number of empirical studies have sought to test the importance of such mechanistic drivers (e.g. Hughes 2000; Cowley et al. 2001; Simková et al. 2002; Heino 2005; Kolb et al. 2006), although the great variation in how this has been done limits the ease with which broad conclusions can be drawn. A plausible but different argument is that occupancy–abundance relationships can arise from the colonization–extinction equilibrium of metapopulation dynamics. According to metapopulation dynamics, occupancy (or the incidence function) of a species can be expressed as a function of colonization and extinction such that

$$p = \frac{C}{C + E} \qquad (11.11)$$

where C and E are colonization and extinction rates, respectively (Hanski 1994, 1997). Whilst C and E may be various functions of mean abundance (μ), the most general forms are $C = a\mu^b$ and $E = e\mu^{-d}$, i.e. colonization increases and extinction decreases with the number of individuals (Hanski 1994). Substituting these two rates into (11.11) leads to

$$p = 1 - \left(1 + \frac{c\mu^z}{1}\right)^{-1} \qquad (11.12)$$

where $c = a/e$ and $z = b + d$. Equation 11.8 is a generalization of equation 11.12, pointing to the connection between metapopulation dynamics and occupancy patterns.

A more interesting approach is to equate equations 11.8 and 11.11, leading to

$$\frac{C}{E} = \left(1 + \frac{c\mu^z}{k}\right)^k - 1 \qquad (11.13)$$

This model postulates a relationship between spatial aggregation as represented by k and colonization–extinction processes. Consider a metapopulation with fixed μ. Under this condition, when k approaches 0 (i.e. the population is extremely aggregated), equation 11.13 equals 0, i.e. $C/E = 0$. This means that spatial aggregation results if colonization is extremely low or extinction is extremely high. This result is consistent with observations that species aggregation can be closely associated with poor colonization ability (Tilman et al. 1997a).

11.2.3 Species occupancy distributions

In isolation, understanding of the form of occupancy–area relationships provides limited insight into the relative frequency with which, at a given spatial resolution, the species in an assemblage will attain different levels of occupancy. A diversity of assumptions have thus been made about the variation amongst species in the scaling of occupancy with area to enable prediction of the shape of species occupancy distributions (e.g. Hui & McGeoch 2007a,b; Šizling & Storch 2007; Storch et al. 2008). In the main, although not exclusively, attention here has focused on very fine spatial resolutions (i.e. a is small), at which point the species occupancy distribution equates to the species abundance distribution (assuming that only a single individual can fit within any given spatial unit). This is because of the great interest in being able to extrapolate from relatively coarse species occupancy data, which are for many species relatively easily obtained (although not necessarily for rare ones), to abundance data, which are much more difficult and expensive to acquire (e.g. Kunin 1998; He & Gaston 2000a; Tosh et al. 2004; Sara 2008; Conlisk et al. 2009; Figueiredo & Grelle 2009). Although species abundance distributions are discussed at greater length elsewhere in this volume (Chapter 10), it is notable that the predictions from occupancy–area relationships can provide particularly good fits to empirical abundance data (e.g. Storch et al. 2008).

Species occupancy distributions will change with spatial resolution, such that those at coarser resolutions may often be of rather different shapes from species abundance distributions. This can be simply illustrated by assuming that (i) the species abundance distribution follows a log-normal distribution

$$f(x) = \frac{1}{\sqrt{2\pi}\sigma x} e^{-\frac{1}{2}\left(\frac{\ln(x)-\mu}{\sigma}\right)^2} \tag{11.14}$$

where x is abundance and μ and σ are the mean and variance of $\log(x)$, and (ii) the occupancy–area relationship takes a Poisson form

$$\frac{y}{A} = 1 - e^{-ax/A} \tag{11.15}$$

where a and A are the spatial resolution and extent, respectively, and y is the occupied area. Our interest is to find out the distribution of y and how the resolution would affect the distribution. By the technique of random variable transformation from x to y, it is easy to show that y has distribution

$$h(y) = \frac{A}{a} f\left(-\frac{A}{a}\log(1 - \frac{y}{A})\right)\frac{1}{A-y} \tag{11.16}$$

Note here that $f(.)$ is the log-normal distribution of equation 11.14. From Fig. 11.4, it is apparent that when a is small, the species occupancy distribution (equation 11.16) is virtually the same as the species abundance distribution. However, as a increases the species occupancy distribution shifts toward the

right. When a increases further, the distribution of more and more species saturate the entire study area, making the occupancy distribution upturn at the far right (right panels of Fig. 11.4). This upturn merely reflects the effect of spatial resolution, with little biology. Note that if other occupancy–area models are used in place of the Poisson model the species occupancy distribution (equation 11.16) can have multiple modes.

Typically, the number of species with low occupancy will increase as spatial resolution increases, and also will increase with the spatial extent of a study and sample number; the opposite will be true for species with high occupancy (McGeoch & Gaston 2002). However, because the details of occupancy–area relationships differ between species, the picture may become rather more complex than this. Indeed, although the potential for marked variation in species occupancy distributions with spatial resolution has been shown to arise both from relatively simple occupancy–area models (Hui & McGeoch 2007a, 2007b) and empirically (Collins & Glenn 1997; Guo et al. 2000; van Rensburg et al. 2000; McGeoch & Gaston 2002), it remains an open question to what extent the wide range of observed forms of species occupancy relationships can be explained on this basis alone. McGeoch & Gaston (2002) observe that across a diversity of spatial resolutions and extents documented forms include unimodal distributions with peaks at low, intermediate, or high levels of occupancy; bimodal distributions with dominant peaks at low, high, or both low and high levels of occupancy; and uniform or apparently random distributions. At the scale of the entire geographic ranges of species, species occupancy distributions tend invariably to be strongly right skewed (Gaston 1996a, 2003).

The importance of spatial resolution for the shape of species occupancy distributions may be reflected in a number of other mechanisms that have been postulated as explanations, including those based on habitat and environmental heterogeneity (see McGeoch & Gaston 2002). The principal alternative set of mechanisms are rooted in colonization/extinction dynamics, which may yield a wide variety of species occupancy distributions, dependent on the assumptions that are made as to

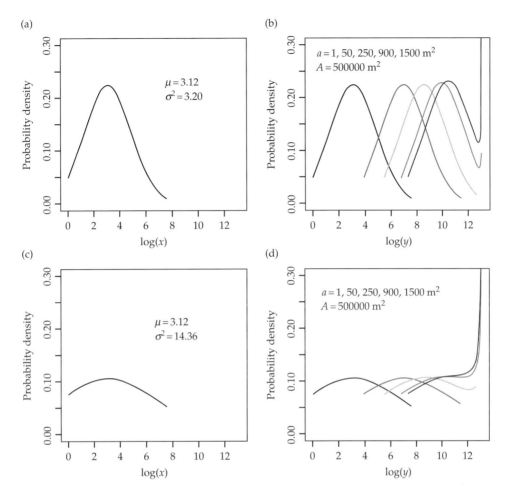

Figure 11.4 The effect of spatial scale on the relationship between species abundance distributions and species occupancy distributions. All the distributions are plotted on a log scale. The left panels are the log-normal species abundance distributions (model 11.14). The first set of log-normal parameters ($\mu = 3.12$, $\sigma^2 = 3.20$) were calculated from the tree species abundances of the 50-ha plot on Barro Colorado Island, Panama (for those trees of size ≥ 10 cm). In the second row, the variance is arbitrarily set to 14.36 to illustrate how variance affects occupancy distribution. The right panels are the respective species occupancy distributions (model 11.16) corresponding to the log-normal distribution. In both cases, the total study area is set to be 50 ha. The density curves from left to right correspond to the cell sizes $a = 1$, 50, 250, 900, and 1500 m^2.

how rates of site colonization and extinction change with overall levels of occupancy and local abundance (Hanski 1982; Gotelli 1991; Warren & Gaston 1997).

11.3 Prospectus

Understanding of the form, determinants, and implications of occupancy–area relationships, occupancy–abundance relationships, and species occupancy distributions has increased markedly in

recent years and doubtless will continue to do so. In this regard, we make four main sets of suggestions:

(i) Predicting abundance from occupancy: Substantial success has been achieved in predicting the abundance of a species from its spatial occupancy for study areas of small extent (e.g. of a few hectares or a small number of sites; He & Gaston 2000a; Sileshi et al. 2006; Conlisk et al. 2009). However, this is of only limited practical benefit, given that it is relatively easy to estimate abundance more directly at such scales. Of far more importance would be an ability to predict abundance from occupancy at scales of hundreds or thousands of square kilometres, where direct estimation is extremely resource demanding and sometimes virtually impossible. Unfortunately, the methods presently available are of limited value for this purpose, commonly leading to under-estimation of numbers of individuals at such scales even by several orders of magnitude. A major challenge is how best to develop methods that are more appropriate. We doubt that occupancy data alone will be sufficient for this purpose, but suggest that some combination of broad-scale occupancy data and fine-scale abundance data from one or a few small areas are probably needed. Together, these will provide a hierarchical understanding of species distribution, which may provide a much more secure basis for the upscaling of abundance to large geographic areas.

(ii) Detectability: As stated at the outset, for ease of presentation throughout this chapter we have ignored issues of differences in the detectability of species in sites, and particularly the frequent under-estimation of levels of occupancy and abundance that result from individuals being overlooked during field sampling. Increasingly sophisticated methods of improving the estimation of both variables are available (see Chapter 3). From the perspective of the estimation of abundance from occupancy, of particular interest is the modelling of detectability probabilities based on time series data on occupancy (MacKenzie et al. 2002, 2003; Royle et al. 2005). Consideration of such approaches highlights that the effective evaluation both of existing and novel methods of predicting abundance may require better estimations of actual occupancy than have in some cases thus far been employed.

(iii) Temporal dynamics: More generally, the contents of this chapter have provided a reasonable reflection of the ecological literature at large in focusing primarily on occupancy–area relationships, occupancy–abundance relationships and species occupancy distributions based on estimations of the occupancy of a

species at a given time or averaged over a given period, and in the main ignoring the temporal dynamics of occupancy (but see Gaston & Lawton 1989; Webb et al. 2007; Heino 2008; Zuckerberg et al. 2009). However, particularly in light of the rapid changes in the distributions of species being wrought as a consequence of anthropogenic pressures (including climate change), a fuller understanding of these patterns is undoubtedly required. Of particular value would be much improved knowledge both of how the different patterns change through time and of how changes in the occupancies of species modify the observed patterns.

(iv) Mechanisms: Among the many factors that can potentially affect species occupancy, species abundance and the spatial distribution of that abundance are the most immediately significant. Other factors do so through their effects on these variables. Given the numbers of possible such variables, and the indirect and scale dependent nature of their effects, their influence may often be difficult to detect other perhaps than under highly controlled circumstances (e.g. microcosms; Gaston & Warren 1997; Warren & Gaston 1997; Holt et al. 2002b, 2004a). This may well in large part explain the great controversies that have raged around the possible influences of niche breadth and position and dispersal abilities on levels of occupancy. In consequence, we do not expect that a single coherent mechanism will be determined that gives rise to occupancy patterns.

11.4   Key points

1. Occupancy is a fundamental measure of the distributions of species in landscapes. It is a function of their abundance and spatial distribution. A locally abundant species typically has higher global occupancy, and vice versa. On the other hand, spatial aggregation reduces occupancy. These two general qualitative patterns are described by the occupancy–abundance and occupancy–area relationships. Although many potential mechanisms give rise

to these relationships, colonization/extinction dynamics play a key role in determining occupancy.

2. Occupancy is scale dependent. The scale not only refers to the spatial resolution at which a species is mapped, but also to the spatial extent over which the species is studied. Because of the effect of scale, the measurement and quantification of occupancy can become complex. Comparison of occupancies for two or more species is irrelevant unless the spatial scales are compatible. Ideally, this should be done using occupancy–area curves, which describe the change of occupancy across the full range of spatial resolutions.

3. The most important application of the occupancy–abundance relationship is to estimate species abundance from occupancy. Present methods have met with a certain degree of success for relatively small spatial extents. Their usefulness in estimating abundance at the regional scale remains to be tested, although it is likely that they will substantially under-estimate regional abundance. It will be a major breakthrough if methods can be developed to estimate abundance from regional occurrence data.

4. Occupancy is the basic unit underlying several macroecological patterns, including species–area curves and gradients in β diversity. Assuming $p_i(a)$ is the occupancy probability of species i in a site of size a, then the species–area curve is simply the sum of probabilities across all species. β diversity can also be formulated by a conditional probability through occupancy: given a species is present in an area, what is the probability that the same species will occur in another area at distance d away?

Acknowledgements

KJG was supported by The Royal Society and The Leverhulme Trust, and FH by the NSERC (Canada).

CHAPTER 12

Measuring the spatial structure of biodiversity

Brian J. McGill

12.1 Introduction

Tobler (1970) coined the first law of geography: 'everything is related to everything else, but near things are more related than distant things'. Put in other words, the second half of Tobler's law is 'far things are less related' or just 'everything varies across space.' Biodiversity certainly follows this law. It is well known that diversity varies latitudinally with the highest diversity in the tropics (Rosenzweig 1992; Kreft & Jetz 2007), but variation in biodiversity occurs at all spatial scales (Lennon et al. 2001; Rahbek & Graves 2001). The abundance of an individual species also varies across space (Brown et al. 1995); even whether a species is present or absent varies across its range (Chapter 11). Of course this should come as no surprise because the underlying environmental variables such as elevation, temperature, and soil properties also vary across space. How can such variation in biodiversity across space be quantified and understood?

For a long time the main method was to develop a checklist—a list of all species found within a geographic entity like a park, county/shire, state/province, or country. But this approach is not particularly strong in capturing the spatial structure. In recent times, there have been increasing numbers of spatially dense biological surveys, especially surveys of birds and trees conducted by national governments. With the advent of GIS technology it is possible to display this data in richly coloured maps (Kreft & Jetz 2007). This allows visual inspection of patterns. This book, however, is mainly focused on the quantification of biodiversity, which requires going beyond maps. Recent decades have seen an explosion of the field of spatial statistics (Cressie 1992; Fortin & Dale 2005). Although spatial statistics received much of its development in applications to mining (ore concentrations measured across space) the tools are applicable to a broad range of fields, including sociology and epidemiology. More relevantly, spatial statistics has a long history of use in the measurement of the biodiversity and abundance of organisms, which is summarized here.

Unfortunately, there has been a great proliferation of spatial statistical techniques, so starting out in spatial statistics can be overwhelming. Books on spatial statistics, whether targeted at statisticians (Cressie 1992) or ecologists (Perry et al. 2002; Fortin & Dale 2005), list dozens of different techniques. There have been a few attempts to find links between the methods (e.g. Dale et al. 2002), but there has been distressingly little effort to emphasize the underlying unity of methods to ease the learning curve for beginners. In this chapter I will adopt the attitude that details of calculations can be left to software and emphasize the conceptual unity of and the interpretation of results for the different methods. To begin to navigate the plethora of spatial statistics methods, I lay out three main axes of importance: what spatial structure is being explored, pattern vs. association, and type of data.

12.1.1 What spatial structure is of interest?

Modern spatial statistics has converged around the model:

$$z(s) = \mu(s) + \eta(s) + \varepsilon$$

where z(s) is the variable of interest (e.g. biodiversity, abundance of a target species), μ(s) is the average value of z in the area of spatial location s, ε is noise or measurement error, which does not depend on spatial position and is independent (uncorrelated) across space, and η(s) is variability about the mean that is spatially structured (i.e. correlated across space). It is common to refer to μ as a first-order effect because it looks only at one point in space at a time and η as a second-order effect because it, by definition, depends on two points in space at once. I extend this semantics to refer to ε as a zeroth-order effect since it does not depend on space at all. Fig. 12.1 explores what the variation in z across space is like with different combinations of zeroth-, first-, and second-order

effects. Conveniently, and not coincidentally, this mathematical organization matches nicely with the two most common questions one asks about the spatial structure of biodiversity.

Question 1: First-order effects—is there variation across space?

The most basic and most useful question is whether there is systematic change in the variable of interest across space. For example, are there regions where diversity or the abundance of a target species is particularly high or particularly low? From a basic research point of view this is interesting because it raises the question of 'why?' Questions of what controls diversity and abundance are central to ecology and exploring how this varies across space

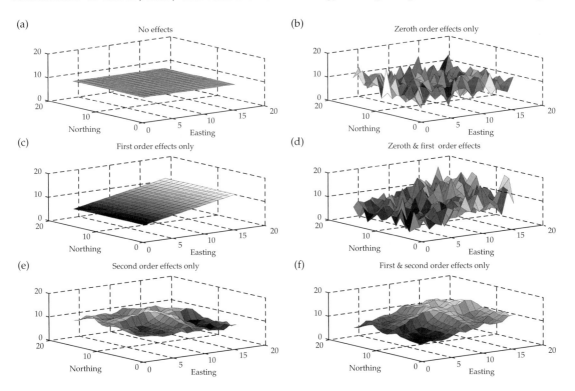

Figure 12.1 Different order effects in spatial modelling. (a) No effects: the measurement variable (possibly abundance of a species, possibly species diversity, possibly soil moisture) is entirely constant. (b) Only zeroth-order (measurement error, innate variability or noise) effects. The variable is on average constant but there is variability. The variability is completely independent, even between adjacent points. (c) First-order effect: a systematic change in the mean of the variable across space. Here a simple linear trend is modelled, but of course if the mean is tracking some underlying variable like soil depth the system can look rugged and irregular even with only first-order effects. (d) Combined zeroth- and first-order effects. Here there is variability due to zeroth-order effects overlayed on top of the same first-order trend in the mean found in (c). (e) Second-order effects only. The mean is constant across space and no measurement error is modelled, but there is autocorrelated variability. When one point is above the mean, adjacent points are more likely (although not guaranteed) to also be above the mean. This starts to give rise to coherent features that are spread across several points, like the peak in the back corner or the trough running across the front corner. (f) Second-order effects (e) overlayed on top of first-order effects (c).

is one of the easiest ways to study these questions. From a management point of view, identifying specific areas of high abundance or diversity can lead immediately to management decisions such as the location of reserves in biodiversity hotspots (Prendergast et al. 1993; Reid 1998) or minimizing human impact from roads and buildings in regions of high abundance for an endangered species. Statistically, these questions all map back to questions about first-order processes—changes in the intensity of a process (the mean value of the variable measured, e.g. biodiversity) across space.

Question 2: Second-order effects—do distant points have effects?

Imagine we have measured the biodiversity at location A. Do we attempt to explain the level of biodiversity at A solely as a function of exogenous variables (temperature, soil, etc.) at A? Or is biodiversity at A in part a function of biodiversity elsewhere in the landscape? If a nearby location B is extraordinarily high in biodiversity might there be a spill-over effect (perhaps B serves as a source and A as a sink, elevating the diversity at A beyond levels the environment there would otherwise support). If B is having a spill-over effect, might location C, which is twice as far away, also be having a spill-over effect on A? Exactly how far from A can we get and still credibly have a spill-over effect? Similarly, for a single species with a given abundance at A, is this abundance only a function of the properties of location A or might the abundance at site B also have an effect? These types of questions are about interactions at a distance. In technical terms, they are question about second-order effects in spatial statistics. When interactions at a distance are positive they tend to create clumping (Fig. 12.3b), while negative interactions tend to create regular distributions (Fig. 12.3c). Interactions can be positive at some scales and negative at other scales (Fig. 12.3e and f).

12.1.2 Number of variables recorded – pattern or association?

As summarized in the last section, to determine which spatial statistical techniques to use, we need to know whether we are studying first-order or second-order effects. We also need to know whether

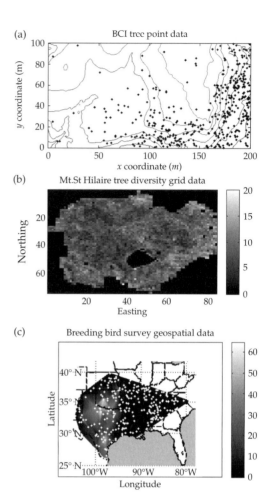

Figure 12.2 Different types of spatial data. (a) Point data from Barro Colorado Island's tropical tree study. This map shows the location of individual trees of the species *Licania platypus* (with a diameter at breast height of 1 cm or greater). Elevation contours are plotted as well, showing the plant is biased towards slopes (Condit et al. 2000; Harms et al. 2001). (b) This plot shows how the species richness of trees varies across the Mt St Hilaire nature reserve. The data are collected on a regular grid of 50 × 50 m cells. (c) This plot shows how the abundance of an individual species of a bird (the scissor-tailed flycatcher) varies across space (notice that the highest abundances are in Texas and Oklahoma, but the range extends all the way east to the Carolinas). The white dots represent routes where the birds were surveyed and are placed irregularly in space. Data from the North American Breeding Bird Survey (Robbins et al. 1986; Patuxent Wildlife Research Center 2001).

one is looking for patterns in one target variable of interest (such as species richness or abundance of a target species) or if one is recording multiple variables (such as other species or environmental variables) and attempting to find associations between the variables. With multiple variables, finding associations can inform about the causes of or lead to predictive models about a variable of interest. Thus, one can build a spatially informed model of which environmental variables increase species richness. Or one can build a predictive model about which habitat factors are associated with high abundance for an endangered species. Such associational analyses have traditionally been done in a non-spatial context, treating measurements across space merely as replicates and using methods such as regression to find the patterns. There is, however, growing awareness that if the replicates are across space then are a number of spe-

cial statistical challenges and opportunities. These are discussed in section 12.2.3 below.

12.1.3   Types of data

Sections 12.1.1 and 12.1.2 lay the main conceptual axes along which geospatial statistics are organized. However, there is also one practical consideration. What type of data is collected? Data on biodiversity across space can take many forms (Fig. 12.2, Table 12.1). As in other areas of statistics, different techniques are required when the data structure differs, even if fundamentally similar questions are

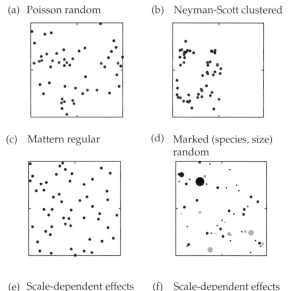

(a) Poisson random

(b) Neyman-Scott clustered

(c) Mattern regular

(d) Marked (species, size) random

(e) Scale-dependent effects

(f) Scale-dependent effects

Figure 12.3   Different kinds of second-order (point interaction) processes give rise to different spatial patterns. (a) A Poisson random process. (b) An example of clustering (attraction between points) simulated by the Neyman–Scott process. (c) An example of regular or over-dispersion (repulsion between points) simulated by the Mattern hard-core process. (d) A process where the locations are Poisson random, but the points are marked by two features: size (e.g. tree diameter) and black/gray (e.g. species). (e) An example of scale-dependent effects: random at small scales, clumped at larger scales, and over-dispersed at very large scales. (f) Another example of scale-dependent effects which appear regular at small scales but random at large scales.

Table 12.1   Major categories of spatial data (section 12.1.3).

Spatial sampling design		Binary variable (present/absent)	Continuous variable (amount/abundance)
Sampler controlled	Regular across space	'Presence/absence quadrat'	Quadrat
	Random across space	'Presence/absence geospatial'	Geospatial
Biology controlled		Point-process	Marked point-process

asked. The single most important question is the nature of the spatial structuring of the data and is described by the dichotomous key below:

(a) The locations recorded are controlled by natural events → **individual point-process data**. Examples include the locations of tree trunks in forest, bird nests, or lightning strikes (Fig. 12.2a).
(b) The locations are chosen by the scientist in the design of the sampling protocol.
  i The locations are spaced regularly across space → **quadrat data**. Examples include quadrats arranged across a line (transects) and quadrats arranged across a rectangular area. In addition to the regularity of the data there is also an assumption that some area (line or rectangle) has been exhaustively covered (Fig. 12.2b).
  ii The locations are spaced irregularly, perhaps apparently randomly across space → **geospatial data**. Examples include counts of abundance of a target species in quadrats where the quadrats are scattered across a large area or soil moisture at irregular spacing across an area. The location may be literally random (a randomization was used in the protocol) or may be just irregular, with the actual locations driven in part by accessibility to roads and trails, etc. (Fig. 12.2c).

Note that there is a gradient as one proceeds from the top (a, individual point processes) to the bottom (b-ii, geospatial data). As one moves down, the amount of information decreases, but the ease of obtaining the information increases. Type a data can be converted to type b-i data, which can be converted to type b-ii data but not in the other direction.

Although it will not affect the type of analysis done, many readers will be aware that the spatial scale at which the data are measured can have profound implications for the results found and the types of questions that can be asked. The scale of the data is usually described by two terms. The grain is the scale of a single measurement. Thus if a single measurement is a 1×1 m quadrat (as is common in grasslands), then the grain is 1 m (or $1\,m^2$ depending on if lineal or areal measurements are used). The

extent is basically the distance between the farthest apart measurements. This can range from metres to thousands of kilometres. The number of sampling units, N, is another key attribute of any survey. These three factors, if grain and extent are measured in areal units, can be combined to describe the coverage of the study (coverage = $N \times$ grain/extent, giving the percentage of the study area actually measured). In point-process and quadrat data (types a and b-i above) it is often assumed that coverage is 100% while the geospatial data survey method is often chosen when the resources available for survey are inadequate to provide 100% coverage of the area of interest. The results of analyzing data can depend heavily on the scales involved (see Fig. 12.3e and f, described later for an example). There is no such thing as a best scale for grain or extent. The goal is that the scales should be chosen to match the question at hand. Thus, if one is studying bird dispersal, then the grain should be small relative to the dispersal distance but the extent should be large relative to the dispersal distance. If one is studying tree mortality, which is a rare event, then the total area covered ($N \times$ grain) needs to be large while the extent should match the question (is one making an assertion about mortality across the geographic range of a species or in a specific park?).

In summary the combination of: (i) two types of question (section 12.1.1), (ii) two options for number of variables recorded (section 12.1.2), and (iii) the three types of data (section 12.1.3), from a $2 \times 2 \times 3$ grid to determine what types of spatial analysis tools can and should be performed (Table 12.2). If one has a spatial dataset but doesn't know what types of analyses to perform, one should start by determining where in this $2 \times 2 \times 3$ grid the data and the questions of interest fall.

12.2 State of the art

Despite the seeming complexity of 12 cells and an implied 12 types of geostatistics, there are really only three basic approaches: one must decide if one is looking at first-order effects, second-order effects, or associations between two variables. From there a single conceptual approach will apply, although the

Table 12.2 Common spatial statistics applied depending on the type of spatial data available, the question asked, and the number of variables measured.

		Point locations	Quadrat counts	Geospatial
One variable only	**What is intensity (interpolation and smoothing)**	Grid, kernel smoothing	Local smoothing	Local smoothing (with interpolation)
			Trend surfaces Kriging	
				Trend surfaces Kriging Covariograms, etc.
	What is effect at distance? Are they aggregated?	Ripley's K	Moran's I	
			Mantel	Spectral Mantel
Two variables (dependent, independent)	**What controls intensity**	Intensity regression	Spatial regression	Spatial regression
	Interactions occur at distance	Cross K	Mantel	Cross-variogram
				Mantel

details of the exact procedure will vary depending on the type of data.

12.2.1 Estimating intensity (first-order effects)

One central goal of spatial analysis (question 1) is simply to create a map of intensity across space where intensity is the value of the variable of interest such as species richness or target species abundance). This then allows exploration of what factors cause high vs low intensity and management decisions based on areas that are favourable (e.g. high intensity of the target organism). Two issues arise in creating such maps. First, if coverage is less than 100% (i.e. the area sampled is a fraction of the area of interest, typically the geospatial data case), then **interpolation** is needed to make a prediction about the areas that are not sampled. Second, whether the coverage is 100% or not, there is a goal to remove the zeroth-order noise and find the underlying 'true' signal. One would hate to locate a critical management resource (e.g. extra food) at a site to find out it appeared to have a high density

due to chance on the day the survey was done with no unusually high abundance ever observed since. This process of removing noise is called **smoothing**. Usually one technique accomplishes both smoothing and, if needed, interpolation. We discuss four broad classes of techniques that can be used.

- **Local surfaces (smoothing):** Many techniques can be grouped together as smoothing (Fig. 12.4b). For any point where a prediction is needed, the predicted value is a weighted average of nearby observed points. If the prediction is to be made where an observation was made then only smoothing is involved, but if the prediction is for where no observation was made then interpolation is also occurring. Typically nearer points are given a greater weight, w_i. This can be captured in the equation:

$$z_p = \frac{\sum_{i \in S} w_i z_i}{\sum_{i \in S} w_i}$$

The predicted value z at point p is a weighted average of the observed values z_i over some subset, S, of all the observed values. The simplest case is nearest neighbour interpolation where $w_i = 1$

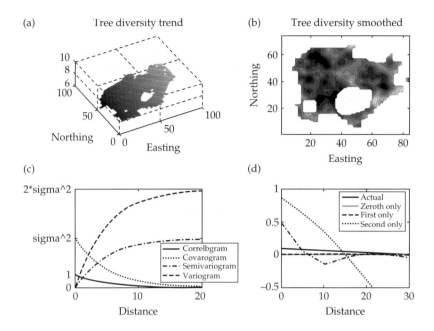

Figure 12.4 Example output from analyses of data discussed in the text. (a) A trend surface (global smoothing) fitted to the data of Fig. 12.2b. Generally, diversity increases from west to east which also matches a transition from active human use to a protected area. (b) The same data kernel-smoothed (Gaussian kernel) and plotted in a coloured contour plot. Considerable variation occurs with peaks on the north and east edges of the lake (large empty region in the centre). (c) Four types of 'grams' on a theoretical data set showing the rescalings that occur. (d) Correlograms on theoretical data (Fig. 12.1) with zeroth-, first- and second-order effects, and then actual data from Fig. 12.2b. Note that the zeroth-order effect shows 0 correlation at all distances—there is no spatial interaction. The first-order effect starts with a very high correlation at short distances and goes to a very negative correlation at long distances due to the trend surface. The second-order effects start with a fairly high correlation in nearby sites, which drops to a negative correlation at the distance at which peaks to valleys are compared and then fades to zero correlation at long distances, indicating no interactions. Thus this analysis gives a clear indication of the scales of interaction. The actual data show a low, but positive, correlation at short distances fading out to zero correlation at longer distances.

if the point i is the closest point to p and $w_i = 0$ otherwise. Moving average is another technique on gridded data where $w_i = 1$ for the cells within h cells of the target cell p. A similar approach used on geospatial data is the moving window, where a box with sides of length h are drawn around each point and $w_i = 1$ if the point i is in the box and zero otherwise. Similar techniques can be used where points are differentially down-weighted the further away they are. Exponential smoothing, where $w_i = \exp(-hd_{ip})$, where d_{ip} is the distance between i and p, is a common choice. The most modern and probably best technique is known as kernel smoothing, which weights the points according to a symmetric probability distribution, $k(d, h)$, centred around the point p and where $w_i = k[||p - i||/h]$. A two-dimensional Guassian bell curve is a common choice for k, so

$w_i = \exp(-d_{ip}^2/h^2)$, as is the quartic kernel, $w_i = 3(1 - d^2/h^2)^2/\pi$ when $d < h$ and 0 if $d > h$. In the quartic case any point further than bandwidth h away has no effect whereas in the Guassian it has an increasingly small effect. Notice that in all of these scenarios the specification of a smoothing parameter h is required where h is a measure of the distance at which effects are still important. As h increases more smoothing occurs. In the limit when h is very large a completely flat surface (Fig. 12.1a) will be produced.

- **Global surfaces (trend surfaces):** In contrast to smoothing approaches, which are local in nature, a trend surface is a global prediction that can be summarized by relatively few parameters. A trend surface is described by a function:

$$z_p = f(x(p), y(p)|\theta)$$

where $x(p)$ and $y(p)$ give the x and y coordinates (possibly latitude and longitude) of the point and θ is a set of parameters (Fig. 12.4a). The function f can vary from simple to quite complicated. The simplest trend surface to fit is a linear model where f is a plane (i.e. $z_p = \beta_1^* x + \beta_2^* y + c$). Such fitting is usually done by a least-squares criterion and is basically just a two-variable regression with the independent variables being spatial coordinates. The next step up is to use a polynomial. A quadratic polynomial would be $z_p = ax + bx^2 + cy + dy^2 + exy + f$. A quadratic polynomial yields a three-dimensional parabola and as such can only represent a unimodal (one-peaked) surface. More commonly cubic or quartic polynomials are used. The number of coefficients that need to be estimated goes up quickly with degree (linear = 3, quadratic = 6, cubic = 10, and generally a polynomial of degree p has $(p+1)(p+2)/2$ coefficients). Care must be used. Fitting a quartic ($p = 4$) polynomial with only 20 data points would leave only 5 (20–15) degrees of freedom, which is probably too low to be reliable. A variety of functions with f more complex than polynomials can also be used. For example, if one is modelling a surface that varies periodically, sine or cosine functions may be appropriate.

- **Kriging:** The first two techniques (local and global surfaces) deal only with first-order effects. However, second-order effects can also impact the predicted values z_p. Over very large distances the second-order effects should decay to zero and a surface based on first-order effects will be unbiased (i.e. be accurate on average). However, on smaller scales second-order effects can significantly affect the predicted values. Knowing that the variable of interest (e.g. abundance) is unusually high at a point p implies that it will usually be unusually high in a neighbourhood around p. First-order processes take this into account to some degree (small bandwidths h and highly flexible global surfaces f are strongly influenced by local conditions). However, a second-order effect is probably a more accurate way to incorporate this information and allows us to make inferences about the nature and distances of interactions. The means to do this is called kriging. Kriging also has the statistically desirable prop-

erty of being a minimum variance estimate. Kriging is the attempt to produce more accurate predictions of intensity by combining first-order and second-order analyses of the data. Further discussion of kriging is postponed to section 12.2.2, where second-order effects are covered in detail.

- **'Let it all hang out':** One approach is to not smooth or interpolate but simply to report the data as it exists. Press and colleagues argue for just this approach (2007). The human mind is naturally good at interpolation. It is only moderately good at smoothing, but certainly it can detect and dismiss outliers.

In comparing these techniques, three things are worth noting. First, the global trend surface approach is effectively making a prediction for all points in the area of interest. The smoothing and kriging techniques only make predictions for a specified set of points $p \in P$. This set can either be a set of target points of interest (e.g. locations under consideration for management decisions) or it can just be a regularly spaced grid of fairly fine resolution placed across the area of interest. Once a trend surface or a grid of predicted points is in hand, the data can be plotted in a number of ways. Three-dimensional surface plots (12.4a) are most commonly used for trend surfaces. Contour maps are probably the most common way to plot smoothed data. In either case colour (or greyscale) intensity can be overlaid.

Secondly, of the four techniques for estimating intensity surfaces, the fourth is the only one directly applicable to point-process data. To estimate intensity surfaces across space from point-process data (e.g. density of tree trunks), two choices are available. The first is to lay a grid over the data and then count the number of points in each grid cell, thereby moving from type i data to type ii-a. Then any of the four techniques can be used. This entails a loss of information and works best when the points are fairly dense in space. Secondly, the local surface method can be modified where instead of using z, the observed intensity at a point, one uses counts of points (replace z_i with n_i) and adjust the weights by area so $n_p = \sum_{i=1}^{n} \frac{1}{h^2} k\left(\frac{p-p_i}{h}\right) / \int_A \frac{1}{h^2} k\left(\frac{p-u}{h}\right) du$ with the intensity at a point p basically being a density weighted average of neighbouring points. Neighbour-based methods to estimate intensity go back to the early days of forestry (Konig 1835), but they are accurate only if complete spatial randomness with no second-order effects holds (see Box 12.1) and are not generally recommended today (see section 12.2.2 for a brief description of one of these methods).

Finally, the first two techniques require the input of a smoothing parameter (degree of smoothing). The smoothing parameter is implicit as the bandwidth, h, in the local smoothing case and implicit in the flexibility of the function f (e.g. degree of polynomial) in the global surface case. If too much smoothing occurs then true variation will be eliminated, but if not enough smoothing occurs then noise will be represented as pattern. Unfortunately, there is no way to determine the mathematically correct smoothing parameter, despite the existence of various guidelines and rules of thumb. The smoothing parameter is ultimately a subjective, human-chosen parameter. The third approach (kriging) essentially derives the degree of smoothing from the data itself and must be considered to have an advantage for this reason. The final approach also avoids a smoothing parameter. Overall, kriging has often been avoided due to its perceived complexity, but with software readily available this argument has lost weight. On the whole I would recommend kriging in combination with always plotting the 'let it all hang out' approach for comparison.

12.2.2 Studying effects at a distance (second-order effects)

Second-order effects assess how the value measured (e.g. biodiversity or abundance) at one point influences the same property at other points some distance away. There are a couple of reasons why one might want to study second-order effects. Most simply, one might wish to make more accurate predictions of intensity (i.e. using kriging). A more involved reason would be to test whether there are effects over distance and whether these effects are positive or negative. An even more informative question is to look at how these effects vary with distance. For example, it is possible that having a high abundance at one site makes sites 10–100 m

away more likely to have a higher than average abundance while making sites 0–10 m away more likely to have a lower than average abundance. This has strong implications for spacing requirements, which in turn has implications for minimal areas to contain a viable population. From a basic research point of view, this then immediately leads into research questions about what processes cause these effects (dispersal limitation, species interactions, resource competition). Additionally, second-order effects are directly related to the goal of measuring whether distributions are clumped or regular. For example, Gaston and He (Chapter 11) describe in detail the study of mean occupancy (percentage of patches occupied) but do not analyze the spatial structure of the occupied cells, specifically whether the occupied cells occur in clumps or not. Second-order effects deal with this problem; positive second-order effects say that knowledge that a species is found at one site implies a greater than average probability of encountering that species at other nearby sites, leading to clumping, while negative second-order effects imply an unusually even spacing (regularity) (see Fig. 12.3).

- **Early approaches:** The oldest method for exploring second-order effects is the variance-to-mean-ratio used on counts taken in quadrats. This test derives from the fact that the variance of the Poisson distribution is equal to the mean of the distribution, μ. This is an unusual and strong property (compare to the normal distribution, where the mean and variance are completely unrelated). Thus we can examine the index of dispersion ID = var(z_i)/average(z_i) = $\left[\sum_{i=1}^{n}(z_i - \overline{z_i})^2/(n-1)\right] / \left[\sum_{i=1}^{n} z_i/n\right]$. Under the null CSR/Poisson assumption (see Box 12.1), ID = 1. When ID > 1, then there are more quadrats with either very low (near zero) or very high (well above average) abundance, which is a sign of a clumped distribution (positive or attractive second-order interactions). Conversely, when ID < 1 then most quadrats have z_i very close to $\overline{z_i}$, which is a sign of regularity. Conveniently, if $n > 6$ and $\overline{z_i} > 1$ then $(n-1) \times$ ID is distributed approximately as a chi-square distribution with $(n-1)$ degrees of freedom, which allows for tests of whether ID is significantly larger or smaller

Box 12.1 Null models and significance tests

With the exception of spatial regression (section 12.2.3), little has been said about the central concern of most statistics: assessing statistical significance. While spatial statistics are frequently used in a purely descriptive fashion, significance tests can be readily fashioned if one has a clear concept of the null model.

Spatial null models

The simplest null model is that the variable of interest is constant across space (see Fig. 12.1a), but this is not particularly useful. Null models need to include statements about variability. The traditional spatial null model goes under varying names such as 'homogenous Poisson process'. The key assumptions of this model (with reference back to equation 12.1) are:

1. First-order: the intensity (expected mean value of the target variable) is constant across space or homogeneous: $\mu(s) = \mu$.
2. Second-order: there are no second-order effects, every location is spatially independent of every other location: $\eta(s) = 0$.
3. Zeroth-order: the noise or error is Poisson distributed: $\mu + \varepsilon \sim Poiss(\mu A)$.

where μ is average density and A is area. This fully specifies a precise mathematical model. Poisson processes have no memory—that is to say the probably of an event occurring is completely independent of whether an event occurred nearby.

Conveniently this single null model applies to both types of data: type a (point process or nature determined locations; see Fig. 12.2a) and type b (measurements at points or grids; see Fig. 12.2b and c) data. Also conveniently, it is trivial to run a computer simulation of this null model:

1) Sample the number of points N from a Poisson distribution with parameter $A\mu$ (A = area).
2) Rescale the spatial coordinates to range from 0 to 1 on both axes and then sample two random uniform numbers over the interval 0–1 (something which nearly every programming language provides).
3) Treat these as the x, y coordinates of the points.

A final convenient fact is that the probability of a non-empty region is given by

$$P(k > 0|\mu A) = 1 - P(0|\mu A) = 1 - e^{-\mu A}.$$

The Poisson model gives a good analytical null model. When a null (randomization) model on empirical data is needed complete spatial randomness (CSR) is used. For sampling data (type b data) where a value z is recorded at different points (or grid cells), simply reshuffle. Take the observed values, z_i, and randomly assign them to a different point or grid cell, i.e. a shuffling or sampling without replacement. This will keep the intensity (μ) constant (point 1 of the null model) and remove second-order effects (point 2 of the null model). The noise (η or point 3 of the model) may or may not be Poisson distributed depending on whether the original data were, but it is usually considered a good thing that the underlying distribution of the data is preserved. To simulate CSR from point data (type a data), just randomly relocate each point individually (independent of the other points). Again assumptions 1 and 2 will be met. Thus the Poisson process serves as an analytical null model while the closely related CSR serves as a Monte-Carlo or randomization null model for empirical data.

Statistical significance on grams and $K(d)$ and $g(d)$ statistics

There are several ways to test the statistical significance of a gram (most commonly whether a correlogram is statistically significantly different from zero at some distance, d). The distribution of Moran's I is known analytically (Box 12.2 and Legendre & Legendre 1998), allowing for a simple analytical test of significance. More generally, a randomization test can be performed. Reshuffle the data as described above to convert the data to a sample from the CSR model. Calculate the correlogram that results. Repeat this, say, 999 times and draw the 95th percentile envelope of these randomizations. Portions of the correlogram that are outside the envelope are significant. Unless one has a prior hypothesis and is testing significance at only one distance bin, any significance test on a correlogram faces a problem of 'multiple tests'; if there are 20 bins there are 20 tests of significance and the probability of making a type I error (believing the null model is rejected when it should not be) is high. All the classic approaches to multiple tests apply. The Bonferroni test (use significance levels of 0.05/n instead of 0.05) is used most commonly, but it is overly conservative (Garcia 2004 and see solutions therein).

Continued

Box 12.1   (*Continued*)

A very similar technique can be used to test for statistical significance on the $K(d)$ and $g(d)$ statistics on point data. Simulate many replicates of CSR on the data (randomly relocate each point) or, equivalently, simulate a Poisson process with the observed number of points. Then calculate the statistic of interest, say $g(d)$, on each simulation. Then the 95th percentile envelopes can be drawn. Places where the statistic goes outside the envelope are significant. Issues of multiple tests arise as in the tests of correlograms.

Mantel tests

A Mantel test (Mantel 1967) is really nothing more than a way of calculating statistical significance on the correlation between two distance matrices. In one scenario, a Mantel test serves as a test for second-order effects. Here, one matrix would hold the physical distance $||i - j||$ between each pair of points in the appropriate cells of the matrix. The other matrix would hold the difference in observed values, $z_i - z_j$. In the other scenario, the Mantel test serves as a test of association at a distance between two variables similar to cross-kriging (section 12.2.3). Here one matrix contains the distance between points in, say, environmental

space (temperature, precipitation, etc.), while the other matrix contains the distance between points in, say, biodiversity, $z_i - z_j$ (or distance in community structure using a measure of dissimilarity like Sorenson or Morisita Horn; see Chapter 6). Once one has two distance matrices, whatever the exact scenario, the process is the same. Each matrix is square with one row and column for each point. One first calculates a correlation coefficient, r, on the $n(n - 1)/2$ cells in the matrix above the diagonal. The calculation can be a Pearson or Spearman correlation. This value r then serves as a measure of association between the two distance matrices just as in traditional correlation analysis (and ranges from -1 to $+1$). The key innovation is in using a permutation test to test significance, which is necessary because of the spatial autocorrelation between the sites. Because a site is represented by both a row and a column, one can not just randomly reshuffle the entries in a matrix, but must simultaneously shuffle rows and columns. Under this constraint, many replicates (e.g. 999) of multiple permutations of one matrix are done and then a new r correlation is calculated between the cells of the two matrices for each replicate. The significance of the unshuffled r value can be assessed as the percentile of the true r vs all of the r values calculated from permuted matrices.

than 1. There has been a great deal of criticism levelled at the ID (Hurlbert 1990) and it is true that ID = 1 does not imply a Poisson process, but ID > 1 or ID < 1 does imply clumping or regularity respectively. A more telling criticism is that this measure has no spatial structure (two quadrats 1 km apart are compared in the same way that two quadrats 10 m apart are), but this is such a quick and dirty measure it belongs in the toolbox of spatial analysis. The first attempts to incorporate spatially explicit measures of second-order interactions (where quadrats far apart are treated differently to those close together) apply only to point-process data and are based on distance to the nearest point. Diggle's function $G(d)$ is defined as the fraction of points p_i where the nearest neighbour of p_i is at a distance less than or equal to d. Under the null hypothesis of CSR, $G(d) = 1 - e^{-\lambda \pi d^2}$ (see Box 12.1) and an empirically observed $G(d)$ can be plotted against the null $G(d)$. First-order information (inten-

sity) can also be derived from nearest-neighbour information under (and only under!) the assumption of CSR, where a maximum likelihood estimate gives $\lambda = 4/(\pi \overline{d^2})$ (Diggle 1983). The related function $F(d)$ gives the probability that the distance from a randomly chosen location in the area (which will usually not coincide with an observed point) to the nearest observed point is less than d. The use of these functions and related ideas based on nearest-neighbour distances, such as the Clark–Evans ratio, the Hopkins ratio, and the Blyth–Ripley ratio, are losing favour because they are poor estimates of second-order effects under some scenarios. Imagine the scenario where every point in a random process is replaced by two points a constant, very small, distance apart. The nearest-neighbour distance will imply perfect regularity (nearest neighbour at a constant distance) even though the data are strongly clumped at a slightly larger scale and generally give a poor picture of overall second-order effects at greater distances (see Fig.12.3e and f). As a result, other than the quick and dirty use of the ID, second-order effects should be estimated using estimates that incorporate all spatial distances, not just nearest neighbours. The exact nature of these estimations depends on whether the data points are nature-controlled (point-process) or human-controlled (quadrat and geospatial).

- **'Grams' and kriging:** We cover the approach for quadrat/geospatial data first, where there are several closely related ways to describe second-order effects (Fig. 12.4c and d). The most direct is the idea of covariance $Cov(z_i, z_j) = \sigma_{ij} = \frac{1}{n}\sum_{k=1}^{n}(z_{i,k} - \bar{z})(z_{j,k} - \bar{z})$. Note that $Cov(z_i, z_i) = Var(z_i) = \sigma_i^2$. Such a definition assumes that we have multiple measures of $z_i(k = 1...n)$ at each spatial location, which is rarely the case (although it could happen if, for example, we take repeated measures over time). This definition is also extremely complex in that a covariance is calculated for each pair of points. Both of these problems can be fixed by studying $C(d) = \sigma_{ij}(d) = \frac{1}{n_d}\sum_{\|i-j\|=d}(z_i - \bar{z})(z_j - \bar{z})$. Here we assume covariance depends only on the distance, d, between two points $\|i - j\|$ and calculate the covariance between all n_d pairs of points that are distance d apart. On gridded data and for discrete distances there are likely to be many points that are exactly d units apart for $d = 1, 2, ...$. On geospatial data, where d is continuous, it is unlikely to find two pairs of points that are exactly the same distance apart. In this case it is common to group data into bins and take all points that are between d and $d + \delta d$ units apart. This binning is similar to what occurs in the creation of a histogram. A rule of thumb (Rossi et al. 1992) is that each bin should have 30–50 data points. Moreover d should typically only go up to half the maximum distance between points (when d is close to the maximum observed distance one is only comparing edges to edges, which may not be representative). A plot of $C(d)$ vs d is called a covariogram. According to the first law of geography, the covariance should decrease with increasing distance, eventually reaching zero, and this is in fact what is observed. Typically $C(0) = \sigma^2$ (the variance in the data) and this decreases

in an exponential- or hyperbolic-like fashion to $C(\infty) = 0$. Certain circumstances can also cause negative covariances. For example, if the data form a peak (e.g. Fig. 12.1e) then distances that match the distance from peak to the valley around it will actually have a negative covariance. Several closely related plots can also be calculated (see Fig. 12.4c). A correlogram $\rho(d)$ is simply the covariogram $C(d)$ rescaled to vary between -1 and 1, just as a correlation coefficient does (the rescaling is based on the fact that Pearsons $r = \sigma_{ij}/[\sigma_i \sigma_j]$). A variogram analyzes not the covariance of two points but the variance of the differences of two points as $V(d) = E\left[(z_i - z_j)^2\right] = \frac{1}{n_d}\sum_{\|i-j\|=d}(z - z_1)^2$ with the same notation as for the covariogram. A factor of two appears because the pair i, j is counted twice in $z_i - z_j$ and $z_j - z_i$. Thus most often the semivariogram defined as $\gamma(d) = V(d)/2$ is more convenient to analyze (so for example $\gamma(\infty) = \sigma^2$ while $V(\infty) = 2\sigma^2$), but is often confusingly just called the variogram. The semivariogram is related to the covariogram as $\gamma(d) = \sigma^2 - C(d)$ (although in practice estimates of $\gamma(d)$ and $C(d)$ do not fit this relationship, for example $\gamma(0)$ is rarely 0 as this formula would require). In general, if the data violate the assumptions of stationarity (discussed in Box 12.2) the equivalences begin to breakdown. Thus all four 'grams' are related linearly (I use 'grams' as a generic term to refer to the set of the four different types of plots: $C(d)$, $\rho(d)$, $V(d)$, and $\gamma(d)$). In summary, correlograms and its relatives provide a simple graph that enables one to determine at what spatial scales the variable of interest is interacting (the regions of d where the highest or lowest regions of the graph occur). They also allow for determination of whether the effects are positive or negative (the sign of the graph). Kriging, which is a spatial form of smoothing, makes use of 'grams' to determine how to weight the points. In a certain technical sense (minimum variance) this is the optimal weighting. See Box 12.2 for more details on kriging.

- **Second-order processes in point-process data:** Earlier in the chapter a fundamental distinction between data where the point locations were driven by nature and where they were chosen by the human was set out. The 'gram' analyses in the

Box 12.2 More details on grams

Because correlograms and related 'gram' techniques are so important (arguably the single most important tool in spatial ecology), more details are given here for the interested reader.

Correlograms or semivariograms?

The main difference between the 'grams' is that the covariogram and correlogram isolate interactions only at distance d, while the (semi)variogram describes an accumulation of effects up to distance d. In this sense the difference is conceptually similar (although not mathematically equivalent to) the difference in probability theory between a probability theory density function (PDF) and a cumulative density function (CDF). The strengths and weaknesses of the different approaches come from this fact. I find the correlogram the easiest to interpret. If the line is above 0 at distance d then there are positive (attractive) second-order effects at distance d and similarly for negative effects. This is less obvious from a (semi)variogram. All regions d of the variogram are positive; where the slope is steep represents high positive correlation while a shallow slope represents low correlation. In other words, a high variance at distance d, $V(d)$, may be due to processes causing high variability near $d = 0$ or to processes causing high variability near to d or at any distance in between. Conversely, however, estimates of the variogram are generally considered more robust to outliers and hence more accurate. This is largely because the first-order process for a variogram, $E(z_i - z_j)$, must equal zero, but the first-order process for a covariogram, $E(z_i)$, is not generally zero and must be estimated.

Grams on gridded/lattice data

The use of 'grams' has come from the world of geospatial data where points are random, continuous distances apart. However, they carry over with little modification to gridded data. Indeed, gridded data can make their application easier in practice. For continuous data one must find an appropriate bin size δ so that enough points occur in each bin. In gridded data, this is not a problem. The natural distance of the grid can be used, where it is guaranteed that there will be many pairs of points that are one cell length apart, two cell lengths apart, etc. Early analyses of

gridded data ignored most diagonal pairs (e.g. a cell three cells North and two cells East), but if each grid cell is located at its centre these distances can also be calculated and the bins can be centred around discrete cell lengths as in 0.5–1.5, 1.5–2.5, 2.5–3.5, etc. cell lengths. Prior to the dominance of the 'gram' format, the Moran's I and Geary's C statistics were used. These were typically applied to gridded data and used only on non-diagonal distances. Interestingly, aside from being designed for gridded data, Moran's I corresponds exactly to the correlogram and Geary's C corresponds to the variogram divided by σ^2 (Fig. 12.5). Moran's I and Geary's C are also often commonly applied to irregular polygon data such as when a variable is known for each county or shire. In these cases an adjacency matrix W is developed that gives the distance between each pair of polygons. Moran's I and Geary's C can then be generalized to use W instead of the classic discrete cell distances. However, in the end all these methods directly relate to the correlogram and variogram. They are treated here as conceptually identical with the difference occurring only in the practicality of the calculations (which can be relegated to software). One minor difference that is important is that, unlike the correlogram, Moran's I can go outside of the interval $(-1, 1)$ and for no correlation (i.e. CSR) has $I = -1/(n-1)$ instead of $I = 0$, where n is the number of observations. As n gets large the difference disappears.

Describing the shape of a gram

Aside from visual inspection of a correlogram or semivariogram, several analyses can be done. Variograms are often described by three measures: $\gamma(0)$ is called the nugget (this is theoretically zero but empirically usually not), the asymptote, $\gamma(\infty) = \sigma^2$ is called the sill, and the distance d at which the sill is hit is called the range. To approximately describe shape over the entire range of distances, one can use a model of the form $\gamma(d) = f(d|\theta)$ or $\rho(d) = G(d|\theta)$, where θ is a set of parameters that can be fit to the empirically estimated grams. This can smooth out some of the noise in estimation. It also allows comparison of the parameters between different 'grams'. The semivariogram is an increasing, decelerating, asymptoting function and is typically fit by the spherical model $f(d|r) = \sigma^2[3d/2r - d^3/(2r^3)]$ if $d \leq r$ or σ^2 if $d > r$, by the exponential $f(d|r) = \sigma^2(1 - e^{-d/r})$, or the Gaussian $f(d|r) = \sigma^2 \left(1 - \exp\left(-d^2/r^2\right)\right)$. All three models pass through (0,0) and asymptote at (∞, σ^2) with one scale parameter r. Offsets can be added to allow for a sill (e.g. $f(d|r) = a + (\sigma^2 - a)(1 - e^{-d/r})$ for the exponential. The correlogram is typically fit by simple exponential decay $G(d|r) = \exp(-d/r)$ and the covariogram by $G(d|r, \sigma^2) = \sigma^2 \exp(-d/r)$.

Kriging (interpolation and smoothing with grams)

Kriging, mentioned in section 12.2.2 as a means of making predictions of intensity that incorporate both first- and second-order effects, builds directly on the fact that the covariogram can be described by only the two parameters, σ^2 and scale r. In the local smoothing methods of section 12.2.3 the question arose of how much weight to give to points at a distance d away, and the only answer was to choose an arbitrary smoothing or bandwidth parameter h. The covariogram and a fitted model $G(d|r, \sigma^2)$ provide an obvious answer: weight points that are a distance d away by the amount $G(d|r, \sigma^2)$! The empirical covariogram curve contains many degrees of freedom and could not be practically estimated, but if we fit a model and boil it down to two parameters, we only lose two degrees of freedom and now get an empirical estimate of how best to incorporate second-order effects.

We can now return to equation 12.1 $(z(s) = \mu(s) + \eta(s) + \varepsilon)$ where μ is some surface (e.g. linear) of spatial location and ε is a function only of the distance between two points and is described completely by the covariogram and its two parameters (η is assumed to be distributed normally with mean zero and variance τ^2, just as in traditional regression). Equation 12.1 essentially now conforms to the generalized least squares (GLS) or mixed model forms of regression. Although not well known, these are standard statistical techniques, and methods for fitting them are readily available (typically involving some iterative solutions and likelihood methods). In practice the semivariogram (which is more stable) is used rather than the covariogram. Conceptually, this is all there is to kriging. The details are left to the software. Several flavours of kriging exist. Simple kriging assumes $\mu(s) = 0$ (or that μ is known instead of estimated) and

is not too common. Ordinary kriging assumes $\mu(s) = c$ with c to be estimated and requires that the user ensure that there are no trends in the data (or that the trends be removed and residuals analyzed; see next paragraph). Universal kriging models the full equation 12.1 with first-order and second-order effects treated simultaneously.

The key assumptions: stationarity and isotropy

The assumption made throughout this section on 'grams' (that second-order effects - i.e. covariance - depends only on d) is in fact an assumption that may be untrue. One common violation is when covariance depends on direction. This could occur if dispersal limitation is a major driver of second-order effects and dispersal depends on prevailing winds or stream currents. When covariance is independent of direction we call it isotropic and we call it anisotropic if covariance is a function of direction. Another violation is when the covariance depends on location. This could occur in the previous scenario if the strength of prevailing winds or currents varies significantly across space. A full definition of stationarity (the usual assumption in spatial statistics) is that the mean is constant (expected value $E(z_i) = \mu$ independent of location i) and that the covariance σ_{ij} depends only on the distance between i and j. The condition on the mean is probably more commonly violated than the condition on the covariance. For example, a simple gradient or trend in z_i across space violates stationarity. It is common to fit a trend surface to the data and then to analyze the second-order structure (covariance) on the residuals, thereby removing the trend. On gridded data, differencing $z'_i = z_{i+1} - z_i$ will also remove a trend. With the exception of some analyses that deal with anisotropy, the covariance condition for stationarity is almost always assumed to be true. If worried, this can be checked using local autocorrelation statistics. Local autocorrelation statistics (Anselin 1995) calculate a measure of correlation for each point just with nearby points but do not average this correlation together with the neighbour correlations of other points (as is done in a global correlogram). The result can be plotted as an intensity of local correlation. If this varies drastically across space, then the assumption of stationarity may not be justified. If a particular process is hypothesized (such as dispersal limitation) to cause the covariance structure, then local autocorrelation statistics can be an indicator of the varying strength of that process across space.

previous section are the dominant tool for study-ing second-order effects in human-driven data. They look at differences in z as a function of dis-tance between the points (d_{ij}). In point-process data, we look instead at the number of points within a neighbourhood of distance d. The F and G statistics mentioned earlier are examples of this but in their focus on nearest neighbours can be dominated by smaller scale second-order effects. The superior approach is known as Ripley's K. This method estimates the average number of points with a neighbourhood of radius d around the points in the point process. This is then nor-malized by dividing by the intensity. By explor-ing various radii around a point, it avoids the problems of nearest-neighbour statistics. $K(d)$ is simple to estimate. If $N(d, p_i)$ is the number of points in a radius d around point p_i (not including the point p_i), then

$$K(d) = \frac{1}{n\mu} \sum_{i=1}^{n} N(d, p_i) \quad L(d) = d - \sqrt{\frac{K(d)}{\pi}}$$

Under the Poisson null hypothesis (Box 12.2), the average number of points in an area A is μA and for a circle of radius d it is $\mu \pi d^2$. $K(d)$ = the aver-age number of points$/\mu = \pi d^2$. This fact is used to create the closely related statistic L, where $L(d) = 0$ for all values of d under CSR. When $L(d) > 0$ then the points are regular at scale d and clumped if $L(d) < 0$. Unfortunately there is not a strong convention for $L(d)$ and some people use $L^*(d) = -L(d)$, so it is important to read carefully when looking at $L(d)$ diagrams. Conceptually, $K(d)$ and $L(d)$ are similar to the semivariogram and the cor-relogram (Fig. 12.5). $K(d)$ and semivariograms are cumulative and monotonically increasing. Correlo-grams and $L(d)$ are referenced relative to zero (with CSR giving a flat line at zero). Locations where the correlogram or $L(d)$ are noticeably above or below the line (equivalently $K(d)$ and semivari-ogram change slope sharply) indicate clumping or regularity at those scales. I prefer an ecologically less-well-known alternative to $L(d)$ that is common in physics and known as the pair correlation func-tion $g(d) = K'(d)/(2\pi d)$ (Wiegand & Moloney 2004). Thus $K(d)$ is a cumulative density function and g(d), being the rescaled derivative to it is related to the probability density function. The rescaling

ensures that $g(d) = 1$ under CSR. Thus, from an interpretation point of view $g(d)$ plays a very sim-ilar role to $L(d)$ and correlograms but it is shifted up to $g(d) = 1$ instead of $L(d) = 0$ or $\rho(d) = 0$. So $g(d) > 1$ equates to clustered patterns and $g(d) < 1$ relates to regular patterns. I prefer $g(d)$ because $L(d)$ is derived from $K(d)$ under the assumption of CSR while $g(d)$ is derived from $K(d)$ more generally with no assumption of pattern. Perhaps the best-known application of $g(d)$ to ecology is by Condit and colleagues (2000), who looked at the spatial aggre-gation of tropical trees; they called their function omega, $\Omega(d)$, but this is just a rescaled version of $g(d)$, which has much longer precedence outside of ecology.

12.2.3 Associations between two variables

Section 12.2.1 dealt with first-order effects with one variable and section 12.2.2 dealt with second-order-effects with just one variable. Of course it is very common to have more than one variable. For example, one might wish to explore how the abundance of one species covaries with the abun-dance of another species or whether large-ranged species covary with a different set of environmental variables than small-ranged species (Jetz & Rahbek 2002). Several techniques are available to address such questions.

Cross-correlograms and other 'cross-' (second-order) associations
Nearly all of the second-order techniques already identified in section 12.2.2 can be applied to two variable problems. So, for example, where a covari-ogram looks at the average value of $(x_i - \bar{x})(x_j - \bar{x})$, the cross-covariogram looks at the average value of $(y_i - \bar{y})(x_j - \bar{x})$ (where y and x are two different variables and and i and j are still two different points). This is called a cross-covariogram. Cross-correlograms, cross-semivariograms, and cross-$K(d)$ and cross-$g(d)$ statistics can also be calculated. These statistics reveal the second-order interactions between two variables, for example does high soil moisture nearby at point B make high species rich-ness more (positive correlogram) or less (negative correlogram) likely at point A. Cross-correlograms can also be used to leverage information from vari-

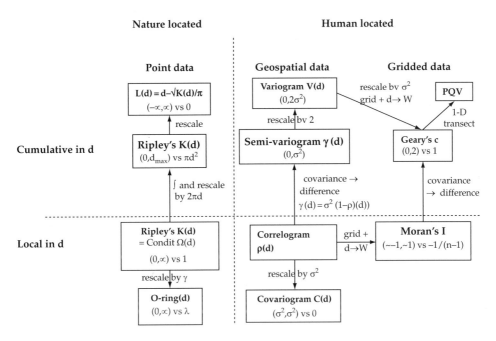

Figure 12.5 The relationships between the most common second-order spatial statistics. In almost all cases, the conversions are simply a matter of linear rescaling ($g(d) = a \times f(d) + b$) or moving between a cumulative vs a local form. Minor adaptations are also needed when moving from continuous space (geospatial data) to discrete space (gridded data) or from two dimensions to one dimension. In this figure, d = distance between two points, λ = intensity (average number of events per area), W = aconnection matrix (on gridded data or on areal data such as a map of states), and $\sigma^2 = Var(z_i)$ the variance of the z value across all points in space. The most commonly used technique for each type of data is in bold print. The phrase 'grid + d $\rightarrow$ W' indicates that the data, instead of being located continuously in space, is located on a grid and consequently the idea of a distance, d, between two observations is replaced by a notion of adjacency, summarized in the matrix W. Note that there are no arrows connecting point data to geospatial data, indicating that the match is conceptual rather than mathematical.

ables that are measured at fewer locations than the target variable of interest in the form of cross-kriging. These models are all analogous to traditional correlation in that there is symmetry between the variables involved.

Spatial regression (first-order associations and possibly second-order associations)

If a more quantitatively predictive model is required and there is a presumption about which variables are dependent and independent, then regression techniques are more appropriate. Imagine trying to predict species richness (S) as a function of temperature (t) and tree height (h), using measurements of all three variables at many sites across space. The simplest approach is a classic multivariate regression $S_i = \beta_0 + \beta_1 \times t_i + \beta_2 \times h_i + \varepsilon_i$ for $i = 1 \ldots n$ fit via ordinary least squares (OLS). The problem with this approach is that a

key assumption is that the errors are independent ($Cov(\varepsilon_i, \varepsilon_j) = 0$). This is almost never true in a spatial context and would technically count as pseudoreplication (Hurlbert 1984). Aside from this worry, we might actively wish to incorporate first-order effects or second-order effects. Further complicating the picture is that the second-order effects might come in as an effect of S_j on S_i (spill-over effects, possibly due to dispersal), t_j on t_i (temperature is nearly always autocorrelated), or by effects of ε_j on ε_i (autocorrelation of errors). At the extreme we could imagine setting up a regression such as:

$$S_i = \beta_0 + \beta_1 \times t_i + \beta_2 \times h_i + \gamma WS + aVt$$

$$+ [x, y]\zeta + \eta + \varepsilon_i \qquad (12.2)$$

where W is a matrix giving spatial distance derived weights (and with 0s on the diagonal so that S_i does

Table 12.3 A summary of symbols used.

$\mu(s)$	Intensity: the average value (first-order effect)
$\eta(s)$	Covariance or effect at a distance (second-order effect)
ε	Uncorrelated error
$z_i, z(s)$	A measured value (e.g. density, temperature) at point i or location s
w_i	A weighting for point i
$k(d,h)$	Kernel (probability density function) used in kernel smoothing
β, θ, ξ	Coefficients in regression models (β, ξ) or parameters (θ) in non-linear functions
h	The smoothing or bandwidth parameter (bigger h smooths over larger areas)
n	The number of points
$\|i - j\|, d_{ij}$	The distance between points i and j
d	Distance
ID	Index of dispersion
$G(d)$	Diggle's function for point processes
$C(d), \rho(d)$	Covariogram and correlogram, respectively; second-order effects for geospatial data
$V(d), \gamma(d)$	Variogram and semivariogram, respectively; cumulative second-order effects for geospatial data
$K(d), L(d), g(d)$	Ripley's K for point processes, $L(d)$ is the null for $K(d)$, $g(d)$ is the pair-correlation function
$f(d|\theta), G(d|\theta)$	Functions fit to (semi)variogram and covariogram/correlogram, respectively
$I(d), C(d)$	Moran's I and Geary's C functions analogous to grams on lattice data
CSR	Complete spatial randomness: a null model for spatial processes
$E[]$	Expected value (mean)
σ, σ^2	Standard deviation and variance

not depend on S_i) and γ indicates the strength of such effects (i.e. is a coefficient to be estimated), similarly for V as a spatial weight matrix and α as a coefficient, $[x,y]$ is a matrix of the spatial coordinates of the points with ζ being coefficients (i.e. fitting a linear trend surface) and η a random term with $E(\eta) = 0$ and $Var(\eta)$ being a covariance matrix of second-order effects (possibly derived from a model of a covariogram). The term $[x, y]\zeta$ incorporates first-order effects (and presumably is capturing the effects of environmental variables that were not measured and used in the model). The terms γWS and αVt capture the second-order effects from the dependent and independent variables and are collectively known as 'lag' (derived from time-series lags) or autocovariate terms while η captures second-order effects as an 'error' term and by depending on a covariance matrix is closely related to the 'gram' techniques above. To my knowledge no one has ever been crazy enough to try and fit the entire model given above, but a variety of techniques have been proposed which fit some subset of the model. Such regression techniques that use some subset of equation 12.2 are known as spa-

tial regression and, being explicitly aware of spatial relationships, are designed to address the shortcomings of OLS on spatial data. A good review of various spatial regression models is by Dormann and colleagues (2007).

Very often when a field sees a new technique introduced, there is a period where methods proliferate and become increasingly confusing and then finally a consolidation phase is reached where the strengths and weaknesses are identified and the toolkit is narrowed back down to one or two techniques. The study of spatial regression (at least in ecology) appears to be just entering this consolidation phase with a robust debate occurring (Lennon et al. 2000; Jetz & Rahbek 2002; Diniz et al. 2003; Dormann 2007a,b; Hawkins et al. 2007; Kissling & Carl 2008). Although it is still early, I will provide my personal recommendation. First, there is growing evidence that the original non-spatial OLS may not be so bad. A regression produces three results, estimates of the coefficients β, a measure of fit (r^2), and a measure of the significance (chance of the null hypothesis of $\beta = 0$ being true). Theory predicts, and studies have shown (Dormann 2007b;

Hawkins et al. 2007; Kissling & Carl 2008), that even in the face of spatial autocorrelation the estimates of β are unbiased (on average correct), almost as efficient (i.e. standard errors of β only slightly larger) as spatial regression estimates, and the r^2 for OLS is lower than in spatial regression but spatial regression has more parameters. The only real problem with OLS is that the p values are very wrong (much more type I error than reported by the p value). If one only cares about prediction and not testing then this is not a problem. If one cares about testing, then there are two choices. Simulations have shown that the p value can be very accurately corrected using Dutelliel's method, which adjusts the degrees of freedom in the model downwards depending on the amount of autocorrelation (more degrees of freedom lost with high autocorrelation) (Dutilleul et al. 1993; Dale & Fortin 2002; Fortin & Dale 2005). The other choice to get accurate p values is to use a spatial regression model. Which one to use? There is growing evidence that lag-based models can be biased and should not be used (Dormann 2007a). This leaves the error approach, where η is incorporated. This has the added advantage of boiling down to the already known general least squares (GLS) or the slightly more general linear mixed model (LMM) approach and the use of covariograms to describe η. A further advantage is that these techniques readily generalize to binomial (logistic) and Poisson regression. So my recommendation is to (i) run an OLS, (ii) calculate a correlogram on the residuals $y_i - \hat{y}_i$, (iii) if the correlogram shows significant autocorrelation in the residuals then do not use the p values from the OLS, and (iv) if you need p values then use spatial regression based on errors (GLS/LMM) if and only if second-order effects are of interest to you but otherwise just use Dutelliel's correction to the OLS p values. This recommendation will be enormously controversial but it is my best read of current evidence combined with an inclination to stick with tried and true methods unless there is a compelling reason not to.

Variance partitioning

As one might imagine, interpreting all of the coefficients in the regression of equation 12.2, even if only a subset of it is used, can be overwhelming. A useful tool is variance partitioning (Borcard et al. 1992). Variables can be lumped into groups (e.g. environmental and spatial), and then the amount of variation explained by each group can be assessed. Of course the environmental and spatial variables are collinear (correlated with each other) and regression does not have the ability to resolve this. The result is that a percentage variance is assigned to each of four categories: environmental only, spatial only, environmental and spatial combined, and unexplained. Together these percentages sum to one (the sum of the first three is the r^2 of the environmental + spatial model). Calculating these numbers is easy. Run three regressions (environment + spatial, environment only, and spatial only) and note the r^2. Then %environment only $= (r^2_{\text{environment+spatial}} - r^2_{\text{spatial}})$, %spatial only $= (r^2_{\text{environment+spatial}} - r^2_{\text{environment}})$, %environment/spatial combined $= r^2_{\text{environment+spatial}} - \%\text{environment only} - \%\text{spatial only} = r^2_{\text{environment}} + r^2_{\text{spatial}} - r^2_{\text{environment+spatial}}$ and %unexplained $= 1 - r^2_{\text{environment+spatial}}$. Very often the combined environment/spatial variance explained is much larger than either factor alone, which is disappointing as this is the least informative category. It is not surprising, but worth noting, that the proportions assigned to each category can depend on how many variables are used in each category. Dozens of environmental variables and just $x - y$ spatial coordinates biases toward environment explaining a higher proportion, and using a few environment variables while using a complex representation of space (e.g. PCNM; Dray et al. 2006) can tilt things the other way (Jones et al. 2008). The variance partitioning approach just described treats each factor as conceptually equal. An alternative approach can treat one factor as having precedence. In this case if we give environment logical primacy over spatial, then %environment $= r^2_{\text{environment}}$ and %spatial $= r^2_{\text{environment+spatial}} - r^2_{\text{environment}}$. This was done for example by Lichstein and colleagues (Lichstein et al. 2003) and also done implicitly when using regression on residuals (e.g. Wilcox 1978). There is considerable controversy again over which is the right approach. Ultimately, however, it is not a question answered by the mathematics, it is a matter of assumptions and appropriateness for the question at hand.

12.2.4 Software available

I have consciously chosen to emphasize the conceptual unity of spatial statistics. However, in doing this I have swept under the rug a large number of issues. The practical calculations can depend heavily on the exact type of data used. Moreover, I have completely ignored the issue of edge effects (the fact that some points are near the 'edge of the earth' or at least the edge of the sampled data raises complications for many methods). There are several methods for dealing with edge effects but they complicate the calculations. Finally, statistical significance tests are most often done by randomization methods, which are not conceptually difficult but require additional computer code. For all of these reasons, I strongly recommend using off-the-shelf software for spatial analysis rather than implementing your own methods. Two excellent and free pieces of software are available for immediate download that handle all of the methods discussed herein. The first is spatial analysis of macroecological (SAM) data (Rangel et al. 2006). This is a custom-built software package targeted at spatial analysis of ecological data. It contains an easy-to-use interface and an impressive list of spatial methods. The more generic (and harder to use) package is R, a general purpose statistical package (R Development Core Team 2005) with the addition of readily available packages (libraries) in R, including spatial, spatstat and splanc (for point processes), gstat (for kriging), and spdep (for gridded data) (Bivand et al. 2008).

12.3 Prospectus

At this point in time spatial statistics probably needs to enter a consolidation phase where the emphasis is on simplification, rejection of outdated techniques, highlighting the underlying unity of methods, and an effort to streamline the communication of these methods. In practice, the scientific community is not well incentivized to do this and it may not happen. Additional development in some areas is needed, such as improved methods of testing statistical significance and better understanding of the strengths of different forms of spatial regression, but these are relatively minor.

There are three new techniques that I believe deserve highlighting. First, is a technique common in the soils literature but that I have seen applied only once in ecology (Kendrick et al. 2008), based on nested models of variograms (also called coregionalisation). Basically the variogram is fit using piecewise regression. This automated breakout of scales immediately suggests (but does not require) distinct processes at these different scales and assigns variance components to make statements about which scales are most important. Unfortunately I am not aware of software commonly used in ecology that performs this test. Another promising technique is geographically weighted regression. This model is basically a regression on spatial points but the coefficients (i.e. the relative importance of different independent variables) is allowed to change across space (Fotheringham et al. 2002; Wimberly et al. 2008). In one example, Wimberly and colleagues (2008) found that climate limited tick abundance in the eastern USA but landscape structure was limiting in the western portions of the range. Instead of treating non-stationarity as a nuisance, this method embraces and measures it. Finally, an increasingly promising alternative to spatial regression and the exploration of causal factors of autocorrelation is the development of process-based models. Houchmandzadeh (2008) recently developed a model that predicts the pair correlation function $g(d)$ under the assumption of simple neutral (diffusive) dispersal. Stronger models of how a species distribution is affected by the environmental context will ultimately allow for the teasing apart of causality.

For the actual application of spatial statistics to ecological data, I believe we are entering an exciting time where software tools can bury the details and let the users focus on interpreting and learning from their data without having to climb a mountain of technical details first.

12.4 Key points

1. Spatial statistics is broadly organized around zeroth-order, first-order and second-order effects.

2. There is a fundamental distinction between data in which the spatial locations are human-chosen versus nature-chosen. Differences within the human-chosen category (e.g. quadrats vs transects vs geospatial data) have important implications for how calculations are performed but conceptually are of little importance and have been exaggerated.

3. Many methods that have been quite popular are now outdated (e.g. F and G functions, variance-to-mean-ratio/ID method, moving average and exponential smoothing) with better alternatives available.

4. Covariograms/kriging/correlograms are probably the single central concept today and users should familiarize themselves with their use and interpretation (although not their precise calculations). Moran's I and Geary's C are members of this set.

5. The most modern methods can be extremely difficult to calculate by hand and naïve implementations in software are likely to be wrong, but fortunately good software is readily available and should be used.

Acknowledgements

I thank Fangliang He for helpful feedback on an earlier draft of this manuscript. I gratefully acknowledge Marty Lechowicz, Marcia Waterway, and Graham Bell for sharing their data on species richness used in Figs 12.2b and 12.4. I also am grateful to McGill University for its stewardship of the Gault Nature Reserve from which the data came and for the many enjoyable hours I personally spent there.

PART IV
Alternative measures of diversity

CHAPTER 13

A primer of trait and functional diversity

Evan Weiher

13.1 Introduction

13.1.1 General definitions

Trait diversity is synonymous with functional diversity and is defined as the degree to which coexisting species vary in terms of their functional traits. Functional traits are observable or operationally defined phenotypic characteristics that influence species performance and/or ecosystem processes (Grime 1973b; Ricklefs & Travis 1980; Díaz & Cabido 2001; Poff et al. 2006). The principal difference between trait diversity and taxonomic-based species diversity is that trait diversity emphasizes the phenotypic differences among taxa while discounting phylogenetic relatedness. Even so, trait diversity is closely allied with phylogenetic diversity (Chapter 14) because functional traits are often phylogenetically conserved and because the two approaches use highly similar numerical methods.

Some have suggested that the term 'functional diversity' be restricted to measures of trait diversity that affect the functions of ecosystems (Tilman 2001; Petchey & Gaston 2006). We should be wary of unnecessarily restrictive definitions for terms that are conceptual, general, and useful (Weiher 2004). In this case, functional traits are widely recognized as having importance for species performance and it is largely for this reason that they also affect ecosystem functioning (Chapin III et al. 2000; Díaz & Cabido 2001; Garnier et al. 2006). It may not be necessary therefore to mark a distinction between trait and functional diversity. However, if the traits used to calculate an index are known to have no bearing on species performance or ecosystem function, then the more generic trait diversity should be used.

13.1.2 General importance

There are two key conceptual areas for which trait diversity has particular importance in ecology. The first area is in community ecology and deals with how local communities are filtered from the larger regional species pool and how this manifests itself in the dispersion of traits across species. The term 'trait dispersion' has been used in community ecology to parallel the study of spatial dispersion patterns in which competition or other processes can lead to spatial over-dispersion, where individuals are more separated from each other than would expected by chance (e.g. Greig-Smith 1957; Ryti & Case 1986). When applied to traits, species can be plotted in trait space (i.e. using one or more traits instead of spatial coordinates) and processes such as competition can similarly lead to resource partitioning, which is expressed as trait over-dispersion (i.e. the species are more spread out in trait space, e.g. Ricklefs & Travis (1980), Moulton & Pimm (1987)). Communities that are over-dispersed in trait space have high trait diversity. Alternatively, if some traits or trait combinations are excluded from some communities (e.g. Grime 1973b), then such communities may have lower trait dispersion and lower trait diversity. Understanding how species are filtered from communities according to their traits remains a fundamental question in community ecology (Keddy 1992; McGill et al. 2007) and there is a growing number of examples of how environmental and biotic constraints vary along environmental gradients to affect trait dispersion and functional diversity (e.g. Weiher & Keddy 1995; Swenson & Enquist 2007; Pausas & Verdú 2008; Filippi-Codaccioni et al. 2009).

The second area is in the linkage between community and ecosystem ecology. A principal question is the degree to which trait or functional diversity matters to ecosystem functioning. A primary mechanism by which biodiversity is thought to influence ecosystem functioning is through complementarity, or the enhancement of ecosystem processes caused by the increased efficiency and thoroughness of resource use by organisms with a high degree of trait dissimilarity. Examples include increased processing of detritus by detritivores that have a range of abilities (Anderson and Sedell 1979; Heemsbergen et al. 2004), and increased primary productivity in plant mixtures with a higher degree of functional diversity compared to monocultures (e.g. Tilman et al. 1997b; Hooper & Vitousek 1997). These ideas have been applied to a wide range of taxa, ecosystem types, and ecosystem services (Hooper et al. 2005; Naeem et al. 2009).

13.1.3   A brief history of trait and functional diversity

We should first recognize that Theophrastus began the functional trait approach in western civilization, and Darwin and Wallace were keenly interested in the centrality of phenotypic variation to evolution and coexistence. In the modern era, Warming (1909) paid careful attention to the idea of the growth forms of plants and the similarities and differences in phenotype among coexisting species. As an example, Warming described how the herbaceous plants growing under a canopy of beech trees were functionally quite similar to each other, even though they came from many different families, and how they were quite functionally distinct from the canopy trees.

The history of trait diversity has been closely tied to the development of niche theory, coexistence and competition theory, and the evolution of closely related species. In the 1930s and 1940s, ecologists first used genus:species ratios as a proxy for trait diversity because congeners are generally more similar to each other than they are to non-congeners. Elton (1946) stated that communities tend to have large genus:species ratios, that is larger than expected trait diversity, because similar species, notably congeners, have a low tendency to

coexist. This idea helped lead Hutchinson (1957) to the idea of a general limiting similarity based on body size ratios. This laid the foundation for the growth in competition-based niche theory in the 1960s and 1970s in which coexistence was seen as dependent on a high degree of dispersion of functional traits among species (e.g. MacArthur & Levins 1967). At that time, a key focal point was the regularity or evenness of body size distributions, which is the equivalent of recent indices of functional evenness (e.g. Mouillot et al. 2005; Villéger et al. 2008). Evolutionary biologists found supporting evidence in the evolution of regular spacing in bill lengths (Lack 1947) and in the over-dispersion of bill sizes among coexisting Darwin's finches (Grant & Schluter 1984). Not all the evidence supported this view, however. Williams (1964) showed that many communities have more species per genus than would be expected by chance. This suggested that communities have lower trait diversity than expected, but his findings were largely overlooked.

By the late 1970s and 1980s, niche theory and the centrality of competition were questioned and criticized as not being adequately tested against null hypotheses (e.g. Connor & Simberloff 1979). This led to a rather heated period of debate in which community null models were used to test if communities were indeed over-dispersed in trait space and therefore structured by competition (Strong et al. 1984). By the 1990s, the methods for using ad hoc null models were largely solved (Gotelli & Graves 1996) and there was growing evidence that some communities are over-dispersed in trait space (e.g. Weiher & Keddy 1995; Dayan & Simberloff 2005). While there was great interest in trait dispersion per se, the idea that trait dispersion was another form of diversity was also overlooked.

In 1980, Ricklefs and Travis developed a functional ecomorphological approach to community ecology that addressed both the degree of similarity of coexisting species and the amount of trait space occupied by communities. The idea of trait space occupation is essentially equivalent to trait diversity, and their approach was especially important because it translated MacArthur's notion of resource partitioning into its manifestation in emergent trait-based community functional parameters. A key area of interest was in how trait space is filled as communities grow in richness, thus forming an early linkage between trait and taxon richness, as well as functional community assembly. Ricklefs and Travis (1980), and later Travis and Ricklefs (1983) used ad hoc methods for estimating the morphological volume occupied by communities, but they also mentioned prim networks, or minimum spanning trees (*MSTs*), and later Moulton and Pimm (1987) used such trees as indices of morphological or trait volume. *MSTs* were used by Moulton and his colleagues in a series of papers in the 1980s and 1990s showing that introduced avifaunas usually have a significantly greater *MST* (greater trait diversity) than what would be expected under neutral community assembly. These results were generally interpreted as evidence for the role of competition in shaping community composition.

Meanwhile, a somewhat separate line of research was building on William's (1964) results and the idea that coexisting species should be phenotypically similar (i.e. communities should have lower than expected trait diversity). These models focused on habitat filtering and habitat-dependent competition causing the exclusion of species which lack certain requisite functional traits, leading to assemblage-wide convergence in traits (Grime 1973b; Southwood 1977; Brown 1987; Keddy 1992).

In the 1990s, Weiher and Keddy (1995) synthesized the competition-niche model and the habitat-filter model of trait dispersion into a general hypothetical model in which the amount of trait dispersion (trait diversity) increased with the importance of competition and decreased with the importance of environmental stress and with increasing scale. In addition, traits associated with habitat filtering can be clumped (with low trait diversity) while traits associated with coexistence can be over-dispersed within the same communities (Weiher et al. 1998). In plant communities, there is limited evidence supporting these ideas (Cavender-Bares et al. 2004; Swenson & Enquist 2007; Pausas & Verdú 2008; de Bello et al. 2009).

Starting in the 1990s, there was a renewed interest in biodiversity effects on ecosystem function (Schulze & Mooney 1994; Kinzig et al. 2001; Loreau et al. 2002). Functional diversity in particular has

emerged from the debate on whether and how biodiversity promotes functioning (Díaz & Cabido 2001). In several high-profile experiments, primary productivity increased with biodiversity and the plant number of functional groups (e.g. Tilman et al. 1997b; Hooper & Vitousek 1997; Hector et al. 1999). A key mechanism by which diverse communities may promote functioning is through complementarity, in which species assemblages are able to more fully utilize resources via niche partitioning, which is expressed through the diversity of functional traits (Hooper et al. (2005) and for a more detailed discussion regarding primary productivity and other mechanisms see Vile et al. (2006) and Fornara and Tilman (2009)). Another mechanism for biodiversity effects is through facilitation, where individual species functioning is enhanced by the presence of non-conspecifics (e.g. Anderson & Sedell 1979; Mulder et al. 2001; Cardinale et al. 2002). Facilitation probably occurred because non-conspecific species had unique traits and this would also add to the functional diversity of the community.

Even though the diversity-function debate has been somewhat controversial, it led to an explosion of interest in the measurement and quantification of trait and functional diversity. A principal driver was the observation that simply counting the number of ad hoc functional types was not a particularly rigorous way of estimating functional diversity (Walker et al. 1999; Petchey & Gaston 2002). Many of the more recent papers have cited Walker et al. (1999) as the start of functional diversity measurement, presumably because they explicitly linked their measure to ecosystem function. The recent work on functional diversity seems to have overlooked much of the literature on trait dispersion in community ecology. This was fortuitous because rather than reinventing the wheel, genuine progress has been made in terms of both creativity and analytical rigor. Important lines of growth have included:

1. the expansion of the distance-based methods to include relative abundance information (Shimitani 2001; Botta-Dukát 2005; Laliberté & Legendre 2010) and the generalization of distance methods that are appropriate for ordinal and other problematic types of trait data (Podani & Schmera 2006; Laliberté & Legendre 2010)

2. the development of dendrogram-based measures, which were adapted from methods for measuring of phylogenetic diversity (Petchey & Gaston 2002, 2006, 2007; Podani & Schmera 2006, 2007; Mouchet et al. 2008; Poos et al. 2009)

3. the expansion of variance-based methods to include both trait information and species abundances (Mason et al. 2003)

4. the development of new measures of trait evenness (Mouillot 2005; Mason et al. 2005; Villéger et al. 2008)

5. the application of convex hull mathematics to the measurement of trait volumes (Cornwell et al. 2006; Villéger et al. 2008)

6. the development of the concept and measurement of functional divergence, which measures the degree to which the most abundant species have extreme trait values in a way that is independent of trait volume (Mason et al. 2005; Villéger et al. 2008)

7. the development of graph-theoretical measures that are independent of species richness (Ricotta & Moretti 2008)

8. some utilitarian testing of functional diversity indices as predictors of ecosystem functioning (e.g. Petchey & Gaston 2004; Díaz et al. 2007).

13.2   State of the field

13.2.1   Overview

We might organize some of the various measures of trait diversity by three criteria (Table 13.1). The first criterion might be whether the index is based on species presences only or if their abundances are incorporated into the index. The second criterion might be the dimensionality of the index in terms of whether we are working with a single trait dimension or multiple traits and hence n-dimensional trait space. We can also recognize that trait diversity might be estimated in the absence of any quantitative trait data by using an a priori functional classification scheme or some measure of phylogenetic relatedness. We can organize the measures a third way, in parallel with the notions of diversity, richness, and evenness (following Mason et al. (2005) and Villéger et al. (2008)). Trait diversity indices that correspond to species richness are based on species presence only and so they focus on the idea

of the utilization or volume of trait space occupied. Trait diversity indices that correspond to diversity indices incorporate abundance information to weight each species' contribution to diversity. Trait diversity indices that parallel the notion of evenness do so by primarily focusing on the evenness or regularity of the distances between the species in trait space, but they can also include evenness in abundance. A further aspect of trait diversity has no simple parallel with taxonomic diversity. These indices measure the relative clumping of species in trait space and were initially developed to address limiting similarity as it relates to species coexistence (Ricklefs & Travis 1980). This idea was further developed to measure the degree to which the most unique species are also most abundant while controlling for the volume of occupied trait space (Mason et al. 2005; Villéger et al. 2008).

13.2.2   Indices of trait and functional diversity

Functional diversity is usually 0 when only one taxon is present. If trait data are available for individuals rather than taxa, this need not be the case. Most of the following indices require only two taxa to be present to calculate a non-zero index. Several (a_{MST}, $FDiv$, $FEve$) require three taxa, one (CHV) requires variable numbers of taxa, depending on the number of traits. The following indices can be calculated using the FD package in R, and R source code is available from many of the authors' webpages.

Convex hull volume (CHV) (Cornwell et al. 2006; *FRic* in Villéger et al. (2008)) is the volume (or area in two dimensions) of trait space occupied by coexisting species. In two trait dimensions, the convex hull is the perimeter of the polygon defined by the most extreme species, ensuring the entire surface of the polygon contains no concave indentations. It is a multidimensional version of range because it collapses to range in the case of a single trait. Individuals that fall inside the convex hull do not add to the total volume or area, and this makes CHV sensitive to only the extreme species that form the vertices at the perimeter of the occupied trait space. Convex hull volume can be expanded to any number of trait dimensions, but the calculations are not trivial. CHV is sensitive to trait units, but Cornwell et al. (2006) found that three rescaling procedures

Table 13.1 A general classification of trait diversity indices.

	Species presences only	Abundances incorporated
Trait richness		
Zero trait dimensions	Genus:species ratio	
	Phylogenetic methods	
	(Chapter 14)	
One trait dimension		
	Range	
	Variance	
	(Platy)kurtosis	
N trait dimensions		
	Minimum spanning tree (*MST*) distance	
	Mean distance, *MD*	
	Sum of distances, *FAD*, *MFAD*	
	Dendrogram-based *FD*	
	Convex hull volume, *FRic*	
	Slope of the cumulative *MST*, a_{MST}	
Trait diversity		
One trait dimension		Variance-based FD_{var}
N trait dimensions		Quadratic entropy, FD_Q
		Functional divergence, *FDiv*
		Functional dispersion, *FDis*
Trait evenness		
One trait dimension		Functional regularity index, *FRO*
N trait dimensions	Evenness in *NND*	Functional evenness, *FEve*
Trait dispersion/density of species packing		
N trait dimensions	Mean *NND*	Abundance-weighted Mean *NND*

Note that any measure that can incorporate *N* trait dimensions can always deal with individual traits. Indices are ordered historically, starting with the oldest. See text for explanation of terms.

were highly reliable ($\bar{r} > 0.93$) when comparing communities with large differences in richness and trait diversity. A critical constraint on *CHV* is the requirement that an analysis with *T* traits requires at least *T* + 1 species, otherwise the volume is 0. (It takes two points to define a distance, three to define an area, four to define a three-dimensional volume, etc.). *CHV* has no simple formula.

Dendrogram-based indices (*FD*) (Faith 1992; Petchey & Gaston 2002) were developed in order to solve the apparent methodological gap suggested by the functional diversity–ecosystem function literature by using tools for measuring phylogenetic diversity (Chapter 14). In the original formulation (Petchey & Gaston 2002), a dendrogram is built from a trait-based distance matrix for each sample, and the total of the branch lengths are summed. The method is therefore somewhat similar to *MST*,

but with additional clustering steps and a different summation procedure. The method was modified (Petchey & Gaston 2006) in order to make the index directly analogous to phylogenetic diversity (PD, Chapter 14). In the modified FD, a single dendrogram is built for the species pool and the total of branch lengths is summed for the species present.

Dendrogram-based measures tend to scale linearly with richness (i.e. they do not meet the monotonicity criterion; Ricotta 2005) and they are sensitive to trait units.

Because dendrogram-based methods require choosing both a distance method and a clustering method, there has been debate regarding methods and sensitivity of the results to methods (Petchey & Gaston 2006, 2007; Podani & Schmera 2006, 2007; Mouchet et al. 2008; Poos et al. 2009). If the data have a wide range of richness and trait diversity, then the various methods tend to be quite reliable (Petchey & Gaston 2006). However, if the trait data are not continuous, or if one is comparing communities with equal numbers of species, then the methods are less reliable (Podani & Schmera 2006, 2007; Poos et al. 2009) and greater care should be taken. Optimal clustering methods cannot be defined a priori, therefore a best practice may be to use a variety of combinations of distance and clustering methods to create consensus dendrograms, and the original and consensus dendrograms should be compared if a single, best method is sought (see Mouchet et al. (2008) for details). Alternatively, one may view the various resultant FD indices as multiple indicators of a latent variable. There is no direct mathematical formula.

Functional dispersion (FDis)(Anderson et al. 2006; Laliberté & Legendre 2010) measures the mean distance to the centroid of the assemblage in trait space, weighted by relative abundances. As such, it is conceptually similar to FD_Q, FD_{var}, and FDiv even though the mechanics of measurement are different. FDis was strongly correlated with FD_Q ($r = 0.96$) and it had a triangular limit function relationship with FDiv (i.e. the upper limit of FDis increased with FDiv) using random data (Laliberté & Legendre 2010). It is worth noting that formal significance tests of FDis values can be determined via homogeneity of multivariate dispersion, if abundance information is not used (Anderson et al. 2006; see Laliberté and Shipley (2009) for details).

Calculations involve the following steps. The weighted centroid is defined as a vector, c, of the weighted mean trait values using the abundance, a, for each of i species and k traits:

$$c = [c_k] = \frac{\sum_{i=1}^{S} a_i t_{ik}}{\sum_{i=1}^{S} a_i}$$

$$FDis = \frac{\sum_{i=1}^{S} a_i z_i}{\sum_{i=1}^{S} a_i}$$

Then FDis is the weighted mean distance, z, from each species to the weighted mean centroid.

Functional divergence (FDiv) (Villéger et al. 2008) was developed to expand the notion of variance-based FD_{var} to multiple dimensions and to standardize the index so that it is independent of both the volume of trait space occupied (CHV) and functional evenness (FEve). It is the degree to which the most abundant taxa are far from the centroid of the assemblage in trait space, standardized to the average distance to the unweighted centroid of the species at the perimeter of the convex hull (c.f. the weighted centroid of all taxa, FDis). FDiv is high when the most abundant species have extreme trait values (i.e. are vertices on the convex hull; sit on the perimeter of the occupied trait space). Although this is common to other measures of trait diversity (e.g. FDis, FD_{var}, and FD_Q), FDiv is standardized so that it is independent of trait volume and therefore it uniquely quantifies this one particular aspect of trait diversity. Three taxa are required.

The calculations require the following steps. First, the centroid (or middle of gravity) of the assemblage is defined using only the V taxa on the perimeter of the convex hull. The centroid G is defined as a vector ($G = g_1, g_2, \ldots, g_k$) of the mean of each of k traits

$$g_k = \frac{1}{V} \sum_{i=1}^{V} t_{i,k}$$

where t is the value of trait k in species i, and V is the number of species on the perimeter of the convex hull (i.e. the vertices). If the number of traits is greater than the number of taxa plus one (if $T > S + 1$), then all the taxa are vertices and S replaces V.

For each species, the distance to the centroid is calculated as the Euclidean distance (see also Box 13.1), and then its mean is found:

$$dG_i = \sqrt{\sum_{k=1}^{T} (t_{i,k} - g_k)^2}$$

$$\overline{dG} = \frac{1}{S} \sum_{i=1}^{S} dG_i$$

From these, two parameters are calculated. The abundance-weighted difference between each taxon's distance to the centroid and the mean distance to the centroid is

$$\Delta d = \sum_{i=1}^{S} p_i \left(dG_i - \overline{dG} \right)$$

Note that Δd is large if abundant taxa have large distances to the centroid, relative to the mean of the assemblage. The total of the weighted differences is summed as

$$\Delta |d| = \sum_{i-1}^{S} p_i \left| dG_i - \overline{dG} \right|$$

Finally,

$$FDiv = \frac{\Delta d + \overline{dG}}{\Delta |d| + \overline{dG}}$$

Therefore, *FDiv* is the abundance-weighted distance by which the most common species tend to be at the periphery of the assemblage in trait space. The maximum possible value for Δd is $\overline{dG}$, so standardizing Δd to its maximum value forces *FDiv* to have a maximum of 1. If all taxa are equidistant from the centroid (and therefore all sit on the perimeter and serve as vertices in the convex hull) and have equal abundance, then *FDiv* is 1. This can occur only if the taxa are arranged at equal distances to the centroid, but regardless of their proximity to each other. *FDiv* is independent of species richness and trait units, but note that trait data should still be rescaled. When there are fewer than three taxa, the index is of questionable meaning or use. *FDiv* will increase as more species are on the perimeter and are vertices, therefore if the number of traits is high relative to the number of taxa, *FDiv* will tend to increase with richness because all the taxa will be vertices of the convex hull until $S + 1 = T$.

Functional evenness (*FEve*) (Villéger et al. 2008) combines both the evenness of species spacing in trait space and the evenness of species relative abundances. It measures the consistency in the branch lengths of the *MST* after weighting the branch lengths by the sum of the relative abundances of the two species at the ends of each branch. The index is 1 if all species have equal abundance and if all the branch lengths have equal length, and it declines toward zero with increasing unevenness in either aspect. This index is different from measuring the standard deviation of the nearest-neighbour distances because it uses the

MST, not just nearest neighbours. By doing so, it truly measures the regularity of spacing in trait space, rather than the regularity of species packing. *FEve* can be used without abundance information, if one wishes to estimate trait evenness separately from evenness in abundance (the simplified methods are provided below). It is independent of species richness and measures of trait diversity such as *CHV* or *MST*. *FEve* is not defined for assemblages with fewer than three taxa because three points are required to assess the regularity of spacing patterns, just as it takes three points to define a plane. Alternatively, one might use the index and conclude that assemblages with fewer than three taxa have high evenness (because there is no variation in the distances between taxa in trait space). Great care should be taken in the interpretation of such values because they at least partly nonsensical.

FEve is calculated from an *MST* where $l_{i,j}$ is the branch length from species i to j, S is the number of species, and p is the relative abundance:

$$FEve = \frac{\sum\limits_{l=1}^{S-1} \min \left(\frac{EW_l}{\sum\limits_{l=1}^{S-1} EW_l}, \frac{1}{S-1} \right) - \frac{1}{S-1}}{1 - \frac{1}{S-1}} \quad \text{where}$$

$$EW_l = \frac{l_{i,j}}{p_i + p_j}$$

In the absence of abundance information, the equation simplifies to:

$$FEve^* = \frac{\sum\limits_{i=1}^{S-1} \min \left(\frac{l_{i,j}}{MST}, \frac{1}{S-1} \right) - \frac{1}{S-1}}{1 - \frac{1}{S-1}}$$

The standardization with the inverse of richness minus 1 is needed for two reasons. First, in the case of perfectly even spacing and abundance, the values within the minimization will always be $1/(S - 1)$, and this forces the index to have a maximum of 1. Second, in cases where there is not perfect evenness, it accounts for bias caused by the fact that there will always be one case where the value in the minimization is less than or equal to $1/(S - 1)$ (Villéger et al. (2008) cite Bulla (1994) for more details). In practice, the standardization may tend to increase the amount by which *FEve* decreases from 1 as the assemblage becomes less even.

Mean distance (*MD*) (Weiher et al. 1998; Heemsbergen et al. 2004) between coexisting taxa measures the average differences among taxa and is a simplistic estimator of trait volume. Mean distance is analogous to the mean phylogenetic distance (*MPD*; Chapter 14). It is sensitive to distance measure, trait units, and the number of traits. Mean distance can decline when intermediate taxa are added to communities and it can similarly increase when intermediate taxa are extirpated or go extinct. This means *MD* does not meet the monotonicity criterion (Ricotta 2005) in that adding species with new combinations of functional traits should increase trait diversity, or at least leave it unchanged. This tendency is most pronounced when comparing assemblages in which all taxa are at the extremes of the trait ranges to assemblages with taxa near the middle:

$$MD = \frac{2!\,(S-2)!}{S!} \sum_{i=1}^{S-1} \sum_{j=i+1}^{S} d_{ij}$$

where S is richness and d_{ij} is the distance between species i and j.

Minimum spanning tree (*MST*) (Ricklefs & Travis 1980; Moulton & Pimm 1987) is the length of the minimum non-recursive (i.e. no loops) tree connecting all species in trait space (i.e. the shortest 'connect-the-dots' distance). *MST* is a multidimensional version of range because it reduces to the range for a single trait. Species that are directly intermediate do not add to the total length, but in practice *MST* tends to increase monotonically with richness, even with random communities (see also Ricotta and Moretti (2008) and a_{MST}). *MST* is conceptually similar to the dendrogram-based methods (*FD*), but it is simpler because it does not require grouping points and recalculating distances. *MST* is sensitive to distance measure, trait units, and the number of traits.

Quadratic entropy (*FD*$_Q$) (Rao 1982; Shimitani 2001; Botta-Dukát 2005) is the sum of the distances between pairs of species in trait space, weighted by the product of their relative abundances. The weighting factor is also the joint probability of choosing an individual of each species. *FD*$_Q$ is conceptually the abundance-weighted mean

distance. Weighting each distance by abundance means that *FD*$_Q$ will increase as the most abundant species have increasingly extreme traits. *FD*$_Q$ is analogous to the weighted mean phylogenetic distance (*MPD*; Chapter 14). *FD*$_Q$ is independent of the number of traits, but it is sensitive to the scale of the traits. It can decline when intermediate taxa are added and increase when intermediate taxa are removed, especially when taxa otherwise load at trait extremes (Pavoine et al. 2005a):

$$FD_Q = \sum_{i=1}^{S-1} \sum_{j=i+1}^{S} d_{ij}\,p_i\,p_j$$

where $d_{i,j}$ is the distance between species i and j, and p is the relative abundance.

Botta-Dukát (2005) suggested using the mean distance (either Euclidean or Manhattan) for each trait divided by the number of traits:

$$d_{i,j} = \frac{1}{T} \sum_{k=1}^{T} \sqrt{\left(t_{i,k} - t_{j,k}\right)^2}$$

$$d_{i,j} = \frac{1}{T} \sum_{k=1}^{T} \left| t_{i,k} - t_{j,k} \right|$$

In this formulation, the distances are always Manhattan. Alternatively, it is possible to use the Euclidean distance divided by the maximum possible distance, $\sqrt{T}$:

$$d_{i,j} = \frac{1}{\sqrt{T}} \sqrt{\sum_{k=1}^{T} \left(t_{i,k} - t_{j,k}\right)^2}$$

In practice, this standardization to ensure that *FD*$_Q$ is bounded to a maximum of 1 is probably unnecessary; one might just as easily use the Euclidean distance for calculating *FD*$_Q$. Using the data described below, the two methods were strongly correlated ($r = 0.97$). However, the use of Euclidean distance with *FD*$_Q$ means that it will reach a maximum when taxa are evenly abundant and each sits at the periphery of the trait space of the species pool (Pavoine et al. (2005a) and cf. *FDiv* and *FEve*). Moreover, the behaviour of *FD*$_Q$ depends on the choice of distance measure (Shimitani 2001). Pavoine et al. (2005a) suggest using ultrametric distance matrices (i.e. distance metrics that come from a tree, such as an *MST*) because this maximizes *FD*$_Q$ when all taxa are included. This approach would avoid the potential problem of recommending that some taxa should be extirpated in order to increase functional diversity.

If all the taxa are completely different (i.e. all $d_{ij} = 1$), then FD_Q reduces to the Simpson diversity index. If all the taxa have equal abundance (of if there is no abundance information), then FD_Q reduces to FAD/S^2. If abundance information is unavailable, it may be better to simply use MD.

Nearest-neighbour metrics:density of species packing (meanNND) (Ricklefs & Travis 1980) **regularity of species packing (sdNND)** (Ricklefs & Travis 1980), and **evenness of species packing (evenNND)** have been used to assess whether there are consistent limits to similarity among coexisting species. $MeanNND$ has been used to assess the degree of trait dispersion in terms of the average limit to similarity within assemblages. Communities with high trait dispersion also have high trait diversity. Mean NND can also be calculated as the abundance-weighted mean (see also Chapter 14). The regularity of species packing has been measured as the standard deviation of the nearest-neighbour distances between coexisting taxa in trait space. Small $sdNND$ indicates regularity or evenness of species spacing in trait space. This approach was borrowed directly from the study of spatial patterning. These methods differ from $FEve$ in that only the nearest-neighbour distances (NND) are considered. Therefore, $sdNND$ measures the evenness in species packing as opposed to the evenness of trait space utilization. Although this may seem to be a subtle difference, the use of NND means that any long gaps in the distribution of species in trait space are ignored.

If we apply the numerical approach of functional evenness ($FEve$) to the evenness in nearest-neighbour distances, then the index will have similar properties (i.e. independence with the amount of occupied trait space and species richness), which should be an improvement over simply measuring the standard deviation of NND:

$$evenNND = \frac{\sum_{i=1}^{S} \min\left(\frac{NND_i}{\sum_{i=1}^{S} NND_i}, \frac{1}{S} \right) - \frac{1}{S}}{1 - \frac{1}{S}}$$

Here, we standardize by the inverse of the number of species because each species has a nearest neighbour.

Slope of the cumulative MST curve (a_{MST}) (Ricotta & Moretti 2008) is the degree to which the MST grows in length as taxa are added, after ranking the branch lengths from smallest to largest. The total lengths of tree-based indices, such as MST and FD_{PG}, have a strong tendency to increase with species richness. The rate of increase as a function of species rank controls for variation in richness because it measures only the degree of increase in MST branch length with the rank of the branch length. This index was specifically designed to be independent of species richness. Low values of this index indicate a high degree of functional redundancy and therefore low functional diversity.

To calculate a_{MST}, rank the branches from the MST from smallest to largest and then calculate the cumulative branch length at each rank. Then a_{MST} can be calculated as the slope of the relationship between the cumulative branch length and rank on a log scale:

$$cbl = c \left(\text{Rank}_{branch.length} \right)^{a}$$

where cbl is the cumulative branch length from the MST after first ranking the branches from smallest to largest.

Sum of distances or functional attribute diversity (FAD) (Walker et al. 1999) and **number of categorical trait states (T)** (Mayfield et al. 2005) are the sum of the distances between coexisting taxa in trait space, while the **modified functional attribute diversity ($MFAD$)** (Schmera et al. 2009) is FAD standardized to the number of functionally unique taxa. FAD is analogous to the sum of the phylogenetic distances (SPD; Chapter 14). FAD is generally not recommended because it does meet the twinning criterion, in that functional diversity should not increase if an identical taxon is added or if a taxon is split into two identical taxa (Weitzman 1992; Mason et al. 2003, 2005). This makes FAD very tightly liked to species richness. In order to address this, the modified FAD ($MFAD$) was developed (Schmera et al. 2009). The approach first lumps taxa with identical trait values (across all traits) into a single functional unit while each unique taxon is considered to be a functional unit. Then the sum of distances between functional units is standardized to the number of functional units (F). This makes *MFAD* similar to the mean distance, but improves on it by removing the cost of functionally equivalent taxa (with zero distance) by lumping them. It is also specifically designed to handle nominal traits:

$$FAD = \sum_{i=1}^{S-1} \sum_{j=i+1}^{S} d_{ij}$$

where d_{ij} is the distance between species i and j.

$$MFAD = \frac{1}{F} \sum_{i=1}^{F-1} \sum_{j=i+1}^{F} d_{i,j}$$

where $d_{i,j}$ is the distance between the unique functional units. If taxa are assigned to functional groups, then *FAD* is the number of groups.

Schmera et al. (2009) suggested using the Marczewski–Steinhaus distance:

$$d_{i,j} = \frac{\sum_{k=1}^{T} |t_{i,k} - t_{j,k}|}{\sum_{k=1}^{T} \max (t_{i,k}, t_{j,k})}$$

or the canberra distance. They found *MFAD* performed very well with both artificial and observed data in which the traits were binomial, ordinal, or fuzzy. Their taxa had a significant amount of functional redundancy and so it is not clear how *MFAD* performs with continuous traits where there is little or no redundancy.

Mayfield et al. (2005) used a similar approach to *FAD* when dealing with sets of categorical traits. They used the number of categorical trait states present in a community for six traits, each of which had as many as 13 states. Their approach was basically univariate, in that they simply summed the number of trait states (i.e. *FAD*) across the six traits, rather than use a multivariate distance measure which would have captured the number of unique combinations of trait states. They found that the number of trait states was not strongly correlated with species richness, nor was there evidence for a rapid saturation of trait states with increasing richness.

Variance-based functional diversity (FD_{var}) (Mason et al. 2003, 2005; Lepš et al. 2006; de Bello et al. 2009) was developed as the abundance-weighted sum of squares of the observed trait values and therefore it is analogous to the calculation of a weighted variance. This method must be applied to each trait singly, and then it can be summed or averaged across traits. Because it employs logarithms, the trait values must be greater than 0. Like several other indices, FD_{var} will increase as the abundance of intermediate species declines to 0.

If there are S species, with a relative abundance, p, and a single trait of values t:

$$FD_{var} = \frac{2}{\pi \arctan \left[5 \sum_{i=1}^{S} p_i \left(\ln t_i - \bar{t}_{aw. \ln} \right)^2 \right]}$$

$$\bar{t}_{aw. \ln} = \sum_{i=1}^{S} p_i \ln t_i$$

where $\bar{t}_{aw. \ln}$ is the abundance-weighted logarithmic mean of the trait.

The dressing around the summation helpfully puts the index into the range of about 0–1 (Mason et al. 2003). Alternatively, the abundance-weighted variance may be calculated without standardization (Lepš et al. 2006; de Bello et al. 2009):

$$FD_{var.2} = \sum_{i=1}^{S} p_i \left(t_i - \bar{t}_{aw} \right)^2$$

$$\bar{t}_{aw} = \sum_{i=1}^{S} p_i t_i$$

13.2.3 Partitioning the components of trait diversity

Inter- and intraspecific components of trait diversity
This is a method that is used to calculate both the among-taxa variance in trait values and the within-taxa variance in trait values, following from the calculations for analysis of variance. This approach explicitly includes intraspecific variation in trait values:

$$s^2_{among} = \sum_{i=1}^{S} p_i \left(t_i - \bar{t} \right)^2$$

$$\bar{t} = \sum_{i=1}^{S} p_i t_i$$

where t_i is the mean trait value for species i and p is its relative abundance. Then,

$$s^2_{within} = \sum_{i=1}^{S} p_i s_i^2$$

where s^2 is the within-taxa variance in trait values (Lepš et al. 2006). Then the sum of among-taxa variance and within-taxa variance can be used as a measure of trait diversity, and the variance components add another level of detail.

Within- (α) and among- (β) community components of trait diversity

Following from Whittaker's concepts of α, β, and γ diversity (see also Chapter 6), one may similarly assess both the within-community α trait diversity and the extent of turnover in traits across communities (β). The partitioning may be done additively (where $\gamma = \alpha + \beta$) or multiplicatively (where $\gamma = \alpha \times \beta$). γ is determined as the trait diversity of the collection of species and their overall relative abundances. Comparing the relative contributions of α and β in terms of species and traits can be particularly enlightening. For example, de Bello et al. (2009) found that α trait diversity accounted for a much larger proportion of γ than species richness-based diversity, which suggests a high degree of functional redundancy in the species pool.

13.2.4 Methodological issues

Traits: selection and measurement

While this issue cannot be reviewed in detail here, the general aim is to capture the functional traits of species or taxa that have particular meaning for the questions of interest, whether they are about constraints on community assembly, effects on ecosystem processes, or something else. One approach includes first identifying the principal challenges or limitations on species performance, and then identifying both the ideal attributes and any simple, measurable phenotypic correlate of the ideal attribute. For example, for plants, key challenges include dispersal, establishment, and persistence, and it was recognized that seed mass, leaf economic traits, and height may serve as a minimal core set of traits, while additional key traits have been identified (Westoby 1999; Weiher et al. 1999; Cornelissen et al.

2003). If the questions relate to ecosystem function, then a subset of these might be of primary interest. A second approach has been to focus on traits associated with life history and resource acquisition in the broadest sense, including the ecomorphology of mobility, feeding structures, and resource use (e.g. Ben-Moshe et al. 2001; Lamouroux et al. 2004; Poff et al. 2006; Gurd 2007). For animals, example traits include body size, mouth size and shape, specialized feeding structures (e.g. dentition in mammals, beaks/bills in birds, mandible parts in arthropods), the ecomorphology of locomotion (e.g. body shape, wing size, shape), phenology (e.g. crepuscular or nocturnal, dormancy or migratory), and life history (e.g. parity, fecundity, egg/offspring size). Some authors have used prey use/trophic level as traits, when they are actually measures of functional role and niche. Similarly, habitat affinity has been used even though this is not a trait, but a measure of realized niche.

When using continuous traits, it is common to use species mean values, even though it is widely recognized that continuous functional traits can have considerable within-species variability. The justification for using species means is based on the observation that species rankings by functional traits tend to be consistent when sampling across time and space (e.g. Garnier et al. 2001) and because the differences between species tend to be larger than the differences within species. For example, Kraft and Ackerly (2009) reported that specific leaf area varied 1.7-fold within species and 9-fold among species. Several approaches have been suggested to deal with intraspecific trait variation. One approach is to measure the continuous traits in each sample or in each individual (e.g. Cianciaruso et al. 2009). A second approach is to use the variability in trait values to estimate the degree of overlap, and then use overlap as the complement of distance (see also section 1.4.3) (e.g. Mason et al. 2003; Lepš et al. 2006). A third approach is to use intraspecific variability as an indicator of niche breadth (e.g. Violle & Jiang 2009), in other words as a trait. Intraspecific trait variation is conceptually problematic because it arises through a combination of both meaningful factors (e.g. genotypic variation, phenotypic plasticity, acclimation, and ontogeny) as well as by measurement error and background noise. Care should be taken when estimating trait variance (because trait data are rarely collected randomly or evenly across taxa, some kind of resampling method should be used to estimate variances, e.g. Rust and Rao (1996)).

Trait scaling and independence

When calculating trait diversity, it is usually important to standardize the trait data because traits are measured with different units and this means they have a variety of ranges and variances. There is currently no simple consensus on the best way to do this. One solution is to z transform quantitative trait data (subtract the mean and divide by the standard deviation). This is appropriate when comparing trait diversity among samples within a study because it gives each trait the same weight by eliminating any effect of measurement units. However, when traits are standardized by their standard deviation, it has the effect of putting them in standard deviation units, and so it is not possible to compare trait diversity across studies (unless the traits have equal variances, which is, of course, extremely unlikely). Furthermore, if some of the traits are not continuous variables, then scaling by the standard deviation makes no sense (Podani & Schmera 2006).

An alternative might be to log transform continuous traits. This would equalize the units of the traits, where one unit would represent a 10-fold change. It would not change any differences in trait range or variance, so the traits would not contribute equally, but it would help in cases where one trait ranges over several orders of magnitude and others do not.

A solution is to standardize the variables to their relevant range by subtracting the minimum then dividing by their range, so that the variables are expressed as a proportion of their entire observed range. This is the standardization used in Gower distances (e.g. Podani & Schmera 2006) and it has been suggested several other times (Botta-Dukát 2005; Mason et al. 2005; Grace 2006). The relevant range may be defined by the observed data set (i.e. the observed minimum and maximum), some regionally appropriate data range or, perhaps ideally, the global range. However, global ranges often suffer from extreme trait values that may have little meaning for a particular study (e.g. mammalian

body size has a maximum of over 30 m and leaf mass per area has a maximum over $1400\,\mathrm{g\,m^{-2}}$). For some traits it might be quite reasonable to know the maximum and minimum global trait (e.g. height or body length), but for lesser-known traits it would helpful to establish clear physical limits (e.g. leaf dry matter content by definition has to be greater than 0 and less than 100, but we don't know its absolute physical limits).

This will not, however, eliminate redundant traits that are not independent of each other and essentially measure a similar function or attribute. For example, many measures of functional morphology and ecophysiology are intrinsically linked to body size (Brown & West 2000) and smaller details, even functional traits of a single organ, such as specific leaf area, leaf dry matter content, leaf thickness, and leaf size, tend to be at least weakly correlated (Wright et al. 2004). If correlated measures of function are used, then those functions or trait axes are over-weighted relative to other functions or trait axes. One solution would be to down-weight correlated or redundant traits (Pavoine et al. 2009) so their total length or input weight would be 1 or equal to other functionally-linked traits.

A more general solution is to collapse the trait axes by using principal components analyses (PCA) or principal coordinates analysis (PCoA). This leads to an equivalent number of uncorrelated trait axes, but if PCA is based on correlation, then the components will be in meaningless standard deviation units. If the traits are first standardized to their relevant range and then collapsed into principal components using covariances rather than correlation, then the resultant components should be uncorrelated and unique, but they will retain their units (percentage of trait range). Alternatively, (PCoA) can be based on any distance measure.

Even though we should be careful about using redundant or correlated traits, we should not necessarily avoid them altogether. Lepš et al. (2006) found that correlated traits do not necessarily produce particularly correlated trait diversities. They also explained that traits can be correlated due to physical constraints, but they may relate to different, or at least distinctive, ecological processes. For example, offspring size and fecundity tend to be negatively related because of a fundamental trade-off, but they relate to different ecological processes (e.g. survivorship and dispersal vs reproductive output). It may therefore be important to include such correlated traits in order to capture particular ecological processes.

Distance/dissimilarity methods

Euclidean distances are commonly used to measure distances between taxa in trait space. This is acceptable as long as the trait data are quantitative and continuous. However, when trait data are ordinal, binomial/nominal (e.g. wings or no wings), fuzzy (e.g. animals that are opportunistically carnivorous, but are often not so), or circular (e.g. phenology by month of year), then Euclidean distances become less meaningful. In addition, such data should not be z transformed. A solution is to use Gower's distance (*GD*; Podani 2005; Pavoine et al. 2009).

Gower's distance is the average Manhattan metric across traits, after rescaling them to their relevant range. The relevant range (R_k) can be defined as either the observed range of trait values or the regional or globally observed range.

$$z_{i,k} = t_{i,k} / R_k$$

$$GD_{i,j} = \frac{1}{T} \sum_{k=1}^{T} |z_{i,k} - z_{j,k}|$$

Gower's distance can be further generalized to adding weighting to each trait. The function gowdis is available in the *FD* package in R.

Matching dissimilarity (*MD*) is a distance approach that estimates niche overlap, and is estimated by the degree of overlap in the distribution of trait values between two taxa (Mason et al. 2003; Lepš et al. 2006):

$$MD_{i,j} = 1 - \left(\frac{1}{T} \sum_{k=1}^{T} O_{i,j} \right)$$

For qualitative or binomial traits with no intraspecific variation, *MD* is the same as Gower's distance. For quantitative traits, is can be estimated by calculating the overlap in the probability density functions of each trait for each pair of coexisting taxa. Lepš et al. (2006) suggest using the trait mean and standard deviation with the approximation of the normal distribution to calculate overlap. Any species pair that has zero overlap will have *MD* = 1

and so there may be considerable loss of distance information when using this metric. One might consider using the matching dissimilarity to downweight other distance measures by the amount of overlap, for example:

$$ED_{i,j}^{O} = ED_{i,j} \times MD_{i,j}$$

Rarefaction

When organisms are sampled incompletely, with variation in sample size or with variation in the spatial arrangement of samples, biodiversity indices are biased and are not readily comparable (see Chapter 2). A solution is to use rarefaction, where unbiased biodiversity indices are either calculated or bootstrapped (see Chapter 4). Rarefaction is usually not necessary with true census data, such as α diversity of sessile organisms in small areas. However, at large spatial grain size, when combining samples to estimate the diversity of large spatial grain sizes, when combining samples with different spatial arrangement of data points, or when sampling motile animals, rarefaction methods are usually necessary.

Walker et al. (2008) provided suggestions for rarefying trait diversity. They described four algorithms for generating species lists for a random sample of *n* individuals or *m* sample units. Gotelli and Colwell (Chapter 4) recommend using sample-based algorithms, with adjustment for the number of individuals sampled. Walker et al.'s study showed how rarefaction was helpful in determining the unbiased change in functional diversity over time and how it also helped to show that extirpated species were functionally redundant.

Abundances are not equivalent

Any index that incorporates abundance information is sensitive to the way in which abundances are measured. Evenness measures are particularly sensitive (see Chapter 5). One cannot compare diversity indices that were calculated using different abundance units. There is a general tendency for biomass-based abundances to have a much greater difference between the maximum abundance and the minimum abundance, with cover estimates intermediate and frequency (i.e. counts of individuals) having the least spread (e.g. Lepš et al. 2006).

This means biomass-based indices will be biased to lower diversity and evenness than the other measures.

Effective numbers transforms of trait diversity
If half the trait diversity is lost, the index should also be reduced by half. The indices of trait richness (CHV, FD, MST) will generally conform to this. However, when abundance information is used, it is often transformed or recombined in a way that distorts the direct interpretation of the index (Jost 2006). A solution is to translate the index back to the 'numbers equivalent' (Jost 2006). For FD_Q, this has been solved because FD_Q reduces to the Simpson diversity if the distance between every species is 1, but more work is needed to assess the other indices.

13.2.5 Conceptual issues

Is functional diversity a unitary latent variable?
One of the principal questions involving functional diversity is whether there is one best measure and there has been considerable debate over which measures and methods are most ideal. In the recent literature, there has been an emphasis on measuring functional diversity in order to capture its potential effects on ecosystem functioning, while much of the earlier interest was in capturing the potential effects of environmental filtering and biotic interactions on community composition (i.e. assembly rules). We should make every effort to be transparent about our goals and be open to the notion that the different measures of trait diversity may be more or less insightful depending on the questions at hand. Even so, we should consider whether the various indices are essentially measuring the same conceptual construct.

Trait diversity is a conceptual construct that we cannot measure directly (cf. temperature), but instead we must use one or more indicators of the concept in order to indirectly measure it. This brings up the question of reliability and whether it is in fact a singular latent variable, or if the various indices are indeed measuring distinct aspects of diversity. To test this, I used principal components analysis to assess the correlation structure among the indices. I calculated the indices using data from

an experimental grassland (524 $1\,m^2$ quadrats with richness from 3 to 15 species, 66 plant species, and two independent functional traits, height and leaf dry matter content rescaled from 0 to 1 (to avoid zero CHV values) and artificial data (equiprobable random richness from 3 to 20 species, with random species abundances, and two random traits)).

There were strong correlations between a core set of trait diversity indices (CHV, FAD, FD_1, FD_2, $FDis$, FD_{var1}, FD_{var2}, FD_Q, $MFAD$, and MST) in both observed plant assemblages and artificial data. These were manifested as nearly equivalent loadings of these indices on the first principal component of both analyses, and each explained over 50% of the variation in the 15 indices (Table 13.2). The mean Pearson correlation between the indices loading heavily on the first principal component was 0.817, suggesting good reliability in their measurement of trait diversity in the observed plant assemblages, but it was less reliable in the artificial data ($\bar{r} = 0.719$).

The PCA suggested that there are about four unique aspects of trait diversity (Fig. 13.1, Table 13.2). The core set that loaded heavily on the first component was separated into those incorporating abundance data and those that did not on the third component in grasslands and on the second component in artificial data. This suggests that in real communities the distinction between trait richness and trait diversity may be unnecessary. A second aspect can be interpreted as the general spacing patterns, as measured by nearest-neighbour metrics, mean distance, and the slope of the cumulative MST curve. The strong correlation between a_{MST} and MD was unexpected ($r = 0.80$ and 0.73 for observed and artificial data, respectively). In grasslands these indices were separated from the others on the second component, while they were separated on the fourth component in random communities. A third aspect was functional evenness ($FEve$ and *evenNND*). They were more strongly correlated with random data ($r = 0.504$) than grassland data ($r = 0.318$). This may have been caused by the random assignment of abundances, which would tend to increase species evenness in comparison to real data. Functional divergence ($FDiv$) was a distinct aspect of trait diversity.

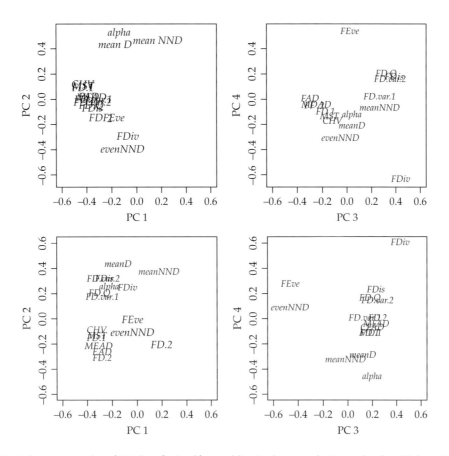

Figure 13.1 Principal components analysis of 16 indices of trait and functional diversity. The upper ordinations are based on 524 observations from an experimental grassland plant community and two traits rescaled to range from 0 to 1, the lower is based on 400 simulated communities with random assembly, random abundance, and two random traits. Both used correlation.

Is trait diversity independent of species richness and should we use a null model to correct for this?

Nearly all of the measures are mathematically independent of richness in that adding a redundant taxon, or splitting a species into two identical taxa, does not cause an increase in trait diversity. Even so, species richness and trait diversity tend to be positively correlated with both simulated and real data (Table 13.3). The trait diversity indices that loaded heavily on PC 1 were also strongly correlated with species richness. There was reasonable concordance between the two data sets. Of the remaining indices, only *meanNND* was negatively correlated with richness, and this was presumably due to the simple requirement that the density of species packing will tend to decline with increasing richness.

A principal cause of the correlations with species richness is the sampling effect: with increasing sample size, there is a greater likelihood of collecting extreme values (e.g. Huston 1997; Lepš et al. 2006). Variance-based indices (FD_{var}) have a tendency to increase with richness for same reason that measures of variance tend to increase with sample size. Distance-based indices (e.g. *FD, MST, MD, FD_Q*) behave similarly. Convex hull volume also tends to increase due to the sampling effect, and because maximal hull volume occurs only when richness is equal to or greater than 2^T where T is the number of traits and when each taxon is on the perimeter (Villéger et al. 2008).

Ricklefs and Travis (1980) interpreted the relationship between trait richness and species richness

Table 13.2 Principal components analysis of 13 trait diversity indices using both observed plant assemblages and artificial data. PC, principal component.

	PC 1	PC 2	PC 3	PC 4
Plant assemblages				
Standard deviation	3.060	1.661	1.027	0.960
Proportion of variance	0.585	0.172	0.066	0.058
Cumulative proportion	0.585	0.757	0.824	0.881
Loadings:				
α_{MST}	−0.138	**0.517**		−0.145
CHV	**−0.304**	0.112	−0.116	−0.160
FAD	**−0.293**		−0.305	
MFAD	**−0.314**		−0.246	
FDis	**−0.285**		0.176	0.176
FDiv		−0.319	0.428	**−0.629**
FD_{PG1}	**−0.312**		−0.183	
FD_{PG2}	**−0.284**	−0.147	−0.268	
FD_Q	**−0.293**		0.323	0.200
FD_{var1}	**−0.290**		0.262	
FD_{var2}	**−0.292**		0.349	0.163
FEve	−0.179	−0.151		**0.541**
MD	−0.158	**0.427**		−0.195
MST	**−0.311**		−0.146	−0.135
meanNND	0.144	**0.457**	0.269	
evenNND	−0.105	**−0.395**		0.190
Artificial data				
Standard deviation	2.915	1.735	1.233	1.063
Proportion of variance	0.531	0.188	0.095	0.071
Cumulative proportion	0.531	0.719	0.814	0.885
Loadings:				
α_{MST}	−0.228	**0.250**		**−0.461**
CHV	**−0.324**			
FAD	**−0.284**	−0.264		
MFAD	**−0.311**	−0.226		
FDis	**−0.285**	0.318		0.233
FDiv		0.252	0.228	**0.615**
FD_{PG1}	**−0.275**	−0.153		−0.109
FD_{PG2}	**−0.267**	−0.303		
FD_Q	**−0.303**	0.204		0.165
FD_{var1}	**−0.275**	0.175		
FD_{var2}	**−0.268**	0.318		0.150
FEve			**−0.660**	0.281
MD	−0.160	**0.372**		−0.288
MST	**−0.326**	−0.136		−0.136
meanNND	0.180	**0.372**	−0.224	**−0.317**
evenNND			**−0.665**	

Table 13.3 Pearson correlations between trait diversity indices and species richness in observed plant assemblages and artificial data.

	Plant assemblages	Artificial data
α_{MST}	0.226	0.399
CHV	0.847	0.803
FAD	0.954	0.972
MFAD	0.965	0.977
FDiv	0.181	0.018
FDis	0.723	0.363
FD_{PG1}	0.905	0.918
FD_{PG2}	0.954	0.938
FD_Q	0.760	0.511
FD_{var1}	0.737	0.428
FD_{var2}	0.727	0.365
FEve	0.496	0.121
MD	0.241	<0.001
MST	0.889	0.904
meanNND	−0.613	−0.696
evenNND	0.356	0.195

as being due to the tendency for species to be added at the periphery of the trait space, rather than internally within the trait space. While this is a reasonable idea, the tendency for random assemblages to also show this pattern suggests an inherent numerical bias. This is one reason why numerous authors have suggested comparing the observed trait diversity to what would be expected under a null model of independent species assortment (e.g. Strong et al. 1984; Villéger et al. 2008; Cornwell et al. 2006). This is probably most important if one wishes to compare trait diversity between regions with different species pools or between taxa at different trophic levels or those with different functional traits. Standardizing to a null model has been useful for investigating patterns of community assembly (see also de Bello et al. (2009)), but it is less clear whether such standardizations will be helpful for understanding the effects of trait diversity on ecosystem processes. Standardized trait diversity can be thought of as the residual diversity, after accounting for neutral processes. If trait diversity, per se, is causally important to ecosystems, then we might not expect the null-standardized index to matter. Alternatively, the null-standardized index may do a better job of catching residual complementarity and actually be more predictive of ecosystem processes than the unstandardized index.

When the correlations between the indices were conditioned on species richness using partial correlation, they tended to decline in the grassland data. This suggests the correlations between the indices are partly due to changes in species richness (Poos et al. 2009). The mean decline in r was only 0.16, however, and this suggests that the correlations between the indices are mainly independent of species richness. *FAD* showed the greatest declines (mean decline in $r = -0.41$), which suggests that approximately half of the information in *FAD* is the same as species richness.

With artificial data, there was no parallel trend, as the mean change in correlation was only -0.01. This means that the reliability of the indices is more strongly dependent on variation in species richness when working with real data than when working with artificial data. It also supports the conclusions of Poos et al. (2009) in which they suggest that greater care must taken when comparing the trait diversity of communities with similar species richness because the methods are less reliable within a narrow range of diversity.

13.3 Prospectus

13.3.1 Recommendations

No single best index
I suggest that are four conceptual aspects to trait diversity: the occupation of trait space, which is measured by the indices associated with trait richness and trait diversity (*CHV*, *FDis*, FD_{PG}, FD_Q, FD_{var}, *MFAD*, *MST*), functional evenness, functional divergence, and the density of species packing. Because the core indices are strongly concordant, it may not matter which is used, but a best practice might be to calculate them all and then use the one(s) that are most instructive. The distinction between trait diversity and trait richness appears to be somewhat artificial and may be unnecessary when using data from extant communities.

Use care, forethought, and hedge your bets when using these indices. There are few, if any, bona fide standard practices at this point in time (but consider Petchey et al. (2009)). First, there is the general question of whether one should use an overall multivariate measure of trait diversity that encompasses all reasonable traits or whether one should calculate trait diversity for each trait separately. The answer depends on one's goal. If the goal is to assess, as thoroughly as possible, the amount of trait diversity in a community, then a multivariate measure is most appropriate. If, however, the goal is to understand the constraints on community assembly, then a trait-by-trait approach may be more enlightening (e.g. Weiher et al. 1998; Cavender-Bares et al. 2004). Similarly, if the goal is to understand effects on ecosystem processes, then choosing a subset of traits that are likely to relate to the process of interest in probably the best approach (e.g. Lepš et al. 2006). Also consider using measures of phylogenetic diversity (Chapter 14), as these are sometimes more predictive of ecosystem processes than trait-based measures (e.g. Cadotte et al. 2009).

We also need to remember that we are dealing with indices of trait and functional diversity, and therefore no individual index should be considered to be the true definition of trait or functional diversity. Trait diversity is a latent variable, that is, it is a conceptual attribute of an assemblage that can only be measured indirectly via one or more indices. The principal method for dealing with latent variables is through confirmatory factor analysis within a structural equation modelling framework (Grace 2006). Such an approach is intellectually honest, in that it generalizes trait diversity by utilizing the common information in a set of parallel indicators.

Consider the indices critically
FD_Q is the most intuitively attractive index of functional diversity because of its simplicity, incorporation of abundance, and parallels with Simpson diversity and *MPD* (see also Lepš et al. (2006) and Chapter 14). Prior to writing this review, I tried to develop my own index from first principles. I was somewhat disappointed to have arrived at FD_Q. *FDis* is similarly intuitive and provides similar values. FD_{var} is also intuitive, but is not truly multivariate. *MD* is conceptually linked to FD_Q

and its phylogenetic analogue, *MPD*. All of these can sometimes produce lower trait diversity when intermediate taxa are added. Perhaps this is only a theoretical issue because both real and artificial data do not show any real problem with declining trait diversity with richness. Care should be taken if one is providing advice on how to maximize diversity; in such cases it is best to follow Pavoine et al. (2005a) and use an ultrametric distance matrix.

The Convex hull volume is very attractive for estimating the volume of trait space occupied by a community. However, as a measure of trait diversity or richness it has three important drawbacks. The first drawback is the requirement that a community have one more species present than it has trait dimensions. This means that communities with few species will have a convex hull volume of 0 if the number of traits is greater than a few. One could state that the convex hull volume in such cases is undefined, but this is more of a semantical dodge than a solution. In geometry, it takes at least four points to define a three-dimensional volume, and so three points in space do not have a volume. So we are left with the fact that if there are three traits of interest, a three-species community has zero trait diversity. One way to avoid this problem is to use only the first two principal components of the trait data and thus communities of three species could have a two-dimensional convex hull area. This still leaves the two-species community in limbo with a volume of 0 and it means we must ignore some of the trait information. Secondly, *CHV* will tend to scale with increasing richness because maximum *CHV* will occur at 2^T species. Lastly, the convex hull volume does not increase if a taxon with intermediate trait values is added to an assemblage. As a measure of trait volume this is reasonable, but as a measure of trait diversity some may view this as inappropriate. This question seems to be a matter of opinion, more than of fact, so we should not privilege one over the other.

MST is the most intuitively attractive of the tree-based methods and it also avoids the question of clustering method. Even so, FD_{PG2} is strictly analogous to *PD*. These methods may be the only solution for estimating the volume of occupied

trait space if the trait dimensionality is more than two or three and some samples have low species richness.

Be aware of critical decisions (Box 13.1)

> ## Box 13.1 Key questions and steps for calculating trait and functional diversity
>
> A. Species by traits data
>   a. Which traits?
>   b. How are traits measured?
>   i. Continuous, ordinal, binomial, or nominal? This has implications for choosing distance measures and trait rescaling.
>   c. More than one trait? If so, rescale traits and collapse correlated traits with PCOA or PCA.
>   i. Rescale to relative range (so that trait values range from 0 to 1 based on the observed trait values), or regional or global range, with z transform, or some other appropriate method.
>   ii. In general, do not z transform ordinal, binomial, or nominal traits.
>   iii. Note that PCoA is more generic and can use a variety of distance methods. PCA on covariance = PCoA if using Euclidean distances, PCA on covariance with z-transformed data = PCA on correlation.
> B. Samples by species data
>   a. How is abundance measured?

13.3.2 Future directions

Some enduring questions remain. There is relatively little understanding of how trait diversity varies along real gradients (but see Swenson and Enquist (2007), Pausas and Verdú (2008), and Filippi-Codaccioni et al. (2009)). Functional ecologists have largely focused on shifts in community mean values (e.g. Cornwell & Ackerly 2009) or have used independent contrasts (i.e. consistent shifts among sets of congeners, e.g. Cunningham et al. (1999)) to assess how functional traits shift along gradients. Historically, community ecologists have focused on how communities differ from neutral communities, rather than applying gradient approaches. If functional diversity is not perfectly correlated with species richness, is it under the same sorts of controls as species richness? If it is not, then what are the controls on it and how do we understand the interrelationships between species richness and functional diversity?

One way to approach the question of how trait diversity is related to species richness is to recognize that the volume of occupied trait space is a simple function of the number of taxa times the average amount of trait space occupied per taxon:

$$Richness_{trait} \approx Richness_{species} \times meanNND$$

This approach could be useful because we can explicitly link MST to richness by

$$MST = meanNND(S-1) + \text{redundancy}$$

$$\text{std.redundancy} = \frac{MST - (meanNND(S-1))}{MST}$$

where the redundancy within a community would be the amount by which average branch length in the MST exceeds the $meanNND$. If each taxon is unique and contributes equally to the MST, then there is no redundancy. As taxa have closer nearest neighbours relative to the average branch length of the MST, then there is increasing redundancy. At the limit, where $meanNND = 0$, then all the taxa are redundant and standard redundancy is 1 (i.e. all of the MST is from redundant taxa).

Does functional diversity affect ecosystem processes? While there is some good evidence that ecosystem processes are indeed promoted by functional diversity (e.g. Petchey & Gaston 2004; Díaz et al. 2007; Cadotte et al. 2009), a general lack of quality functional trait data has hampered progress in this area, as many studies simply used the number of functional types in lieu of traits.

How do these measures vary as a function of realistic changes in functional diversity, that is, if we double trait diversity, do we double the index of trait diversity? Do we need some kind of 'effective numbers' transforms for the indices that use abundance information?

How can phylogenetic and functional approaches be combined to increase understanding, for example consider Cavender-Bares et al. (2009) and Pavoine et al. (2009)?

13.4 Key points

1. Many of the indices have shortcomings because of their intrinsic relationships with species richness, their capacity to decrease when intermediate taxa are added, and their requirements for three or more taxa, for the number of taxa per trait, for needing non-zero trait values, or for less than clear standard methods. In addition, the indices represent at least four components of diversity, therefore no best index for calculating trait diversity can be singled out. Multiple indices should be used and compared.

2. A subset of the indices of trait diversity was strongly correlated, even after accounting for variation in species richness, therefore many of the indices may be roughly equivalent indicators of trait diversity, especially if species richness and trait diversity have notable variation among the samples. This also suggests that trait diversity and trait richness may be largely a singular latent variable that can be measured with good reliability.

3. Several indices measure distinctive aspects of trait diversity. These include: (a) functional divergence ($FDiv$), (b) functional evenness ($FEve$ and $evenNND$), and (c) nearest-neighbour metrics (a_{MST} and $meanNND$).

4. Like other diversity indices, trait diversity is sensitive to a variety of methodological choices and there is no sound way to compare trait diversities except when produced using absolutely parallel methods.

5. There are great opportunities for the further development of trait diversity indices, for understanding the environmental controls on trait diversity, and for understanding the effects of trait diversity on ecosystems. These questions remain open.

Acknowledgements

EW thanks Will Cornwell for helpful suggestions, and Tali Lee and 18 undergraduates who contributed to the trait data. EW was supported by NSF DEB-0415383.

Measuring phylogenetic biodiversity

Mark Vellend, William K. Cornwell, Karen Magnuson-Ford,
and Arne Ø. Mooers

14.1 Introduction

14.1.1 Overview

Biodiversity has been described as the 'biology of numbers and difference' (Gaston 1996). Because species are different from one another, traditional metrics of biodiversity such as species richness or evenness increase when there are more species or when abundance is more equally apportioned among these species (see Chapters 4 and 5). Not only are species different from one another, the magnitude of these differences varies tremendously depending on the set of species in question. Consider two hypothetical islands, each with only two species of vertebrate animals in equal abundance: two birds in one case and a bird plus a mammal in the other. Both islands have species richness = 2 (for vertebrates) and the same maximal value of species evenness. However, our intuition tells us that a bird plus a mammal represents more biodiversity than does two birds (Purvis & Hector 2000). Metrics of phylogenetic diversity quantify the difference.

Differences among species can be characterized by measuring any number of traits, such as body size and shape, dietary requirements, physiological tolerance of various stressors, etc. (see Chapter 17). Particular traits may be of special interest to a researcher for various reasons, such as their hypothesized role in mediating species interactions (e.g. beak size in birds) or their importance in tolerating different environmental conditions (e.g. leaf thickness in plants). However, the degree of similarity or difference among species will depend strongly on the choice of traits measured, and many traits are only applicable to particular groups of organisms (e.g. photosynthetic rate in plants). A far more general method for quantifying diversity among species is an assessment of the species' evolutionary relationships, in the form of either taxonomy or a phylogeny. Modern phylogenies are derived from DNA-sequence data, which can be acquired for all organisms on the tree of life. The phylogenetic distance between two species is an estimate of the amount of time since the most recent common ancestor of both species, in other words the time that each has evolved independently of the other. While individual traits may show 'convergence', that is, similar values evolving in distantly related lineages, the phylogenetic distance represents a proxy for the magnitude of phenotypic differences (across a large number of traits) expected between any two species (Cavender-Bares et al. 2009).

Biologists have been interested in the phylogenetic component of biodiversity for two main reasons: (i) to explicitly incorporate species differences (via a common currency applicable to all taxa from bacteria to primates), rather than just species numbers, into conservation prioritization and (ii) to yield insights into the structure of ecological communities. In the first case, recognizing that difficult prioritization decisions need to be made concerning the investment of limited resources for conservation, it has been argued that the aim should not be just to protect the greatest number of species possible, but to protect sets of species that are most taxonomically distinct or that represent the greatest possible variety of biological features (Vane-Wright et al. 1991; Faith 1992; Mooers et al. 2005; Isaac et al. 2007). To this end, considerable effort has been aimed at quantifying the evolutionary distinctness (and therefore conservation value) of individual species, or the 'phylogenetic diversity' of a group of species (Vane-Wright et al. 1991; Faith 1992; Altschul & Lipman 1990; Nixon & Wheeler 1992; Pavoine et al. 2005b; Redding and Mooers 2006).

In terms of analyses in community ecology, the incorporation of phylogenetic information has a relatively long history. Darwin (1859) first hypothesized that competition should be strongest between close relatives (e.g. congeners), leading subsequent researchers to explore ratios of species-to-genus numbers (or genus-to-family, etc.) as potentially indicative of the role of competition in structuring ecological communities (e.g, Elton 1946). More recently, the same conceptual question has been approached using modern phylogenies, which contain far more information on evolutionary relationships than taxonomic categories (reviewed in Webb et al. (2002), Vamosi et al. (2009), and Cavender-Bares et al. (2009)). If indeed close relatives compete most strongly, local communities should contain species that are relatively distantly related to one another. Alternatively, species membership in a local community might be most constrained by tolerance of abiotic environmental conditions, and if close relatives share similar tolerances, local communities should contain species that are relatively closely related to one another. To test these hypotheses, researchers have employed some of the phylogenetic diversity metrics from the conservation literature and also introduced some additional metrics of their own (Webb et al. 2008).

As applied to issues in both conservation biology and community ecology, phylogenetic diversity has been a topic of tremendous interest in the recent literature. As such, a large number of metrics to quantify phylogenetic diversity have been introduced, and for some subsets of these metrics analyses have been done to assess their redundancy or the degree to which they meet certain pre-set criteria (e.g. Pavoine et al. 2005b; Kraft et al. 2007; Hardy 2008; Schweiger et al. 2008). In this chapter, we aim to provide guidance to researchers and practitioners for selecting particular metrics and for interpreting published results based on different metrics. After providing some important definitions (see Box 14.1) and a conceptual overview, we will first offer a categorization of metrics found

in the literature, according to the functional form of the calculation and the nature of the input data (e.g. species presence–absence vs abundance data). Next we report results of simulation analyses, in which artificial communities were created under different assumptions about the processes by which phylogenies arise, and by which membership and abundance in local communities are determined. The goals here were to assess quantitative relationships among different metrics (e.g. which behave similarly?) and to assess the sensitivity of different metrics to underlying evolutionary and ecological processes. We will then discuss the qualitative and quantitative relationships among metrics and how researchers can go about choosing metrics for different purposes.

14.1.2 Approaching the study of phylogenetic diversity

The choice of metrics of phylogenetic diversity in empirical studies is entirely under the control of the researcher, but will be influenced by three key aspects of a particular system, which are typically not (or only partially) under a researcher's control: underlying processes, related patterns (other than phylogenetic diversity), and data constraints.

A variety of evolutionary and ecological processes influence the values of phylogenetic diversity metrics, either indirectly or directly. Macroevolutionary processes will create patterns that matter a great deal for phylogenetic community structure and the choice of metric. For example, the extent to which speciation is 'ecological' (i.e. driven by divergent selection) will affect the shape of the phylogeny and the phylogenetic conservatism of different traits. Both of these will in turn affect the extent to which species coexistence may be influenced by relatedness (Mooers & Heard 1997; Kembel & Hubbell 2006; Kraft et al. 2007; McPeek 2007, 2008). Ecological processes influencing community assembly, such as environmental constraints on fitness or competition for resources, will also influence phylogenetic diversity metrics (Webb et al. 2002).

Some empirical patterns, including the distribution of species numbers and abundances among sites, and the degree of balance in a phylogenetic tree (see Box 14.1), may influence the range of

Box 14.1 Definitions of attributes of phylogenetic trees

A rooted phylogenetic tree summarizes hypothesized evolutionary relationships among species or other biological units such as lineages within species. Phylogenetic trees can be estimated using a variety of methods (see Felsenstein 2004), the details of which are beyond the scope of this chapter. For the purposes of this discussion we will assume that the **tips** (sometimes referred to as 'leaves') of the tree represent species (see Figure Box 14.1). A **node** represents the most recent common ancestor of all species descending from that point in the tree (i.e. where branches split) and the **root node** (often referred to simply as the root) is a single point from which it has been inferred that all species descend, thus giving the entire tree temporal directionality. The simplest type of phylogenetic tree represents only the topology, with no information on the lengths of branches connecting the nodes (e.g. taxonomies based on morphological data and some types of molecular data). We refer to such trees as **node-based trees**.

A branch in the phylogenetic tree (also referred to as an 'edge' in graph theory), and its associated **branch length**, may represent the accumulation of evolutionary change, in which case the tips may not line up because the rate of evolutionary change is not constant across all branches. Alternatively, branch lengths may be scaled to represent the passage of time, such that all tips line up in the same place. Each of these two types of phylogenetic trees are considered **additive**, and the latter type is additionally called **ultrametric** (all distances from root to tip are the same). We refer to trees with quantitative branch lengths as **distance-based trees**.

Nodes are usually bifurcating, such that lineages split into two. **Polytomies** are nodes where this is not the case, and the lineage splits into three or more. This arises most commonly due to data limitations. The **degree** of a node is the number of branches, both ancestral and descendant, connected to that node (three for a bifurcating node).

The shape of phylogenetic trees can be characterized by two key properties: their degree of balance and the degree to which divergence events happened predominantly early (divergence decelerating) or late (divergence accelerating) during the evolution of the group (the latter is characterized by the γ statistic). In a perfectly **balanced tree**, all tips are separated from the root by the same number of nodes, which is equivalent to saying that all lineages bifurcate the same number of times. In a perfectly **imbalanced tree**, one lineage descending from each node connects directly to a tip with no further bifurcations. In a tree with low γ divergence events are concentrated early during the evolution of the group, and vice versa.

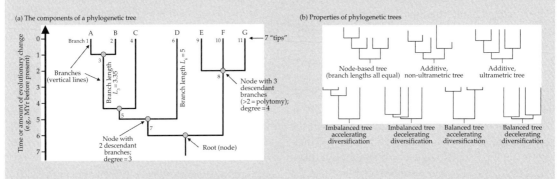

Figure Box 14.1 The components of a phylogenetic tree (a), and different representations and shapes of trees illustrating their properties (b).

possible values different metrics can take. The same factors may affect the degree to which particular metrics are distinct from others (e.g. Redding et al. 2008; Schweiger et al. 2008). These 'other' patterns may be influenced by some of the same processes as phylogenetic diversity, but they can be quantified independently and may on their own influence

phylogenetic diversity metrics regardless of what processes created them.

Finally, there may be data constraints. Specifically, the nature of the phylogenetic information may only allow representation of the topology of a phylogenetic tree, or it may allow estimation of branch lengths connecting nodes in the tree (see

Box 14.1). In addition, data might be available only on the presence or absence of species in particular places without relative abundances. Unlike the processes and patterns mentioned under the first two considerations, these constraints are, in theory, under the control of the researcher, but, in practice, many studies are based on existing data, which may impose such constraints.

In this chapter we do not discuss the first consideration of the link between process and pattern (e.g. *why* do locally co-occurring species represent a non-random subset of a regional phylogeny?), which has been thoroughly reviewed elsewhere (Webb et al. 2002; McPeek 2008; Vamosi et al. 2009; Cavender-Bares et al. 2009). Instead we focus on the practical issue of what quantitative information is reflected in different metrics and on the latter considerations of how properties of the existing data may influence the choice or interpretation of different metrics. We restrict our attention to calculations of phylogenetic diversity within focal sets of species or local communities, rather than partitioning diversity among hierarchical levels (e.g. α, β, γ; Graham & Fine 2008).

14.2   State of the field

All empirical studies of phylogenetic diversity begin with an estimated phylogeny for the group of species of interest. The scope of this phylogeny varies—it may include all known species across some broader region (e.g. all birds of South America or of the world) or only those species present in particular surveyed areas (e.g. the birds found in a survey of five tropical forest plots). For convenience, we refer to these two options as a 'regional' phylogeny and a 'local' phylogeny, respectively. It is then typically of interest to quantify the relative magnitude of phylogenetic diversity among focal subsets of species, which may be defined as those co-occurring in a local area (e.g. the birds in one tropical forest plot) or a candidate set of species proposed for special conservation attention (e.g. the bird species listed as endangered in Brazil). We refer to the portion of the regional or local phylogeny that includes only the focal subset of species as the 'subset' phylogeny.

Two qualitatively different types of metrics of phylogenetic diversity have been developed. We refer to type I metrics as those that begin by calculating a distinctness score for all species in a regional phylogeny and then calculating some function of these scores (typically the sum) for particular focal subsets of species to yield a metric of phylogenetic diversity. Type II metrics start with a local phylogeny (or possibly a regional phylogeny), and for a focal subset of species they depend only on properties of the subset phylogeny. Type I metrics have been used largely in conservation biology, while community ecologists have mostly employed type II metrics, but some have been used in both fields. For type I metrics, the motivation behind first calculating fixed individual species scores, rather than effectively allowing these to depend on the focal species set (as in type II metrics), is to permit individual species to be ranked in a way that does not depend on the status of other species (e.g. whether or not they are already protected).

Type I metrics of phylogenetic diversity are calculated in two stages. First, an index of distinctness is calculated for each species and second, these values are entered into a separate function to summarize the scores for a focal subset of species. In stage one, five different indices of species' distinctness have been used in the literature: taxonomic distinctness (TD), species originality (SO), pendant edge (PE), species evolutionary history (SEH), and originality of species within a set (OSS; see Table 14.1). The first two (TD, SO) are based only on node-based phylogenetic trees, and the other three (PE, SEH, OSS) are based on distance-based trees. In stage two, the most common function is simply the sum, which is obviously intended to incorporate species richness into the metric (all else being equal, more species represent more phylogenetic diversity). With species' abundance data it is also possible to apply a procedure similar to rarefaction (see Chapter 4) to yield an index that reflects the expected sum in a sample of x individuals chosen randomly from the community (Ricotta 2004), but this is seldom used in the literature. In theory it is also possible to calculate the mean of distinctness values, although this is also seldom done.

At first glance, the number of different type II metrics in the literature appears rather large, but the

Table 14.1   Indices of species distinctness for use in type I metrics of phylogenetic diversity.

Index	Description	Reference
Taxonomic distinctness (*TD*)	Reciprocal of number of nodes between species and root of tree (standardized by dividing by the sum of these scores across species and multiplying by 100)	Vane-Wright et al. (1991)
	Modification: To account for polytomies, count number of descendants at each node rather than number of nodes	May (1990)
Species originality (*SO*)	Assign each node in a tree a value of 1 if more species descend from that node than its sister node, and 0 otherwise; sum the values at the nodes between a species and the root; smaller values indicate greater distinctness	Nixon & Wheeler (1992)
	Modification: As above, but assign each node a value equal to the number of species that descend from that node; referred to as weighted species originality (*WSO*)	Nixon & Wheeler (1992)
Pendant edge (*PE*)	The length of the branch connecting a species to the rest of the regional tree	Altschul & Lipman (1990)
Species evolutionary history (*SEH*)	The portion of a phylogenetic tree attributable to a species; shared branches are apportioned equally among descendant lineages ('equal splits'), for example in a tree with no polytomies, the portion of a branch that is assigned to a species that is n nodes away from that branch is equal to $1/2^n$.	Redding & Mooers (2006)
	Modification: As above, but shared branches are apportioned equally among descendant species ('fair proportions', *SEH*_fair); referred to as species evolutionary distinctiveness	Redding et al. (2008)
Originality of species within a set (*OSS*)	Values for each species that 'maximize the expected dissimilarity between two species randomly drawn from the set' There is no simpler way of describing this metric	Pavoine et al. (2005b)

Capitalized short forms are used in the text. Equations are not shown because in most cases either verbal descriptions are very simple (*TD*, *PE*) or it is not possible to write an equation that clarifies any further the meaning of the metric (*SO*, *OSS*). Original publications can be consulted for details.

distinction between many of these is based only on the nature of the input data rather than the equation into which the data enter. Two data characteristics in particular allow different sets of metrics to be aggregated. First is the nature of the phylogenetic tree (see Box 14.1). If only the tree topology has been estimated, 'distances' within the tree are quantified simply by counting the nodes along the path of interest (e.g. between two tips). Quantitative branch lengths allow distances to take a continuous range of values. Metrics based on counting nodes are effectively special cases of distance-based metrics in which all branch lengths are set equal to one. Second is the nature of species abundance data. There may be quantitative estimates of species' abundances, or only of species' presence or absence; metrics based on the latter are special

cases of the former in which each species has the same abundance. Four distinct kinds of type II metric have been proposed (described in Table 14.2). Each of these can incorporate abundance data if available, and may also be expressed as deviations from expected values based on null models.

14.2.1   Null models

Any of the metrics we have described thus far can be expressed in their raw form or as deviations from an expectation derived from a null model. In practice, null models have not been employed in the conservation literature, but are commonplace in the community ecology literature. In addition, null models are almost always used only with presence–absence data at the smallest scale. The

Table 14.2 Type II metrics of phylogenetic diversity.

Metric	Presence–absence (PA) version	Abundance-weighted (AW) version	Equation	References
Phylogenetic diversity (PD)	Sum of all branch lengths in the portion of a phylogenetic tree connecting the focal set of species (PD, PDn)	For the subset tree, the number of branches multiplied by the weighted mean branch length, with weights equal to the average abundance of species sharing that branch* (PDaw, PDnaw)	$B \times \dfrac{\sum\limits_{i}^{B} L_i A_i}{\sum\limits_{i}^{B} A_i}$	PA: Faith (1992) AW: Barker (2002)
Mean phylogenetic distance (MPD)[†]	Mean phylogenetic distance between each pair of species in the focal set (MPD, MPDn)	Mean phylogenetic distance between pairs of individuals (or other units of abundance), excluding same-species pairs (MPDaw, MPDnaw)	$\dfrac{\sum\sum_{m<n} d_{mn} a_m a_n}{\sum\sum_{m<n} a_m a_n}$	PA: Webb (2000) AW: Warwick & Clarke (1995)
		Modification: Mean phylogenetic distance between pairs of individuals (or other units of abundance), including same-species pairs	$\dfrac{\sum\limits_{m}\sum\limits_{n} d_{mn} a_m a_n}{\sum\limits_{m}\sum\limits_{n} a_m a_n}$	Rao (1982); Warwick & Clarke (1995)
Sum of phylogenetic distances (SPD)[‡]	Sum of phylogenetic distances between each pair of species Equivalent to MPD multiplied by the number of species pairs	Abundance-weighted MPD multiplied by the number of species pairs	$\left(\dfrac{S(S-1)}{2}\right) \times$ $\dfrac{\sum\sum_{m<n} d_{mn} a_m a_n}{\sum\sum_{m<n} a_m a_n}$	PA: Crozier (1997); Helmus et al. (2007) AW: none
Mean nearest neighbour distance (MNND)	Mean phylogenetic distance from each species to its closest relative in the focal species set (MNND, MNNDn)	Weighted mean phylogenetic distance from each species to its closest relative, with weights equal to species' abundance (MNNDaw, MNNDnaw)	$\sum\limits_{m}^{S} \min(d_{mn}) a_m$	PA: Webb (2000) AW: none

Short forms correspond to labels in PCA plots (see Fig. 14.1); n = node-based metric. B, number of branches in tree; L_i, length of branch i; A_i, average abundance (measured in any units) of species that share branch i; d_{mn}, phylogenetic distance between species m and n; a_m, abundance of species m (with presence–absence data all species have the same abundance); S, number of species in the focal set; aw, abundance-weighted metric.

*This is our interpretation of how Barker's iterative method (for unrooted trees) would be applied most simply to a rooted tree.

[†] For ultrametric trees, the presence–absence version of MPD is equivalent to twice the phylogenetic species variability (PSV) metric of Helmus et al. (2007), which was derived as the expected variance among species in a neutrally evolved trait. The phylogenetic species evenness (PSE) metric of Helmus et al. is a rescaled version of abundance-weighted MPD (both PSV and PSE are calculated using a phylogenetic tree with branch lengths scaled so that all root-to-tip distances are 1).

[‡] Helmus et al. (2007) calculate phylogenetic species richness (PSR) by multiplying MPD by the number of species, rather than the number of species pairs, although the two options scale monotonically with one another.

principle goal in constructing a null model is to ask what distribution of values is expected for focal sets of species in which there is no phylogenetic structure, but in which all other properties (e.g. species richness) are the same.

Two main classes of null models have been used. First, for a focal set of S species, one can take repeated draws of S species chosen randomly from the regional phylogenetic tree. In essence, this is like shuffling the species identities randomly among tips in the phylogenetic tree. Alternatively,

with a species-by-site data matrix, one can repeatedly shuffle the species' presences among sites to essentially randomize which species co-occur while retaining each species' frequency across sites. It is also possible to place a variety of additional constraints on the shuffling procedure, such as retaining both the species richness of each site and the frequency of each species (Gotelli & Graves 1996).

Once a null model has been constructed, the metrics of interest are calculated for each simulated set of species, and observed values can be expressed either as the number of standard deviations away from the expected mean (Webb et al. 2008) or the probability of obtaining a lower (or higher) value than that observed solely by chance. Since in many cases the distribution of values will depend on species richness, metrics expressed in this way are usually not monotonic transformations of the initial values. For example, phylogenetic diversity (PD) might be equivalent in two different communities with different numbers of species, but the one with fewer species will have a lower null expectation, and therefore the re-expressed value will be higher in the community with fewer species.

14.2.2 Simulation analyses

Different metrics can be compared and evaluated both qualitatively and quantitatively. In terms of qualitative comparisons, a researcher's choice of metric may depend on what information they want reflected in the metric (e.g. species' closest relatives or their full set of relationships), rather than any predetermined quantitative criteria (e.g. sensitivity to a non-random community assembly). Both qualitative and quantitative considerations are addressed in the Prospectus section, and to make quantitative comparisons we conducted a set of simulation analyses. The simulations were aimed at addressing the following three questions: (1) which metrics are redundant with one another, (2) how do metrics compare with respect to their sensitivity to different non-random community assembly processes, and (3) how does tree shape influence the answers to questions 1 and 2?

We simulated sets of species ('communities') under a number of scenarios that vary in the following respects: the degree of balance in the regional phylogenetic tree, the change or lack thereof in diversification rate through time in the regional phylogeny (decelerating or accelerating, according to the 'γ' parameter, *sensu* Pybus & Harvey 2000), the nature of (non)randomness in the community assembly process, and the number of species in the community. All regional phylogenetic trees were rooted, ultrametric, contained 100 species, and were created in five ways: (1) by a pure birth ('Yule') process (constant rate of diversification

through time and across all lineages), (2) entirely imbalanced with decelerating diversification, (3) entirely imbalanced with accelerating diversification, (4) entirely balanced, decelerating diversification, and (5) entirely balanced, accelerating diversification. In order to span the range of empirical values of change in diversification rate, we rescaled the branch length of both the balanced and imbalanced trees to match the most extreme observations (measured via the γ statistic; see McPeek 2008). For each tree, we simulated local communities either by randomly selecting species or via algorithms that created phylogenetically clustered or over-dispersed sets of species, with each of the latter done in two ways. For phylogenetic over-dispersion, the first species was chosen randomly and each subsequent species was chosen with a probability proportional to the square root of its average phylogenetic distance to either species (method 1) or individuals (method 2) already in the community. Using the square root of phylogenetic distances approximates the expected trait difference based on a Brownian motion model of trait evolution (Felsenstein 1985). For method 2, the mean phylogenetic distances were calculated by weighting the distance to each already-chosen species by the abundance of that species. Phylogenetically clustered sets of species were created in an identical way, except that the mean phylogenetic distance to already-chosen species or individuals determined the probability of a species *not* being chosen. Abundances were either considered to be equivalent across species (presence–absence based metrics) or drawn from a log-normal distribution and assigned from highest to lowest in the sequence that species were chosen. Sets of species were selected with species richness of 10, 20, 30, or 40. For each of the five tree types, we simulated 500 sets of species for each of the four levels of species richness in each of the five community assembly processes, for a total of 20 000 sets of species.

We focused our analyses on two groups of metrics, which correspond to those of interest to conservation biologists and those of interest to community ecologists. The 'conservation' group consisted of all type I metrics (sums of species distinctness values), plus Faith's (1992) phylogenetic diversity (PD) because type I metrics are often

Table 14.3 Correlations among sums of type I metrics, as well as species richness (*SR*) and phylogenetic diversity (*PD*), for 10 000 simulated species sets selected from a pure birth phylogenetic tree. Short forms correspond to those in Table 14.1.

TD	0.92						
SO	0.95	0.91					
WSO	0.94	0.92	0.98				
PE	0.93	0.83	0.91	0.87			
SEH	0.95	0.96	0.94	0.95	0.86		
SEH_fair	0.97	0.96	0.95	0.95	0.87	1.00	
OSS	0.73	0.91	0.76	0.79	0.62	0.88	0.87
PD	0.87	0.90	0.85	0.86	0.78	0.94	0.94	0.87
	SR	TD	SO	WSO	PE	SEH	SEH_fair	OSS

evaluated with respect to their ability to capture PD (e.g. Redding et al. 2008). Because community ecologists are typically interested in assessing non-random phylogenetic structure in sets of species, rather than phylogenetic diversity per se, the 'community ecology' group of metrics included only the null-model corrected versions of each type II metric. These were calculated as the number of standard deviations from the mean across randomly assembled communities (described above). In addition, since the value of the summed phylogenetic distance (*SPD*) and the modified mean phylogenetic distance (*MPD*; see Table 14.2) differ from unmodified *MPD* only due to species richness or the species abundance distribution, both of which are accounted for in the null model, the null-model corrected versions of these are redundant. Thus, we focused on the four versions of *PD*, *MPD*, and *MNND*, depending on the combination of node- vs distance-based trees and presence–absence vs abundance data, for a total of 12 metrics in the community ecology group. To calculate these metrics, we drew on publicly available functions in the ape (v2.3), picante (v0.7), and ade4 (v1.4) libraries for R. New phylogenetic functions coded specifically for this analysis are available within the Picante library for R (http://picante.r-forge.r-project.org/).

14.2.3   Simulation results

Correlations among type I metrics, and between these metrics and phylogenetic diversity (*PD*), were typically very high. Principal component analyses for each tree type revealed that the variation among these metrics is essentially one dimensional, with >90% of the variance explained by the first principal component in all cases (figures not shown). Table 14.3 shows the correlation structure among these metrics (as well as species richness) for the pure birth tree, where $r > 0.7$ for all pairwise comparisons except one (for which $r > 0.6$). Correlations among metrics were even higher for all other tree types, with the one exception arising for balanced trees with accelerating diversification. In this case, all species receive highly similar distinctness scores (see example of this tree type in Box 14.1), such that type I sums give virtually identical results to each other and to species richness ($r > 0.99$). However, *PD* varies considerably depending on how many basal clades are included in a given sample of species, such that correlations between *PD* and the type I sums were relatively low ($r \approx 0.45$). For pure birth or balanced trees, correlations of these metrics with species richness were high (mean $r > 0.9$), whereas for imbalanced trees correlations with species richness were considerably lower (mean $r = 0.62$ for decelerating diversification, mean $r = 0.45$ for accelerating diversification).

Type II metrics also gave broadly similar results to one another for pure birth or balanced trees, but not for imbalanced trees (Table 14.4). For pure birth and imbalanced trees, correlations tended to be higher within distance-based or node-based groups of metrics than across these groups (Fig. 14.1). For imbalanced trees the correlations across the two groups were actually negative (Fig. 14.1), a result that can be explained as follows. Commu-

Table 14.4   Correlations of distance-based (*D*) vs. node-based (*N*), and presence-absence (PA) vs. abundance-weighted (AW) versions of each of the three main type II metrics, in all cases expressed as deviations from a null model.

	Presence–absence version	Abundance-weighted version	Distances	Nodes	
	D vs. N	D vs. N	PA vs. AW	PA vs. AW	
Metric					
PD	0.79	0.68	0.89	0.85	Pure birth tree
MPD	0.69	0.80	0.91	0.79	
MNND	0.84	0.83	0.88	0.89	
PD	−0.75	−0.55	0.83	0.35	Imbalanced tree
MPD	−0.25	−0.15	0.95	0.84	Decelerating diversification
MNND	−0.10	0.02	0.96	0.53	
PD	−0.68	−0.45	0.86	0.40	Imbalanced tree
MPD	−0.71	−0.69	0.91	0.88	Accelerating diversification
MNND	−0.26	0.05	0.93	0.56	
PD	0.99	0.96	0.92	0.96	Balanced tree
MPD	0.98	0.98	0.95	0.97	Decelerating diversification
MNND	0.99	0.98	0.95	0.95	
PD	0.96	0.93	0.97	0.95	Balanced tree
MPD	0.96	0.97	0.91	0.95	Accelerating diversification
MNND	0.98	0.96	0.92	0.93	

nity assembly was based on a tree with quantitative distances along branches, such that over-dispersed sets of species contain many of the species that connect to the rest of the tree via long branches (early-divergent or 'basal' species). Although these species are relatively distantly related to most others, they are separated from one another by relatively few nodes, such that over-dispersed sets of species actually appear clustered on a node-based tree. For clustered community assembly, if the first species chosen (randomly) is relatively basal, then most other species will be equidistant from the first and therefore have similar probabilities of joining the community next. For the resulting set of species, the value of node-based metrics will actually be higher than when over-dispersed species were chosen during community assembly. This creates the observed negative correlations. Within the distance-based type II metrics (null-model corrected), variation among sets of species was largely one dimensional, with >85% of the variation in each PCA explained by the first axis (Fig. 14.1).

Sensitivity to non-random community assembly processes varied considerably among metrics and among types of phylogenetic trees (Fig. 14.2), with several notable patterns. First, for imbalanced trees, node-based metrics are either insensitive to non-random community assembly or they actually deviate from the null model in the opposite direction than expected (Fig. 14.2b and 14.2c). In particular, over-dispersed communities had *lower* node-based metric values than expected, for the reasons explained above with respect to negative correlations between distance-based and node-based metrics on imbalanced trees.

The amount of variance among species in their phylogenetic distinctness mediated the effect of tree shape on the sensitivity of different metrics. We focus here only on distance-based metrics (the first and third panels from the left in Fig. 14.2). For balanced trees (Fig. 14.2d and 14.2e) there are relatively few basal clades, each with many species, such that overall, variance among species in their phylogenetic distinctness is small. In other words, on balanced trees most species in the phylogeny have very similar distribution of relatedness to other species on the tree and also very similar type I scores. In this evolutionary context, clustered assembly leads to sets of species that may be concentrated in only one of a few clades. In contrast, randomly assembled communities (which contained at least 10 species) will probably have members from across many or all deep clades, leading to large deviations from random expectation in metrics for clustered communities. In contrast, over-dispersed communities have representatives from many clades just as randomly assembled communities often do, with the non-random selection of species within clades only capable of creating relatively small deviations from random expectation. In imbalanced trees with accelerating diversification (Fig. 14.2c), a relatively small proportion of species are far more phylogenetically distinct than most others, leading to large deviations of over-dispersed communities (which include these species) from random sets of species. With the first species in each simulation chosen randomly, even clustered communities will sometimes include basal species, and after the first species is chosen all more derived species are equally related and have an equal chance of being selected, such that clustered communities deviate from random to a lesser extent than over-dispersed communities despite symmetry in the ecological community assembly processes. In pure birth trees there is sufficiently little variation among species in distinctness that over-dispersion is easier to detect than clustering (Fig. 14.2a), and in imbalanced trees with decelerating diversification over-dispersed and clustered communities show approximately equal deviations from the null expectation.

The final point to make concerning Fig. 14.2 is that in some cases the sensitivity to non-random community assembly varies among metrics. Again focusing only on distance-based metrics, for pure birth or balanced trees, *MPD* was more sensitive than *PD* or *MNND*, while for imbalanced trees the differences among metrics were relatively small.

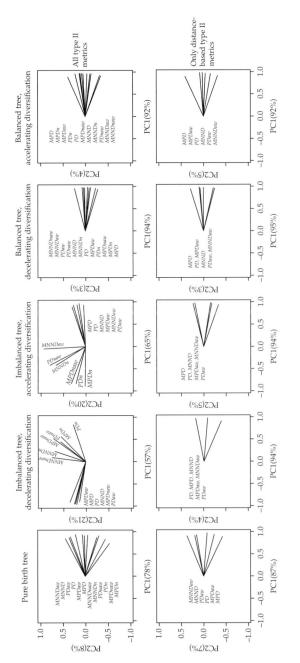

Figure 14.1 Principal component analyses for 12 type II null-model corrected metrics (top row) and for the six of these based on quantitative branch length information (distance-based metrics, bottom row). Labels correspond to those in Table 14.2 and the ordering in lists corresponds to the factor score for the relevant metric on PC2. The percentage variance accounted for by each axis is shown in the axis label.

14.3 Prospectus

14.3.1 Phylogenetic diversity in conservation

To the extent that assigning individual species distinctness scores is itself of value in conservation biology, researchers and practitioners should continue to find type I metrics useful. The sums across

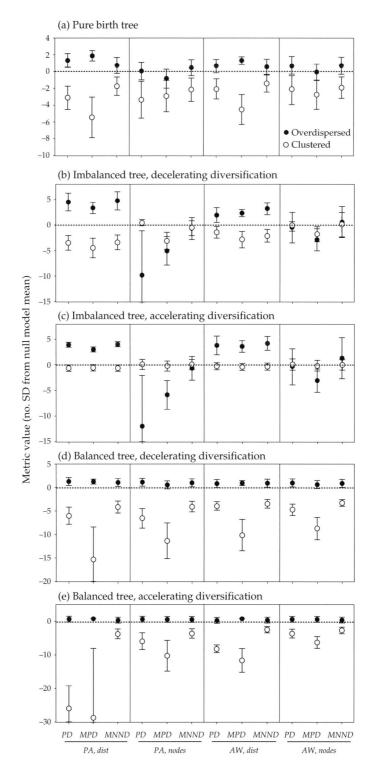

Figure 14.2 Sensitivity of each type II metric to over-dispersed or clustered phylogenetic community assembly processes. The *y*-axis shows the mean ±1 standard deviation for each type II metric, expressed as the number of standard deviations from a null-model mean, in 2000 focal species sets. Results are shown for community assembly processes in which species abundance was not part of the process (results were very similar for both versions of the community assembly process).

species for any of the type I metrics correlate fairly strongly with each other and with *PD*. Distance-based trees more completely represent evolutionary relationships than node-based trees, and since the use of node-based metrics appears to be motivated largely by logistical considerations (i.e. the lack of a distance-based tree), distance-based metrics seem clearly preferable. Within node-based and distance-based metrics, redundancy is quite high ($r > 0.9$ for most pairs of metrics across all tree types). As such, an appropriate criterion for choosing among metrics is their conceptual and mathematical simplicity. For node-based metrics, we recommend the taxonomic distinctness (*TD*) metric as it is more straightforward than either version of the species originality metrics (*OS*, *WOS*; see Table 14.1). For distance-based metrics, the originality-of-species-in-a-set (*OSS*) metric is conceptually less straightforward, requires an ultrametric tree, is mathematically much more complicated, and captures less *PD* than do the others (Redding et al. 2008), so we do not yet recommend its use, despite the fact that it shows relatively low correlations with *some* other metrics. The pendant-edge (*PE*) and species evolutionary history (*SEH*) metrics are both simple conceptually and mathematically (*PE* more so). Although *PE* and *SEH* are largely redundant on most tree shapes, *SEH* contains more information and will, for example, identify as evolutionarily distinct each species in a pair of close relatives when the species pair itself is evolutionarily distinct, whereas *PE* would be quite small in this case. It does not matter which method of apportioning shared branches is used in the calculation of *SEH* ($r \geq 0.98$ for all tree types).

In some cases a conservation biologist may not be interested in prioritizing species, but in prioritizing sites based on the species they contain (e.g. Forest et al. 2007) or in understanding how ecosystem processes depend on the phylogenetic diversity, rather than only the richness, of the species in a community (e.g. Cadotte et al. 2008). In such cases, there is no need to assign individual scores and it is more appropriate to use PD as a straightforward proxy for the quantity of evolutionary history and therefore trait variation in a community.

14.3.2 Phylogenetic diversity in community ecology

When community ecologists are interested in using phylogenetic information to assess the degree to which community assembly has been non-random with respect to species traits or relatedness, it is most appropriate to use null-model corrected versions of type II metrics. The mean value of some metrics (in their raw form) is correlated with species richness (e.g. *MNND* decreases as species are added to a community), and even for those that are not (e.g. *MPD*) the variance among randomly assembled communities may well be correlated with species richness. The range of possible *MPD* values, for example, declines as the number of species increases. As such, the extent to which the members of a community represent non-random selections from a phylogeny cannot generally be assessed using the raw values for type II metrics. In terms of null models, shuffling species among phylogeny tips seems most straightforward, as this most directly randomizes the key data attribute of interest—the phylogenetic positions of species in the community.

Perhaps the most striking result from our simulations was the faulty performance of node-based metrics on imbalanced phylogenetic trees. At best they are insensitive to non-random community assembly, and at worst they could lead to seriously flawed conclusions. For example, if community membership depends on a species being phylogenetically distinct from others, a node-based metric may actually suggest lower rather than higher phylogenetic diversity than expected based on a random selection of species (Fig. 14.2b, and 14.2c). Even for pure birth or balanced trees there is little to no power to detect over-dispersion using a node-based representation of a phylogenetic tree. As such, we recommend against the use of node-based trees in studies of phylogenetic community assembly and advocate great caution for researchers who nonetheless decide to proceed with studies of this kind.

For distance-based metrics, *MPD* showed greater power than *PD* or *NMMD* to detect non-random community assembly. However, the probability of species being added to communities in our simulations was a function of their mean phylogenetic distance to already-chosen species, so this result is unlikely to generalize across different kinds of non-random community assembly processes. In theory, the relative magnitudes of different metrics' deviation from a null model might itself reveal something about underlying processes (e.g. does community membership depend on having few very close relatives or on average relatedness?), but more work is needed to determine whether such differences might also arise as artefacts of the nature of underlying data.

A more pronounced concern than which distance-based metric to select is how the shape of the phylogenetic tree itself influences the likelihood of detecting non-random community assembly. Balanced trees make it easy to detect phylogenetic clustering but quite difficult to detect phylogenetic over-dispersion, whereas the opposite is true for imbalanced trees with accelerating diversification (Fig. 14.2). Fortunately, many phylogenetic trees are more imbalanced than a pure birth tree with decelerating diversification (Mooers and Heard 1997; McPeek 2008), in which case clustering and over-dispersion have similar chances of being detected (Fig. 14.2b). Statistics exist for quantifying both balance (Heard 1992) and trends in diversification (Pybus & Harvey 2000); these statistics should be calculated by researchers interested in phylogenetic community structure, used to interpret the statistical power of the analysis, and reported with empirical results. Our most general recommendation is for researchers to think carefully about this issue when drawing conclusions, especially when making the explicit or implicit assumption that phylogenetic similarity is a proxy for trait similarity. For example, even a small degree of convergent evolution in a balanced tree (e.g. one or two species in one clade evolve similar phenotypes as a different clade) could lead to phylogenetic over-dispersion when really the species in a set are highly clustered in trait space (see also Kraft et al. (2007)). Exploring some simulation results using the empirical phylogeny of interest seems warranted in this case, despite the non-trivial burden this places on the researcher.

14.3.3 Abundance vs presence–absence data

The vast majority of empirical studies on phylogenetic diversity have not incorporated data on species' abundances. In conservation, some effort has been made to combine phylogenetic distinctness and extinction risk in prioritizing species (Redding & Mooers, 2006; Isaac et al. 2007), which effectively assigns greater weight to species with *lower* abundance. Given the many criteria, in addition to phylogenetic distinctness, that might enter into the equation for conservation prioritization we did not explore the explicit incorporation of abundance data into type I measures of phylogenetic diversity.

One of the underlying premises of many studies in phylogenetic community ecology is that the fitness of individual organisms depends on their similarity to other organisms in the community, in which case species' abundances should be an important consideration. To an individual organism, if several species in the community are close relatives, it should matter far more if those species are abundant than if they are rare. In our simulations, non-randomly assembled communities were created either with abundance taken into consideration or not, but this had virtually no influence on the values of different null-corrected type II metrics or their dependence on tree shape (comparison not shown; Fig. 14.2 shows only the case in which abundances were not incorporated into community assembly). This was counter to our expectation that abundance-weighted metrics would be more sensitive to abundance-weighted community assembly.

The reason appears to be that the particular nature of the phylogeny obscures the abundance-weighted metrics' ability to recover the pattern. Consider the clustering assembly process: in our assembly algorithm, the first and most abundant species was chosen randomly from the phylogeny of potential species, and that species' lineage may or may not have close relatives. If that most abundant species does have close relatives, those closely related species are very likely to be chosen and the abundance-weighted metrics will detect a closely related community. However, in many trials the most abundant species will not have close relatives and so weighting the selection process by this species abundance will have little effect. The second most abundant species may be the most abundant species' closest relative, but in the context of the broader phylogeny those species could be relatively distantly related. In this case, despite the abundance-weighted assembly process, the abundance-weighted metrics perform poorly. Thus, the particular location on the phylogeny of the most abundant species adds considerable random variation to the performance of the abundance-weighted metrics, making them generally less sensitive to non-random assembly (Fig. 14.2). There was one exception to the general pattern: abundance-weighted MNND was more sensitive to abundance-weighted over-dispersion compared to the non-abundance-weighted measure.

For different kinds of non-random community assembly, for example if abundance is the outcome of competitive interactions rather than determined based on assembly order, we might expect abundance data to reveal more than presence–absence data. Another case in which abundance seems likely to be important is when ecosystem function depends on phylogenetic diversity (as a proxy for trait variation; see, for example, Cadotte et al. (2008)), as these ecosystem functions are performed by individual organisms rather than species per se. Comparison of abundance-weighted metrics with their presence–absence counterparts appears to be a potentially fruitful avenue of future research.

14.4 Key points

1. Metrics of phylogenetic diversity are used in conservation biology, where it is desirable to first assign individual species distinctness scores, and in community ecology, where it is of interest to assess the degree to which the species in a community represent a non-random subset of the species in a reference phylogenetic tree.

2. The metrics used in conservation biology show a high degree of redundancy (i.e. strong correlations) with one another and with total phylogenetic diversity (the sum of branch lengths connecting the species in a focal set). For a node-based phylogenetic tree (i.e. no information on branch lengths), the taxonomic diversity (TD) measure is conceptually the most straightforward, and for a distance-based tree, the pendant-edge (PE) and species evolutionary history (SEH) metrics are both conceptually straightforward and mathematically simple.

3. In tests of non-random community assembly, metrics need to be standardized based on null models to remove inherent dependence on species richness. For such null-corrected metrics, those calculated from node-based trees can be seriously misleading. Redundancy is fairly high among those calculated from distance-based trees. We recommend against the use of node-based trees in phylogenetic community ecology.

4. The sensitivity of phylogenetic diversity metrics depends strongly on the shape of the phylogenetic tree, with phylogenetic clustering far more detectable in some cases (balanced trees) and phylogenetic over-dispersion far more detectable in others (e.g. imbalanced trees with accelerating diversification). It is important for empirical researchers to take the effect of their particular tree shape on statistical power into account.

CHAPTER 15

Genetic methods for biodiversity assessment

Melanie Culver, Robert Fitak, and Hans-Werner Herrmann

15.1 Introduction

Biodiversity encompasses the extant diversity of plants, animals, fungi, and microorganisms; including the genes they contain and the community in which they live. There are three fundamental levels of biological diversity to consider: genetic diversity, species diversity, and community diversity (Primack et al. 1998). Genetic diversity is the sum of the genetic variation within a species, species diversity refers to the number of species present and their relative abundance, and community diversity is the collection of organisms co-existing in their physical environment. Recently, genetics has become a valuable tool for investigating biodiversity. Although all three levels of biodiversity can benefit from genetic methods, in this chapter our attention is focused on using these methods to assess both genetic and species diversity.

Genetic diversity is a critical component of biodiversity for two reasons: first, genetic diversity is the essence of all biodiversity, and second, genetic and biological diversity are mutually dependent (Lankau & Strauss 2007). In other words, the diversity between species (biological diversity) is dependent on the diversity within a species (genetic diversity) and vice versa. Therefore, techniques to monitor the long-term changes in and distribution of genetic diversity are essential (Drayton & Primack 1996; Wilson et al. 1996b; Manley et al. 2004). In the past, techniques to assess genetic diversity included restriction fragment length polymorphism (RFLP) analyses and the comparison of DNA sequences from single or multiple genes. Recently, techniques to analyse thousands of locations across whole genomes have become more commonly used. These whole genomes and genome-wide scans focus on a variety of unlinked co-dominant genetic markers such as **single nucleotide polymorphisms (SNPs)** and **microsatellite DNA loci (STR)**. At the population level, genetic diversity is more difficult to assess. Gene flow occurs at varying levels and may result in complex genetic patterns that can extend from completely panmictic to mostly isolated populations. Fairly isolated populations with a unique genetic/phenotypic signature and evolutionary trajectory are generally referred to as subspecies or **evolutionarily significant units (ESUs)**.

Species diversity is a measure commonly used to represent biological diversity. This is because species are a comparatively well-defined biological category; a trait that cannot be claimed for above-species systematic categories (genera, families, orders, etc.) or the lower subspecies category. However, as biological species are, by definition, isolated gene pools (no exchange of genetic material), the actual 'units of evolution', the precursors of species, are populations (see DeQuiroz 2007 for a detailed discussion). These more-or-less isolated gene pools (populations) contain unique signatures that can at times only be identified using genetic methods. Genetic methods are also an advantage when taxonomists are unable to classify species using morphological characters, such as in species-rich groups like Coleoptera, or when species are rare, cryptic, or otherwise difficult to identify.

Why are we interested in measuring and assessing biodiversity? The answer is two-fold: (i) to determine how many species are present and (ii) to estimate what ('biodiversity') is required to maintain the integrity of evolutionary processes.

In the following, we discuss the application of genetics in examining these key topics in biodiversity assessments. After a short description of the methods currently used, we review how phylogenies, non-invasive monitoring, **DNA barcoding**, and **genomics** have been employed to measure, maintain, and (potentially) revive biodiversity.

15.2   Genetic methods in biodiversity assessment

As a tool to investigate biological diversity, **molecular genetics** has gained high resolving power in the last two decades with the rapid innovation of biotechnological methods (Palumbi & Cipriano 1998) and the development of computer-based tools to manage large amounts of genetic data. Here we only consider the areas of molecular genetics that are important for examining biological diversity. These areas are concentrated around methods which utilize the two primary sources of DNA: **organellar DNA** and **nuclear DNA**.

15.2.1   Mitochondrial, chloroplast, and nuclear DNA

For the purpose of this chapter genetic data consists of DNA sequence variation in mitochondrial DNA (mtDNA), chloroplast (cpDNA), or nuclear DNA (nDNA). This variation can be quantified in different ways depending on the question addressed and the level of resolution required. Generally, nuclear genes, which have the slowest evolutionary rate, reveal more ancient evolutionary resolution than mitochondrial or chloroplast genes, which have more rapid evolutionary rates. Non-coding regions of DNA, however, are the most rapidly evolving relative to nuclear, chloroplast, and mitochondrial genes (Table 15.1).

DNA sequence variation is characterized as allelic variation for co-dominant markers such as SNPs and microsatellites in a **diploid** (or higher) system or as **haplotypes** on a section of haploid DNA such as found in mitochondria, chloroplasts, Y-**chromosomes** (or other heterogametic sex chromosomes), or some organisms without sexual reproduction. The observed sequence variation for an organism can either be unique or shared with other organisms. Depending on the question asked, the appropriate **molecular (genetic) marker** must be examined. Usually, sets of genetic markers with varying degrees of resolution due to differing evolutionary rates are used.

15.2.2   Genome technologies

New high-throughput sequencing technologies (e.g. 454 pyrosequencing) have largely reduced the cost of genome-scale sequencing (for a review of novel sequencing technologies, see Ansorge (2009)), therefore analyses at the genomic level are now within the financial reach of typical genetic projects. Researchers have recently employed high-throughput (next-generation) sequencing to extract thousands of SNP markers (Vera et al. 2008) for subsequent microarray development, and microsatellite markers (Castoe et al. 2009) for population genetic analyses. The search for large numbers of genetic markers is enhanced by the potential to simultaneously sequence multiple 'tagged' samples in the same reaction (Roche Diagnostics 2009). The considerable increase in the number of markers will improve the resolution and precision of genotyping efforts, and thus the ability to examine biodiversity. Also, these genomic-level analyses are not limited to the taxon sequenced but, depending on phylogenetic distance and questions addressed, may result in other, 'genome-enabled' taxa (Kohn et al. 2006).

15.3   Biodiversity assessments

15.3.1   Phylogenies for biodiversity assessment using mtDNA and nuclear DNA

One of the greatest contributions of genetics to wildlife conservation is through resolving taxonomic uncertainties. Cryptic species are those with few morphological differences, but identified as separate taxonomic units based on other types of data (e.g. genetic, behavioural, vocalizations). Without genetic studies cryptic species could remain unknown or become extinct without ever being recognized. Conversely, genetic data may prompt the pooling of phenotypic variants to the same species or population, reducing the number of

Table 15.1 Representative molecular genetic markers used for biodiversity assessments across the animal and plant kingdom.

Genome	Marker	Description	Length/coverage	Rate	Resolution
Mitochondria	COI	Cytochrome oxidase I gene	~ 1552 bp in eutherian mammals	0.07%bp/Myr	species, populations
	Cytb	Cytochrome B gene	~ 1149 in eutherian mammals	0.19% bp/Myr	species, populations
	D-loop	Control region for the mitochondria	~ 1600 bp in eutherian mammals	0.81% bp/Myr	species, populations, individuals
	16S rRNA	16S ribosomal RNA gene	~ 1676 in eutherian mammals	0.23% bp/Myr	species, populations
Chloroplasts	trnH-psbA	Highly variable chloroplast intergenic region		2.4% variability	species, populations
	Introns and intergenic spacers	Untranslated part of a gene or between genes	26753bp	(Average) 3.09–4.12% variab	species, populations
	rpoC1	γ subunit of chloroplast DNA-dependent RNA polymerase	?	?	species, populations
	matK	MaturaseK	?	?	species, populations
	rbcL	Rubisco large subunit	?	?	species, populations
	rpoB	β subunit of chloroplast DNA-dependent RNA polymerase	?	?	species, populations
Nuclear	Microsatellites	Tandemly repeated units of two to six base pairs	100– 400 bp/1000–10 000 genome-wide	1.0^{-4}/locus	populations, individuals
	SNPs	Single nucleotide polymorphisms	1 bp, limitless number genome-wide	10.6/Mb/genome	species, populations, individuals
	Transposons	DNA that has been moved from other places	10–300 bp/thousands genome wide	1.0^{-3}–1.0^{-4}/locus	genera, species
	Numt	DNA transposed from mitochondrial genome	variable	1.0^{-9}/locus	species
	Genes	DNA that codes for functional proteins	Average 3000 bp/60–80 000 genome- wide	1.0^{-12}/locus	genera, species, populations
	Y chromosome	Mammalian sex chromosome	60 million bp	1.0^{-12}/locus	species
	introns	Part of a gene not translated into the protein	10–100bp/millions genome wide	1.0^{-9}/locus	species, populations

Mitochondrial mutation rates are from Lopez et al. (1997) and are based on eutherian mammals.

Chloroplast rates are from Shaw et al. (2007) and are based on angiosperms and the CBOL Plant Working Group (2009).

Nuclear rates are from Frankham et al. (2002) and are based on mammals.

?, unknown.

recognized species. Genetic analyses are a powerful tool for revealing the evolutionary history and taxonomic position of species.

New species discovery in large mammals using genetic techniques is rare and has been exemplified twice in recent years in the Felidae and Proboscidae. Molecular evidence has shown a distinct clouded leopard species occurring on the islands of Borneo and Sumatra (*Neofelis diardi*). The previously described species, *N. nebulosa*, is now considered to be restricted to the Asian mainland. Two studies using mtDNA, microsatellite markers, nuclear DNA sequences, and cytogenetics revealed a deep historical partition between these populations, warranting species-level status (Buckley-Beason et al. 2006; Wilting et al. 2007). This finding was further supported by a morphometric investigation of pelage features (Kitchener et al. 2006). In this case molecular markers led to the description of a new species. Another molecular study distinguished forest and savannah elephants from each other as different species (*Loxodonta africana*, forest; *Loxodonta cyclotis*, savannah) (Roca et al. 2001). This study used 1732 nucleotides from four nuclear genes to describe these distinct species, which show as much divergence as Asian elephants to African elephants, and is an example of adaptive evolution to forest versus savannah habitat types.

Genetic analyses may also suggest the opposite, that is, that populations or phenotypes previously considered to be different species are found to be so genetically similar that they are more accurately classified as one species. For example, also in mammals, the *Felis silvestris* complex (including *F. silvestris*, *F. catus*, *F. libyca*, and *F. bieti*), has low levels of genetic differentiation, suggesting that they are more appropriately classified as a single species (Driscoll et al. 2007).

Because conservation efforts often focus at the species or subspecies level (e.g. IUCN Red List, US Endangered Species Act) a population's protection status may be directly related to its taxonomic status. As evolution is a slow, gradual process, species assignments are not always unambiguous. During a speciation event, there will be a period where the genetic difference is deemed insufficient to warrant subspecies or species status. Such vari-ation may still comprise local adaptations of significant ecological and evolutionary importance, or differentiation caused by genetic drift, perhaps leading to speciation (the *Felis silvestis* complex may be an example of this). Where to draw the line for the level of genetic differentiation worth protecting is often debatable. As the resolution and population coverage of genetic analyses increase, such dilemmas will become increasingly common and conservation decisions will have to be guided by more clearly defined conservation goals.

15.3.2   Non-invasively monitoring for biodiversity

Genetic monitoring programmes are often amenable to non-invasively collected samples (e.g. hair, feces, urine), which is appealing for investigating elusive animals. For example, hairs collected by birds to reinforce or insulate their nests can be used to efficiently census rare and elusive mammals (Toth 2008). Genetic methods can also be used to analyse diets and disease, typically from faecal analysis. While morphological analysis of scat contents typically identifies to genus level, molecular identification can often identify individual species (Dee et al. in review). Animal scat is used to indicate the presence of a species, although visual identification of scat is frequently ambiguous even for experts (Halfpenny 1986; Foran et al. 1997). Recent advances in molecular genetics, however, allow species to be identified reliably from both animal scat (Farrell et al. 2000) and bone samples (Taberlet & Fumagalli 1996).

Because carnivore scat contains bone material from prey, and both prey and predator species can be identified from a single scat sample, this illustrates carnivore scat as a source for assessing vertebrate biodiversity. Taberlet and Fumagalli (1996) described a similar method for monitoring small-mammal communities using DNA extracted from bone material removed from owl pellets. In general, scat from mammalian predators is more ubiquitous in the environment than owl pellets and may contain a higher variety of prey items (Farrel et al. 2000), therefore analyzing predator scat samples and the bone material within them could effectively maximize the number of species detected while minimizing the number of samples.

Molecular scatology has been applied to the field of biodiversity assessment through identification of rare species (e.g. Kohn et al. 1995 ; Palomares et al. 2002) and diet analyses (e.g. Kvitrud et al. 2005; Parsons et al. 2005). Although molecular scatology has been applied to several sympatric species simultaneously and to the diet analysis of predators, it has yet to be applied at broader community levels such as the measurement of species richness. As molecular techniques become easier to use, less expensive, and more available to biologists and managers, techniques such as those described here should better address community-level questions in wildlife biology and in estimating community-level parameters such as species richness.

15.3.3   DNA barcoding for biodiversity assessment

DNA barcoding is a technique using a short sequence, usually a haploid gene fragment in mitochondria or chloroplasts, to help classify the species of the organism from which the DNA originated. This technique has been designated as a tool to not only identify existing diversity from 'unidentified' specimens, but also as a tool to discover new biodiversity (species) and therefore to gain new genetic information. DNA barcoding is intended to become a universal biodiversity tool with an open- access database that allows for the identification of specimens by non-taxonomists and follows a standardized, minimalistic procedure. Its benefits include protecting endangered species, sustaining natural resources, discovering hidden biodiversity, discovering biodiversity in difficult to access scenarios (i.e, eggs, larvae, etc.), controlling agropests, and becoming a powerful environmental monitoring tool. Conceptually, DNA-based biodiversity assessment tools have merit over morphology as phenotypic divergence is driven by selection and confounded by **homoplasy**, whereas genetic divergence is driven by stochastic processes that are quasi neutral (Winker 2009). In this context genetic data are of tremendous value. That neutral characters are not drivers of speciation is critical. How

continuous is the nature of these neutral characters and are 'bins' appropriate?

The promise of (single-**locus**) DNA barcoding

DNA barcoding originated when Paul Herbert and colleagues from the University of Guelph published a paper on the technique (Hebert et al. 2003). They demonstrated that it was possible to reliably assign samples to the correct higher systematic groups of hexapods and to identify closely related lepidopterans down to the species level. The study examined DNA sequence differences in an approximately 650 bp fragment of the mitochondrial cytochrome c oxidase I (COI) gene. Taxonomic expertise is collapsing and a standardized procedure is required to evaluate the millions of species encompassed within biological diversity. Only a DNA-based procedure is financially feasible while additionally providing the large throughput work-flow required. Such a system overcomes the limitations of morphology-based identification and is independent of systematic expertise or different states of phenotypes (i.e. life history stage or sex). COI was chosen because it is haploid, without recombination, and insertions/deletion mutations (indels) are rarely observed. Additionally, there are conserved regions for which universal primers that work across many taxa can be designed. Most importantly, the mutation rate of COI exhibits resolution at the species level.

Single-locus barcoding has proven useful in a large dataset of about 100 000 specimens of 3500 morphologically defined species of moths, butterflies, tachinid flies, and parasitoid wasps. Only a small percentage (<1%) could not be distinguished by their COI barcode (Janzen et al. 2009). The COI barcode did, however, assist in discovery of many cryptic species, later confirmed by morphological features previously assumed to be within species variation boundaries.

Extensive sampling over large geographic areas covering whole taxonomic groups show that the observed power of species differentiation is not a sampling artefact. In a large study of 353 species of central Asian butterflies, allopatric species did not have less sequence diversity than sympatric species (Lukhtanov et al. 2009). The large geographical coverage did substantially increase intraspecific variation, thus reducing the barcoding gap (Fig. 15.1). However, this did not impede the use of barcoding for species identification, which had a success rate of >90%.

In well-studied animal groups, such as birds, closely related sister species could be identified, and later confirmed by a coalescent test, with the single-locus COI barcoding approach (Tavares & Baker 2008). However, a universal distance-based 'cutoff' approach was invalid based on variation of times to common ancestry among sister species and in rates of evolution.

COI barcodes work well in birds and fishes, with birds providing a more defined species pattern than fishes (Ward 2009). The latter is caused by species diversity being less understood in fishes, including numerous cryptic species. DNA barcoding is clearly superior to morphological approaches to define species because, unlike barcoding, morphological approaches are often distorted by homoplasy (Packer et al. 2009).

Plant mitochondria, however, demonstrate very slow mutation rates and cannot be used for DNA barcoding. Another organelle found in plants, chloroplasts, exhibit slower evolutionary rates in their genomes than mitochondrial genomes in animals. Despite slower evolutionary rates, portions of the chloroplast *matK* gene and *trnH-psbA* spacer are useful barcoding genes in South African and Costa Rican plants (Lahaye et al. 2008). Notably, *matK* exhibited a barcoding gap between intra- and interspecific variants (with some overlap, see Figure 15.1) and has enough resolution to identify more than 1000 Mesoamerican orchids. The identified orchids included cryptic species, some of which are listed as endangered in the Convention on International Trade of Endangered Species (CITES). Adding *trnH-psbA* sequence variation to the *matK* data only slightly improves the power of the analysis.

Recently, the CBOL (Consortium for the Barcoding of Life) Plant Working Group (2009) announced standardized DNA barcoding loci for plants using the chloroplast genes *matK* and *rbcL*. Despite the use of two loci, the species discrimination was only 72% in a sample set of 259 specimens comprising 95 species from 34 genera. This clearly performs

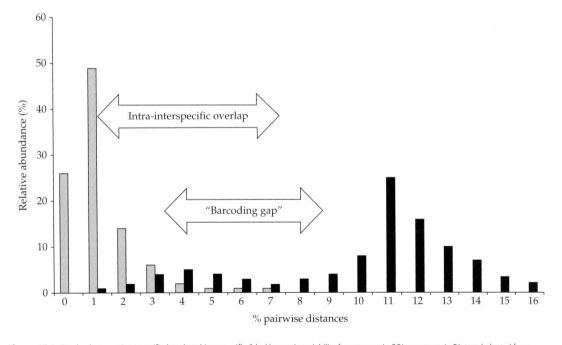

Figure 15.1 Overlap between intraspecific (grey) and interspecific (black) genetic variability for congeneric COI sequences in Diptera (adapted from Meier et al. 2006). 'Barcoding gap' indicates the approximate position and range of an expected barcoding gap.

worse than the COI locus in animals. Kress et al. (2009) used a three-locus approach ($matK + rbcL + trnH - psbA$) and the BLAST algorithm to correctly identify >98% of the 296 species of woody plants in their study plot in Panama, but three genes can be expensive and time-consuming, thus challenging some of the basic barcoding objectives.

Ecological applications have shown that barcoding can identify the organisms contained in wild animal diets through sequencing the stomach extracts of species such as krill (Passmore et al. 2006). Another projected advantage of the 'Barcode of Life' project was its ability to account for the diversity of unicellular life. As of yet, the barcoding of eukaryotic microorganisms has been poorly studied, but with emerging genomic technologies there is more promise in this field (Trezal and Leblois 2008).

The pitfalls of (single-locus) barcoding

Although COI is a good barcoding gene in a number of animal groups (Hebert et al. 2003), there is evidence that COI barcoding does not always perform as well in amphibians, for example (Vences et al. 2005a). COI divergence in amphibians is generally high (7–14% within a species with a maximum of 18%) and overlaps with interspecific divergence rates. This introduces high variation at the priming sites, making the successful amplification of COI fragments a challenge. The observed high divergence of COI in amphibians is not caused by excessive substitution rates but by deep mitochondrial divergence and is intensified by frequently observed introgression and incomplete lineage sorting. This leads to common discordance between geographical signatures. High mitochondrial divergence within species has also been described for pulmonate land snails (Thomaz et al. 1996). Vences et al. (2005b) recommend the use of the mitochondrial 16S rRNA gene as the barcoding locus for amphibians (and possibly other vertebrates). They show that 16S rRNA primer sites have fewer substitutions and amplify DNA fragments more reliably than COI primers. Additionally, 16S rRNA is able to recover major monophyletic clades of vertebrates, distinguish between sibling species, and characterize individual populations whereas COI cannot. In land snails, 16S rRNA performs better

than COI (Steinke et al. 2005). Jansen et al. (2009) were unable to use COI barcodes to delimitate Nearctic ant species and found a large overlap of intra- and inter-specific distances in Palaearctic ant species. Davison et al. (2009) emphasized that it is very important to have good baseline data in order to assign species. If that baseline is not available, species assignment will be incorrect. In Porifera and Anthozoa, mtDNA evolution is much slower than in other metazoans (Huang et al. 2008). In these groups, it is impossible to use COI to distinguish between species because several well-characterized species share the same barcode.

Sequence units (genes) that exhibit good barcoding properties can vary in size and location between taxa. This decreases the usefulness of one single barcoding locus. Roe and Sperling (2007) investigated the COI and II loci and assessed their usefulness for barcoding efforts. For both subunits they included the entire 2.3 Kb region and used a 600 bp sliding window to analyse patterns of evolution. They found that locations of maximum divergence between taxa were highly variable and not confined to the DNA barcoding region of COI. Like others before them they found a major overlap of divergence within and between species. They also found areas of mutation saturation indicated by transition/transversion indices with only limited association to levels of DNA divergence. They concluded that no single 600 bp region of the COI and II genes is optimally informative across taxa and recommended pilot studies in the taxonomic areas of interest to identify the most informative regions. Additionally, they recommended analyzing several specimens from different populations to increase taxon sampling.

For similar reasons criticism can also be directed towards the analysis of barcoding data as implemented in the Barcode of Life Datasystems (BOLD, www.barcodinglife.org). This database is characterized by a number of improvements to other genetic databases, i.e. the requirement of trace data submission, quality control of trace data, deposition of voucher specimens from which genetic data originated, photo vouchers, etc. (Ratnasingham & Hebert 2007). The most common criticism is the use of distance methods to identify and delineate species. In a paper analyzing 1333 COI sequences for 449 species of Diptera, Meier et al. (2006) found a relatively low species identification success rate (<70%) with tree-based identification criteria. They illustrated that pairwise distances or other similarity measures can lead to logically inconsistent results and that the often-applied neighbour-joining (NJ) clustering methods are insufficient to resolve data ambiguity as NJ methods generally result in only one tree and disregard other potential trees. In their dataset they found a wide overlap of intra- and interspecific COI sequences and found the species' COI divergence threshold (proposed at 3%) problematic. However, DNA barcoding can be successful in taxa where taxon sampling is nearly complete (i.e. *Aedes* and *Anopheles*).

Can single-gene/single-threshold criteria for species discovery work theoretically for biological species with reproductive isolation? To answer this question Hickerson et al. (2006) employed reciprocal monophyly in tree-based analyses and a formerly proposed 10 times rule (Hebert et al. 2004), meaning that average pairwise genetic differences between two species must be at least 10 times greater than the differences observed within each species. Theoretically, these criteria can identify reproductively isolated species with an error rate of less than 10%, but only if the isolation happened at least 4 million generations ago. For more recent species, this method is useless.

To compute barcoding gaps, the intra- and interspecific sequence variability for congeneric COI sequences and mean interspecific genetic distances are commonly used. Instead of mean interspecific genetic distance, the smallest distance should be used (Meier et al. 2008). This is necessary because the closest relatives within a genus need to be separated. This approach will render species identification more difficult as the number of species sampled per genus increases. Non-distance-based 'character' methods can help to circumvent this problem. Instead of using distance-based methods to delimitate species from single-locus mtDNA sequences, coalescence model-based methods may be more appropriate. In a dataset encompassing 1614 individuals of insects from 12 families in four orders such a model was able to delineate 370 putative species, which were confirmed by nuclear DNA variation and/or morphological characters

(Monaghan et al. 2009). The taxa delineated represent evolutionary coherent entities rather than similarity-based operational units.

Nuclear mitochondrial pseudogenes (numts) can introduce ambiguity into DNA barcoding. Numts are easily coamplified with orthologous mtDNA, and barcoding with COI led to overestimating the number of unique species in grasshoppers and crayfish (Song et al. 2008). Even after rigorous quality control for numts, such as screening for indels, in-frame stop codons, and nucleotide composition, not all numts were identified. Such observations call for rigorous quality control in barcoding studies, including a number of approaches such as the use of mitochondria-rich tissue, the amplification of long DNA fragments, or the use of multiple loci not physically located near each other in the genome. Because no simple or rapid adjustment has been found, numts pose a serious challenge to DNA barcoding and will have to be considered in order to reduce incorrect molecular inferences.

That universal primers frequently do not perform well in metazoan groups, leading to the usage of degenerate primers combined with very low annealing temperatures, which decreases the stringency of DNA-fragment amplification, is another serious shortcoming in the light of incorrect molecular inference and fast, inexpensive DNA barcoding (Siddall et al. 2009). The loss of specificity can lead to amplification of contaminants, which then find their way into databases and confound the barcoding effort.

Beyond (single-locus) DNA barcoding
Frezal and Leblois (2008) provide an excellent review of the DNA barcoding field. They discuss the progress made and clearly point out the limitations of barcoding. As discussed earlier, these limitations include sampling shortage across taxa ('sampling gaps'), nuclear copies of mitochondrial genes ('numts'), mtDNA based assignments, and the false assignment of sequences using distance methods. Additionally, there are inherent problems associated with describing new species from only a ~ 600 bp fragment of mtDNA, without having an actual specimen 'in hand.' For example, mtDNA is not an adequate source of species-defining DNA

in cases of reduced populations size, introgression, inconsistent mutation rate, or **heteroplasmy**. Many of these conditions may be a common occurrence in populations being sampled for biodiversity (Rubinoff et al. 2006). Because it is unlikely that the single-locus approach can be used across all eukaryotic systems, the idea of a multi-locus barcoding approach has been proposed. For example, in plants one could use an 'identifier' to provide for correct assignments to higher taxonomic categories and varying 'identifiers' for species-level resolution. While the value of the barcoding technique is less controversial when applied to the identification of species previously defined by other criteria, the application of DNA barcodes is still a contentious issue for defining novel biodiversity (Blaxter et al. 2005; Rubinoff et al. 2006; Frezal & Leblois 2008).

Parallel to the DNA barcoding initiative another large effort to assess biodiversity in the sea was initiated by Craig Venter (Venter et al. 2004; Rusch et al. 2007). His group chose a different approach, both in targeted organisms and technique. They collected marine microbial populations in water samples and used shotgun cloning to sequence libraries. In their first attempt, Venter et al. were able to identify 1800 genomic species based on sequence relatedness, including 148 previously unknown bacterial phylotypes. It is important to realize that the methods used here are expensive, not standardized, and far from minimalistic. Venter et al. predicted that the economics of sequencing will change dramatically and make large-scale genetic biodiversity assessments feasible.

Single-locus DNA barcoding is not a silver bullet to genetically measure and assess biodiversity. It is successful in a few well- studied groups but is characterized by numerous limitations ranging from primers to analyses and is not applicable in some organism groups. The genetic barcoding system of the future should preferably include numerous independent (unlinked) loci with a genome-wide distribution. Additionally, markers should show different levels of resolution. Venter et al. (2004) came closest to this approach but were restricted by the inhibitive cost of shotgun cloning and Sanger sequencing. Next-generation sequencing technology will enable genome-wide barcoding in the near future.

15.3.4 Genome technologies for biodiversity assessment

The increased sequencing capacity offered by next-generation technologies will continue to expand our knowledge of biodiversity. Although most commonly used in the description of microbial biodiversity (see Chapter 16), genome technologies will facilitate future research in three key areas of biodiversity assessment: (i) the measurement of biodiversity, (ii) the maintenance of biodiversity, and (iii) the revival of biodiversity.

The ability to identify species from DNA sequences is critical for measuring biodiversity. Whether using DNA barcodes or other loci, next-generation sequencing provides a diagnostic tool for rapid species detection. In a single reaction, next-generation technologies can analyse over 1 million sequences (www.454.com). When screening samples containing multiple species, individual sequences are compared with existing sequences to identify the species. For example, Valentini et al. (2009) and Deagle et al. (2009) used this approach to examine the biodiversity in the diet of herbivores and fur seals, respectively. Next-generation sequencing is also valuable for characterizing ancient biodiversity by sequencing DNA fragments from historical specimens (Millar et al. 2008). Using pyrosequencing, Blow et al. (2008) were able to classify an unidentified 69 000- year-old tooth as belonging to an ancestor of steppe bison. While the identification of species is important for measuring past and current biodiversity, the analysis of complete genomes and genetic variation will benefit the maintenance of existing biodiversity.

The maintenance, or conservation, of biodiversity is principally concerned with endangered or declining species. Recently, one of the first complete genome sequences for an endangered species was released, that of the giant panda (*Ailuropoda melanoleuca*; Ruiqiang et al. 2010). The authors were the first to demonstrate the *de novo* assembly of a eukaryotic genome strictly from next-generation sequencing methods. In addition to the assessment of several unique evolutionary traits, the authors identified > 2.7 million SNPs. SNPs, or other genome-wide sets of genetic markers, are valuable for conserving biodiversity. For instance,

SNPs have already been used to suggest a 'marker-assisted' captive breeding strategy for the European and American bison (Pertoldi et al. 2009). Marker-assisted breeding strategies will reduce inbreeding, thus decreasing the expression of lethal **alleles**, such as chondrodystrophy in the California condor (Romanov et al. 2009). Genomics will also facilitate studies of adaptive differences between populations. Compared to neutral markers, like most SNPs and microsatellites, adaptive loci can provide better estimates of evolutionary differentiation resulting from ecological pressures (Gebremedhin et al. 2009). Genomic studies of adaptive loci in amphibians have been predicted to shed light on the variation responsible for certain populations' susceptibility to causes of decline (Storfer et al. 2009). In the future, projects such as the initiative to sequence 10 000 vertebrate genomes (Genome 10K Community of Scientists; Hayden 2009) will not only provide more neutral and adaptive markers, but advance our understanding of the mechanisms underlying the evolution of biodiversity.

The final, and most controversial, application of genome technologies to studies of biodiversity is the revival of extinct species. The resurrection of extinct species became a reality when the Pyrenean ibex (*Capra pyrenaica pyrenaica*), extinct as of 2000, became un-extinct for several minutes in 2009 before the cloned newborn died of lung failure (Folch et al. 2009). Albeit nuclear-transfer techniques were performed to clone the ibex; it may soon be possible to regenerate biodiversity simply with a genome sequence. Nicholls (2009) pointed out the inherent difficulties in resurrecting the extinct woolly mammoth from a genome sequence, although its feasibility was not entirely ruled out. The revival of extinct biodiversity raises many contentious biological and ethical concerns, but its impact on biological diversity cannot be ignored (for a review see Piña-Alguilar et al. 2009).

15.4   Prospectus

Biodiversity assessments from genetic methods in the near future will certainly continue to rely on technologies such as DNA barcoding and whole-genome sequencing, or even a combination of the two where DNA barcoding takes on a more whole-genome character.

For DNA barcoding the silver lining on the not too far away horizon is next-generation sequencing, with its precipitous drop in sequencing cost. This cost reduction equalled four orders of magnitude for the last decade and leads to proposals like the 10 000 genome project in which scientists are aiming for 10 000 complete genomes across representative vertebrate species (Genome 10K Community of Scientists 2009). Proposals like this one would have been science fiction a few years ago but are now in close reach, only requiring one more order of magnitude drop in cost before realization. Now it is easy to imagine DNA barcodes that are based on SNPs with a genome-wide coverage.

The availability of whole genomes represents a quantum leap in genetic biodiversity assessment, as did the complete human genome for medical research. As these whole-genome sequences become available they will advance our understanding of the genetic variation that has been so elusive for the past several decades, that of adaptive variation. With this increased understanding of adaptive variation will come a better understanding of the evolutionary process that generated the existing biodiversity. The question of whether biodiversity should be measured in 'species' or 'genotypes' becomes philosophical. In reality we will work with genotypic data as it will be readily available. Finally, the future holds the controversy of whether or not to use genomic technologies to resurrect extinct biodiversity.

15.5   Key points

1. The genetic diversity of individuals and populations is an important component of species diversity, as it is important to the diversity of the biological community.
2. Genetic diversity is measured using a variety of molecular genetic markers, each with a different evolutionary rate giving them different resolving power. Markers with the appropriate resolution are selected for different biodiversity questions.
3. Genetic analyses are a powerful tool for revealing the evolutionary history and taxonomic

position of species, particularly the cryptic ones that cannot be detected by other means.

4. Non-invasive methods to assess biodiversity in the wild become more important as newer technologies allow us to retrieve increasingly more information from less sample. As molecular techniques become easier to use and less expensive, they will become more available to biologists and managers.

5. The value of barcoding has been widely accepted when applied to the identification of species previously defined by other criteria, but is controversial when used for novel species identification. However, barcoding is an emerging technology that shows promise in the field of genetic biodiversity assessment, especially once genome-wide barcodes can be implemented.

6. The developing genomic technologies are important for measuring past and current biodiversity, as well as measuring existing biodiversity of neutral and adaptive variation. Quite possibly, in the future it might be possible to regenerate extinct biodiversity by generating an entire genome sequence.

PART V

Applications

CHAPTER 16

Microbial diversity and ecology

Lise Øvreås and Thomas P. Curtis

16.1 Introduction

Microbial diversity is surely the outermost frontier of the exploration of diversity. The scale and inscrutability of the microbial world have deceived some into thinking there is nothing very interesting there!

> ... "I do not discuss the biodiversity of microorganisms at all. From the point of view of diversity, they are probably the most poorly known of taxa. Perhaps their diversity shows many patterns but I am unaware of them."

Michael Rosenzweig 'Species Diversity in Space and Time' Rosenzweig (1995)

Nothing could be further from the truth. However, the exploration of this frontier presents the investigator with multiple challenges, which are, little by little, being considered, constrained, and obviated. Although great progress has been made there seems little doubt that the golden age of microbial diversity lies before us and not behind.

Microorganisms are not only the oldest and most diverse living organisms on the planet, but they also represent the vast majority of the Earth's biodiversity and are the driving forces in major biogeochemical processes. For approximately 4.5 billion years the Earth has been evolving from an unproductive volcanic landscape into the lively globe full of life that it is today. The first forms of life, prokaryotes, have been found in fossils from 3.5 billion years ago, and evidence for photosynthesis and earliest life have been reported back at 3.8 billion years in the Isua Greenstone Belt in Greenland (Rosing & Frei 2004). For more than 2 billion years life, and evolution, on the planet was solely prokaryotic. Microorganisms began to evolve with the changing environmental conditions of the planet. New environmental conditions created by microorganisms created new selective pressures driving the evolutionary process and creating, over millennia, new orders, families, genera, and species. Yet we know very little about microbial diversity—we have only the slenderest notion of its extent and know still less about how it is generated and maintained. The assessment of biodiversity is one of the most challenging and fascinating aspects of microbiology. The scale of our ignorance is reflected by the range of estimates of the number of bacterial species that exist on Earth today, varying between 10^4 and 10^9. Our lack of enlightenment is partly due to the isolation of microbial diversity studies from the general study of biodiversity, but is also perhaps because of microbial diversity's shear inscrutability: the absence of a species concept, the impossibility of morphological examination, and the inadequacy of culture-based methods has forced microbial ecologists into the arms of the molecular biologists, whose methods have traditionally been applied to a narrow range of conserved genes. The tools of molecular ecology are only partially suited to the scale of the microbial communities microbial world and can offer an at best limited, and at worst totally false, view of the microbial world. Although great strides are being made by focusing on the occurrence and diversity of a handful of genes (typically 16S rRNA) there is so much more to the microbial world than this molecule.

Times are changing, however, and the rational structured and adequate use of molecular tools to explore ecology is foreseeable, and in certain instances possible. The proper determination of microbial diversity is a key part of that change. We will in this chapter lay out the bare bones of the conceptual foundations, laboratory techniques, and mathematical methods required, but this is only a

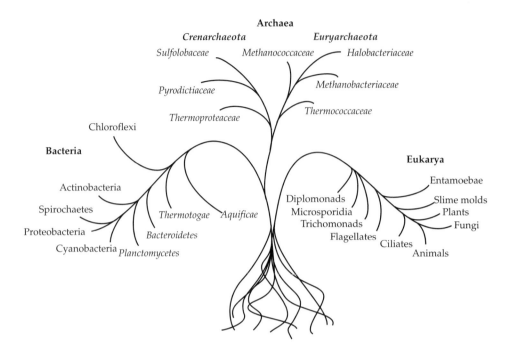

Figure 16.1 The tree of life shows how much greater the diversity of the microbial world is compared to the diversity of larger organisms. The Archaea and the Bacteria in particular account for the bulk of the tree.

beginning. This is science not accountancy. It would be a mistake to collapse all microbial ecology into a number or even a few numbers for they could not possibly capture the wonder and complexity of the microbial world.

Our most primitive scratchings at the surface of the problem have amazed us. It is not only the great diversity that is surprising (Fig. 16.1) but also the revealing of completely new forms of life. Who knows what treasures future generations will find when they explore systematically, and in earnest, equipped with a sound grasp of the microbial diversity around them.

The focus in this chapter will be on prokaryotic microorganisms. Their importance is noticeable as they represent by far the largest phylogenetic diversity on Earth, are vehicles for all the biogeochemical cycles, and regulate nutrient cycling and nutrient pools for eukaryotes.

16.2 The diversity concept

The term 'microbial diversity' describes different aspects of complexity and variability within microbial populations and communities. This includes genetic variability within taxa (species), variability in community composition, and complexity of interactions, trophic levels, and number of guilds. Traditionally biodiversity is based on the 'species' as a unit. In microbial ecology the species concept is useless as the species concept for bacteria is obscure. In microbiology the term 'diversity' is used to describe qualitative variation among microorganisms as we draw on more abstract and arbitrary measures of evolution.

Because of difficulties with classification, numerical taxonomy (using mathematical algorithms like cluster analysis) is often used for bacterial systematics. With this method the differences between bacterial isolates are calculated and are then clustered into biotypes. A biotype is an operational taxonomic unit (OTU) that can be used instead of a species to describe and compare microbial populations and communities. Diversity may also be represented as phylogenetic trees, or appreciated from the number of functional groups.

16.3 Phylogeny

The measurement of microbial diversity is rooted in evolutionary relationships as comparative analyses of specific genes can be used to infer the evolutionary pathways of organisms (see Chapter 14). This approach, termed molecular phylogeny, reveals the history of organismal lineages as they change through time, and is based on the number and location of differences in the nucleotide sequences of homologous genes from different organisms. The prime goal of molecular phylogeny is to establish a framework into which organisms are grouped according to their evolution, and show that all life is genetically connected via a vast phylogenetic tree (see Chapter 15). It is generally assumed that early life forms originated from a gene pool representing common evolutionary ancestry. Classification of microorganisms should be explicit and follow accepted nomenclature guidelines. Individuals showing high degrees of similarity are grouped, defining the lowest unit of classification. In biology the basic taxonomic unit is the species, however a problem herein is that the classification of prokaryotic microorganisms has been rather ambivalent and the species concept ambiguous. Still, the tree of life provides an accurate framework to direct research in all biological sub-disciplines, and represents an ideal model for the organization of biological knowledge at different levels.

16.4 rRNA as an evolutionary chronometer

There are several evolutionarily conserved genes that are present in most organisms and certain criteria are important for a molecule to be regarded as an evolutionary chronometer. In order to determine the evolutionary relationship it is essential that the gene chosen will (i) be universally distributed between organisms, (ii) have a defined structure and function, (iii) be present in large numbers per cell, (iv) keep stable with time, and (v) have a sequence that changes at a rate corresponding with the evolutionary distance being measured (Zuckerka & Pauling 1965; Olsen et al. 1986). The most favoured, and thus most important, gene specifies the sequence for the ribosomal RNA molecule and it encodes a specific component

of the protein-synthesising ribosomes. By comparing ribosomal RNA (rRNA) sequences Carl Woese established a molecular sequence based phylogenetic tree that could be used to relate all organisms and reconstruct the history of life (Woese 1987). The rRNA molecule evolves at a particular rate and some parts of the molecule are more important to its function than others. As a result the functional regions of the molecule are almost identical in sequence from the smallest bacterium to the largest animal. rRNA has attracted considerable interest and is today the primary tool for measuring diversity and the proxy for the species concept for microorganisms. When rRNA sequences from different organisms are compared to each other, the number of changes in the sequence can be used to create a phylogenetic tree.

16.5 Methods for assessing diversity

The insight that sequences rather than cultures could be used to infer differences between organisms has been liberation for microbial ecologists. Unlike macroorganisms, most microbes cannot be taxonomically and metabolically categorized according to directly visible phenotypes. Traditionally, to identify an organism it was necessary to obtain a pure culture and to conduct a battery of tests to determine its core identities and physiological properties. This is not only very laborious but a highly partial process as most species cannot (or have not) been cultivated in the laboratory (Pace 1997). Culturing conditions select for a distinct subpopulation of the bacteria present in the given environment (Staley & Konopka 1985) Cultivation-dependent methods therefore only give information about those few organisms able to grow under the given conditions. This is a highly biased approach and only a limited fraction of microorganisms have, or ever will be, fully characterized in this manner (Amann et al. 1995). This challenge in cultivation has skewed our knowledge of microbial diversity and limited our understanding of the microbial world.

16.5.1 PCR-based methods

The most common approach for assessing microbial diversity is to use polymerase chain reaction

(PCR) to amplify 16S rRNA genes (rDNA) from the community (Pace et al. 1986) The amplified genes can then be cloned, into *E. coli*, and identified by sequencing using classical sequencing technologies and then compared, by alignments (Hugenholtz & Pace 1996) to other taxa. The advantage of this method is that a large fragment of the gene can be unequivocally analysed. The disadvantage is that the cloning and sequencing is time consuming and labour intensive. Although clone libraries of hundreds or more are technically feasible they are seldom undertaken for more than a site or two in most studies and most laboratories can, or could, only manage tens of clones per sample if more than a handful of samples were to be analysed.

Consequently, community fingerprinting techniques have gained favour. These methods are quick, simple and cheap, and as such can be used to study many sites in space and time. They include denaturant gradient gel electrophoresis (DGGE; Muyzer et al. 1993), terminal restriction fragment length polymorphism (T-RFLP; Liu et al. 1997), single stand conformation polymorphism (SSCP; Schwieger & Tebbe 1998), ribosomal intergenic spacer region (RISA; Ranjard et al. 2000), and automated RISA (ARISA; Cardinale et al. 2004). All these methods provide information about the numerically dominant community members based on sequence differences in the genes of interest. Differences in sequences are detected manually by eye or automatically by machine and the sequence variations are governed by both the detection limit and the resolution level of the method. Thus only the most abundant taxa will be characterized by these methods (see flow diagram of the methods, Fig. 16.2, and detection limits and thresholds, Table 16.1). Although all such methods are flawed in some respect, they may nevertheless be tentatively used.

These intermediate resolution methods resolve the diversity of microbial communities and are based on differences in conserved genes like 16S rRNA genes and functional genes. Such molecular methods give qualitative information about the organisms present and have revolutionized our understanding of the diversity and distribution of bacteria, archaea and microbial eukaryotes. The results obtained using these methods has demon-strated that the analysis of microbial model systems can provide important insights into ecosystem function and stability. However, the terminology and metrics used in macroecology must be applied with great caution because the methods available to characterize microbial communities are still in their infancy.

The ability of microbial ecologists to quantify diversity and test hypotheses regarding patterns and processes in microbial communities depends to a great extent on their ability to characterize the diversity and distribution of microbes in a wide range of habitats. Typically, investigators are interested in the relative diversities of communities across a gradient of stress, disturbance and other biotic or abiotic differences. It is difficult with current techniques to study the true diversity since we do not know what is present and we have no way of determining the accuracy of our extraction or detection methods. Current studies on the diversity of prokaryotes often employ methods based on the analyses of 16S rRNA genes, as these allow investigators to detect and quantify phylotypes that are inaccessible by culture in the laboratory. In this way a more comprehensive assessment of diversity can be obtained than was previously possible, leading to the improved understanding of the extraordinary richness of prokaryotic biodiversity (Woese 1987; DeLong & Pace 2001; Wellington et al. 2003; Oremland et al. 2005; Nakatsu 2007). Although progress has been made towards an understanding of microbial diversity, it has been faltering and in many ways it is flawed. Sample sizes are still dictated by what is feasible, not what is required. Attempts to mathematically extrapolate data are often inconsistent, with the inherent limitations of sample sizes ignored and the crucial difference between a sample and the environment typically unacknowledged. The application of these contemporary methods has demonstrated that the extent of prokaryotic diversity in most habitats is almost beyond our understanding, with complex habitats containing an estimated 10^4–10^6 taxa in a single gram (Dykhuizen 1998; Torsvik et al. 1998; Øvreås et al. 2003; Gans et al. 2005). The Earth's biosphere contains more than 10^{30} individuals (Whitman et al. 1998) and an untold number of species. The key to the efforts to characterize this extraordinary diversity is that the

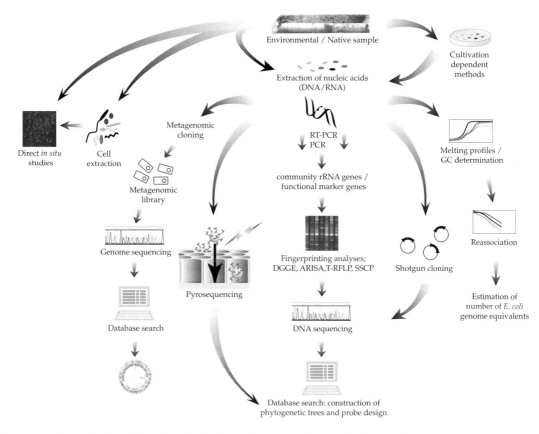

Figure 16.2 The array of tools available to the microbial ecologist exploring microbial diversity. The relationships between them are large and increasing. See Table 16.1 for more details on the performance of each method.

observed and inferred rank abundance distribution for most communities show a long tail of numerically minor species or phylotypes (MacArthur 1960; Curtis & Sloan 2004). This means that most native microbial communities are dominated by a small number of species whereas the vast majority of populations are rather uncommon.

16.5.2 Pyrosequencing

Novel sequencing technologies such as massively parallel pyrosequencing have brought sequencing to yet another level, with a throughput of up to 400 million high-quality bases in 10 hours. This is the sequencing scale we require to explore the extent of microbial diversity. A few years ago 'pyrosequencing' (http://www.454.com) was developed as a remarkably inexpensive approach

to shotgun style studies. The advantage of this pyrosequencing is its significantly lower price and the higher number of sequences that can be obtained quickly. Recent dramatic advances in DNA sequencing technology, including the 454 Life Science pyrosequencing techniques, have made metagenomic analysis of environmental samples an achievable reality. Because of this, an exponential increase in sequencing data has been generated. A traditional Sanger sequencer produces (per run) approximately 70 Kbp, whereas a 454 pyrosequencer produces 100 Mbp. The bottleneck will therefore rapidly become computational. In order to make sense of these massive data sets, mathematical modelling will assume a central role in microbial ecology. These newer methods are prone to sequencing error and this may have distorted the number of singletons in early reports of

Table 16.1 Summary of the available technology for determining diversity in microbial samples.

Method	Sequences	Advantages	Disadvantages	Sample size	Detection threshold	Selected references
Guanine plus cytosine	No	No PCR, includes all extracted DNA	Requires large quantities of DNA Dependent on lysis of cells and extraction efficiency Low resolution level	$1–10^{10}$	Depends on reassociation time Torsvik et al. (1990a,b) Øvreås (2000)	Nusslein & Tiedje (1999)
Nucleic acid reassociation	No	No PCR, total DNA extraction, includes all Gives an estimate of the total diversity	Requires large quantities of DNA Sequences needs to be in high copy number to be recorded Dependent on lysis of cells and extraction efficiency Low resolution level	$1–10^{10}$	Depends on reassociation time	Torsvik et al. (1990a, b) Øvreås & Torsvik (1998) Torsvik et al. (2002)
Metagenomics library	Yes Usually Sanger	No PCR, excellent read quality	Very laborious Low sample size	1–4000	1/number of target sequences	Tyson et al. (2004) Venter et al. (2004) Tringe et al. (2005)
Metatranscriptome analyses	Yes Sanger	Simultaneously obtain information on structure and function	Requires high quality RNA RT-PCR for generation of cDNA	$10^{4}–10^{6}$	1/number of target sequences	Urich et al. (2008)
Classical clone library	Yes Sanger	High sequence quality, lengthy reads	PCR biases Laborious, low sample size	20–1000	1/sample size	Hugenholtz & Pace (1996)
Denaturant gradient gel electrophoresis (DGGE)	Optional	Quick and cheap Large number of samples can be analysed simultaneously	PCR biases Accessible Low resolution Only most abundant taxa One band can represent more than one species	$\sim 10^{5}$	$\sim 1\%$ biomass	Muyzer et al. (1993), Nakatsu (2007)

Method	Novel	Advantages	Disadvantages			References
Terminal restriction fragment length polymorphism (T-RFLP)	No	Quick and cheap Can be automated and large number of sequences processed Highly reproducible Compare differences in microbial communities	PCR biases Accessible Low resolution Only most abundant taxa Choice of primers and restriction enzymes will influence on the fingerprint	$\sim 10^5$	$\sim 1\%$ biomass	Osborn et al. 2000
Amplified ribosomal DNA restriction analysis (ARDRA)	No	Quick and cheap Detect structural changes in microbial community	PCR bias Low resolution	$\sim 10^5$	1% biomass	Liu et al. (1997), Tiedje et al. (1999).
(Automated) ribosomal intergenic spacer analysis (ARISA)/(RISA)	No	Quick and cheap Highly reproducible community profiles	PCR biases Accessible Low resolution Only most abundant taxa	$\sim 10^5$	$\sim 1\%$ biomass	Fisher & Triplett (1999) Garcia-Martinez et al. (1999)
Pyrosequencing	Yes Novel	Huge sample sizes	Short reads Sequencing errors	10^4–10^6	1/sample size	Sogin et al. (2006) Huber et al. (2007)

diversity using this technology. However, this is not an insuperable problem (Quince et al. 2009) and seems unlikely to affect the scale of estimates of diversity using this technology (Øvreås et al., in preparation).

The advent of 454 sequencing could finally place the rational exploration of microbial diversity on a scale corresponding with the magnitude of the task. The technology permits the deep sequencing of a specific gene amplified from community DNA. The diversity of this gene is an indicator of the underlying diversity of the community. The analysis of the few very large datasets generated using this technology has been relatively unsophisticated and the results only qualitatively confirm long-standing theoretical estimates that the diversity would be big. Quince and collaborators (Quince et al. 2008) recently presented a more rational and systematic approach to the exploration of microbial diversity in which significant samples were analysed using appropriate sample sizes.

16.5.3 Metagenomics

In principle the analysis of total DNA extracted directly from a community generates information derived from all the community members, providing estimates of the microbial diversity and a broad picture of the native microbial community composition. Diversity information stored in nucleic acids can give information at different resolution levels. DNA extracted directly from an environmental sample can be regarded as one large microbial community genome—often called the metagenome. The metagenome approach represents a different whole community DNA-based analysis. Not only does it circumvent the cultivation anomaly, but it also avoids the PCR biases by cloning and sequencing genes directly from the environmental DNA. Metagenomics provides a relatively unbiased view not only of the community structure (species richness and distribution) but also the functional (metabolic) potential of a community. In practice such information is hard to obtain and hard to analyse.

The first metagenomic analysis presented is that of Torsvik and collaborators (Torsvik et al. 1990b), in which the prokaryotic community from soil

was analysed based on its DNA composition. This method makes the assumption that the extracted community genome contains all information about the diversity in that specific community. The total genetic diversity was therefore measured by rean-nealling of DNA, as this rate is dependent on the amount of homologous DNA in a given sample. This rate can then be used to calculate genome size or more precisely genome complexity in that sample, and is referred to as the community DNA reassociation method. The main advantage of the reassociation method is that it offers an estimate of the extent of diversity in the prokaryotic community. The method basically provides information about the total number of completely different genomes present in the environmental sample but it also tells us something about the distribution of different genomes based on the slope of the curve. This method is a broad-scale, low-resolution, cultivation-independent approach for assessing the diversity of microbial communities.

Another metagenome approach involves construction of complex community libraries by direct cloning of large genomic DNA fragments (40–80 kb) from environmental samples into fosmid or bacterial artificial chromosome (BAC) vectors. This approach can be used to generate information on the potential functioning of individual microbial species in natural environments in order to study the broader role of microorganisms in the ecosystem (Rondon et al. 2000; Tyson et al. 2004; Tringe et al. 2005).

Although still in its infancy, such metagenomic analyses have already contributed to our knowledge of genome structure, population diversity, gene content and the composition of naturally occurring microbial assemblages. In low complexity populations, metagenomic studies have led to the assembly of almost complete genomes from the abundant genotypes and have provided composite genomic representation of the abundant genotype. Extreme environments such as acid mine drainage (Tyson et al. 2004), anaerobic methane oxidizing zones in the deep-sea (Hallam et al. 2004) and geothermal environments (Bhaya et al. 2007) have played a leading role in the metagenomics area. In many cases the restrictive geochemistry of these environments limits microbial phylogenetic diversity. Such relatively low diversity systems are excellent templates for using metagenomics to explore the roles of microheterogeneiety in ecosystem resilience and stability. One of the most interesting studies has been focused on the marine environment: the largest metagenomic study to date is the Global Ocean sampling expedition, which followed the voyage of Darwin's ship HMS Beagle.

Early metagenomic analyses provided some very significant insights into ecosystem function. Perhaps the most striking example is that of the discovery of proteorhodopsin. Proteorhodopsin are retinal-binding photoproteins that function as light-driven protonpumps. The genes encoding proteorhodopsin were originally found in the marine environmental BAC library (Beja et al. 2001), resulting in the detection of a novel type of phototrophic organism in the ocean. Later comparisons of genomic approaches have demonstrated that proteorhodopsin are widely distributed among divergent bacterial taxa in marine environments and that this process contributes significantly to the phototrophic processes in the ocean. Metagenomic studies have also led to the recognition of the novel anaerobic methane oxidization metabolism or 'reverse methanogenesis' performed by Archaea in deep-sea sediments (Hallam et al. 2004) and to the prediction that non-thermophilic archaea from soil and marine plankton gain energy through the oxidation of ammonia (Schleper et al. 2005).

Another approach is to look into the functional genes in a microbial community using proteomics. Proteomics provide direct information on the dynamic protein expression in tissue or whole cells. Together with the significant accomplishment of genomics and bioinformatics, the systematic analysis of all expressed cellular components has become a reality in the post-genomic era, and attempts to grasp a comprehensive picture of the biology have become possible. One important aspect of proteomics is to characterize proteins differentially expressed by dissimilar cell types or cells imposed to different environmental conditions. In this way changes in protein expression under different growth conditions can be studied. Proteins induced under exposure to external stress

factors, such as pH stress, nutrient limitation or the presence of metals, have been reported (Amaro et al. 1991; Seeger & Jerez 1992; Vera et al. 2003).

In almost all of the metagenomic and proteomic studies a separate accompanying molecular typing method—usually based on the PCR-amplified 16S rRNA gene—is needed to characterize the gene discovery in the context of the microbial phylogenetic diversity of the sample (Venter et al. 2004; Tringe et al. 2005; Gill et al. 2006; Huber et al. 2007). However, DNA-based metagenomic and diversity studies do not allow us to draw the conclusions on the expression state of the genes, and therefore the functional role of genes or organisms in the investigated environments remains uncertain. A logical next step in the metagenomic area therefore includes metatranscriptomics technology (Urich et al. 2008). In this study the total RNA pool of a soil microbial community of both functional and taxonomically relevant molecules, i.e. mRNA and rRNA, was enriched and analysed in a 'double RNA' approach. In this way Urich and his co-workers were able to link community structure and function in one single experiment. Using this approach they found a high level of activity not withstanding the relative low abundance of the Crenarchaeota in the ecosystem (Urich et al. 2008).

16.6 Sampling, scale, and thresholds

Sampling is of central importance to the estimation of diversity at all living things (see Chapter 2 and 3). However, the disparity between the number of individuals in the microbial world and the number of sequences we can examine deserves special consideration. The species patterns seen in a sample, even quite a large sample, may look nothing like the community from which they are drawn. The advent of much larger sample sizes has not necessarily obviated this problem (Fig. 16.3). This plainly casts doubt on the naive use of species abundance curves, diversity and similarity indices, and the other paraphernalia of macroecology. In addition to the problem of sample size, one must also consider the detection threshold. For clone libraries and analogous methods such as pyrosequencing the threshold is simply the reciprocal of the size of the library.

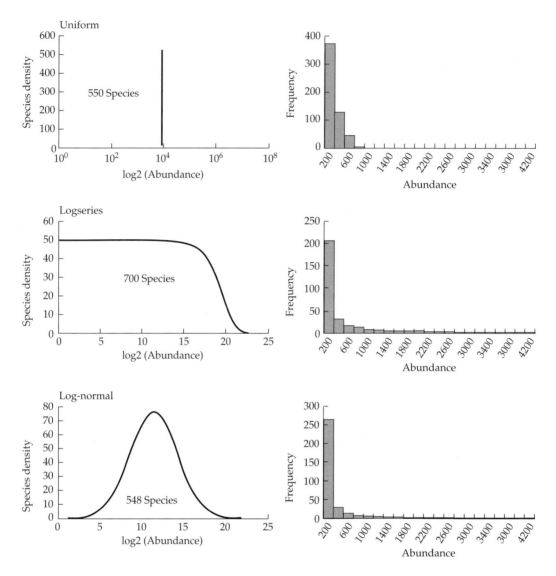

Figure 16.3 Simulated samples (left column) from artificial communities (right column) with similar diversities and very different species abundance curves (uniform, log-series, and log-normal). The sample distributions are superficially similar even with an apparently large sample size of 15 000 reads (with thanks to Steve Woodcock for running the simulations).

Thus a library of 1000 sequences has a detection limit of 1/1000. However, molecular fingerprinting techniques such as DGGE, ARISA and T-RFLP are subject to a detection threshold of about 1% abundance (Muyzer et al. 1993; Bent et al. 2007). Thus, when we naively attempt to infer changes in species richness using these methods we are really just evaluating the number of taxa occurring above or below

this threshold. The number of species above or below the detection limit the detection limit reflects a change in the distribution of taxa in the sample, which may, or may not, be associated with a change in richness. It could just be a change in distribution. Moreover, whilst a reduction in the number of detectable taxa is assumed to be associated with a loss of diversity, it could also be associated with an increase in diversity as the associated increase in evenness drops more taxa below the threshold.

Thresholds and sampling issues cast a pall over all contemporary studies of microbial diversity (Woodcock et al. 2007). Microbial ecologists would do well to be cautious and qualified in their claims. It will be interesting to see how much of what we think we know will survive re-examination with adequate sample sizes supported by adequate statistical analysis.

16.7 Mathematical tools for estimating diversity

It should now be apparent that we can virtually never measure diversity directly. Rather, it must be estimated or inferred from the data available to us. The excitement of the outstanding insights of the latest batch of sequencing technology should not blind us to the fact that these methods cannot, as currently deployed, directly determine the diversity of a community. However, the new generation of sequencing does mean that these estimates are now far more credible and can, in principle at least, be rationally verified.

The mathematical tools we can use can be divided into four groups:

1. collectors' curves
2. Chao and Chao-type non-parametric estimators
3. parametric estimators that assume a distribution
4. parametric estimators that infer a distribution.

16.7.1 Collectors curves

A simple and intuitive way to evaluate a collection of sequences is to plot the number of different sequences on the y-axis against the total number of sequences examined. The asymptote of the curve is then estimated and taken to represent the total diversity (Colwell & Coddington 1994). This method, reviewed in detail in Chapter 4, is quite incapable of dealing with the scale of diversity of the microbial world. The logarithmic nature of the distribution of the microbial world means that the asymptote is apparently approached long before all the diversity is sequenced. This may not be obvious at first. Imagine a sample with 7000 species. Now imagine that species of modal rank abundance are

10 000 times less abundant than the most abundant taxon. When only half the taxa have been discovered, a new sequence is only going to be found once every 10^4 sequences. This would be a very flat collectors curve! The estimation or inference of such asymptotes has been very deceptive, leading authors to quite incorrectly believe they have nearly all the diversity in a sample (Roesch et al. 2007). These and allied methods are in principle and in practice a wholly inadequate way of determining species richness.

16.7.2 Chao's non-parametric estimators

There are a number of related methods, developed by Anne Chao, that are in many ways one of the intellectually most pleasing tools in the toolbox (Chao 1987). Their primary advantages are that they make mathematically infallible estimates of the lower bounds of the diversity (i.e. the diversity, whatever it is, cannot be less than the value estimated) and they are very simple to execute. This robustness arises because they make no assumption about the underlying distribution of the taxa (which is why they are termed non-parametric). This approach is described in more detail in Chapter 4 and exemplified by the Chao 1 method that determines S_T, a lower bound estimator for the total diversity, from S, the number of species observed in the sample and the number of taxa observed once (f_1) and observed twice (f_2):

$$\hat{S}_T = S + \frac{f_1^2}{2f_2} \qquad (16.1)$$

There are a number of such methods but the estimates they make are all sensitive to the underlying distribution. This sensitivity to distribution can be quite profound. Schloss and Handelsmann (Schloss & Handelsman 2006b) used simulations to show that a sample with 5000 species and a log-normal distribution could require anything between 18 000 and 40 000 clones to find the species richness. However, only 150 clones would be required if the distribution was even. Thus, although in principle this estimator requires a sample size of at least the square root of twice the diversity, in reality much, much larger sample sizes are usually required. The sensitivity to distribution varies slightly from method to method so it is better to choose one method and stick to it. For the microbial ecologist, these are great, quick and dirty tools for the estimation of the lower bounds of diversity in a sample, as long as one remembers that this is a lower bound. At present it appears that, even with pyrosequencing and sample sizes of the order of tens or even hundreds of thousands these methods underestimate, but typically by less than an order of magnitude (Quince et al. 2008). It is not possible to use these methods to determine if you should take a bigger sample or to say how big a sample you should take in a subsequent study or to extrapolate to sample sizes for metagenomic studies. They will also be particularly sensitive to sequencing error, increasing the number of apparent singletons. This is a particular problem with the new generation of sequencing technologies. Thus, as a rule of thumb one can never go wrong with non-parametric estimators, equally one can never know if one is right. One can only be sure that the diversity, whatever it is, is very probably bigger than the estimate of these non-parametric estimators.

16.7.3   Parametric estimators that assume a distribution

Parametric estimators assume that the relative abundance follows a particular distribution. The best known is probably that of Curtis and coworkers (Curtis et al. 2002) and was inspired by, but is distinct from, the method of Preston mentioned in Chapter 4. This procedure assumes a log-normal taxa abundance distribution and is, in principle, very simple. A taxa abundance distribution self-evidently describes the number of taxa occurring at a given abundance. One way to describe this relationship is as a graph in which the abundance is plotted on the y-axis and the number of taxa at that abundance is plotted on the x-axis. The number of species or taxa is simply the area under this curve. Thus, to determine the total diversity in the sample or environment of interest it is not necessary to count every species, merely to know the taxa abundance pattern and then determine the area under the curve. The disparity between the size of the microbial world and the sample sizes deployed to describe it is such that the no-one has directly

observed the taxa abundance curve of any microbial sample or community (but see below). We can, however, assume a distribution and there are plausible reasons for assuming that species abundance curves for rapidly growing organisms are typically log-normal (MacArthur 1960; Curtis et al. 2002) and this distribution appears to be the most likely in at least some microbial communities (Quince et al. 2008).

To estimate the diversity of a community one must first estimate the area under the species abundance curve using the data available. Fortunately there is a relationship between the area under a species abundance curve (which we don't know) and the total number of individuals in a sample, which we do know.

It is possible to show that there is a mathematical relationship between the diversity of the sample or environment (S_T) and the ratio of the total number of individuals in a sample (N_T) and the abundance of the most abundant taxon (N_{max}). The one unknown in this relationship is the standard deviation of the species abundance curve, which is dictated by the abundance of the least abundant taxon or N_{min} and is typically assumed to be one species at an abundance of one. This is patently a blind assumption, but the value of S_T is not very sensitive to modest departures from this guesstimate.

The upshot of this approach is that one can, under these assumptions, infer the diversity of any community or sample as long as one can estimate the total number of individuals the proportional abundance of the most abundant taxon. One can thus consider the diversity of an entire sea or a diversity of a drop thereof (Fig. 16.4).

The estimates produced on this basis are crude ballpark estimates that lack statistical rigour. However, they were and are consistent with the estimates of the Bergen group based on DNA:DNA hybridization showing that the diversity of soil massively exceeds the diversity of samples of seawater and that the latter could easily exceed 3–4000 taxa in a few grams of soil (Torsvik et al. 1990b).

In principle the next generation of sequencing technology should obviate the need for assumptions about taxa abundance curves.

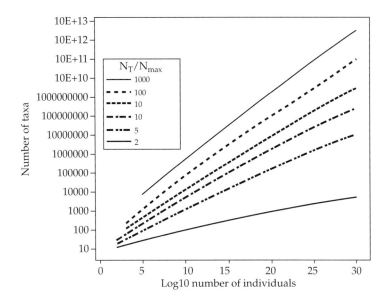

Figure 16.4 The relationship between species richness and the total number of individuals over 30 orders of magnitude for various ratios of N_T/N_{max} by assuming that N_{min} is equal to 1 and a log-normal taxa area curve (Curtis et al. 2002). As a rule of thumb, soil has an N_T/N_{max} ratio of 10 and seas and lakes a ratio of 4. There are about 10^{30} bacteria in the world (Whitman et al. 1998).

16.7.4 Estimating diversity by inferring a distribution from the data

Of course, in an ideal world one would not assume or ignore the distribution of the data, but infer it from the data. However, to do so one must confront the problem of sample size. If the sample size is too small there is so much uncertainty attached to the parameters of the distribution as to render the estimates useless. One would do far better to fall back on assumed distributions or simpler nonparametric methods. It is only very recently that sample sizes have become large enough to permit credible estimates to be made. An early attempt to circumvent the issue by fitting a taxa abundance curve to reassociation data (Gans et al. 2005) gave very large ($\sim 10^6$ species per gram) estimates of diversity. It was subsequently criticized because the variance in these estimates proved too high to allow a meaningful estimate to be made (Bunge et al. 2006; Hong et al. 2006).

Robust methods for determining the diversity from robust estimates of the distribution of the taxa rest on approaches pioneered by (Chao & Bunge 2002), who looked at the γ distributions of species.

Hong, Bunge and colleagues applied this approach to microbes and considered a wider variety of distributions (Hong et al. 2006). They could only obtain a suitable fit by using a subset of the data available to them, a stratagem that was perhaps necessary because their dataset was also too small. Most recently Quince et al. (2008) have exploited the new generation of pyrosequencing data and extended Bunge's likelihood approach and demonstrated how it can be used to determine the sample sizes required to capture a specified fraction of the abundance of a particular gene or indeed all the genetic material in an environment. The microbial literature has been well reviewed by Sloan et al. (2008) and Connolly and Dornelas have written a very accessible introduction to Bayesian methods in Chapter 10. Those seeking a deeper understanding of Bayesian statistics can find guidance elsewhere (Gelman 2003).

The core of the new approach is the use of a likelihood function. A likelihood function in essence allows the estimation of particular model parameters from a given distribution given a particular dataset (in our case observed taxa abundances). The beauty of such an approach is that it not only allows one to estimate the parameters of a particular species distribution and thus the diversity, but it also allows one to estimate the uncertainty around those parameters and thus the diversity estimated. However, what a likelihood function cannot tell you is which distribution to choose. That is still a question of judgement or intuition. Nevertheless, one's choice of distribution can be evaluated.

This likelihood function can then be used in conjunction with Monte–Carlo–Markov chain protocols to generate a distribution of the model parameters given the data. The choice of species abundance distribution is at present arbitrary. A comparison of number of data sets by Quince et al. (2008) found the log-normal to give a good fit for many, but not all, data sets and the inverse Gaussian, log-t, and Sichel all gave good fits in some cases. However, the exponential, γ, and a mixture of exponential were found to be unsatisfactory. Not surprisingly, the estimates of diversity tended to converge to within a factor of 2 in the better sampled environments (Fig. 16.5). This suggests that the best strategy is to take a large enough sample and choose from a range of distributions to obtain a satisfactory fit.

16.8   Estimation of required sample size

Once one has some idea about the distribution one can make an estimate of the sample size required to obtain a particular fraction of the diversity. A conceptually simple way to do this is to generate artificial communities with the best estimated taxa abundance distributions and sample from them (Schloss & Handelsman 2006b). This approach is laborious and requires the size of the community to be defined. A slightly more elegant approach is to exploit the Bayesian approach to examine the effect of sample size on the unobserved proportion of the taxa (Chao & Bunge 2002).

Such estimates are very dependant on an ability to determine the true nature of the species abundance curve, and thus are sensitive to under-sampling and maybe substantially distorted by sequencing error (Fig. 16.5).

16.9   In-depth metagenome analyses

Traditionally, metagenomic studies have been something of a shot in the dark. However, if we know, or think we know, the abundance distribution of a sample we can determine how many reads are required to capture a specified fraction of the metagenome and/or to capture all the genetic material of an organism of specified abundance. The procedure is described in greater detail elsewhere (Sloan et al. 2008; Quince et al. 2008) but it is a very simple extension of the estimation of the sample size for a specified fraction of the diversity. If the mean genome length is G and it is sequenced with a method yielding genome fragments of DNA (reads) of size R then the number of reads required to span a genome γ is G/R. Quince et al. (2008) show that to calculate the expected sample size to capture a given fraction of the genomic material one must simply multiply γ by the expected sample size required to capture the same fraction of the species diversity. Thus the best-fitting distribution for the Global Ocean Survey that 90% of the diversity could be captured with 35 million reads. The estimates are highly sensitive to the underlying taxa abundance curve. If the underlying distribution was log-normal nearly 10^{10} reads might be required to capture most of the genomic material. The ability to correctly determine the taxa abundance patterns will be of strategic importance to the rational exploration of the microbial world in years to come.

16.10   Prospectus

For the last 30 years microbial diversity studies have relied on molecular tools to liberate this field from the constraints of culture and we have marvelled at what they have found. In the coming decades the new generations of sequencing technology and associated mathematical and computational developments will liberate us from the woefully inadequate sample sizes of the first generation of molecular methods. In so doing they will allow us to put the exploration of this frontier on a rational basis. We do not yet know what we will find; most likely new and fascinating molecules and processes

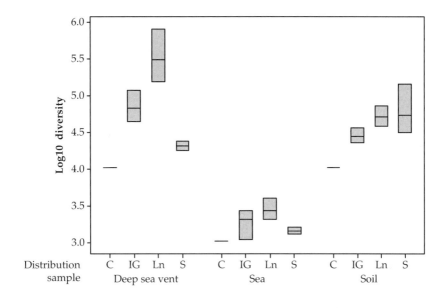

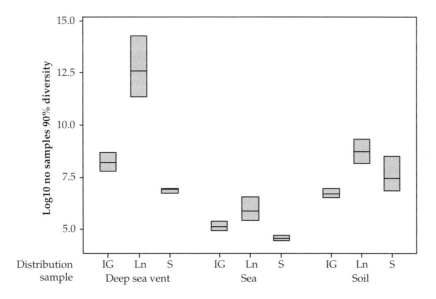

Figure 16.5 Upper panel: Bayesian parametric diversity estimates from fits of abundance distributions of samples from the sea (Global Ocean Survey), a Canadian soil, and a deep-sea vent. Estimates are given as medians with a 95% confidence interval. LN, log-normal; IG, inverse Gaussian; S, Sichel. The Chao estimates (C) and are also shown. Lower panel: the sampling effort (as 16S reads) necessary to sample 90% of taxa present. Adapted from Quince et al. (2008). The deep-sea vent is sample FS 396B in this paper.

will be uncovered. We do know that the unexplored exceeds the explored by orders of magnitude. It seems likely that much of what we think we know will be changed and revaluated as new molecules and patterns emerge and sampling artefacts are seen for what they are. We need to create a new generation of numerate and computer savvy molecular microbial ecologists to explore this immense frontier. They will no doubt regard much of which has done in the past 30 years as quaint and primitive.

16.11 Key points

1. Microbial ecology is one of the most awe-inspiring frontiers in any science, and microbial diversity estimates are just the beginning.

2. The traditional species concept is useless in microbial ecology; we must draw on more abstract and arbitrary measures of evolution.

3. We use evolutionary relationships inferred from changes in molecules to determine differences between microorganisms.

4. rRNA is the molecule of choice for inferring phylogeny. However, it gives only a partial view of the diversity of a community, the true extent of which can only be inferred by considering all of the genetic material.

5. Microbial diversity studies have shifted from a culture-based approach to a molecular view of microbial diversity and the biosphere.

6. Sampling is of central importance to the estimation of microbial diversity, yet the disparity between the number of microbes and the number of sequences we can examine deserves special consideration.

7. Diversity can virtually never be measured directly, but rather it must be estimated or inferred from available data. Our estimates are anchored in the sample itself and the community or environment from which it was drawn.

8. The advent of novel massive parallel sequencing could finally place the rational exploration of microbial diversity on a scale corresponding with the magnitude of the task.

CHAPTER 17

Biodiversity and disturbance

Maria Dornelas, Candan U. Soykan, and Karl Inne Ugland

17.1 Introduction

Disturbances play a fundamental role in shaping biodiversity patterns and ecosystem processes. Some disturbances completely destroy a community by killing all of its inhabitants. However, periodically disturbing ecological communities may enhance biodiversity by releasing resources (Holt 2008) and by promoting the coexistence of species adapted to different conditions (Connell 1978). Given the importance of biodiversity for ecosystem functioning (Hooper et al. 2005) and specifically for ecosystem resilience (Folke et al. 2004), accurately measuring the effects of disturbances on biodiversity is a fundamental step in the management of natural resources and conservation efforts. Here we review biodiversity metrics and their ability to detect the effects of disturbances.

Considerable effort has gone towards measuring the effects of disturbances on ecosystem properties, with many metrics being developed for quantifying ecological integrity (Rice 2000; Costello et al. 2004; Jorgensen et al. 2005). There are available metrics for properties at different levels of organization, ranging from individual health to ecosystem function. Given the focus of this book on species diversity, we restrict our discussion to community-level metrics, noting that a considerable body of work addresses individual-, population-, and ecosystem-level metrics (see Jorgensen et al. (2005)). Even at the community level, the sheer number of choices available makes it difficult to select an appropriate metric or suite of metrics for a specific purpose. Moreover, a lack of rigorous comparative studies means that the relative merits of the full range of community-level metrics is yet to be determined (but see Abella et al. (2006), Patrício et al. (2006), Salas et al. (2006a), Salas et al. (2006b), and Ware et al. (2008) for examples comparing selected metrics).

Although it represents an important research objective in the field of applied ecology, a full evaluation of the various community-level metrics used to measure the effects of human disturbance on ecological communities is beyond the scope of this chapter. Instead, our objectives are to organize existing metrics around a logical framework, describe their strengths and limitations, highlight important areas for future research, and make some recommendations based on current knowledge. Along these lines, in the sections that follow we group the various metrics into three categories with increasing preservation of information: univariate metrics, abundance distribution-based metrics, and multivariate analyses. From each of these categories we describe selected metrics that are commonly used, effective, and/or novel.

17.2 What is a disturbance?

Before we can measure the effects of disturbance on biodiversity, it is useful to consider what we mean by disturbance. The term 'disturbance' is broadly used, and has a variety of meanings. One definition is that an ecological disturbance is any condition that causes mortality or loss of biomass (Huston 1994). Another definition includes any event that kills, displaces, or damages individuals (Sousa 1984). Often a disturbed ecosystem is thought of as one damaged by anthropogenic actions, and disturbance is used interchangeably with human threat. Here we use the broader meaning of disturbance and consider both 'natural' and anthropogenic disturbances, although most of our examples are linked to human actions. We also try to refrain from assigning any judgment about whether disturbances are 'good' or 'bad' for biodiversity, and focus merely on measuring their effects. Ultimately, disturbances temporarily change the rules that govern community dynamics, potentially affecting biodiversity. However, disturbances come in many forms and influence communities in different ways. We will begin by briefly discussing an overview of disturbances according to their source, time scale, spatial scale, intensity, and specificity.

17.2.1 Source of the disturbance

Disturbances may be classified as physical, chemical, or biological. Examples of physical disturbances include fire, waves, drought, floods, ice, and wind. Chemical disturbances are usually associated with the presence of a substance the community is not adapted to. Examples include most types of pollutants, as well as freshwater in a marine environment, or salt water in a freshwater community (although neither would really be a disturbance in an estuarine environment). Biological disturbances include population outbreaks of predators, competitors, or diseases, as well as the introduction of invasive species.

Disturbances are often classified as either natural or anthropogenic. Some disturbances easily fall under one of these classes. For example, a volcanic eruption is clearly a natural disturbance and an oil spill an anthropogenic one. However, the distinction is not always obvious: forest fires can either be a natural disturbance or the result of human action; a cyclone is a natural phenomenon, but human effects on climate change seem to be increasing their frequency and intensity (Schiermeier 2005). Furthermore, human action sometimes prevents natural disturbances, like floods for example, and this also has important ecosystem consequences. In fact, given the influence humans have on the planet it is increasingly difficult to find pristine communities and to know whether or not a disturbance is 'natural'. Hence, from a practical point of view it may be more useful to classify disturbances according to whether or not humans can manipulate them to maximize biodiversity as well as ecosystem services. In this review we will focus primarily on

disturbances that are either produced by or can be manipulated by humans.

17.2.2 Timescale

As ecologists became aware that communities are continually being perturbed and rarely if ever are at equilibrium (Connell & Sousa 1983), the concept of disturbance evolved from that of a discrete event to that of a disturbance regime. Consequently, timescale is now recognized as an essential facet of disturbance characterization. There are two main aspects of disturbance timing to be taken into consideration: duration and frequency. Duration regards how long the disturbance affects a community. Duration is a continuous variable, with disturbances at the two extremes often known as press (chronic disturbances with very long durations) and pulse (short and discrete disturbances) (Bender et al. 1984). Arguably, the former eventually can no longer be considered a disturbance, once the community acclimatizes to the new conditions, but the resulting community may be very different from the one before the disturbance. Disturbance frequency is how often a community is disturbed. Both duration and frequency determine the effects of disturbances on biodiversity patterns. For example, reef corals react to temperature stress by expelling their symbiotic algae, a process known as coral bleaching. Bleaching events that are either very long or very frequent can result in the death of an entire reef, whereas corals can recover from shorter bleaching events given enough time between them (Anthony et al. 2009).

17.2.3 Spatial scale

The effects of a disturbance, as well as the community's ability to recover, are strongly linked to its spatial scale. Some disturbances are localized, some are patchy, and some are regional. Large and spatially homogeneous disturbances usually have detrimental effects on biodiversity, whereas smaller or patchy disturbances can actually enhance regional diversity (Huston 1994). In fact, the homogenization of environmental conditions in modified landscapes such as agroecosystems can be a threat to biodiversity (Dornelas et al. 2009). Most importantly, spatial scale determines how effective management tools can be in preventing and/or protecting a community from disturbances. For example, reserves can effectively deter hunting or fishing within them, but do not protect communities from pollution dispersed from other areas or from climate change.

17.2.4   Intensity

Communities are constantly undergoing all sorts of perturbations, both ecological and environmental. We can think of disturbances as intense perturbations with significant consequences to the community. The intensity of a disturbance can be measured as the strength of the disruptive force in action or as the extent of the damage it creates (Sousa 1984). The more intense a disturbance is, the greater its effects on biodiversity patterns. However, even apparently subtle changes in the community can have drastic effects on ecosystem services (Hooper et al. 2005). Because species abundances are typically highly asymmetric, the loss of a single species may correspond to dramatic reductions in total biomass (Gaston & Fuller 2008). By the same token, the loss of only a small proportion of individuals can correspond to the disappearance of many species because most species are rare. We therefore need powerful biodiversity metrics to be able to detect even subtle effects of disturbances.

17.2.5   Specificity

Species vary in their ability to withstand disturbances, and disturbances also vary in whether they affect most species or only some. Some disturbances, like a fire, are relatively indiscriminate in which species are affected. Others, such as disease outbreaks, affect a single species. Hence, the effects of disturbances on biodiversity sometimes are drastic reductions in the number of species, other times are shifts in the identity of the species that dominate the community, and often are a combination of the two. Additionally, disturbances often have both direct and indirect effects. For example, a fire in a forest may directly remove trees and indirectly affect all the species that depended on the trees for

habitat or that are able to exploit the resources freed by the tree removal.

17.2.6   Summary

Different disturbances lead to different effects on biodiversity, therefore it is not surprising that there is no single ideal biodiversity metric to detect the effects of disturbances. When measuring these effects it is important to be as specific as possible about the nature of the disturbance being investigated, and to make predictions about the effects we expect it to have on the community. Specifying these expectations allows the choice of appropriate biodiversity metrics to detect the effects of the disturbance. In the next section we will explore the available methods for detecting such effects.

17.3   State of the field: measuring the effects of disturbance on biodiversity

Biodiversity metrics can be organized according to how much information is preserved. Univariate metrics are the easiest to use and the most general, but retain the least information by concentrating it into a single value. Metrics based on abundance distributions attempt to retain more information while remaining general by ignoring species identities (and consequently allowing the comparison of communities in different biogeographic regions and even habitats). Finally, multivariate metrics retain the most information, including species identities, and therefore allow the detection of compositional changes. In this chapter we review available metrics and discuss their advantages and disadvantages (Table 17.1). We do not attempt an exhaustive overview of all metrics available, but focus instead on representative examples.

17.3.1   Univariate metrics

Univariate metrics are often grouped into three main categories: species richness-, species evenness-, and species diversity-based metrics. We refrain from a detailed description of how they can be calculated because Chapters 4 and 5 are dedicated to species richness estimation and the comparison of diversity and evenness measures,

Table 17.1 Examples of methods available to quantify the effects of disturbance on biodiversity.

Method	Advantages	Disadvantages	Comments	Useful software
Univariate Species richness Species evenness Species diversity Phylogenetic diversity Trait diversity	Simple to interpret, easy to calculate, general	Insensitive to more subtle changes	Species richness and evenness complement one another Diversity indices may mask differences in components Phylogenetic and trait diversity are promising	EstimateS, Primer, EcoSim
SADs *Non-parametric* Slope of rank abundance eCDF *k* dominance ABC curves Q statistic Size spectra *Parametric* Log-series α Log-normal Gambin α	General, more powerful, flexible, allow testing for several different effects: rare species, dominant species, community structure	Many approaches proposed but not standardized, not often used	Promising area with more methods emerging Comparisons among methods needed	
Multivariate analysis R-mode approach Q-mode approach	Powerful, flexible Allow testing for several different effects: rare species, dominant species, species composition	Site specific and sometimes difficult to interpret	R mode allows the identification of the contribution of different species to overall patterns Q mode approach often yields more interpretable results	Vegan package in R Primer CANOCO

respectively. To these three categories we add phylogenetic and trait diversity, discussed at length in Chapters 13 and 14, respectively, but worthy of mention because of their potential application in environmental assessment (Warwick & Clarke 1998; Rosenfeld 2002).

Just as it is the most commonly used diversity metric in basic studies, so too species richness is the most popular of the metrics used to measure the effects of human disturbance on ecological communities (Costello et al. 2004). Although species richness often declines at high levels of disturbance, several issues interfere with its performance. Firstly, under certain circumstances richness is relatively insensitive to disturbance, often showing little change in spite of considerable human influence (Chapin III et al. 2000; Hillebrand et al. 2008). Secondly, richness often follows a unimodal,

or hump-shaped, pattern, peaking at intermediate levels of disturbance (Grime 1973a; Horn 1975; Connell 1978; Huston 1979; Sousa 1979). Finally, species richness estimates are proportional to the area sampled, sample size, and the number of samples collected, complicating comparisons among sites that differ in sampling intensity (Gotelli & Colwell 2001; Magurran 2004; see also Chapter 4). These caveats aside, its ease of calculation (only presence–absence data are required) and its intuitive appeal make species richness a fundamental biodiversity metric that should be used in studies on the effects of disturbances.

Species evenness—the relative asymmetry in abundance of species in a community—responds more rapidly to human disturbance than species richness (Hillebrand et al. 2008). Moreover, empirical evidence that evenness metrics complement patterns revealed by species richness is accumulating (Death & Zimmerman 2005; Pillans et al. 2007; see the example in Box 17.1). The momentum for the use of evenness indices has also come from an influential review by Smith & Wilson (1996), who identified a set of preferred metrics. Specifically, the authors conclude their study by recommending four indices, Simpson evenness, Carmago evenness, the Nee et al. index (E_Q), and what many are now calling the Smith–Wilson evenness index (E_{var}), as best meeting a set of required and desirable criteria for any index that purports to measure evenness. The combination of these factors has piqued interest in measuring changes in evenness due to human disturbance, encouraging numerous authors to include an evenness measure in their study (see, for example, Stewart et al. (2005), Todd (2006), and Dampier et al. (2007)). Empirical studies that report changes in evenness are accumulating, but the implications and causes of such changes remain poorly understood. An important, and as yet nearly unexplored, research theme will involve developing a theoretical framework for explaining the patterns that emerge, as well as predicting future changes in evenness as a result of human activity (see Drobner et al. (1998) for a promising first step).

Species diversity (sensu Hurlbert (1971)), also referred to as heterogeneity (sensu Peet (1974)), indices attempt to combine evenness and species richness into a single entity. A number of diversity metrics have been developed with this goal including the commonly used Shannon index (other popular ones include Shannon evenness, Simpson's dominance, Hill's diversity indices, and the Brillouin index). These metrics differ in the degree to which they emphasize richness versus evenness (Huston 1994; Magurran 2004), but all confound them to some degree. As a result different community states can have the same value of a given diversity metric, and these metrics as a whole have been shown to perform poorly under a variety of circumstances (Magurran 2004). In spite of decades of admonitions against the use of these metrics (see, for example, Hurlbert (1971)), they remain popular. So that there is no confusion in the reader's mind, we urge caution when using any univariate metric that combines richness and evenness into a

single value—the two components of diversity are often orthogonal and should usually be treated as such (Stirling & Wilsey 2001). In Box 17.1 we show how the two metrics complement each other and provide an example where species richness allows the detection of the effects of one type of disturbance, whereas evenness allows the detection of another.

Recognizing the fact that heterogeneity measures combines species richness and evenness, Buzas & Hayek (1996) developed a method to decompose the Shannon diversity metric into its two components, species richness and evenness. A major advantage of this approach is that it allows researchers to interpret changes in diversity. Thus, a decrease in diversity as a result of human activity can be attributed to a loss of richness, evenness, or both. Termed SHE analysis, this decomposition can also be used to analyse changes in community structure along a gradient (Buzas & Hayek 1998). Specifically, as samples are accumulated, species richness will increase; this, in turn, will affect values for Shannon diversity and evenness. The ways in which diversity and evenness change along a gradient can be used to look for breaks in the pattern that indicate a change in the community.

The phylogenetic metrics of biodiversity were developed in a bid to incorporate differences among species and evolutionary history into biodiversity metrics. These metrics and their relative performance are reviewed by Vellend et al. in Chapter 14. Typically, the magnitude of phylogenetic diversity (estimated from the position of species in a phylogenetic tree) of a community or set of communities is compared with that of a reference (the regional phylogenetic diversity). One example of this type of metrics that has been used to detect the effects of disturbances is taxonomic distinctness, which uses taxonomic hierarchy as a proxy for phylogenetic information (Clarke & Warwick 1998; Warwick & Clarke 1998). Taxonomic distinctness tends to decline with increasing human disturbance, is extremely robust in the face of variations in sampling effort, requires only incidence data, and is one of the few phylogenetic measures that is unbiased by species richness (Schweiger et al. 2008). A drawback is the fact that taxonomic distinctness

Box 17.1 The complementary nature of species richness and evenness

Death & Zimmerman (2005) studied aquatic invertebrate biodiversity patterns in 10 New Zealand streams that differed in substrate movement (a natural disturbance). For each stream they compared communities under native forest canopy and at sites surrounded by grassland (a human disturbance). Their main conclusion, that 'invertebrate communities in these mountain streams were strongly influenced by both the stability of the streambed and the presence or absence of a forest canopy', was influenced by their use of multiple, complementary diversity metrics.

For each sample these authors calculated rarefied species richness (species richness estimates standardized for sampling effort (see Chapter 4) and evenness (using the

Smith and Wilson evenness index, E_{var} (see also Chapter 5). Species richness allowed the authors to detect an effect of increasing natural disturbance (measured as stone movement). However, rarefied richness did not differ between forest canopy and grassland sites (Fig. 17.1a) and therefore did not allow the detection of the human disturbance. E_{var} differed significantly between forest canopy and open grassland sites, with greater evenness under undisturbed native forests (Fig. 17.1b). This example illustrates well the complementary nature of species richness and evenness, therefore demonstrating the value of measuring both rather than combining them into a single metric.

(a)

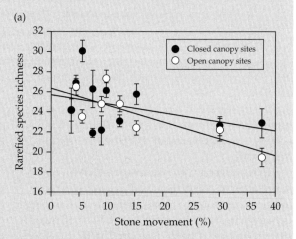

(b)

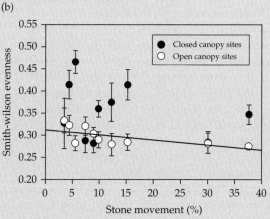

Figure 17.1 (a) Rarefied species richness for aquatic invertebrates along a gradient of natural disturbance (measured using stone movement); closed circles represent sites with a native forest canopy, while open circles represent open grassland sites. (b) Species evenness along the same gradient. Note that rarefied richness declines with increasing natural disturbance for both types of sites, however, it does not differ between closed and open sites. In contrast, evenness differs between closed and open sites, but only declines with increasing natural disturbance at the open sites.

is often less sensitive than other indices (Clarke & Warwick 1998) and may be influenced by natural environmental gradients (Abella et al. 2006). Despite its faults (see Hall & Greenstreet (1998), Abella et al. (2006), Salas et al. (2006b), and Ware et al. (2008)), it is a promising metric for the assessment of disturbances to ecological communities (Clarke & Warwick 1998). Because it measures a fundamentally different aspect of diversity, taxonomic distinctness should be seen as complementing, rather than replacing, the other metrics described in this section.

An alternative way of incorporating differences among species into biodiversity metrics is trait diversity. Under this approach evolutionary and taxonomic relationships are ignored, and we focus instead on species functional traits, linking community dynamics to ecosystem functioning (Hooper et al. 2005). Historically, trait (or functional) diversity was estimated by aggregating species into groups representing distinct functional niches (Rosenfeld 2002). Because this classification is necessarily a subjective step, recently numerous alternative approaches have emerged (e.g. Petchey & Gaston 2002; Cornwell et al. 2006; Podani & Schmera 2006) and their relative merits are discussed by Weiher in Chapter 13. As with species and taxonomic diversity, trait diversity can be decomposed into functional richness, evenness, and diversity (Mouillot et al. 2005). Functional richness is the amount of functional space occupied by the species of the community, functional evenness of a community depends on how regular species positions are in trait space, and functional diversity incorporates species abundance to weigh their contribution to the community attributes. The novel metrics of trait diversity are leading to the rapid expansion of this field. For example, recent studies have shown how trait diversity buffers ecosystem functioning from human perturbations (Hooper et al. 2005). Using trait diversity to quantify the effects of disturbances is a promising approach, which we predict will be fruitful.

The metrics described in this section complement each other, as they quantify different aspects of biodiversity. We can illustrate this with a hypothetical example. Let's imagine a plant assemblage with four species: an abundant grass, a common shrub,

and two rare mosses. Let's imagine that an invasive shrub (phylogenetically distant from all the other species) is introduced in this assemblage and becomes the dominant species by out-competing the grass and the other shrub. In this scenario species richness and phylogenetic diversity would increase (because of the invasive species), evenness would decrease (because the assemblage would have one very abundant and four rare species), and trait diversity would decrease (because the community becomes dominated by the invasive shrub).

17.3.2 Species abundance distribution-based metrics

As with the univariate indices, species abundance distributions (SADs) are covered in other chapters of this book. These metrics are discussed by McGill in Chapter 9 while Connolly and Dornelas (Chapter 10) describe how to best fit models to SADs. Here we discuss non-parametric metrics based on SAD shape and the application of parametric models to the study of human disturbance. We start by discussing non-parametric measures, namely the slope of the rank abundance distribution, the empirical cumulative distribution function, k dominance plots, abundance/biomass comparison (ABC) curves and size spectra. We then focus on the use of models fitted to SADs to detect effects of disturbances and specifically discuss the log-series, log-normal and gambin models, as well as the Q statistic (not to be confused with Q-mode multivariate analysis, which is described in the following section).

One of the first approaches suggested for comparing communities was the shape of rank abundance distribution (RAD) plots (Whittaker 1965; Frontier 1985), also known as dominance/diversity curves (Wilson 1991). RAD plots have the ranks of the species plotted on the x-axis in descending order (from most abundant to least abundant) and their abundances plotted on the y-axis (Figure 17.2a). The slope of the RAD measures evenness, with a shallower slope indicative of a more even distribution of abundances among species. While they offer a useful and appealingly simple visual check of community structure, the slopes

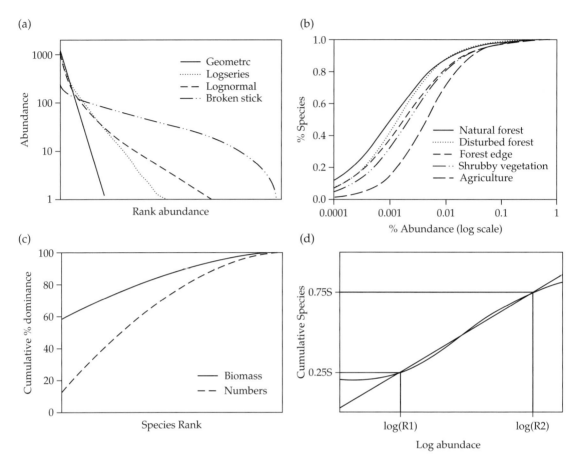

Figure 17.2 Graphical approaches for measuring species diversity. (a) Rank abundance distributions (RADs); (b) the empirical cumulative distribution function (eCDF); (c) abundance biomass comparison (ABC) curves; (d) the Q statistic, calculated as the interquartile slope of the cumulative species abundance curve.

of RAD curves are influenced by the number of species in the community, confounding interpretation (thus, it is really a diversity index, rather than an evenness index). We therefore caution against the use of RAD slopes to compare communities that differ in species richness. Note, however, that an evenness index proposed by Nee et al. (1992) and modified by Smith and Wilson (1996), E_Q, corrects for the problems encountered with the slope of the RAD. Specifically, ranks are scaled by dividing by the maximum rank, and independence from species richness is achieved by taking the inverse of the usual RAD slope (Smith & Wilson 1996).

The empirical cumulative distribution function (eCDF) (Chapter 9) is a graphical method that uses

the visual appeal of RADs as inspiration, while addressing their analytical shortcomings. The CDF is commonly used in mathematics and quantitative sciences. It is interpreted as the proportion of points with a value (here abundance) less than a given value. The eCDF is generated by sorting species from smallest to largest abundance, and then calculating the cumulative abundances. Both axes are standardized by dividing by species richness and total abundance (Figure 17.2b). In so doing, a richness-independent, mathematically familiar, yet conceptually simple graph is generated for comparing ecological communities along gradients of human activity (Soykan et al. in preparation). In particular, both the slope of the eCDF and the intercept of the inflection point can be used to compare curves of disturbed and undisturbed communities. The slope is indicative of evenness, whereas the intercept of the inflection point indicates the fraction of rare species. Fig. 17.2b shows how the eCDF curve changes through a gradient of disturbance from an undisturbed forest to an agriculture plot.

Another approach that builds on the RAD concept is the k-dominance plot, where the cumulative abundance of species in an assemblage is plotted against log-species rank (Lambshead et al. 1983; Platt et al. 1984). As with the RAD, the species are ranked along the x-axis from most to least abundant, but it is their cumulative abundance that is plotted, rather than their individual abundances. Noting that dominance is often affected by pollution; Platt et al. (1984) demonstrate the application of k-dominance plots for discriminating among meoifaunal assemblages exposed to different levels of pollution. Plots that are straighter (less convex) indicate a community with greater evenness that has been less disturbed than plots that are curved (more convex). In general, if the curve representing one assemblage lies entirely above another, the former assemblage can be said to be less diverse (and thus more affected by human activity) than the latter (Lambshead et al. 1983). However, complications arise when the two curves cross, making it impossible to say which community is more diverse. Lambshead et al. (1983) insightfully point out that such a situation results in different univariate diversity indices producing conflicting diversity rankings (because they weight different aspects of diversity differentially, i.e. abundant versus rare species).

One variation of the k-dominance plot, ABC curves does not rely on the presence of multiple communities for comparison (Warwick 1986). Instead, two k-dominance curves are generated for each assemblage, one based on abundance and one on biomass. The two curves are then compared and their relative positions used to infer the state of the community (Fig. 17.2c). Several metrics, including the W, d, and R statistics, have been developed to quantify the difference between abundance and biomass curves (Clarke 1990). The W statistic, which measures the total distance of each curve from the x-axis, has become the most pop-

ular (although Clarke himself recommends the i or R statistics, which measure the area between the curves, suggesting that they are more likely to detect differences between communities). The value of W ranges between -1 and 1, with positive values indicative of undisturbed communities and negative values indicative of disturbance. Fig. 17.2c illustrates the use of ABC curves to detect the effects of disturbances.

Related to k-dominance plots are what is known in the fisheries literature as community size spectra (Rice 2000) and in the terrestrial literature as body-size distributions (Brown 1999). The size spectrum refers to the smooth relationship of aggregate numbers, biomass, or diversity to size interval across the sampled size range of the community (i.e. how many individuals, how much biomass, or what is the diversity of the different size classes of organisms that make up the community). Size spectra have been shown to vary with habitat changes (White et al. 2004) and fishing pressure (Bianchi et al. 2000). This is likely due to the greater susceptibility of large-bodied individuals to fishing pressure and habitat modification (Gislason & Rice 1998). These changes can be used as an indicator of human disturbance that can be calculated over time for a given system or spatially across communities. Like trait diversity, size spectra focus on community trait distributions rather than taking a strictly taxonomic approach to measuring biodiversity. Given the links between body size and metabolism, changes in size spectra have significant implications for ecosystem fluxes and thus potentially ecosystem services. We therefore feel this is a promising approach to detecting community changes with important ecological consequences.

A potentially efficient way to detect changes in the shape of SADs is to compare parameter estimates or the goodness of fit of models to these types of data. However, with the exception of the log-series α, parametric measures have rarely been applied to detect the effects of disturbances. This may be due, in part, to the computational difficulties previously associated with estimating parameters. Given the widespread availability of appropriate software (Table 17.1), this is no longer a problem. With the main obstacle to their use removed, the study of parametric diversity indices represents a promising, relatively unexplored area of research. Fig. 17.2a shows a RAD plot of some models that have been used to detect the effects of disturbances. There are over 30 models currently available that can be used for this purpose, and there is no consensus as to which models are best (McGill et al. 2007). We will focus only on some of the models that have been used in this context and appear to be effective: the log-series, log-normal and gambin models. We note that, although model parameters may be able to detect the effects of disturbances regardless of the goodness of fit of the model to the data (Kempton & Taylor 1976) (i.e. even if a model does not fit the data very well, its parameter estimates may reflect changes in the distribution), following best practices in parameter estimation and goodness-of-fit testing (Chapter 10) is likely to enhance any method's efficiency.

Log-series α, also known as Fisher's α in honour of its developer (Fisher et al. 1943), is a measure of diversity that has occasionally been used in applied studies (see, for example, Fiedler & Schulze (2004), Wolf (2005), and Hilt et al. (2006)). It is a parametric measure calculated in order to fit the log-series distribution. However, regardless of whether a given community fits the log-series distribution well or not, log-series α can be used as a measure of diversity (Kempton & Taylor 1974, 1976; Taylor 1978). Like all measures of diversity, it confounds species richness and evenness to some extent. Nevertheless, unlike the diversity measures mentioned in the previous section, it is relatively unaffected by sample size and confidence intervals can be calculated easily (Anscombe 1950).

The log-normal distribution is probably the most commonly used SAD model, and deviations from this model have been suggested to be indicative of disturbance (Kempton & Taylor 1974; Ugland & Gray 1982; Gray 1987). For example, Kevan et al. (1997) fitted log-normal curves to pollinator abundance data in areas with and without insecticide application. They found that the undisturbed sites had an SAD that resembled a log-normal distribution, while the disturbed sites did not. Ugland & Gray (1982) argue that the log-normal is a good descriptor of undisturbed habitats, but under disturbance the single log-normal breaks down into several independent curves. In

fact, there is evidence of changes in species abundance due to human disturbance resulting in multimodal SADs (Ugland & Gray 1982; Dornelas et al. 2009). It has, therefore, been suggested that the log-normal model provides an objective standard by which ecosystem health can be evaluated, in contrast with most metrics, which require a reference or control for comparison with the disturbed community (Gray 1981, 1983). However, there is substantial controversy surrounding the log-normal as a SAD model (e.g. McGill 2003b; Volkov et al. 2003; Williamson & Gaston 2005). Nevertheless, we believe this to be a promising approach that merits both more empirical tests and theoretical explanation. A way to quantify these effects is to fit different parametric distributions to SADs. For example, Gray (1987) points out that the geometric series of Motomura fits communities that are poor in species, such as those under extreme pollution, while the log-series fits moderately disturbed communities and the log-normal best describes SADs for undisturbed sites. However, using different models to measure a gradient in human disturbance is difficult to justify theoretically and presents practical challenges regarding the selection of the most appropriate model for each SAD.

An alternative is to use a flexible distribution that can accommodate variability in shape within a single framework. An example is the gambin model (named for the two distributions, γ and binomial, used to fit the model) recently proposed by Ugland et al. (2007). Despite its compound nature, the model has only a single parameter, α, for which the authors provide a biological interpretation. Specifically, Ugland et al. (2007) suggest that α is related to niche space and the number of processes structuring ecological assemblages. Lower values indicate few structuring processes, as might be expected in stressed or disturbed systems. Thus, Ugland et al. (2007) conclude that gambin α might be useful for the assessment of ecosystem health (see the example in Box 17.2).

The Q statistic (Kempton & Taylor 1976) is based on the cumulative species abundance curve (not to be confused with the eCDF). It can be calculated by plotting the cumulative abundance curve and measuring the interquartile slope (see Fig. 17.2d). The fact that the most common and rarest species are excluded from the calculation of Q means it is less

Box 17.2 Using changes in the species abundance distributions to measure the effects of disturbance

Graham et al. (2004) examined the effects of habitat disturbance on the abundance of ants in the southeastern USA. Certain parts of the study area were heavily disturbed by mechanized infantry training. Tanks and other vehicles had denuded large areas of most of their vegetation. However, relatively undisturbed forest was found adjacent to the training areas. It was therefore possible to study ant communities across a disturbance gradient, and the area was divided into three classes: low, medium, and high disturbance. Lightly disturbed areas had minimal disturbance to soils, extensive woody vegetation and canopy cover. Moderately disturbed areas had an intact canopy but active erosion was often observed. Gullies were present in these areas and there was evidence of surface soil loss. Heavily disturbed areas had greatly reduced plant cover. There were large patches of bare ground and many signs of active erosion. Ant communities were sampled at each level of disturbance.

SADs are often presented as histograms with log-2 abundance classes (octaves), known as Preston plots. Binning the ant abundance data into octaves containing 1,

2–3, 4–7, 8–15, etc. individuals/species yields the three sets of histograms shown in Fig. 17.3a–17.3c. The effects of this type of disturbance are immediately apparent, with community structure showing a classical response: an initial log-normal-like species abundance curve gradually changes into a log-series-like curve. These changes can be quantified by fitting the gambin model to the data (Fig. 17.3; Ugland et al. 2007). The model is fitted by maximum likelihood estimation of the parameter α. Differences among disturbance regimes are clearly reflected in the gambin α parameter, which takes the values $\alpha_{Low} = 5.0$, $\alpha_{Medium} = 3.2$ and $\alpha_{High} = 1.5$. In the lightly disturbed areas the number of processes structuring the ant community is large and therefore the species abundance curve appears log-normal. At high levels of disturbance the α parameter drops down to 1.5 because the main process structuring the community under these conditions is 'tolerance' to sandy eroded soils. Only a few species maintain a large population size while most of the species abundances drop dramatically, with a substantial fraction disappearing from the habitat.

variable to changes in dominance or the number of rare species, which are much affected by sampling effort. For this same reason, however, the Q statistic is a relatively insensitive metric of biodiversity change. Importantly, the Q statistic can be calculated using parametric SAD models such as the log-series, log-normal, or γ distributions. For example, Q equals the log-series diversity parameter α (Kempton & Taylor 1976). Although not strictly a parametric metric, we mention the Q statistic here because calculating it using the fitted models yields more precise estimates than doing it directly from the data.

Finally, we want to emphasize that SADs often provide powerful illustrations of the effects of disturbances on community structure. SAD plots can be visually compared among various communities in order to detect changes brought about by human disturbance. Showing dramatic changes in community structure visually (see Fig. 17.3) is a useful addition to any quantitative analysis.

17.3.3   Multivariate analysis

So far, with the exception of phylogenetic and trait diversity, we have discussed metrics that are independent of species identities. However, because species have different susceptibilities, community composition is usually modified by disturbance. That is, along a disturbance gradient robust species usually replace species that are more sensitive to that particular disturbance. Therefore, tracking communities through multivariate space, where species abundances are the multiple variables, allows the detection of subtle effects of disturbances on community composition. Several techniques can be used to this effect, and we will give a brief overview of some of the options available. We recommend consulting more comprehensive descriptions of multivariate analysis (e.g. Legendre & Legendre 1998; Quinn & Keough 2002; Leps & Smilauer 2003) to readers unfamiliar with this type of approach.

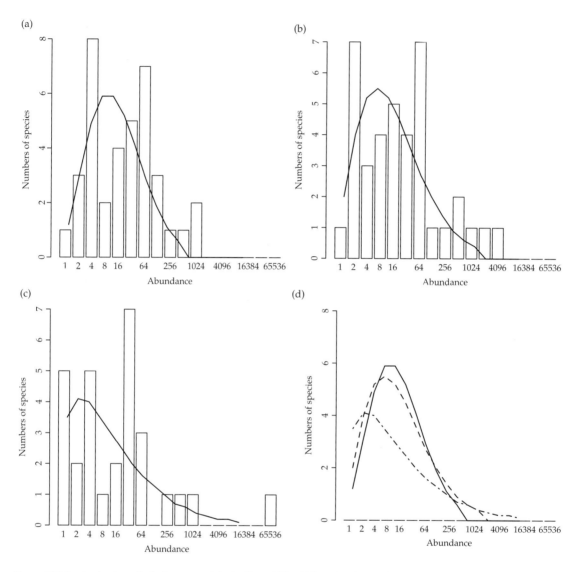

Figure 17.3 Species abundance distribution curves and the Gambin model for pitfall samples of ants in the southeastern USA (Graham et al. 2004) for three regimes of habitat destruction (the significance probability (P) is based on 1000 simulations see Ugland et al. (2007)). (a) low, $P = 0.32$; (b) medium, $P = 0.46$; (c) high, $P = 0.13$; (d) comparison of the three fitted curves: low, solid line; medium, dashed line; high, point dashed line.

Multivariate analysis aims to reduce the number of dimensions in data while preserving as much information as possible. We will mention two approaches, often known as R-mode and Q-mode analysis (Quinn & Keough 2002). In the context of community composition, R-mode analysis rearranges the data based on associations between species; whereas Q-mode analysis is based on similarities between sampling units. That is, in R-mode analysis the structure in the covariances (or correlations) among species is analysed to extract new synthetic variables that concentrate the original variance in fewer variables. Some commonly used methods that follow the R-mode approach are principal component analysis (PCA), redundancy analysis (RDA), and correspondence analysis (CA). In Q-mode analysis, a matrix of pair-wise similarities among all sampling units is calculated

Box 17.3 Detecting the effects of disturbances on community composition

Magurran and Phillip (2001) collected an extensive dataset of freshwater fish communities from Trinidad and Tobago. From these data, we selected seven pairs of sites in similar freshwater streams, which included an undisturbed site and a heavily polluted site. At each site Magurran and Phillip (2001) took a standardized sample and identified all fish caught to species. Here we investigate if disturbed communities (i.e. communities from polluted sites) differ in composition from undisturbed communities.

We use non-metric multidimensional scaling available in the R-package vegan (Oksanen et al. 2008; a good source of more detailed advice on these methods can be found in the vegan tutorial). We begin by transforming the species × site matrix using a Wisconsin double standardization. This standardization consists of dividing each species by its maximum and each site by its total. It often improves the results because it prevents the dominant species from overwhelming distance measures, as well as preventing differences in community size from confounding the results. Secondly we calculate a site × site Bray–Curtis distance matrix. Finally we re-scale ranked distances onto new dimensions using Kruskal's non-metric multidimensional scaling (Kruskal 1964). This ordination method finds the coordinates of each site on synthetic dimensions, so that the order of distances among sites is as close as possible to the original matrix. The success of the ordination can be checked by looking at the R^2 of a regression between observed and ordination distances (which measures the amount of variance explained by the ordination). A linear fit between the Bray–Curtis distances we calculated and the ordination distances has an R^2 of 0.953 and a non-metric fit has an R^2 of 0.991. Hence, we can be confident that the ordination has not distorted the observed distances excessively.

A plot of the results shows that the first dimension separates most disturbed and undisturbed sites (Fig. 17.4), but there are two polluted sites and two clean sites that are in between the two clusters. The second dimension separates these four sites, so that clean sites cluster in the bottom right corner and polluted sites in the upper left corner. Performing an analysis of similarity would allow testing of whether the effects of disturbance on the species composition of these freshwater fish communities are statistically significant in a classical hypothesis testing fashion.

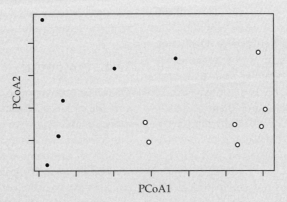

Figure 17.4   NMDS ordination plot of polluted (black circles) and unpolluted (white circles) sites from freshwater fish communities in Trinidad and Tobago (data from Magurran and Phillip (2001)).

using species abundances. The sampling units are then re-scaled onto new dimensions that minimize the distortion of the original distances. The methods that follow Q-mode analysis most commonly used in community ecology are principal coordinate analysis (PCoA) and multidimensional scaling (MDS) Box 17.3.

In Q-mode analysis the choice of similarity measure is crucial, and there is a vast array of measures available (see, for example, Legendre & Legendre (1998)) for detailed descriptions. Two commonly used measures in this context based on presence–absence data are the Sørensen and Jaccard distances, which differ only on the weight given to shared vs unshared species. Modifications of these distances to be used with abundance data are known as Bray–Curtis (Bray & Curtis 1957) (also known as Steinhaus similarity) and Chao distances (Chao et al. 2005), respectively. It is important to note that using presence–absence data gives equal weight to all species in the communities, regardless of whether they are represented by a single individual or thousands. Since the majority of species are rare in most communities, using presence–absence based distances emphasizes the importance of rare species. In contrast, since the abundance of dominant species is typically orders of magnitude greater than that of the rarest species, abundance-based similarities tend to be mostly driven by the most abundant species. Anderson et al. (2006) propose a flexible similarity measure that can be used to tune the weight of abundances. These authors also recommend running analyses with both compositional (i.e. presence–absence based) and abundance changes to distinguish the effects of each facet on the patterns.

Both R- and Q-mode approaches can be used to compare communities with different levels of disturbance, and in some cases they allow different questions to be addressed (see Legendre et al. (2008) for an example). However, R-mode methods, and to some extent PCoA, are particularly affected by the 'arch effect', where linear gradients are represented as a curve with extremes scaled as close together (Minchin 1987). This is a consequence of the joint absence of species, and there is debate about whether it is an artefact of the scaling techniques or a real pattern (Wartenberg et al. 1987). From a practical point of view, the arch effect is problematic because it can make gradients impossible to recognize without prior knowledge of site order. Simulation studies have shown that MDS, and in particular non-metric MDS, are the methods most robust to this effect (Minchin 1987).

Multivariate analysis is extremely versatile and can be used to detect effects of disturbances on community composition in several ways. Communities can be tracked through time as they undergo a disturbance and through the recovery trajectory (Warwick & Clarke 1993). We can analyse sampling units distributed across a disturbance gradient to test whether community composition and species abundances reflect the level of disturbance (Hewitt

et al. 2005). The effects of disturbances can also be quantified by a community disturbance index (CDI), which compares disturbed sites to previously scaled boundaries of undisturbed communities (Flaten et al. 2007). Loss of β diversity (i.e. homogenization of the landscape) can be detected by comparing the dispersion of sampling units in multivariate space (Anderson et al. 2006).

The application of multivariate analysis to detect the effects of disturbances on biodiversity is potentially very powerful. This approach can detect effects not reflected by metrics, like species richness or diversity, because it takes into account the identity of species (Hewitt et al. 2005). However, for this same reason multivariate approaches are highly site specific. Thus, biogeographic influence and habitat specificity can hide the effects of disturbances when large or isolated regions are included in the same analysis. Consequently, multivariate approaches are not suitable for generalizations about the effects of a disturbance at global scales (although some approaches have been proposed (Warwick & Clarke 1993)) or across habitats. Additionally, multivariate analysis is conceptually complex and sometimes difficult to interpret. Consequently, a good understanding of these techniques is a fundamental prerequisite to successfully using this approach.

17.4 Prospectus

There is a vast array of methods available to measure the effects of disturbance on biodiversity patterns. In this review we grouped metrics into three categories: univariate indices condense all information about each community into a single number, SAD-based metrics consider distributions of abundance or traits in the communities, and multivariate approaches retain information regarding species identities. In principle, the ability to detect disturbances should increase along these groups. However, there are trade-offs between metric sensitivity and both the generality and the interpretability of the results, therefore the best metric is not necessarily the most sensitive.

In fact, there is no single best metric to detect the effects of disturbances on biodiversity. This is because both disturbance and biodiversity are complex concepts that include multiple processes and patterns. The best metric depends both on the type of disturbance (see Introduction) and the type of effects we are interested in detecting (see below). Nevertheless, from the vast array of metrics available, some perform better than others and some are more suited to certain types disturbances, available data, or to detect specific effects. Table 17.1 summarizes the metrics reviewed in this chapter and highlights some of their advantages and disadvantages. Although some studies compare the relative performance of different biodiversity metrics (e.g. Abella et al. 2006; Patrício et al. 2006; Salas et al. 2006a,b; Ware et al. 2008), further synthetic research is needed so that best approach standards emerge.

One conclusion that emerges from this review is the importance of explicitly identifying what type of effects a study is aiming to detect. The aim of detecting *any* effects of a disturbance is too vague to allow the selection of an appropriate method. Specifically, we may be interested in measuring whether the total number of species in a community is affected by a disturbance, in which case species richness is the obvious metric. If we are particularly concerned with the fate of rare species, because they are of special conservation interest for example, we should probably use a SAD-based metric. Some studies will focus on particular or dominant species to assess the risk posed by pests or species invasions, and need to use metrics that include composition information. We may also be interested in how biodiversity relates to ecosystem services, and need to consider metrics that include species traits. Once the type of effect we are trying to detect is identified, the choice of biodiversity metric follows. Moreover, using a range of different metrics to capture different aspects of diversity will often be important. Thanks to the development of computing abilities and software, computational difficulties are no longer a constraint. We note that promoting the use of novel methods will hinge on the availability of the software needed to compute them.

We want to highlight a few metrics that in our opinion are particularly promising. Firstly, trait-based metrics allow the detection of changes that may be subtle at a taxonomic level, but have crucial implications for ecosystem functioning and services. Secondly, although SAD-based metrics have been around since the 1970s, we feel their full potential is yet to be explored and encourage their use in the context of detecting the effects of disturbances. The eCDF in particular, because of its simplicity and independence from any parametric model, is a promising approach. Thirdly, multivariate metrics are extremely versatile and ideal to target questions where species identities are important. Non-metric MDS (NMDS) seems to be the most robust method for the type of data typical in this field. Finally, we believe it is important to report standard metrics, and species richness in particular, for comparative purposes.

On a final note we call for theoretical development in this area. Ultimately, rather than measure destruction we aim to predict the effects of disturbances before they occur, in order to manage natural resources in the most effective way. For that, we need to develop theory for how aspects of diversity other than species richness are affected by disturbances. We feel that much more needs to be done on this front.

17.5   Key points

1. The biodiversity metric most appropriate to quantify the effects of disturbance depends on the nature of the disturbance, the type of effect, and the data available. Often the use of multiple metrics is necessary for a good understanding of the consequences of disturbances.
2. Species richness and evenness are two standard univariate metrics that complement each other.
3. Trait diversity is an important metric because it allows the consequences of disturbances to ecosystem services to be explored.
4. From the SAD-based metrics, the eCDF is a promising new approach. It is mathematically familiar, simple to interpret, and easy to use.
5. NMDS seems to be the multivariate approach most appropriate for the type of data typically available in disturbance studies.
6. More theoretical work is needed to understand the effects of disturbances on biodiversity metrics other than species richness.

Acknowledgements

We are grateful to Melodie McGeoch, Miguel Barbosa, and Nick Graham for comments on earlier versions of this manuscript. MD thanks the Australian Research Council for funding and dedicates this book chapter to her son Manuel.

CHAPTER 18

Measuring biodiversity in managed landscapes

Steven L. Chown and Melodie A. McGeoch

18.1 Introduction

One thing that is clear is that the majority of land-scapes, in a physical sense, are the result of interaction between man and nature, and of man's use and misuse of nature.

Gunnarsson 2006
A Mirror of Nature
Nordic Landscape Painting 1840–1910

If one wishes to explain the distribution and numbers of a certain species of animal, here is one way of going about the job which we have found especially profitable. It is best to describe the method as if it were done in three stages, although, in practice, it is usually best to have the three stages going forward at the same time.

a) The physiology and behaviour of the animal must be investigated . . .
b) The physiography, climate, soil and vegetation in the area must be investigated . . .
c) The numbers of individuals in the population that has been selected for study must be measured as accurately as practicable.

Andrewartha & Birch 1954
The Distribution and Abundance of Animals

Over the past century the human population has grown from an estimated 1.66 billion to 6.79 billion. It is projected to reach *c.* 9 billion by 2050 with a current growth rate of, on average, 1.17% p.a. (Anonymous 1999; CIA Fact Book 2009). Despite considerable spatial and temporal fluctuations in birth and death rates, often correlated with changing climates (Zhang et al. 2007), the human population has seen increasing growth since the black

death that ravaged much of Eurasia in the 14th century (Cohen 1995; Anonymous 1999; Marriott 2002). This growth has been supported by and stimulated ongoing changes in the ways in which humans interact with the world, including the agricultural and industrial revolutions (Harrison 1992; Cohen 1995). These changes have led to modification of a substantial proportion of the planet's surface, including its atmosphere, and freshwater and marine systems. Indeed, somewhere between one-third and a half of the land surface has been transformed by human activities, and marine systems have seen similar, although less visible, changes (Vitousek et al. 1997; Watling & Norse 1998; Jackson et al. 2001; Klein Goldewijk 2001; Milesi et al. 2005; Ellis & Ramankutty 2008). Even those areas that might at first appear largely untransformed are being affected indirectly, either by human influences on the global climate (Parmesan 2006; le Roux & McGeoch 2008; Chen et al. 2009) or through the introduction of self-sustaining and often increasing populations of invasive alien species (Foxcroft et al. 2004; Dawson et al. 2009). Moreover, many of these apparently untransformed areas have long histories of human influence (e.g. Mabunda et al. 2003) and are currently subject to some form of management. The latter is certainly true of all but the globe's largest protected areas. Even there, management policies that in several instances involve direct management (e.g. fire and herbivore management) have typically been formulated (DuToit 2003; Govender et al. 2006). In consequence, when biodiversity is measured, more often than not it is measured in or across landscapes under some form of management or exposure to human-induced transformation (see Gaston (2006) for further discussion).

A major consequence of this preponderance of managed and modified landscapes is that much of what is known about how and why biodiversity varies through space and time, and how this variation should be quantified, refers either directly or indirectly to such landscapes. Indeed, it might be argued that for many purposes, the kinds of methods developed for measuring biodiversity more generally (as reviewed throughout this book and elsewhere, e.g. Blackburn and Gaston (1998); Epperson (2003); Magurran (2004); and Gaston et al. (2009)) are as much applicable to modified and managed landscapes as they are to all others. No particularly special set of methods is required. However, as with all such work, the form, structure, grain, and varying age of the elements of the landscape should be considered carefully, as should the scale or scales at which the study should be undertaken and the sampling methods required to address the issues at hand (see Chapters 2–15). When biodiversity is measured in what is more typically considered a managed landscape (such as a set of fields with hedgerows or wheat fields with small remnant patches of Renosterveld (Samways 1989; Donaldson et al. 2002)) the goals often concern questions about the management of particular features of the landscape, be they individuals, populations, metacommunities, or system functioning. In a conservation context, the goals of measurement are often how to manage to reduce levels of transformation or the impact thereof.

From this perspective, modification of the landscape and management thereof can be considered orthogonal axes, along which different regimes can clearly be set out and for which the overall goals of biodiversity measurement may differ substantially (Fig. 18.1). Therefore, in this chapter, rather than specifically reviewing the methods that might be used for measuring biodiversity, which are dealt with elsewhere in the book, we shift the focus to: (i) the ways in which the goals of biodiversity measurement vary with the extent of modification and management of landscapes, which is partly also a question of resolution and extent of the investigation, (ii) specific examples of approaches that have been successful in addressing these goals, and (iii) the benefits of adopting $r \times c$ matrices for integrating biodiversity measures and

understanding across several levels of the biological hierarchy.

18.2   State of the field

18.2.1   Variation in biodiversity measurement goals

Across the range of variation in the extent of landscape modification and management (Fig. 18.1), the goals of biodiversity measurement typically differ substantially. Moreover, the spatial scale (extent and resolution) of the studies tends to covary along the axes of modification and management. For example, investigations of the patterns in and mechanisms underlying large-scale variation in biodiversity (usually richness, but also turnover, abundance, range size, and body size, e.g. Chown et al. (1998); Pautasso & Gaston (2005); Buckley & Jetz (2008); Dunn et al. (2009); and Olson et al. (2009)) usually assume that the signal of human landscape transformation has not markedly influenced the patterns detected at large spatial extents and resolutions, and the mechanisms thought to underlie them (see discussion in Gaston (2006)). More often the concerns lie with the influence of different kinds of data (e.g. range maps vs museum specimen records, see Hurlbert & White (2005), Graham & Hijmans (2006), Rondinini et al. (2006), and McPherson & Jetz (2007)), and spatial extent and resolution (Rahbek & Graves 2001; van Rensburg et al. 2002; Hurlbert & Jetz 2007; Mora et al. 2008) on the outcomes of the work, and on how the measurement approach varies with extent and resolution (e.g. the census area effect; Gaston et al. (1999)).

At global and continental scales the assumption that the non-human signal still predominates seems justified (although poorly explored, but see Ellis & Ramankutty (2008) for a different perspective), but at somewhat smaller scales, such as for particular countries or sub-regions, landscape transformation certainly does appear to affect patterns of richness, composition, abundance, and their interactions (e.g. Fisher & Frank 2004; Evans et al. 2006a; Gaston 2006; Leprieur et al. 2008). Because the goals of sub-regional or country studies typically are to investigate the form of macro-scale variation and the mechanisms underlying it (including variation

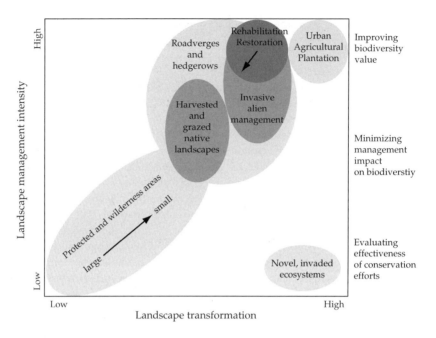

Figure 18.1 The relationship between landscape management intensity, transformation, land-use type, and (right axis) varying objectives for biodiversity measurement.

in single species, e.g. Moodley & Bruford (2007) and Evans et al. (2009)), understanding covariation between human activities, population density, and measures of biodiversity must form a component thereof (Chown et al. 2003; Gaston 2006). In this context it is important to recognize that human population density and species richness are often positively related, largely because both respond similarly to environmental drivers such as productive energy availability and elevation (Chown et al. 2003; Milesi et al. 2005; Luck 2007). Moreover, these relationships are likely to change markedly as productivity continues to increase in a spatially variable manner (Nemani et al. 2003), as human population size continues to increase more in areas where net primary productivity is water limited (Milesi et al. 2005), and, in many countries, as urbanization continues to exert an increasing influence on the landscape (Latimer et al. 2004; McKinney 2006; Evans et al. 2006b; Tratalos et al. 2007; McDonald et al. 2008).

As the levels of landscape transformation and management increase, so the variety of research questions posed, and approaches adopted, tends

to become larger, and often also more context specific. For example, at the scale of whole, very large protected areas (those above 1 million ha) or catchments (scales where management intensities might be considered intermediate (Fig. 18.1)), the questions may vary from those concerned with variation in the richness of indigenous and/or invasive species (McKinney 2002; Stohlgren et al. 2006; Foxcroft et al. 2009), to those dealing with population variation and the environmental and management influences thereon (Ogutu & Owen-Smith 2003; Owen-Smith et al. 2006). Alternatively, questions may concern the influence of particular management regimes on assemblage structure and composition, such as the impact of fire regimes on biodiversity in savanna parks (Parr et al. 2004; Govender et al. 2006). In addition to the usual recommendations for biodiversity measurement in such studies, much more context-dependent measurement problems arise. For example, despite the significance of understanding the impacts of different burning regimes on biodiversity in fire-prone systems in southern Africa (e.g. Govender et al. 2006), much of the work on animals has been characterized by inadequate replication, lack of attention to fire duration, season, and time of day, poor reporting of spatial extent and sample unit size, and poor representation of invertebrates, amphibians, and reptiles in these investigations (Parr & Chown 2003). Often the need to address these kinds of problems extends to other geographic areas and represents a more general recognition of the value of increased experimental rigour or new approaches. In some instances, the concerns lie with the application of extant and readily accessible theory and techniques (e.g. the take up of information theoretic approaches to model selection; review in Johnson & Omland (2004)). In others, relatively recent theoretical and technological developments are rapidly extending the scope of current understanding. For example, developments in theory and computer technology that have enabled spatially explicit approaches to be adopted are bringing about major changes in such areas as population viability assessment and the assessment of how populations are likely to respond to changes in landscape variation over time (Porter et al. 2002; Akçakaya et al. 2004; Carroll 2006; McRae et al. 2008). In essence, these developments form a component of the $r \times c$ matrix approach that will be discussed below.

At the greatest levels of modification and management (Fig. 18.1), especially in intensive agriculture or small, intensively managed reserves, the nature of biodiversity measurement is often similar, albeit focused simply on either increasing or otherwise manipulating diversity and population sizes. For example, the assessment of population dynamics may be aimed at either controlling a problem species (population reduction) or conserving a rare one (population maintenance or increase). Thus, invasive species may be the subject of control in conservation areas, whereas the conservation of functionally significant species may be the goal in an agricultural context. Whether these opposing goals are being realized in a protected area or intensively farmed landscape, the methods adopted are often similar and incorporate work across almost the full range of the biological hierarchy, from the level of genes to the level of landscapes and ecosystems. The former may involve the assessment of the risks of introgression from genetically modified

organisms to crop or to wild species (e.g. Zapiola et al. 2008; Piñeyro-Nelson et al. 2009; McGeoch et al. 2009), whilst the latter may concern the effects of the spatial arrangement of patches and corridors on the diversity of assemblages (Damschen et al. 2006), the ways different ecosystems interact to affect local diversity (Knight et al. 2005), or the most appropriate management actions for restoring diversity at the landscape level (e.g. Rand et al. 2006; Richardson et al. 2007). By its very nature, much of this measurement concerns the use of subsets of biodiversity that are representative of broader responses, and the use of these subsets to monitor changes in environmental state or the status of biodiversity per se.

18.2.2   Bioindicators and monitoring

Bioindication and monitoring have long been features of pest management, ecotoxicology, and conservation (van Straalen & Verhoef 1997; McGeoch et al. 2002; Bockstaller & Girardin 2003). Bioindicators that readily reflect and represent the state of the environment are considered an effective and necessary approach to gathering sufficient information whilst minimizing the resources required to do so (McGeoch 1998). In conservation, they are considered especially appropriate for addressing the challenges of understanding and mitigating human influences on biodiversity. Three main categories of bioindication can be recognized, each of which has its own goals (Table 18.1). Nonetheless, they overlap to some extent and share several methodological principles. Key amongst these is the predictability of the relationship between the bioindicator and the environmental variable of interest (abiotic or biotic, i.e. in biodiversity indication this could be the relationship between the abundance of a single species and the diversity of an assemblage, e.g. Fleishman et al. (2005)). Thus the indicator and variable of interest should (i) have a significant and strong relationship (statistical significance should preferably be accompanied by large effect size) and (ii) be characterized by a robust relationship, i.e. the relationship should remain constant within the spatial and temporal context of inference, or should be consistent and repeatable (McGeoch 2007; Table 18.2). The value of the indicator will

Table 18.1 The three categories of bioindication, distinguished by their distinct objectives, and their application in measuring biodiversity in managed and transformed landscapes.

Category

Environmental indicator

A species or group of species that responds predictably, in ways that are readily observed and quantified, to often abiotic environmental disturbance or to a change in environmental state.
  Related terms: Sentinel, exploiter, bioassay, accumulator, biomarker.
  Example   The community structure of soil arthropods is indicative of soil properties (e.g. pH) and the impact of human activities (van Straalen 1998).

Ecological indicator

A species or group of species that demonstrate the effects of environmental change (such as habitat alteration and fragmentation and climate change) on biota or biotic systems.
  Example   The abundance and richness of trap-nesting bees are indicative of habitat quality and ecological change in European agricultural landscapes (Tscharntke et al. 1998).

Biodiversity indicator

A biodiversity indicator is a group of taxa (e.g. genus, tribe, family, or order, or a selected group of species from a range of higher taxa) or functional group, the diversity of which reflects some measure of the diversity (e.g. character richness, species richness, level of endemism) of other higher taxa in a habitat or set of habitats.
  Related terms: Surrogate, umbrella, flagship, focal species or taxon.
  Example   Occurrence patterns of selected butterfly species are indicative of substantial, significant variation in combined bird and butterfly species richness in the Central Great Basin (Fleishman et al. 2005).

increase if the additional criteria of representivity and generality are met (Fig. 18.2). If the bioindicator, or bioindication system (van Straalen & Verhoef 1997), does not comply with these criteria, including clear objectives, ease of sampling, cost-efficacy, and taxonomic knowledge (McGeoch 1998, Lawton & Gaston 2001; Chapter 2), then, irrespective of the methodological correctness of the sampling and/or measurement approaches, it is unlikely to prove useful. Much biodiversity measurement in the context of bioindication is aimed at quantifying and testing these ideas.

The value of bioindicators ultimately lies in their adoption and application in monitoring programmes, e.g. for monitoring the success of restoration efforts (Albrecht et al. 2007), the effect of river flow management on fish diversity (Taylor et al. 2008), or the effectiveness of protected areas in conserving biodiversity (Jackson & Gaston 2008). The functions of monitoring programmes are nonetheless clearly closely allied with the functions of bioindicators (McGeoch 1998, 2007). Importantly, where monitoring systems are established to detect the influence of change on any particular level of the biological hierarchy, thresholds and their

identification become particularly significant (Biggs et al. 2009). Here it is important to distinguish between ecological thresholds (values of system state variables) and decision thresholds (thresholds at which management actions are taken and which may be determined by societal values rather than ecological thresholds per se) (Martin et al. 2009).

Much attention has rightly been given to the establishment of monitoring programmes for biodiversity management in both control and conservation settings (Mace & Baillie 2007; Regan et al. 2008; Foxcroft et al. 2009). However, some of the most useful detections of long-term change in biodiversity have emerged from biodiversity measurement activities that initially did not have these goals in mind. For example, much useful information has arisen from recent repetitions of surveys previously conducted 20–40 years ago, especially on long-term, climate change-related alterations in patterns of diversity, from genetic to assemblage levels. Insights from such work include shifts in the latitudinal cline in the alcohol dehydrogenase polymorphism in *Drosophila melanogaster* (Umina et al. 2005), changes in body size patterns in one or more populations (Gilchrist et al. 2004), declines in abundance

Table 18.2 Procedural steps in the development of a bioindication system for use in managed and transformed landscapes (adapted from McGeoch 1998).

Step	Action	Explanation
1	Determine broad objective as environmental, ecological or biodiversity indication	See Table 18.1
2	Refine objective and clarify endpoint	Place broad objective into specific context of interest and define context-specific objectives, e.g. to detect changes in environmental quality as a result of changing pesticide usage or to detect the impacts of increasing habitat fragmentation on ecosystem functioning
3	Select potential indicator based on accepted a priori selection criteria, e.g. cost-effectiveness, usefulness demonstrated in other regions, taxonomically well known	Select appropriate species, higher level taxon, assemblage, or community (decision will be scale dependent)
4	Accumulate data on the relationship between the putative bioindicator and the environmental (relational) variable/stressor of interest	For example, measure the response of the indicator to the disturbance or environmental variable of interest by measuring both the response and the environmental variable(s)
5	Establish statistically the relationship between the putative bioindicator and the environmental (relational) variable	Determine both the significance and the strength of the relationship (Fig. 18.2)
6	Based on the nature of the relationship, either accept (preliminarily) or reject the species, taxon, or assemblage as a bioindicator	Is the relationship significant and strong (e.g. high coefficient of determination)? If yes, then move on to step 7, if not, repeat from step 3
7	Establish the robustness of the bioindicator by developing and testing relevant hypotheses	For example, test the relationship established in step 6 in following years, different seasons, or in the same context but at different sites or regions (Fig. 18.2)
8	If the null hypotheses are rejected, make specific recommendations based on the original objectives for the application of the bioindicator	Develop the bioindicator as a tool for use in monitoring programmes for management, for example by the development of user guides, pictorial keys, and decision-support systems
9	Establish the generality of the bioindicator (optional)	Test the same set of hypotheses developed in step 7 in different contexts, for example different agroecosytems, different bioregions (temperate versus tropics), or different disturbance or management regimes (Fig. 18.2)

of particular sensitive groups, such as salamanders (Rovito et al. 2009), and alterations in the ranges and assemblage composition of plants and insects (Kelly & Goulden 2008; le Roux & McGeoch 2008; Raxworthy et al. 2008; Chen et al. 2009). Often such studies draw attention to deficiencies in the earlier surveys that constrain current understanding, but which of course, importantly, serve to inform the way in which new surveys should be designed. Where a set of sites is to be re-surveyed given historical data, much merit lies in assessing carefully how best to replicate the past work to ensure as much comparability as possible, whilst also providing an approach that may prove to be more valuable to those in the future who might wish to survey the site again.

These examples show how thoughtful consideration of previous work (where the full data set was often published; see Lawton (1999a)) can provide insights that might otherwise not have been possible. Indeed, substantial scope exists for the combination of innovative approaches and extant data to provide further understanding of biodiversity changes in modern landscapes and of ecological questions more generally. Although such approaches might not be considered 'monitoring' in the conventional sense, they certainly provide the kinds of information that monitoring approaches seek to deliver. A few additional examples readily illustrate the point. First, the latitudinal gradient in richness is one of the most well known biological patterns. Typically it is seen as a pattern that

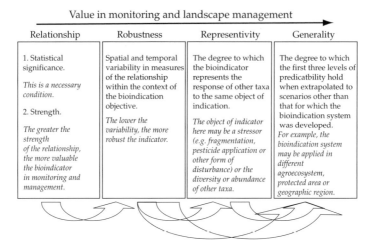

Figure 18.2 The predictability gradient in bioindication. As a biological relationship moves along the predictability gradient (left to right), so its value as a bioindicator increases and hence its value for assessing the status of, and monitoring changes in, biodiversity in managed and transformed landscapes (adapted from McGeoch (2007)). Note that representivity is not relevant in all bioindication contexts.

demonstrates relatively long-term changes (Crame 2001), but which shows the bulk of its variation among taxa, systems, and regions (Gaston 1996b; Hillebrand 2004). Recent work using long-term fisheries data collected in the northwest Atlantic has shown not only that the gradient exhibits interannual variation, but also that this variation is strongly related to changes in the sign and strength of the North Atlantic Oscillation (Fisher et al. 2008). Second, the extent to which the phenotypic response to climate change (such as advances in arrival dates or changes in phenology; see Parmesan (2006)) have a microevolutionary basis or are the result mostly of environmental responses is a significant question for understanding the likely responses of organisms to further change (Davis & Shaw 2001; Chown & Terblanche 2007; Gienapp et al. 2008). To disentangle these processes, information on the relatedness of individuals is usually required. Recently, Gienapp et al. (2007) proposed an approach using phenotypic measurements through time, converted to haldanes, which provides at least an estimate of whether the rates of change are within those expected from theory and empirical studies of evolutionary change (e.g. Lynch & Lande 1993; Hendry & Kinnison 1999). If rates of phenotypic change

lie above a few per cent of 1 haldane, then the change is probably not only a consequence of microevolutionary change in the trait mean. Finally, owing to the substantial and rapid effects humans may have on phenotypic change in animals (Hendry et al. 2008), and on the apparently rapid response of size to changes in the environment (e.g. Gilchrist et al. (2004), although not always associated with genetic change; see Teplitsky et al. (2008)), utilization of size data, which can often be obtained readily from museum specimens, may provide considerable insight into environmental change in the absence of specific monitoring programmes.

18.2.3   Measuring biodiversity for management

Having established that the goals of biodiversity measurement in modified and managed landscapes vary with the extent of management and modification, and clearly with the scale of the study or question being addressed, we provide here several sets of examples that have used a variety of methods to address these goals. Our aim is not to suggest that these are the definitive measurement approaches that should be adopted, but rather to illustrate the variety of methods that can usefully be applied to biodiversity measurement in modified landscapes.

Human influences on avian species richness

That humans have an influence on diversity is widely accepted. However, the extent to which conservation areas might mitigate this influence is often not explicitly demonstrated, despite the fact that doing so is of considerable significance (Gaston et al. 2008b). This is especially the case with species for which protected areas were not primarily intended. Moreover, the converse also applies: studies of broad-scale patterns in biodiversity should consider human influences more generally (see section 18.2.1). Using bird atlas species richness data, at a quarter degree square resolution for South Africa, energy availability estimated in the form of the normalized difference vegetation index, proportion of a grid square covered by a formally protected area, and a generalized linear modelling approach, Evans et al. (2006a) demonstrated that conservation areas are effective. In low-energy areas, species richness typically increases from 64 to 85 species as protection increases from 0 to 100%. By contrast, in higher energy areas, the increase is larger—from 213 to 250 species. This broader scale work prompted the local-scale investigation of three protected areas (established for purposes other than avian conservation) and the landscapes surrounding them, demonstrating that these protected areas were indeed effective in conserving both avian richness and particular foraging guilds (Greve 2007).

Enhancing biodiversity in agricultural and forestry landscapes

Measurement of biodiversity in landscapes managed for forestry or agriculture is generally aimed at either (i) enhancing ecosystem services provided by biodiversity that are of value in such settings (e.g. biological control via natural enemies, pollination and provision of host plants and habitats for such species) (Bianchi et al. 2006) or (ii) improving the general biodiversity conservation value of regions that are largely transformed and have a long history thereof (e.g. Kleijn et al. 2006; McGeoch et al. 2007). Work on the general

goal of enhancing biodiversity in European agro-ecosystems has revealed that much more targeted objectives are required to achieve specific biodiversity outcomes (Box 18.1). Different management measures were shown to be required for the alternative goals of benefiting common species (often those performing important roles as predators and pollinators in fields) versus improving the conservation value of agro-ecosystems by providing suitable habitat for rare species (Kleijn et al. 2006).

The work of Tscharntke et al. (2005) also clearly illustrates the importance of the relationship between landscape transformation and management shown in Fig. 18.2. In highly transformed agricultural settings, management interventions to enhance biodiversity are not very effective (because there is little available source habitat), whereas less transformed landscapes are more responsive to biodiversity-oriented management practices (Box 18.1). Furthermore, the species richness of human-dominated landscapes provides insight into the functional characteristics of such landscapes. For example, Tscharntke et al. (2008) showed that tropical agricultural landscapes not only supported fewer species of birds and insects than semi-natural habitats, but that functional diversity also differed between them. Thus, more frugivores and nectivores but fewer insectivores occurred in the agroforest avian assemblage compared with unmanaged forests. Furthermore, for both birds and insects, assemblages were more similar across agricultural landscapes (lower beta diversity) than they were across natural landscapes. The study also demonstrated that the scale of landscape structures is an important determinant of biodiversity across managed landscapes, as the distance between managed and unmanaged patches of habitat has a significant effect on richness and functional diversity.

Further significant insights have been gained by adopting spatially scaled approaches to measuring biodiversity across mixed-use landscapes (Steffan-Dewenter et al. 2002; Box 18.1). For example, spider diversity in cereal crops responded to both local (higher diversity at field edges than centres) and landscape (more diverse in complex than in simple) scale structures (Clough et al. 2007). This scale dependence of diversity patterns and drivers

Box 18.1 Measuring biodiversity in agricultural landscapes: objectives and insights

Significant insight has been gained from the measurement of biodiversity in agricultural landscapes on the patterns and drivers of biodiversity in managed landscapes, as well as their scale dependence. The interdependence of the dual goals of maximizing biodiversity and function in managed landscapes is also well illustrated from work done in this area.

The figures below, for example, illustrate the positive relationships between biodiversity and ecosystem functioning in an agricultural context, how management effectiveness is determined by landscape structure, and a successful sample design for understanding the scale dependence of these relationships.

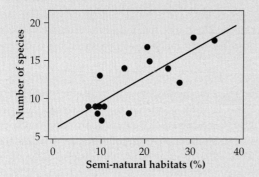

Figure Box 18.01a   The number of flower-visiting bee species increases as the proportion of semi-natural habitat in the pre-dominantly agricultural landscape increases (redrawn from Tscharntke et al. (2005), but see Steffan-Dewenter et al. (2002)).

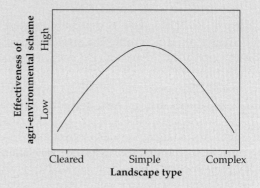

Figure Box 18.01c   The hump-shaped relationship between the degree of landscape transformation (from cleared to complex) and the effectiveness of managed schemes aimed at enhancing biodiversity (redrawn from Tscharntke et al. (2005); see text for explanation).

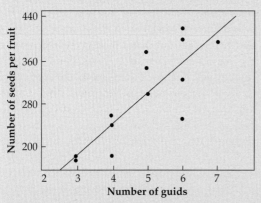

Figure Box 18.01b   The number of pumpkin seeds per fruit increases as the number of pollinating bee guilds increases (redrawn from Hoehn et al. (2008)), a clear illustration of the functional importance of biodiversity.

Figure Box 18.01d   A schematic of the hierarchically scaled sampling design (extending radii of 250 m) used by Steffan-Dewenter et al. (2002) and others to demonstrate the importance to biodiversity not only of the amount of habitat, but also the spatial characteristics of such habitat, including the distribution, size, and total area of land under different levels of management intensity (from natural, unmanaged to intensively managed).

is one of the fundamental considerations during the design and analysis of biodiversity measurement studies (Box 18.1; see also Chapters 11 and 12).

The bioindication value of taxa for reflecting the functional status of such settings has also been examined, for example using trap-nesting bees and wasps. A range of independent studies has demonstrated that aculeate bees (specifically their richness and abundance), and to a lesser extent wasps, respond significantly and consistently to habitat isolation and plant diversity (the latter indicative of food and nest site availability) (Tscharntke et al. 1998). This group of Hymenoptera has additional value as a bioindicator because its members are functionally significant in agro-ecosystems (as pollinators and in biological control). Monitoring groups such as this is therefore likely to be essential for evaluating the biodiversity value and functional status of many agricultural and mixed-use landscapes (Schulze et al. 2004).

Several of these relationships between biodiversity, landscape structure, and management have been measured and tested not only across sites within regions, but also across European and tropical systems, and have been found to be similar (i.e. the ideas have gained some degree of generality; Fig. 18.2). In consequence, the importance of heterogeneity for maintaining biodiversity in landscapes managed for agriculture and forestry is now well supported.

A macroecological approach to measuring biodiversity in managed landscapes

Recently, an alternative, macroecological, approach to understanding the impact of management on biodiversity has been proposed. It is based on the rationale that given the contingencies associated with each management system and managed landscape, an approach that is able to be applied to the measurement of any system, in comparable units, may better reveal general assemblage responses to management intensity than those that focus on assemblage diversity and composition. Dornelas et al. (2009) thus proposed that the shape of species abundance distributions (SADs, the frequency distribution of species abundances in an assemblage expressed as a histogram, see Chapters 9 and 17) may be used to infer the relative degree of environmental heterogeneity. Although, for sufficiently large sample sizes, SADs are approximately log-normal, the authors propose that the deviation from log-normal is systematically related to the degree of environmental heterogeneity. Specifically they hypothesized that

heterogeneity increases multimodality in SADs and that this effect of the shape of SADs is produced regardless of the mechanism generating that heterogeneity. Using weed, seed-bank communities subjected to a range of agronomic treatments (e.g. fertilization, ploughing and different cover crops), Dornelas et al. (2009) demonstrated that environmental heterogeneity does indeed, as predicted, generally produce more multimodal SADs. This hypothesis is ripe for further testing across a range of management intensity gradients, and if supported will add substantially to our current understanding of biodiversity in managed landscapes.

18.2.4 Matrices for measurement

The quote by Andrewarth and Birch (1954) at the start of the chapter nicely reflects early recognition that to understand pattern in and mechanisms underlying abundance variation, measures of the environment, the physiological and behavioural responses of individuals, and of abundance are required. The same could be said of many, if not most, levels in the biological hierarchy. Although the fields typically occupied with such measurements developed separately over much of the 20th century (Gaston et al. 2009), current work shows that they are being re-integrated, especially with substantial modern efforts to understand the effects of human-mediated climate and landscape change (Chown & Terblanche 2007; Soberón 2007; Chown & Gaston 2008; Kearney & Porter 2009; Gaston et al. 2009).

Perhaps the major differences between early integrated work and current approaches are those that have resulted from an increase in computing power which, in turn, has enabled integration to take place in a spatially explicit manner. The modern emphasis on spatial ecology not only recognizes the importance of spatial scale and structure, but also the significance of dispersal processes in affecting everything from the extent of phenotypic plasticity to the position of range edges and the structure of assemblages (Hubbell 2001; Holt et al. 2004b; Veldtman & McGeoch 2004; Chown & Terblanche 2007; Angilletta 2009; Gaston 2009; Chapter 11). Indeed, a spatially explicit approach may prove to be one of the most useful ways of integrating biodiversity measurements across a range of hierarchical levels (Hui et al. 2006). Such an approach is proving necessary not only to understand patterns of biodiversity variation and the mechanisms underlying it, but also to understand how both may change through time owing to landscape change, landscape management, responses to unintended or intentional human influences, or to evolution in response to these changes.

In the context of biodiversity surveys, Bell (2003) recognized the value of between-site differences in providing information on spatial variation in traits in the biodiversity matrix. A substantial amount of information may be obtained from considering row and column totals and variances from a species by sites ($r \times c$) matrix, including richness variation, variation in abundances of species, and the extent to which assemblages may be nested (see Chapter 11 and Simberloff & Connor (1979) for an earlier and related matrix approach, i.e. Q-mode and R-mode analysis). Although Bell's (2003) assessment was concerned with either presence–absence or abundance data, the cells of the matrix may also take the form of other characters, such as body size. Indeed, when this is done it immediately becomes apparent that the $r \times c$ approach provides a means of distinguishing between spatial variation in traits at the intraspecific, interspecific, and assemblage levels, and understanding the relationships among them (Gaston 2008a; Fig. 18.3). For example, whilst intraspecific clinal variation in size probably has to do with temperature, water availability, season length, organism size, and generation time (Chown & Gaston 2010), interspecific variation is also influenced by range position and taxonomic replacement, whilst assemblage variation includes these influences as well as variation in species richness (Greve et al. 2008; Olson et al. 2009). Dray and Legendre (2008) take the matrix approach a step further by demonstrating how the linkage (using an extension of the fourth-corner method) of a species abundance matrix with an environmental and phenotypic matrix (behavioural or other trait matrix of interest) can be used to describe the multivariate relationships between species, species traits, and the environment.

The $r \times c$ approach can also be applied to physiological variables, such as desiccation resistance,

metabolic rate, or thermal tolerance (Gaston et al. 2009). Likewise, the complexities of responses in the presence of other species may be incorporated into the $r \times c$ approach (see de Mazancourt et al. (2008) and Angilletta (2009) for examples). Once this is done, and it is recognized that the site columns can readily be decomposed into two or three spatial dimensions (x, y, z coordinates) (i.e. be made spatially explicit; see Hui et al. (2010) and Chapter 11), it rapidly becomes clear that the matrix approach can be used to represent landscape variation (e.g. variation in mean daily maximum temperature or soil type), a function that relates this variation to survival, reproductive rate, or abundance (Chown & Gaston 2008; Angilletta 2009), and finally to represent abundance variation within and across taxa (Fig. 18.3). Moreover, the function relating the environment to abundance may also take some other form, such as the approach set out as the fourth-corner problem (Legendre et al. 1997; Dray & Legendre 2008) or as a spatially explicit population viability model. In turn, the matrices may be stepped through time, as spatially explicit population models often do, with the landscape matrix changing, the functional matrix evolving, or both, to provide predictions of what the outcome of these changes might be. At large scales this approach is very similar to mechanistic niche modelling developed by Kearney and Porter (2009); at smaller scales it is equivalent to spatially explicit population viability assessment, whilst at the field scale it can be seen as similar to pest forecasting models. Because the spatial autocorrelation structure of the environment, and how individuals respond to it, may also lie at the heart of larger-scale patterns, such as the species–area relationship, species abundance distributions, and the occupancy–area relationship (e.g. Hui & McGeoch et al. 2007a,c; Storch et al. 2008), this approach also provides a means to understand how environmental variation may be responsible for generating these macroecological generalities. In this regard, perhaps the most well-acknowledged risk of inferring process from spatial pattern is that both different and multiple processes may generate similar patterns. McIntire and Fajardo (2009) outline an approach for linking spatial pattern and process, and maximizing the inference that can be achieved using space as a surrogate for unmeasured

(a)

Species by sites matrix for critical thermal minimum (°C)						Interspecific variation	
i Sites / *j* Species	Site A (40°S)	Site B (38°S)	Site C (35°S)	Site D (30°S)		Mean CTmin	Mean site position
					Intraspecific variation		
Sp. 1	4.0	5.0	6.0	8.0		5.8	35.8
Sp. 2	3.0	4.0	7.0			4.7	37.7
Sp. 3	3.0	4.0				3.5	39.0
Sp. 4	2.0					2.0	40.0
Mean assemblage value	3.0	4.3	6.5	8.0			
Assemblage variance	0.7	0.3					

(b)

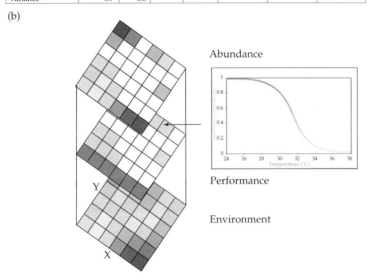

Figure 18.3 (a) An *r* × *c* matrix of species by sites indicating how physiological variables may be included in such a matrix and can provide insight into intraspecific, interspecific, and assemblage-level variation. The variable here is critical thermal minimum (see Chown & Terblanche (2007)). The italics indicate intraspecific variation across space. Interspecific variation is calculated as a mean value for the species at the centre of its range, whilst assemblage characteristics are the mean and variance of a trait across all species at a given site (see Gaston et al. (2008a)). (b) A schematic indication of how the former matrix may be made spatially explicit to investigate the relationships between environmental variation (shown in the lower matrix), performance (an upper lethal temperature figure is shown), and abundance variation.

environmental variables. Likewise, a null model approach based on *r* × *c* matrices, which may be used as an alternative or complementary one to that described above, has been elaborated by Gotelli et al. (2009).

Managed landscapes represent excellent opportunities for understanding biodiversity pattern and process and its maintenance, as well as for testing new methods of biodiversity measurement because possibilities for replication and semi-controlled experimentation are often more practicable than in more natural settings. How useful these new developments in matrix approaches might prove to be in the context of understanding biodiversity

in managed landscapes is yet to be determined. However, given their considerable utility in other settings, we are of the view that they will provide considerable insight.

18.3 Prospectus

By 2050 the human population is expected to reach 9 billion, and along with this increase our influence on the planet will also rise (Millennium Ecosystem Assessment 2005). In consequence, biodiversity measurement seems set to be undertaken in an increasingly human-dominated world, a world that has fewer species, less available energy for those that remain, and sharper edges, as more areas are managed for agriculture and for fuel production (Sutherland et al. 2008). Some areas will also become home to entirely novel ecosystems—those which are highly modified but not highly managed (and to which we have admittedly paid little attention here; see Hobbs et al. (2006)). Future biologists undertaking biodiversity measurement will no doubt have to cope with these challenges. Perhaps the best lesson that current measures of biodiversity in modified landscapes has taught us is that much more attention should be given to mitigation of our impacts, rather than to attempts to adapt to them.

18.4 Key points

1. Humans currently dominate much of the globe, both on land and at sea. In consequence, the measurement of biodiversity often concerns biodiversity in managed landscapes.
2. Objectives for measuring biodiversity typically differ depending on land-use type and its associated degree of landscape transformation and management intensity.
3. In managed landscapes, the biodiversity to be measured may range from the level of genes and transcripts, through populations, to assemblages and metacommunities. No particularly special set of methods is required for managed landscapes, beyond those typically advised for a particular level of the biological hierarchy.

However, the form, structure, grain, and varying age of the elements of the landscape should be considered carefully, as should the scale or scales at which the study should be undertaken and the sampling methods required to address the issues at hand.

4. Bioindicators should be developed with a focus on clear objectives, ease of sampling, cost-efficacy, and taxonomic knowledge. The indicator and variable of interest should have a significant, strong, and robust relationship, and the value of the former will be enhanced if it is representative and general.
5. An $r \times c$ approach to biodiversity measurement, across the full range of managed and relatively unmanaged landscapes, provides a means to explore and integrate both patterns in and the mechanisms underlying variation in biodiversity across the full biological hierarchy. Several complementary approaches now exist that are based on such matrices, which at the finest resolution can be thought of as continuous data.

Acknowledgements

We thank an anonymous reviewer for comments on a previous version of the chapter, and the editors for the invitation to contribute to this volume. SLC was partly supported by a Stellenbosch University Overarching Strategic Plan grant to the Centre for Invasion Biology.

CHAPTER 19

Estimating extinction with the fossil record

Peter J. Wagner and S. Kathleen Lyons

19.1 Introduction

Many ecological and palaeontological studies focus on extinction. The fossil record is particularly important for studying long-term patterns in extinction: although analyses of extant phylogenies can estimate extinction rates (e.g. Alfaro et al. 2009) and even suggest mass extinctions (e.g. Crisp & Cook 2009), they cannot imply trilobites ever existed or that sphenodonts (now represented only by the tuatara) were once as diverse as lepidosaurs (lizards and snakes). However, workers also use the fossil record to test ideas about the pace of major extinction events that use methods similar to those that conservation biology might use. Here we will review current palaeobiological methods for inferring extinction patterns, spanning 'traditional' methods using stratigraphic ranges to methods using more exact information about distributions of finds within stratigraphic ranges.

Palaeontological studies of diversity patterns also focus extensively on standing richness and origination rates. We do not focus on either of these parameters for their own sake. However, standing richness (usually referred to simply as 'diversity' in palaeontological studies) is an important parameter when discussing extinction as extinction metrics necessarily rely on changes in standing richness. Origination rates also can be an important parameter as the distribution of originations within time spans (i.e. evenly throughout the interval vs concentrated in the beginning) have small but important effects on the predictions of extinction rate hypotheses. Moreover, palaeontological techniques for estimating origination rates

are essentially identical to those for estimating extinction, save that they are done 'in reverse'. Thus, discussions of *how* one estimates extinction rates using fossil data can almost double for discussion of how one estimates origination from fossil data.

The other parameter that will be important throughout this review is preservation (i.e. sampling) rate. Just as ecologists know that incomplete sampling affects sampled richness (e.g. Hurlbert 1971) and implied extinction (e.g. Solow 1993a), palaeontologists know that incomplete sampling affects the first and last appearances of fossils, both in local sedimentary sections (Signor & Lipps 1982) and globally (Sepkoski 1975). Workers have expressed concern that major extinctions are exaggerated by or possibly even illusions of intervals of poor preservation (Raup 1979; Smith et al. 2001; Peters & Foote 2002). Because sampling intensity is of interest to both fields, we shall also discuss how palaeontological studies address sampling when estimating diversity and diversity dynamics.

19.2 State of the field

19.2.1 Basic metrics

Palaeontological studies of richness and diversity dynamics (i.e. extinction and origination) date back to the 19th century (Phillips 1860). Traditional palaeontological studies use *synoptic databases* (e.g. Sepkoski 1982, 2002), which catalogue the first and last appearances of taxa. These almost always are binned into chronostratigraphic units: typically stages and substages, but sometimes as fine as

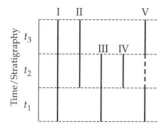

Figure 19.1   Chronostratigraphic ranges of five hypothetical taxa. Each *t* gives a separate chronostratigraphic unit, with t_1 the oldest. Dashed vertical line for V indicates that taxon V is not actually found in unit t_2. Modified from Foote (2000), Fig. 1.

faunal zones. (We use 'intervals' to refer chronostratigraphic units because of the correspondence between units of time and strata; see Gradstein et al. (2005)). For numerous reasons, synoptic studies typically use supraspecific taxa, with genera being the most common taxon since the mid 1980s.

Fig. 19.1 presents a simple example. We use last appearances in each unit t to infer rates of extinction. Two types of metrics commonly are used: per taxon (pt) and per capita (pc; see Foote (2000)). Per-taxon metrics measure the proportion of standing richness, S, that have their last appearance in an interval. Per-taxon extinction thus is:

$$\mu_{\text{pt}} = \frac{S_L}{S} \qquad (19.1)$$

where S_L is the number of taxa last appearing in an interval. In Fig. 19.1, taxa III and IV last appear in t_2, so $S_L = 2$. S is not the sum of taxa sampled in an interval, but the sum of taxa with chronostratigraphic ranges spanning the interval. Taxon V in t_2 illustrates the difference: because it first appears before t_2 and last appears after t_2, we assume that it existed in t_2 even though V is not sampled in t_2. This assumption is unsound only if taxon V is polyphyletic. As the synoptic data for taxa I and V are identical, we need a more detailed database to recognize cases like taxon V. Thus, $S_{t2} = 5$ regardless of how many 'range-through' taxa (e.g. I and V) actually are sampled in t_2, and $\mu_{\text{pt}} - 0.40$. (Per-taxon origination, λ_{pt}, simply replaces S_L with S_F, the taxa first appearing in t_2).

Per-capita extinction rate measures the survivorship of taxa present at the outset of an interval. This is:

$$\mu_{\text{pc}} = \ln\left(\frac{S_a}{S_{az}}\right) \qquad (19.2)$$

where S_a is the number of taxa crossing the boundary from the prior interval and S_{az} is the number of the taxa also crossing through both the base and the top (i.e. the range-through taxa). Note that 'per capita' here refers not to individuals within a species, but to taxa as operational units. For t_2 in Fig. 19.1, S_a is 3 (taxa I, III, and V) and S_{az} is 2 (taxa I and V), giving $\mu_{\text{pc}} = 0.41$. The most likely probability of a taxon becoming extinct in an interval is now $1 - e^{\mu_{\text{pc}}}$. However, this is identical to μ_{pc} if we restrict per-taxon rates to only boundary crossers.

Chronostratigraphic intervals vary considerably in temporal length (Gradstein et al. 2005). Accordingly, workers often divide rates by interval length to get rates per million years instead of rates per interval. This is appropriate if extinction is distributed throughout an interval. One expectation of continuous turnover rates is that longer intervals should have higher extinction rates. However, Foote (1994) showed that 'raw' extinction metrics are random with respect to the length of chronostratigraphic units, whereas per million year rates show a negative correlation. We will return to this issue below when we summarize tests of pulsed vs continuous rates.

The distribution of extinctions and originations plays a role in whether we should prefer per-taxon or per-capita extinction rates. If extinction and origination happen throughout an interval, then per-taxon rates overestimate immediate extinction risk as well as exaggerating S from any one slice of time. 'Singletons,' that is those taxa known from only one interval, such as taxon IV in Fig. 19.1, exacerbate this problem. Singletons often reflect differences in research effort and/or available fossils (Raup & Boyajian 1988) and excluding singletons greatly reduces the volatility of per-taxon rates (Alroy 1996). Although per-capita rates are excellent for describing continuous rates, they still can accurately reflected pulsed extinction.

19.2.2 Survivorship curves

Per-capita rates lead conceptually to survivorship curves. The per-capita rate for any one interval reflects the proportion of taxa expected to survive the entire interval into the next interval. Survivorship curves reflect the proportion of taxa that survive multiple successive intervals. Some survivorship analyses contrast rates among higher taxa in order to assess whether extinction rates in some groups differ markedly from those in other groups (e.g. Simpson 1944, 1953) or whether there are common patterns among higher taxa (Van Valen 1973, 1979; Raup 1991). Alternatively, cohort analyses contrast sets of taxa that originate in the same interval (i.e. Raup 1978; Foote 1988) to examine whether extinction rates change markedly over time. Given a per-taxon extinction rate, we expect the proportion of taxa that survive N intervals, $f(N)$, to be:

$$f(N) = \mu_{pc} = e^{-N\mu_{pc}} \qquad (19.3)$$

Given $\mu_{pc} = -\ln(\frac{3}{2})$ from our example above, we expect 66.7% of the taxa to survive 1+ intervals, 44.4% to survive 2+ intervals, etc., and thus 33.3% of the taxa to have durations of 1 interval, 22.2% to have durations of 2 intervals, etc. Of course, in reality this will vary even if extinction rates are constant simply by chance. However, the slope of the logged frequency of taxa with durations of 1, 2, 3, etc. intervals plotted against duration approximates the average μ_{pc}.

Foote (1988) uses Monte Carlo simulations to demonstrate that survivorship slopes for cohorts of Cambrian trilobites are significantly steeper than those for cohorts of Ordovician trilobites. (Subsequent revisions to the timescale greatly reduced the average longevity of Cambrian trilobites, making the pattern more pronounced than Foote reports; Bowring et al. 1993). Raup (1991) also uses this approach to demonstrate that survivorship slopes for Phanerozoic cohorts fit the expectations of a general 'kill curve' of extinction rates.

19.2.3 The importance of sampling

For three reasons, equation 19.3 will not predict the distributions of stratigraphic ranges even if μ_{pc} is

constant over time and among taxa. First, if we measure stratigraphic ranges in discrete bins (as is almost always done), then $f(N=1) = e^{-\mu_{pc}}$ only if all taxa originate at the very base of intervals. If origination is continuous throughout intervals, then we expect (for example) half of the taxa lasting one half an interval to span from t_x to t_{x+1}. Thus, only the slope from taxa with ranges of 2+ intervals will reflect μ_{pc} under continuous diversification. Second, extinction rates do not make predictions about the ages of extant taxa: instead, the age distribution of contemporaneous taxa (i.e. a 'backwards survivorship' curve *sensu* Pease (1988) or a 'prenascence' curve *sensu* Foote (2001b)) reflects origination rates (Foote 2001b).

The third reason is the most critical: extinction rates make predictions about temporal durations, but we can observe only stratigraphic ranges. As preservation rates strongly affect stratigraphic ranges, 'survivorship' curves using fossil ranges actually reflect both preservation and extinction (Sepkoski 1975; Pease 1988; Foote & Raup 1996). Consider a simple example of two clades where origination and extinction occur at the beginning and end of each interval, and for which $\bar{\mu}_{pc} = 0.69$ (Fig. 19.2). For one clade, the probability of recov-

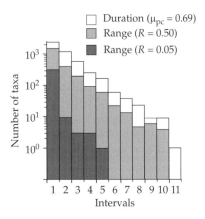

Figure 19.2 The relationship between durations (time from birth to death) and stratigraphic ranges (= number of chronostratigraphic units from first to last appearances). This simulation of 5000 taxa uses $\mu_{pc} = 0.69$, which predicts half of the taxa present at the outset of an interval to go extinct in that interval. Sampled stratigraphic ranges reflect sampling intensity (R) of 0.5 and 0.05 per interval. Following palaeontological studies, both durations and ranges are binned into discrete intervals.

ery, R, is 0.5 per interval; for the other, $R = 0.05$ per interval. These illustrate two patterns emphasized by Foote and Raup (1996). First, the slopes of the logged survivorship curves *after* the first interval parallel each other quite well. Second, the proportion of taxa sampled from 1 interval to those sampled over 2+ intervals increases as R decreases. At sufficiently low R, all taxa are known from single finds (and thus single intervals) only. From this, Foote and Raup derived preservation intensity as:

$$R_{FR} = \frac{S^2_{sr=2}}{S_{sr=1} \times S_{sr=3}} \qquad (19.4)$$

where $S_{sr=x}$ is the number of taxa with stratigraphic ranges of x intervals. In our example here, $R_{FR} = 0.53$ when true $R = 0.50$ and $R_{FR} = 0.09$ when true $R = 0.05$.

The ability to contrast preservation rates over time or among taxa obviously interests palaeontologists. However, subsequent work embraced the fact that joint hypotheses of preservation and extinction make exact predictions about distributions of stratigraphic ranges. This led to a shift from contrasting slopes of survivorship curves to contrasting the likelihoods of hypothesized extinction and preservation rates (Solow & Smith 1997; Foote 1997). Consider a simple system where origination and extinction occur at the beginning and end of intervals. Extinction here is a per-taxon metric giving the proportion of taxa expected to become extinct at the end of each interval. The expected proportion of taxa with a stratigraphic range (sr) of 1 interval is:

$$f[sr = 1] = \frac{\sum\limits_{d=sr}^{w} \left[P[\mu](1 - P[\mu])^{(d-1)} \times d(1 - R)^{(d-sr)} R\right]}{1 - \sum\limits_{d=1}^{w} \left[P[\mu](1 - P[\mu])^{(d-1)} \times (1 - R)^d\right]}$$

$$(19.5a)$$

while the expected proportion of taxa known from $x - 2, \ldots, w$ intervals (where w is the maximum possible) is:

$$f[sr] = \sum_{d=sr}^{w} \left[P[\mu](1-P[\mu])^{(d-1)} \times (1 + d - sr)(1-R)^{(d-sr)} \right.$$
$$\left. \times \sum_{n=0}^{sr-2} \binom{sr-2}{n} (1-R)^{(sr-2-n)} R^{(n+2)} \right] \Big/$$
$$1 - \sum_{d=1}^{w} \left[P[\mu](1 - P[\mu])^{(d-1)} \times (1 - R)^d \right] \quad (19.5b)$$

where d is the true duration and n is the number of intervals between the first and last interval in which a taxon might be found (Foote 1997). The three important recurring terms here are:

$\mu(1 - \mu)^{d-1}$: the probability of avoiding extinction for $d - 1$ intervals and becoming extinct in interval d, where μ is equivalent to μ_{pc} for boundary crossers only;

$(1 - R)^x$: the probability of being unsampled for x intervals;

R^y: the probability of being sampled in y intervals.

The denominator in both equations estimates the proportion of taxa that are sampled as one minus the proportion that are unsampled, i.e. the probability of having duration d times the probability of going unsampled for d intervals summed over the entire range of possible durations (w). This is because we can test hypotheses based only on their predictions about *sampled* taxa. The numerator also sums over the range of possible durations. The second part of both numerators reflects the number of ways a stratigraphic range of sr fits within a duration of d, which is simply $1 + (d - sr)$. For example, there is only one way to fit $sr = 4$ within $d = 4(t_1, \ldots, t_4)$ and two ways to fit $sr = 4$ within $d = 5(t_1, \ldots, t_4$ and $t_2, \ldots, t_5)$, etc. The final term in equation 19.5a, $\sum\limits_{n=0}^{sr-2} \binom{sr-2}{n} (1-R)^{(sr-2-n)} R^{(n+2)}$, sums the probabilities given R of all of the different stratigraphic records that match a synoptic range of sr. All taxa with $sr = 4$ are found in at least two intervals (the first and last). However, there are four possible stratigraphic records consistent with that synoptic range (Fig. 19.3), therefore the likelihood function must sum the probabilities of all four possibilities given any R.

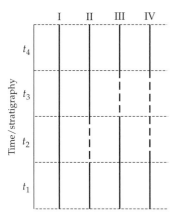

Figure 19.3 Four exact stratigraphic distributions resulting in a synoptic range of four intervals.

Foote (1997) presents more complex variations of equation 19.5 for continuous stratigraphic ranges. As most palaeontological studies use discrete bins, we will not cover this in detail. However, we will return to the effects of continuous μ and λ (origination) on the expectations for stratigraphic ranges below. At this point, equation 19.5 gives us an expected observed survivorship curve given any combination of μ and R. Multinomial probability then gives the probability of the data given that combination. However, this obviously is not wholly satisfactory for several reasons. In particular, this approach is useful for contrasting general differences in average extinction rates between taxa while controlling for the possibility of different average preservation rates. Most of the interesting palaeoecological questions concern differences in extinction rates in particular intervals. We also have ample evidence that sampling varies over time (e.g. Peters 2006; McGowan & Smith 2008), which might affect our estimates of extinction.

19.2.4 Relevant studies

Foote (2001c, 2003) modifies the approach outlined above to estimate interval-by-interval rates of μ, λ and R. One applies variations of equation 19.5 on 'birth' and 'death' cohorts, that is, how long do taxa first appearing in an interval last and how old are the taxa that last appear in an interval? In other words, instead of analysing a vector of ages at last appearance, one now analyses a matrix X where each cell X_{ij} gives the number of taxa first appearing in t_i and last appearing in t_j. Now, one can apply separate μ_i and R_i (and λ_i) at each t_i on variations of equation 19.5. The expected number of taxa originating in t_i with $d = j$ now is affected by variation in μ from i to j, and the probability of any given $sr \leq d$ is affected by variation in R from i to j. Because the best R_i for any t_i must accommodate both the backwards survivorship curves as well as the forwards survivorship curve, λ_i is relevant for estimating μ_i. The algorithms to find the collection of parameters maximizing the probability of the observed matrix are computationally intensive. Foote's (2003) analysis of Sepkoski's (2002) compendium of marine genera shows, for example, that the major loss of taxa at the Big Five mass extinction events (Raup & Sepkoski 1982) and the high turnover of the Cambrian taxa (Sepkoski 1979) require high rates of extinction even in those cases where preservation rates were low.

Finally, estimates of extinction and preservation from equation 19.5 effectively assume that taxa extant are present throughout all intervals within their durations. This can be true only if both origination and extinction are pulsed, that is, concentrated in some particular interval. However, if they are continuous, then true durations will span fractions of the first and last intervals for most taxa. This has two effects (Foote 2005). One, if origination probabilities are uniform throughout intervals, then there is a 70% chance that a taxon with a true duration of 2.7 intervals exists in all or part of four intervals. Two, the probability of sampling a taxon in its first or last interval is not R, but $1 - (1 - R)^x$, where x is the fraction of the first/last interval in which the taxon occurs. Given this subtle difference, Foote (2005) found strong support for pulsed extinctions and origination in most intervals. One implication of this is that the tradition of standardizing extinction rates by millions of years often is highly misleading.

19.2.5 Occurrence-based diversity estimates

We require approaches such as outlined in the prior section when synoptic ranges are our only

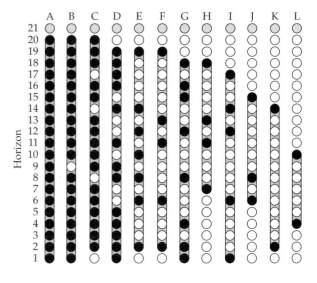

Figure 19.4   Hypothetical distribution of finds in a section, based on a single simulation. 'Horizons' represent fossiliferous beds. Black circles indicate that the species is sampled. White circles indicate that it is unsampled. Hatched circles represent the first fossiliferous horizon following the extinction event. Gray ellipses give the observed stratigraphic ranges. Although all 12 species are extant throughout the time represented, they appear to go extinct (and originate) gradually.

data. However, in many cases we have data concerning the distributions of finds within stratigraphic ranges, such as the Paleobiology Database (http://pbdb.org; see, for example, Alroy et al. (2001)). This provides us with an independent means of estimating R_i using range-through taxa for any t_i. In Fig. 19.4, four taxa are known to be extant during t_2 and t_3 because they were sampled before and after those intervals. This leads to a simple estimate (Connolly & Miller 2001b):

$$R_i = \frac{S_{i,\text{obs}}}{S_{i,\text{az}}} \qquad (19.6)$$

where $S_{i,az}$ is the number of range-through taxa for t_i (see Fig. 19.1) and $S_{i,\text{obs}}$ is the subset of those taxa that we actually observe. If one uses empirical estimates of R_i instead of solving for R_i at the same time as μ_i (and λ_i), then it becomes much easier to solve for the diversity parameters.

Foote (2007a) uses the Paleobiology Database to measure R with range-through taxa and then assess the effect of preservation on recalibrated extinction rates. This suggested that extinction is *less* continuous through the Phanerozoic than previously thought, as immediate R_i explains the last appearances in many low extinction intervals. A corresponding result is that extinction rates of subsequent intervals increase, with the end result being that intervals with high extinction given 'face value'

data have even higher extinction after optimizing for R. In particular, Foote's analysis suggested that extinction rates in the intervals preceding the end-Permian, end-Triassic, end-Ordovician, and end-Devonian were lower than suggested by the 'face value' fossil record. Thus, accommodating preservation elevates rather than erases mass extinction episodes. Nevertheless, and as Foote emphasizes in that work, the 'face value' data leads to the same conclusions, for example estimates of discontinuity of extinction rates separating a few intervals of mass extinctions from other intervals remains (see Wang 2003).

Connolly and Miller (2001b) use the distribution of genus finds over time to estimate preservation, extinction, and origination likelihoods using a capture–mark–recapture (CMR) approach. This represents a modification of the CMR methods used to estimate the same parameters for Recent taxa given conservation data (Pradel 1996). One obvious advantage of this sort of approach is that one can estimate diversity parameters for separate environments or biogeographic units from the same stages (see, for example, Miller & Foote (1996) and Connolly & Miller (2001a)). Alroy (2000) uses likelihood estimates of these parameters to construct faunal ordinations that maximize the probability of observed species lists. The further development of such techniques in conjunction with the expansion of large occurrence-based databases (e.g. the PBDB) represents an important future direction for palaeobiological studies (see Prospectus section below).

19.2.6   Gap analyses

The use of exact numbers of finds within stratigraphic ranges and the issue of continuous versus pulsed extinction rates points the way to the most exact methods for evaluating the timing of extinctions. This is perhaps best known in association with Alvarez et al.'s (1980) proposal that the end-Cretaceous extinction is a sudden event triggered by a major asteroid impact. However, the idea that extinction events are pulsed rather than gradual is not new (see, for example, Erwin (2006)). Some theory suggests that lower-level turnovers often are pulsed (Vrba 1985; Morris et al. 1995) and many of our concepts about stratigraphic zones tacitly assume pulsed turnovers (e.g. Shaw 1964). Foote's (2005) study argues against 'gradual' extinction mechanisms that distribute extinctions through entire stages. However, chronostratigraphic stages and substages typically are millions of years long whereas the 'gradual' extinction hypotheses often predict extinction over hundreds of thousands of years. Thus, although the 'pulsed' hypotheses of extinctions predict extinctions over tens of thousands of years or less, both 'pulsed' and 'gradual' might make the same predictions about synoptic data. We therefore must focus on the distributions of finds within chronostratigraphic units to find different predictions between gradual and pulsed extinction hypotheses.

Preservation again is very important when ascertaining the expectations of pulsed and gradual extinction hypotheses. The probabilistic nature of preservation and sampling means that we expect gradual disappearances of taxa from the fossil record even if all of the taxa share the same time of extinction (Signor & Lipps 1982). Simple simulations illustrate the Signor–Lipps effect (Fig. 19.4). Consider the first and last occurrences of 12 taxa over 21 fossiliferous beds (horizons), with the 12 taxa forming a Zipf abundance distribution ($\gamma = 2.0$) and having equal preservation probability per specimen. Although all 12 taxa are present throughout

the section, they appear to phase out gradually simply because of sampling failure: although the common taxa are sampled up to the top of the section, the less common taxa have highly truncated ranges. Solow (1993a) notes a similar problem for conservation biologists: it is easy to miss rare species for 5+ years by chance alone, so failing to sample one for a long period of time is weak evidence that it is extinct; conversely, it is difficult to miss a common species for any length of time, so failing to sample one is strong evidence that it is extinct.

One advantage that palaeontologists have that conservation biologists do not is that they can continue to sample all of the time planes. Ultimately, elevated sampling should reveal the rare taxa. However, this is too labour intensive and expensive to be done at many sites. Thus, we need solutions using the available data. This, in turn, leads to gap analyses, which attempt to use estimates of expected gaps between samples to evaluate both extinction and the Signor–Lipps effect.

Strauss and Sadler (1989; see also Marshall (1990)) use a Dirichlet distribution to assess possible gaps between last appearance and true extinction at any given confidence interval (CI) as:

$$g = sr \times \left([1 - C_1]^{-\frac{1}{H-1}} - 1 \right) \qquad (19.7)$$

where g is the hypothesized gap, sr is the observed stratigraphic range, H is the number of horizons, and C_1 is the CI on one end of the stratigraphic range. Note that if we use continuous meters (e.g. Strauss & Sadler 1989) or time (e.g. Marshall 1990), then the stratigraphic range would be the last horizon minus the first horizon and single samples have no range; however, with binned horizons, the minimum range is 1. We use horizons here simply because the non-random distribution of horizons within units of strata or time require further modifications to these approaches (Marshall 1994, 1997; but see Prospectus section below). Thus, for taxon E, $g_{50\%}$ is 18 horizons $\times ([1 - 0.5]^{-\frac{1}{7-1}} - 1) = 2.2$ horizons beyond the last appearance. In other words, there is a 50% chance that the true extinction happened between the last appearance and this point and a 50% chance that the true extinction happened after this point.

Marshall (1995) proposes using 50% confidence intervals to test the null hypothesis of simultaneous extinction. Marshall uses the range that is above $g_{50\%}$ for half of the species as the optimal extinction zone. In Fig. 19.4, half of the taxa have $g_{50\%} \leq 2.2$ and half have $g_{50\%} \geq 3.1$. Thus, the 22nd horizon would be the optimum extinction horizon. As that follows the last appearance of all of the taxa, we cannot reject a single extinction. Using metres of sediment rather than fossiliferous horizons, Marshall (1995) shows that Cretaceous ammonoids not only fail to reject the simultaneous extinctions, but that the $g_{50\%}$ values do an excellent job of predicting the iridium layer terminating the Cretaceous. Conversely, Marshall and Ward (1996) demonstrate that the 50% line for Late Cretaceous inoceramid bivalves precedes the last appearance of nearly half the species. As many species clearly existed after the optimal extinction time for half the species, there almost certainly are multiple extinction events for inoceramids.

Marshall's basic approach lends itself well to likelihood tests of numbers of extinction events. Building on a model initially presented by Solow (1996), Wang and Everson (2007) consider the likelihood of the hypothesized extinctions, $\zeta_{1\ldots S}$, of S taxa, noting that:

$$L[\zeta_{1\ldots S}|sr_{1\ldots S}, H_{1\ldots S}] \propto \prod_{i=1}^{S} \left(\frac{sr_i}{\zeta_i - FA_i + 1} \right)^{H_i} \quad (19.8a)$$

where FA_i is the first appearance of taxon i, and therefore:

$$\zeta_i - FA_i + 1 = g_i + sr_i \quad (19.8b)$$

(i.e. the observed stratigraphic range, sr, plus the gap, g, implicit to the hypothesized extinction ζ). Again, the '+1' is necessary only when stratigraphic ranges are in discrete rather than continuous units. Note also that the likelihood is 0 rather than a negative number if $g < 0$ as this is an impossible hypothesis. For any taxon i, the likelihood decreases as g_i increases. The number of parameters is equal to the number of different extinction events. Thus, the simplest (minimum varying parameter) hypothesis has all taxa sharing the same extinction events and the most likely single-parameter (single-extinction) hypothesis sets all ζ_i to the latest last appearance

(e.g. horizon 20 in Fig. 19.4). Conversely, the most complex possible hypothesis posits a separate extinction for each taxon. The single most likely version of this basic model is one in which $g_i = 0$ for all taxa, and thus can have as many differing ζ values (and thus as many different parameters) as there are taxa. The support (log-likelihood rescaled to the maximum) for this hypothesis is 0. There are a large number of alternatives of intermediate complexity, for example one can examine a two-parameter hypothesis that posits two separate extinctions giving $\zeta_{A\ldots F}$ at horizon 20 and $\zeta_{G\ldots L}$ at horizon 19.

Log-likelihood ratio tests (e.g. Edwards 1992) now can assess whether the more complex hypothesis predicts the data significantly better than the simpler hypothesis. In Fig. 19.4, the support (i.e. the log-likelihood rescaled to the most likely hypothesis) for $\zeta_{A\ldots L} = -7.34$. Whether we can reject this in favour of continuous extinction depends on how many parameters we ascribe to the best 'continuous' hypothesis. Wang and Everson (2007) use S on the grounds that there is one extinction for each of the S taxa. However, in this example there are only seven last appearance beds. This means that we need only seven extinction events to eliminate all 12 taxa, and that the degrees of freedom should be 6 $(7 - 1)$ rather than 11. This is important because we would not reject the null hypothesis of a single extinction if we assume that the overall most likely hypothesis requires 12 parameters ($p = 0.20$) whereas we would if we assume that the overall most-likely hypothesis requires seven parameters ($p = 0.02$). However, a two-parameter hypothesis ($\zeta_{A\ldots C} = 20$, $\zeta_{D\ldots L} = 19$) represents a significant improvement over the one-parameter hypothesis (support $= -4.45$; $p = 0.02$) while withstanding rejection from the overall most likely hypothesis given the assumption of either 12 parameters ($p = 0.54$) or seven parameters ($p = 0.11$) or from the most-likely three-parameter hypothesis ($\zeta_{A\ldots C} = 20$, $\zeta_{D\ldots F} = 19$, $\zeta_{G\ldots L} = 18$; support $= -3.13$, $p = 0.10$). This clearly is erroneous given that all 12 taxa share the same time of extinction in the simulations, but restricting all 12 extinctions to the final two beds strongly contradicts the idea of a prolonged extinction event.

Information theory criteria give an alternative means for assessing the hypothesis. An appealing aspect is that these criteria can lead one to conclude that the simpler hypothesis is superior to the more complex hypothesis rather than simply unrejected (Burnham & Anderson 2002). Here, Akaike's information criteria (AIC; Akaike 1973), modified for sample size (Burnham & Anderson 2002), is:

$$\text{AICc} = -2 \ln \text{L}[\zeta_{A...L}] + 2K \left(\frac{S}{S - K - 1} \right)$$

where K is the number of parameters and the taxon richness, $S = 12$, is the number of data points. Because the $\text{AICc}[\zeta_{A...L} = 20] = 17.1$ whereas $\text{AICc}[7$ separate $\zeta_i] = 42$, we now prefer the single extinction to the mostly-likely seven-extinction hypothesis. However, we still prefer the best two-parameter hypothesis ($\text{AICc}[\zeta_{A...C} = 20, \zeta_{D...L} = 19] = 14.2$) to the best single-extinction hypothesis. On one hand, one might fault the method for failing to corroborate the correct hypothesis that all of the extinctions happened after the last bed. However, it is reassuring that the favoured hypothesis is a near miss that concentrates all of the extinctions in the last two beds.

Huelsenbeck and Rannala (1997) estimate the probability of zero finds over some interval given preservation rate, R. Although this is intuitively reasonable, R itself is an unknown. R is not explicitly addressed in the Wang and Everson approach, but uncertainty about R should be a concern there too. An intuitive estimate of R is simply:

$$R = \frac{H}{sr} \quad (19.9a)$$

As Fig. 19.4 illustrates, this is biased towards overestimating preservation rates because the denominator under-estimates the true duration (Wagner 2000; Foote 2001a). Instead, an unbiased estimate is given by the finds *within* the known range, i.e.:

$$R = \frac{H - 2}{sr - 2} \quad (19.9b)$$

Even so, we should *not* estimate the likelihood of hypothesized extinction as:

$$\text{L}[\zeta \mid H, sr, R] = \left(1 - \frac{H - 2}{sr - 2} \right)^g$$

First, the uncertainty around the most likely R can be very large, especially for taxa sampled from a few beds over a short duration. Although the probability of the stratigraphic data is maximized with equation 19.7b, the joint probability of the observed data and the hypothesized gap (and thus the joint likelihood of ζ and R; Wagner 2000) is maximized at:

$$R' = \frac{H - 1}{g + sr - 1} \quad (19.10)$$

giving the maximum:

$$\max \text{L}[\zeta, R \mid sr, H] \propto (1 - R)^g \times ([1 - R]^{sr - H} \times R^{H-1})$$
$$(19.11a)$$

$$\propto (1 - R)^{g + sr - H} \times R^{H-1} \quad (19.11b)$$

where the first term in equation 19.9a is the probability of zero finds over the gap and the second term is the sufficient statistic from the binomial probability of $H - 1$ finds over the observed stratigraphic range after the first find. (The binomial combinatoric is constant for all hypotheses.) Note that we now subtract only one horizon as one end of the 'true' duration is implicit to the hypothesis and we truncate only the base.

We now can estimate the likelihood of one or more extinction events using the product of equation 19.11 for all species with $H \geq 2$. Returning to our example in Fig. 19.4, the log-likelihood of a single extinction at horizon 20 for the 10 species with $H_i \geq 2$ is -18.70. The log-likelihood of each species going extinct at its last appearance increases only to -14.65, which is insufficient to reject the single ζ hypothesis even when assuming only seven-parameters ($p = 0.23$) and which fares far worse given information theory ($\text{AICc}[\zeta_{A...L} = 20] = 39.8$ vs $\text{AICc}[\zeta_{A...L} = LA_{A...L}] = 71.3$). However, a hypothesis of extinctions at horizons 19 and 20 still is preferable ($\ln \text{L} = 16.25$) given either log-likelihood ratio tests ($p = 0.03$) or AIC ($\text{AICc}[\zeta_{A...C} = 20, \zeta_{D...L} = 19] = 37.8$).

The potential advantage of this approach over the approach of Solow/Wang and Everson is that it allows one to assess whether preservation rates change within a stratigraphic range. If so, then change in R can be explicitly accommodated (see Solow 1993b; Wagner 2000). For example, a simple test of linearly increasing/decreasing R over horizons would simply test the exact sequence of finds and misses with changing probabilities of finds and misses. Alternatively, one might posit a sudden shift in preservation rate. If the frequency of misses increases/decreases, then the gap between last appearance and extinction will increase/decrease. For example, taxon I in Fig. 19.4 shows an increasing recovery rate over time: it is found once over 10 horizons (2–11) then twice over the next five horizons (12–16). The most likely single R, $\frac{5-2}{17-2} = 0.2$ (equation 19.7b) has a support of $-7.51 (= \ln[0.2^3 \times 0.8^{12}])$. The best gradually shifting R, with $R_2 = 0.05 \rightarrow R_{16} = 0.34$, increases the support only to -7.14. The best two-phase R, $R_{2...11} = 0.1$ and $R_{12...16} = 0.4$, increases the support only to -6.86. In neither case would we reject the idea that sampling was homogeneous throughout taxon I's range and thus we have no particular reason to distrust the likelihood given sampling over those 20 horizons. However, Wagner (2000) presents empirical examples where this approach does reject homogeneous R and thus leads to different likelihoods on hypothesized extinctions.

19.3 Prospectus

The study of extinction can proceed in many directions, many of which workers have tentatively explored already. In particular, the use of databases such as the PBDB to ascertain more exact tests of extinction pacing and preservation rates within taxa represents the logical next steps to the methods described above. For example, using observed range-through taxa to estimate R provides an average sampling intensity within an interval. This obviously will not represent all genera. With higher taxa in particular, species richness within a genus or family will strongly affect preservation rate, as will other factors, such as the geographic distributions of the species within the taxa. Foote (2007b) shows that the occurrences of genera typically follow a bell curve over time, that is, occurrences are low both in the early and late intervals of a genus' range and typically peak in the middle. Because genera originate throughout time, this means that different genera will be at different points in their bell curves in any given interval. Moreover, the peaks of these

distributions (i.e. the maximum numbers of occurrences) differ among genera. These two factors combined means that it should be possible to derive a distribution of preservation intensities within each interval rather than a single R 'per genus'. What is most intriguing is that we might use the bell curves themselves in a Bayesian context to assess extinction risk (see, for example, Solow (1993b)). In other words, extinction risk should be relatively low at the peak of an occurrence distribution, when a genus typically is widespread and fairly speciose (see, for example, Foote et al. (2008)). Conversely, the extinction risk should be relatively high near the tail. Whether or not we wish to assume normal curves for occurrences over time requires further testing; however, data such as the PBDB make it possible to assess whether 'commonness' of genera is linked to extinction risk.

Part of the reason why we should expect common genera to be less extinction prone than uncommon genera is that we expect geographically wide-ranging genera to be more common in the fossil record than contemporaneous geographically narrow-ranging genera (e.g. Jablonski 2000). However, because sampling is not randomly distributed over geography, we cannot simply equate occurrences with geographic range. Instead, we need to actually examine occurrences in particular geographic units (see, for example, Foote et al. (2008)). Alroy (in Alroy et al. (2008)) presents methods for accommodating geographic dispersal in sampling standardized estimates of richness over time. We should adopt similar approaches for summarizing geographic distributions when examining the predictions of alternative extinction models.

Even occurrences within temporal and geographic units obscure important information about abundances within localities. In general, there is a good correlation between abundances and occurrences, in that taxa that are abundant anywhere within their geographic range tend to have many occurrences (Buzas et al. 1982; Alroy et al. 2008). However, in gap analyses of particular sections, variation in abundances of specimens has an important effect on the plausibility of missing an extant species (see, for example, Hurlbert (1971)). The simulations sample equal numbers of 'specimens' per bed. However, in reality, all beds are not equal: due to access, taphonomy, weathering, etc., some beds in the same section will yield many more specimens than others. Weiss and Marshall (1999) explicitly accommodate this when examining extinction boundaries for late Cambrian trilobites. Similarly, McElwain et al. (2009) examine the end-Triassic extinction in plants not in loss of richness, but in shifts on most likely relative abundance distributions. A combination of the two approaches would assess the likelihoods of hypothesized abundances over time/strata, with extinction being an abundance of 0. The logic of shifting R over a section would apply here, except that we now would ask whether we could sample X specimens without finding a species given that it is known from n of N specimens prior to that.

Another promising avenue of research involves the use of ordination techniques to describe fossil turnover without assuming a particular chronostratigraphic scale (e.g. Alroy 1992, 1994, 2000; Sadler and Cooper 2003). Although presented as techniques for repeatable, high-resolution chronostratigraphy, these methods also describe fossil distributions in the same manner needed for confidence interval studies, but at the geographic and geologic scales of synoptic studies.

Finally, one might ask whether gap analyses of extinction events frame the basic hypotheses properly. As done above, the 'complexity' of the hypotheses is the number of extinction events. A single-extinction event thus is the null because it is only one event. Statistically, this is also appropriate because a single event necessarily is less likely than (as in Fig. 19.4) seven events, as it maximizes the minimum number of necessary gaps. However, this is not quite the appropriate null hypothesis if we look at extinction *rates*. A single event requires two rates: a 'background' rate of no extinction and a single pulsed rate of (nearly) 100% extinction. Thus, we can ask, what is the probability of X extinctions from Y remaining taxa given a hypothesized extinction rate per bed? As Weiss and Marshall (1999) note, the extinction rate provides a prior probability of a lineage existing 1, 2, 3, etc., beds after its last find. This multiplied by likelihood of the gap gives a posterior probability of the taxon existing 1, 2, 3, etc., beds after its last finds. The sum of these posterior probabilities is what we would use as the count of the number of extinctions per bed. For example, in Fig. 19.4, we would have numerous extinctions in the last two beds given a hypothesis of uniform extinction rates and the sampling data. This would be strong evidence against a gradual hypothesis. However, if last appearances were distributed more evenly throughout the section, then it would be much more difficult to extend the durations to the top of the section as not only would they become increasingly improbable, but the plausibility of the taxon still being extant also would become increasingly improbable.

19.4 Key points

1. The fossil record provides data capable of testing a wide variety of extinction hypotheses.
2. This can be done at very broad temporal scales as well as over intervals closer to 'ecological time'.
3. Accommodating preservation is critical at all temporal scopes of palaeontological analyses of extinction.

CHAPTER 20

Estimating species density

Michael L. Rosenzweig, John Donoghue II, Yue M. Li, and Chi Yuan[1]

20.1   Introduction

20.1.1   The problem: what is the density of species?

In 1969, students of biodiversity were astonished by the conclusion that the highest plant species diversities in the world were not in tropical rainforests, but in the evergreen heathlands of Australia and South Africa (Richards 1969). This conclusion was based on estimates of species density obtained by taking total number of species, S, and dividing by total area, A. However, the conclusion was reversed by Parsons and Cameron (1974), who realized that the right way to compare diversities was to compare species–area curves: the system with the higher species–area curve is the more diverse—at any particular area, it has more species. In contrast, as the reader will see below, species densities obtained by simply dividing the number of species by area can be extremely misleading.

Yet, despite the high profile of the plant diversity discussion (above and repeated in Rosenzweig 1995), we still find ourselves reading important papers that estimate species densities with the same faulty, linear method of division. For example, Stein et al. (2008) produced a valuable analysis of all the public lands in the USA. One of their goals was to compare the concentrations of species of concern in different types of public land. They concluded that lands belonging to the US Department of Defense (DoD) bear far more of the burden for species conservation than any other type of public land, including US national parks and forests. Much of the impact of that conclusion comes from a stunning bar graph (their Fig. 3) whose y-axis is species

density. DoD lands appear to have roughly three times the density of species of concern compared to lands of the US National Park Service (which are in second place). However, the species densities of that bar graph come from dividing the number of species by the amount of land, and they mislead badly.

Indeed, the DoD does bear a heavy responsibility for conservation of the nation's species diversity. Stein et al. show that about 23% of species of concern reside on DoD land. The DoD must shoulder its responsibility in environments where it is extremely difficult to avoid habitat disruption (owing to target practice, tank training, etc.), but, proportionally, its responsibility is not nearly as close to overwhelming as the bar graph suggests because the DoD manages only 12.1×10^6 ha whereas the Park Service manages 33.8×10^6 ha and the Forest Service 78.1×10^6 ha. Take any number of species, S, and divide it by those areas; it will seem the DoD has 2.8 times the Park Service's job and 6.5 times that of the Forest Service.

20.1.2   Defining the density of species

How can we get it right? How can we define species density so that our estimates of it will permit meaningful comparisons? The answer lies in using the very non-linear relationship SPAR that causes the problem to begin with.

SPAR stands for SPecies–ARea relationship: As area increases, so does the number of species found in the area. Ecologists have investigated this relationship for more than two centuries. It is so well established and so general that ecologists have called it a law (Lawton 1999b).

---

[1] Equal participants listed in random order.

A SPAR is usually reported as a straight line in logarithmic space:

$$\log S = c + z \log A$$

where A is the area, S is the number of species, and the other two parameters are coefficients of the regression. Several exciting contributions have now demonstrated mathematically that SPARs, although they come close to being straight lines in logarithmic space, do in fact have some curvature (Leitner & Rosenzweig 1997; Allen & White 2003; McGill & Collins 2003). Nonetheless, they are straight enough to justify our continuing to approximate SPARs with straight lines and to capitalize on the benefits of that approximation. One of these is that because the logarithmic version of the SPAR is linear, we can use it to measure species density.

Consider the fact that a density or concentration of something is a quantity that stays the same no matter how much area or volume is surveyed. Thus, a population density of three gerbils per hectare means that 10 ha will have 30 gerbils, 100 ha will have 300 gerbils, 1000 ha will have 3000 gerbils, etc. One cannot do this for species density, however, without taking into consideration the fact that SPARs are strongly curved in arithmetic space. Suppose, for example, that the number of beetle species

fits the formula $\log S = 1.3 + 0.177 \log A$. Then 10 ha will have 30 beetle species, 100 ha will have 45 beetle species, 1000 ha will have 68 species, etc. If we were to calculate the density of beetle species using simple division, S/A, we would obtain densities of 3, 0.45, and 0.068, respectively. Yet all of these results would have come from a taxon whose species diversity follows one single, simple equation, i.e. $\log S = 1.3 + 0.177 \log A$, so all three actually have the same species density! Fig. 20.1 shows a graphical example of the misleading effects of using division to calculate species densities.

Now we use the SPAR itself to recognize the quantitative property that stays constant in different amounts of area. That property is the coefficient c. To make this property most closely resemble an arithmetic density, we transform it to its antilog (being careful to use a single base of logarithms for all operations—we use 10). Now we can define a useful species density, C:

$$C = 10^c = S/A^z$$

The two coefficients of SPARs, C and z, are very different. The value z reflects the scale of the SPAR (Rosenzweig 2003). Values of z that come from comparisons of biogeographical provinces exceed 0.55 and often return numbers close to unity. Values of

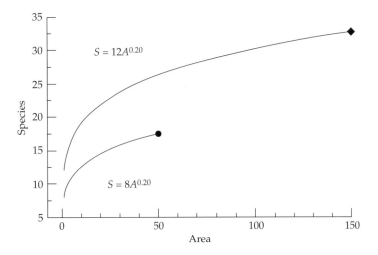

Figure 20.1 Comparison of two hypothetical samples. Both were generated by a SPAR with z of 0.20. The lower one, with $C = 8$, was sampled at 50 units of area and yielded 17.5 species. The upper one, with $C = 12$, was sampled at 150 units of area and yielded 32.7 species. Because SPARs are curvilinear, raw density, S/A, varies with the value of A at which one takes the sample. In this case, S/A is 0.350 and 0.218, respectively, that is, it is greater for the lower curve! S/A reveals nothing of the underlying biological properties of the samples. In contrast, the species density, S/A^z, is independent of A. In these two cases, it is $17.5/50^{0.20}(= 8.0)$, and $32.7/150^{0.20}(= 12.0)$.

z from different sized areas of a single region are generally less than 0.23 and usually more than 0.12. Values from archipelagoes exceed the latter range but are less than those of provinces. This difference among z values makes theoretical sense and reflects the different biological processes at work at the different scales.

Other than varying with scale however, z values vary little. Perhaps we could use a convention to estimate C? Perhaps we should simply set all z values to 0.2, then estimate species density as $S/A^{0.2}$? This already would have been a great improvement, but herein we shall try to do better than that by obtaining a data-based estimate of z.

20.1.3 Species density takes on new importance in an era of environmental concern

The importance of being able to make meaningful comparisons between species densities grew with the recommendation of the National Research Council (2000) (NRC) to rely on species densities for some basic environmental indicators. The NRC wanted these indicators to give policymakers a thumbnail sketch of the environmental state of the USA. The subtext is one of concern. Many fear our environment is spiralling out of control and that without transparent, simple, and objective indicators, policymakers will be hard-pressed to do anything about it.

The NRC did not endorse the erroneous estimation of species density by linear division. Instead, it adopted a definition, C, based on SPARs and suggested by one of us (Rosenzweig) and restated above:

$$C = S/A^z$$

The NRC recommendation was expanded by Rosenzweig (2004).

Neither publication, however, laid out a practical method for estimating species densities. In this chapter, you will come to appreciate that estimating C is far from trivial. We shall use a large plant dataset taken in Virginia to reveal the challenges of estimating species densities from field data. We shall also explore ways to circumvent the problems and arrive at reliable estimates, and we shall test our result.

We begin with a description of the dataset and a first analysis that we conduct as if there were no challenges. Then we advance to recognize and confront them.

20.2 Data set

20.2.1 Data description

Our data come from the Virginia Natural Heritage Program (VNHP), which aims to save Virginia's native plant, animal life, and ecosystems. We analysed its plant data only (Virginia Natural Heritage Program 2006; DCR-DNH vegetation plots database, ver. 3.0. Virginia Department of Conservation and Recreation, Division of Natural Heritage. Richmond). The plant data set has three parts (see Table 20.1):

- A list of all 4205 plant species ever recorded in Virginia. Each species listing includes its Latin name, common name, family name, global element rank, state element rank, and existing status.
- Details of 652 study plots sampled by VNHP. Details include plot area, latitude, longitude, elevation, slope, ecoregion, ecological community

Table 20.1 The Virginia Natural Heritage Program's plots have six different areas and belong to seven different ecoregions.

Area (m²)	1000	800	400	300	200	100
Number of plots	50	1	588	2	5	6

Ecoregion	Number of plots	Ecoregion	Number of plots
Unknown	1	Cumberland/Southern Ridge &Valley	17
Central Appalachian Forest	444	Chesapeake Bay Lowlands	10
Piedmont	155	Lower New England/Northern Piedmont	8
Southern Blue Ridge	13	Mid-Atlantic Coastal Plain	4

Box 20.1 WS2M

EstimateS is far and away the most widely used software for reducing sample size bias when estimating diversity. However, we used our own software, WS2M, for our analyses. WS2M is based on EstimateS, yet, running on a Windows platform, it provides some features not available in EstimateS. These include estimates based on several extrapolation formulae—which once again have proved their usefulness in our studies—as well as the version of the Michaelis–Menten extrapolator (MMf) that is fit by non-linear regression (rather than by maximum likelihood). WS2M computes jack-knife estimates based on all five jack-knife orders as specified in Burnham and Overton (1979). It also allows for analysis of presence–absence data.

WS2M requires one of three pure ASCII input file types. In this work, we used a matrix input: each species is a column; each plot is a row. Each entry is the abundance of a particular species in a particular plot. Each entry is separated from the next by a space. The matrix is preceded by two ASCII lines, the first is any set of ASCII characters; we usually use it for a matrix name and to specify special goals for that matrix. The second is a pair of numbers specifying the matrix size, with number of columns (species) first. For example:

Butterflies of Willow Slough

34 6
1 1 42 53 44 9 1 837
4 1 7 5 9 2 2 2 50 13 1 1 1 11 14 5 5 2 0 0 0 0 0 0 0
19 6 0 188 126 36 0 7 5 1
23 29 43 50 3 3 257 26 9 0 5 5 9 5 24 10 1 2 2 3 0 0 0 0
2 0 0 44 474 18 0 167 1 0
9 8 19 21 2 9 552 30 12 0 7 9 13 15 19 6 1 0 0 1 0 0 0 0
6 0 0 175 293 14 0 16
4 0 0 20 12 6 24 20 50 7 15 3 3 0 2 25 4 2 2 0 1 1 1 0 0 0
27 0 0 52 743 31 1 363 1 0 10 7 11
25 4 11 1041 18 38 21 18 12 19 11 15 3 1 1 0 3 0 0 0 0
4 0 0 128 146 38 0 18
6 1 9 7 13 4 19 1 132 2 11 1 3 0 6 31 45 3 0 0 0 0 0 0 0

The example above has the abundances of 34 species in six plots. (In this case a plot happens to be a year.) A second example shows the same records converted to incidence data (i.e. presence or absence):

Butterflies of Willow Slough (presence or absence)

34 6
1 1 1 1 1 1 1 1 1 1 1 1 1 1 1 1 1 1 1 1 1 1 1 1 1 1 1 1 1 0 0 0
0 0 0 0 0
1 1 0 1 1 1 0 1 1 1 1 1 1 1 1 1 1 1 0 1 1 1 1 1 1 1 1
1 0 0 0 0

1 0 0 1 1 1 0 1 1 0 1 1 1 1 1 1 1 1 1 0 1 1 1 1 1 1 1 0 0
1 0 0 0 0
1 0 0 1 1 1 0 1 1 0 0 1 1 1 1 1 1 1 1 1 0 1 1 1 1 1 0 1
1 1 0 0 0
1 0 0 1 1 1 1 1 0 1 1 1 1 1 1 1 1 1 1 1 1 1 1 1 1 1 1 1 0
1 0 0 0 0
1 0 0 1 1 1 0 1 1 1 1 1 1 1 1 1 1 1 1 0 1 1 1 1 0 0
0 0 0 0 0

You must give all matrix files the 'prn' file extension and place them in the same folder as the program. WS2M depends on you to do those things.

WS2M also does not know whether you are inputting an abundance or an incidence file. You must tell it by setting certain flags after you load your data matrix:

- On the Actions tab, check 'Shuffle Sample Order' and 'Shuffle Individuals'.
- Then check 'Make Exchangeable' and UNcheck 'Shuffle Individuals'.
- On the Advanced Options tab, check 'Shuffle Incidences Only'.

The few settings above are those required for the analysis of presence–absence data. Other settings are explained in the user manual available online at http://eebweb.arizona.edu/diversity/, where you will also find the program itself to download (ws2mb.exe).

WS2M is research software. It is not commercial and not for the blithe. WS2M will automatically warn you of some mistakes and automatically correct others, but not many. It relies on your professionalism, especially your willingness to decide in advance what you really want to do. It will not replace a magic wand.

WS2M produces an output file that will allow you to design stunning presentations with your own favourite graphics package, but the graphs that it generates internally may not seem so useful. (One of the authors is colour-blind and the other two got tired of resetting the output colours of the software to compensate!) Also, the software exploits Windows at a very low level. That makes it very powerful and fast, but it also means that it inevitably runs into one of those infamous unfixed Windows bugs: when you close the program Windows will tell you of an error. Ignore the warning. It's a Windows colour bug and has no effect on the output values.

And, yes, WS2M runs under Windows Vista, too, at least on the 32-bit versions.

group, and detailed soil characteristic (pH, N, S, P, etc.). In all, 1001 plant species were recorded in the 652 plots. Each plot had 11.3 species on average.

- A list of species in each plot and each species coverage score in each plot where it was recorded. Coverage score is a measure of abundance (which we discuss below), but no other measure of abundance is provided. Some species, 3402 to be precise, were not recorded in any plot, but of the 1001 species that were recorded, each species occurred in 7.4 plots on average.

20.2.2 Data manipulation

All data were in Microsoft Access, so we wrote code to build tables from which we could estimate SPAR. (All code for this chapter is available at evolutionary-ecology.com/data/speciesdensity.)

One function of the code was to eliminate the coverage variable. All coverage values are integers from 0 to 9. They are not abundances. So the code converted all values greater than 1 into 1. Thus the data sets became presence–absence matrices.

20.2.3 *NP*: our surrogate for *A*

If we had abundance data, we could use them as a surrogate for area. The *x*-axis would be log *N*, that is, the logarithm of the number of individuals. But we do not have abundance data. Although coverage score is indeed a rough measure of abundance, we have no information about how it scales with abundance nor even whether the quantitative meaning of a unit increase in score from 1 to 2 (say) is equivalent to one of increase from 3 to 4.

In data subsets where all plots had the same area, the number of plots, *NP*, was a perfect measure of *A* and we used it. But we also used *NP* as a surrogate for *A* in the entire data set, even though plots have six different *A* values. We did the same when analysing the plots of a single ecoregion. This is justified because we can and did accumulate plots in random order over 1000 replications per analysis. Thus we obtained SPAR for the average area of a plot. The reader should realize, however, that the area added by each additional unit of *NP* varied between analyses. It depended on the average

area of the plots in a single plot of that particular analysis. Knowing that allowed us to replace *NP* with *A* when needed.

To obtain each accumulation curve, we added plots one by one and counted the number of unique species at each step (with 1000 replications and using the WS2M software discussed in Box 20.1). Then, using linear regression, we analysed the mean values of log *S* vs log *NP* at each step to get our SPAR for that accumulation curve.

20.3 Density estimates

20.3.1 First density estimate

For our first analysis, we lumped together all 652 plots in the complete dataset regardless of their size or ecoregion. The average plot had 43.8 plant species. The result of the linear regression was log $S = 2.06 + 0.34 \log NP$. So the plant species density is 114.8 (i.e. $10^{2.06}$). Its units are not spp/area, but spp/plot$^{0.34}$. The R^2 of this SPAR is 0.96 and both its coefficients have probabilities in the region of 10^{-15}.

However, Fig. 20.2 shows that we must refine our analysis because of systematic deviation from linearity. Predicted *S* values are much too large over small *NP* and too small over larger *NP*. Thus, the very high R^2 is misleading; it comes from the fact that *NP* is on a logarithmic scale so that very few points occur on the left side, where the fit is rather bad.

In addition, we still have to deal with the lack of abundance data in plots of four different areas. We now turn to this.

20.3.2 Density estimates for subsets with a uniform plot size

Our *x* variable is *NP*, 'number of plots in the sample'. Absence of a species in a plot of 1000 m^2 may not mean the same as its absence in a plot of 200 m^2. The obvious and appropriate solution is to restrict each analysis to a set of plots of uniform area.

The set of 588 plots of 400 m^2 is the largest and that of 50 plots of 1000 m^2 is the second largest. Let us analyse them separately and see how their results compare to those of the entire set of 652 plots.

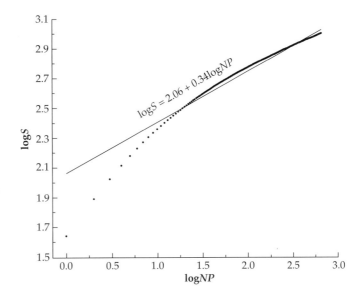

Figure 20.2   Naive estimate of plant species density in Virginia. All 652 sampling plots are included, although they have various areas and come from seven different ecoregions. Each plot is added in random order to an accumulation curve, the process is repeated 1000 times, and averages obtained. The result is a pronounced convex-upward curve with an estimated z value of 0.34 and a plant species density of 114.8 per $A^{0.34}$.

Density estimates for 400-m^2 plots

The average plot of 400 m^2 had 42.25 species. The set of 558 400-m^2 plots had 931 of the 1001 species in the entire data set. The linear regression was $\log S = 2.04 + 0.34 \log NP$, so the plant species density is 109.6 (i.e. $10^{2.04}$), almost the same as 114.8, that is, that of the entire set of 652 plots (above).

The R^2 of this SPAR is 0.96 and both its coefficients have probabilities in the region of 10^{-15} or even less.

Density estimates for 1000-m^2 plots

There were 50 plots of 1000-m^2. Together they had 551 of the 1001 species in the intire data set. The linear regression was $\log S = 1.92 + 0.50 \log NP$, so the plant species density is 82.4 (i.e. $10^{1.92}$), lower than either set that contains the 400-m^2 plots (above).

The R^2 of this SPAR is 0.98 and both its coefficients also have probabilities in the region of 10^{-15} or even less.

Despite the impressive R^2 values, however, Fig. 20.3 shows a systematic deviation of the regressions from linearity just like Fig. 20.2. Predicted S values are too large over small NP and too small over large NP, but the deviations from the regression of the 1000-m^2 plots are smaller than those of the 400-m^2 plots. That is because the 400-m^2

plots cover a much greater range of NP values and include a large number of points far to the right-hand side of the graph where the relationship is not so steep.

We confirm our explanation by reanalysing the first 50 points of the 400-m^2 results. We did not re-do the analysis; we just truncated it at 50 points. Now $\log S = 1.76 + 0.55 \log NP (R^2 = 0.98)$—a result much closer to that with the fifty 1000-m^2 plots than with the very data set from which the fifty 400-m^2 plot points came. Species density is 57.6, that is, less than that for the fifty 1000-m^2 plots, a result that seems reasonable as we should expect fewer species in a smaller plot.

The lesson of the 400- and 1000-m^2 plots

The z value of the 1000-m^2 plots was 0.50 rather than the 0.34 of the 400-m^2 plots, but the first step in calculating a species density is to raise A (or its surrogate) to the power z. So if two sets of samples come from different segments of a single curve, they will generate different z values (such as 0.50 and 0.34 above) and thus different species densities. That is not acceptable. Hence, for species densities to be meaningful, all must be founded on the same z value.

Thus, examination of the two plot areas separately has uncovered two problems:

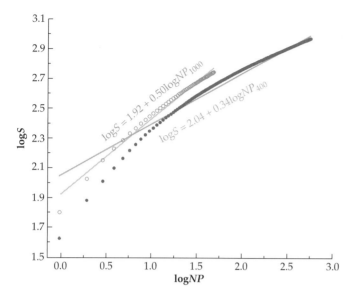

Figure 20.3   An analysis for the set of 1000-m^2 plots and another for the set of 400-m^2 plots. The 400-m^2 plots yielded results similar to those Fig. 20.2, but the 1000-m^2 plots showed a steeper z and a lower species density. The accumulation curves of both analyses retain a convex-upward shape, which leads to variable estimates of z.

- the definition of species density implicitly requires that comparisons be made between entities that share a z value
- curvature in the data points from which SPAR is obtained will lead to different estimates of species density if samples encompass different ranges of the curvature.

Yet both these issues have curvature at their heart. Curvature is a serious problem. If logarithmic data follow a curve, a z value estimated from one part of the data set will differ from a z value estimated from another part. What causes curvature and how might one remove it? That is the topic of the following section.

20.4   Curvature in SPARs

SPARs arise from four sets of processes (Rosenzweig 2003). Two of them are at work in the Virginia plant plots:

- As area grows, so does the number of habitats included in the area.
- Results from larger areas almost always contain more individuals in the cumulative sample.

Thus, when we measure the diversity of a place such as a 400-m^2 plant plot, two signals influence the result: the actual diversity and the sample size that we obtained to estimate that diversity. The

smaller the sample size, the smaller the proportion of species we discover. Unfortunately, that creates a nagging statistical issue, sample-size bias. We wish to estimate the actual diversity and to suppress the negative bias of small sample sizes. This problem affects all efforts to measure diversity and diversity density.

An accumulation curve that comes from studying one area by adding to its dataset over time reflects only its growing sample size. A SPAR based on such data is linear in logarithmic space (Rosenzweig 1995). Similarly, a SPAR from a set of areas in which one has species lists that are virtually 100% complete is also linear in logarithmic space. However, when the two processes combine to determine a data set, the result will not be linear in logarithmic space. Its diversity, log S, will grow very fast over small sample sizes because log S reflects both signals. As sample size grows, bias declines, leaving only the signal of actual growth in diversity with area. We need to remove the sample size signal as much as possible so as to lay bare the true SPAR and thus the underlying species density C.

20.5   Reducing the bias

Fisher et al. (1943) were the first to address the problem of sample-size bias. Their solution yields an index (Fisher's α) of the number of species independent of sample size. But Fisher's α does not estimate the number of species itself. It remains a powerful investigative tool, especially to discover trends in local data, but it offers no standard to use for interpretation.

Since Fisher, a number of other biologists and biometricians have addressed the sample-size problem. (In fact, it has assumed a life that is independent of its biological origins, for example Efron & Thisted 1976.) One approach, rarefaction, has treated the problem by imposing a similar bias on all results (Chapter 4). Generally speaking, rarefaction reduces the data available for comparisons by removing data from larger samples until all samples suffer equal bias. Thus, rarefaction does not so much reduce sample-size bias as surrender to it. In addition, its comparisons come from the data-poor portion of a sample, the portion whose attributes mostly reflect the bias-freighted signal and have little to do with the diversity signal.

Methods that do strive for bias reduction approach the problem in two very different ways. Some investigators work with estimators based on extrapolating S to an asymptote while others base their estimates on the frequency of scarce species.

20.5.1 Extrapolation

As sample size grows, the number of observed species rises monotonically towards an asymptote. This phenomenon is the accumulation curve itself. It is convex upward. The asymptote (or plateau) is the true number of species.

Extrapolation attempts to estimate the diversity at the plateau by fitting an appropriate equation template to the known part of the accumulation curve. Here are the minimal requirements for an appropriate template Rosenzweig et al. (2003), regardless of the values of its coefficients:

- It traverses the point (1,1) because a single individual can belong only to a single species.
- It has a positive first derivative for all sample sizes.
- It has a negative second derivative for all sample sizes.
- It has an upper asymptote.

Michaelis–Menten extrapolation
The first to suggest and use an extrapolation template was Holdridge et al. (1971). He noticed the similarity of the Michaelis–Menten formula to diversity accumulation curves. Holdridge fitted some data to this template and noted that they fit very well.

The Michaelis–Menten formula has several other names in ecology but their parameters can always be manipulated to produce a Michaelis–Menten equation of the form:

$$y = kx/(h + x)$$

For purposes of diversity estimation, Michaelis–Menten becomes:

$$S_O = SN/(h + N)$$

where S is the true number of species, S_O is the observed number of species, N is sample size (NP in our case) and h is a coefficient of curvature termed the half-saturation constant.

Michaelis–Menten satisfies all but one of the criteria for an acceptable extrapolation formula. It does not traverse the point (1,1). Nevertheless, we include Michaelis–Menten in our set of methods. When data matrices are converted from abundance to presence–absence (as we have done for the Virginia plant data), Michaelis–Menten often seems to work quite powerfully (Rosenzweig et al. 2003).

An alternative set of extrapolators
A set of extrapolation formulae that do satisfy all criteria belong to the following family:

$$S_O = S \wedge (1 - N^{-f(N)}) \tag{20.1}$$

where $f(N)$ is any positive, unbounded, monotonically increasing function of N (which again is NP in our case). As N rises towards infinity, equation 20.1 converges on S. In other words, the asymptote of equation 20.1 is S, the true diversity of the system.

We used two functions $f(N)$ in this study. We substituted them into equation 20.1 to produce two extrapolation estimators, F3 and F5:

F3 uses $f(N) = q \ln N$
F5 uses $f(N) = q N^q$.

Like Michaelis–Menton, F3 and F5 have, in no sense, been derived from first principles. They simply offer a template with the appropriate properties. Unlike MM they even traverse the point (1,1).

20.5.2 Estimators based on the frequency of scarce species

The estimates of this class of methods come from looking at the accumulated total diversity and the number of locations in which each species occurs.

Burnham and Overton (1979) introduced estimators of this type based on jack-knifing the data. They developed five different orders of the jack-knife, but they also recommended not selecting just a single order. Instead, they advocate calculating all five orders and choosing among them with certain statistical criteria. We followed their recommendation in our work.

Chao and her colleagues introduced another series of estimators (Chao 1984; Chao & Lee 1992; Chao et al. 1996). The first two have now clearly been superseded by the more recent ones. In our work, we used the incidence coverage estimator (ICE), but that is not to say we believe it to be the best one. It simply fitted the needs of our data in this case, allowed us to demonstrate the use of the Chao class of estimators, and was the most convenient to use.

All estimators in this group have the common goal of estimating the number of species in a complete sample of a defined sampling universe. In contrast, the extrapolators can also include unsampled habitats (if sampled ones are carefully arranged) (Rosenzweig et al. 2003).

We employed these bias-reducing tools and they improved the estimate of C, as the reader will see. We are not, however, trying to write the last word on the matter. No doubt there will be further advances. However, we did want to explore how one might go about the task of measuring species density in practice. We trust that future and better bias reducers will fit well into the framework that we are about to describe.

20.6 Applying bias reduction

Using WS2M (Turner et al. 2000), we obtained bias-reduced SPARs from five overlapping data

Table 20.2 Using bias-reduction estimators to generate z values, species densities (C values), and R^2 values for Virginia plants. 'Raw' signifies that no bias-reduction was used to generate that row of results. 'CAF' are the 444 plots from the Central Appalachian Forest. See text for meaning of other treatment abbreviations. Bias reduction reduces SPAR-curvatures and z-values, and increases estimated species densities.

z values	All	400s	1000s	CAF	Piedmont
Raw	0.342	0.344	0.503	0.350	0.379
ICE	0.248	0.243	0.375	0.229	0.201
B&O	0.303	0.283	0.503	0.299	0.297
F3	0.265	0.260	0.348	0.258	0.299
F5	0.218	0.210	0.248	0.204	0.257
MM	0.215	0.207	0.217	0.198	0.227

log C	All	400s	1000s	CAF	Piedmont
Raw	2.06	2.04	1.92	1.98	1.93
ICE	2.44	2.43	2.34	2.41	2.41
B&O	2.34	2.36	2.16	2.28	2.24
F3	2.35	2.34	2.30	2.29	2.19
F5	2.48	2.48	2.49	2.43	2.28
MM	2.43	2.42	2.47	2.39	2.29

R^2	All	400s	1000s	CAF	Piedmont
Raw	0.962	0.961	0.983	0.959	0.974
ICE	0.912	0.894	0.717	0.987	0.937
B&O	0.927	0.900	0.872	0.903	0.817
F3	0.986	0.985	0.995	0.984	0.988
F5	0.998	0.998	0.999	0.998	0.991
MM	1.000	0.999	0.994	0.998	0.998

sets (Table 20.2). Three are the same as previously analysed above. We took the fourth and fifth from the two ecoregions with more plots than the rest: the Central Appalachian Forest and Piedmont. The ecoregional data are already contained in the largest data set and many are also in the 400-m^2 and 1000-m^2 plots. Grouping them specially by ecoregion should avoid any heterogeneity in z values that might accompany plant association patterns in different ecoregions.

Table 20.2 reveals some reassuring conclusions. First, the bias reducers eliminated most of the deviations from linearity. In fact, the R^2 values generated by both F5 and Michaelis–Menten are remarkable. All but two are 0.998 or more. The smallest is 0.991. Figs 20.4a and c show the SPARs for two of these 10 cases and Figs 20.4b and d show two others that did not remove as much curvilinearity.

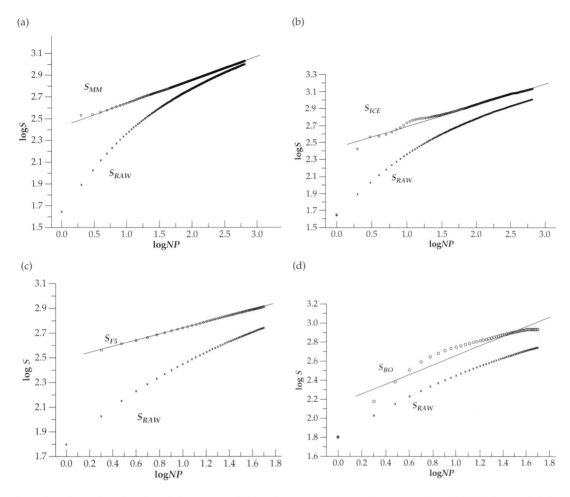

Figure 20.4 The sample-size bias of raw SPARs is reduced, which in the best cases removes most of its curvature. (a) and (b) All 652 plots are included. (c) and (d) Only the 50 plots of area 1000 m² are included. (a) Correction by Michaelis–Menten template. (b) Correction by Chao incidence coverage estimator. (c) Correction by F5 template. (d) Correction by Burnham and Overton jack-knife estimator. In each graph we also plot the raw accumulation curve for comparison.

Also reassuring was the uniform reduction of z values compared to the five uncorrected SPARs. Only the estimate from Burnham and Overton's jack-knife (0.503) is as large as that of the raw SPAR, and then only for the 1000-m² plots. Furthermore the z values produced by F5 and Michaelis–Menten (0.198–0.257) are quite similar to each other and also to what ecologists have come to expect of z values in nested samples within mainland regions (Rosenzweig 1995). Quite possibly, matrices of presence–absence will be useful for generating z estimates in ecoregions.

The log C values generated by F5 and Michaelis–Menten are also rather similar. We would perhaps be justified in concluding (for example) that the species density of plants in Central Appalachian Forest is about 257 species per (Area of plot)$^{0.2}$. (Note: $257 = 10^{2.41}$.)

20.7   Checking our results on the scale of all of Virginia

We begin by determining the area of one unit of NP. The entire Commonwealth of Virginia has

$110\,785\,\text{km}^2$. The average plot in the dataset had $442.1\,\text{m}^2$. So there are $110\,785\,000/442.1 = 262\,470$ plot units in the entire state.

Extrapolating the Michaelis–Menten estimates for all sample plots to the area of the entire state we obtain:

$$\log S = 2.43 + 0.215 \log 262470 = 3.595$$

so $S = 3936$ plant species

Extrapolating the F5 estimates, we obtain:

$$\log S = 2.48 + 0.218 \log 262470 = 3.66$$

so $S = 4585$ plant species

Virginia has 4205 known plant species. Neither the F5 estimate (4585 species) nor the Michaelis–Menten estimate (3936 species) is very far from that. We note without comment that if we use their average coefficients (2.455 and 0.2165), the result is 4248 species, only 1% different from 4205.

In short, using the extrapolation estimators the method succeeded even in the face of three serious obstacles:

- no abundance data
- disparate plot sizes
- inadequate samples of five of Virginia's seven ecoregions.

20.8   Why species density?

20.8.1   Species density as an environmental indicator

Policymakers need a reliable, efficient way to take the pulse of the environment. For this purpose, they need a very small set of environmental indicators. These indicators will not be exactly parallel to economic indicators, but they will be similar in number (about 10), similar in being general, and similar in being able to reflect a nation's overall environmental condition without necessarily enumerating all its details. Species density promises to provide practical indicators of environmental condition that policymakers will be able to use.

A committee of the NRC began work on this project in the 1990s and soon published its list of indicators, its reasons for choosing them, and its hopes to have them adopted (National Research Council 2000). But the NRC's hopes were not fulfilled.

After the NRC began its work, the Heinz Center undertook a parallel project. Unlike the NRC committee, Heinz implemented its own recommendations and began publishing widely anticipated reports on the state of the nation's environment (The H. John Heinz III Center for Science 2008). Perhaps as a cost of getting the necessary cooperation of environmental professionals all over the country, the Heinz list of indicators is roughly 10 times as long as that of the NRC, so its reports are thick, data-rich, complex books rather than the one-page summary-style reports envisioned by the NRC committee. Although there is much overlap between the two lists, they differ substantially in the ways that they handle and report matters associated with biological diversity.

NRC's indicators include two that are based on species density and use the same definition of it that we use here, then they compare densities to a standard. The standard is the density revealed by the taxon-specific SPAR of the natural landscape in the ecoregion.

NRC's strategy is to estimate C for a particular taxon in an unexploited (read 'natural') habitat of an ecoregion, then to do the same for one type of land use. Let p signify pristine habitat and i any land use. Now consider the NRC indicator for native species density. C in the unexploited habitat, C_p, will be the expected value of native species density. C in the utilized habitat, C_i, will be the observed native species density. The NRC indicator is simply C_i/C_p.

Thus, the diversity-density indicators of the NRC explore new ground. This creates problems for their implementation. It will not be immediately clear to professionals how to measure their components, how to combine them, or how to interpret them. In addition, the NRC report was published with a serious typographical error in the main formula for the most important indicator, an error which makes this indicator not just irrelevant, but impossible even to calculate.

Although the error was corrected in a subsequent publication (Rosenzweig 2004), that publication also fails to address the problems of implementation. This chapter has tried to explain how to calculate diversity density—what data need to be collected, what problems those data will present, and how the data may be processed.

One might fairly ask whether an indicator that requires so much initial effort has much value. We believe it does for several reasons.

- There is nothing inherently difficult about the indicator. Instead, it relies on one of ecology's most familiar rules: larger areas have more species. Thus the initial familiarization period will probably be followed by a sense of comfort on the part of professionals.
- Software is currently available to support implementation.
- The indicator closely parallels those in the River Invertebrate Prediction and Classification System (RIVPACS) family (Moss et al. 1987; Wright 2000) now in use in the UK, Australia, Canada, New Zealand, Sweden and the USA (Hawkins et al. 2000), but RIVPACS is much more labour intensive and so far has been demonstrated and used only in freshwater habitats. In contrast, the NRC indicator builds on patterns found in every habitat.

The RIVPACS diversity indicator parallels the NRC indicator because RIVPACS is the ratio of the number of species found in a place to the number of species expected to be found there. In other words, the indicator is the ratio <observed/expected>, O/E. The NRC indicator uses this idea exactly.

However, the RIVPACS determines E with detailed examinations of the habitat distributions of each species. This is hard work, requiring expert attention, the measurement of many habitat variables, and the separate analysis of each species' habitat distribution with respect to those habitat variables.

In contrast, the NRC indicator relies on a well-established shortcut, the species–area relationship.

20.8.2   Species density as a topic of study

People—including ecologists—do like to make comparisons. Being able to state, with some confidence, that the butterflies (say) of ecoregion A have a higher species density than those of ecoregion B will surely please some of us. Being able to conclude that a planned change in the style of human use in ecoregion X has improved its species density of birds (say) will please even more of us.

Having a working method for estimating C, we will be encouraged to search for C patterns among taxa, among biogeographical provinces, and among ecoregions. We know already that, unlike z, C varies a lot. We are already certain that (say) beetles of the Neotropics have a denser diversity than plants of New Zealand, but with our new quantitative tool, we should be able to make much more refined and interesting distinctions. How does aridity or productivity—or any other environmental property of an ecoregion—influence its C value? What characteristics might predispose a taxon to unusual C values? Do C values behave similarly in different biogeographical provinces, and so on? If we do find patterns, will we not be inspired to uncover their explanations? C opens a new book of macroecological investigations.

20.9   Key points

- To account for the curvature of SPAR (species–area curves), species density C is defined as $C = S/A^z$, where S is the number of species, A is the area sampled, and z is the curvature of SPAR.
- All values of S on a single SPAR have the same C value.
- SPARs from raw counts of species reflect two signals: negative sample-size bias and true increase in S with A.
- Bias reducers straighten SPARs if those bias reducers rely on extrapolation of S to an asymptote.
- The straightened SPARs yield a reasonable estimate of the total S in an area that can be considerably larger than the area in which the SPAR data were obtained.
- C is a useful indicator of environmental condition and an interesting property for basic research.

Acknowledgements

Thanks to the Virginia Natural Heritage Program, Virginia   Department   of   Conservation   and

Recreation, Division of Natural Heritage for a copy of and permission to work with their vegetation plot database, and to Anne Marsh, Director, Observation and Understanding Programs, The H. John Heinz III Center for Science, Economics and Environment for help in locating and accessing it. Thanks to the Heinz Center also for supporting part of the analysis work. Finally, thanks for useful criticism of the manuscript from John Hall, Program Manager, Sustainable Infrastructure, SERDP/ESTCP, and from Brian McGill, School of Natural Resources, University of Arizona.

PART VI
Conclusions

CHAPTER 21

Conclusions

Brian J. McGill and Anne E. Magurran

'A society is defined not only by what it creates, but by what it refuses to destroy.'

—*John Sawhill, former president/CEO of The Nature Conservancy*

As already reviewed in the Foreword and Chapter 1, measuring biodiversity could not be more urgent or important. Diversity is being lost at a rate orders of magnitude higher than baseline 'natural' extinctions (Millenium Ecosystem Assessment 2005). Society is concerned enough about this to band together and commit to preventing the loss of biodiversity with concrete goals by 2010 (the United Nations Convention on Biodiversity (CBD); available at http://www.cbd.int/convention/convention.shtml). The CBD specifies what to measure (biodiversity) but does not specify exactly how to measure it. This presumably is the job of ecologists such as those reading this book.

Something not really recognized in the CBD but evidenced by this book is that the measurement of biodiversity is an active area of research—it is not a static technique that is well understood. In her 2004 book *Measuring Biodiversity*, one of us (Anne Magurran) surveyed the field of biodiversity measurement in five core chapters (excluding introduction and conclusions) but predicted that measurements of β diversity, functional diversity, phylogenetic diversity and genetic diversity would see rapid growth. This 2010 book on measuring biodiversity, albeit slightly different in intent and audience, confirms these predictions. In comparison, the present book has 14 core chapters and another five chapters of specific applications. The additional chapters include the prophesied topics as well as several unforeseen topics.

In this book, and in the literature in general, we identify the following as some important trends in recent biodiversity research:

1. **Synthetic frameworks:** One way to resolve the proliferation of different measures of biodiversity is to find the underlying mathematical unity that ties together many different approaches. The use of Hill numbers (Hill 1973) to join together many different measures of evenness and diversity partitioning as described and extended by Jost et al (Chapter 6) is one example. Information and variance views of evenness given by Maurer and McGill (Chapter 5) is another.

2. **Special cases:** It should not be overlooked that the enormous diversity of the tree of life itself presents challenges. Different groups of organisms are more or less amenable to the standard paradigm of field-based censuses performed by the human eye on a community that is well defined in space and time. Different taxonomic groups and counting conditions require modified methods (Chapters 16 and 19).

3. **Statistical approach:** The recognition (Smith & Wilson 1996; Etienne 2005; Green & Plotkin 2007) that even the data that come out of traditional biotic censuses on traditional groups of organisms (e.g. birds, trees, fish) are not 'the reality' but an approximation of reality that needs appropriate statistical treatment is growing (Chapters 2, 3, 5, 9 and 10).

4. **Spatial/temporal context:** Biodiversity changes over time and space. This is part of what makes biodiversity fascinating. Quantifying this and placing biodiversity into its spatiotemporal framework is increasingly important. This parallels the growing importance of space in ecology broadly, where we are beginning to deal with

the fact that systems are not closed (Magurran & Henderson 2003; McGill 2003a; Zillio & Condit 2007) and that it is a mistake to study points in isolation. Accordingly, biodiversity studies increasingly are exploring the relationships in biodiversity between points in space or time (e.g. Chapters 7, 11, 12 and 20).

5. **Comparative approach:** We would argue that many biodiversity measures are most meaningful not in an absolute sense (what does a Simpson evenness of 0.75 mean) but rather become meaningful mostly in a comparative sense (e.g. disturbed sites have lower evenness) (McGill et al. 2007; Chapter 9). Kempton and Taylor (1974) gave us a simple statistical tool to identify methods with maximum discriminatory power and Gray (1979) showed the efficacy of this approach for applied problems decades ago, but uptake has been slow. We are starting to see movement towards using biodiversity metrics in a comparative fashion that makes them increasingly useful in an applied context (Chapters 9, 10, 17, and 18).

6. **Non-species-centric measures:** The study of the distribution and abundance of species has been a cornerstone of ecology (Krebs 1972; Andrewartha & Birch 1984), but as the limits of such an approach have become apparent (Lawton 1999) ecologists are increasingly looking elsewhere for meaningful assessments of diversity that are not species centric (Webb et al. 2002; McGill et al. 2006b). This distinction is implicit in the organization of this book, with several non-species-specific measures emerging (Chapters 13, 14 and 15).

7. **Continued emphasis and education on the most basic measures:** Because of the societal importance of biodiversity, ecologists should not lose the simple, intuitive ideas of biodiversity just because more complex approaches exist. Specifically, we must continue to emphasize and educate on the proper use of such basic aspects of biodiversity as species richness (Chapter 4) and the existence of many rare species (Chapter 8).

8. **Process based:** One trend that we haven't seen but would like to see is a greater tie between processes that control biodiversity and the metrics that measure biodiversity. Nearly all the metrics described in this book are basically descriptive in nature, and if they tie to any process at all it is a grossly oversimplified null process such as Poisson spatial randomness (Chapters 11 and 12). Aspects of biodiversity as distinct as β diversity over space, species abundance distributions, and species–area relationships are being unified under quantitative predictive theories (Hubbell 2001; Harte 2008; Morlon et al. 2008; McGill 2010). This suggests that there may be key parameters in these models that could at once subsume a panoply of metrics and provide metrics that are in some sense more fundamental. We hope that these types of measures will be identified.

Comparing to the last book on biodiversity measurement, reviewing the eight trends listed above, and noticing the well over 100 metrics of biodiversity described in this book all make it inescapable that the toolkit for measuring biodiversity has become bigger, more sophisticated, and more complex over time. And it will continue to get even bigger and more sophisticated and complex. Is bigger better? The honest answer is, 'it depends.' It depends on at least three factors, which are covered in the next three paragraphs.

On one hand, it is natural and good that as the field of biodiversity studies matures, it will become more refined and nuanced in its ability to measure biodiversity. The Convention on Biological Diversity (CBD) defines biodiversity broadly: ' "biological diversity" means the variability among living organisms from all sources including, inter alia, terrestrial, marine and other aquatic ecosystems and the ecological complexes of which they are part; this includes diversity within species, between species and of ecosystems.' It would be odd if scientists had a more simplistic approach to biodiversity than politicians and were unable to measure all the aspects and nuances described in the CBD. Moreover, a nuanced view of biodiversity allows the choice of measures that are appropriate for given questions. For example, the effects of biodiversity on ecosystem function are probably more related to measures of functional diversity than species richness (Tilman et al. 1997b), but the resilience to successfully respond to long-term change probably would depend most on genetic diversity and phylogenetic diversity.

On the other hand, bigger and more complex is not good if it is a consequence of laziness. Specifically, if there is no pruning, no rejection and removal of failed attempts, then it is certain that much of the current large complex edifice of measuring biodiversity should not be there. For example, in the field of species abundance distributions, MacArthur proposed the broken-stick model in 1957 (MacArthur 1957) and already by 1960 (MacArthur 1960) had clearly stated in print that he considered the model a failed attempt that should not receive further attention. However, it continues to be studied (Wilson 1993) and taught in basic textbooks (Morin 1999; Begon et al. 2006). Similarly, a number of authors have attempted to compare the relative performance of different measures, especially evenness measures (Smith & Wilson 1996), but the rejected measures continue to be popular. It seems unavoidable to conclude that ecologists have not done a good job of simplifying as we go. Many of the chapters in this book have performed rigorous studies comparing different approaches and measures leading to specific recommendations about what should be used and not used going forward.

The above two 'it depends' qualifications are the traditional give and take of science—continuously expanding the frontiers while hopefully showing progress through identifying ideas that work and don't work. However, for better and worse, ecologists' efforts to measure biodiversity do not play out solely on the scientific stage. Societal interest in and policy debates over how to measure biodiversity and what aspects of biodiversity are important can be found everywhere. Given this, we must avoid the common mistake made by scientists of revelling in our ability to achieve complexity and subtlety. We must be unmistakably clear that despite internal debate and ever-increasing complexity, there is a clear and meaningful concept of biodiversity. Right now, today, we can make definitive statements about the fact that biodiversity

is decreasing at historically unprecedented rates (Millennium Ecosystem Assessment 2005), that some places have more biodiversity than others (Pianka 1989; Reid 1998), that certain policies and management practices maintain biodiversity better than others (Bawa & Seidler 1998; Tscharntke et al. 2005), and that biodiversity has benefits for society (Daily et al. 1997; Loreau et al. 2002). The overview of this book (Chapter 1) invoked the analogy of blind people trying to understand an elephant and returning a complex, multifaceted answer, which is accurate, but at the same time it seems unlikely that the people in the room were unaware that there was a big impressive thing also in the room! This ability to be multifaceted while not losing sight of the basic storyline must be how we approach the measurement of biodiversity going forward when all eyes of society are on us.

In conclusion, in addition to the eight specific research agendas identified above, future work on biodiversity needs to be guided by broader principles: (i) continue to refine our ability to measure different facets of biodiversity even while (ii) pruning the failed ideas and (iii) keeping firm the reality and measurability of biodiversity to the general public.

This book set out to provide an accessible description of the frontiers of measuring biodiversity. We hope the reader has found the journey as exciting, inspiring, and important as we do. We end, as we began, by quoting Charles Darwin's *On the Origin of Species* (1859); specifically we quote his last sentence which is a meditation on whether scientific understanding of biodiversity increases or decreases the ability of the planet's diverse creatures to inspire awe in us. Although Darwin speaks of the improved understanding of evolution, we would suggest his conclusion applies to the improved measurement of biodiversity as well.

> 'There is grandeur in this view of life, with its several powers, having been originally breathed into a few forms or into one; and that, whilst this planet has gone cycling on according to the fixed law of gravity, from so simple a beginning endless forms most beautiful and most wonderful have been, and are being, evolved.'

References

Abbot, I. (1983) The meaning of z in species/area regression and the study of species turnover in island biogeography. Oikos, 41, 385–390.

Abella, P., Bilton, N. D., Millan, A., Sanchez-Fernandez, D., & Ramsay, P. M. (2006) Can taxonomic distinctness assess anthropogenic impacts in inland waters? A case study from a Mediterranean river basin. Freshwater Biology, 51, 1744–1756.

Abrams, P. A. (2001) A world without competition. Nature, 412, 858–859.

Adler, P. B. (2004) Neutral models fail to reproduce observed species-area and species-time relationships in Kansas grasslands. Ecology, 85, 1265–1272.

Adler, P. B. & Lauenroth, W. K. (2003) The power of time: spatiotemporal scaling of species diversity. Ecology Letters, 6, 749–756.

Adler, P. B., White, E. P., Lauenroth, W. K., Kaufman, D. M., Rassweiler, A., & Rusak, J. A. (2005) Evidence for a general species-time-area relationship. Ecology, 86, 2032–2039.

Agosti, D., Majer, J., Alonso, E., & Schultz, T. R. (eds) (2000) Ants: Standard Methods for Measuring and Monitoring Biodiversity. Smithsonian Institution Press, Washington, DC.

Akaike, H. (1973) Information theory and an extension of the maximum likelihood principle. International Symposium on Information Theory, 2, 267–281.

Akçakaya, H. R., Radeloff, V. C., Mladenoff, D. J., & He, H. S. (2004) Integrating landscape and metapopulation modeling approaches: viability of the sharp-tailed grouse in a dynamic landscape. Conservation Biology, 18, 526–537.

Albrecht, M., Duelli, P., Schmidm, B., & Muller, C. B. (2007) Interaction diversity within quantified insect food webs in restored and adjacent intensively managed meadows. Journal of Animal Ecology, 76, 1015–1025.

Alfaro, M. E., Santini, F., Brock, C., Alamillo, H., Dornburg, A., Rabosky, D. L., Carnevale, G., & Harmon, L. J. (2009) Nine exceptional radiations plus high turnover explain species diversity in jawed vertebrates. Proceedings of the National Academy of Sciences, 106, 13410–13414.

Alldredge, M. W., Pollock, K. H., Simons, T. R., & Shriner, S. A. (2007) Multiple-species analysis of point count data: a more parsimonious modelling framework. Journal of Applied Ecology, 44, 281–290.

Allen, A. P., & E. P. White. 2003. Effects of range size on species–area relationships. Evolutionary Ecology Research, 5, 493–499.

Allen, B., Kon, M., & Bar-Yam, Y. (2009) A new phylogenetic diversity measure generalizing the Shannon index and its application to phyllostomid bats. The American Naturalist, 174, 236–243.

Alonso, D. & McKane, A. J. (2004) Sampling Hubbell's neutral theory of biodiversity. Ecology Letters, 7, 901–910.

Alroy, J. (1992) Conjunction among taxonomic distributions and the Miocene mammalian biochronology of the Great Plains. Paleobiology, 18, 326–343.

Alroy, J. (1994) Appearance event ordination: a new biochronologic method. Paleobiology, 20, 191–207.

Alroy, J. (1996) Constant extinction, constrained diversification, and uncoordinated stasis in North American mammals. Palaeogeography, Palaeoclimatology, Palaeoecology, 127, 285–311.

Alroy, J. (2000) New methods for quantifying macroevolutionary patterns and processes. Paleobiology, 26, 707–733.

Alroy, J., Marshall, C. R., Bambach, R. K., Bezusko, K., Foote, M., Fürsich, F. T., Hansen, T. A., Holland, S. M., Ivany, L. C., Jablonski, D., Jacobs, D. K., Jones, D. C., Kosnik, M. A., Lidgard, S., Low, S., Miller, A. I., Novack-Gottshall, P. M., Olszewski, T. D., Patzkowsky, M. E., Raup, D. M., Roy, K., John, J., Sepkoski, J., Sommers, M. G., Wagner, P. J., & Webber, A. (2001) Effects of sampling standardization on estimates of Phanerozoic marine diversity. Proceedings of the National Academy of Sciences USA, 98, 6261–6266.

Alroy, J., Aberhan, M., Bottjer, D. J., Foote, M., Fürsich, F. T., Harries, P. J., Hendy, A. J. W., Holland, S. M.,

Ivany, L. C., Kiessling, W., Kosnik, M. A., Marshall, C. R., McGowan, A. J., Miller, A. I., Olszewski, T. D., Patzkowsky, M. E., Peters, S. E., Villier, L., Wagner, P. J., Bonuso, N., Borkow, P. S., Brenneis, B., Clapham, M. E., Fall, L. M., Ferguson, C. A., Hanson, V. L., Krug, A. Z., Layou, K. M., Leckey, E. H., Nürnberg, S., Powers, C. M., Sessa, J. A., Simpson, C., Tomasovych, A., & Visaggi, C. C. (2008) Phanerozoic trends in the global diversity of marine invertebrates. Science, 321, 97–100.

Altermatt, F., Baumeyer, A., & Ebert, D. (2009) Experimental evidence for male biased flight-to-light behavior in two moth species. Entomologia experimentalis et applicata, 130, 259–265.

Altschul, S. F. & Lipman, D. J. (1990) Equal animals. Nature, 348, 493–494.

Alvarez, L. W., Alvarez, W., Asaro, F., & Michel H. V. (1980) Extraterrestrial cause for the Cretaceous–Tertiary extinction. Science, 208, 1095–1108.

Amann, R. I., Ludwig, W., & Schleifer, K. H. (1995) Phylogenetic identification and in-situ detection of individual microbial-cells without cultivation. Microbiological Reviews, 59, 143–169.

Amaro, A. M., Chamorro, D., Seeger, M., Arredondo, R., Peirano, I., & Jerez, C. A. (1991) Effect of external pH perturbations on invivo protein-synthesis by the acidophilic bacterium thiobacillus-ferrooxidans. Journal of Bacteriology, 173, 910–915.

Anderson, S. (1977) Geographic ranges of North American terrestrial mammals. American Museum novitates, 2629, 1–15.

Anderson, N. H. & Sedell, J. R. (1979) Detritus processing by macroinvertebrates. Annual Review of Entomology, 24, 351–357.

Anderson, M. J., Ellingsen, K. E., & McArdle, B. H. (2006) Multivariate dispersion as a measure of beta diversity. Ecology Letters, 9, 683–693.

Andrewartha, H. G. & Birch, L. C. (1954) The Distribution and Abundance of Animals. University of Chicago Press, Chicago.

Andrewartha, H. G. & Birch, L. C. (1984) The Ecological Web: More on the Distribution and Abundance of Animals. University of Chicago Press, Chicago.

Angilletta, M. J. (2009) Thermal Adaptation. A Theoretical and Empirical Synthesis. Oxford University Press, Oxford.

Anonymous (1999) The World at Six Billion. United Nations Population Division, New York.

Anscombe, F. J. (1950) Sampling theory of the negative binomial and logarithmic series distributions. Biometrika, 37, 358–382.

Anselin, L. (1995) Local indicators of spatial association-LISA. Geographical Analysis, 27, 93–115.

Ansorge, W. J. (2009) Next-generation DNA sequencing techniques. New Biotechnology, 25, 195–203.

Anthony, K. R. N., Hoogenboom, M. O., Maynard, J. A., Grottoli, A. G., & Middlebrook, R. (2009) Energetics approach to predicting mortality risk from environmental stress: a case study of coral bleaching. Functional Ecology, 23, 539–550.

Arita, H. T., Christen, J. A, Rodríguez, P., & Soberón, J. (2008) Species diversity and distribution in presence-absence matrices: mathematical relationships and biological implications. The American Naturalist, 172, 519–532.

Arntz, W. E. & Rumohr, H. (1982) An experimental study of macrobenthic colonization and succession, and the importance of seasonal variation in temperate latitudes. Journal of Experimental Marine Biology and Ecology, 64, 17–46.

Barker, G. M. (2002) Phylogenetic diversity: a quantitative framework for measurement of priority and achievement in biodiversity conservation. Biological Journal of the Linnean Society, 76, 165–194.

Baselga, A., Jiménez-Valverde, A., & Niccolini, G. (2007) A multiple-site similarity measure independent of richness. Biology Letters, 3, 642–645.

Bawa K. S. & Seidler R. (1998) Natural forest management and conservation of biodiversity in tropical forests. Conservation Biology, 12, 46–55.

Bayley P. B. & Herendeen R. A. (2000) The efficiency of a seine net. Transactions of the American Fisheries Society, 129, 901–923.

Bazzaz, F. A. (1975) Plant species diversity in old-field successional ecosystems in southern Illinois. Ecology, 56, 485–488.

Beals, E. W. (1984) Bray–Curtis ordination: An effective strategy for analysis of multivariate ecological data. Advances in Ecological Research, 15, 1–55.

Begon, M., Harper, J. L., & Townsend, C. R. (2006) Ecology: From Individuals to Ecosystems, 4th edn. Sinauer Associates, Sunderland, MA.

Beja, O., Spudich, E. N., Spudich, J. L., Leclerc, M., & DeLong, E. F. (2001) Proteorhodopsin phototrophy in the ocean. Nature, 411, 786–789.

Bell, G. (2000) The distribution of abundance in neutral communities. The American Naturalist, 155, 606–617.

Bell, G. (2001) Neutral macroecology. Science, 293, 2413–2418.

Bell, G. (2003) The interpretation of biological surveys. Proceedings of the Royal Society London, 270, 2531–2542.

Bender, E. A., Case, T. J., & Gilpin, M. E. (1984) Perturbation experiments in community ecology: theory and practice. Ecology, 65, 1–13.

Ben-Moshe, A., Dayan, T., & Simberloff, D. (2001) Convergence in morphological patterns and community organization between Old and New World rodent guilds. The American Naturalist, 158, 484–495.

Bent, S. J., Pierson, J. D., & Forney, L. J. (2007) Measuring species richness based on microbial community fingerprints: The emperor has no clothes. Applied and Environmental Microbiology, 73, 2399–2399.

Berger, W. H. & Parker, F. L. (1970) Diversity of planktonic foraminifera in deep-sea sediments. Science, 168, 1345.

Bersier, L. F. & Sugihara, G. (1997) Species abundance patterns: the problem of testing stochastic abundance models. Journal of Animal Ecology, 66, 179–774.

Bettoli, P. W. & Maceina, M. J. (1996) Sampling with toxicants. In: Fisheries Techniques, Murphy, B. R. & Willis, D. W. (eds). American Fisheries Society Bethesda, MD, pp. 303–333.

Bhaya, D., Grossman, A. R., Steunou, A.-S., Khuri, N., Cohan, F. M., Hamamura, N., Melendrez, M. C., Bateson, M. M., Ward, D. M., & Heidelberg, J. F. (2007) Population level functional diversity in a microbial community revealed by comparative genomic and metagenomic analyses. The ISME Journal, 1, 703–713.

Bianchi, G., Gislason, H., Graham, K., Hill, L., Jin, X., Koranteng, K., Manickchand-Heileman, S., Paya, I., Sainsbury, K., Sanchez,F., & Zwanenburg, K. (2000) Impact of fishing on size composition and diversity of demersal fish communities. ICES Journal of Marine Science, 57, 558–571.

Bianchi, F., Booij, C. J. H., & Tscharntke, T. (2006) Sustainable pest regulation in agricultural landscapes: a review on landscape composition, biodiversity and natural pest control. Proceedings of the Royal Society London B, 273, 1715–1727.

Bibby, C. J. (1999) Making the most of birds as environmental indicators. Ostrich, 70, 81–88.

Biggs, R., Carpenter, S. R., & Brock, W. A. (2009) Turning back from the brink: detecting an impending regime shift in time to avert it. Proceedings of the National Academy of Sciences USA, 106, 826–831.

Bivand, R. S., Pebesma, E. J., & Gómez-Rubio, V. (2008) Applied spatial data analysis with R. Springer, Düsseldorf.

Blackburn, T. M. & Gaston, K. J. (1998) Some methodological issues in macroecology. The American Naturalist, 151, 68–83.

Blackburn, T. M., Cassey, P., & Gaston, K. J. (2006) Variations on a theme: sources of heterogeneity in the form of the interspecific relationship between abundance and distribution. Journal of Animal Ecology, 75, 1426–1439.

Blake, J. & Loiselle, B. (2000) Diversity of birds along an elevational gradient in the Cordillera Central, Costa Rica. The Auk, 117, 663–686.

Blaxter, M., Mann, J., Chapman, T., Thomas, F., Whitton, C., Floyd, R., & Eyualem-Abebe (2005) Defining operational taxonomic units using DNA barcode data. Philosophical Transactions of the Royal Society London B, 360, 1935–1943.

Blow, M. J., Zhang, T., Woyke, T., Speller, C. F., Krivoshapkin, A., Yang, D. Y., Derevianko, A., & Rubin, E. M. (2008) Identification of ancient remains through genomic sequencing. Genome Research, 18, 1347–1353.

Bockstaller, C. & Girardin, P. (2003) How to validate environmental indicators. Agricultural Systems, 76, 639–653.

Boik, R. J. (2004) Commentary on: Why Likelihood? In: The Nature of Scientific Evidence: Statistical, Philisophical, and Empirical considerations, Taper, M. L. & Lele, S. R. (eds). University of Chicago Press, Chicago, pp. 167–180.

Bonar, S. A. & Hubert, W. A. (2002) Standard sampling of inland fish: Benefits, challenges, and a call for action. Fisheries, 27, 10–16.

Bonar, S. A., Thomas, G. L., Thiesfeld, S. L., & Pauley, G. B. (1993) Effect of triploid grass carp on the aquatic macrophyte community of Devils Lake, Oregon. North American Journal of Fisheries Management, 13, 757–765.

Bonar, S. A., Divens, M., & Bolding, B. (1997) Methods for sampling the distribution and abundance of bull trout and Dolly Varden. Washington Department of Fish and Wildlife, Fish Management Program, Inland Fisheries Investigations, Resource Assessment Division, Olympia, WA.

Bonar, S. A., Hubert, W. A., & Willis, D. W. (2009a) The North American freshwater fish standard sampling project: Improving fisheries communication. Fisheries, 34, 340–344.

Bonar, S. A., Hubert, W. A., & Willis, D. W. (2009b) Standard methods for sampling North American freshwater fishes. American Fisheries Society, Bethesda.

Bonham, C. D. (1989) Measurements for terrestrial vegetation. Wiley, New York.

Borcard, D., Legendre, P., & Drapeau, P. (1992) Partialling out the spatial component of ecological variation. Ecology, 5, 1045–1055.

Borchers, D. L., Buckland, S. T., & Zucchini, W. (2002) Estimating animal abundance: closed populations. Springer, London.

Borregaard, M. K. & Rahbek, C. (2006) Prevalence of intraspecific relationships between range size and abundance in Danish birds. Diversity & Distributions, 12, 417–422.

Boswell, M. T. & Patil, G. P. (1970) Chance mechanisms generating the negative binomial distribution. In: Random Counts in Scientific Work, Vol 1, Patil, G. P. (ed). Pennsylvania State, University Press, University Park, pp. 3–22.

Botta-Dukát, Z. (2005) Rao's quadratic entropy as a measure of functional diversity based on multiple traits. Journal of Vegetation Science, 16, 33–540.

Boulinier, T., Nichols, J., Sauer, J., Hines, J., & Pollock, K. (1998) Estimating species richness: the importance of heterogeneity in species detectability. Ecology, 79, 1018–1028.

Bowring, S. A., Grotzinger, J. P., Isachsen, C. E., Knoll, A. H., Pelechaty, S. M., & Kolosov, P. (1993) Calibrating rates of early Cambrian evolution. Science, 261, 1293–1298.

Bray, J. R. & Curtis, J. T. (1957) An ordination for the upland forest communities of southern Wisconsin. Ecological Monographs, 27, 325–349.

Brewer, A. & Williamson, M. (1994) A new relationship for rarefaction. Biodiversity and Conservation, 3, 373–379.

Brook, B., Sodhi, N., & Ng, P. (2003) Catastrophic extinctions follow deforestation in Singapore. Nature, 424, 420–426.

Brose, U., Martinez, N. D., & Williams, R. J. (2003) Estimating species richness: sensitivity to sample coverage and insensitivity to spatial patterns. Ecology, 84, 2364–2377.

Brown, J. H. (1987) Variation in desert rodent guilds: patterns, processes, and scales. In: Organization of Communities: Past and Present, Gee, J. H. R. & Giller, P. S. (eds). Blackwell, London, pp. 185–203.

Brown, J. H. (1999) Macroecology: progress and prospect. Oikos, 87, 3–14.

Brown, J. H. & Kodric-Brown, A. (1977) Turnover rates in insular biogeography: effect of immigration on extinction. Ecology, 58, 445–449.

Brown, J. H. & West, G. B. (2000) Scaling in Biology. Oxford University Press, Oxford.

Brown, J. H., Mehlman, D. H., & Stevens, G. C. (1995) Spatial variation in abundance. Ecology, 76, 2028–2043.

Buckland, S. T., Anderson, D. R., Burnham, K. P., Laake, J. L., Borchers, D. L., & Thomas, L. (2001) Introduction to Distance Sampling. Oxford University Press, Oxford.

Buckland, S. T., Anderson, D. R., Burnham, K. P., Laake, J. L., Borchers, D. L., & Thomas, L. (2004) Advanced Distance Sampling. OUP, Oxford.

Buckland, S. T., Magurran, A. E., Green, R. E., & Fewster, R. M. (2005) Monitoring change in biodiversity through composite indices. Philosophical Transactions of the Royal London B, 360, 243–254.

Buckley, L. B. & Jetz, W. (2008) Linking global turnover of species and environments. Proceedings of the National Academy of Sciences. USA, 105, 17836–17841.

Buckley-Beason, V. A., Johnson, W. E., Nash, W. G., Stanyon, R., Menninger, J. C., Driscoll, C. A., Howard, J., Bush, M., Page, J. E., Roelke, M. E., Stone, G., Martelli, P. P., Wen, C., Ling, L., Duraisingam, R. K., Lam, P. V., O'Brien, S. J. (2006) Molecular evidence for species-level distinctions in clouded leopards. Current Biology, 16, 2371–2376.

Bulla, L. (1994) An index of evenness and its associated diversity measure. Oikos, 70, 167–171.

Bulmer, M. G. (1974) Fitting Poisson Lognormal Distribution to species-abundance data. Biometrics, 30, 101–110.

Bunge, J., Epstein, S. S., & Peterson, D. G. (2006) Comment on 'Computational improvements reveal great bacterial diversity and high metal toxicity in soil'. Science, 313, 918.

Burnham, K. P. & Anderson, D. R. (1998) Model Selection and Inference, a Practical Information-Theoretic Approach. Springer, New York.

Burnham, K. P. & Anderson, D. R. (2002) Model Selection and Inference: A Practical Information-Theoretic Approach, 2nd edn. Springer, New York.

Burnham, K. P. & Overton. W. S. (1979) Robust estimation of population size when capture probabilities vary among animals. Ecology, 60, 927–936.

Bush, A. & Bambach, R. (2004) Did alpha diversity increase during the Phanerozoic? Lifting the veils of taphonomic, latitudinal, and environmental biases in the study of paleocommunities. Journal of Geology, 112, 625–642.

Butler, B. J. & Chazdon, R. L. (1998) Species richness, spatial variation, and abundance of the soil seed bank of a secondary tropical rain forest. Biotropica, 30, 214–222.

Buzas, M. A. & Hayek, L. -A. C. (1996) Biodiversity resolution: an integrated approach. Biodiversity Letters, 3, 40–43.

Buzas, M. A. & Hayek, L. -A. C. (1998) SHE Analysis for biofacies identification. Journal of Foraminiferal Research, 28, 233–239.

Buzas, M. A., Koch, C. F., Culver, S. J., & Sohl, N. F. (1982) On the distribution of species occurrence. Paleobiology, 8, 143–150.

Byrd, I. B. (1973) Homer Scott Swingle, 1902–1973. Wildlife Society Bulletin, 1, 157–159.

Cadotte, M. W., Cardinale, B. J., & Oakley, T. H. (2008) Evolutionary history and the effect of biodiversity on plant productivity. Proceedings of the National Academy of Sciences. USA, 105, 17012–17017.

Cadotte, M. W., Cavender-Bares, J., Tilman, D., & Oakley, T. H. (2009) Using phylogenetic, functional, and trait diversity to understand patterns of plant community productivity. PLoS One, 4, e5695.

Cadotte, M. W., Davies, T. J., Regetz, J., Kembel, S. W., Clevand, E., & Oakley, T. (2010) Phylogenetic diversity metrics for ecological communities: integrating species richness, abundance and evolutionary history. Ecology Letters, 13(1), 96–105.

Cam, E., Nichols, J., Hines, J., Sauer, J., Alpizar-Jara, R., & Flather, C. (2002) Disentangling sampling and ecological explanations underlying species-area relationships. Ecology, 83, 1118–1130.

Camargo, J. A. (1993) Must dominance increase with the number of subordinate species in competitive interactions? Journal of Theoretical Biology, 161, 537–542.

Cardinale, B. J., Palmer, M. A., & Collins, S. L. (2002) Species diversity enhances ecosystem functioning through interspecific facilitation. Nature, 415, 426–429.

Cardinale, M., Brusetti, L., Quatrini, P., Borin, S., Puglia, A. M., Rizzi, A., Zanardini, E., Sorlini, C., Corselli, C., & Daffonchio, D. (2004) Comparison of different primer sets for use in automated ribosomal intergenic spacer analysis of complex bacterial communities. Applied and Environmental Microbiology, 70, 6147–6156.

Carroll, C. (2006) Interacting effects of climate change, landscape conversion, and harvest on carnivore populations at the range margin: marten and lynx in the northern Appalachians. Conservation Biology, 21, 1092–1104.

Caruso, T. & Migliorini, M. (2006) A new formulation of the geometric series with applications to oribatid (Acari, Oribatida) species assemblages from human-disturbed Mediterranean areas. Ecological Modelling, 195, 402–406.

Casas, F., Mougeot, F., Viñuela, J., & Bretagnolle, V. (2009) Effects of hunting on the behaviour and spatial distribution of farmland birds: importance of hunting-free refuges in agricultural areas. Animal Conservation, 12, 346–354.

Castoe, T. A., Poole, A. W., Gu, W., Jason de Koning, A. P., Daza, J. M., Smith, E. N., & Pollock, D. D. (2009) Rapid identification of thousands of copperhead snake (*Agkistrodon contortrix*) microsatellite loci from modest amounts of 454 shotgun genome sequence. *Molecular Ecology Resources*, 341–347.

Cavender-Bares, J., Ackerly, D. A., Baum, D., & Bazzaz, F. A. (2004) Phylogenetic overdispersion in Floridean oak communities. The American Naturalist, 163, 823–843.

Cavender-Bares, J., Kozak, K. H., Fine, P. V.A., & Kembel, S. W. (2009) The merging of community ecology and phylogentic biology. Ecology Letters, 12, 693–715.

CBOL Plant Working Group. (2009) A DNA barcode for land plants. Proceedings of the National Academy of Sciences, 106, 12794–12797.

Chao, A. (1984) Non-parametric estimation of the number of classes in a population. Scandinavian Journal of Statistics, 11, 265–270.

Chao, A. (1987) Estimating the population-size for capture recapture data with unequal catchability. Biometrics, 43, 783–791.

Chao, A. (2001) An overview of closed capture-recapture models. Journal of Agricultural, Biological and Environmental Statistics, 6, 158–175.

Chao, A. (2005) Species estimation and applications. In: Encyclopedia of Statistical Sciences, Balakrishnan, N., Read, C. B., & Vidakovic, B. (eds), 2nd edn. Wiley, New York, Vol. 12, pp. 7907–7916.

Chao, A. & Bunge, J. (2002) Estimating the number of species in a Stochastic abundance model. Biometrics, 58, 531–539.

Chao, A. & Lee, S. -M. (1992) Estimating the number of classes via sample coverage. Journal of the American Statistical Association, 87, 210–217.

Chao, A. & Shen, T. -J. (2003a) SPADE: Species Prediction And Diversity Estimation. Program and user's guide at http://chao.stat.nthu.edu.tw/softwareCE.html.

Chao, A. & Shen, T. -J. (2003b) Nonparametric estimation of Shannon's index of diversity when there are unseen species. Environment and Ecological Statistics, 10, 429–443.

Chao, A., Yip, P., & Lin, H. S. (1996) Estimating the number of species via a martingale estimating function. Statistica Sinica, 6, 403–418.

Chao, A., Chazdon, R. L., Colwell, R. K., & Shen, T. -J. (2005) A new statistical approach for assessing similarity of species composition with incidence and abundance data. Ecology Letters, 8, 148–159.

Chao, A., Chazdon, R. L., Colwell, R. K., & Shen, T. -J. (2006) Abundance-based similarity indices and their estimation when there are unseen species in samples. Biometrics, 62, 361–371.

Chao, A., Jost, L., Chiang, S. -C., Jiang, Y. -H., & Chazdon, R. (2008) A two-stage probabilistic approach to multiple-community similarity indices. Biometrics, 64, 1178–1186.

Chao, A., Colwell, R. K., Lin, C. -W., & Gotelli, N. (2009) Sufficient sampling for asymptotic minimum species richness estimators. Ecology, 90, 1125–1133.

Chapin III, F. S., Zavaleta, E. S., Eviner, V. T., Naylor, R. L., Vitousek, P. M., Reynolds, H. L., Hooper, D. U., Lavorel, S., Sala, O. E., Hobbie, S. E., Mack, M. C., & Díaz, S. (2000) Consequences of changing biodiversity. Nature, 405, 234–242.

Chave, J., Muller-Landau, H. C., & Levin, S. A. (2002) Comparing classical community models: theoretical consequences for patterns of diversity. The American Naturalist, 159, 1–23.

Chen, I. C., Shiu, H., Benedick, S., Holloway, J. D., Chey, V. K., Barlow, H. S., Hill, J. K., & Thomas, C. D. (2009) Elevation increases in moth assemblages over 42 years on a tropical mountain. Proceedings of the National Academy of Sciences. USA, 106, 1479–1483.

Chiarucci, A., Wilson, J. B., Anderson, B. J., & De Dominicis, V. (1999) Cover versus biomass as an estimate of species abundance: does it make a difference to the conclusions? Journal of Vegetation Science, 10, 35–42.

Chiarucci, A., Bacaro, G., Rocchini, D., & Fattorini, L. (2008) Discovering and rediscovering the sample-based rarefaction formula in the ecological literature. Community Ecology, 9, 121–123.

Chivian, D., Brodie, E. L., Alm, E. J., Culley, D. E., Dehal, P. S., DeSantis, T. Z., Gihring, T. M., Lapidus, A., Lin, L. -H., Lowry, S. R., Moser, D. P., Richardson, P. M., Southam, G., Wanger, G., Pratt, L. M., Andersen, G. L., Hazen, T. C., Brockman, F. J., Arkin, A. P., & Onstott, T. C. (2008) Environmental genomics reveals a single-species ecosystem deep within Earth. Science, 322, 275–278.

Chown, S. L. & Gaston, K. J. (2008) Macrophysiology for a changing world. Proceedings of the Royal Society London, B, 275, 1469–1478.

Chown, S. L. & Gaston, K. J. (2010) Body size variation in insects: a macroecological perspective. Biological Reviews, 85, 139–169.

Chown, S. L. & Terblanche, J. S. (2007) Physiological diversity in insects: ecological and evolutionary contexts. Advances in Insect Physiology, 33, 50–152.

Chown, S. L., Gaston, K. J., & Williams, P. H. (1998) Global patterns in species richness of pelagic seabirds: the Procellariiformes. Ecography, 21, 342–350.

Chown, S. L., van Rensburg, B. J., Gaston, K. J., Rodrigues, A. S. L., & van Jaarsveld, A. S. (2003) Energy, species richness, and human population size: conservation implications at a national scale. Ecological Applications, 13, 1233–1241.

Chytrý, M., Sedláková, I., & Tichý, L. (2009) Species richness and species turnover in a successional heathland. Applied Vegetation Science, 4, 89–96.

CIA Fact Book. (2009) https://www.cia.gov/library/publications/the-world-factbook/geos/XX.html. Accessed 12 July 2009 12h17 UTC.

Cianciaruso, M. V., Batalha, M. A., Gaston, K. J., & Petchey, O. L. (2009) Including intraspecific variability in functional diversity. Ecology, 90, 81–89.

Clarke, K. R. (1990) Comparisons of dominance curves. Journal of Experimental Marine Biology and Ecology, 138, 143–157.

Clarke, J. A, & May, R. M. (2002) Taxonomic bias in conservation research. Science, 297, 191–192.

Clarke, K. R. & Warwick, R. M. (1998) A taxonomic distinctness index and its statistical properties. Journal of Applied Ecology, 35, 523–531.

Clarke, K. R. & Warwick, R. M. (2001) Change in Marine Communities: An Approach to Statistical Analysis and Interpretation (PRIMER-E). Plymouth Marine Laboratory, Plymouth.

Clifford, H. T. & Stephenson, W. (1975) An Introduction to Numerical Classification. Academic Press, New York.

Clough, Y., Holzschuh, A., Gabriel, D., Purtauf, T., Kleijn, D., Kruess, A., Steffan-Dewenter, I., & Tscharntke, T. (2007) Alpha and beta diversity of arthropods and plants in organically and conventionally managed wheat fields. Journal of Applied Ecology, 44, 804–812.

Cochran, W. G. (1977) Sampling Techniques. Wiley, New York.

Coddington, J. A., Agnarsson, I., Miller, J. A., Kuntner, M., & Hormiga, G. (2009) Undersampling bias: the null hypothesis for singleton species in tropical arthropod surveys. Journal of Animal Ecology, 78, 573–584.

Cohen, J. E. (1995) How Many People Can the Earth Support? W. W. Norton, New York.

Coleman, B. D., Mares, M. A., Willig, M. R., & Hsieh, Y. -H. (1982) Randomness, area, and species richness. Ecology, 63, 1121–1133.

Collins, S. L. & Glenn, S. M. (1997) Effects of organismal and distance scaling on analysis of species distribution and abundance. Ecological Applications, 7, 543–551.

Collins, S. L., Micheli, F., & Hartt, L. (2000) A method to determine rates and patterns of variability in ecological communities. Oikos, 91, 285–293.

Collins, S. L., Suding, K. N., Cleland, E. E., Batty, M., Pennings, S. C., Gross, K. L., Grace, J. B., Gough, L., Fargione, J. E., & Clar, C. M. (2008) Rank clocks and plant community dynamics. Ecology, 89, 3534–3541.

Colwell, R. K. (2009) Estimates: Statistical Estimation of Species Richness and Shared Species from Samples User's Guide and application published at: http://purl.oclc.org/estimates.

Colwell, R. K. & Coddington, J. A. (1994) Estimating terrestrial biodiversity through extrapolation. Philosophical Transactions of the Royal Society, London, Series B, 345, 101–118.

Colwell, R. K., Mao, C. X., & Chang, J. (2004) Interpolating, extrapolating, and comparing incidence-based species accumulation curves. Ecology, 85, 2717–2727.

Colwell, R. K., Brehm, G., Cardelús, C., Gilman, A. C., & Longino, J. T. (2008) Global warming, elevational range shifts, and lowland biotic attrition in the wet tropics. Science, 322, 258–261.

Condit, R., Hubbell, S. P., LaFrankie, J. V., Sukumar, R., Manokaran, N., Foster, R. B., & Ashton P. S. (1996) Species-area and species-individual relationships for tropical trees: a comparison of three 50-ha plots. Journal of Ecology, 84, 549–562.

Condit, R., Ashton, P. S., Baker, P., Bunyavejchewin, S., Gunatilleke, S., Gunatilleke, N., Hubbell, S. P., Foster, R. B., Itoh, A., LaFrankie, J. V., Lee, H. S., Losos, E., Manokaran, N., Sukumar, R., & Yamakura, T. (2000) Spatial patterns in the distribution of tropical tree species. Science, 288, 1414–1418.

Conlisk, E., Bloxham, M., Conlisk, J., Enquist, B., & Harte, J. (2007) A new class of models of spatial distribution. Ecological Monographs, 77, 269–284.

Conlisk, E., Conlisk, J., Enquist, B., Thompson, J., & Harte, J. (2009) Improved abundance prediction from presence-absence data. Global Ecology and Biogeography, 18, 1–10.

Connell, J. H. (1978) Diversity in tropical rain forests and coral reefs. Science, 199, 1302–1310.

Connell, J. H. & Sousa, W. P. (1983) On the evidence needed to judge ecological stability or persistence. The American Naturalist, 121, 789–824.

Connolly, S. R. & Miller, A. I. (2001a) Global Ordovician faunal transitions in the marine benthos: proximate causes. Paleobiology, 27, 779–795.

Connolly, S. R. & Miller, A. I. (2001b) Joint estimation of sampling and turnover rates from fossil databases: capture-mark-recapture methods revisited. Paleobiology, 27, 751–767.

Connolly, S. R., Hughes, T. P., Bellwood, D. R., & Karlson R. H. (2005) Community structure of corals and reef fishes at multiple scales. Science, 309, 1363–1365.

Connolly, S. R., Dornelas, M., Bellwood, D. R., & Hughes, T. P. (2009) Testing species abundance models: a new bootstrap approach applied to Indo-Pacific coral reefs. Ecology, 90, 3138–3149.

Connor, E. F. & Simberloff, D. (1979) The assembly of species communities: chance or competition? Ecology, 60, 1132–1140.

Constanza, R. et al. (1997) The value of the world's ecosystem services and natural capital. Nature, 387, 253–257 .

Cornelissen, J. H. C., Lavorel, S., Garnier, E., Díaz, S., Buchmann, N., Gurvich, D. E., Reich, P. B., Ter, Morgan, H. D., van der Heijden, M. G. A., Pausas, J. G., and Poorter, H. (2003). A handbook of protocols for standardised and easy measurement of plant functional traits worldwide. Australian Journal of Botany, 51, 335–380.

Cornwell, W. K. & Ackerly, D. D. (2009) Community assembly and shifts in plant trait distributions across an environmental gradient in coastal California. Ecological Monographs, 79, 109–126.

Cornwell, W. K., Schwilk, D. W., & Ackerly, D. D. (2006) A trait-based test for habitat filtering: convex hull volume. Ecology, 87, 1465–1471.

Costello, M. J., Pohle, G., & Martin, A. (2004) Evaluating biodiversity in marine environmental assessments. In: Research and Development Monograph Series, Series RaDM (ed.), Ottawa.

Cowley, M. J.R., Thomas, C. D., Wilson, R. J., León-Cortés, J. L., Gutiérrez, D., & Bulman, C. R. (2001) Density-distribution relationships in British butterflies: II. An assessment of mechanisms. Journal of Animal Ecology, 70, 426–441.

Crame, J. A. (2001) Taxonomic diversity gradients through geological time. Diversity & Distributions, 7, 175–189.

Cressie, N. (1992) Statistics for Spatial Data. Wiley Interscience, Chichester.

Crisp, M. D. & Cook, L. G. (2009) Explosive radiation or cryptic mass extinction? Interpreting signatures in molecular phylogenies. Evolution, 63, 2257–2265.

Crist, T. O. & Veech, J. A. (2006) Additive partitioning of rarefaction curves and species-area relationships: unifying alpha, beta, and gamma diversity with sample size and area. Ecology Letters, 9, 923–932.

Crist, T. O., Veech, J. A., Gering, J. C., & Summerville, K. S. (2003) Partitioning species diversity across landscapes and regions: a hierarchical analysis of alpha, beta, and gamma diversity. The American Naturalist, 162, 734–743.

Crozier, R. H. (1997) Preserving the information content of species: genetic diversity, phylogeny, and conservation worth. Annual Review of Ecology and Systematics, 28, 243–268.

Cunningham, S. A., Summerhayes, G., & Westoby, M. (1999) Evolutionary divergences in leaf structure and chemistry, comparing rainfall and soil nutrient gradients. Ecology, 69, 569–588.

Curtis, T. P. & Sloan, W. T. (2004) Prokaryotic diversity and its limits: microbial community structure in nature and implications for microbial ecology. Current Opinion in Microbiology, 7, 221–226.

Curtis, T. P., Sloan, W. T., & Scannell, J. W. (2002) Estimating prokaryotic diversity and its limits. Proceedings of the National Academy of Sciences of the United States of America, 99, 10494–10499.

Daily, G. C., Alexander, S., Ehrlich, P. R., Goulder, L., Lubchenco, J., Matson, P. A., Mooney, H. A., Postel, S., Schneider, S. H., & Tilman, D. (1997) Ecosystem services: benefits supplied to human societies by natural ecosystems. Issues in Ecology, 1, 1–18.

Dale, M. R.T. & Fortin, M. J. (2002) Spatial autocorrelation and statistical tests in ecology. Ecoscience, 9, 162–167.

Dale, M. R.T., Dixon, P., Fortin, M.-J., Legendre, P., Myers, D. E., & Rosenberg, M. S. (2002) Conceptual and mathematical relationships among methods for spatial analysis. Ecography, 25, 558–577.

Dalton, H. (1920) The measurement of the inequality of incomes. Economic Journal, 119, 348–361.

Dampier, J. E. E., Luckai, N., Bell, F. W., & Towill, W. D. (2007) Do tree-level monocultures develop following Canadian boreal silviculture? Tree-level diversity tested using a new method. Biodiversity and Conservation, 16, 2933–2948.

Damschen, E. I., Haddad, N. M., Orrock, J. L., Tewksbury, J. J., & Levey, D. J. (2006) Corridors increase plant species richness at large scales. Science, 313, 1284–1286.

Darwin, C. (1859) On the origin of species by means of natural selection, or the preservation of favoured races in the struggle for life. John Murray, London.

Dauvin, J. C. (1984) Dynamique d'écosystèmes macrobenthiques des fonds sédimentaires de la baie de Morlaix et leur perturbation par les hydrocarbures de l'Amoco Cadiz'. Thèse d'Etat, Université de Paris, Paris, 456pp.

Davis, M. B. & Shaw, R. G. (2001) Range shifts and adaptive responses to Quaternary climate change. Science, 292, 673–679.

Davison, A., Blackie, R. L. E., & Scothern, G. P. (2009) DNA barcoding of stylommatophoran land snails: a test of existing sequences. Molecular Ecology Research, 9, 1092–1101.

Dawson, W., Burslem, D. F. R. P., & Hulme, P. E. (2009) The suitability of weed risk assessment as a conservation tool to identify invasive plant threats in East African rainforests. Biological Conservation, 142, 1018–1024.

Dayan, T. & Simberloff, D. (2005) Ecological and community-wide character displacement: the next generation. Ecology Letters, 8, 875–894.

Deagle, B. E., Kirkwood, R., & Jarman, S. N. (2009) Analysis of Australian fur seal diet by pyrosequencing prey DNA in faeces. Molecular Ecology, 18, 2022–2038.

Death, R. G. & Zimmerman, E. M. (2005) Interaction between disturbance and primary productivity in determining stream invertebrate diversity. Oikos, 111, 392–402.

de Bello, F., Thuiller, W., Lepš, J., Choler, P., Clément, J. -C., Macek, P., Sebastià, M. T., & Lavorel, S. (2009) Partitioning of diversity reveals the scale and extent of trait convergence and divergence. Journal of Vegetation Science, 20, 475–486.

DeLong, E. E. & Pace, N. R. (2001) Environmental diversity of Bacteria and Archaea. Systematic Biology, 50, 470–478.

de Mazancourt, C., Johnson, E., & Barraclough, T. G. (2008) Biodiversity inhibits species' evolutionary responses to changing environments. Ecology Letters, 11, 380–388.

DeQuiroz, K. (2007) Species concepts and species delimitations. Systematic Biology, 56, 879–886.

Dewdney, A. K. (1998) A general theory of the sampling process with applications to the "veil line". Theoretical Population Biology, 54, 294–302.

Dewdney, A. K. (2000) A dynamical model of communities and a new species-abundance distribution. The Biological Bulletin, 198, 152–165.

Diamond, J. M. & May, R. M. (1977) Species turnover rates on islands: dependence on census intervals. Science, 197, 266–270.

Díaz, S. & Cabido, M. (2001) Vive la différence: plant functional diversity matters to ecosystem processes. Trends in Ecology and Evolution, 16, 646–655.

Díaz, S., Lavorel, S., de Bello, F., Quétier, F., Grigulis, K., & Robson, T. M. (2007) Incorporating plant functional diversity effects in ecosystem service assessments. Proceedings of the National Academy of Sciences, 104, 20684–20689.

Diggle, P. J. (1983) Statistical Analysis of Spatial Point Patterns. Academic Press, London.

Diniz, J. A. F., Bini, L. M., & Hawkins, B. A. (2003) Spatial autocorrelation and red herrings in geographical ecology. Global Ecology and Biogeography, 12, 53–64.

Diserud, O. H. & Engen, S. (2000) A general and dynamic species abundance model, embracing the lognormal and the gamma models. The American Naturalist, 155, 497–511.

Diserud, O. H. & Ødegaard, F. (2007) A multiple-site similarity measure. Biology Letters, 3, 20–22.

Dobyns, J. R. (1997) Effects of sampling intensity on the collection of spider (Araneae) species and the estimation of spider richness. Environmental Entomology, 26, 150–162.

Donaldson, J., Nänni, I., Zachariades, C., & Kemper, J. (2002) Effects of habitat fragmentation on pollinator diversity and plant reproductive success in renosterveld shrublands of South Africa. Conservation Biology, 16, 1267–1276.

Dormann, C. F. (2007a) Assessing the validity of autologistic regression. Ecological Modelling, 207, 234–242.

Dormann, C. F. (2007b) Effects of incorporating spatial autocorrelation into the analysis of species distribution data. Global Ecology and Biogeography, 16, 129–138.

Dormann, C. F., McPherson, J. M., Araújo, M. B., Bivand, R., Bolliger, J., Carl, G., Davies, R. G., Hirzel, A., Jetz, W., & Kissling, W. D. (2007) Methods to account for spatial autocorrelation in the analysis of species distributional data: a review. Ecography, 30, 609.

Dornelas, M. & Connolly, S. R. (2008) Multiple modes in a coral species abundance distribution. Ecology Letters, 11, 1008–1016.

Dornelas, M., Connolly, S. R., & Hughes, T. P. (2006) Coral reef diversity refutes the neutral theory of biodiversity. Nature, 440, 80–82.

Dornelas, M., Moonen, A. C., Magurran, A. E., & Barberi, P. (2009) Species abundance distributions reveal environmental heterogeneity in modified landscapes. Journal of Applied Ecology, 46, 666–672.

Dornelas, M., Phillip, D. A. T., and Magurran, A. E. (2010) Abundance and dominance become less predictable as species richness decreases. Global Ecology and Biogeography, in press.

Doroghazi, J. R. & Buckley, D. H. (2008) Evidence from GC-TRFLP that bacterial communities in soil are lognormally distributed. Plos One, 3, e2910.

Dray, S. & Legendre, P. (2008) Testing the species traits-environment relationships: the fourth-corner problem revisited. Ecology, 89, 3400–3412.

Dray, S., Legendre, P., & Peres-Neto, P. R. (2006) Spatial modelling: a comprehensive framework for principal coordinate analysis of neighbour matrices (PCNM). Ecological Modelling, 196, 483–493.

Drayton, B. & Primack, R. B. (1996) Plant species lost in an isolated conservation area in metropolitan Boston from 1894 to 1993. Conservation Biology, 10, 30–39.

Driscoll, C. A., Menotti-Raymond, M., Roca, A., Hupe, K., Johnson, W. E., Geffen, E., Harley, E. H., Delibes, M., Pontier, D., Kitchener, A. C., Yamaguchi, N., O'Brien, S. J., & Macdonald, D. W. (2007) The near eastern origin of cat domestication. Science, 317, 519–523.

Drobner, U., Bibby, J., Smith, B., & Wilson, J. B. (1998) The relation between community biomass and evenness: What does community theory predict, and can these predictions be tested? Oikos, 82, 295–302.

Dunn, R. R., Sanders, N. J., Menke, S. B., Weiser, M. D., Fitzpatrick, M. C., Laurent, E., Lessard, J. -P., Agosti, D., Andersen, A., Bruhl, C., Cerda, X., Ellison, A., Fisher, B., Gibb, H., Gotelli, N., Gove, A., Guénard, B., Janda, M., Kaspari, M., Longino, J. T., Majer, J., McGlynn, T. P., Menke, S. B., Parr, C., Philpott, S., Pfeiffer, M., Retana, J., Suarez, A., & Vasconcelos, H. (2009) Climatic drivers of hemispheric asymmetry in global patterns of ant species richness. Ecology Letters, 12, 324–333.

Dutilleul, P., Clifford, P., Richardson, S., & Hemon, D. (1993) Modifying the t test for assessing the correlation between two spatial processes. Biometrics, 49, 305–314.

DuToit, J. T. (2003) Large herbivores and savanna heterogeneity. In: The Kruger Experience: Ecology and Management of Savanna Heterogeneity, DuToit, J. T., Rogers, K. H., & Biggs, H. C. (eds). Island Press, Washington, pp. 292–309.

Dykhuizen, D. E. (1998) Santa Rosalia revisited: Why are there so many species of bacteria? Antonie Van Leeuwenhoek International Journal of General and Molecular Microbiology, 73, 25–33.

EASAC. (2009) Ecosystem Services and Biodiversity in Europe. The Royal Society, London.

Economo, E. & Kiett, T. (2008) Species diversity in neutral metacommunities: a network approach. Ecology. Letters 11, 52–62.

Edwards, A. W.F. (1992) Likelihood – Expanded Edition. Johns Hopkins University Press, Baltimore.

Efron, B. & Thisted, R. (1976) Estimating the number of unseen species: how many words did Shakespeare know? Biometrika, 63, 35–41.

Efron, B. & Tibshirani, R. J. (1993) An Introduction to the Bootstrap. Chapman & Hall/CRC, Boca Raton, FL.

Elith, J., Graham, C. H., Anderson, R. P., Dudik, M., Ferrier, S., Guisan, A., Hijmans, R. J., Huettmann, F., Leathwick, J. R., Lehmann, A., Li, J., Lohmann, L. G., Loiselle, B. A., Manion, G., Moritz, C., Nakamura, M., Nakazawa, Y., Overton, J. M. M., Peterson, A. T., Phillips, S. J., Richardson, K., Scachetti-Pereira, R., Schapire, R. E., Soberon, J., Williams, S., Wisz, M. S., & Zimmermann, N. E. (2006) Novel methods improve prediction of species' distributions from occurrence data. Ecography, 29, 129–151.

Ellis, E. C. & Ramankutty, N. (2008) Putting people in the map: anthropogenic biomes of the world. Frontiers in Ecology and the Environment, 6, 439–447.

Ellison, A. M., Record, S., Arguello, A., & Gotelli, N. J. (2007) Rapid inventory of the ant assemblage in a temperate hardwood forest: species composition and assessment of sampling methods. Environmental Entomology, 36, 766–775.

Elton, C. (1946) Competition and the structure of ecological communities. Journal of Animal Ecology, 15:54–68.

Elzinga, C. L., Salzer, D. W., & Willoughby, J. W. (1998) Measuring & Monitoring Plant Populations. US Dept.

of the Interior, Bureau of Land Management; Nature Conservancy, Denver, CO.

Engen, S. & Lande, R. (1996a) Population dynamic models generating species abundance distributions of the gamma type. Journal of Theoretical Biology, 178, 325–331.

Engen, S. & Lande, R. (1996b) Population dynamic models generating the lognormal species abundance distribution. Mathematical Biosciences, 132, 169–183.

Engen, S., Lande, R., Walla, T., & DeVries, P. J. (2002) Analyzing spatial structure of communities using the two-dimensional Poisson lognormal species abundance model. The American Naturalist, 160, 60–73.

Engen, S., Saether, B. E., Sverdrup-Thygeson, A., Grotan, V., & Odegaard, F. (2008) Assessment of species diversity from species abundance distributions at different localities. Oikos, 117, 738–748.

Epperson, B. K. (2003) Geographical Genetics. Princeton University Press, Princeton.

Erickson, R. O. (1945) The Clematis fremontii var. riehlii population in the Ozarks. Annals of the Missouri Botanical Garden, 32, 413–460.

Erwin, D. H. (2006) Extinction: How life on Earth Nearly Ended 250 Million Years Ago. Princeton University Press, Princeton.

Etienne, R. S. (2005) A new sampling formula for neutral biodiversity. Ecology Letters, 8, 253–260.

Etienne, R. S. (2007) A neutral sampling formula for multiple samples and an 'exact' test of neutrality. Ecology Letters, 10, 608–618.

Etienne, R. S. & Alonso, D. (2005) A dispersal-limited sampling theory for species and alleles. Ecology Letters, 8, 1147–1156.

Etienne, R. S. & Olff, H. (2004) A novel genealogical approach to neutral biodiversity theory. Ecology Letters, 7, 170–175.

Etienne, R. S. & Olff, H. (2005) Confronting different models of community structure to species-abundance data: a Bayesian model comparison. Ecology Letters, 8, 493–504.

Etienne, R. S., Latimer, A. M., Silander, J. A., & Cowling, R. M. (2006) Comment on "Neutral ecological theory reveals isolation and rapid speciation in a biodiversity hot spot". Science, 311, 610.

Etienne, R. S., Alonso, D., & McKane, A. J. (2007a) The zero-sum assumption in netural biodiversity theory. Journal of Theoretical Biology, 248, 522–536.

Etienne, R. S., Apol, M. E. F., Olff, H., & Weissing, F. J. (2007b) Modes of speciation and the neutral theory of biodiversity. Oikos, 116, 241–258.

Evans, K. L., Rodrigues, A. S. L., Chown, S. L., & Gaston, K. J. (2006a) Protected areas and regional avian species richness in South Africa. Biology Letters, 2, 184–188.

Evans, K. L., van Rensburg, B. J., Gaston, K. J., & Chown, S. L. (2006b) People, species richness and human population growth. Global Ecology and Biogeography, 15, 625–636.

Evans, K. L., Gaston, K. J., Sharp, S. P., McGowan, A., & Hatchwell, B. J. (2009) The effect of urbanisation on avian morphology and latitudinal gradients in body size. Oikos, 118, 251–259.

Evans, M., Hastings, N., & Peacock, B. (1993) Statistical Distributions, 2nd edn. Wiley, New York.

Faith, D. P. (1992) Conservation evaluation and phylogenetic diversity. Biological Conservation, 61, 1–10.

Fargione, J., Brown, C. S., & Tilman, D. (2003) Community assembly and invasion: an experimental test of neutral versus niche processes. Proceedings of the National Academy of Sciences of the United States of America, 100, 8916–8920.

Farrell, L. E., Roman, J., & Sunquist, M. E. (2000) Dietary separation of sympatric carnivores identified by molecular analysis of scats. Molecular Ecology, 9, 1583–1590.

Felsenstein, J. (1985) Phylogenies and the comparative method. The American Naturalist, 125, 1–15.

Felsenstein, J. (2004) Inferring Phylogenies. Sinauer Associates, Sunderland, MA, USA.

Feng, M. C., Nowierski, R. M., & Zeng, Z. (1993) Populations of Sitobion avenae and Aphidius ervi on sprint wheat in the northwestern United States. Entomologia Experimentalis et Applicata, 67, 109–117.

Fewster, R. M., Buckland, S. T., Siriwardena, G. M., Baillie, S. R., & Watson, J. D. (2000) Analysis of population trends for farmland birds using generalized additive models. Ecology, 81, 1970–1984.

Fiedler, K. & Schulze, C. H. (2004) Forest modification affects diversity (but not dynamics) of speciose tropical pyraloid moth communities. Biotropica, 36, 615–627.

Figueiredo, M. S. L. & Grelle, C. E. V. (2009) Predicting global abundance of a threatened species from its occurrence: implications for conservation planning. Diversity & Distributions, 15, 117–121.

Filippi-Codaccioni, O., Clobert, J., & Julliard, R.. (2009) Urbanization effects on the functional diversity of avian agricultural communities. Acta Oecologia, 35, 705–710.

Finch, S., Skinner, G., & Freeman, G. H. (1975) The distribution and analysis of cabbage root fly egg populations. The Annals of Applied Biology, 79, 1–18.

Fisher, J. A. D. & Frank, K. T. (2004) Abundance-distribution relationships and conservation of exploited marine fishes. Marine Ecology Progress Series, 279, 201–213.

Fisher, M. M. & Triplett, E. W. (1999) Automated approach for ribosomal intergenic spacer analysis of microbial diversity and its application to freshwater bacterial communities. Applied and Environmental Microbiology, **65**, 4630–4636.

Fisher, R. A., Corbet, A. S., & Williams, C. B. (1943) The relation between the number of species and the number of individuals in a random sample of an animal population. Journal of Animal Ecology, 12, 42–58.

Fisher, J. A. D., Frank, K. T., Petrie, B., Leggett, W. C., & Shackell, N. L. (2008) Temporal dynamics within a contemporary latitudinal diversity gradient. Ecology Letters, 11, 883–897.

Flaten, G. R., Botnen, H., Grung, B., & Kvalheim, O. M. (2007) Quantifying disturbances in benthic communities – comparison of the community disturbance index (CDI) to other multivariate methods. Ecological Indicators, 7, 254–276.

Flather, C. (1996) Fitting species-accumulation functions and assessing regional land use impacts on avian diversity. Journal of Biogeography, 23, 155–168.

Fleishman, E., Thomson, J. R., Mac Nally, R., Murphy, D. D., & Fay, J. P. (2005) Using indicator species to predict species richness of multiple taxonomic groups. Conservation Biology, 19, 1125–1137.

Folch, J., Cocero, M. J., Chesné, P., Alabart, J. L., Dominguez, V., Cognié , Y., Roche, A., Vernández-Áriaz, A., Marti, J. I., Sánchez, P., Echegoyen, E., Beckers, J. F., Sánchez Bonastre, A., & Vignon, X. (2009) First birth of an animal from an extinct subspecies (Capra pyrenaica pyrenaica) by cloning. Theriogenology, 71, 1026–1034.

Folke, C., Carpenter, S., Walker, B., Scheffer, M., Elmqvist, T., Gunderson, L., & Holling, C. S. (2004) Regime shifts, resilience, and biodiversity in ecosystem management. Annual Review of Ecology Evolution and Systematics, 35, 557–581.

Foote, M. (1988) Survivorship analysis of Cambrian and Ordovician trilobites. Paleobiology, 14, 258–271.

Foote, M. (1994) Temporal variation in extinction risk and temporal scaling of extinction metrics. Paleobiology, 20, 424–444.

Foote, M. (1997) Estimating taxonomic durations and preservation probability. Paleobiology, 23, 278–300.

Foote, M. (2000) Origination and extinction components of taxonomic diversity: general problems. In: Deep time – Paleobiology's perspective, Erwin, D. H. & Wing, S. L. (eds). Paleobiology Memoir, Paleontological Society and University of Chicago Press, pp. 74–102.

Foote, M. (2001a) Estimating completeness of the fossil record. In: Paleobiology II, Briggs, D. E. G. & Crowther, P. R. (eds). Blackwell, Oxford, pp. 500–504.

Foote, M. (2001b) Evolutionary rates and the age distribution of living and extinct taxa. In: Evolutionary Patterns – Growth, Form, and Tempo in the Fossil Record, Jackson, J. B. C., Lidgard, S., & McKinney, F. K. (eds). The University of Chicago Press, Chicago, pp. 245–294.

Foote, M. (2001c) Inferring temporal patterns of preservation, origination, and extinction from taxonomic survivorship analysis. Paleobiology, 27, 602–630.

Foote, M. (2003) Origination and extinction through the Phanerozoic: a new approach. The Journal of Geology, 111, 125–148.

Foote, M. (2005) Pulsed origination and extinction in the marine realm. Paleobiology, 31, 6–20.

Foote, M. (2007a) Extinction and quiescence in marine animal genera. Paleobiology, 33, 261–272.

Foote, M. (2007b) Symmetric waxing and waning of marine invertebrate genera. Paleobiology, 33, 517–529.

Foote, M. & Raup, D. M. (1996) Fossil preservation and the stratigraphic ranges of taxa. Paleobiology, 22, 121–140.

Foote, M., Crampton, J. S., Beu, A. G., & Cooper, R. A. (2008) On the bidirectional relationship between geographic range and taxonomic duration. Paleobiology, 34, 421–433.

Foran, D. R., Crooks, K. R., & Minta, S. C. (1997) Species identification from scat: an unambiguous genetic method. Wildlife Society Bulletin, 25, 835–839.

Ford, N. B. & Lancaster, D. L. (2007) The species-abundance distribution of snakes in a bottomland hardwood forest of the southern United States. Journal of Herpetology, 41, 385–393.

Forest, F., Grenyer, R., Rouget, M., Davies, T. J., Cowling, R.M, Faith, D. P., Balmford, A., Manning, J. C., Proches, S., van der Bank, M., Reeves, G., Hedderson, T. A. J., & Salvolainen, V. (2007) Preserving the evolutionary potential of floras in biodiversity hotspots. Nature, 445, 757–760.

Fornara, D. A. & Tilman, D. (2009) Ecological mechanisms associated with the positive diversity – productivity relationship in an N-limited grassland. Ecology, 90, 408–418.

Fortin, M. J. & Dale, M. R.T. (2005) Spatial Analysis: A Guide for Ecologists. Cambridge University Press, Cambridge.

Foster, S. D. & Dunstan, P. K. (2009) The analysis of biodiversity using rank abundance distributions. Biometrics, 661, 186–195.

Fotheringham, A. S., Brunsdon, C., & Charlton, M. (2002) Geographically Weighted Regression: The Analysis of Spatially Varying Relationships. Wiley, Chichester.

Foxcroft, L. C., Rouget, M., Richardson, D. M., & Mac-Fadyen, S. (2004) Reconstructing 50 years of Opuntia stricta invasion in the Kruger National Park, South Africa: environmental determinants and propagule pressure. Diversity & Distributions, 10, 427–437.

Foxcroft, L. C., Richardson, D. M., Rouget, M., & Mac-Fadyen, S. (2009) Patterns of alien plant distribution at multiple spatial scales in a large national park: implications for ecology, management and monitoring. Diversity & Distributions, 15, 367–378.

Frankham, R., Ballou, J. D., & Briscoe, D. A. (eds) 2002. Introduction to Conservation Genetics. Cambridge University Press.

Freckleton, R. P., Gill, J. A., Noble, D., & Watkinson, A. R. (2005) Large-scale population dynamics, abundance-occupancy relationships and the scaling from local to regional population size. Journal of Animal Ecology, 74, 353–364.

Freeman, S. N., Noble, D. G., Newson, S. E., & Baillie S. R. (2007) Modelling population changes using data from different surveys: the Common Birds Census and the Breeding Bird Survey. Bird Study, 54, 61–72.

Freese, L., Auster, P. J., Heifetz, J., & Wing, B. L. (1999) Effects of trawling on seafloor habitat and associated invertebrate taxa in the Gulf of Alaska. Marine Ecology-Progress Series, 182, 119–126.

Frezal, L. & Leblois, R. (2008) Four years of DNA barcoding: current advances and prospects. Infection, Genetics and Evolution, 8, 727–736.

Frontier, S. (1985) Diversity and structure in aquatic ecosystems. Oceanography and Marine Biology – An Annual Review, 23, 253–312.

Gans, J., Wolinsky, M., & Dunbar, J. (2005) Computational improvements reveal great bacterial diversity and high metal toxicity in soil. Science, 309, 1387–1390.

Garcia, L. V. (2004) Escaping the Bonferroni iron claw in ecological studies. Oikos, 105, 657.

Garcia-Martinez, J., Acinas, S. G., Anton, A. I., & Rodriguez-Valera, F. (1999) Use of the 16S-23S ribosomal genes spacer region in studies of prokaryotic diversity. Journal of Microbiological Methods, **36**, 55–64.

Gardner, T. A., Cote, I. M., Gill, J. A., Grant, A., & Watkinson, A. R. (2003) Long-term region-wide declines in Caribbean corals. Science, 301, 958–960.

Gardner, T. A., Barlow, J., Aruajo, I. S., Ávila-Pires, T. C., Bonaldo, A. B., Costa, J. E., Esposito, M. C., Ferreira, L. V., Hawes, J., Hernandez, M. I. M., Hoogmoed, M. S., Lieite, R. N., Lo-Man-Hung, N. F., Malcolm, J. R., Martins, M. B., Mestre, L. A. M., Miranda-Santos, R., Overal, W. L., Parry, L., Peters, S. L., Roberio-Junior, M. A., da Silva, M. N. F., Motta, C. D. S., & Peres, C. A. (2007) The cost-effectiveness of biodiversity surveys in tropical forests. Ecology Letters, 11, 139–150.

Garnier, E., Laurent, G., Bellmann, A., Debain, S., Berthelier, P., Ducout, B., Roumet, C., & Navas, M.-L. (2001) Consistency of species ranking based on functional leaf traits. The New Phytologist, 152, 69–83.

Garnier, E., Lavorel, S., Ansquer, P., Castro, H., Cruz, P., Dolezal, J., Eriksson, O., Fortunel, C., Freitas, H., Golodets, C., Grigulis, K., Jouany, C., Kazakou, E., Kigel, J., Kleyer, M., Lehsten, V., Lepš, J., Meier, T., Pakeman, R., Papadimitriou, M., Papanastasis, V. P., Quested, H., Quétier, F., Robson, M., Roumet, C., Rusch, G., Skarpe, C., Sternberg, M., Theau, J.-P., Thébault, A., Vile, D., & Zarovali, M. P. (2006) Assessing the effects of land-use change on plant traits, communities and ecosystem functioning in grasslands: a standardized methodology and lessons from an application to 11 European Sites. Annals of Botany, 99, 967–985.

Gaston, K. J. (1991) How large is a species' geographic range? Oikos, 61, 434–438.

Gaston, K. J. (1994) Rarity. Chapman & Hall, London.

Gaston, K. J. (ed) (1996) Biodiversity: A biology of numbers and difference. Wiley, New York.

Gaston, K. J. (1996a) Species-range size distributions: patterns, mechanisms and implications. Trends in Ecology and Evolution, 11, 197–201.

Gaston, K. J. (1996b) Biodiversity – latitudinal gradients. Progress in Physical Geography, 20, 466–476.

Gaston, K. J. (2003) The Structure and Dynamics of Geographic Ranges. Oxford University Press, Oxford.

Gaston, K. J. (2006) Biodiversity and extinction: macroecological patterns and people. Progress in Physical Geography, 30, 258–269.

Gaston, K. J. (2009) Geographic range limits: achieving synthesis. Proceedings of the Royal Society London, B, 276, 1395–1406.

Gaston, K. J. & Blackburn, T. M. (2000) Pattern and Process in Macroecology. Blackwell, Oxford.

Gaston, K. J. & Fuller, R. A. (2008) Commonness, population depletion and conservation biology. Trends in Ecology and Evolution, 23, 14–19.

Gaston, K. J. & Fuller, R. A. (2009) The sizes of species' geographic ranges. Journal of Applied Ecology, 46, 1–9.

Gaston, K. J. & Lawton, J. H. (1989) Insect herbivores on bracken do not support the core-satellite hypothesis. The American Naturalist, 134, 761–777.

Gaston, K. J. & Lawton, J. H. (1990) Effects of scale and habitat on the relationship between regional distribution and local abundance. Oikos, 58, 329–335.

Gaston, K. J. & He, F. (2002) The distribution of species range size: a stochastic process. Proceedings of the Royal Society London, B, 269, 1079–1086.

Gaston, K. & May, R. M. (1992) The taxonomy of taxonomists. Nature, 356, 281–283.

Gaston, K. J. & McArdle, B. H. (1994) The temporal variability of animal abundances: measures, methods and patterns. Philosophical Transactions of the Royal Society, London Lond. B, 345, 335–358.

Gaston, K. J. & Warren, P. H. (1997) Interspecific abundance-occupancy relationships and the effects of disturbance: a test using microcosms. Oecologia, 112, 112–117.

Gaston, K. J., Blackburn, T. M., & Lawton, J. H. (1997) Interspecific abundance-range size relationships: an appraisal of mechanisms. Journal of Animal Ecology, 66, 579–601.

Gaston, K. J., Blackburn, T. M., & Gregory, R. D. (1998a) Interspecific differences in intraspecific abundance-range size relationships of British breeding birds. Ecography, 21, 149–158.

Gaston, K. J., Blackburn, T. M., Gregory, R. D., & Greenwood, J. J.D. (1998b) The anatomy of the interspecific abundance-range size relationship for the British avifauna: I. Spatial patterns. Ecology Letters, 1, 38–46.

Gaston, K. J., Blackburn, T. M., & Gregory, R. D. (1999a) Does variation in census area confound density comparisons? Journal of Applied Ecology, 36, 191–204.

Gaston, K. J., Blackburn, T. M., & Gregory, R. D. (1999b) Intraspecific abundance-range size relationships: case studies of six bird species in Britain. Diversity & Distributions 5, 197–212.

Gaston, K. J., Blackburn, T. M., Greenwood, J. J.D., Gregory, R. D., Quinn, R. M., & Lawton, J. H. (2000) Abundance-occupancy relationships. Journal of Applied Ecology, 37 (Suppl. 1), 39–59.

Gaston, K. J., Borges, P. A.V., He, F., & Gaspar, C. (2006) Abundance, spatial variance, & occupancy: species distribution in the Azores. Journal of Animal Ecology, 75, 646–656.

Gaston, K. J., Chown, S. L., & Evans, K. L. (2008a) Ecogeographic rules: elements of a synthesis. Journal of Biogeography, 35, 483–500.

Gaston, K. J., Jackson, S. F., Cantú-Salazar, L., & Cruz-Piñón, G. (2008b) The ecological performance of protected areas. Annual Review of Ecology, Evolution and Systematics, 39, 93–113.

Gaston, K. J., Chown, S. L., Calosi, P., et al. (2009) Macrophysiology: a conceptual re-unification. The American Naturalist, 174, 595–612.

Gebremedhin, B., Ficetola, G. F., Naderi, S., Rezaei, H. R., Maudet, C., Rioux, D., Luikart, G., Flagstad, Ø., Thuiller, W., & Taberlet, P. (2009) Frontiers in identifying conservation units: from neutral markers to adaptive genetic variation. Animal Conservation, 12, 107–109.

Gelman, A. (2003) A Bayesian formulation of exploratory data analysis and goodness-of-fit testing. International Statistical Review, 71, 369–382.

Genome 10K Community of Scientists. (2009) Genome 10K: a proposal to obtain whole-genome sequence for 10000 vertebrate species. Journal of Heredity, 100, 659–674.

Gerrodette, T. (1993) TRENDS: Software for a power analysis of linear regression. Wildlife Society Bulletin, 21, 515–516.

Gibbs, J. E. (1995) MONITOR: Software for power analysis in population monitoring programs. In. USGS Pautuxent Wildlife Research Center Laurel, Maryland.

Gibbs, J. P., Droege, S., & Eagle, P. (1998) Monitoring populations of plants and animals. BioScience, 48, 935–940.

Gienapp, P., Leimu, R., & Merilä, J. (2007) Responses to climate change in avian migration time – microevolution versus phenotypic plasticity. Climate Research, 35, 25–35.

Gienapp, P., Teplitsky, C., Alho, J. S., Mills, J. A., & Merilä, J. (2008) Climate change and evolution: disentangling environmental and genetic responses. Molecular Ecology, 17, 167–178.

Gilchrist, G. W., Huey, R. B., Balanyá, J., Pascual, M., & Serra, L. (2004) A time series of evolution in action: a latitudinal cline in wing size in South American *Drosophila subobscura*. Evolution, 58, 768–780.

Gill, S. R., Pop, M., DeBoy, R. T., Eckburg, P. B., Turnbaugh, P. J., Samuel, B. S., Gordon, J. I., Relman, D. A., Fraser-Liggett, C. M., & Nelson, K. E. (2006) Metagenomic analysis of the human distal gut microbiome. Science, 312, 1355–1359.

Gillespie, T. W., Foody, G. M., Rocchini, D., Giorgi, A. P., & Saatchi S. (2008) Measuring and modelling biodiversity from space. Progress in Physical Geography, 32, 203–221.

Gislason, H. & Rice, J. (1998) Modelling the response of size and diversity spectra of fish assemblages to changes in exploitation. ICES Journal of Marine Science, 55, 362–370.

Gleason, H. A. (1929) The significance of Raunkiaer's law of frequency. Ecology, 10, 406–408.

Golicher, D. J., O'Hara, R. B., Ruiz-Montoya, L., & Cayuela, L. (2006) Lifting a veil on diversity: a Bayesian approach to fitting relative-abundance models. Ecological Applications, 16, 202–212.

Good, I. J. (1953) The population frequencies of species and the estimation of population parameters. Biometrika, 40, 237–264.

Good, I. J. (2000) Turing's anticipation of empirical Bayes in connection with the cryptanalysis of the naval

Enigma. Journal of Statistical Computation and Simulation, 66, 101–111.

Goßner, M., Chao, A., Bailey, R., & Prinzing, A. (2009) Native fauna on exotic trees: phylogenetic conservatism and geographic contingency in two lineages of phytophages on two lineages of trees. The American Naturalist, 173, 599–614.

Gotelli, N. J. (1991) Metapopulation models: the rescue effect, the propagule rain, and the core-satellite hypothesis. The American Naturalist, 138, 768–776.

Gotelli, N. J. (2008) A Primer of Ecology, 4th edn. Sinauer Associates, Sunderland, MA.

Gotelli, N. J. & Colwell, R. K. (2001) Quantifying biodiversity: procedures and pitfalls in the measurement and comparison of species richness. Ecology Letters, 4, 379 391.

Gotelli, N. & Entsminger, G. L. (2009) EcoSim: Null Models Software for Ecology. Version 7. Acquired Intelligence Inc. & Kesey-Bear, Jericho, VT 05465. http://garyentsminger.com/ecosim.htm.

Gotelli, N. J. & Graves, G. R. (1996) Null Models in Ecology. Smithsonian Institution Press, WA, USA.

Gotelli, N., Anderson, M. J., Arita, H. T., Chao, A., Colwell, R. K., Connolly, S. R., Currie, D. J., Dunn, R. R., Graves, G. R., Green, J. L., Grytnes, J. A., Jiang, Y.-H., Jetz, W., Lyons, S. K., McCain, C. M., Magurran, A. E., Rahbek, C., Rangel, T. F.L. V.B., Soberon, J., Webb, C. O., & Willig, M. R. (2009) Patterns and causes of species richness: a general simulation model for macroecology. Ecology Letters, 12, 873–886.

Govender, N., Trollope, W. S. W., & van Wilgen, B. W. (2006) The effect of fire season, fire frequency, rainfall and management on fire intensity in savanna vegetation in South Africa. Journal of Applied Ecology, 43, 748–758.

Gower, J. C. (1971) A general coefficient of similarity and some of its properties. Biometrics, 27, 857–871.

Gower, J. C. (1985) Measures of similarity, dissimilarity and distance. In Enclopedia of Statistical Sciences, Kotz, S. & Johnson, N. L. (eds). Wiley, New York, Vol. 5, pp. 397–405.

Grace, J. B. (2006) Structural Equation Modeling and Natural Systems. Cambridge University Press, Cambridge.

Gradstein, F., Ogg, J., & Smith, A. (2005) A geological Times Scale 2004. Cambridge University Press, Cambridge.

Graham, C. H. & Fine, P. V. A. (2008) Phylogenetic beta diversity: linking ecological and evolutionary processes across space in time. Ecology Letters, 11, 1265–1277.

Graham, C. H. & Hijmans, R. J. (2006) A comparison of methods for mapping species ranges and species richness. Global Ecology and Biogeography, 15, 578–587.

Graham, J. H., Hughie, H. H., Jones, S., Wrinn, K., Krzysik, A. J., Duda, J. J., Freeman, D. C., Emlen, J. M., Zak, J. C., Kovacic, D. A., Chamberlin-Graham, C., & Balbach, H. (2004) Habitat disturbance and the diversity and abundance of ants (Formicidae) in the Southeastern Fall-Line Sandhills – art. no. 30. Journal of Insect Science, 4, 30–30.

Grant, P. R. & Schluter, D. (1984) Interspecific competition inferred from patterns of guild structure. In: Ecological Communities: Conceptual Issues and the Evidence, Strong, D. R., Simberloff, D., Abele, L. G., & Thistle, A. B. (eds). Princeton University Press, Princeton, USA, pp. 201–233.

Grassle, J. F. & Smith, W. (1976) A similarity measure sensitive to the contribution of rare species and its use in investigation of variation in marine benthic communities. Oecologia, 25, 13–22.

Gray, J. S. (1979) Pollution-induced changes in populations. Philosophical Transactions of the Royal Society of London B, 286, 545–561.

Gray, J. S. (1981) Detecting pollution induced changes in communities using the log-normal distribution of individuals among species. Marine Pollution Bulletin, 12, 173–176.

Gray, J. S. (1983) Use and misuse of the log-normal plotting method for detection of effects of pollution – a reply. Marine Ecology-Progress Series, 11, 203–204.

Gray, J. S. (1987) Species-abundance patterns. In: Organization of communities – past and present, Gee, J. H. R. & Giller, P. S. (eds). Blackwell, Oxford, pp. 53–67.

Gray, J. S. & Mirza, F. B. (1979) Possible method for the detection of pollution-induced disturbance on marine benthic communities. Marine Pollution Bulletin, 10, 142–146.

Gray, J. S., Clarke, K. R., Warwick, R. M., & Hobbs, G. (1990) Detection of the initial effects of pollution on marine benthos: an example from the Ekofisk and Eldfisk oilfields, North Sea. Marine Ecology Progress Series, 66, 285–299.

Gray, J. S., Bjogesaerter, A., & Ugland, K. I. (2005) The impact of rare species on natural assemblages. Journal of Animal Ecology, 74, 1131–1139.

Gray, J. S., Bjorgesaeter, A., & Ugland, K. I. (2006) On plotting species abundance distributions. Journal Of Animal Ecology, 75, 752–756.

Green, J. L. & Plotkin, J. B. (2007) A statistical theory for sampling species abundances. Ecology Letters, 10, 1037–1045.

Gregorius, H. R. (1987) The relationship between the concepts of genetic diversity and differentiation. Theoretical and Applied Genetics, 74, 397–401.

Gregorius, H. R. (1996) Differentiation between populations and its measurement. Acta Biotheoretica, 44, 23–36.

Gregorius, H. R. (2010) Linking diversity and differentiation. Diversity, 2, 370–394.

Gregory, R. D., Noble, D., Field, R., Marchant, J., Raven, M., & Gibbons, D. W. (2003) Birds as indicators of biodiversity. Ornis Hungarica, 12–13, 11–24.

Greig-Smith, P. (1957) Quantitative Plant Ecology. Butterworth, London.

Greig-Smith, P. (1983) Quantitative Plant Ecology, 3rd edn. Blackwell, London.

Greve, M. (2007) Avifaunal responses to environmental conditions and land-use changes in South Africa: diversity, composition and body size. M.Sc. Thesis, Stellenbosch University, 185pp.

Greve, M., Gaston, K. J., van Rensburg, B. J., & Chown, S. L. (2008) Environmental factors, regional body size distributions, and spatial variation in body size of local avian assemblages. Global Ecology and Biogeography, 17, 514–523.

Grime, J. P. (1973a) Control of species density in herbaceous vegetation. Journal of Environmental Management, 1, 151–167.

Grime, J. P. (1973b) Competitive exclusion in herbaceous vegetation. Nature, 242, 344–347.

Grinnell, J. (1922) The role of the 'accidental'. Auk, 39, 373–380.

Groves, R. M. (1989) Survey Errors and Survey Costs. Wiley, New York.

Gunnarsson, T. (2006) A Mirror of Nature: Nordic Landscape Painting 1840–1910. Statens Museum for Kunst, Copenhagen, pp. 11–37.

Guo, Q., Brown, J. H., & Valone, T. J. (2000) Abundance and distribution of desert annuals: are spatial and temporal patterns related? The Journal of Ecology, 88, 551–560.

Gurd, D. B. 2007. Predicting resource partitioning and community organization of filter-feeding dabbling ducks from functional morphology. The American Naturalist, 169, 334–343.

Halfpenny, J. 1986. A Field Guide to Mammal Tracking in Western America. Johnson Books, Boulder, CO, pp. 134–148.

Hall, S. J. & Greenstreet, S. P. (1998) Taxonomic distinctness and diversity measures: responses in marine fish communities. Marine Ecology Progress Series, 166, 227–229.

Hallam, S. J., Putnam, N., Preston, C. M., Detter, J. C., Rokhsar, D., Richardson, P. M., & DeLong, E. F. (2004) Reverse methanogenesis: testing the hypothesis with environmental genomics. Science, 305, 1457–1462.

Hannah, L. & Kay, J. A. (1977) Concentration in the modern industry: theory, measurement, and the U. K. experience. MacMillan, London.

Hanski, I. (1982) Dynamics of regional distribution: the core and satellite species hypothesis. Oikos, 38, 210–221.

Hanski, I. (1994) A practical model of metapopulation dynamics. Journal of Animal Ecology, 63, 151–162.

Hanski, I. (1997) Metapopulation dynamics, from concepts and observations to predictive models. In: Metapopulation Biology, Hanski, I. & Gilpin, M. E. (eds). Academic Press, San Diego, pp. 69–91.

Hanski, I. & Gyllenberg, M. (1997) Uniting two general patterns in the distribution of species. Science, 275, 397–400.

Hardy, O. J. (2008) Testing the spatial phylogenetic structure of local communities: statistical performances of different null models and test statistics on a locally neutral community. The Journal of Ecology, 96, 914–926.

Hardy, O. J. & Jost, L. (2008) Interpreting and estimating measures of community phylogenetic structuring. The Journal of Ecology, 96, 849–852.

Hardy, O. J. & Senterre, B. (2007) Characterizing the phylogenetic structure of communities by additive partitioning of phylogenetic diversity. The Journal of Ecology, 95, 493–506.

Harms, K. E., Condit, R., Hubbell, S. P., & Foster, R. B. (2001) Habitat associations of trees and shrubs in a 50-ha neotropical forest plot. Journal of Ecology, 89, 947–959.

Harper, J. L. (1981) The meanings of rarity. In: The Biological Aspects of Rare Plant Conservation, Synge, H. (ed). Wiley, New York, pp. 189–203.

Harrison, P. (1992) The Third Revolution. Population, Environment and a Sustainable World. Penguin Books, London.

Harrison, S., Ross, S. J., & Lawton, J. H. (1992) Beta diversity on geographic gradients in Britain. Journal of Animal Ecology, 61, 151–158.

Harte, J. (2008) From spatial pattern in the distribution and abundance of species to a unified theory of ecology: the role of maximum entropy methods. Applied Optimization, 102, 243.

Harte, J., Kinzig, A., & Green, J. (1999) Self-similarity in the distribution and abundance of species. Science, 284, 334–336.

Harte, J., Conlisk, E., Ostling, A., Green, J. L., & Smith, A. B. (2005) A theory of spatial structure in ecological communities at multiple spatial scales. Ecological Monographs, 75, 179–197.

Harte, J., Zillio, T., Conlisk, E., & Smith, A. B. (2008) Maximum entropy and the state variable approach to macroecology. Ecology, 89, 2700–2711.

Hartley, S., Kunin, W. E., Lennon, J. J., & Pocock, M. J. O. (2004) Coherence and discontinuity in the scaling of species' distribution patterns. Proceedings of the Royal Society London, B, 271, 81–88.

Hassell, M. P., Southwood, T. R. E., & Reader, P. M. (1987) The dynamics of the viburnum whitefly (*Aleurotrachelus jelinekii*): a case study of population regulation. Journal of Animal Ecology, 56, 283–300.

Hauer, R. F. & Resh, V. H. (2006) Macroinvertebrates. In: Methods in Stream Ecology, Hauer, F. R. & Lamberti, G. A. (eds). Academic Press/Elsevier San Diego, CA, pp. 435–463.

Hawkins, C. P., Norris, R. H., Hogue, J. N., & Feminella, J. W. (2000) Development and evaluation of predictive models for measuring the biological integrity of streams. Ecological Applications, 10, 1456–1477.

Hawkins, B. A., Diniz-Filho, J. A. F., Bini, L. M., De Marco, P., & Blackburn, T. M. (2007) Red herrings revisited: spatial autocorrelation and parameter estimation in geographical ecology. Ecography, 30, 375.

Hayden, E. C. (2009) 10,000 genomes to come. Nature, 462, 21.

He, F. & Condit, R. (2007) The distribution of species: occupancy, scale, and rarity. In: Scaling Biodiversity, Storch, D., Marquet, P. A., & Brown, J. H. (eds). Cambridge University Press, Cambridge, pp. 32–50.

He, F. & Gaston, K. J. (2000a) Estimating species abundance from occurrence. The American Naturalist, 156, 553–559.

He, F. & Gaston, K. J. (2000b) Occupancy-abundance relationships and sampling scales. Ecography, 23, 503–511.

He, F. & Gaston, K. J. (2003) Occupancy, spatial variance and the abundance of species. The American Naturalist, 162, 366–375.

He, F. & Tang, D. (2008) Estimating the niche preemption parameter of the geometric series. Acta Oecologica, 33, 105–107.

He, F., Gaston, K. J., & Wu, J. (2002) On species occupancy-abundance models. Écoscience, 9, 119–126.

Heard, S. B. (1992) Patterns in tree balance among cladistic, phenetic, and randomly generated phylogenetic trees. Evolution, 46, 1818–1826

Hebert, P. D. N., Cywinsky, A., Ball, S. L., & deWaard, J. R. (2003) Biological identifications through DNA barcodes. Proceedings of the Royal Society London, B, 270, 313–321.

Hebert, P. D. N., Stoeckle, M. Y., Zemlak, T. S., & Francis, C. M. (2004) Identification of birds through DNA barcodes. PLoS, Biology, 2, 1657–1663.

Heck, K. L., Jr., van Belle, G., & Simberloff, D. (1975) Explicit calculation of the rarefaction diversity measurement and the determination of sufficient sample size. Ecology, 56, 1459–1461.

Hector, A., Schmid, B., Beierkuhnlein, C., Caldeira, M. C., Diemer, M., Dimitrakopoulos, P. G., Finn, J. A., Freitas, H., Giller, P. S. Good, J., Harris, R., Högberg, P., Huss-Danell, K., Joshi, J., Jumpponen, A., Körner, C., Leadley, P. W., Loreau, M., Minns, A., Mulder, C. P.H., O'Donovan, G., Otway, S. J., Pereira, J. S., Prinz, A., Read, D. J., Scherer-Lorenzen, M., Schulze, E.-D., Siamantziouras, A.-S. D., Spehn, E. M., Terry, A. C., Troumbis, A. Y., Woodward, F. I., Yachi, S., & Lawton, J. H. (1999) Plant diversity and productivity in European grasslands. Science, 286, 1123–1127.

Heemsbergen, D. A., Berg, M. P., Loreau, M., van Hal, J. R., Faber, J. H., & Verhoef, H. A. (2004) Biodiversity effects on soil processes explained by interspecific functional dissimilarity. Science, 306, 1019–1020.

Heino, J. (2005) Positive relationship between regional distribution and local abundance in stream insects: a consequence of niche breadth or habitat niche position? Ecography, 28, 345–354.

Heino, J. (2008) Temporally stable abundance-occupancy relationships and occupancy frequency patterns in stream insects. Oecologia, 157, 337–347.

Helmus, M. R., Bland, T. J., Williams, C. K., & Ives, A. R. (2007) Phylogenetic measures of biodiversity. The American Naturalist, 169, E68–E83.

Heltshe, J. & Forrester, N. E. (1983) Estimating species richness using the jackknife procedure. Biometrics, 39, 1–11.

Henderson, P. A. (2007) Discrete and continuous change in the fish community of the Bristol Channel in response to climate change. Journal of the Marine Biological Association, 87, 589–598.

Henderson, P. A. & Holmes, R. H. A. (1991) On the population dynamics of dab, sole and flounder within Bridgwater bay in the lower severn Estuary, England. Netherlands Journal of Sea Research, 27, 337–344.

Henderson, P. A. & Magurran, A. E. (2010) Linking species abundance distributions in numerical abundance and biomass through simple assumptions about community structure. Proceedings of the Royal Society London, published online, 277, 1561–1570.

Hendry, A. P. & Kinnison, M. T. (1999) The pace of modern life: measuring rates of contemporary microevolution. Evolution, 53, 1637–1653.

Hendry, A. P., Farrugia, T. J., & Kinnison, M. T. (2008) Human influences on rates of phenotypic change in wild populations. Molecular Ecology, 17, 20–29.

Hengeveld, R. (1990). Dynamic Biogeography. Cambridge University Press, Cambridge.

Hesse, R., Allee, W. C., & Schmidt, K. P. (1937) Ecological Animal Geography. Wiley, New York.

Hewitt, J. E., Anderson, M. J., & Thrush, S. F. (2005) Assessing and monitoring ecological community health in marine systems. Ecological Applications, 15, 942–953.

Hickerson, M. J., Meyer, C. P., & Moritz, C. (2006) DNA barcoding will often fail to discover new animal species over broad parameter space. Systems Biology, 55, 729–739.

Hicks, G. R. F. (1980) Structure of phytal harpacticoid copepod assemblages and the influence of habitat complexity and turbidity. Journal of experimental marine Biology and Ecology, 44, 157–192.

Hilborn, R. & Mangel, M. (1997) The Ecological Detective, Confronting Models with Data. Princeton University Press, New Jersey.

Hill, M. O. (1973) Diversity and evenness: a unifying notation and its consequences. Ecology, 54, 427–432.

Hillebrand, H. (2004) On the generality of the latitudinal diversity gradient. The American Naturalist, 163, 192–211.

Hillebrand, H., Bennett, D. M., & Cadotte, M. W. (2008) Consequences of dominance: a review of evenness effects on local and regional ecosystem processes. Ecology, 89, 1510–1520.

Hilt, N., Brehm, G., & Fiedler, K. (2006) Diversity and ensemble composition of geometrid moths along a successional gradient in the Ecuadorian Andes. Journal of Tropical Ecology, 22, 155–166.

Hinsley, S. A., Pakeman, R., Bellamy, P. E. & Newton, I. (1996) Influences of habitat fragmentation on bird species distributions and regional population size. Proceedings of the Royal Society London, B, 263, 307–313.

Hobbs, R. J., Arico, S., Aronson, J., et al. (2006) Novel ecosystems: theoretical and management aspects of the new ecological world order. Global Ecology and Biogeography, 15, 1–7.

Hoehn, P., Tscharntke, T., Tylianakis, J. M., & Steffan-Dewenter, I. (2008) Functional group diversity of bee pollinators increases crop yield. Proceedings of the Royal Society London, B, 275, 2283–2291.

Holdridge, L. R., Grenke, W. C., Hatheway, W. H., Liang, T., & Tosi, J. A. (1971) Forest Environments in Tropical Life Zones. Pergamon Press, Oxford.

Holmes, S. (2003) Bootstrapping phylogenetic trees, theory and methods. Statistical Science, 18, 241–255.

Holt, R. (2008) Theoretical perspectives on resource pulses. Ecology, 89, 671–681.

Holt, A. R., Gaston, K. J., & He, F. (2002a) Occupancy-abundance relationships and spatial distribution. Basic and Applied Ecology , 3, 1–13.

Holt, A. R., Warren, P. H., & Gaston, K. J. (2002b) The importance of biotic interactions in abundance-occupancy relationships. Journal of Animal Ecology, 71, 846–854.

Holt, A. R., Warren, P. H., & Gaston, K. J. (2004a) The importance of habitat heterogeneity, biotic interactions and dispersal in abundance-occupancy relationships. Journal of Animal Ecology, 73, 841–851.

Holt, R. D., Knight, T. M., & Barfield, M. (2004b) Allee effects, immigration, and the evolution of species' niches. The American Naturalist, 163, 253–262.

Holyoak, M., Jarosik V., & Novak, I. (1997) Weather-induced changes in moth activity bias measurement of long-term population dynamics from light trap samples. Entomologia Experimentalis et Applicata, 83, 329–335.

Holyoak, M., Leibold, M., & Holt, R. (2005) Metacommunities: Spatial Dynamics and Ecological Communities. University of Chicago Press, Chicago.

Hong, S. H., Bunge, J., Jeon, S. O., & Epstein, S. S. (2006) Predicting microbial species richness. Proceedings of the National Academy of Sciences of the United States of America, 103, 117–122.

Hooper, D. U. & Vitousek, P. M. (1997) The effects of plant composition and diversity on ecosystem processes. Science, 277, 1302–1305.

Hooper, D. U., Chapin, F. S., Ewel, J. J., Hector, A., Inchausti, P., Lavorel, S., Lawton, J. H., Lodge, D. M., Loreau, M., Naeem, S., Schmid, B., Setala, H., Symstad, A. J., Vandermeer, J., & Wardle, D. A. (2005) Effects of biodiversity on ecosystem functioning: a consensus of current knowledge. Ecological Monographs, 75, 3–35.

Horn, H. S. (1966) Measurement of "overlap" in comparative ecological studies. The American Naturalist, 100, 419–424.

Horn, H. I. (ed.) (1975) Markovian Properties of Forest Succession. Harvard University Press, Cambridge, MA.

Horner-Devine, M. C., Lage, M., Hughes, J. B., & Bohannan, B. J. M. (2004) A taxa – area relationship for bacteria. Nature, 432, 750–753.

Hortal, J., Borges, P. A. V., & Caspar, C. (2006) Evaluating the performance of species richness estimators: sensitivity to sample grain size. Journal of Animal Ecology, 75, 274–287.

Houchmandzadeh, B. (2008) Neutral clustering in a simple experimental ecological community. Physical Review Letters, Aug 15, 101(7), 078103. Epub 2008.

Huang, D., Meier, R., Todd, P. A., & Chou, L. M. (2008) Slow mitochondrial COI evolution at the base of the metazoan tree and its implications for DNA barcoding. Journal of Molecular Evolution, 66, 167–174.

Hubalek, Z. (1982) Coefficients of association and similarity, based on binary (presence-absence) data: an evaluation. Biological Reviews, 57, 669–689.

Hubbell, S. P. (2001) A Unified Theory of Biodiversity and Biogeography. Princeton University Press, Princeton.

Hubbell, S. P., Foster, R. B., O'Brien, S. T., Harms, K. E., Condit, R., Wechsler, B., Wright, S. J., & De Lao, S. L. (1999) Light-gap disturbances, recruitment limitation, and tree diversity in a neotropical forest. Science, 283, 554.

Huber, J. A., Mark Welch, D., Morrison, H. G., Huse, S. M., Neal, P. R., Butterfield, D. A., & Sogin, M. L. (2007) Microbial population structures in the deep marine biosphere. Science, 318, 97–100.

Huelsenbeck, J. P. & Rannala, B. (1997) Maximum likelihood estimation of topology and node times using stratigraphic data. Paleobiology, 23, 174–180.

Hugenholtz, P. & Pace, N. R. (1996) Identifying microbial diversity in the natural environment: a molecular phylogenetic approach. Trends in Biotechnology, 14, 190–197.

Hughes, R. G. (1986) Theories and models of species abundance. The American Naturalist, 128, 879–899.

Hughes, J. B. (2000) The scale of resource specialization and the distribution and abundance of lycaenid butterflies. Oecologia, 123, 375–383.

Hughes, J. B., Hellmann, J. J., Ricketts, T. H., & Bohannan, B. J. M. (2000) Counting the uncountable: statistical approaches to estimating microbial diversity. Applied and Environmental Microbiology, 67, 4399–4406.

Hui, C. & McGeoch, M. A. (2007a) A self-similarity model for the occupancy frequency distribution. Theoretical Population Biology, 71, 61–70.

Hui, C. & McGeoch, M. A. (2007b) Modeling species distributions by breaking the assumption of self-similarity. Oikos, 116, 2097–2107.

Hui, C. & McGeoch, M. A. (2007c) Capturing the "droopy-tail" in the occupancy-abundance relationship. Ecoscience, 14, 103–108.

Hui, C. & McGeoch, M. A. (2008) Does the self-similar distribution model lead to unrealistic predictions? Ecology, 89, 2946–2952.

Hui, C., McGeoch, M. A., & Warren, M. (2006) A spatially explicit approach to estimating species occupancy and spatial correlation. The Journal of Animal Ecology, 75, 140–147.

Hui, C., Veldtman, R., & McGeoch, M. A. (2010) Measures, perceptions and scaling patterns of aggregated species distributions. Ecography, 33, 95–102.

Hurlbert, S. H. (1971) The nonconcept of species diversity: a critique and alternative parameters. Ecology, 52, 577–586.

Hurlbert, S. H. (1984) Pseudoreplication and the design of ecological field experiments. Ecological Monographs, 54, 187–211.

Hurlbert, S. H. (1990) Spatial distribution of the montane unicorn. Oikos, 58, 257–271.

Hurlbert, A. H. & Jetz, W. (2007) Species richness, hotspots, and the scale dependence of range maps in ecology and conservation. Proceedings of the National Academy of Sciences. USA, 104, 13384–13389.

Hurlbert, A. H. & White, E. P. (2005) Disparity between range map – and survey-based analyses of species richness: patterns, processes and implications. Ecology Letters, 8, 319–327.

Huston, M. A. (1979) A general hypothesis of species diversity. The American Naturalist, 113, 81–101.

Huston, M. A. (1994) Biological Diversity: The Coexistence of Species on Changing Landscapes. Cambridge University Press, Cambridge.

Huston, M. L. (1997) Hidden treatments in ecological experiments: re-evaluating the ecosystem function of biodiversity. Oecologia, 110, 449–460.

Hutchings, J. A. (2000) Collapse and recovery of marine fishes. Nature, 406, 882–885.

Hutchinson, G. E. (1957) Homage to Santa Rosalia; or why are there so many kinds of animals? The American Naturalist, 93, 145–159.

Isaac, N. J. B., Turvey, S. T., Collen, B., Waterman, C., & Baillie, J. E. M. (2007) Mammals on the EDGE: conservation priorities based on threat and phylogeny. PLoS ONE, 2, e296.

Izsak J. (2006) Some practical aspects of fitting and testing the Zipf-Mandelbrot model – a short essay. Scientometrics, 67, 107–120.

Jablonski, D. (2000) Micro- and macroevolution: scale and hierarchy in evolutionary biology and paleobiology. In: Deep time – Paleobiology's Perspective, Erwin, D. H. & Wing, S. L. (eds). Paleobiology Memoir, Paleontological Society and University of Chicago Press, Chicago, pp. 15–52.

Jaccard, P. (1900) Contribution an Problème de l'immigration post-glaciaire de la flore alpine. Bulletin de la Société Vaudoise des Sciences Naturelles, 36, 87–130.

Jaccard, P. (1901) Etude compararative de la distribution florale dans une portion des Alpes et du Jura. Bulletin de la Société Vaudoise des Sciences Naturelles, 37, 647–579.

Jackson, S. F. & Gaston, K. J. (2008) Land use change and the dependence of national priority species on protected areas. Global Ecology and Biogeography, 14, 2132–2138.

Jackson, J. B. C., Kirby, M. X., Berger, W. H., et al. (2001) Historical overfishing and the recent collapse of coastal ecosystems. Science, 293, 629–638.

James, F. C. & Wamer, N. O. (1982) Relationships between temperate forest bird communities and vegetation structure. Ecology, 63, 159–171.

Janson, S. & Vegelius, J. (1981) Measures of ecological association. Oecologia, 49, 371–376.

Jansen G, Savolainen R, & Versäläinen K. (2009) DNA barcoding as a heuristic tool for classifying undescribed Nearctic Myrmica ants (Hymenoptera: Formicidae). Zoologica Scripta, 38, 527–536.

Janzen, D. H., Hallwachs, W., Blandin, P., Burns, J. M., Cadiou, J.- M., Chacon, I., Dapkey, T., Deans, A. R., Epstein, M. E., Espinoza, B., Franclemont, J. G., Haber, W. A., Hajibabei, M., Hall, J. P. W., Hebert, P. D. N., Gauld, I. D., Harvey, D. J., Hausmann, A., Kitching, I. J., Lafontaine, D., Landry, J. -F., Lemaire, C., Miller, J. Y., Montero, J., Munroe, E., Green, C. R., Ratnasingham, S., Rawlins, J. E., Robbins, R. K., Rodriguez, J. J., Rougerie, R., Sharkey, M. J., Smith, M. A., Solis, M. A., Sullivan, J. B., Thiaucourt, .P, Wahl, D. B., Weller, S. J., Whitfield, J. B., Willmott, K. R., Wood, D. M., Woodley, N. E., & Wilson, J. J. (2009) Integration of DNA barcoding into an ongoing inventory of complex tropical biodiversity. Molecular Ecology Research, 9(Suppl. 1), 1–26.

Järvinen, O. (1982) Species-to-genus ratios in biogeography: a historical note. Journal of Biogeography, 9, 363–370.

Jetz, W. & Rahbek, C. (2002) Geographic range size and determinants of avian species richness. Science, 297, 1548–1551.

Johnson, J. B. & Omland, K. S. (2004) Model selection in ecology and evolution. Trends in Ecology and Evolution, 19, 101–108.

Jones, M. M., Tuomisto, H., Borcard, D., Legendre, P., Clark, D. B., & Olivas, P. C. (2008) Explaining variation in tropical plant community composition: influence of environmental and spatial data quality. Oecologia, 155, 593–604.

Jorgensen, S. E., Xu, F. -L., Salas, F., & Marques, J. C. (eds.) (2005) Application of indicators for the assessment of ecosystem health. CRC Press, Boca Raton, FL.

Jost, L. (2006) Entropy and diversity. Oikos, 113, 363–375.

Jost, L. (2007) Partitioning diversity into independent alpha and beta components. Ecology, 88, 2427–2439.

Jost, L. (2008) GST and its relatives do not measure differentiation. Molecular Ecology, 17, 4015–4026.

Jost, L. (2009) Mismeasuring biological diversity: response to Hoffman and Hoffman (2008). Ecological Economics, 68, 925–927.

Jost, L., DeVries, P., Walla, T., Greeney, H., Chao, A., & Ricotta, C. (2010) Partitioning diversity for conservation analyses. Diversity and Distributions, 16, 65–76.

Jurasinski, G., Retzer, V., & Beierkuhnlein, C. (2009) Inventory, differentiation, and proportional diversity: a consistent terminology for quantifying species diversity. Oecologia, 159, 15–26.

Karjalainen, J., Rahkola, M., Viljanen, M., Andronikova, I. N., & Avinskii, V. A. (1996) Comparison of methods used in zooplankton sampling and counting in the joint Russian-Finnish evaluation of the trophic state of Lake Ladoga. Hydrobiologia, 322, 249–253.

Kearney, M. & Porter, W. P. (2009) Mechanistic niche modelling: combining physiological and spatial data to predict species' ranges. Ecology Letters, 12, 334–350.

Keating, K. A. & Quinn, J. F. (1998) Estimating species richness: the Michaelis-Menten model revisisted. Oikos, 81, 411–416.

Keddy, P. A. (1992) Assembly and response rules: two goals for predictive community ecology. Journal of Vegetation Science, 3, 157–164.

Kelly, A. E. & Goulden, M. L. (2008) Rapid shifts in plant distribution with recent climate change. Proceedings of the National Academy of Sciences. USA, 105, 11823–11826.

Kembel, S. W. & Hubbell, S. P. (2006) The phylogenetic structure of a neotropical forest tree community. Ecology, 87, S86–S99.

Kempton, R. A. (1979) The structure of species abundance and measurement of diversity. Biometrics, 35, 307–321.

Kempton, R. A. & Taylor, L. R. (1974) Log-series and log-normal parameters as diversity discriminants for Lepidoptera. Journal of Animal Ecology, 43, 381–399.

Kempton, R. A. & Taylor, L. R. (1976) Models and statistics for species diversity. Nature, 262, 818–820.

Kempton, R. A. & Taylor, L. R. (1978) The Q-statistic and the diversity of floras. Nature, 275, 252–253.

Kempton, R. A. & Wedderburn, R. W.M. (1978) A comparison of three measures of species diversity. Biometrics, 34, 25–37.

Kendrick, G. A., Holmes, K. W., & Van Niel, K. P. (2008) Multi-scale spatial patterns of three seagrass species with different growth dynamics. Ecography, 31, 191.

Kennedy, C. E. J. & Southwood, T. R. E. (1984) The number of species of insects associated with British trees: a reanalysis. Journal of Animal Ecology, 53, 455–478.

Kevan, P. G., Greco, C. F., & Belaoussoff, S. (1997) Log-normality of biodiversity and abundance in diagnosis and measuring of ecosystemic health: pesticide stress on pollinators on blueberry heaths. Journal of Applied Ecology, 34, 1122–1136.

King, T. A., Williams, J. C., Davies, W. D., & Shelton, W. L. (1981) Fixed versus random sampling of fishes in a large reservoir. Transactions of the American Fisheries Society, 110, 563–568.

Kinzig, A., Tilman, D., & Pacala, S. (2001) The Functional Consequences of Biodiversity: Empirical Progress and Theoretical Extensions. Princeton University Press, Princeton, NJ.

Kissling, W. D. & Carl, G. (2008) Spatial autocorrelation and the selection of simultaneous autoregressive models. Global Ecology and Biogeography, 17, 59–71.

Kitchener, A. C., Beaumont, M. A., & Richardson, D. (2006) Geographical variation in the clouded leopard, *Neofelis nebulosa*, reveals two species. Current Biology, 16, 2377–2383.

Kleijn, D., Baquero, R. A., Clough, Y., et al. (2006) Mixed biodiversity benefits of agri-environment schemes in five European countries. Ecology Letters, 9, 243–254.

Klein Goldewijk, K. (2001) Estimating global land use change over the past 300 years: the HYDE database. Global Biogeochemical Cycles, 15, 417–33.

Knight, T. M., McCoy, M. W., Chase, J. M., McCoy, K. A., & Holt, R. D. (2005) Trophic cascades across ecosystems. Nature, 437, 880–883.

Kobayashi, S. & Kimura, K. (1994) The number of species occurring in a sample of a biotic community and its connections with species-abundance relationship and spatial distribution. Ecological Research, 9, 281–294.

Koch, L. F. (1957) Index of biotal dispersity. Ecology, 38, 145–148.

Kohn, M., Knauer, F., Stoffella, A., Schröder, W., & Pääbo, S. (1995) Conservation genetics of the European brown bear – a study using excremental PCR of nuclear and mitochondrial sequences. Molecular Ecology, 4, 95–103.

Kohn, M. H., Murphy, W. J., Ostrander, E. A., & Wayne, R. K. (2006) Genomics and conservation genetics. Trends in Ecology and Evolution, 21, 629–637.

Kolasa, J. (1989) Ecological systems in hierarchical perspective: breaks in community structure and other consequences. Ecology, 70, 36–47.

Kolb, A., Barsch, F., & Diekmann, M. (2006) Determinants of local abundance and range size in forest vascular plants. Global Biogeochemical Cycles, 15, 237–247.

Koleff, P., Gaston, K. J., & Lennon, J. J. (2003) Measuring beta diversity for presence – absence data. Journal of Animal Ecology, 72, 367–382.

Konig, G. (1835) Die Forst-Mathematik. Beckersche Buchhandlung, Gotha.

Kosso, P. (1992) Reading the book of nature: an introduction to the philosophy of science. Cambridge University Press, Cambridge.

Kraft, N. J. B. & Ackerly, D. D. (2009) Response to Comment on "Functional Traits and Niche-Based Tree Community Assembly in an Amazonian Forest". Science, 324, 1015.

Kraft, N. J. B., Cornwell, W. K., Webb, C. O., & Ackerly, D. D. (2007) Trait evolution, community assembly, and the phylogenetic structure of ecological communities. The American Naturalist, 170, 271–283.

Krausman, P. R. (2002) Introduction to Wildlife Management: The Basics. Prentice-Hall, Upper Saddle River, NJ.

Krebs, C. J. (1972) Ecology. Harper & Row, New York.

Krebs, C. J. (1989) Ecological Methodology. Harper and Row, New York.

Krebs, C. J. (1999) Ecological Methodology, 2nd edn. Addison Wesley Longman, Menlo Park, CA.

Kreft, H. & Jetz, W. (2007) Global patterns and determinants of vascular plant diversity. Proceedings of the National Academy of Sciences, 104, 5925.

Kress, W. J., Erickson, D. L., Jones, F. A., Swenson, N. G., Perez, R., Sanjur, O., & Bermingham, E. (2009) Plant DNA barcodes and a community phylogeny of a tropical forest dynamics plot in Panama. Proceedings of the National Academy of Sciences, 106, 18621 18626.

Kruskal, J. (1964) Nonmetric multidimensional scaling: a numerical method. Phychometrika, 29, 115–129.

Kulczynski, S. (1928) Die Pflanzenassoziationen der Pieninen. Bulletin international de l'Academie Polonaise des Sciences et des Lettres, Classe des sciences mathématiques et naturelles, Série B Suppl 2, 57–203.

Kunin, W. E. (1998) Extrapolating species abundance across spatial scales. Science, 281, 1513–1515.

Kunin, W. E. & Gaston, K. J. (eds) (1997) The Biology of Rarity: Causes and Consequences of Rare-Common Differences. Chapman & Hall, London.

Kuno, E. (1986) Evaluation of statistical precision and design of efficient sampling for the population estimates based on frequency of sampling. Research in Population Ecology, 28, 305–319.

Kvitrud, M. A., Riemer, S. D., Brown, R. F., Bellinger, M. R., & Banks, M. A. (2005) Pacific harbor seals (*Phoca vitulina*) and salmon: genetics presents hard numbers for elucidating predator-prey dynamics. Marine Biology, 147, 1459–1466.

Lack, D. L. (1947) Darwin's Finches. Cambridge University Press, Cambridge.

Lahaye, R., van der Bank, M., Bogarin, D., Warner, J., Pupulin, F., Gogot, G., Maurin, O., Duthoit, S., Barraclough, T. G., & Savolainen, V. (2008) DNA barcoding in floras of biodiversity hotspots. Proceedings of the National Academy of Sciences, 105, 2923–2928.

Laliberté, E. & Legendre, P. (2010) A distance-based framework for measuring functional diversity from multiple traits. Ecology, 91, 299–305.

Laliberté, E. and Shipley, W. (2009) http://ftp3.ie. freebsd.org/pub/CRAN/web/packages/FD/FD.pdf.

Lambshead, P. J. D., Platt, H. M., & Shaw, K. M. (1983) The detection of differences among assemblages of marine benthic species based on an assessment of dominance and diversity. Journal of Natural History, 17, 859–874.

Lamouroux, N., Doledec, S., & Gayraud, S. (2004) Biological traits of stream macroinvertebrate communities: effects of microhabitat, reach, and basin filters. Journal of North American Benthic Society, 23, 449–466.

Lance, G. N. & Williams, W. T. (1967) Mixed-data classificatory programs. I. Agglomerative systems. Australian Computational Journal, 1, 15–20.

Lande, R. (1996) Statistics and partitioning of species diversity, and similarity among multiple communities. Oikos, 76, 5–13.

Lande, R., Engen, S., & Saether, B. -E. (2003) Stochastic Population Dynamics in Ecology and Conservation. Oxford University Press, Oxford.

Lankau, R. A. & Strauss, S. Y. (2007) Mutual feedbacks maintain both genetic and species diversity in a plant community. Science, 317, 1561–1563.

Larsen, D. P., Kincaid, T. M., Jacobs, S. E., & Urquhart, N. S. (2001) Designs for evaluating local and regional scale trends. BioScience, 51, 1069–1078.

Larsen, D., Kaufmann, P., Kincaid, T., & Urquhart, N. (2004) Detecting persistent change in the habitat of salmon-bearing streams in the Pacific Northwest. Canadian Journal of Fisheries and Aquatic Sciences, 61, 283–291.

La Sorte, F. A. & Boecklen, W. J. (2005) Temporal turnover of common species in avian assemblages in North America. Journal of Biogeography, 32, 1151–1160.

Latimer, A. M., Silander, J. A., Gelfand, A. E., Rebelo, A. G., & Richardson, D. M. (2004) Quantifying threats to biodiversity from invasive alien plants and other factors: a case study from the Cape Floristic Region. South African Journal of Science, 100, 81–86.

Lauer, T. E. & Spacie, A. (2004) Space as a limiting resource in freshwater systems: competition between zebra mussels (Dreissena polymorpha) and freshwater sponges (Porifera). Hydrobiologia, 517, 137–145.

Lawes, J., Gilbert, J., & Masters, M. (1882) Agricultural, botanical and chemical results of experiments on the mixed herbage of permanent meadow, conducted for more than twenty years on the same land. II. The botanical results. Philosophical Transactions of the Royal Society, London B., 173, 1181–1413.

Lawton, J. H. (1990) Species richness and population dynamics of animal assemblages. Patterns in body size: abundance space. Philosophical Transactions of the Royal Society, London, Series B, 330, 283–291.

Lawton, J. H. (1999a) http://www.worries. Oikos, 85, 190–192.

Lawton, J. H. (1999b) Are there general laws in ecology? Oikos, 84, 177–192.

Lawton, J. H. & Gaston, K. J. (2001) Indicator species. In: Encyclopedia of Biodiversity, Levin, S. A. (ed). Academic Press, New York, Vol. 3, pp. 437–450.

Lawton, J. H., Bignell, D. E., Bolton, B., Bloemers, G. F., Eggleton, P., Hammond, P. M., Hodda, M., Holt, R. D., Larsen, T. B., Mawdsley, N. A., Stork, N. E., Srivastava, D. S., & Watt, A. D. (1998) Biodiversity inventories, indicator taxa and effects of habitat modification in tropical forest. Nature, 391, 72–76.

Legendre, P. & Legendre, L. (1998) Numerical Ecology 2nd edn. Elsevier, Amsterdam.

Legendre, P., Galzin, R., & Harmelin-Vivien, M. L. (1997) Relating behaviour to habitat: solutions to the fourth-corner problem. Ecology, 78, 547–562.

Legendre, P., Borcard, D., & Peres-Neto, P. R. (2008) Analyzing or explaining beta diversity? Comment. Ecology, 89, 3238–3244.

Leger, E. A. & Forister, M. L. (2009) Colonization, abundance, and geographic range size of gravestone lichens. Basic and Applied Ecology, 10, 279–287.

Leitner, W. A. & Rosenzweig, M. L. (1997) Nested species-area curves and stochastic sampling: a new theory. Oikos, 79, 503–512.

Lekve, K., Boulinier, T., Stenseth, N. C., Gøsaeter, J., Fromentin, J. -M., Hines, J. E., & Nichols, J. D. (2002) Spatio-temporal dynamics of species richness on coastal fish communities. Proceedings of the Royal Society London, 269, 1781–1789.

Lennon, J. J. (2000) Red-shifts and red herrings in geographical ecology. Ecography, 23, 101–113.

Lennon, J. J., Koleff, P., Greenwood, J. J.D., & Gaston, K. J. (2001) The geographical structure of British bird distributions: diversity, spatial turnover and scale. Journal of Animal Ecology, 70, 966–979.

Lennon, J. J., Kunin, W. E., Hartley, S., & Gaston, K. J. (2007) Species distribution patterns, diversity scaling and testing for fractals in southern African birds. In: Scaling Biodiversity, Storch, D., Marquet, P. A., & Brown, J. H. (eds). Cambridge University Press, Cambridge, pp. 51–76.

Leprieur, F., Beauchard, O., Blanchet, S., Oberdorff, T., & Brosse, S. (2008) Fish invasions in the world's river systems: when natural processes are blurred by human activities. PLoS Biology, 6, e28 (1–7).

Lepš, J. & Smilauer, P. (2003) Multivariate Analysis of Ecological Data using CANOCO. Cambridge University Press, Cambridge.

Lepš, J., de Bello, F., Lavorel, S., & Berman, S. (2006) Quantifying and interpreting functional diversity of natural communities: practical considerations matter. Preslia, 78, 481–501.

le Roux, P. C. & McGeoch, M. A. (2008) Rapid range expansion and community reorganization in response to warming. Global Change Biology, 14, 2950–2962.

Lichstein, J. W., Simons, T. R., Shriner, S. A., & Franzreb, K. E. (2003) Spatial autocorrelation and autoregressive models in ecology. Ecological Monographs, 72, 445–463.

Limpert, E., Stahel, W. A., & Abbt, M. (2001) Log-normal distributions across the sciences: keys and clues. BioScience, 51, 341–352.

Liu, W. T., Marsh, T. L., Cheng, H., & Forney, L. J. (1997) Characterization of microbial diversity by determining terminal restriction fragment length polymorphisms of genes encoding 16S rRNA. Applied and Environmental Microbiology, 63, 4516–4522.

Locke, J. W. (1991) Statistical measurement control. In: Quality and Statistics: Total Quality Management, Kowalewski, M. J. (ed). ASTM Philadelphia, PA, pp. 30–42.

Loehle, C. (2006) Species abundance distributions result from body size-energetics relationships. Ecology, 87, 2221–2226.

Loehle, C. & Hansen, A. (2005) Community structure and scaling relations for the avifauna of the US pacific and inland northwest. Ecological Complexity, 2, 59–70.

Loh, J., Green, R. E., Ricketts, T., Lamoreux, J., Jenkins, M., Kapos, V., & Randers, J. (2005) The Living Planet Index: using species population time series to track trends in biodiversity. Philosophical Transactions of the Royal Society, London, Series B, 360, 289–295.

Longino, J. T., Coddington, J., & Colwell, R. K. (2002) The ant fauna of a tropical rain forest: estimating species richness three different ways. Ecology, 83, 689–702.

Lopez, J. V., Culver, M., Stephens, J. C., Johnson, W. E., & O'Brien, S. J. (1997) Rates of nuclear and cytoplasmic mitochondrial DNA sequence divergence in mammals. Molecular Biology and Evolution, 14, 277–286.

Loreau, M. (2010) Linking biodiversity and ecosystems: towards a unifying ecological theory. Philosophical Transactions of the Royal Society, London, Series B, 365, 49–60.

Loreau, M., Naeem, S., & Inchausti, P. (2002) Biodiversity and Ecosystem Functioning: Synthesis and Perspectives. Oxford University Press, USA.

Luck, G. W. (2007) A review of the relationships between human population density and biodiversity. Biological Reviews, 82, 607–645.

Lukhtanov, V. A., Sourakov, A., Zakharov, E. V., & Hebert, P. D.N. (2009) DNA barcoding Central Asian butterflies: increasing geographical dimension does not significantly reduce the success of species identification. Molecular Ecology and Research, 9, 1302–1310.

Lynch, M. & Lande, R. (1993) Evolution and extinction in response to environmental change. In: Biotic Interactions and Global Change, Kareiva, P. M., Kingsolver, J. G., & Huey, R. B. (eds). Sinauer Associates, Sunderland, pp. 234–250.

Lyons, J. (1986) Capture efficiency of a beach seine for seven freshwater fishes in a north-temperate lake. North American Journal of Fisheries Management, 6, 288–289.

Mabunda, D., Pienaar, D. J., & Verhoef, J. (2003) The Kruger National Park: a century of management and research. In: The Kruger Experience: Ecology and Management of Savanna Heterogeneity, DuToit, J. T., Rogers, K. H., & Biggs, H. C. (eds). Island Press, Washington, pp. 3–21.

MacArthur, R. (1957) On the relative abundance of bird species. Proceedings of the National Academy of Sciences, 43, 293–295.

MacArthur, R. (1960) On the relative abundance of species. The American Naturalist, 94, 25–36.

MacArthur, R. H. (1965) Patterns of species diversity. Biological Reviews, 40, 510–533.

MacArthur, R. H. (1972) Geographical Ecology: Patterns in the Distribution of Species. Princeton University Press, Princeton, NJ.

MacArthur, R. & Levins, R. (1967) The limiting similarity, convergence, and divergence of coexisting species. The American Naturalist, 101, 377–385.

MacArthur, R. H. & Wilson, E. O. (1967) The Theory of Island Biogeography. Princeton University Press, Princeton.

Mace, G.M & Baillie, J. E. M. (2007) The 2010 biodiversity indicators: challenges for science and policy. Conservation Biology, 21, 1406–1413.

Mace, G. M., Collar, N. J., Gaston, K. J., Hilton-Taylor, C., Akçakaya, H. R., Leader-Williams, N., Milner-Gulland, E. J., & Stuart, S. N. (2008) Quantification of extinction risk: IUCN's system for classifying threatened species. Conservation Biology, 22, 1424–1442.

MacKenzie, D. I., Nichols, J. D., Lachman, G. B., Droege, S, Royle, J. A, & Langtimm, C. A. (2002) Estimating site occupancy rates when detection probabilities are less than one. Ecology, 83, 2248–2255.

MacKenzie, D. I., Nichols, J. D., Hines, J. E., Knutson, M. G., & Franklin, A. B. (2003) Estimating site occupancy, colonization, and local extinction when a species is detected imperfectly. Ecology, 84, 2200–2207.

MacKenzie, D. I., Nichols, J. D., Royle J. A., Pollock, K. H., Bailey, L. L., & Hines, J. E. (2006) Occupancy Estimation and Modeling: Inferring Patterns and Dynamics of Species Occurrence. Academic Press, San Diego.

MacNally, R. (2007) Use of the abundance spectrum and relative-abundance distributions to analyze assemblage change in massively altered landscapes. The American Naturalist, 170, 319–330.

Magurran, A. E. (1988) Ecological Diversity and its Measurement. Princeton University Press, Princeton, NJ.

Magurran, A. E. (2004) Measuring Biological Diversity. Blackwell Science, Oxford.

Magurran, A. E. (2005) Evolutionary Ecology: The Trinidadian Guppy. Oxford University Press, Oxford.

Magurran, A. E. (2007) Species abundance distributions over time. Ecology Letters, 10, 347–354.

Magurran, A. E. (2008) Diversity over time. Folia Geobotanica, 43, 319–327.

Magurran, A. E. (2009) Threats to freshwater fish. Science, 325, 1215–1216.

Magurran, A. E., Baillie, S. R., Buckland, S. T., Dick, J. McP., Elston, D. A., Scott, E. M., Smith, R. I., Somerfield, P. J., Watt, A. D. (2010) Long-term data sets in biodiversity research and monitoring: assessing change in ecological communities through time. Trends in Ecology and Evolution, in press.

Magurran, A. E. & Henderson, P. A. (2003) Explaining the excess of rare species in natural species abundance distributions. Nature, 422, 714–716.

Magurran, A. E. & Phillip, D. A. T. (2001) Implications of species loss in freshwater fish assemblages. Ecography, 24, 645–650.

Mandelbrot, B. B. (1963) New methods in statistical economics. Journal of Political Economy, 71, 421–440.

Mandelbrot, B. B. (1982) The fractal geometry of nature. W. H. Freeman and Co, New York.

Manly, B. F. J. (1991) Randomisation and Monte Carlo Methods in Biology. Chapman & Hall, London.

Manly, B. F. J. (2004) Multivariate Statistical Methods: A Primer. Chapman & Hall/CRC.

Manley, P. N., Zielinski, W. J., Schlesinger, M. D., & Mori, S. R. (2004) Evaluation of a multiple-species approach to monitoring species at the ecoregional scale. Ecological Applications, 14, 296–310.

Mantel, N. (1967) The detection of disease clustering and a generalized regression approach. Cancer Research, 27, 209–220.

Mao, C. X. & Colwell, R. K. (2005) Estimation of species richness: mixture models, the role of rare species, and inferential challenges. Ecology, 86, 1143–1153.

Mao, C. X. & Li, J. (2009) Comparing species assemblages via species accumulation curves. Biometrics, 65, 1063–1067.

Mao, C. X., Colwell, R. K., & Chang, J. (2005) Estimating species accumulation curves using mixtures. Biometrics, 61, 433–441.

Marques, T. A., Thomas, L., Fancy, S. G., & Buckland, S. T. (2007) Improving estimates of bird density using multiple covariate distance sampling. The Auk, 124, 1229–1243.

Marquet, P. A., Keymer, J. A., & Hernan, C. (2003) Breaking the stick in space: of niche models, metacommunities and patterns in the relative abundance of species. In: Macroecology: Concepts and Consequences, Blackburn, T. M. & Gaston, K. J. (eds). Blackwell Science, Oxford, pp. 64–86.

Marriott, E. (2002) The Plague Race. A Tale of Fear, Science and Heroism. Picador, London.

Marshall, C. R. (1990) Confidence intervals on stratigraphic ranges. Paleobiology, 16, 1–10.

Marshall, C. R. (1994) Confidence intervals on stratigraphic ranges: partial relaxation of the assumption of randomly distributed fossil horizons. Paleobiology, 20, 459–469.

Marshall, C. R. (1995) Distinguishing between sudden and gradual extinctions in the fossil record: predicting the position of the iridium anomaly using the ammonite fossil record on Seymour Island, Antarctica. Geology, 23, 731–734.

Marshall, C. R. (1997) Confidence intervals on stratigraphic ranges with nonrandom distributions of fossil horizons. Paleobiology, 23, 165–173.

Marshall, C. R. & Ward, P. D. (1996) Sudden and gradual molluscan extinctions in the latest Cretaceous of western European Tethys. Science, 274, 1360–1363.

Martin, J., Runge, M. C., Nichols, J. D., Lubow, B. C., & Kendall, W. L. (2009) Structured decision making as a conceptual framework to identify thresholds for conservation and management. Ecological Applications, 19, 1079–1090.

Martinez, W. L. & Martinez, A. R. (2002) Computational Statistics Handbook with MATLAB. Chapman & Hall/CRC, Boca Raton.

Mason, N. W.H., MacGillivray, K., Steel, J. B., & Wilson, J. B. (2003) An Index of functional diversity. Journal of Vegetation Science, 14, 571–578.

Mason, N. W.H., Mouillot, D., Lee, W. G., & Wilson, J. B. (2005) Functional richness, functional evenness and functional divergence: the primary components of functional diversity. Oikos, 111, 112–118.

Maurer, B. A. (1999) Untangling Ecological Complexity. University of Chicago Press, Chicago.

May, R. M. (1975) Patterns of species abundance and diversity. In: Ecology and Evolution of Communities, Cody, M. L. & Diamond, J. M. (eds). Harvard University Press Cambridge, MA, pp. 81–120.

May, R. M. (1990) Taxonomy as destiny. Nature, 347, 129–130.

May, R. M. (2007) Unanswered questions and why they matter. In Theoretical Ecology: Principles and

Applications, 3rd edn, May, R. M. & McLean, A. R. (eds), pp. 205–215. Oxford University Press, Oxford.

Mayfield, M., Boni, M., Daily, G., & Ackerly, D. D. (2005) Species and functional diversity of native and human-dominated plant communities. Ecology, 86, 2365–2372.

Mazancourt, C. (2001) Consequences of community drift. Science, 293, 1772.

McDonald, R. I., Kareiva, P., & Forman, R. T. T. (2008) The implications of current and future urbanization for global protected areas and biodiversity conservation. Biological Conservation, 141, 1695–1703.

McElwain, J. C., Wagner, P. J., & Hesselbo, S. P. (2009) Fossil plant relative abundances indicate sudden loss of Late Triassic biodiversity in Greenland. Science, 324, 1554–1556.

McGeoch, M. A. (1998) The selection, testing and application of terrestrial insects as bioindicators. Biological Reviews, 73, 181–201.

McGeoch, M. A. (2007) Insects and bioindication: theory and practice. In: Insect Conservation Biology, Stewart, A. J., New, T. R., & Lewis, O. T. (eds), CABI, Wallingford, pp. 144–174.

McGeoch, M. A. & Gaston, K. J. (2002) Occupancy frequency distributions: patterns, artefacts and mechanisms. Biological Reviews, 77, 311–331.

McGeoch, M. A., Van Rensburg, B. J., & Botes, A. (2002) The verification and application of bioindicators: a case study of dung beetles in a savanna ecosystem. Journal of Applied Ecology, 39, 661–672.

McGeoch, M. A., Kalwij, J. M., & Rhodes, J. I. (2009) A spatial assessment of Brassica napus gene flow potential to wild and weedy relatives in the Fynbos Biome. South African Journal of Science, 105, 109–115.

McGeoch, M. A., Schroeder, M., Ekbom, B., & Larsson, S. (2007) Saproxylic beetle diversity in a managed boreal forest: importance of stand characteristics and forestry conservation measures. Diversity & Distributions, 13, 418–429.

McGill, B. (2003a) Does Mother Nature really prefer rare species or are log-left-skewed SADs a sampling artefact? Ecology Letters, 6, 766–773.

McGill, B. J. (2003b) A test of the unified neutral theory of biodiversity. Nature, 422, 881–885.

McGill, B. J. (2003c) Strong and weak tests of macroecological theory. Oikos, 102, 679–685.

McGill, B. J. (2006) A renaissance in the study of abundance. Ecology, 314, 770–772.

McGill, B. J. (2010) Towards a unification of unified theories of biodiversity. Ecology Letters, 13, 627–642.

McGill, B. & Collins, C. (2003) A unified theory for macroecology based on spatial patterns of abundance. Evolutionary Ecology Research, 5, 469–492.

McGill, B. J. & Nekola, J. C. (2010) Mechanisms in macroecology: AWOL or purloined letter? Towards a pragmatic view of mechanism. Oikos, 119, 591–603.

McGill, B. J., Hadly, E. A., & Maurer, B. A. (2005) Community inertia of quaternary small mammal assemblages in North America. Proceedings of the National Academy of Sciences of the United States of America, 102, 16701–16706.

McGill, B. J., Maurer, B. A., & Weiser, M. D. (2006a) Empirical evaluation of the neutral theory. Ecology, 87, 1411–1423.

McGill, B. J., Enquist, B. J., Weiher, E., & Westoby, M. (2006b) Rebuilding community ecology from functional traits. Trends in Ecology and Evolution, 21, 178–185.

McGill, B. J., Etienne, R. S., Gray, J. S., Alonso, D., Anderson, M. J., Benecha, H. K., Dornelas, M., Enquist, B. J., Green, J. L., He, F., Hurlbert, A. H., Magurran, A. E., Marquet, P. A., Maurer, B. A., Ostling, A., Soykan, C. U., Ugland, K. I., & White, E. P. (2007) Species abundance distributions: moving beyond single prediction theories to integration within an ecological framework. Ecology Letters, 10, 995–1015.

McGowan, A. J. & Smith, A. B. (2008) Are global Phanerozoic marine diversity curves truly global? A study of the relationship between regional rock records and global Phanerozoic marine diversity. Paleobiology, 34, 80–103.

McIntire, E. J. B. & Fajardo, A. (2009) Beyond description: the active and effective way to infer processes from spatial patterns. Ecology, 90, 46–56.

McIntosh, R. P. (1962) Raunkiaer's "Law of Frequency". Ecology, 43, 533–535.

McIntosh, R. P. (1967) An index of diversity and the relation of certain concepts of diversity. Ecology, 48, 392–404.

McKinney, M. L. (2002) Influence of settlement time, human population, park shape and age, visitation and roads on the number of alien plant species in protected areas in the USA. Diversity & Distributions, 8, 311–318.

McKinney, M. L. (2006) Urbanization as a major cause of biotic homogenization. Biological Conservation, 127, 247–260.

McKinney, M. L. & Lockwood, J. L. (1999) Biotic homogenization: a few winners replacing many losers in the next mass extinction. Trends in Ecology and Evolution, 14, 450–453.

McNaughton, S. J. & Wolf, L. L. (1970) Dominance and the niche in ecological systems. Science, 167, 131–139.

McPeek, M. A. (2007) The macroevolutionary consequences of ecological differences among species. Paleontology, 50, 111–129.

McPeek, M. A. (2008) The ecological dynamics of clade diversification and community assembly. The American Naturalist, 172, E270–E284.

McPherson, J. M. & Jetz, W. (2007) Type and spatial structure of distribution data and the perceived determinants of geographical gradients in ecology: the species richness of African birds. Global Ecology and Biogeography, 16, 657–667.

McRae, B. H., Schumaker, N. H., McKane, R. B., Busing, R. T., Solomon, A. M., & Burdick, C. A. (2008) A multimoldel framework for simulating wildlife population response to land-use and climate change. Ecological Modelling, 219, 77–91.

Meier, R., Shiyang, K., Vaidya, G., & Ng, P. K. L. (2006) DNA barcoding and taxonomy in Diptera: a tale of high intraspecific variability and low identification success. Systematic Biology, 55, 715–728.

Meier, R., Zhang, G., & Ali, F. (2008) The use of mean instead of smallest interspecific distances exaggerates the size of the "Barcoding Gap" and leads to misidentification. Systematic Biology, 57, 809–813.

Mercado-Silva, N. & Escandon-Sandoval, D. S. (2008) A comparison of seining and electrofishing for fish community bioassessment in a Mexican Atlantic slope montane river. North American Journal of Fisheries Management, 28, 1725–1732.

Milesi, C., Hashimoto, H., Running, S. W., & Nemani, R. W. (2005) Climate variability, vegetation productivity and people at risk. Global and Planetary Change, 47, 221–231.

Millar, C. D., Huynen, L., Subramanian, S., Mohandesan, E., & Lambert, D. M. (2008) New developments in ancient genomics. Trends in Ecology and Evolution, 23, 386–393.

Millennium Ecosystem Assessment. (2005) Ecosystems and Human Well-being: Biodiversity Synthesis. World Resources Institute, Washington, DC.

Miller, A. I. & Foote, M. (1996) Calibrating the Ordovician Radiation of marine life: implications for Phanerozoic diversity trends. Paleobiology, 22, 304–309.

Minchin, P. R. (1987) An evaluation of the relative robustness of techniques for ecological ordination. Vegetatio, 69, 89–107.

Misra, M. K. & Misra, B. N. (1981) Species diversity and dominance in a tropical grassland community. Folia Geobotanica, 16, 309–316.

Monaghan, M. T., Wild, R., Elliot, M., Fujisawa, T., Balke, M., Inward, D. J. G., Lees, D. C., Ranaivosolo, R., Eggleton, P., Barraclough, T. G., & Vogler, A. P. (2009) Accelerated species inventory on Madagascar using coalescent-based models of species delineation. Systematic Biology, 58, 298–311.

Montroll, E. & Shlesinger, M. F. (1982) On 1/f noise and other distributions with long tails. Proceedings of the National Academy of Sciences, 79, 3380–3383.

Moodley, Y. & Bruford, M. W. (2007) Molecular biogeography: towards an integrated framework for conserving pan-African biodiversity. PLoS ONE, 5, e454.

Mooers, A. O. & Heard, S. B. (1997) Evolutionary process from phylogenetic tree shape. The Quarterly Review of Biology, 72, 31–54.

Mooers, A. O., Heard, S. B., & Chrostowski, E. (2005) Evolutionary heritage as a metric for conservation. In: Phylogeny and Conservation, Purvis, A., Brooks, T. L., & Gittleman, J. L. (eds). Oxford University Press, Oxford, pp. 120–138.

Mora, C., Tittensor, D. P., & Myers, R. A. (2008) The completeness of taxonomic inventories for describing the global diversity and distribution of marine fishes. Proceedings of the Royal Society London, B, 275, 149–155.

Moreno, C. E. & Halffter, G. (2001) Spatial and temporal analysis of α, β and γ diversity of bats in a fragmented landscape. Biodiversity and Conservation, 10, 367–382.

Morin, P. J. (1999) Community Ecology. Wiley-Blackwell, Malden, PA.

Morisita, M. (1959) Measuring of interspecific association and similarity between communities. Memoires of the Faculty of Science, Kyushu University, Series E (Biolology), 3, 65–80.

Morlon, H., Chuyong, G., Condit, R., Hubbell, S., Kenfack, D., Thomas, D., Valencia, R., & Green, J. L. (2008) A general framework for the distance – decay of similarity in ecological communities. Ecology Letters, 11, 904.

Morlon, H., White, E. P., Etienne, R. S., Green, J. L., Ostling, A., Alonso, D., Enquist, B. J., He, F., Hurlbert, A., Magurran, A. E., Maurer, B. A., McGill, B. J., Olff, H., Storch, D., & Zillio T. (2009) Taking species abundance distributions beyond individuals. Ecology Letters, 12, 488–501.

Morris, P. J., Ivany, L. C., Schopf, K. M., & Brett, C. E. (1995) The challenge of paleoecological stasis: reassessing sources of evolutionary stability. Proceedings of the National Academy of Sciences, USA, 92, 11269–11273.

Moss, D., Furse, M. T., Wright, J. F., & Armitage, P. D. (1987) The prediction of the macroinvertebrate fauna of unpolluted running-water sites in Great Britain using environmental data. Freshwater Biology, 17, 41–52.

Motomura, I. (1932) On the statistical treatment of communities. Zoological Magazine, Tokyo, 44, 379–383.

Mouchet, M., Guilhaumon, F., Villéger, S., Mason, N. W. H., Tomasini, J. A., & Mouillot, D. (2008) Towards a consensus for calculating dendrogram-based functional diversity indices. Oikos, 117, 794–800.

Mouillot, D., Mason, N. W. H., Dumay, O., & Wilson, J. B. (2005) Functional regularity: a neglected aspect of functional diversity. Oecologia, 142, 353–359.

Moulton, M. P. & Pimm, S. L. (1987) Morphological assortment in introduced Hawaiian passerines. Evolutionary Ecology, 1, 113–124.

Mulder, C. P. H., Uliasi, D. D., & Doak, D. F. (2001) Physical stress and diversity-productivity relationships: the role of positive interactions. Proceedings of the National Academy of Sciences USA, 98, 6704–6708.

Murphy, B. R. & Willis, D. W. (1996) Fisheries Techniques. American Fisheries Society, Bethesda, MD, USA.

Murray, R. D., Holling, M., Dott, H. E. M., & Vandome, P. (1998) The Breeding Birds of South-East Scotland. A tetrad atlas 1988–1994. The Scottish Ornithologists Club, Edinburgh.

Murray, B. R., Rice, B. L., Keith, D. A., Myerscough, P. J., Howell, J., Floyd, A. G., Mills, K., & Westoby, M. (1999) Species in the tail of rank-abundance curves. Ecology, 80, 1806–1816.

Muyzer, G., Dewaal, E. C., & Uitterlinden, A. G. (1993) Profiling of complex microbial-populations by denaturing gradient gel-electrophoresis analysis of polymerase chain reaction-amplified genes-coding for 16s ribosomal-RNA. Applied and Environmental Microbiology, 59, 695–700.

Nachman, G. (1981) A mathematical model of the functional relationship between density and spatial distribution of a population. Journal of Animal Ecology, 50, 453–460.

Nachman, G. (1984) Estimates of mean population density and spatial distribution of Tetranychus urticae (Acarina: Tetranychidae) and Phytoseiulus persimilis (Acarina: Phytoseiidae) based upon the proportion of empty sampling units. Journal of Applied Ecology, 21, 903–913.

Naeem, S., Bunker, D. E., Hector, A., Loreau, M., & Perrings, C. (2009) Biodiversity, Ecosystem Functioning, and Human Wellbeing: An Ecological and Economic Perspective. Oxford University Press, Oxford.

Nakatsu, C. H. (2007) Soil microbial community analysis using denaturing gradient gel electrophoresis. Soil Science Society of America Journal, 71, 562–571.

Nanney, D. L. (2004) No trivial pursuit. BioScience, 54, 720–721.

National Research Council. (2000) Ecological Indicators for the Nation. National Academy Press, Washington, DC.

Nee, S. (2003) The unified phenomenological theory of biodiversity. In: Macroecology: Concepts and Consequences, Blackburn, T. M. & Gaston, K. J. (eds). Blackwell Science, Oxford, pp. 31–44.

Nee, S., Harvey, P. H., & Cotgreave, P. (1992) Population persistence and the natural relationship between body size and abundance. In Conservation of Biodiversity for Sustainable Development, Sandlund, O. T., Hindar, K., & Brown, A. H. D. (eds). Scandavanian University Press, Oslo, pp. 124–136.

Nemani, R., Keeling, C. D., Hashimoto, H., Jolly, W. M., Piper, S. C., Tucker, C. J., Myneni, R. B., & Running, S. W. (2003) Climate-driven increases in global terrestrial net primary production from 1982 to 1999. Science, 300, 1560–1563.

Newson, S. E., Woodburn, R., Noble, D. G., & Baillie, S. R. (2005) Evaluating the breeding bird survey for producing national population size and density estimates. Bird Study, 52, 42–54.

Newson, S. E., Evans, K. L., Noble, D. G., Greenwood, J. J. D., & Gaston, K. J. (2008) Use of distance sampling to improve estimates of national population sizes for common and widespread breeding birds in the UK. Journal of Applied Ecology, 45, 1330–1338.

Nicholls, H. (2009) Darwin 200: Let's make a mammoth. Nature, 456, 310–314.

Nixon, K. C. & Wheeler, Q. D. (1992) Measures of phylogenetic diversity. In: Extinction and Phylogeny, Novacek, M. J. & Wheeler, Q. D. (eds). Columbia University Press, New York, pp. 216–234.

Norden, N., Chazdon, R., Chao, A., Jiang, Y. -H., & Vilchez-Alvarado, B. (2009) Resilience of tropical rain forests: rapid tree community reassembly in secondary forests. Ecology Letters, 12, 385–394.

Nusslein, K. & Tiedje, J. M. (1999) Soil bacterial community shift correlated with change from forest to pasture vegetation in a tropical soil. Applied and Environmental Microbiology, 65, 3622–3626.

Ochiai, A. (1957) Zoogeographic studies on the soleoid fishes found in Japan and its neighboring regions. Bulletin of the Japanese Society of Scientific Fisheries, 22, 526–530.

O'Dwyer, J. P., Lake, J. K., Ostling, A., Savage, V. M., & Green, J. L. (2009) An integrative framework for stochastic size-structured community assembly. Proceedings of the National Academy of Science, 106, 6170–6175.

Ogutu, J. O. & Owen-Smith, N. (2003) ENSO, rainfall and temperature influences on extreme population declines among African savanna ungulates. Ecology Letters, 6, 412–419.

O'Hara, R. B. (2005) Species richness estimators: how many species can dance on the head of a pin. Journal of Animal Ecology, 74, 375–386.

Oksanen, J., Kindt, R., Legendre, P., O'Hara, B., Simpson, G.L., & Stevens, M. H. H. (2008) vegan: Community Ecology Package. In: R package version. http://cran.r-project.org.

Olden, J. D. (2006) Biotic homogenization: a new research agenda for convervation biogeography. Journal of Biogeography, 33, 2027–2039.

Olsen, G. J., Lane, D. J., Giovannoni, S. J., Pace, N. R., & Stahl, D. A. (1986) Microbial ecology and evolution – a ribosomal-RNA approach. Annual Review of Microbiology, 40, 337–365.

Olson, V. A., Davies, R. G., Orme, C. D. L., Thomas, G. H., Meiri, S., Blackburn, T. M., Gaston, K. J., Owens, I. P. F., & Bennett, P. M. (2009) Global biogeography and ecology of body size in birds. Ecology Letters, 12, 249–259.

Oremland, R. S., Capone, D. G., Stolz, J. F., & Fuhrman, J. (2005) Whither or wither geomicrobiology in the era of 'community metagenomics'. Nature Reviews Microbiology, 3, 572–578.

Osborn, A. M., Moore, E. R. B., & Timmis, K. N. (2000) An evaluation of terminal-restriction fragment length polymorphism (T-RFLP) analysis for the study of microbial community structure and dynamics. Environmental Microbiology, **2**, 39–50.

Øvreås, L. (2000) Population and community level approaches for analyzing microbial diversity in natural environments. Ecology Letters, 3, 236–251.

Ovreas L. & Torsvik, L. Microbial diversity and community structure in two different agricultural soil communities. Microbial Ecology, 36, 303–315.

Øvreås, L., Daae, F. L., Torsvik, V., & Rodriguez-Valera, F. (2003) Characterization of microbial diversity in hypersaline environments by melting profiles and reassociation kinetics in combination with terminal restriction fragment length polymorphism (T-RFLP). Microbial Ecology, 46, 291–301.

Owen-Smith, N., Kerley, G. I. H., Page, B., Slotow, R., & van Aarde, R. J. (2006) A scientific perspective on the management of elephants in the Kruger National Park and elsewhere. South African Journal of Science, 102, 389–394.

Pace, N. R. (1997) A molecular view of microbial diversity and the biosphere. Science, 276, 734–740.

Pace, N. R., Stahl, D. A., Lane, D. J., & Olsen, G. J. (1986) The analysis of natural microbial-populations by ribosomal-RNA sequences. Advances in Microbial Ecology, 9, 1–55.

Packer, L., Gibbs, J., Sheffield, C., & Hanner, R. (2009) DNA barcoding and the mediocrity of morphology. Molecular Ecology and Research, 9(Suppl. 1), 42–50.

Palomares, F., Godoy, J. A., Piriz, A., O'Brien, S. J., & Johnson, W. E. (2002) Faecal genetic analysis to determine the presence and distribution of elusive carnivores: design and feasibility of the Iberian Lynx. Molecular Ecology, 11, 2171–2182.

Palumbi, S. R. & Cipriano, F. (1998) Species identification using genetic tools: the value of nuclear and mitochondrial gene sequences in whale conservation. The Journal of Heredity, 89, 459–464.

Pan, H. Y., Chao, A., & Foissner, W. (2009) A nonparametric lower bound for the number of species shared by multiple communities. Journal of Agricultural, Biological and Environmental Statistics, 14, 452–468.

Pardo, L. (2006) Statistical Inference Based on Divergence Measures. Chapman & Hall/CRC, Taylor & Francis Group, Boca Raton, FL.

Parmesan, C. (2006) Ecological and evolutionary responses to recent climate change. Annual Review of Ecology, Evolution and Systematics, 37, 637–669.

Parr, C. L. & Chown, S. L. (2003) Burning issues for conservation: a critique of faunal fire research in Southern Africa. Austral Ecology, 28, 384–395.

Parr, C. L., Robertson, H. G., Biggs, H. C., & Chown, S. L. (2004) Response of African savanna ants to long-term fire regimes. Journal of Applied Ecology, 41, 630–642.

Parsons, R. F. & Cameron, D. G. (1974) Maximum plant species diversity in terrestrial communities. Biotropica, 6, 202–203.

Parsons, K. M., Piertney, S. B., Middlemas, S. J., Hammond, P. S., & Armstrong, J. D. (2005) DNA-based identification of salmonid prey species in seal faeces. Journal of Zoology, 266, 275–281.

Passmore, A. J., Jarman, S. N., Swadling, K. M., Kawaguchi, S., McMinn, A., & Nicol, S. (2006) DNA as a dietary biomarker in Antarctic krill, Euphausia superba. *Journal of Marine Biotechnology*, 8, 686–696.

Patrício, J., Salas, F., Pardal, M. A., Jørgensen, S. E., & Marques, J. C. (2006) Ecological indicators performance during a re-colonisation field experiment and its compliance with ecosystem theories. Ecological Indicators, 6, 43–57.

Patuxent Wildlife Research Center (2001) Breeding Bird Survey FTP site. URL ftp://www.mp2-pwrc.usgs.gov/pub/bbs/Datafiles/

Pausas, J. G. & Verdú, M. (2008) Fire reduces morphospace occupation in plant communities. Ecology, 89, 2181–2186.

Pautasso, M. & Gaston, K. J. (2005) Resources and global avian assemblage structure in forests. Ecology Letters, 8, 282–289.

Pavoine, S., Ollier, S., & Pontier, D. (2005a) Measuring diversity from dissimilarities with Rao's quadratic entropy: are any dissimilaries suitable? Theoretical Population Biology, 67, 231–239.

Pavoine, S., Ollier, S., & Dufour, A. B. (2005b) Is the originality of a species measurable? Ecology Letters, 8, 579–586.

Pavoine, S., Love, M., & Bonsall, M. B. (2009) Hierarchical partitioning of evolutionary and ecological patterns in the organization of phylogenetically-structured species assemblages: application to rockfish (genus: Sebastes) in the Southern California Bight. Ecology Letters, 12, 898–908.

Payton, M. E., Greenstone, M. H., & Schenker, N. (2003) Overlapping confidence intervals or standard error intervals: What do they mean in terms of statistical significance? 6 pp. Journal of Insect Science, 3, 34, available online: insectscience.org/3.34.

Pearson, T. H. (1975) The benthic ecology of Loch Linnhe and Loch Eil, a sea loch system on the west coast of Scotland. IV. Changes in the benthic fauna attributable to organic enrichment. Journal of Experimental Marine Biology and Ecology, 20, 1–41.

Pease, C. M. (1988) Biases in the survivorship curves of fossil taxa. Journal of Theoretical Biology, 130, 31–48.

Peet, R. K. (1974) The measurement of species diversity. Annual Review of Ecology and Systematics, 5, 285–307.

Perry, J. N., Liebhold, A. M., Rosenberg, M. S., Dungan, J., Miriti, M., Jakomulska, A. & Citron-Pousty, S. (2002) Illustrations and guidelines for selecting statistical methods for quantifying spatial pattern in ecological data. Ecography, 25, 578.

Perry, J. N. & Woiwod, I. P. (1992) Fitting Taylor's power law. Oikos, 65, 538–542.

Perry, J. N. & Taylor, L. R. (1985) Adès: new ecological families of species-specific frequency distributions that describe repeated spatial samples with an intrinsic power-law variance-mean property. Journal of Animal Ecology, 54, 931–953.

Perry, J. N. & Taylor, L. R. (1986) Stability of real interacting populations in space and time: implications, alternatives and the negative binomial kc. Journal of Animal Ecology, 55, 1053–1068.

Pertoldi, C., Wójcik, J. M., Malgorzata, T., Kawalko, A., Kristensen, T. N., Loeschcke, V., Gregersen, V. R., Coltman, D., Wilson, G. A., Randi, E., Henryon, M., & Bendixen, C. (2009) Genome variability in European and American bison detected using the BovineSNP50 BeadChip. Conservation Genetics, 11, 627–634. doi: 10.1007/s10592–009–9977-y.

Petchey, O. L. & Gaston, K. J. (2002) Functional diversity (FD), species richness and community composition. Ecology Letters, 5, 402–411.

Petchey, O. L. & Gaston, K. J. (2004) How do different measures of functional diversity perform? Ecology, 85, 847–857.

Petchey, O. L. & Gaston, K. J. (2006) Functional diversity: back to basics and looking forward. Ecology Letters, 9, 741–758.

Petchey, O. L. & Gaston, K. J. (2007) Dendrograms and measuring functional diversity. Oikos, 116, 1422–1426.

Petchey, O. L., O'Gorman, E. J., & Flynn, D. F. B. (2009) A functional guide to functional diversity measures. In: Biodiversity, Ecosystem Functioning, and Human Wellbeing: An Ecological and Economic Perspective, Naeem, S., Bunker, D. E., Hector, A., Loreau, M., & Perrings, C. (eds). Oxford University Press, Oxford, pp. 49–59.

Peters, S. E. (2006) Genus extinction, origination, and the durations of sedimentary hiatuses. Paleobiology, 32, 387–407.

Peters, S. E. & Foote, M. (2002) Determinants of extinction in the fossil record. Nature, 416, 420–424.

Peterson, J. T. & Paukert, C. P. (2009) Converting nonstandard fish sampling data to standardized data. In: Standard Methods for Sampling North American Freshwater Fishes, Bonar, S. A., Hubert, W. A., & Willis, D. W. (eds). American Fisheries Society, Bethesda, MD.

Phillips, J. (1860) Life on Earth: its Origin and Succession. Macmillan, Cambridge.

Phillip, D. A. (1998) Biodiversity of freshwater fishes of Trinidad and Tobago, West Indies. In: School of Biology. University of St Andrews, St Andrews, p. 99.

Pianka, E. R. (1989) Latitudinal gradients in species diversity. Trends in Ecology and Evolution, 4, 223.

Pielou, E. C. (1975) Species abundance distributions. In: Ecological Diversity. Wiley Interscience, New York, pp. 19–31.

Pielou, E. C. (1977) Mathematical Ecology. Wiley, New York.

Pillans, S., Ortiz, J.-C., Pillans, R. D., & Possingham, H. P. (2007) The impact of marine reserves on nekton diversity and community composition in subtropical eastern Australia. Biological Conservation, 136, 455–469.

Piña-Alguilar, R. E., Lopez-Saucedo, J., Sheffield, R., Ruiz-Galaz, L. I., Barroso-Padilla, J. J., & Gutiérrez-Gutiérrez, A. 2009. Revival of extinct species using nuclear transfer: hope for the mammoth, true for the Pyrenean ibex, but is it time for "conservation cloning"?. Cloning and Stem Cells, 11, 341–346.

Piñeyro-Nelson, A., Van Heerwaarden, J., Perales, H. R. et al. (2009) Transgenes in Mexican maize: molecular evidence and methodological considerations for GMO detection in landrace populations. Molecular Ecology, 18, 750–761.

Platt, J. R. (1964) Strong inference. Science, 146, 347–353.

Platt, H. M., Shaw, K. M., & Lambshead, P. J.D. (1984) Nematode species abundance patterns and their use in the detection of environmental perturbations. Hydrobiologia, 118, 59–66.

Plotkin, J. B. & Muller-Landau, H. C. (2002) Sampling the species composition of a landscape. Ecology, 83, 3344–3356.

Podani, J. (2005) Multivariate exploratory data analysis of ordinal data in ecology: pitfalls, problems and solutions. Journal of Vegetation Science, 16, 497–510.

Podani, J. & Schmera, D. (2006) On dendrogram-based measures of functional diversity. Oikos, 115, 179–185.

Podani, J. & Schmera, D. (2007) How should a dendrogram based measure of functional diversity function? A rejoinder to Petchey and Gaston. Oikos, 116, 1427–1430.

Poff, N. L., Olden, J. D., Vieira, N. K. M., Finn, D. S., Simmons, M. P., & Kondratieff, B. C. (2006) Functional trait niches of North American lotic insects: traits-based ecological applications in light of phylogenetic relationships. Journal of North American Benthic Society, 25, 730–755.

Pollard, E. (1979) A national scheme for monitoring the abundance of butterflies. The first three years. Proceedings and Transactions of the British Entomological and Natural History Society, 12, 77–90.

Poon, E. L. & Margules, C. R. (2004) Searching for new populations of rare plant species in remote locations. In: Sampling Rare or Elusive Species, Thompson, W. L. (ed). Island Press, Washington, DC, pp. 189–207.

Poos, M. S., Walker, S. C., & Jackson, D. A. (2009) Functional-diversity indices can be driven by methodological choices and species richness. Ecology, 90, 341–347.

Popper, K. R. (1959) The Logic of Scientific Discovery. Hutchinson.

Porter, W. P., Sabo, J. L., Tracy, C. R., Reichman, O. J., & Ramankutty, N. (2002) Physiology on a landscape scale: plant-animal interactions. Integrative and Comparative Biology, 42, 431–453.

Pradel, R. (1996) Utilization of Capture-Mark-Recapture for the study of recruitment and population growth rate. Biometrics, 52, 703–709.

Prendergast, J. R., Quinn, R. M., Lawton, J. H., Eversham, B. C., & Gibbons, D. W. (1993) Rare Species, the Coincidence of Diversity Hotspots and Conservation Strategies. Nature, 365, 335–337.

Press, W. H., Teukolsky, S. A., Vetterling, W. T., & Flannery, B. P. (2007) Numerical Recipes: The Art of Scientific Computing. Cambridge University Press, Cambridge.

Preston, F. W. (1948) The commonness and rarity of species. Ecology, 29, 254–283.

Preston, F. W. (1960) Time and space and the variation of species. Ecology, 41, 612–627.

Preston, F. W. (1962) The canonical distribution of commonness and rarity: Parts 1 and 2. Ecology, 43, 185–215, 410–432.

Price, P. W., Diniz, I. R., Morais, H. C., & Marques, E. S. A. (1995) The abundance of insect herbivore species in the tropics: the high local richness of rare species. Biotropica, 27, 468–478.

Primack, R. B. (1998). Essentials of Conservation Biology, 2nd edn. Sinauer Associates, Sunderland, MA.

Pueyo, S. (2006) Diversity: between neutrality and structure. Oikos, 112, 392–405.

Pueyo, Y., Alados, C. L., & Ferrer-Benimeli, C. (2006) Is the analysis of plant community structure better than common species-diversity indices for assessing the effects of livestock grazing on a Mediterranean arid ecosystem? Journal of Arid Environments, 64, 698–712.

Purvis, A. & Hector, A. (2000) Getting the measure of biodiversity. Nature, 405, 212–219.

Pybus, O. G. & Harvey, P. H. (2000) Testing macroevolutionary models using incomplete molecular phylogenies. Proceedings of the Royal Society London, B, 267, 2267–2272.

Quince, C., Curtis, T. P., & Sloan, W. T. (2008) The rational exploration of microbial diversity. The ISME Journal, 2, 997–1006.

Quince, C., Lanzen, A., Curtis, T. P., Davenport, R. J., Hall, N., Head, I. M., Read, L. F., & Sloan, W. T. (2009) Accurate determination of microbial diversity from 454 pyrosequencing data. Nature Methods 6, 639–641.

Quinn, G. P. & Keough, M. J. (2002) Experimental Design and Data Analysis for Biologists. Cambridge University Press, Cambridge.

R Development Core Team. (2005) R: A Language and Enviornment for Statistical Computing. R Foundation for Statistical Computing, Vienna, Austria.

Rabeni, C. F., Peterson, J. T., Lyons, J., & Mercado-Silva, N. (2009) Sampling fish in warmwater wadeable streams. In: Standard Methods for Sampling North American Freshwater Fishes, Bonar, S. A., Hubert, W. A., & Willis, D. W. (eds). American Fisheries Society, Bethesda.

Rabinowitz, D. (1981) Seven forms of rarity. In: Biological Aspects of Rare Plant Conservation, Synge, H. (ed.). Wiley, Chichester, pp. 205–217.

Rabinowitz, D., Cairns, S., & Dillon, T. (1986) Seven forms of rarity and their frequency in the flora of the British Isles. In: Conservation Biology: The Science of Scarcity and Diversity, Soulé, M. J. (ed). Sinauer, Sunderland, MA, pp. 182–204.

Rahbek, C. & Graves, G. R. (2001) Multiscale assessment of patterns of avian species richness. Proceedings of the National Academy of Sciences. USA, 98, 4534–4539.

Rand, T. A., Tylianakis, J. M., & Tscharntke, T. (2006) Spillover edge effects: the dispersal of agriculturally subsidized insect natural enemies into adjacent natural habitats. Ecology Letters, 9, 603–614.

Rangel, T., Diniz-Filho, J. A. F., & Bini, L. M. (2006) Towards an integrated computational tool for spatial analysis in macroecology and biogeography. Global Ecology and Biogeography, 15, 321–327.

Ranjard, L., Poly, F., Combrisson, J., Richaume, A., Gourbiere, F., Thioulouse, J., & Nazaret, S. (2000) Heterogeneous cell density and genetic structure of bacterial pools associated with various soil microenvironments as determined by enumeration and DNA fingerprinting approach (RISA). Microbial Ecology, 39, 263–272.

Rao, C. R. (1982) Diversity and dissimilarity coefficients: a unified approach. Theoretical Population Biology, 21, 24–43.

Rapoport, E. H. 1982. Areography: Geographical Strategies of Species. Pergamon, Oxford.

Ratnasingham, S. & Hebert, P. D. N. (2007) BOLD: the barcode of life data system (www.barcodinglife.org). Molecular Ecology Notes 7:355–364.

Raunkaier, C. (1909) Formationsundersogelse og Formationsstatistik. Svensk Botanisk Tidskrift, 30, 20–132.

Raunkaier, C. (1934) Life Forms and Statistical Plant Geography. Oxford University Press, Oxford.

Raup, D. M. (1975) Taxonomic diversity estimation using rarefaction. Paleobiology, 1, 333–342.

Raup, D. M. (1978) Cohort analyses of generic survivorship. Paleobiology, 4, 1–15.

Raup, D. M. (1979) Size of the Permo-Triassic bottleneck and its evolutionary implications. Science, 206, 217–218.

Raup, D. M. (1991) A kill curve for Phanerozoic marine species. Paleobiology, 17, 37–48.

Raup, D. M. & Boyajian, G. E. (1988) Patterns of generic extinction in the fossil record. Paleobiology, 14, 109–125.

Raup, D. M. & Sepkoski, J. J., Jr. (1982) Mass extinctions in the marine fossil record. Science, 215, 1501–1503.

Raxworthy, C. J., Pearson, R. G., Rabibisoa, N., Rakotondrazafy, A. M., Ramanamanjato, J.-B., Raselimanana, A. P., Wu, S., Nussbaum, R. A., & Stone, D. A. (2008) Extinction vulnerability of tropical montane endemism from warming and upslope displacement: a preliminary appraisal for the highest massif in Madagascar. Global Change Biology, 14, 1703–1720.

Redding, D. W. & Mooers, A. O. (2006) Incorporating evolutionary measures into conservation prioritisation. Conservation Biology, 20, 1670–1678.

Redding, D. W., Hartmann, K., Mimoto, A., Bokal, D., DeVos, M., & Mooers, A. O. (2008) Evolutionarily distinctive species often capture more phylogenetic diversity than expected. Journal of Theoretical Biology, 251, 606–615.

Regan, H. M., Hierl, L. A., Franklin, J., Deutschman, D. H., Schmalbach, H. L., Winchell, C. S., & Johnson, B. S. (2008) Species prioritization for monitoring and management in regional multiple species conservation plans. Diversity & Distributions, 14, 462–471.

Reid, W. V. (1998) Biodiversity hotspots. Trends in Ecology and Evolution, 13, 275–280.

Renkonen, O. (1938) Statistisch-ökologische Untersuchungen über die terrestrische Käferwelt der finnischen Bruchmoore. Annale Zoologici Societatis Zoologicae-Botanicae Fennicae Vanamo, 6, 1–231.

Rice, J. C. (2000) Evaluating fishery impacts using metrics of community structure. ICES Journal of Marine Science, 57, 682–688.

Richards, P. W. 1969. Speciation in the tropical rain forest and the concept of the niche. Biological Journal of the Linnean Society, 1, 149–153.

Richardson, D. M., Holmes, P. M., Esler, K. J., Galatowitsch, S. M., Stromberg, J. C., Kirkman, S. P., Pyšek, P., & Hobbs, R. J. (2007) Riparian vegetation: degradation, alien plant invasions, and restoration prospects. Diversity & Distributions, 13, 126–139.

Ricklefs, R. E. 2008. Disintegration of the ecological community. The American Naturalist, 172, 741–750.

Ricklefs, R. E. & Travis, J. (1980) A morphological approach to the study of avian community organization. Auk, 97, 321–338.

Ricotta, C. (2004) A parametric diversity measure combining the relative abundances and taxonomic distinctiveness of species. Diversity & Distributions, 10, 143–146.

Ricotta, C. (2005) A note on functional diversity measures. Basic and Applied Ecology, 6, 479–486.

Ricotta, C. & Moretti, M. (2008) Quantifying functional diversity with graph-theoretical measures: advantages and pitfalls. Community Ecology, 9, 11–16.

Ricotta, C. & Szeidl, L. (2009) Diversity partitioning of Rao's quadratic entropy. Theoretical Population Biology, 76, 299–302.

Riitters, K. H., O'Neill, R. V., Hunsaker, C. T., Wickham, J. D., Yankee, D. H., Timmins, S. P., Jones, K. B., & Jackson, B. L. (1995) A factor analysis of landscape pattern and structure metrics. Landscape Ecology, 10, 23–39.

Robbins, C. S., Bystrak, D., & Geissler, P. H. (1986) The Breeding Bird Survey: Its First Fifteen Years, 1965–1979. US Dept of the Interior, Fish and Wildlife Service, Washington, DC.

Roca. A. L., Georgiadis, N., Pecon-Slattery, J., & O'Brien, S. J. (2001) Genetic evidence for two species of elephant in Africa. Science, 293, 1747–1477.

Roche Diagnostics. (2009) Using Multiplex Identifier (MID) Adaptors for the GS FLX Titanium Chemistry – Basic MID Set. Technical Bulletin Genome Sequencer FLX System, Mannheim, Germany, pp. 1–11.

Rodrigues, A. S. L., Gregory, R. D., & Gaston, K. J. (2000) Robustness of reserve selection procedures under temporal species turnover. Proceedings of the Royal Society London, 267, 49–55.

Roe, A. D. & Sperling, F. A. H. (2007) Patterns of evolution of mitochondrial cytochrome c oxidase I and II DNA and implications for DNA barcoding. Molecular Phylogenetics and Evolution, 44, 325–345.

Roesch, L. F., Fulthorpe, R. R., Riva, A., Casella, G., Hadwin, A. K. M., Kent, A. D., Daroub, S. H., Camargo, F. A. O., Farmerie, W. G., & Triplett, E. W. (2007) Pyrosequencing enumerates and contrasts soil microbial diversity. The ISME Journal, 1, 283–290.

Romanov, M. N., Tuttle, E. M., Houck, M. L., Modi, W. S., Chemnick, L. G., Karody, M. L., Stremel Mork, E. M., Otten, C. A., Renner, T., Jones, K. C., Dandekar, S., Papp, J. C., Da, Y., NISC Comparative Sequencing Program, Green, E. D., Magrini, V., Hickenbotham, M. T., Glasscock, J., McGrath, S., Mardis, E. R., & Ryder, O. A. (2009) The value of avian genomics to the conservation of wildlife. BMC Genomics, 10: doi:10.1186/1471-2164-10-S2-S10.

Romanuk, T. N. & Kolasa, J. (2001) Simplifying the complexity of temporal diversity dynamics: a differentiation approach. Ecoscience, 8, 259–263.

Rondinini, C., Wilson, K. A., Boitani, L., Grantham, H., & Possingham, H. P. (2006) Tradeoffs of different types of species occurrence data for use in systematic conservation planning. Ecology Letters, 9, 1136–1145.

Rondon, M. R., August, P. R., Bettermann, A. D., Brady, S. F., Grossman, T. H., Liles, M. R., Loiacono, K. A., Lynch, B. A., MacNeil, I. A., Minor, C., Tiong, C. L., Gilman, M., Osburne, M. S., Clardy, J., Handelsman, J., & Goodman, R. M. (2000) Cloning the soil metagenome: a strategy for accessing the genetic and functional diversity of uncultured microorganisms. Applied and Environmental Microbiology, 66, 2541–2547.

Rosenfeld, J. S. (2002) Functional redundancy in ecology and conservation. Oikos, 98, 156–162.

Rosenzweig, M. L. (1992) Species diversity gradients: we know more and less than we thought. Journal of Mammalogy, 73, 715–730.

Rosenzweig, M. L. (1995) Species Diversity in Space and Time. Cambridge University Press, Cambridge.

Rosenzweig, M. L. (1998) Preston's ergodic conjecture: the accumulation of species in space and time. In: Biodiversity Dynamics: Turnover of Populations, Taxa, and Communities, McKinney, M. L. & Drake, J. A. (eds). Columbia University Press New York, pp. 311–348.

Rosenzweig, M. L. (2003) Reconciliation ecology and the future of species diversity. Oryx, 37, 194–205.

Rosenzweig, M. L. (2004) Applying species-area relationships to the conservation of species diversity. In: Frontiers of Biogeography: New Directions in the Geography of Nature, Lomolino, M. V. & Heany, L. (eds). Sinauer Associates, Sunderland, MA, pp. 325–343.

Rosenzweig, M. L., Turner, W. R. Cox, J. G., & Ricketts, T. H.. (2003) Estimating diversity in unsampled habitats of a biogeographical province. Conservation Biology, 17, 864–874.

Rosewell, J., Shorrocks, B., & Edwards, K. (1990) Competition on a divided and ephemeral resource: testing the assumptions. I. Aggregation. Journal of Animal Ecology, 59, 977–1001.

Rosing, M. T. & Frei, R. (2004) U-rich Archaean sea-floor sediments from Greenland – indications of > 3700 Ma oxygenic photosynthesis. Earth and Planetary Science Letters, 217, 237–244.

Rossi, R. E., Mulla, D. J., Journel, A. G., & Franz, E. H. (1992) Geostatistical tools for modeling and interpreting ecological spatial dependence. Ecological Monographs, 62, 277–314.

Roughgarden, J. (2009) Is there a general theory of community ecology? Biology and Philosophy, 24, 521–529.

Routledge, R. (1979) Diversity indices: which ones are admissible? Journal of Theoretical Biology, 76, 503–515.

Routledge, R. D. & Swartz, T. B. (1991) Taylor's power law reexamined. Oikos, 60, 107–112.

Rovito, S. M., Parra-Olea, S., Vásquez-Almazán, C. R., Papenfuss, T. J., & Wake, D. B. (2009) Dramatic declines in neotropical salamander populations are an important part of the global amphibian crisis. Proceedings of the National Academy of Sciences. USA, 106, 3231–3236.

Royal Society. (2003) Measuring Biodiversity for Conservation. The Royal Society, London.

Royle, R. A., Nichols, J. D., & Kéry, M. (2005) Modelling occurrence and abundance of species when detection is imperfect. Oikos, 110, 353–359.

Rubinoff, D., Cameron, S., & Will, K. (2006) A genomic perspective on the shortcomings of mitochondrial DNA for "barcoding" identification. The Journal of Heredity, 97, 581–594.

Li, R., Fan, W., Tian, G., Zhu, H., He, L., Cai, J., Huang, Q., Cai, Q., Li, B., Bai, Y., Zhang, Z., Zhang, Y., Wang, W., Li, J., Wei, F., Li, H., Jian, M., Li, J., Zhang, Z., Nielsen, R., Li, D., Gu, W., Yang, Z., Xuan, Z., Ryder, O. A., Leung, F. C.-C., Zhou, Y., Cao, J., Sun, X., Fu, Y., Fang, X., Guo, X.,

Wang, B., Hou, R., Shen, F., Mu, B., Ni, P., Lin, R., Qian, W., Wang, G., Yu, C., Nie, W., Wang, J., Wu, Z., Liang, H., Min, J., Wu, Q., Cheng, S., Ruan, J., Wang, M., Shi, Z., Wen, M., Liu, B., Ren, X., Zheng, H., Dong, D., Cook, K., Shan, G., Zhang, H., Kosiol, C., Xie, X., Lu, Z., Zheng, H., Li, Y., Steiner, C., Lam, T., Lin, S., Zhang, Q., Li, G., Tian, J., Gong, T., Liu, H., Zhang, D., Fang, L., Ye, C., Zhang, J., Hu, W., Xu, A., Ren, Y., Zhang, G., Bruford, M. W., Li, Q., Ma, L., Guo, Y., An, N., Hu, Y., Zheng, Y., Shi, Y., Li, Z., Liu, Q., Chen, Y., Zhao, J., Qu, N., Zhao, S., Tian, F., Wang, X., Wang, H., Xu, L., Liu, X., Vinar, T., Wang, Y., Lam, T.-W., Yiu, S.-M., Liu, S., Zhang, H., Li, D., Huang, Y, Wang, X., Yang, G., Jiang, Z., Wang, J., Qin, N., Li, L., Li, J., Bolund, L., Kristiansen, K., Wong, G. K.-S., Olson, M., Zhang, X., Li, S., Yang, H., Wang, J., & Wang, J. (2010). The sequence and de novo assembly of the giant panda genome. Nature, 463, 311–317.

Rusch, D. B., Halpern, A. L., Sutton, G., Heidelberg, K. B., Williamson, S., Yooseph, S., Wu, D., Eisen, J. A., Hoffman, J. M., Remington, K., Beeson, K., Tran, B., Smith, H., Baden-Tillson, H., Stewart, C., Thorpe, J., Freeman, J., Andrews-Pfannkoch, C., Venter, J. E., Li, K., Kravitz, S., Heidelberg, J. F., Utterback, T., Rogers, Y. -H., Falcón, L. I., Souza, V., Bonilla-Rosso, G., Eguiarte, L. E., Karl, D. M., Sathendranath, S., Platt, T., Bermingham, E., Gallardo, V., Tamayo-Castillo, G., Ferrari, M. R., Strausberg, R. L., Nealson, K., Friedman, R., Frazier, M., & Venter, J. C. (2007) The Sorcerer II global ocean sampling expedition: Northwest Atlantic through Eastern tropical Pacific. PLoS Biology, 5, 398–431.

Russell, G. J., Diamond, J. M., Pimm, S. L., & Reed, T. M. (1995) A century of turnover: community dynamics at three timescales. Journal of Animal Ecology, 64, 628–641.

Rust, K. F. & Rao, J. N. K. (1996) Variance estimation for complex surveys using replication techniques. Statistical Methods in Medical Research, 5, 283–310.

Ryti, R. T. & Case, T. J. (1986) Overdispersion of ant colonies: a test of hypotheses. Oecologia, 69, 446–453.

Sachs, J. D. (2008) Common Wealth: Economics for a Crowded Planet. Penguin Press, London.

Sadler, P. M. & Cooper, R. A. (2003) Best-fit intervals and consensus sequences: a comparison of the resolving power of traditional biostratigraphy and computer assisted correlation. In: High-Resolution Stratigraphic Approaches in Paleontology, Harries, P. (ed). Plenum Press, New York, pp. 49–94.

Saint-Germain, M., Buddle, C. M., Larrivée, M., Mercado, A., Motchula, T., Reichert, E., Sackett, T. E., Sylvain, Z., & Webb, A. (2007) Should biomass be considered more frequently as a currency in terrestrial arthropod community analysis. Journal of Applied Ecology, 44, 330–339.

Salas, F., Marcos, C., Neto, J. M., Patrício, J., Perez-Ruzafa, A., & Marques, J. C. (2006a) User-friendly guide for using benthic ecological indicators in coastal and marine quality assessment. Ocean and Coastal Management, 49, 308–331.

Salas, F., Patrício, J., Marcos, C., Pardal, M. A., Perez-Ruzafa, A., & Marques, J. C. (2006b) Are taxonomic distinctness measures compliant to other ecological indicators in assessing ecological status? Marine Pollution Bulletin, 52, 162–174.

Samways, M. J. (1989) Insect conservation and the disturbance landscape. *Agriculture, Ecosystems & Environment*, 27, 183–194.

Sanders, H. (1968) Marine benthic diversity: a comparative study. The American Naturalist, 102, 243.

Sara, M. (2008) Breeding abundance of threatened raptors as estimated from occurrence data. The Ibis, 150, 776–778.

Sawyer, A. J. (1989) Inconstancy of Taylor's b: simulated sampling with different quadrat sizes and spatial distributions. Research in Population Ecology, 31, 11–24.

Scharff, N., Coddington, J. A., Griswold, C. E., Hormiga, G., & De Place Bjørn, P. (2003) When to quit? Estimating spider species richness in a northern European deciduous forest. Journal of Arachnology, 31, 246–273.

Scheaffer, R. L., Mendenhall, W., & Ott, L. (2006) Elementary Survey Sampling. Thomson Brooks/Cole, Southbank, Vic., Belmont, CA.

Schechtman, E. & Wang, S. (2004) Jackknifing two-sample statistics. Journal of statistical Planning and Inference, 119, 329–340.

Scheiner, S. M., Cox, S. B., Willig, M., Mittelbach, G. G., Osenberg, C., & Kaspari, M. (2000) Species richness, species-area curves and Simpson's paradox. Evolutionary Ecology Research, 2, 791–802.

Schiermeier, Q. (2005) Hurricane link to climate change is hazy. Nature, 437, 461–461.

Schleper, C., Jurgens, G., & Jonuscheit, M. (2005) Genomic studies of uncultivated archaea. Nature Reviews Microbiology, 3, 479–488.

Schloss, P. D. & Handelsman, J. (2006a) Introducing SONS, a tool for operational taxonomic unit-based comparisons of microbial community memberships and structures. Applied Environmental Microbiology, 72, 6773–6779.

Schloss, P. D. & Handelsman, J. (2006b) Toward a census of bacteria in soil. Plos Computational Biology, 2, 786–793.

Schmera, D., Erös, T., & Podani, J. (2009) A measure for assessing functional diversity in ecological communities. Aquatic Microbial Ecology, 43, 157–167.

Schulze, E. -D. & Mooney, H. A. (1994) Biodiversity and Ecosystem Function. Springer, Berlin, Germany.

Schulze, C. H., Waltert, M., Kessler, P. J. A., et al. (2004) Biodiversity indicator groups of tropical land-use systems: comparing plants, birds, and insects. Ecological Applications, 14, 1321–1333.

Schwarz, G. (1978) Estimating the dimension of a model. Annals of Statistics, 6, 461–464.

Schwieger, F. & Tebbe, C. C. (1998) A new approach to utilize PCR-single-strand-conformation polymorphism for 16s rRNA gene-based microbial community analysis. Applied and Environmental Microbiology, 64, 4870–4876.

Schweiger, O., Klotz, S., Durka, W., & Kühn, I. (2008) A comparative test of phylogenetic diversity indices. Oecologia, 157, 485–495.

Seeger, M. & Jerez, C. A. (1992) Phosphate limitation affects global gene-expression in Thiobacillus-ferrooxidans. Geomicrobiology Journal, 10, 227–237.

Seigel, A. F. & German, R. Z. (1982) Rarefaction and taxonomic diversity. Biometrics, 38, 235–2411.

Selmi, S. & Boulinier, T. (2004) Distribution-abundance relationship for passerines breeding in Tunisian oases: test of the sampling hypothesis. Oecologia, 139, 440–445.

Sepkoski, J. J., Jr. (1975) Stratigraphic biases in the analysis of taxonomic survivorship. Paleobiology, 1, 343–355.

Sepkoski, J. J., Jr. (1979) A kinetic model of Phanerozoic taxonomic diversity. II. Early Phanerozoic families and multiple equilibria. Paleobiology, 5, 222–251.

Sepkoski, J. J., Jr. (1982) A compendium of fossil marine families. Milwaukee Public Museum Contributions in Biology and Geology, 51, 139.

Sepkoski, J. J. Jr. (1988) Alpha, beta, or gamma: where does all the diversity go? Paleobiology, 14, 221–234.

Sepkoski, J. J., Jr. (2002) A compendium of fossil marine animal genera. Bulletins of American Paleontology, 363, 1–563.

Shaw, A. B. (1964) Time in Stratigraphy. McGraw-Hill, New York.

Shaw, J., Lickey, E. B., Schilling, E. E., & Small, R. L. (2007) Comparison of whole chloroplast genome sequences to choose noncoding regions for phylogenetic studies in angiosperms: the tortoise and the hare III. American Journal of Botany, 94, 275–288.

Shen, T., Chao, A., & Lin, C. (2003) Predicting the number of new species in further taxonomic sampling. Ecology, 84, 798–804.

Sherwin, W. B., Jabot, F., Rush, R., & Rossetto, M. (2006) Measurement of biological information with applications from genes to landscapes. Molecular Ecology, 15, 2857–2869.

Shimida, A. (1984) Whittaker's plant diversity sampling method. Israel Journal of Botany, 33, 41–46.

Shimitani, K. (2001) On the measurement of species diversity incorporating species differences. Oikos, 93, 135–147.

Shorrocks, B. & Rosewell, J. (1986) Guild size in drosophilids: a simulation model. Journal of Animal Ecology, 55, 527–541.

Shurin, J. B. (2007) How is diversity related to species turnover through time? Oikos, 116, 957–965.

Siddall, M. E., Fontanella, F. M., Watson, S. C., Kvist, S., & Erséus, C. (2009) Barcoding bamboozled by bacteria: convergence to metazoan mitochondrial primer targets by marine microbes. Systematic Biology, 58, 445–451.

Signor, P. W., III & Lipps, J. H. (1982) Sampling bias, gradual extinction patterns and catastrophes in the fossil record. Geological Society of America Special Paper, 190, 291–296.

Sileshi, G., Hailu, G., & Mafongoya, P. L. (2006) Occupancy-abundance models for predicting densities of three leaf beetles damaging the multipurpose tree Sesbania sesban in eastern and southern Africa. Bulletin of Entomological Research, 96, 61–69.

Simberloff, D. S. (1972) Properties of the rarefaction diversity measurement. The American Naturalist, 106, 414–418.

Simberloff, D. (1978) Use of rarefaction and related methods in ecology. In: Biological Data in Water Pollution Assessment: Quantitative and Statistical Analyses, Dickson, K. L., Cairns, J., Jr., & Livingston, R. J. (eds). American Society for Testing and Materials, Philadelphia, pp. 150–165.

Simberloff, D. & Connor, E. F. (1979) Q-mode and R-mode analyses of biogeographic distributions: null hypotheses based on random colonization. In: Contemporary Quantitative Ecology and Related Econometrics, Patil, G. P. & Rosenzweig, M. L. (eds), International Cooperative Publishing House, Fairland, pp. 123–128.

Simková, A., Kadlec, D., Gelnar, M., & Morand, S. (2002) Abundance-prevalence relationship of gill congeneric ectoparasites: testing the core satellite hypothesis and ecological specialisation. Parasitology Research, 88, 682–686.

Simpson, E. H. (1949) Measurement of diversity. Nature, 163, 688.

Simpson, G. G. (1944) Tempo and Mode in Evolution. Columbia University Press, New York.

Simpson, G. G. (1953) The Major Features of Evolution. Columbia University Press, New York.

Singh, J., Behal, A., Singla, N., Joshi, A., Birbian, N., Singh, S., Bali, V., & Batra, N. (2009) Metagenomica: concept, methodology, ecological inference and recent advances. Biotechnology Journal, 4, 480–494.

Sitran, R., Bergamasco, A., Decembrini, F., & Guglielmo, L. (2009) Microzooplankton (tintinnid ciliates) diversity: coastal community structure and driving mechanisms in the southern Tyrrhenian Sea (Western Mediterranean). Journal of Plankton Research, 31, 153–170.

Šizling, A. L. & Storch, D. (2004) Power-law species – area relationships and self-similar species distributions within finite areas. Ecology Letters, 7, 60–68.

Šizling, A. L. & Storch, D. (2007) Geometry of species distributions: random clustering and scale invariance. In: Scaling Biodiversity, Storch, D., Marquet, P. A., & Brown, J. H. (eds). Cambridge University Press, Cambridge, pp. 77–100.

Šizling, A. L., Šizlingová, E., Storch, D., Reif, J., & Gaston, K. J. (2009) Rarity, commonness and the contribution of individual species to species richness patterns. The American Naturalist, 174, 82–93.

Sloan, W. T., Quince, C., & Curtis, T. P. (2008) The Uncountables. In: Accessing Uncultivated Microorganisms: from the Environment to Organisms and Genomes and Back, Zengler, K. (ed). ASM Press: Washington, DC, pp. 35–54.

Smith, M. D. & Knapp, A. K. (2003) Dominant species maintain ecosystem function with non-random species loss. Ecology Letters, 6, 509–517.

Smith, W. & Grassle, F. (1977) Sampling properties of a family of diversity measures. Biometrics, 33, 283–292.

Smith, B. & Wilson, J. B. (1996) A consumer's guide to evenness indices. Oikos, 76, 70–82.

Smith, E. P. & Zaret, T. M. (1982) Bias in estimating niche overlap. Ecology, 63, 1248–1253.

Smith, K. W., Dee, C. W., Fearnside, J. D., Fletcher, E. W., & Smith, R. N. (1993) The Breeding Birds of Hertfordshire. The Hertfordshire Natural History Society, Hertfordshire.

Smith, W., Solow, A. R., & Preston, P. E. (1996) An estimator of species overlap using a modified beta-binomial model. Biometrics, 52, 1472–1477.

Smith, A. B., Gale, A. S., & Monks, N. E. (2001) Sea-level change and rock-record bias in the Cretaceous: a problem for extinction and biodiversity studies. Paleobiology, 27, 241–253.

Smith, D. R., Brown, J. A., & Lo, N. C.H. (2004) Applications of adaptive sampling to biological populations. In: Sampling for Rare or Elusive Species: Concepts, Designs, and Techniques for Estimating Population Parameters, Thompson, W. L. (ed). Island Press, Washington, pp. 77–122.

Sobek S., Steffan-Dewenter I., Scherber C., & Tscharntke T. (2009) Spatiotemporal changes of beetle communities across a tree diversity gradient. Diversity & Distributions, 15, 660–670.

Soberón, J. (2007) Grinnellian and Eltonian niches and geographic distributions of species. Ecology Letters, 10, 1115–1123.

Soberón, J. & Llorente, J. (1993) The use of species accumulation functions for the prediction of species richness. Conservation Biology, 7, 480–488.

Sogin, M. L., Morrison, H. G., Huber, JA., Welch, D. M., Huse, S. M., Neal, P. R., Arrieta, J. M., & Herndl, G. J., (2006) Microbial diversity in the deep sea and the underexplored "rare biosphere". Proceedings of the National Academy of Sciences, 103, 12115–12120.

Solow, A. R. (1993a) Inferring extinction from sighting data. Ecology, 74, 962–963.

Solow, A. R. (1993b) Inferring extinction in a declining population. Journal of Mathematical Biology, 32, 79–82.

Solow, A. R. (1996) Tests and confidence intervals for a common upper endpoint in fossil taxa. Paleobiology, 22, 406–410.

Solow, A. R. & Smith, W. K. (1997) On fossil preservation and the stratigraphic ranges of taxa. Paleobiology, 23, 271–277.

Song, H., Buhay, J. E., Whiting, M. F., & Crandall, K. A. (2008) Many species in one: DNA barcoding overestimates the number of species when nuclear, mitochondrial pseudogenes are coamplified. Proceedings of the National Academy of Sciences, 105, 13486–13491.

Sørensen, T. (1948) A method of establishing groups of equal amplitude in plant sociology based on similarity of species content and its application to analyses of the vegetation on Danish commons. Biologiske Skrifter, 5, 1–34.

Sorensen, L. L., Coddington, J. A., & Scharff, N. (2002) Inventorying and estimating subcanopy spider diversity using semiquantitative sampling methods in an Afromontane forest. Environmental Entomology, 31, 319–330.

Soule, M. E. (1986) Conservation Biology: The Science of Scarcity and Diversity. Sinauer Associates, Sunderland, MA.

Sousa, W. P. (1979) Disturbance in marine intertidal boulder fields: the nonequilibrium maintenance of species diversity. Ecology, 60, 1225–1239.

Sousa, W. P. (1984) The role of disturbance in natural communities. Annual Review of Ecology and Systematics, 15, 353–391.

Southwood, T. R. E. (1977) Habitat: the templet for ecological strategies. Journal of Animal Ecology, 46, 337–365.

Southwood, T. R. E. (1978) Ecological Methods. Chapman & Hall, London.

Southwood, T. R. E. (1996) The Croonian Lecture 1995. Natural communities: structure and dynamics. Philosophical Transactions of the Royal Society, London Lond. B., 351, 1113–1129.

Southwood, R. & Henderson, P. A. (2000) Ecological Methods. 3rd edn. Blackwell Science, Oxford.

Soykan, C., McGill, B., Magurran, A., Dornelas, M., Bahn, V., Ugland, K., & Gray, J. S. (in prep.) An Assessment of Indicator Performance along Human Disturbance Gradients.

Spiegelhalter, D., Best, N., Calin, B., & van der Linde, A. (2002) Bayesian measures of model complexity and fit. Journal of the Royal Statistical Society, Series B, 64, 583–639.

Staley, J. T. & Konopka, A. (1985) Measurement of in-situ activities of nonphotosynthetic microorganisms in aquatic and terrestrial habitats. Annual Review of Microbiology, 39, 321–346.

Steffan-Dewenter, I., Muenzenberg, U., Buerger, C., Thies, C., & Tscharntke, T. (2002) Scale-dependent effects of landscape context on three pollinator guilds. Ecology, 83, 1421–1432.

Stein, B. A., Scott, C., & Benton, N. (2008) Federal lands and endangered species: the role of military and other federal lands in sustaining biodiversity. Bioscience, 58, 339–347.

Steinke, D., Vences, M., Salzburger, W., & Meyer, A. (2005) TaxI: a software tool for DNA barcoding using distance methods. Philosophical Transactions of the Royal Society, London B, 360, 1075–1980.

Stewart, J. G., Schieble, C. S., Cashner, R. C., & Barko V. A. (2005) Long-term Trends in the Bogue Chitto River Fish Assemblage: a 27 Year Perspective. Southeastern Naturalist, 4, 261–272.

Stirling, G. & Wilsey, B. (2001) Empirical relationships between species richness, evenness, and proportional diversity. The American Naturalist, 158, 286–299.

Stohlgren, T. J. (2007) Measuring Plant Diversity: Lessons from the Field. Oxford University Press, Oxford, New York.

Stohlgren, T. J., Jarnevich, C., Chong, G. W., & Evangelista, P. H. (2006) Scale and plant invasions: a theory of biotic acceptance. Preslia, 78, 405–426.

Storch, D. & Šizling, A. L. (2002) Patterns in commonness and rarity in Central European birds: reliability of the core-satellite hypothesis. Ecography, 25, 405–416.

Storch, D., Šizling, A., Reif, J., Polechová, J., Šizlingová, E., & Gaston, K. J. (2008) The quest for a null model for macroecological patterns: geometry of species distributions at multiple spatial scales. Ecology Letters, 11, 771–784.

Storfer, A., Eastman, J. M., & Spear, S. F. (2009) Modern molecular methods for amphibian conservation. BioScience, 59, 559–571.

Strauss, D. & Sadler, P. M. (1989) Classical confidence intervals and Bayesian probability estimates for ends of local taxon ranges. Mathematical Geology, 21, 411–427.

Strong, D. R., Simberloff, D., Abele, L. G., & Thistle, A. B. (1984) Ecological Communities: Conceptual Issues and the Evidence. Princeton University Press, Princeton, USA.

Sugihara, G. (1980) Minimal community structure: an explanation of species abundance patterns. The American Naturalist, 116, 770–787.

Sugihara, G., Bersier, L. F., Southwood, T. R. E., Pimm, S. L., & May, R. M. (2003) Predicted correspondence between species abundances and dendrograms of niche similarities. Proceedings of the National Academy of Sciences of the United States of America, 100, 5246–5251.

Sutherland, W. J., Bailey, M. J., Bainbridge, I. P., et al. (2008) Future novel threats and opportunities facing UK biodiversity identified by horizon scanning. Journal of Applied Ecology, 45, 821–833.

Swenson, N. G. & Enquist, B. J. (2007) Ecological and evolutionary determinants of a key plant functional trait: wood density and its community-wide variation across latitude and elevation. American Journal of Botany, 94, 451–459.

Swingle, H. S. (1950) Relationships and Dynamics of Balanced and Unbalanced Fish Populations. Agricultural Experiment Station of the Alabama Polytechnic Institute, Auburn, AL.

Swingle, H. S. (1952) Farm pond investigations in Alabama. Journal of Wildlife Management, 16, 243–249.

Taberlet, P. & Fumagalli, L. (1996) Owl pellets as a source of DNA for genetic studies of small mammals. Molecular Ecology, 5, 301–305.

Taper, M. L. & Lele, S. R. (2004) The Nature of Scientific Evidence: Statistical, Philosophical, and Empirical Considerations.. University of Chicago Press, Chicago.

Tavares, E. S. & Baker. A. J. (2008) Single mitochondrial gene barcodes reliably identify sister-species in diverse clades of birds. BMC Evolutionary Biology, 8, 81.

Taylor, L. R. (1961) Aggregation, variance and the mean. Nature, 189, 732–735.

Taylor, L. R. (ed.) (1978) Bates, Williams, Hutchinson – A Variety of Diversities. Blackwell Publishing, Oxford.

Taylor, L. R. (1984) Assessing and interpreting the spatial distributions of insect populations. Annual Review of Entomology, 29, 321–357.

Taylor, L. R., Kempton, R. A., & Woiwod, I. P. (1976) Diversity statistics and the log series model. Journal of Animal Ecology, 45, 255–271.

Taylor, L. R., Woiwod, I. P., & Perry, J. N. (1978) The density-dependence of spatial behaviour and the rarity of randomness. Journal of Animal Ecology, 47, 383–406.

Taylor, L. R., Woiwod, I. P., & Perry, J. N. (1979) The negative binomial as a dynamic ecological model for aggregation and the density dependence of k. Journal of Animal Ecology, 48, 289–304.

Taylor, C. M., Millican, D. S., Roberts, M. E., & Slack, W. T. (2008) Long-term change to fish assemblages and the flow regime in a southerneastern U. S. river system after extensive aquatic ecosystem fragmentation. Ecography, 31, 787–797.

Teplitsky, C., Mills, J. A., Alho, J. S., Yarrall, J. W., & Merilä, J. (2008) Bergmann's rule and climate change revisited: disentangling environmental and genetic responses in a wild bird population. Proceedings of the National Academy of Sciences. USA, 105, 13492–13496.

Terborgh, J. T. (1983) Five New World Primates: a Study in Comparative Ecology. Princeton University Press, Princeton, NJ.

Terborgh, J., Foster, R. B., & Núñez, V. P. (1996) Tropical tree communities: a test of the nonequilibrium hypothesis. Ecology, 77, 561–567.

The H. John Heinz III Center for Science, Economics, and the Environment (2008) The Nation's Ecosystems: core Indicators, Pn: The State of the Nation's Ecosystems 2008; Measuring the Land, Waters, and Living Resources of The United States. Island Press, Washington, DC., 13–62.

Thibault, K., White, E., & Ernest, S. K.M. (2004) Temporal dynamics in the structure and composition of a desert rodent community. Ecology, 85, 2649–2655.

Thomas, C. D. & Mallorie, H. C. (1985) Rarity, species richness and conservation: butterflies of the Atlas Mountains of Morocco. Biological Conservation, 33, 95–117.

Thomas, L., Buckland, S. T., Rexstad, E. R., Laake, J. L., Strindberg, S., Hedley, S. L., Bishop, J. R. B., Marques, T. A., & Burnham, K. P. (2010) Distance software: design and analysis of distance sampling surveys for estimating population size. Journal of Applied Ecology, 47, 5–14.

Thomaz, D., Guiller, A., & Clarke, B. (1996) Extreme divergence of mitochondrial DNA within species of pulmonate land snails. Proceedings of the Royal Society London, B, 263, 363–368.

Thompson, W. L. (2004) Sampling Rare or Elusive Species: Concepts, Designs, and Techniques for Estimating Population Parameters. Island Press, Washington.

Thrush, S. F., Hewitt, J. E., Dayton, P. K., Coco, G., Lohrer, A. M., Norkko, A., Norkko, J., & Chiantore, M. (2009) Forecasting the limits of resilience: integrating empirical research with theory. Proceedings of the Royal Society London, 276, 3209–3217.

Tiedje, J. M., Asuming-Brempong, S., Nusslein, K., Marsh, T. L., & Flynn, S. J. (1999) Opening the black box of soil microbial diversity. Applied Soil Ecology, 13, 109–122.

Tilman, D. (2001) Functional diversity. In: Encyclopaedia of Biodiversity, Levin, S. A. (ed). Academic Press, San Diego, CA, pp. 109–120.

Tilman, D., Lehman, C. L., & Kareiva, P. (1997a) Population dynamics in spatial habitats. In: Spatial Ecology, Tilman, D. & Kareiva, P. (eds). Princeton University Press, New Jersey, pp. 3–20.

Tilman, D., Knops, J., Wedin, D., Reich, P., Ritchie, M., & Siemann, E. (1997b) The influence of functional diversity and composition on ecosystem processes. Science, 277, 1300.

Tipper, J. C. (1979) Rarefaction and rarefiction—the use and abuse of a method in paleoecology. Paleobiology, 5, 423–434.

Tobler, W. R. (1970) A computer movie simulating urban growth in the Detroit region. Economic Geography, 46, 234–240.

Todd, S. W. (2006) Gradients in vegetation cover, structure and species richness of Nama-Karoo shrublands in relation to distance from livestock watering points. Journal of Applied Ecology, 43, 293–304.

Tokeshi, M. (1990) Niche apportionment or random assortment: species abundance patterns revisited. Journal of Animal Ecology, 59, 1129–1146.

Tokeshi, M. (1993) Species abundance patterns and community structure. Advances in Ecological Research, 24, 112–186.

Tokeshi, M. (1996) Power fraction: a new explanation of relative abundance patterns in species-rich assemblages. Oikos, 75, 543–550.

Tokeshi, M. (1999) Species Coexistence. Blackwell Sciences Ltd, Oxford.

Tomašových, A. & Kidwell, S. M. (2009) Fidelity of variation in species composition and diversity partitioning by death assemblages: time-averaging transfers diversity from beta to alpha levels. Paleobiology, 35, 94–118.

Torsvik, V., Goksoyr, J., & Daae, F. L. (1990a) High diversity in DNA of soil bacteria. Applied and Environmental Microbiology, 56, 782–787.

Torsvik, V., Salte, K., Sorheim, R., & Goksoyr, J. (1990b) Comparison of phenotypic diversity and DNA heterogeneity in a population of soil bacteria. Applied and Environmental Microbiology, **56**, 776–781.

Torsvik, V., Daae, F. L., Sandaa, R. A., & Ovreas, L. (1998) Novel techniques for analysing microbial diversity in natural and perturbed environments. Journal of Biotechnology, 64, 53–62.

Torsvik, V., Ovreas, L., & Thingstad, T. F. (2002) Prokaryotic diversity – magnitude, dynamics, and controlling factors. Science, **296**, 1064–1066.

Tosh, C. A., Reyers, B., & van Jaarsveld, A. S. (2004) Estimating the abundances of large herbivores in the Kruger National Park using presence-absence data. *Animal Conservation*, 7, 55–61.

Toth, M. 2008. A new noninvasive method for detecting mammals from birds' nests. Journal of Wildlife Management, 72, 1237–1240.

Tratalos, J., Fuller, R. A., Evans, K. L., Davies, R. G., Newson, S. E., Greenwood, J. J.D., & Gaston, K. J. (2007) Bird densities are associated with household densities. Global Change Biology, 13, 1685–1695.

Travis, J. & Ricklefs, R. E. (1983) A morphological comparison of island and mainland assemblages of Neotropical birds. Oikos, 41, 434–441.

Tringe, S. G., von Mering, C., Kobayashi, A., Salamov, A. A., Chen, K., Chang, H. W., Podar, M., Short, J. M., Mathur, E. J., Detter, J. C., Bork, P., Hugenholtz, P., & Rubin, E. M. (2005) Comparative metagenomics of microbial communities. Science, 308, 554–557.

Tscharntke, T., Gathmann, A., & Steffan-Dewenter, I. (1998) Bioindication using trap-nesting bees and wasps and their natural enemies: community structure and interactions. Journal of Applied Ecology, 35, 708–719.

Tscharntke, T., Klein, A., Kruess, A., Steffan-Dewenter, I., & Thies, C. (2005) Landscape perspectives on agricultural intensification and biodiversity – ecosystem service management. Ecology Letters, 8, 857–874.

Tscharntke, T., Sekercioglu, C. H., Dietsch, T. V., Sodhi, N. S., Hoehn, P., & Tylianakis, J. M. (2008) Landscape constraints on functional diversity of birds and insects in tropical agroecosystems. Ecology, 89, 944–951.

Tuomisto, H. (2010) A diversity of beta diversities: straightening up a concept gone awry. Part 1. Defining beta diversity as a function of alpha and gamma diversity. Ecography, 33, 2–22.

Tuomisto, H., Ruokolainen, K., Kalliola, R., Linna, A., Danjoy, W., & Rodriguez, Z. (1995) Dissecting Amazonian biodiversity. Science, 269, 63–66.

Turner, W., Leitner, W. A., & Rosenzweig, M. L. (2000) Ws2m.exe. http://eebweb.arizona.edu/diversity.

Tylianakis, J. M., Klein, A. -M., & Tscharntke, T. (2005) Spatiotemporal variation in the diversity of hymenopters across a tropical habita gradient. Ecology, 86, 3296–3302.

Tyson, G. W., Chapman, J., Hugenholtz, P., Allen, E. E., Ram, R. J., Richardson, P. M., Solovyev, V. V., Rubin, E. M., Rokhsar, D. S., & Banfield, J. F. (2004) Community structure and metabolism through reconstruction of microbial genomes from the environment. Nature, 428, 37–43.

Ugland, K. I. & Gray, J. S. (1982) Lognormal distributions and the concept of community equilibrium. Oikos, 39, 171–178.

Ugland, K. I., Gray, J. S., & Ellingsen, K. E. (2003) The species – accumulation curve and estimation of species richness. Journal of Animal Ecology, 72, 888–897.

Ugland, K. I., Lambshead, F. J. D., McGill, B., Gray, J. S., O'Dea, N., Ladle, R. J., & Whittaker, R. J. (2007) Modelling dimensionality in species abundance distributions: description and evaluation of the Gambin model. Evolutionary Ecology Research, 9, 313–324.

Ulrich, W. & Buszko, J. (2003) Self-similarity and the species-area relation of Polish butterflies. Basic and Applied Ecology, 4, 263–270.

Ulrich, W. & Ollik, M. (2004) Frequent and occasional species and the shape of relative-abundance distributions. Diversity & Distributions, 10, 263–269.

Ulrich, W. & Zalewski, M. (2006) Abundance and co-occurrence patterns of core and satellite species of ground beetles on small lake islands. Oikos, 114, 338–348.

Umina, P. A., Weeks, A. R., Kearney, M. R., McKechnie, S. W., & Hoffmann, A. A. (2005) A rapid shift in a classic clinal pattern in *Drosophila* reflecting climate change. Science, 308, 691–693.

Urich, T., Lanzen, A., Qi, J., Huson, D. H., Schleper, C., & Schuster, S. C. (2008) Simultaneous assessment of soil microbial community structure and function through analysis of the Meta-Transcriptome. PLoS ONE, 3, e2527.

Urquhart, N. S. & Kincaid, T. M. (1999) Designs for detecting trend from repeated surveys of ecological resources. Journal of Agricultural, Biological, and Environmental Statistics, 4, 404–414.

Urquhart, N. S., Paulsen, S. G., & Larsen, D. P. (1998) Monitoring for policy-relevant regional trends over time. Ecological Applications, 8, 246–257.

Valentini, A., Miquel, C., Nawaz, M. A., Bellemain, E., Coissac, E., Pompanon, F., Gielly, L., Cruaud, C., Nascetti, G., Wincker, P., Swenson, J. E., & Taberlet, P. (2009) New perspectives in diet analysis based on DNA barcoding and parallel pyrosequencing: the trnL approach. Molecular Ecology Research, 9, 51–60.

Vamosi, S. M., Heard, S. B., Vamosi, J. C., & Webb, C. O. (2009) Emerging patterns in the comparative analysis of phylogenetic community structure. Molecular Ecology, 18, 572–592.

van der Gast, C. J., Ager, D., & Lilley, A. K. (2008) Temporal scaling of bacterial taxa is influences by both stochastic and deterministic ecological factors. Environmental Microbiology, 10, 1411–1418.

Vandermeer, J., Granzow de la Cerda, I., Perfecto, I., Boucher, D., Ruiz, J. & Kaufmann, A. (2004) Multiple basins of attraction in a tropical forest: evidence for a nonequilibrium community structure. Ecology, 85, 575–579.

van Rensburg, B. J., McGeoch, M. A., Matthews, W., Chown, S. L., & van Jaarsveld, A. S. (2000) Testing generalities in the shape of patch occupancy frequency distributions. Ecology, 81, 3163–3177.

van Rensburg, B. J., Chown, S. L., & Gaston, K. J. (2002) Species richness, environmental correlates, and spatial scale: a test using South African birds. The American Naturalist, 159, 566–577.

van Straalen, N. M. (1998) Evaluation of bioindicator systems derived from soil arthropod communities. Applied Soil Ecology, 9, 429–437.

van Straalen, N. M. & Verhoef, H. A. (1997) The development of a bioindicator system for soil acidity based on arthropod pH preferences. The Journal of Applied Ecology, 34, 217–232.

Van Valen, L. (1973) A new evolutionary law. Evolutionary Theory, 1, 1–30.

Van Valen, L. (1979) Taxonomic survivorship curves. Evolutionary Theory, 4, 129–142.

Vane-Wright, R. I., Humphries, C. J., & Williams, P. H. (1991) What to protect? – Systematics and the agony of choice. Biological Conservation, 55, 235–254.

Veech, J. A., Summerville, K. S., Crist, T. O., & Gering, J. C. (2002) The additive partitioning of species diversity: recent revival of an old idea. Oikos, 99, 3–9.

Veldtman, R. & McGeoch, M. A. (2004) Spatially explicit analyses unveil density dependence. Proceedings of the Royal Society London, B, 271, 2439–2444.

Vellend, M. (2001) Do commonly used indices of β-diversity measure species turnover? Journal of Vegetation Science, 12, 545–552.

Vellend, M., Harmon, L. J., Lockwood, J. L., Mayfield, M. M., Hughes, A. R., Wares, J. P., & Sax, D. F. (2007) Effects of exotic species on evolutionary diversification. Trends in Ecology and Evolution, 22, 481–488.

Vences, M., Thomas, M., Bonett, R. M., & Vieites, D. R. (2005a) Deciphering amphibian diversity through DNA barcoding: chances and challenges. Philosophical Transactions of the Royal Society, London B 360: 1859–1868.

Vences, M., Thomas, M., van der Meijden, A., Chiari, Y., & Vieites, D. R. (2005b) Comparative performance of the 16S rRNA gene in DNA barcoding of amphibians. Frontiers in Zoology, 2, 5.

Venier, L. A. & Fahrig, L. (1998) Intraspecific abundance-distribution relationships. Oikos, 82, 438–490.

Venter, J. C., Remington, K., Heidelberg, J. F., Halpern, A. L., Rusch, D., Eisen, J. A., Wu, D. Y., Paulsen, I., Nelson, K. E., Nelson, W., Fouts, D. E., Levy, S., Knap, A. H., Lomas, M. W., Nealson, K., White, O., Peterson, J., Hoffman, J., Parsons, R., Baden-Tillson, H., Pfannkoch, C., Rogers, Y. H., & Smith, H. O. (2004) Environmental genome shotgun sequencing of the Sargasso Sea. Science, 304, 66–74.

Vera, M., Guiliani, N., & Jerez, C. A. (2003) Proteomic and genomic analysis of the phosphate starvation response of Acidithiobacillus ferrooxidans. Hydrometallurgy, 71, 125–132.

Vera, J. C., Wheat, C. W., Fescemyer, H. W., Frilander, M. J., Crawford, D. L., Hanski, I., & Marden, J. H. (2008) Rapid transcriptome characterization for a nonmodel organism using 454 pyrosequencing. Molecular Ecology, 17, 1636–1647.

Vile, D., Shipley, B., & Garnier, E. (2006) Ecosystem productivity can be predicted from potential relative growth rate and species abundance. Ecology Letters, 9, 1061–1067.

Villéger, S., Mason, N. W.H., & Mouillot, D. (2008) New multidimensional functional diversity indices for a multifaceted framework in functional ecology. Ecology, 89, 2290–2301.

Violle, C. & Jiang, L. (2009) Towards a trait-based quantification of species niche. Journal of Plant Ecology, 2, 87–93.

Virginia Natural Heritage Program. (2006) DCR-DNH vegetation plots database, ver. 3.0. Virginia Department of Conservation and Recreation, Division of Natural Heritage, Richmond.

Vitousek, P. M., Ehrlich, P. R., Ehrlich, A. H., & Matson, P. A. (1986) Human appropriation of the products of photosynthesis. BioScience, 36, 368–373.

Vitousek, P. M., Mooney, H. A., Lubchenco, J., & Melillo, J. M. (1997) Human domination of Earth's ecosystems. Science, 277, 494–499.

Volkov, I., Banavar, J. R., Hubbell, S. P., & Maritan, A. (2003) Neutral theory and relative species abundance in ecology. Nature, 424, 1035–1037.

Volkov, I., Banavar, J. R., Hubbell, S. P., & Maritan, A. (2007) Patterns of relative species abundance in rainforests and coral reefs. Nature, 450, 45–49.

Vrba, E. S. (1985) Environment and evolution: alternative causes of the temporal distribution of evolutionary events. South African Journal of Science, 81, 229–236.

Wagner, P. J. (2000) Likelihood tests of hypothesized durations: determining and accommodating biasing factors. Paleobiology, 26, 431–449.

Walker, B., Kinzig, A., & Langridge, J. (1999) Plant attribute diversity, resilience, and ecosystem function: the nature and significance of dominant and minor species. Ecosystems, 2, 95–113.

Walker, S. C., Poos, M. S., & Jackson, D. A. (2008) Functional rarefaction: estimating functional diversity from field data. Oikos, 117, 286–296.

Walther, B. A. & Moore, J. L. (2005) The concepts of bias, precision and accuracy, and their use in testing the performance of species richness estimators, with a literature review of estimator performance. Ecography, 28, 815–829.

Walther, B. A. & Morand, S. (1998) Comparative performance of species richness estimation method. Parasitology, 116, 395–405.

Wang, S. C. (2003) On the continuity of background and mass extinction. Paleobiology, 29, 455–467.

Wang, S. C. & Everson, P. J. (2007) Confidence intervals for pulsed mass extinction events. Paleobiology, 33, 324–336.

Ward, R. D. (2009) DNA barcoding divergence among species and genera of birds and fishes. Molecular Ecology Research, 9, 1077–1085.

Ward, S. A., Sunderland, K. D., Chambers, R. J. & Dixon A. F. G. (1986) The use of incidence counts for estimation of cereal aphid populations. 3. Population development and the incidence-density relation. Netherlands Journal of Plant Pathology, 92, 175–183.

Ware, D. M. & Thomson, R. E. (2005) Bottom-up ecosystem trophic dynamics determine fish production in the northeast Pacific. Science, 308, 1280–1284.

Ware, S. J., Rees, H. L., Boyd, S. E., & Birchenough, S. N. (2008) Performance of selected indicators in evaluating the consequences of dredged material relocation and marine aggregate extraction. Ecological Indicators, 9, 704–718.

Warming, E. 1909. Oecology of Plants. Clarendon Press, Oxford.

Warren, P. H. & Gaston, K. J. (1997) Interspecific abundance-occupancy relationships: a test of mechanisms using microcosms. Journal of Animal Ecology, 66, 730–742.

Wartenberg, D., Ferson, S., & Rohlf, F. J. (1987) Putting things in order: a critiqye of detrended correspondence analysis. The American Naturalist, 129, 434–448.

Warwick, R. M. (1986) A new method for detecting pollution effects on marine macrobenthic communities. Marine Biology, 92, 557–562.

Warwick, R. M. & Clarke, K. R. (1991) A comparison of some methods for analysing changes in benthic community structure. Journal of the Marine Biological Association of the United Kingdom, 71, 225–244.

Warwick, R. M. & Clarke, K. R. (1993) Comparing the severity of disturbance: a meta-analysis of marine macrobenthic community data. Marine Ecology Progress Series, 92, 221–231.

Warwick, R. M. & Clarke, K. R. (1994) Relearning the ABC – taxonomic changes and abundance biomass relationships in disturbed benthic communities. Marine Biology, 118, 739–744.

Warwick, R. M. & Clarke, K. R. (1995) New 'biodiversity' measures reveal a decrease in taxonomic distinctness with increasing stress. Marine Ecology Progress Series, 129, 301–305.

Warwick, R. M. & Clarke, K. R. (1998) Taxonomic distinctness and environmental assessment. Journal of Applied Ecology, 35, 532–543.

Watling, L. & Norse, E. A. (1998) Disturbance of the seabed by mobile fishing gear: a comparison to forest clearcutting. Conservation Biology, 12, 1180–1197.

Webb, C. O. (2000) Exploring the phylogenetic structure of ecological communities: an example for rain forest trees. The American Naturalist, 156, 145–155.

Webb, C. O., Ackerly, D. D., McPeek, M. A., & Donoghue, M. J. (2002) Phylogenies and community ecology. Annual Review of Ecology and Systematics, 33, 475–505.

Webb, T. J., Noble, D., & Freckleton, R. P. (2007) Abundance-occupancy dynamics in a human-dominated environment: linking interspecific and intraspecific trends in British farmland and woodland birds. Journal of Animal Ecology, 76, 123–134.

Webb, C. O., Ackerly, D. D., & Kembel, S. W. (2008) Phylocom: software for the analysis of phylogenetic community structure and trait evolution. Bioinformatics, 24, 2098–2100.

Weiher, E. (2004) Why should we constrain stress and limitation? – Why conceptual terms deserve broad definitions. Journal of Vegetation Science, 15, 569–571.

Weiher, E. & Keddy, P. A. (1995) Assembly rules, null models, and trait dispersion, new questions from old patterns. Oikos, 74, 159–164.

Weiher, E., Clarke, G. D.P., & Keddy, P. A. (1998) Community assembly rules, morphological dispersion, and the coexistence of plant species. Oikos, 81, 309–322.

Weiher, E., van der Werf, A., Thompson, K., Roderick, M., Garnier, E., & Eriksson, O. (1999) Challenging Theophrastus: a common core list of plant traits for functional ecology. Journal of Vegetation Science, 10, 609–620.

Weiss, R. E. & Marshall, C. R. (1999) The uncertainty in the true end point of a fossil's stratigraphic ranges when stratigraphic sections are sampled discretely. Mathematical Geology, 31, 435–453.

Weitzman, M. L. (1992) On diversity. Quarternary Journal of Economics, 107, 363–405.

Wellington, E. M. H., Berry, A., & Krsek, M. (2003) Resolving functional diversity in relation to microbial community structure in soil: exploiting genomics and stable isotope probing. Current Opinion in Microbiology, 6, 295–301.

Westoby, M. (1999) A leaf-height-seed (LHS) plant ecology strategy scheme. Plant and Soil, 199, 213–227.

White, E. P. (2007) Spatiotemporal scaling of species richness: patters, processes, and implications. In: Scaling Biodiversity, Storch, D., Marquet, P. A., & Brown, J. H. (eds). Cambridge University Press, Cambridge, pp. 325–346.

White, G. C., Burnham, K. P., & Anderson, D. R. (2001) Advanced features of Program MARK. In: Wildlife, Land, and People: Priorities for the 21st Century, Field, R., Warren, R. J., Okarma, H., & Sievert, P. R. (eds). The Wildlife Society, Bethesda, MD, pp. 368–377.

White, E. P., Ernest, S. K. M., & Thibault, K. M. (2004) Trade-offs in community properties through time in a desert rodent community. The American Naturalist, 164, 670–676.

White, E. P., Adler, P. B., Lauenroth, W. K., Gill, R. A., Greenberg, D., Kaufman, D. M., Rassweiler, A., Rusak, J. A., Smith, M. D., Steinbeck, J. R., Waide, R. B., & Yao, J. (2006) A comparison of the species-time relationship across ecosystems and taxonomic groups. Oikos, 112, 185–195.

White, E. P., Enquist, B. J., & Green, J. L. (2008) On estimating the exponent of power-law frequency distributions. Ecology, 89, 905–912.

Whitman, W. B., Coleman, D. C., & Wiebe, W. J. (1998) Prokaryotes: the unseen majority. Proceedings of the National Academy of Sciences of the United States of America, 95, 6578–6583.

Whittaker, R. H. (1952) A study of summer foliage insect communities in the Great Smoky Mountains. Ecological Monographs, 22, 1–44.

Whittaker, R. H. (1960) Vegetation of the Siskiyou mountains, Oregon and California. Ecological Monographs, 30, 279–338.

Whittaker, R. H. (1965) Dominance and diversity in land plant communities. Science, 147, 250–260.

Whittaker, R. H. (1972) Evolution and measurement of species diversity. Taxon, 12, 213–251.

Whittaker, R. H. (1975) Communities and Ecosystems. 2nd edn. MacMillan Publishers, New York.

Wiegand, T. & Moloney, K. A. (2004) Rings, circles, and null-models for point pattern analysis in ecology. Oikos, 104, 209.

Wilcox, B. A. (1978) Supersaturated island faunas: a species-age relationship for lizards on post-pleistocene land-bridge islands. Science, 199, 996–998.

Williams, C. B. (1964) Patterns in the Balance of Nature and Related Problems in Quantitative Ecology. Academic Press, London.

Williams, B. K., Nichols, J. D., & Conroy, M. J. (2002) Analysis and Management of Animal Populations. Academic Press, San Diego.

Williamson, M. & Gaston, K. J. (2005) The lognormal distribution is not an appropriate null hypothesis for the species-abundance distribution. Journal of Animal Ecology, 74, 409–422.

Willis, J. C. (1922) Age and Area: A Study in Geographical Distribution and Origin of Species. Cambridge University Press, Cambridge.

Willis, D. W. & Murphy, B. R. (1996) Planning for sampling. In: Fisheries Techniques, Murphy, B. R. & Willis, D. W. (eds). American Fisheries Society, Bethesda, MD, USA, pp. 1–15.

Wilsey, B. J., Chalcraft, D. R., Bowles, C. M., & Willig, M. R. (2005) Relationships among indices suggest that richness is an incomplete surrogate for grassland biodiversity. Ecology, 86, 1178–1184.

Wilson, J. B. (1991) Methods for fitting dominance/diversity curves. Journal of Vegetation Science, 2, 35–46.

Wilson, J. B. (1993) Would we recognise a broken-stick community if we found one? Oikos, 67, 181–183.

Wilson, L. T. & Room, P. M. (1983) Clumping patterns of fruit and arthropods in cotton, with implications for binomial sampling. Environmental Entomology, 12, 296–302.

Wilson, J. B., Wells, T. C. E., Trueman, I. C., Jones, G., Atkinson, M. D., Crawley, M. J., Dodd, M. E., & Silvertown, J. (1996a) Are there assembly rules for plant species abundance? An investigation in relation to soil resources and successional trends? Journal of Ecology, 84, 527–538.

Wilson, D. E., Nichols, J. D., Rudran, R., & Southwell, C. (1996b) Introduction. In: Measuring and Monitoring Biological Diversity, Standard Methods for Mammals, Wilson, D. E., Cole, R. F., Nichols, J. D., Rudran, R., & Foster, M. S. (eds). Smithsonian Institution Press, Washington, DC, pp. 1–7.

Wilting, A., Buckley-Beason, V. A., Feldhaar, H., Gadau, J., O'Brien, S. J., & Linsenmair, K. E. (2007) Clouded leopard phylogeny revisited: support for species recognition and population division between Borneo and Sumatra. Frontiers in Zoology, 4, 15.

Wimberly, M. C., Yabsley, M. J., Baer, A. D., Dugan, V. G., & Davidson, W. R. (2008) Spatial heterogeneity of climate and land-cover constraints on distributions of tick-borne pathogens. Global Ecology and Biogeography, 17, 189–202.

Winemiller, K. O. (1990) Spatial and temporal variation in tropical fish trophic networks. Ecological Monographs, 60, 331–367.

Winker, K. (2009) Reuniting phenotype and genotype in biodiversity research. BioScience, 59, 657–665.

Woese, C. R. (1987) Bacterial evolution. Microbiological Reviews, 51, 221–271.

Wolda, H. (1981) Similarity indices, sample size and diversity. Oecologia, 50, 296–302.

Wolda, H. (1983) Diversity, diversity indices and tropical cockroaches. Oecologia, 58, 290–298.

Wolf, J. H. D. (2005) The response of epiphytes to anthropogenic disturbance of pine-oak forests in the highlands of Chiapas, Mexico. Forest Ecology and Management, 212, 376–393.

Woodcock, S., van der Gast, C. J., Bell, T., Lunn, M., Curtis, T. P., Head, I. M., & Sloan, W. T. (2006) Neutral assembly of bacterial communities. In: Joint Symposium of the Environmental-Microbiology-Group/British-Ecological-Society/Society-for- General-Microbiology, York, pp. 171–180.

Woodcock, S., van der Gast, C. J., Bell, T., Lunn, M., Curtis, T. P., Head, I. M., & Sloan, W. T. (2007) Neutral assembly of bacterial communities. FEMS Microbiology Ecology, 62, 171–180.

Wootton, J. T. (2005) Field parameterization and experimental test of the neutral theory of biodiversity. Nature, 433, 309–312.

Wright, S. (1951) The genetic structure of populations. Annals of Eugenics, 15, 323–354.

Wright, D. H. (1991) Correlations between incidence and abundance are expected by chance. Journal of Biogeography, 18, 463–466.

Wright, I. J., Reich, P. B., Westoby, M., Ackerly, D. D., Baruch, Z., Bongers, F., Cavender-Bares, J., Chapin, T., Cornelissen, J. H., Diemer, M., Flexas, J., Garnier, E., Groom, P. K., Gulias, J., Hikosaka, K., Lamont, B. B., Lee, T., Lee, W., Lusk, C., Midgley, J. J., Navas, M. L., Niinemets, U., Oleksyn, J., Osada, N., Poorter, H., Poot, P., Prior, L., Pyankov, V. I., Roumet, C., Thomas, S. C., Tjoelker, M. G., Veneklaas, E. J., & Villar, R. (2004) The worldwide leaf economics spectrum. Nature, 428, 821–827.

Wright, J. F. (2000) An introduction to RIVPACS. In: Assessing the Biological Quality of Fresh Waters: RIVPACS and Other Techniques, Wright, J. F., Sutcliffe, D. W., & Furse, M. T. (eds). Freshwater Biological Association, Ambleside, Cumbria, pp. 1–24.

Yang, L. H. (2004) Periodical cicadas as resource pulses in North American forests. Science, 306, 1565–1567.

Yin, Z. Y., Ren, H., Zhang, Q. M., Peng, S. L., Guo, Q. F., & Zhou, G. Y. (2005) Species abundance in a forest community in south China: a case of Poisson lognormal distribution. Journal of Integrative Plant Biology, 47, 801–810.

Yoccoz, N. G., Nichols, J. D., & Boulinier, T. (2001) Monitoring of biological diversity in space and time. Trends in Ecology and Evolution, 16, 446–453.

Zahariev, M., Dahl, V., Chen, W., & Lévesque, C. A. (2009) Efficient algorithms for the discovery of DNA oligonucleotide barcodes from sequence databases. Molecular Ecology Research, 9(Suppl. 1), 58–64.

Zamora, J., Verdú, J. R., & Galante, E. (2007) Species richness in Mediterranean agroecosystems: spatial and temporal analysis for biodiversity conservation. Biological Conservation, 134, 113–121.

Zapiola, M. L., Campbell, C. K., Butler, M. D., & Mallory-Smith, C. A. (2008) Escape and establishment of transgenic glyphosate-resistant creeping bentgrass Agrostis stolonifera in Oregon, USA: a 4-year study. Journal of Applied Ecology, 45, 486–494.

Zar, J. H. (1996) Biostatistical Analysis, 3rd edn. Prentice-Hall, Upper Saddle River, New Jersey, USA

Zhang, D. A., Brecke, P., Lee, H. F., He, Y.-Q., & Zhang, J. (2007) Global climate change, war, and population decline in recent history. Proceedings of the National Academy of Sciences. USA, 104, 19214–19219.

Zillio, T. & Condit, R. (2007) The impact of neutrality, niche differentiation and species input on diversity and abundance distributions. Oikos, 116, 931–940.

Zuckerberg, B., Porter, W. F., & Corwin, K. (2009) The consistency and stability of abundance-occupancy relationships in large-scale population dynamics. Journal of Animal Ecology, 78, 172–181.

Zuckerka, E. & Pauling, L. (1965) Molecules as documents of evolutionary history. Journal of Theoretical Biology, 8, 357.

Index

Boldface indicates a definition of the term. Italics indicates the term appears in a figure, table, or figure legend.

niche: 185, 187
   competition-niche model: 177
   mechanistic niche modeling: 262
   niche apportionment: 97, 100, **124**,
      126, 137
   niche partitioning: 99, 177
   niche preemption: 106
   niche similarity: 123
   realized niche: 185
nonthermophilic: 229
normalizing: 75, **128**, 136
North Atlantic Oscillation: 258
NRC (*see National Research Council*)
nuclear DNA: 209
null model: 176, 189, 190, 198, **199**,
   205, 206, 263

occupancy: 15, 59, **98**, 141, 142,
   148–**150**, 160
   absence: **280**
occupancy-abundance relationship:
   143, 145–147, 150, 151
occupancy-area relationship: 141,
   143, 148–150, 262
occurrence: 2, 141, 143
Ochiai index: *68*, 70
OLS (*see ordinary least squares*)
operational taxonomic unit: 222
orders of magnitude: 1, 3, 232, *232*,
   235
ordinary least squares: 167
ordination: 113
organism size: (*see species size*)
origination distribution: 265, 266
origination rate: **265**, 267
orthogonality: **114**, 115
OTU (*see operational taxonomic unit*)
overdispersed: *155*

palaeontological: 86, **265**, *267*
Paleobiology Database: 270
parameter: 55, *56*, *58*, *59*, 62, 63,
   126, 127
   estimates: 127, 129, 130
   migration parameter: **131**
   neutral model parameter: 134
   parameter bootstrapping: **133**,
      134
   parameter estimation: 126, 128,
      130, 137, 139
   rate parameter: **126**
   scale parameter: 126
   smoothing parameter: 158, 160
   shape parameter: 126
Pareto distribution (*see also Power
   distribution*): **111**, 113
partitioning

additive partitioning: 79, 81,
   82, 84
multiplicative partitioning: 79,
   81, 84
passenger pigeon: xvi, 99
PBDB database: 270, 271, 274
PCA (*see principle components
   analyses*)
PCoA (*see principle coordinates
   analysis*)
PCR (*see polymerase chain reaction*)
PctRare
   1%: *58*
   5%: *58*
   N/S: *58*
PD (*see phylogenetic diversity*)
PDF (*see probability density function*)
Pearson's χ^2 test statistic: 131–134
Pearson correlation: 162, 188, *190*
Phanerozoic: 267, 270
phenotypic: 172
   phenotypic change: 258
   phenotypic plasticity: 185, 261
   phenotypic variation: 176
phototrophic: 229
phylogenetic: 5, 84, 86, 133, 175
phylogenetic clusters: **200**, 206, 207
phylogenetic diversity: 5, 92, 175,
   179, 195, 197, *199*, 207, 240, 241,
   291
   MNND (*see mean nearest neighbor
      distance*)
   MPD (*see mean phylogenetic
      distance*)
   mean nearest neighbor distance:
      183, 193, *199*, 201, *203*, 205
   mean phylogenetic distance: 182,
      199, 201, *203*, 205
   SPD (*see sum of phylogenetic
      distance*)
   sum of phylogenetic distance: *199*,
      201
phylogenetic overdispersion: 200,
   203, 206, 207
phylogenetic tree: *196*, 197, 199, 207,
   222, 223
   balanced tree: *196*, 200, 202–*204*,
      206, 207
   imbalanced tree: *196*, 200, 201, *203*,
      204, 206, 207
phylogeny: 209
   local phylogeny: 197
   regional phylogeny: 197, 200
   subset phylogeny: 197
physiological properties: 223
physiological variables: 262, *263*
   desiccation resistance: 262

metabolic rate: 262
   thermal tolerance: 262
pilot surveys: 16, **18**, 24
plot: 11, 13, 15, 17–23
   nested: 18, *19*, 22, 23
   number of plots: 280
   modified Whittaker: 18
   Whittaker: 18, *19*
population: 11, 13–*16*, 17–19, 21,
   23, 24, 30–**35**, 208,
   210, 211, 216
   human population: 252, 254,
      263
   population density: 254
   population maintenance: 255
   population reduction: 255
Poisson algorithm: **128**, *129*
Poisson distribution: *58*, *112*, 125,
   133, 146, 160, *161*
Poisson lognormal: 53, *112*, 115, *118*,
   125, 126, 128, *129*
Poisson variability: 131
polymerase chain reaction: 223
posterior distribution: 135–137
posterior odds ratio: 136
PowBend distribution: *111*, *115*,
   119
Power distribution (*see also Pareto
   distribution*): *111*, 114
power law model: 143, 144, **146**
precision: 14, *16*–18, 24, 52, 138
presence: **41**, 48
Preston's data smoothing method:
   107
Preston's lognormal: 110
Preston plots: **99**, 109
Preston's temporal scales: **86**
principle components analyses: 186,
   192, 248
principle coordinates analysis: 186,
   192, *249*, 250
probability density function: 107,
   164, 166, 168
probability of detection: 25, 28, *30*,
   33, 36
prokaryote: **221**, 224, 228
prop LN: *58*
proteomics: **229**
proteorhodopsin: **229**
Pyrenean ibex (*Capra pyrenaica
   pyrenaica*): 217
pyrosequencing: 225, *227*, 229, 232

quadrat data: 156, 163
quadratic entropy: *179*, **182**
quadratic polynomial: **159**
qualitative: 195, 197, 200